# The Known World

## OCEAN OF LAMENTATIONS

Krek'kaos

Noxeran Steppe

River Crao

Seleno

Krek Mountains

GLADIOPOLIS

SEPTRA

Asijawi

Plains and

Deserts

of the

East

URANOPOLIS

THEREMA

Terakos

ISHAMAR

ASHMIR

NARATMAJAH

Nir

Manel

FRAGRANCE

Al-Mamlakah
Jabali

ALBAGDIR

PIORTAM'N

Gulf of
Oxyrhynchus

SAGRADA

RASSINE

Capharnaum

SEMZAROT

VILLAGE OF
THE PROPHETS

MESSARA

Lazyrina Sea

AILHUN MUNJHAM

OPONA

AL-KASIR

Aramla
El-Nar

ISHANKTI

KATHRAT

MADINA
AL-MUHIT

Kh'saaba

Isle of
Agramatra

JERGATH THE GREAT

# Credits

## FOR STUDIO DEADCROWS (FRENCH VERSION)

**Conceived and edited** by Raphaël Bardas and François Cedelle.

**Written** by Raphaël Bardas, François Cedelle, Pierre Coppet, Boris Courdesses, Nadège Debray, Matthias Haddad, Frédéric Hubleur, Romain d'Huissier, Julien Laroche, Didier Kurth, François Labrousse, Emmanuelle Lemasson, Yann Machurey, Willem Peerbolte, Silvère Popoff, Samuel Zonato.

**Artwork** by Emmanuel Bouley, Mélodie Cisinksi, Hélène Galtier, Mathieu Gasperin, Benoit Gillaumot, Angélique Grevet, Sébastien Lhotel, Lohran, Marc Simonetti, Frédéric Sintes, Ysha, Christophe Zerr.

**Calligraphy** by Gildas Malassinet-Tannou.

**Colour Insert** by Boris Courdesses and Mathieu Gasperin.

**Layout** by François Labrousse

**Edited** by Raphaël Bardas and François Cedelle.

**Cover Art** by Boris Courdesses.

**Proofreading** by Raphaël Bardas, François Cedelle, Boris Courdesses, Nadège Debray, Laurent Devernay, Romain d'Huissier, Frederic Hubleur, Yann Machurey, Neko, Stephen Nogret, Christophe Zerr, Samuel Zonato.

**Capharnaüm – L'Héritage des Dragons** is published by Studio Deadcrows.

© 2008 Studio Deadcrows. All rights reserved.

Le Studio Deadcrows, 6 rue Henri René, 34000 Montpellier, France.

www.deadcrows.net

## FOR MINDJAMMER PRESS (ENGLISH VERSION)

**Line Development** by Sarah Newton.

**Additional writing** by Sarah Newton.

**Translated** by Sarah Newton and José Luis Porfirio.

**Layout and Graphic Design** by Jason Juta.

**Art Direction** by Jason Juta.

**Art Colouring and Additional Artwork** by Jason Juta.

**Edited** by Sarah Newton.

**Proofreading** by Sarah Newton.

**Produced** by Chris McWilliam and Sarah Newton.

**Enquiries:** info@mindjammerpress.com.

**ISBN (ebook):** 978-1-911380-31-3

**ISBN (physical version):** 978-1-911380-30-6

**Product Code:** MUH042601

**Published** by Mindjammer Press Ltd, 35 Altham Grove, Harlow, Essex, CM20 2PQ, United Kingdom.

**Distributed** by Modiphius Entertainment Ltd, 35 Harwood Road, London SW6 4PQ.

**Publicity and Promotion** by Modiphius Entertainment. For publicity and promotion details contact pr@modiphius.com.

Find out more about *Capharnaum – The Tales of the Dragon-Marked* and other Mindjammer Press games and fiction at www.mindjammerpress.com and www.facebook.com/mindjammerpress

*With great thanks to our art master backers Mathias Green and David Poppel, the inspirations behind Avienus Morcilius Gorgo (page 145) and Don Alfonso Diago Infanzo de Sarajon (page 146). All Hail the Dragon-Marked!*

# Capharnaüm

### The Tales of the Dragon-Marked

## A Fantasy Roleplaying Game

## MINDJAMMER PRESS

# Contents

# - Part One -
# Playing Capharnaum

# INTRODUCTION
# WELCOME TO THE LAND OF 1001 GODS

*Capharnaum – The Tales of the Dragon-Marked* is a roleplaying game set in a "fantasy Arabian" cosmos. The heroes you'll play are people with a legendary destiny, chosen by the dragons, guardians of the celestial gates, to quest to gain entry to the kingdom of the gods.

Bearing the mystical **Dragon Mark**, your characters will have to show strength, cunning and bravery to one day be worthy to take their place beside Hubal, Shirad or Aether, the mighty Lords of Creation.

Wait no longer! Seize your scimitar, the fate of Capharnaum is in your hands!

## An Epic World

Capharnaum is a land at the world's heart, close by a sunlit sea. At the crossroads of the trade routes, it's a strategic focal point for whoever would control access between its lands and peoples. It's a place where history is made and unmade, where the threads of the world's fate are woven.

The known world is vast. Far to the west, the Quarterian nations—worshippers of the Quartered God—prepare their next Crusade. North of the Inner Sea, the Agalanthian city states are a shadow of their past grandeur, once an empire that ruled the world. But here, in Jazirat, the peninsular land burned by the sun of Hubal, life is punctuated by the comings and goings of the caravans of the Saabi and the Shiradim, and of mercenaries mistrustful of the peace that has reigned in Capharnaum since the end of the Crusade of the Knights of the Quarter.

Farther away, the continent of Al-Fariq'n jealously guards its secrets, while from Nir Manel and Asijawi in the distant East come commodities that make fortunes for the merchants of Jazirat— silks, spices, and more. But only the maddest sailors and criminals with nothing to lose dare sail the dangerous Southern Seas.

Finally, far from the sea lanes, the Northern Marches are home to the barbarian tribes of the Krek'kaos. Although disorganised, the inhabitants of these hostile steppes and the mountain ranges of their cold-scoured fastnesses raid the sunny southlands every year.

## A World of Sorcery and Mystery

It's said the gods inspire men and women and guide the arms of the faithful when they go to war. It's also said they take on human form to seduce us, interfere in our feuds, fight at our sides. All this is true! In *Capharnaum*, mythology is real and being made right now. Gods and demons, djinn and mirages: everything exists. A minor god fallen into madness manipulates men and women to

## A Roleplaying Game?

A roleplaying game is a tabletop game where a group of friends participate in imaginary adventures. One of the players, usually called the Gamemaster or GM, is in charge of setting up the story. She describes the action, creates the plot the other players will be faced with, and, during the game, plays the roles of all the "non-player characters" (the extras in the story) they encounter.

In **Capharnaum – The Tales of the Dragon-Marked**, the Gamemaster is called **Al-Rawi**, "the one who tells stories" or "the Storyteller".

Each of the other players creates one or more imaginary characters, and describes their actions and words in the situations set up by Al-Rawi. Here's an example:

**Al-Rawi:** *Nicholas, your character, Haji Ibn Tufiq, sees a strange man approaching the rich merchant you're supposed to protect.*

**Nicholas:** *I say to the merchant: "Your excellency, watch out!" and draw my scimitar to stop the assassin dead!*

**Al-Rawi:** *OK, grab your dice! Let's see if you manage it...*

Next in the action, Nicholas and Al-Rawi simulate a conflict using dice rolls and the rules in this book to work out what happens. The adventure unfolds: the assassin is stopped, there's an investigation into who commanded the attack, and the merchant's life is saved once again. Nicholas's character basks in success and good fortune—at least, that is, until Al-Rawi calls him to adventure again...

This book provides you with all you need to play adventures in the lands of **Capharnaum**. It also provides lots of information which is specifically for Al-Rawi, the Storyteller (in particular **Part Three: Al-Rawi's Guide to Capharnaum**), so if you're intending to be a player, you might want to skip those sections until you're ready to run adventures yourself across the lands of Jazirat!

## Capharnaum isn't a historical game!

It's worth saying this up front. Although they often recall our own world, and may even be partly inspired by it, the places and events described in **Capharnaum – The Tales of the Dragon-Marked** are fictional. A historian will be hard put to track down exact cultural references for its peoples: the Jazirati and the Kh'saaba have as much of Arabia Felix in their veins as the people of the mysterious Queen of Sheba; Capharnaum is Mesopotamian, but also Maghrebian, Iraqi, and sometimes Ottoman. Sagrada is the enchanted child of Jerusalem, Baghdad and Mecca; and the Agalanthians are fallen Atlanteans, with strong Greco-Roman tendencies. And Jason Quartered, of course, is not Jesus Christ!

Drawing from the tales of the Arabian Nights, but also from the world of the ancient Mediterranean and the Crusades, Capharnaum is a cornucopia of inspirations. It's inspired by the best the Mediterranean world has seen through the ages: that spellbinding canvas that mixes sun, spice, sand, mystery—and blood.

---

follow his ravings; a mirage leads a caravan into the limbo of the magical world; a djinn gives you a flying carpet if only you free him from a lamp. All these ingredients and more are found in a game of *Capharnaum – The Tales of the Dragon-Marked*.

## A World of Conflict and Adventure!

Religion and ideology are often at the heart of events in *Capharnaum*. The world is divided into realms, often at war, who tell the most horrendous (and often incorrect...) tales about each other. However, *Capharnaum* is a game of fun and adventure—and it's up to you, Al-Rawi and players alike, to ensure these themes are treated appropriately during play. It's good to have characters who are passionate—but it can be miserable if those passions are purely negative, filled with hatred, prejudice, or resentment. Sure, in the wider world, many Saabi look down on the Shiradim, and in turn lots of them think Agalanthians are degenerate thugs, and the Quarterians think they have to fight against anyone who doesn't revere Aether and Jason, their gods. Add in religious zealots like the Tarekids, marauding barbarians like the Krekhin, and it's a potent mix. But that doesn't mean your characters think that way!

You'll see something similar when it comes to social class and the sexes in *Capharnaum*. As the game tries to refract historical themes into a fantasy world, many (even most) of its societies have some pretty rigid ideas of how people are supposed to behave, depending on their social status, their birth, their sex. Our own societies are still grappling with many of these issues and resolving them, but in *Capharnaum*, they can be in your face, obvious, and unjust.

How should you handle this? Quite simply, we've set up the world and peoples of *Capharnaum* to generate exciting and adventure-filled conflict, not hatred and bigotry. This is a fantasy game, where dragons and sorcerers are real. That means that some of the appalling features of our own culture's histories don't necessarily have to apply quite as ruthlessly in *Capharnaum* as they often have in our own world. Yes, women often lead lives of relative unfree-

## A Capharnaum Glossary

In these pages you'll find terms which are specific to the lands and rules of **Capharnaum**. Don't worry—they'll become clear as you read. If you ever want a quick refresher, though, we've included a **Glossary** right at the back of this book, on page 366.

dom in some of *Capharnaum's* societies: but that doesn't mean *all* women. People always find ways to express themselves, to rebel, to go beyond society's strictures, and *Capharnaum's* women are no exception. For every meek Occidentian daughter waiting for an arranged marriage, there's a Gitanillan horsemistress armed with a rapier fighting against the invader and ignoring the opprobrium of her peers, an Agalanthian oracle ekeing out a precarious existence in the wilderness in ecstatic communion with her goddess, a Shiradi spy-mistress whose tentacles control the underworld of a Jazirati city and even influence the politics of its court.

Leave the negative emotions to the bad guys in play: your characters are *heroes*, motivated by comradeship, nobility, and a love of adventure! From your very first session, your characters, often from radically different—and even enemy—backgrounds, will find themselves thrust together, and will have to cooperate to succeed. And, more than that, they'll find they share a common destiny which transcends any petty human concerns, and which must unite them if they're to fulfil their potential: the **Dragon Mark**.

## A World of Heroes!

In *Capharnaum*, your character isn't an ordinary mortal. From the dawn of time, special children have been born bearing the **Dragon Mark** on their backs, just behind their hearts. Destined for greatness, people say these **Dragon-Marked** are blessed by the gods—or marked by demons! Which is the truth? Perhaps you'll find out, leading your character through the burning paths of *Capharnaum*, wielding sword and sorcery, charm and wisdom, and—perhaps—rising to the dizzy heights of power and rivalling the gods!

## How This Book is Structured

You don't have to read this whole book to play *Capharnaum*! In fact, we've structured it so you can learn what you need quickly and get playing right away. This book has three parts. We've colour-coded the pages to make them easy to find:

- **Part One: Playing Capharnaum:** That's this part, the four core chapters detailing character creation, how to play the game, and magic. This is really all you need to read to get started.
- **Part Two: The World of Capharnaum.** Starting on page 147, this describes the setting of *Capharnaum* in detail. It's part-encyclopedia, part-gazetteer. Give it a glance through to begin with, and then maybe read some of the sections which catch your eye or which you think might be cool to bring into your game.
- **Part Three: Al-Rawi's Guide to Capharnaum.** If you're going to be a player in *Capharnaum*, don't read this! Part Three is the game master's section—it contains campaign secrets, monsters, and more. If you're going to be game master—or **Al-Rawi** in *Capharnaum* parlance—then look through this section and familiarise yourself with what's there.

That's it! *Capharnaum* is a deep and detailed game, but it's a setting that will be familiar to you from countless books, movies, and ancient tales. Grab your scimitar, mount your camel, and enter the djinn-haunted ruins in the desert wastes. Adventure awaits!

---

## "He" and "She"

*Some of the societies and organisations in this book might seem to have very strict roles for men and women. This reflects the prevailing customs in those groups. However, it most certainly does* **not** *mean that you have to follow those customs for your characters.*

*Your heroes are by definition extraordinary people: they combat injustice, they fight to change the world, to discover the meaning of their Dragon Mark. Don't treat the inequalities of the world as a straitjacket, but as an impulse to heroism and adventure. The world is looking for heroes!*

*Whenever we say "he" in the descriptions below, we could just as well mean "she", and when we say "she" we could mean "he". There are always men and women that break the mould, and the history of* **Capharnaum** *is filled with stories of heroic female warriors who prevailed in battle, sensual male houris whose seductions and espionage helped bring a tyrant low, revolutionary priestesses and female scholars whose insights changed the world forever. Many of the societies of* **Capharnaum** *may seem to be imprisoned by the shackles of their past traditions: you, as a player, are certainly not!*

---

## What You Need to Play

*Capharnaum is a roleplaying game, so there isn't a whole lot you need to play. You'll find some or all of the following useful:*

- *A copy of this book!*
- *At least 12 six-sided dice (also called D6).*
- *At least 1 six-sided die which is different from the others—maybe larger, or a different colour. This is a* **dragon die** *(page 48), and it's good to have one for each player.*
- *A character sheet (see page 364) for each player.*
- *Scratch paper and pencils.*
- *A way of determining "yes / no" answers, such as a flipped coin. The best is two identically-sized stones, one black, one white, in a pouch—see page 77.*
- *Optionally, miniature figurines or tokens. They're not necessary, but can be great fun and a cool aid for visualisation!*
- *Optionally, a copy of the Arcana of Adventure Player's Guide for each player.*

# CHAPTER ONE
# POLYMNIA – CREATING CHARACTERS

## The Cut-Throat and the Razor

*B*y the thrice-sacred prophets! Hafiz Thufir Jamil Ibn Rashid Abd-al-Hassan hated the feeling of a sharpened blade against his throat! The slight pressure on his Adam's apple sent a shiver down his spine. Vulnerable at that moment like no other, he felt the seductive caress of danger mingle with the fear of death. Feelings all too familiar—he had slashed so many jugulars himself.

One of Prince Mammud's bodyguards, Thufir handled the dirty work. Expert at silencing his master's enemies, he would lure them into a shadowy alcove or dark corridor, then draw his khanjar and strike with lightning speed and accuracy. He worked cleanly—a point of honour. No blood ever soiled his spotless dishdasha.

The blade withdrew from his throat. Thufir fought down the memories of his victims collapsing to the floor, and summoned sweeter ones. Whenever his work was done, he would reappear at the receptions his master organised, quickly forgetting his revulsion in the arms of the most beautiful women of Carrassine.

As Prince Mammud's henchman, Thufir was better known for his amorous exploits than for the dismal work he performed for his master. Everywhere people praised his handsomeness, the perfection of his poems. Green-eyed and fine-featured, blessed with elegance of form and attire, a subtleness of melody and rhyme, he was one of the court's greatest lovers. He seduced coveted damsels without ever asking for their hand, received delicious concubines from a master whose life he had saved many times, who could refuse him nothing. He found solace in the embrace of the most elegant widows of Carrassine, many of whom owed their unfortunate state to him...

Each Altarek—the ninth day of the Jazirati week—the assassin with the face of a courtier bared his throat to the expert hand of Master Benyamin Bar Chemed. Thufir enjoyed the irony. Any one of his enemies could pay the friendly old man to slip his blade—people said money could make a Shiradi do anything—but Thufir doubted he would ever accept. A thousand times he had taken that chance, a thousand times his trust had been rewarded. The master barber was no stranger to Thufir's glory, and his tender ministrations gilded the fineness of his features.

Done with the razor, the barber massaged Thufir's face with aromatic oils, the secret of his trade. Thufir paid him and took his leave, losing himself among the crowds of the Al-Dhumma medina. The throng ushered him east through the spice market. Avoiding Pepper Street, hating how it had been invaded by Quarterian wine merchants (delicious though their wine was), he dove into the incense souk. There, tribeswomen threw pinches of precious blends into burners, and their heady fumes intoxicated him. At the market's edge, he took the gate of the Sixth Terrace to the Al-Wudu medina. It was only right that he should be at the side of his master, Prince Mammud, on the day of his fourth wedding...

of such a chosen one, the dragons appear to the pregnant mother and place their seal on her belly. Although the mother bears no trace of it, the child within her is born with a birthmark in the shape of a dragon's claw on its back, just behind its heart.

Many refuse to believe the mother. Sometimes the child is considered a monster. But behind the Dragon-Marked a dragon waits, ready to guide them. Some Dragon-Marked succumb to evil. Others—far more numerous—perish along the way. A large majority refuse their heritage, or don't believe it exists. But some make it, to enter the Kingdom of Heaven and take their place among the stars at the side of Hubal, Shirad, Aether, and Kalos.

Six hundred years ago, a mysterious event occurred. No one knows why, but the Dragon-Marked suddenly stopped being born. It was as if the dragons had turned their attentions elsewhere. Only during the last century have things changed, and new Dragon-Marked started to appear again. Some claim something big happened forty years ago to mark their return, but no-one really knows. Even now, the return of the Dragon-Marked has been a modest affair, and fewer than a thousand have been born.

**Every** player character in *Capharnaum – The Tales of the Dragon-Marked* is one of them.

Recently, the pace of events has begun to accelerate. Everywhere, *kahini* and *kahanim*—priests of all types—have become aware of an inexplicable reality: since the end of the Holy Crusade of the Quarterians, a few years ago, Dragon-Marked children have been born by the score!

Your character has been chosen by the dragons, servants of the gods. You have a purpose in the world, a mission to accomplish. But what is it? What are the stakes? The only thing you know for sure is that you have the potential to become a hero. A great hero, who may be feared and rejected. Who may even be worshipped...

To create your *Capharnaum* character, follow the steps below. You can jot down your decisions on a piece of paper: we've provided a **character sheet** on page 364 specifically for this purpose. An example character is shown on the facing page, and in text boxes throughout this chapter.

In *Capharnaum – The Tales of the Dragon-Marked,* players play the roles of the extraordinary heroes known as the **Dragon-Marked**. Men and women chosen from the descendants of the gods, they are divine agents who may one day win their place in the Kingdom of Heaven. However, not even the gods can decide mortal destinies. The Dragon-Marked, though chosen by the gods, make their own fate.

At first, your character led a normal life. You grew up at home, maybe went to school, learned a trade, raised a family. The **character creation system** below focusses on your family and social life: you'll choose your Dragon-Marked's **blood** (your family and geographic origin) as well as your **path** (the martial, magical or social discipline you follow), and finally your **occupation**.

# PLAYING A DRAGON-MARKED

There are common mortals, and there are those who rise above them. These are the heroes, the war chiefs, the great thinkers and legendary lovers of the world. Even among heroes, some shine even brighter—or have the potential to do so. These are the **Dragon-Marked**.

Since the dawn of time, the mystical **dragons** have watched over the world's peoples. Psychopomps and guardians of celestial secrets, they serve the gods, their mission to guide the best of men and women through the tortuous paths of mortal adventure. Just before the birth

# STEP I: BLOOD AND PATH

In this first step, you choose your **blood**: the social and geographic origin of your character, as well as your place in the world. Bloods include Saabi **clans**, Shiradi **tribes**, Agalanthian **city-states**, and Quarterian **kingdoms**. You can find short descriptions of these bloods below (page 13), and much more detail in **Chapter Seven: Euterpe – Peoples and Societies**, on page 232.

Choosing your blood gives you +1 point in one **attribute**, representing one of the five physical and mental qualities of Strength (STR), Constitution (CON), Dexterity (DEX), Intelligence (INT), and Charisma (CHA); and +1 point in three specific **skills**, representing the things you know how to do, described in each blood below. See pages 23 and 25 for more on attributes and skills.

At the same time, you should choose the discipline you've devoted your life to in your clan, tribe, city-state, or kingdom. This is called your **path**. It's a generic term: the Agalanthians call it a **school** and the Quarterians an **academy**. Your choice of path opens the doors of that organisation to you—fighting schools, warrior sects, sorcerous colleges, mystical traditions, and so on.

Each path provides you with +1 point in one attribute point, +1 point in three skills, and a special ability called your **first path ability**, also described in each blood, below. When you're creating your character, you can only chose the first path ability of your path, but each path has **six** path abilities which you can eventually aspire to: see **Chapter Two: Thalia – Word and Deed**, page 81, for more. There are many more paths than are presented in this book.

Note also that, although paths are presented below associated with specific bloods, you don't have to choose the path from your blood. You can choose another path, as long as it's connected to your clan (for the Saabi) or your people in general. See the section on "Rebels, Dissidents, Mixed-Bloods, Cousins and Traitors" on page 11 for more.

Choosing a blood and path gives you a rapid and concise summary of your character's cultural and social references. However, don't feel this has to restrict how you see or play your character: a Hassanid *mujahid* (sacred warrior) living in Kh'saaba and his cousin, a mercenary at Carrassine, will have very different points of view. Likewise, a Quarterian Templar who stayed behind in Capharnaüm after the end of the Holy Crusade may well now be defrocked and living a life of debauchery.

Note also that your path isn't your character's profession, but rather a discipline you've decided to follow, a code of conduct, a vocation. Your mujahid warrior following the path of the Suspicion of Traitors (page 17) may have the Sage as his main **archetype** or occupation (see Step 4, page 26), and may have been delegated by Kh'saaba as ambassador to Fragrance. Or, your character from the Aragonian academy of San Llorente de Valladon (your path) may be a wandering artist, belonging to a travelling theatre troupe (the Poet archetype).

# Capharnaüm
## The Tales of the Dragon-Marked

| | |
|---|---|
| **Name** Jaziya the Demon Huntress | **Path** The Sand Preachers |
| **Blood** Saabi - The Clan of Yazid, Tribe of the Tarekids / Bint Yazid Abd-al-Tarek | |
| **Status** Wandering Mujahid Zealot | **Occupation** Demon Hunter |

**Strength** 2
**Constitution** 3
**Dexterity** 4
**Bravery** 3
**Heroism** 3
**Intelligence** 3
**Faith** 5
**Loyalty** 2
**Charisma** 1
**Max Init** 4
**Dragon Dice** 1
**Adventure Points**
**Soak** 6

### Passive Defence
16

| | |
|---|---|
| First Weapon | Damage |
| Shimshir Long Scimitar 9/4 | +10 |
| Second Weapon | Damage |
| Jambiya Dagger 9/4 | +7 |
| Third Weapon | Damage |
| Javelin 9/4 | +10 |

### Armour
Light Armour (AV: 3)

### Hit Points
30

| The Adventurer | | The Poet | | The Rogue | | The Sorcerer | |
|---|---|---|---|---|---|---|---|
| Athletics | 6 | Acting | | Assassination | 1 | Prayer | 5 |
| Riding | 2 | Music | 1 | Intrusion | 2 | Sacred Word | 2 |
| Storytelling | 2 | Oratory | | Stealth | 1 | Sacrifice | 1 |
| Survival | 4 | Poetry | | Thievery | 1 | Willpower | 2 |
| The Labourer | | The Prince | | The Sage | | The Warrior | |
| Agriculture | 1 | Elegance | | History & Peoples | | Combat Training | 4 |
| Craft | 1 | Flattery | | Instruction | | Command | 3 |
| Endurance | 2 | Save Face | | Notice | 1 | Fighting | 5 |
| Solidarity | 1 | Unctuous Bargaining | 1 | Science | | Intimidate | 4 |

## Path Abilities

The Sand Preachers
The Path of Yazid, Servant of Tarek
Level 1
When Jaziya commits a hands-on assassination, she may use her Prayer skill instead of Assassination. If she lights up a constellation, she gains a damage bonus equal to twice her Faith score (+10 points).

Level    1

## Magic

Sacred Word    2

○ Create    ○ Transform    ○ Destroy

| Element | Type | Element | Type |
|---------|------|---------|------|
| *Mundane World:* | | *Phantasmal World:* | |
| Flames | | Courage | |
| | | Demon | |
| | | Jahannam | |

## Character Portrait

## Personal Legend

As the daughter of Jazir the Kahini, Jaziya seemed destined to become a temple servitor. However, she was also the bastard great-granddaughter of a famed Hassanid mujahid, whose family had no male heir, and so by royal decree she was sent to a Hassanid military academy. Insubordinate and rebellious, she was flogged and sentenced to death by starvation in a hellhole prison cell buried twenty feet underground, but managed to escape. Using an assumed identity, she hid for a year in a troupe of wandering artists until, one day, a mysterious veiled figure appeared to her. Since then, the Dragon Mark on her back has lit up with a strange aura whenever danger has approached. It was thanks to this aura that Jaziya was alerted when a demonic horde attacked her wandering troupe. Terrified by the aura, Jaziya fled, only to find later, when she returned, that all her friends had been killed. She swore to find the demons which had done this foul deed and destroy them all!

Contacts:

- Jazir the Kahini, Father (level 2 contact)
- Hakim the Caravaneer (level 1 contact)
- Uncle Jibril (level 2 contact)

## Equipment

Shimshir Mujahid Scimitar (4 lbs)
Jambiya (2lbs)
Javelin (2lbs)
Light Armour (20lbs)
Set of urban clothing (3lbs)
Set of desert clothing (3lbs)
Comfortable Shoes
Camel, carries:
   Tent (9lbs), 50ft rope (9lbs), 3 large leather sacks (3lbs),
   5 torches (10lbs), portable incense burner.

Wt. carried: 31lbs

Wealth Level     0    Money    2 ounces of cumin

## Blood, Path, Dragon-Marked, Archetypes...

How can you picture your *Capharnaum* character to yourself? What kind of character can you play in the game? Can you play bad guys? Characters who aren't human?

A *Capharnaum* player character is a human being who is extraordinary for several reasons.

First of all, for some reason he doesn't fully understand, the gods, and their servants the dragons, have picked him out. He has received the Dragon Mark, a mysterious birthmark that indicates he is bound for greatness. All Dragon-Marked have some attributes better than the run-of-the-mill mortal, being stronger, cleverer, more agile, and so on. Some even come from a lineage of Dragon-Marked: your father or mother, grandfather or grandmother, and many others before you, may have been chosen by the celestial powers. For more on this, see Table 1-17: Legends of the Dragon-Mark on page 41.

Second of all, for reasons of your own, your character has been following a special discipline known as a path, perhaps belonging to an academy, fighting school, or mystical order, usually attached to an important figure in your people's history. Paths aren't the preserve of the Dragon-Marked—indeed, most of their members are not Dragon-Marked—but you're both. You can find out much more about paths in **Chapter Two: Thalia – Word and Deed** (page 81).

Remember to check out the Glossary on page 366 whenever you want a summary of these *Capharnaum* terms.

## Summary of Step 1:

a. Choose your **blood** (your geographic origin) from page 13, and note down the attribute and skill points it gives you on your character sheet.

b. Choose your **path** (the discipline you follow) from page 17, and note down its attribute and skill point bonuses, as well as your first path ability and its parameters, on your character sheet.

c. If the blood and path you've chosen are unconnected, see "Rebels, Dissidents, Mixed-Bloods, Cousins and Traitors" below.

## Jaziya the Demon Huntress! An Example of Character Creation

*Sarah's about to create her first Dragon-Marked character. Al-Rawi briefly introduces the setting, and Sarah takes a look through the setting chapters of Capharnaum: The Tales of the Dragon-Marked to better visualise its different peoples and the atmosphere of the game. She decides she wants to play a demon-hunting desert warrior who follows her quarry to the ends of the earth—and even into hell if needs be! In the text boxes which follow, let's see just how Sarah goes about creating her Dragon-Marked hero…*

## Rebels, Dissidents, Mixed-Bloods, Cousins and Traitors

Most of the time, your *Capharnaum* character will follow a path connected to your blood. That's the simplest way to create a character, and we recommend it when you're starting out. It's not mandatory, though, and it may be that your Dragon-Marked has broken with his past, that he was raised by others, that his culture is completely different.

If you're choosing a "dissident" destiny like this for your character, assume your blood remains the same but your path comes from a blood not your own. Be sure to justify this with a good story: maybe you're the son of an Agalanthian lord and a Saabi courtesan; or you have Agalanthian blood but you've followed the path of Mimun Abd-al-Tarek; or maybe you're a Shiradi traveller who has converted and become a Quarterian Templar.

Having this kind of dissident destiny has the following effects:

❖ Even if you decide your character has completely broken with your blood or path (or both), you still get the benefits of the blood and path in question during character creation. Create your character normally, except that your Loyalty heroic virtue (page 22) is set to 0. It may rise above this during play, but may never exceed 4. Additionally, you have only 7 points to distribute between your two other heroic virtues.

❖ You get your first path ability as normal (page 17), but you may not automatically acquire subsequent paths, unless, during your adventures (and subject to Al-Rawi's judgement), you somehow reconnect or renew contact with your people.

If you decide your character has always followed a path other than that of your blood (you're a mixed-blood, or you've been fostered by a family friend or cousin, or you ran away at an early age and were raised by foreigners), then the following points apply:

❖ **If you were raised in the same tribe but you follow a path from a different clan of that tribe (such as an Ibn Malik fol-**

## Character Creation Checklist

*Step One: Blood and Path (page 8)*

    *a. Choose your **blood** (your geographic origin) from page 13, and note down the attribute and skill points it gives you on your character sheet.*

    *b. Choose your **path** (the discipline you follow) from page 17, and note down its attribute and skill point bonuses, as well as your first path ability and its parameters, on your character sheet.*

    *c. If the blood and path you've chosen are unconnected, see "Rebels, Dissidents, Mixed-Bloods, Cousins and Traitors" on page 11.*

*Step Two: Heroic Virtues (page 22)*

    *a. Distribute 10 points between Bravery, Faith, and Loyalty, with a minimum score of 1 and a maximum of 6.*

    *b. The average of your Bravery, Faith, and Loyalty, rounded down, is your Heroism score. This is usually 3 for beginning characters, unless your scores were modified in Step 5 (page 35).*

*Step Three: Attributes (page 23)*

    *a. Assign 1 point to each of your five attributes (Strength, Constitution, Dexterity, Intelligence, Charisma).*

    *b. Then, allocate 6 additional points between them, and add any bonuses gained from your blood and path in Step 1. No attribute score may exceed 4 at this point.*

*Step Four: Archetypes and Skills (page 25)*

    *a. To begin with, increase the following skills by +1: Endurance, Prayer, Unctuous Bargaining, and Willpower.*

    *b. Then, rank the eight archetypes in descending order of relevance to your character. Increase the skills belonging to those archetypes by +3, +2, +1, +1, +1, and then +0, +0, +0 respectively.*

    *c. Total up the scores in each of your skills, including any bonuses acquired in Step 1 (page 8). If any skill score exceeds 5 at this point, reduce it to 5 and set aside the excess points to use as **freely distributed points** in Step 5 (page 35).*

*Step Five: Finishing Touches (page 35)*

    *a. Freely distribute 5 points among your skills, adding no more than 2 points to any one skill, and with no skill exceeding 5.*

    *b. Roll for your Legend, rolling twice on the Legend table for your blood, once on the Legend table for your main archetype, twice on Table 1-16: Legendary Archetypes, and once on Table 1-17: Legends of the Dragon-Mark.*

    *c. Create a back story for your character, incorporating your Legend roll results.*

    *d. Determine your contacts and acquaintances.*

    *e. Calculate your Soak, Hit Points, Max Init and Passive Defence.*

    *f. Determine your equipment and your Wealth Level.*

## Dragons and Civilisations

*Dragons are important in* **Capharnaüm**. *They're present in all the world's cultures, but they're not always viewed the same way. This means that the Dragon-Marked—your characters and their fellows—can be treated completely differently in different places and times. What did your family think when they saw your Dragon Mark? How did your town or village react? How did you grow up? Answering these questions helps you pin down how your culture views dragons and the Dragon-Marked. You don't have to restrict yourself to the typical views of your people: there are always exceptions, and you're free to imagine any crazy story you want, since—as always—a good story justifies any madness...*

❖ *The* **Shiradim** *(page 15) know that the constellations of the night sky are the heavenly manifestations of dragons, the spirits of those ancient, benevolent advisors subject to the will of* **Shirad** *(page 263). They live in a world beyond the world, and carry on their own feuds, incomprehensible to mere mortals. They have chosen the Dragon-Marked to serve Shirad and spread his wisdom.*

❖ *The* **Quarterians** *(page 16) see dragons as creatures sent by Aether to punish the unvirtuous. Diseases, madness, storms and earthquakes are manifestations of their wrath and power. They're the punitive arm of their god, Aether, and of Mira and Jason, the other members of his Trinity. The Dragon-Marked are servants of the dragons and thus of Aether, whether as the god of love or the god of conquest.*

❖ *The* **Agalanthians** *(page 15) revere dragons as ancient heroes who have joined the gods. During their earthly lives, they made the world live and advance, writing its histories, making great discoveries, solving human dramas. Upon their (usually) heroic deaths, they became dragons, servants of the gods and guides for new heroes. For the Agalanthians, the terms "Hero" and "Dragon-Marked" are the same thing, although they tend to prefer the former.*

❖ *For the* **Saabi**, *dragons are kin, allies, and servants of the gods—but sometimes also their rivals and enemies. In different regions and tribes it's not uncommon to encounter widely differing views, but nevertheless everyone agrees the dragons are guides, companions and patrons—whether for good or ill. Like the Agalanthians, they believe the Dragon-Marked have been chosen by the dragons to become the servants of their own masters, the gods. If they rise to this glorious destiny, the Dragon-Marked become dragons in turn. That's why the Saabi affix a dragon's name with an adjective or animal name symbolising their past mortal existence: Hassan the King Dragon, Salif the Night Dragon, Tarek the Lion Dragon, and so on.*

*Whatever your origin, your Dragon-Marked character feels apart from and above other mortals. You know the Dragon Mark is proof the gods exist—all the gods, since there are Dragon-Marked from every land. Even if your character is a religious fanatic, you'll grant at least some respect to any Dragon-Marked, even if they worship gods other than your own.*

---

lowing an Ibn Mussah path—see page 17): Character creation is unchanged. The same applies for a Shiradim choosing a Shiradi path from a different tribe (an Ashkenim following a Pharati path, for example).

❖ **If you were raised among the same people but you follow a path from another tribe, kingdom, or city-state of that people (such as an Occidentian in an Orkadian Academy, a Fragrantine in a Thereman School, or a Hassanid following a Salifah path):** Your character is frowned upon, and your beginning Loyalty is 0 and can never exceed 4. You only have 7 points to divide among your other two heroic virtues (see Step 2: Heroic Virtues, page 22).

❖ **Whether or not you were raised by your people, you follow a path from another people (such as a Saabi following a Shiradi path, or a Quarterian in an Agalanthian school):** Your character is unpopular, often attacked or run out of town by members of either people. Your beginning Loyalty is 0 and can never exceed 2. You have only 7 points to divide among your other two heroic virtues (see Step 2: Heroic Virtues, page 22).

## Other Destinies...

You may not even want your character to follow a path at all. To be honest, we don't really recommend this, at least not all the time, but it's possible to do it if you have a particularly awesome story for your character you want to tell (a good story always trumps the rules). Here's how to create an "independent" Dragon-Marked:

❖ Add 1 point to the attribute of your choice.

❖ Add only 2 skill points: no skill may exceed 4, and you may not allocate the 2 points to the same skill.

❖ Your character is considered one of the common folk, although you still have the heroic virtues of a Dragon-Marked.

❖ You don't have any of the special path abilities you get when you follow a path, but you can still become a great warrior, a renowned sage, an infamous bandit or a mysterious sorcerer.

# THE SAABI TRIBES AND CLANS

Dragon-Marked characters of Saabi blood come from one of the Three Great **Tribes** descended from one of the **Three Prophets**, and belong to a **clan** within that tribe. You're considered nobility, with different levels of proximity to the crown (your choice), regardless of your character's occupation.

## The Hassanid Tribe

Hassan was the greatest warrior of the Saabi. His line boasts the finest sword and spear fighters. It's a sedentary tribe, living in cities and oases, and most Saabi generals belong to it.

## The Clan of Malik, Servant of Hassan

### Ibn Malik Abd-al-Hassan

This is the Hassanid bloodline which the king of Kh'saaba belongs to. It breeds the greatest generals, the most honourable scions, the most admired leaders of troops, and popular heroes of boundless faith and courage. Many *mujahidin* (page 235) come from this clan.

- ❖ **Attribute and Skill Bonuses:** DEX or STR +1; Combat Training +1, Command +1, Fighting +1.
- ❖ **Suggested Path:** One of the paths of Malik, Servant of Hassan, such as the Fire Scimitars (page 17).

## The Clan of Mussah, Servant of Hassan

### Ibn Mussah Abd-al-Hassan

The Ibn Mussah are the powers behind the throne, those who advise and conspire, whose political and commercial ability is devoted to strengthening the Kingdom of Kh'saaba.

- ❖ **Attribute and Skill Bonuses:** CHA +1; Elegance +1, Flattery +1, Save Face +1.
- ❖ **Suggested Path:** One of the paths of Mussah, Servant of Hassan, such as the Alchemists of Men (page 17).

## The Clan of Rashid, Servant of Hassan

### Ibn Rashid Abd-al-Hassan

The Ibn Rashid are an ambiguous bloodline. They're the most faithful bodyguards, yet the most merciless assassins when their job demands it.

- ❖ **Attribute and Skill Bonuses:** CON +1; Assassination +1, Fighting +1, Poetry +1.
- ❖ **Suggested Path:** One of the paths of Rashid, Servant of Hassan, such as the Suspicion of Traitors (page 17).

## The Salifah Tribe

The Salifah have the skills that bring order to Jazirat: those of travel and commerce. Merchants or caravaneers, explorers or criminals, the Salifah defy easy categorisation.

### The Clan of Yussef, Servant of Salif

#### Ibn Yussef Abd-al-Salif

Traders, merchants, and caravaneers par excellence, the children of Yussef are found throughout Jazirat, and are sedentary as well as nomadic. They're everywhere you'd expect them to be, and even where you wouldn't, turning up as local rulers, stewards of the powerful, or simple desert caravaneers. The clan has a strong feeling of cohesion and family spirit for the whole of the tribe, and is the cement which holds the children of Salif together. In the pure tradition of Saabi caravaneers, they are the greatest merchants, owning endless caravans, wealthy trading posts, oases, and more. Some even master trading magic (page 115).

- ❖ **Attribute and Skill Bonuses:** CHA or INT +1; Flattery +1, Survival +1, Unctuous Bargaining +1.
- ❖ **Suggested Path:** One of the paths of Yussef, Servant of Salif, such as the Saffron Dunes (page 18).

### The Clan of Aziz, Servant of Salif

#### Ibn Aziz Abd-al-Salif

If it wasn't bound by a certain code of honour, the clan of Aziz would bring forth the very worst kind of people. It's divided into two parts: the first took part in the founding of Carrassine, and specialises in the hiring out of mercenaries; the second is its shady counterpart, the Princes of Thieves who are behind most of the illegal activities in Jazirat, including organised crime, kidnapping, and the slave trade to the Agalanthians.

- ❖ **Attribute and Skill Bonuses:** DEX +1; Fighting +1, Thievery +1, Unctuous Bargaining +1.
- ❖ **Suggested Path:** One of the paths of Aziz, Servant of Salif, such as the Children of the Souk (page 18).

### The Clan of Khalil, Servant of Salif

#### Ibn Khalil Abd-al-Salif

Unusually for the Saabi, the Ibn Khalil are mostly of Al-Fariqani origin, and many have black or deep-tanned skin. They are famous for their fighters, who ride **abzulim** (page 307), small dragons as large as two oxen, and who sell their services for exorbitant fees. Originating along the coasts and in Al-Fariq'n, it's not uncommon to find one elsewhere: they're famous explorers, travelling far to East and West. They know otherworldly mysteries, and often seem aloof.

- ❖ **Attribute and Skill Bonuses:** CON +1; Agriculture +1, Riding +1, Survival +1.
- ❖ **Suggested Path:** One of the paths of Khalil, Servant of Salif, such as the Walad Badiya (page 18).

## The Tarekid Tribe

The poorest and most violent of the three tribes of the Saabi, and the greatest religious zealots, the Tarekids live in the desert in small groups, waging constant war against the Salifah, who they believe have succumbed to debauchery and decadence.

### The Clan of Tufiq, Servant of Tarek

#### Ibn Tufiq Abd-al-Tarek

An extraordinarily violent clan of warriors and religious zealots who preach the word of Hubal at swordpoint. Calling themselves the **Desert Jackals**, they are nomads of the Aramla El-Nar (the Desert of Fire), warring constantly against the "decadent and unclean" Salifah. They're so terrifying that the Hassanids always consult with them before making important decisions. The arrival of an Ibn Tufiq prince in a town is quickly followed by inquisition, the righting of wrongs, and purges and death.

- ❖ **Attribute and Skill Bonuses:** STR +1; Combat Training +1, Fighting +1, Prayer +1.
- ❖ **Suggested Path:** One of the paths of Tufiq, Servant of Tarek, such as the Walkers on Bloodied Feet (page 18).

### The Clan of Mimun, Servant of Tarek

#### Bint Mimun Abd-al-Tarek

This clan, dominated by women, was founded by Mimun, the originator of an exotic magical art called the **Kitaba Nader** or the Book of Essences (page 256). Its devotees, called the **Paper Virgins,** practice their art by stealing the bodily essences of their victims to make magical concoctions capable of manipulating their minds and behaviours. Zealots like the Ibn Tufiq, the Bint Mimun are artist-courtesans who voluntarily embark upon lives of corruption to bring the decadent cities of Jazirat down from within. Male Paper Virgins exist just as well as female, although they are perhaps lower profile...

The Ibn Mimun also field agents who adopt the roles of pimps and organised gangs working for the Paper Virgins. They are fiercely opposed to the Salifah (see page 14, above).

- ❖ **Attribute and Skill Bonuses:** CHA +1; Assassination +1 or Flattery +1, Sacred Word +1, Stealth +1.
- ❖ **Suggested Path:** One of the paths of Mimun, Servant of Tarek, such as the Beloved of Agushaya (page 19).

## The Clan of Yazid, Servant of Tarek

### Ibn Yazid Abd-al-Tarek

The founder of the third Tarekid clan is a distant descendant of Mustafah, one of the three disciples of Tarek. Yazid and his followers are mad mystics who live in caves and practice extreme forms of meditation and asceticism deep in the Desert of Fire. Most members are lone pilgrims, or small groups found in Jazirati cities. Following their leader's example, they have an unsettling stare that seems to justify rumours that the Ibn Yazid have been gifted with strange powers of revelation. They oppose the Ibn Tufiq, from whom they originally descended.

- ❖ **Attribute and Skill Bonuses:** CHA or DEX +1; Prayer +1, Sacred Word +1, Survival +1.
- ❖ **Suggested Path:** One of the paths of Yazid, Servant of Tarek, such as the Sand Preachers (page 19).

## The Tribes of the Shiradim

Physically and culturally close to their Saabi cousins, the Shiradim pray to a single deity: Shirad, the One But Many God. The Shiradi tribes were long persecuted by other peoples, and always fought to keep their dignity; the most obvious examples are the Great Exile from Kh'saaba to Capharnaum, led by Mogda, and the founding of the city of Jergathine (now known as Sagrada—see page 183).

### The Tribe of the Ashkenim

The Ashkenim are the elite warriors of the Shiradim. Their way of combat is almost like a dance, graceful but deadly. The most fearsome among them perform a "dance of death" which follows the rhythms of the sacred texts of the One God to find divine inspiration.

- ❖ **Attribute and Skill Bonuses:** CHA or DEX +1; Elegance +1, Fighting +1, Save Face +1.
- ❖ **Suggested Path:** One of the paths of the Ashkenim, such as the Red Lions of Shirad (page 19).

### The Tribe of the Pharatim

Priests, scholars, teachers: the Pharatim are that and much more. They are the living memory of the Shiradim, the guardians of the holy words of the One God, who created the Jazirati alphabet to transcribe Shirad's commandments.

- ❖ **Attribute and Skill Bonuses:** INT +1; History & Peoples +1, Instruction +1, Science +1.
- ❖ **Suggested Path:** One of the paths of the Pharatim, such as the Heavenly Voice of Shirad (page 19).

### The Tribe of the Salonim

The Salonim are renowned physicians who take the Oath of Salone, a sacred bond to heal the children of Shirad and protect them from all ills. If the physicians apply the first part of their Oath (to heal), the second (to protect from all ills) is sometimes used by certain Salonim to create poisons and deal out death.

- ❖ **Attribute and Skill Bonuses:** INT +1; Assassination +1, Science +2.
- ❖ **Suggested Path:** One of the paths of the Salonim, such as the Sacred Heart of Shirad (page 20).

## The Agalanthian City-States

Once upon a time, the Agalanthians dominated the lands and seas, thanks to their now-forgotten science, a gift of the dragons. Jazirat, like everywhere else in the known world, was under their dominion. But, one day, three hundred years ago, when their Empire was already in its long decline, their capital of flamboyant Therema collapsed. Faced with the wrath of the gods, the Agalanthians' pride was laid low. The Empire fragmented, so that now there remain only independent city-states experimenting with ideas of democracy.

### The City-State of Therema

The ancient Agalanthian capital, it's said that Therema trains the best elite soldiers in the Empire. It's known for its theatres, its monuments to the glory of the gods, its senate, and its circus games, but also for its old town, drowned by the swamp in the cataclysmic earthquake of 5666 and now in the hands of beggars.

- ❖ **Attribute and Skill Bonuses:** DEX +1; Elegance +1, Fighting +1, Riding +1.
- ❖ **Suggested Path:** One of the military schools of Therema, such as the Order of the Thereman Myrmidons (page 20).

### The City-State of Fragrance

The city of spices and perfumes is located in Capharnaum, and is the oldest Agalanthian bastion in Jazirati lands. Left partly ruined by the Holy Crusade of the Quarterians, the "Gateway to the East" is still the city of pleasures. The greatest charioteers in the world are trained here.

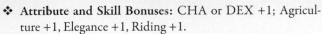

- **Attribute and Skill Bonuses:** CHA or DEX +1; Agriculture +1, Elegance +1, Riding +1.
- **Suggested Path:** One of the military schools of Fragrance, such as the Fragrantine Charioteers' School (page 20).

### The City-State of Etrusia

An island city where East meets West, where Jazirat meets Al-Fariq'n, Etrusia is a colourful city blessed by the gods. It's even said some of the gods were born here! It's famous for its schools of sorcery and its fine wine.

- **Attribute and Skill Bonuses:** CHA or CON +1; Agriculture +1, Elegance +1, Endurance +1.
- **Suggested Path:** One of the Agalanthian mystical-philosophical sorcery schools, such as the Etrusian Bacchantes (page 21).

# The Quarterian Kingdoms

The execution by quartering of the hero Jason by the Agalanthians some centuries ago, and especially the fact that he survived the execution attempt, inspired certain individuals so much that a new religion was born—a new religion that shook many lands and peoples to their foundations and led to the emergence of a new form of civilisation. Worshipping Jason the Quartered God, the Son of Aether and Mira, the people of the West are now organised into three feudal kingdoms, who recently attacked Capharnaum on a quest for the mortal remains of the Son of Aether, Jason the Undefeated. Although peace has returned and the Holy Crusade is over, many Quarterians remain in Jazirat. Sagrada is currently in their hands.

## Aragon

A people inhabiting the southernmost of the western lands, Aragonians are accustomed to arid country, rocky mountains and great journeys on horseback. As pious as they are brave and proud, they are horse tamers and great horsemen, loving riding to war just as much as their noisy family gatherings, where wine flows deep into the night, and wives and sisters abandon themselves to the dance of the wild Gitanilla.

- **Attribute and Skill Bonuses:** CHA or DEX +1; Agriculture +1, Elegance +1, Riding +1.
- **Suggested Path:** The Aragonian academy of the Duellists of San Llorente de Valladon (page 21).

## Orkadia

A unified empire for only the last two centuries, Orkadia is made up of many petty kingdoms. Although the centre is civilised, the outskirts, long exposed in the east to Agalanthian attacks, and in the north to the cold and the raids of the Krek'kaos barbarians, are a patchwork of brutal and bloodthirsty tribes. Tough warriors used to the harsh climate, Orkadians are one of the most fearsome peoples of the known world.

---

### Jaziya the Demon Huntress! Step 1(a): Jaziya's Blood

*Sarah decides Jaziya will be Saabi, from the Tarekid tribe. Wanting a bit of social and religious rebelliousness, she decides she'll be from the clan of Yazid. This means her full formal name will be Jaziya Bint Yazid Abd-al-Tarek. Looking at the write-up for the clan of Yazid, she writes down the following bonuses on her character sheet: DEX +1 (Jaziya's more of a fighter than a preacher!), Prayer +1, Sacred Word +1, Survival +1.*

---

### First Path Abilities and Lighting Up Constellations

*The path your character follows provides you with certain special abilities. In the following section, we present the first such ability provided by each path, used by characters (Dragon-Marked or not) at the beginnings of their careers. Collectively we're calling these the **first path abilities**. Each path has five more abilities, presented in the complete descriptions of the paths on page 81, which your characters may learn during play.*

*Note that all first path abilities must be **activated** in play in order to make use of them, by rolling at least three identical numbers on a dice roll, known as **lighting up a constellation** (page 48). If you don't roll three such numbers, you may spend one point (or "star") of one of your heroic virtues (see page 22) to make up the difference. For example, if you only rolled two identical dice, you may spend 1 star of heroic virtue to light up the constellation; if you didn't even roll doubles, you may spend 2. The specific heroic virtue you spend depends on the first path ability in question, described below. Note that each point of heroic virtue may comprise up to five stars: when you've spent five stars in a level, your heroic virtue score drops by 1. Starting characters begin with heroic virtue scores as determined on page 22, and zero stars; as soon as they spend a single star in a virtue, that heroic virtue score drops by one, and they then have 5 stars in that score.*

- **Attribute and Skill Bonuses:** CON or STR +1; Athletics +1, Fighting +1, Survival +1
- **Suggested Path:** The Orkadian academy of the Order of Saint Gerda Dragonslayer (page 22).

### Occidentia

The central lands of the West are also the most advanced and civilised. Famous for their sophistication, literature and wines, the Occidentians were also the instigators of the attack on Sagrada, at the initiative of King Simeon IV, supported by the Quarterian Magister (page 289).

- ❖ **Attribute and Skill Bonuses:** INT or STR +1; Agriculture +1, Elegance +1, Save Face +1.
- ❖ **Suggested Path:** The Occidentian academy of the Order of the Temple of Sagrada (page 22).

# FIRST PATH ABILITIES OF THE SAABI

Reserved for the Saabi elite, the following paths are organisations whose members are drawn almost exclusively from the three Great Tribes.

## The Fire Scimitars

### Path of Malik, Servant of Hassan

- ❖ **Social Status:** Your character is a *mujahid* sacred warrior and member of the royal family; you should determine your degree of proximity to the king in discussion with Al-Rawi. Being close to the king will give you great responsibility and power, but leave you with little freedom for adventuring.
- ❖ **Attribute Bonus:** DEX +1.
- ❖ **Skill Bonuses:** Athletics +1, Fighting +1, Sacred Word +1.
- ❖ **First Path Ability:** The Fire Scimitar *mujahid* is a war dancer, a combat fury capable of whirling into melee as fast as a flame, dealing wounds without ever being touched. If you're in combat against more than two **Babouche-Draggers** or **Valiant Captains** (page 65) and you light up a constellation on an attack action where you take out at least one opponent, you automatically take out an additional number of opponents equal to your Bravery score. Note that this does not apply to the powerful opponents called **Champions**.
- ❖ **Heroic Virtue:** Bravery.
- ❖ **Style:** As catlike as you are strong, you unite strength and finesse in all your gestures. Elegant even when wounded, you're as much lion as monkey.

## The Alchemists of Men

### Path of Mussah, Servant of Hassan

- ❖ **Social Status:** *Al-kimyat* sorcerer and man of science.
- ❖ **Attribute Bonus:** INT +1.
- ❖ **Skill Bonuses:** Sacred Word +1, Science +1, Willpower +1.

- ❖ **First Path Ability:** You're an *al-kimyat* sorcerer, plying your trade in classrooms, universities, gardens and palaces. Whenever you light up a constellation when using magic for social purposes (helping, healing, reconciling people, etc), you gain a magnitude bonus on your dice roll (page 46) equal to your CHA score.
- ❖ **Heroic Virtue:** Loyalty.
- ❖ **Style:** Charismatic and poised, you're a determined humanist, often even altruistic. You have goodness in your eyes and your gestures express kindness. As a symbol of wisdom, you usually sport a large, elegantly braided beard, its tip dyed with henna.

## The Suspicion of Traitors

### Path of Rashid, Servant of Hassan

- ❖ **Social Status:** *Mujahid* sacred warrior and bodyguard.
- ❖ **Attribute Bonus:** INT +1.
- ❖ **Skill Bonuses:** Assassination +1, Elegance +1, Stealth +1.
- ❖ **First Path Ability:** As a *mujahid* of the Suspicion of Traitors, you can detect traitors and assassins. If you suspect someone, you may make an INT + Assassination roll (page 27) with a difficulty equal to 3 times the Assassination score of the target, plus 6 (Assassination x 3 + 6).

 On a success, you confirm your suspicions about the target. If you light up a constellation (page 48), you also gain a result bonus on your Active Defence roll, or a bonus to your Passive Defence (page 55), equal to your Loyalty score in combat against that target at any point in time thereafter.

Note that your suspicions are always directed at those you **suspect** of being a possible traitor. You may not make this roll when facing someone you already know to be a confirmed enemy. The path requires great concentration, and may only be attempted against any given target once per game session.

❖ **Heroic Virtue:** Loyalty.
❖ **Style:** The best bodyguards, like the best assassins, are unsuspected. You have no specific style, no distinctive signs. You appear to be a courtier, adventurer, or soldier, just like anyone else.

## The Saffron Dunes

### Path of Yussef, Servant of Salif

❖ **Social Status:** *Al-kimyat* sorcerer and master trader.
❖ **Attribute Bonus:** INT +1.
❖ **Skill Bonuses:** Flattery +1, Sacred Word +1, Unctuous Bargaining +1.
❖ **First Path Ability:** If you light up a constellation on an opposed Unctuous Bargaining roll to sell something (food, jewels, palaces...), the price you receive is increased by +50%. If you light up a constellation on an Unctuous Bargaining roll to buy something, the price you pay is reduced by -50%.
❖ **Heroic Virtue:** Faith.
❖ **Style:** You dress richly and with many jewels, each one larger than the other. You wear a gold signet ring representing a dune, by which everyone can identify you as a member of the path.

## The Children of the Souk

### Path of Aziz, Servant of Salif

❖ **Social Status:** No particular honorific status (mercenary or thief).
❖ **Attribute Bonus:** CHA +1.
❖ **Skill Bonuses:** Intrusion +1, Stealth +1, Thievery +1.
❖ **First Path Ability:** As a Child of the Souk, if you light up a constellation on a difficulty 9 INT + Thievery roll when attempting to set up a robbery, ambush or any other risky, secret, but not necessarily illegal operation (freeing a hostage, relieving a Prince of Thieves of his goods, etc.) in urban territory, you may recruit in half a day a number of henchmen equal to your CHA score multiplied by your Loyalty

(CHA x Loyalty). The henchmen will be reliable, working for your cause and only asking for a share of the take (Al-Rawi's discretion).

❖ **Heroic Virtue:** Loyalty.
❖ **Style:** You have no particular style; you prefer dark clothes, and a veil hiding your hair and cheeks but not your face.

## The Walad Badiya

### Path of Khalil, Servant of Salif

❖ **Social Status:** *Mujahid* sacred warrior and adventurer.
❖ **Attribute Bonus:** DEX +1.
❖ **Skill Bonuses:** Fighting +1, Riding +1, Storytelling +1.
❖ **First Path Ability:** In combat, you ride an *abzul* (a huge, reptilian steed—see page 307) with which you form a single being—the Walad Badiya. If you light up a constellation when attacking or defending, you may:
  ❖ Add the STR of your abzul to your damage (if attacking); against Babouche-Draggers (page 65), double your magnitude instead.
  ❖ Subtract your abzul's DEX from the damage you suffer, as long as you're performing an Active Defence (see page 54).
❖ **Heroic Virtue:** Bravery.
❖ **Style:** You live, sleep and eat in the saddle of your abzul. You wear symbolic tattoos on your faces, shoulders and arms, reinforcing your bond with your saurian half. The spear, a good weapon for mounted combat, is your preferred weapon.
❖ **Special:** You should also create statistics for the abzul that is your mount and alter-ego. See page 308.

## The Walkers on Bloodied Feet

### Path of Tufiq, Servant of Tarek

❖ **Social Status:** *Mujahid* sacred warrior and bedouin.
❖ **Attribute Bonus:** STR +1.
❖ **Skill Bonuses:** Fighting +1, Intimidate +1, Prayer +1.
❖ **First Path Ability:** In combat, you may use your Prayer skill instead of Fighting for all your attack and defence actions. If you light up a constellation when doing so, you gain a damage bonus to any damage you do on your attack, or a result bonus on your Active Defence roll, equal to your Faith score.
❖ **The main disadvantage of this path is that, by using your Prayer skill in combat, you may not specialise in a weapon (see "Specialisation and Expertise", page 74), unlike when you use the Fighting skill.**
❖ **Heroic Virtue:** Faith.

- **Style:** You have the fearsome custom of chopping off your victims' private parts and shoving them in their mouths when they're dead. No one messes with you lightly.

## The Beloved of Agushaya

### Path of Mimun, Servant of Tarek

- **Social Status:** *Al-kimyat* sorcerer and Paper Virgin (page 254).
- **Attribute Bonus:** CHA +1.
- **Skill Bonuses:** Acting +1 or Poetry +1 or Music +1, Flattery +1, Thievery +1.
- **First Path Ability:** As an artist, courtesan, lover and killer of the Beloved of Agushaya, you worship the Goddess of Love and War, the source of your power. During lovemaking, if you light up a constellation on a CHA + Flattery roll against a difficulty equal to 3 times your partner's INT (INT x 3), you gain 1 point of temporary Heroism (to a maximum of 6) which must be spent in the current session.
- **Heroic Virtue:** Faith.
- **Style:** You devote your life to pleasure, both intellectual and physical. You frequent places of culture as well as classes and bathhouses. Your only distinguishing mark, other than your uncommon beauty or handsomeness, is a small dot tattooed at the base of your spine.

## The Sand Preachers

### Path of Yazid, Servant of Tarek

- **Social Status:** Wandering near-heretic *mujahid* sacred warrior.
- **Attribute Bonus:** INT +1.
- **Skill Bonuses:** Athletics +1, Prayer +1, Survival +1.
- **First Path Ability:** When you commit a "hands-on" assassination (stabbing, garrotting, slitting the throat, etc, but not poisoning), you may use your Prayer skill instead of Assassination. If you light up a constellation, you gain a damage bonus equal to twice your Faith score (Faith x 2).
- **The main disadvantage of this path is that, because you attack with your Prayer skill instead of Assassination, you may not specialise (see "Specialisation and Expertise" on page 74).**
- **Heroic Virtue:** Faith.
- **Style:** You affect an ascetic, spartan style, devoid of any sign of wealth.

# FIRST PATH ABILITIES OF THE SHIRADIM

Paths are as sacred to the Shiradim as they are to the Saabi. However, they're not considered to be the inventions of men and women, but rather interpretations of Shirad's commandments pertaining to war, learning and magic. They're official cults, whose more eminent members play political roles in Shiradi society. This makes them strict and sacred institutions which are difficult to join.

## The Red Lions of Shirad

### Ashkenim Path

- **Social Status:** A *macchabah*, a holy warrior of Shirad and elite soldier.
- **Attribute Bonus:** DEX +1.
- **Skill Bonuses:** Combat Training +1, Fighting +1, Prayer +1.
- **First Path Ability:** By means of a quick prayer at the beginning of combat (a free action—see page 50), you may enter a mystical trance making your combat actions (even magical ones) more effective. If you light up a constellation on a difficulty 9 CON + Prayer roll, you gain a result bonus on all your combat actions, whether for attack, defence, movement, casting spells, and so on, equal to your Faith score.
- **Heroic Virtue:** Faith.
- **Style:** Highly coloured, the raiment of the Red Lions of Shirad contrasts sharply with the usual modesty of the Shiradim. You prefer purple clothes and gold jewellery, especially earrings and pearl eyebrow studs.

## The Heavenly Voice of Shirad

### Pharatim Path

- **Social Status:** A *kahan* priest and popular, recognised sage.
- **Attribute Bonus:** CHA +1.
- **Skill Bonuses:** History & Peoples or Science +1, Instruction +1, Sacred Word +1.
- **First Path Ability:** You can extract a fact or anecdote from the accumulated knowledge of centuries at your disposal, to help you answer a question or solve a problem. If you light up a constellation on a roll of INT + History & Peoples or INT + Science, you gain a result bonus equal to your Faith score on any dice rolls made that day to solve the problem, which may relate to military strategy (Command), diplomacy (any of the Prince archetype skills—see page 26), survival (Endurance, Survival), medical treatment (Science), and so

on. In rare cases these may even be combat or sorcery rolls, but Al-Rawi should take care that this path doesn't become systematically abused in this manner: it's about receiving a flash of insight to solve a major problem, not a trick to be used to enhance your own attack action successes.

- ❖ **If the problem isn't solved the same day, you must make a new roll the next day if you want to benefit from the bonus again.**
- ❖ **Heroic Virtue:** Faith.
- ❖ **Style:** You have a tattoo in the palm of your left hand depicting the sun of knowledge (a symbolic rather than religious representation, which doesn't transgress the Shiradi dogma prohibiting iconic portrayals of god).

## The Sacred Heart of Shirad

### Salonim Path

- ❖ **Social Status:** A *kahan* priest and popular physician.
- ❖ **Attribute Bonus:** INT +1.
- ❖ **Skill Bonuses:** Science +3, or Science +2 and Stealth +1 (see Special, below).
- ❖ **First Path Ability:** If you light up a constellation when making a Science roll to operate on a wounded person, diagnose a disease, or heal anyone (page 70), you gain a result bonus equal to your Loyalty score.
- ❖ **Heroic Virtue:** Loyalty.
- ❖ **Style:** You have a tattoo over your heart depicting the sun of knowledge (a symbolic rather than religious representation, which doesn't transgress the Shiradi dogma prohibiting portrayals of god).
- ❖ **Special:** If you choose a +2 Science and +1 Stealth instead of a +3 Science, you are expert at using your knowledge of medicine and the human body to cause death. In this case, Al-Rawi has more details for how you can develop your character (see page 344).

# FIRST PATH ABILITIES OF THE AGALANTHIANS

The Agalanthian city-states, although they no longer enjoy the splendour and greatness of yore, still have reputations for excellence. In part, this is due to their **schools**, whose teachings often rest upon millennia of experience. Unlike Jazirati paths, Agalanthian schools are open to everyone, as long as families can afford to pay their children's tuition fees. It's not uncommon to see schools recruit from the masses by organising tournaments and contests, where youths from the four corners of the known world fight to secure places in these prestigious institutions.

## The Thereman Myrmidons

### Agalanthian School of the City-State of Therema

- ❖ **Social Status:** Elite *myrmidon* legionary.
- ❖ **Attribute Bonus:** DEX +1.
- ❖ **Skill Bonuses:** Combat Training +1, Command +1.
- ❖ **First Path Ability:** You're a *myrmidon*, a member of an elite unit founded during the ages of Agalanthian glory and a terrifyingly effective warrior. If you light up a constellation on a CON + Combat Training roll with the intention of obtaining bonus dice (page 49) for a round, you gain additional bonus dice equal to half your Heroism score (round down).
- ❖ **Heroic Virtue:** Loyalty.
- ❖ **Style:** Legend says the first myrmidons were soldier ants that Cthonos transformed into men to defend the gates of hell. Some escaped into the mortal world and founded this order. This is why, when you create a myrmidon character, you're presented with a suit of **myrmidon armour** (page 64), black armour which evokes an insect's shell or carapace and which contributes to your fearsome reputation for being a demonic insect!

## The Fragrantine Charioteers

### Agalantian School of the City-State of Fragrance

- ❖ **Social Status:** A talented celebrity, a popular idol, and an object of fascination for the rich.
- ❖ **Attribute Bonus:** DEX +1.
- ❖ **Skill Bonuses:** Flattery +1, Riding +2.
- ❖ **First Path Ability:** If you light up a constellation when performing a Charge Attack (page 53) when driving your chariot, it takes you only 2 actions instead of 3 (page 56)!
- ❖ **Heroic Virtue:** Bravery.
- ❖ **Style:** Your school has no distinctive sign. However, as a charioteer, you'll often wear the colours of your stable or sponsor, or even your owner if you're a slave. You have access to a chariot (you may even own one!)—see page 56 for what to do with it.

## The Etrusian Bacchantes

### Agalanthian School of the City-State of Etrusia

- ❖ **Social Status:** A popular sorcerer, hermit, and drunk.
- ❖ **Attribute Bonus:** CON +1.
- ❖ **Skill Bonuses:** Agriculture +1, Flattery +1, Sacrifice +1.
- ❖ **First Path Ability:** As a bacchant, debauchery, alcohol and the decadent arts are your main concerns. Transcending mere ecstasy, your devotion to these activities lets you draw upon an energy which simplifies your practice of magic. If you light up a constellation on a CHA + Flattery roll during an orgy, or on a CON + Endurance roll during a drunken debauch, you receive a result bonus equal to your Faith score to all subsequent Sacred Word rolls. This bonus lasts a number of hours equal to the constellation die (so if you roll three 2s, the bonus lasts 2 hours).
- ❖ **Heroic Virtue:** Faith.
- ❖ **Style:** As a bacchant, you're probably overweight, with the stigmata of alcoholism (a blotchy complexion, red nose, etc).

# FIRST PATH ABILITIES OF THE QUARTERIANS

For many years the Quarterian peoples were nothing more than geographical neighbours, worshipping different gods and waging hereditary wars to obtain the tiniest territorial advantages. Although some of their academies today derive from ancient traditions and date back centuries, most are recent. This is the case for the three academies described below. Military orders as much as prestigious schools, they're the preserve of the nobility, or those the nobility sponsor. To join a Quarterian academy, you must be of noble Quarterian extraction, or must have accomplished a glorious feat (your choice) granting you membership.

## Common Paths

There are many more paths than are presented here. Some of these are described in other **Capharnaum** products. You can even create your own; if you're interested in doing so, take a look at the "Common Paths" section on page 98 for ideas and guidelines.

## Jaziya the Demon Huntress! Step 1(b): Jaziya's Path

Next, Sarah decides that Jaziya will follow the path of Yazid, the Sand Preachers, recommended for a character from her clan. She notes down the bonuses for INT +1, Athletics +1, Prayer +1, and Survival +1. She also jots down her first path ability, as well as her social status: a wandering mujahid zealot with almost heretical beliefs. She notes that her Faith will be her replacement heroic virtue (meaning she can burn stars of Faith to make up dice when she needs to light up a constellation to activate her path ability—see page 73).

## The Duellists of San Llorente de Valladon

### Aragonian Academy

- ❖ **Social Status:** *Hidalgo* (the nobility of the sword) or *campeador* (the nobility of the cape), depending upon how you view your character. See page 285 for more.
- ❖ **Attribute Bonus:** DEX +1.
- ❖ **Skill Bonuses:** Agriculture +1, Fighting +1, Riding +1.
- ❖ **First Path Ability:** If you light up a constellation when attacking with a whip, you may immediately make a second attack against the same target with another weapon (a sword, axe, spear, fist, etc.) as a **Free Attack** (page 53). This second weapon need not have been readied: drawing the weapon is part of the free action. The attack is resolved as part of the same action as the whip attack. If you aren't in range for this second attack (for example, a whip is longer than a dagger or a sword), then the move to close range is also free and takes place in the same action. If your target is out of range of the whip attack (about 3 paces or 15 feet), then this ability may not be used.
- ❖ **Heroic Virtue:** Loyalty.
- ❖ **Style:** You often wear a theatre mask depicting a weeping face. Otherwise, you wear the tattoo or face-painting of a tear beneath your left eye (on the side of the heart, the symbol of sincerity).

## The Order of Saint Gerda Dragonslayer

### Orkadian Academy

- ❖ **Social Status:** Knight.
- ❖ **Attribute Bonus:** STR +1.
- ❖ **Skill Bonuses:** Combat Training +1, Fighting +1, Intimidate +1.
- ❖ **First Path Ability:** You can draw upon Saint Gerda's strength to promote justice. If you light up a constellation in combat, you gain a damage bonus equal to your STR score (this is in addition to your usual STR damage bonus, ie you add STR twice).
- ❖ **Heroic Virtue:** Bravery.
- ❖ **Style:** You brand yourself with the Quarterian cross, usually on the wrist, although you may also choose to wear the mark on your forehead. If you're especially fanatical or fervent, you may bear an enormous brand on your back.

## The Order of the Temple of Sagrada

### Occidentian Academy

- ❖ **Social Status:** Knight Monk.
- ❖ **Attribute Bonus:** DEX +1.
- ❖ **Skill Bonuses:** Fighting +1, Prayer +1, Sacred Word +1.
- ❖ **First Path Ability:** As comfortable with matters of war as with the magical uses of the Holy Scriptures, if you light up a constellation on either a combat roll (whether an attack or a defence) or on a Sacred Word roll, you gain a magnitude bonus equal to your Faith score.
- ❖ **Heroic Virtue:** Faith.
- ❖ **Style:** You're both a knight and a monk, and wear the religious tonsure as well as the heavy armour of the warrior. Your military raiment is finished with a tabard bearing the red cross of your order.

# STEP 2: HEROIC VIRTUES

The four **heroic virtues** quantify the dramatic qualities of your character. There are four such virtues: Bravery, Faith, Loyalty, and Heroism. Each has a score, ranging from 1 to 6 for the Dragon-Marked, and from 1 to 3 for normal mortals. Heroic virtue scores may vary during play. They're important not only for indicating how your character is viewed in society, but also for influencing your **path abilities** (page 73).

## The Heroic Virtues

### Bravery

Bravery measures your behaviour in the face of danger. A high Bravery score indicates a character who doesn't hesitate to take risks in combat and place himself at risk for others.

### Faith

Faith measures your devotion and religious observance. Do you pray? Do you sacrifice to the gods? Do you go out of your way to spread the faith?

### Loyalty

Loyalty measures your devotion to your clan, ancestors, family, city, and so on, as well as to your adventuring companions (Dragon-Marked or not).

---

### Jaziya the Demon Huntress! Step 2: Jaziya's Heroic Virtues

*Sarah wants to be able to activate her path ability when she doesn't roll enough constellation dice, so she puts as many points as she can into her Faith heroic virtue. Moreover, she decides that, because Jaziya doesn't have many friends right now, she's probably not the type to sacrifice herself for strangers. Sarah notes down that Jaziya's Faith is 5, her Loyalty is 2, and her Bravery is 3. Averaging these three values, her Heroism score is 3.*

### Heroism

Your Heroism score is calculated. It's the average of the three heroic virtues mentioned above, rounded down. Heroism is recalculated at the start of each session of play, and is used to determine the number of **Adventure Points** (see page 78) you gain. It also plays a role in the calculation of **Hit Points** (page 42), and limits how much your character can **swagger** (page 49) when performing an action.

Sometimes you may spend points of Heroism in play. This is the case when you consult **Urim and Turim**, the "Stones of Fate" (page 77), when you activate certain path abilities (page 16), and when you wish to avoid major wounds (page 67), environmental damage (page 67), and encumbrance penalties (page 78).

## Calculating Your Heroic Virtues

When creating a Dragon-Marked character, you have 10 points to divide between Bravery, Faith, and Loyalty, with a minimum score of 1 and a maximum of 6. Your Heroism score is equal to the average of these three scores, rounded down; that means beginning characters will usually have a Heroism score of 3.

## Summary of Step 2

a. Distribute 10 points between Bravery, Faith, and Loyalty, with a minimum score of 1 and a maximum of 6.
b. The average of your Bravery, Faith, and Loyalty, rounded down, is your Heroism score. This is usually 3 for beginning characters, unless your scores were modified in Step 5 (page 35).

# Step 3: Attributes

All characters have five **attributes**: Strength, Constitution, Dexterity, Intelligence, and Charisma. We usually abbreviate these as STR, CON, DEX, INT, and CHA, to make them easily distinguishable from the names of skills (see below).

Attributes represent your character's inner faculties, the things you didn't have to learn. An attribute is something you "are"; a **skill**, described below, is something you "know". You can say "My character is smart!", meaning he has a high Intelligence (INT) score, but he may have never set foot in a university. On the other hand, you can say "My character knows a lot of stuff!", meaning he has a high Science or History & Peoples skill; he may be as thick as a brick, but at least he studied at school.

The same analogy applies to your character's physical capabilities. You can say "My character is strong!", meaning he has a high Strength (STR) attribute; and "My character can handle himself in combat", meaning he has a high Fighting skill.

These two aspects are often linked, of course: educated characters may be intelligent, and characters who are good at combat may be strong.

When you create your character, you begin with a score of 1 in each of your five attributes. You then have 6 points to distribute between them, in addition to any attribute bonus you may have received in Step 1 (page 8). At this point, you may not raise any attribute above 4.

## Summary of Step 3

a. Assign 1 point to each of your five attributes (Strength, Constitution, Dexterity, Intelligence, Charisma).
b. Then, allocate 6 additional points between them, and add any bonuses gained from your blood and path in Step 1. No attribute score may exceed 4 at this point.

## Strength (STR)

Strength measures your character's raw power, striking force, and your ability to inflict damage.

| WHAT YOUR STRENGTH MEANS... | |
|---|---|
| **SCORE** | **DESCRIPTION** |
| 1 | You have the sleek body of a bureaucrat or academic. You can lift a whole waterskin of water, sometimes without breaking a sweat. |
| 2 | You're average. You can lift one and a half times your weight. |
| 3 | You can fight shirtless without being ashamed. Your sword blows are starting to hurt, too. |
| 4 | You have some pretty muscles rippling under that tunic! You've everything it takes to make a village wrestling champion or a good city guard. |
| 5 | You've all the muscle necessary to make a good blacksmith. Metal almost twists itself in your hands. |
| 6 | Some people just get called "one-punch" or "iron-fist". With this level of strength, you've a more than impressive set of muscles. In fact, you're so big and strong it's cold in your shadow. |

# Constitution (CON)

Constitution measures your character's resistance to pain and wounds, your defence against disease, and your capacity just to keep going before exhaustion sets in. Sometimes it also determines your pugnaciousness and determination.

| WHAT YOUR CONSTITUTION MEANS... | |
|---|---|
| SCORE | DESCRIPTION |
| 1 | You can run almost a full league non-stop, in only an hour. |
| 2 | You're average. You can run one league in half an hour without stopping. Even partying all night before a long day's desert march is not beyond your grasp. |
| 3 | As a child, you asked your friends to throw stones at you to see if it hurt. |
| 4 | You're like an Agalanthian athlete! Untiring, solid as a rock, never too cold, never too hot. |
| 5 | Whenever anyone needs a messenger to run between two cities more than ten leagues apart right in the middle of a war, they come to you. |
| 6 | Five minutes underwater wrestling with a kraken? Bring it on! |

# Dexterity (DEX)

Dexterity measures your character's coordination, speed, agility, and suppleness.

| WHAT YOUR DEXTERITY MEANS... | |
|---|---|
| SCORE | DESCRIPTION |
| 1 | You're not really used to using your body, although you can usually survive a village dance. |
| 2 | You're average, but you'll need a bit of training if you're going to participate in any tournaments. |
| 3 | Now you're starting to worry your opponents. Your admirers love the way you roll your hips. |
| 4 | Your sword is your favourite possession. It feels the same way about you. |
| 5 | You have the soul of an acrobat or duellist! |
| 6 | Walking a tightrope over the city rooftops while dodging missiles from every angle? Let's do this! |

## Jaziya the Demon Huntress! Step 3: Jaziya's Attributes

*Jaziya's going to be a fighter, but Sarah decides she's going to emphasise her deftness and endurance above her simple ability to do damage. Her five attributes begin at a default score of 1, and then she adds her bonuses gained in Step 1. This gives her Strength 1, Constitution 1, Dexterity 2, Intelligence 2, Charisma 1. Now she allocates her 6 points, noting that no attribute may exceed 4. She favours Constitution, Dexterity, and Intelligence, which allow for a good Maximum Initiative score (page 51), but is also careful not to neglect her Strength, also key for fighters. She ends up with: Strength 2, Constitution 3, Dexterity 4, Intelligence 3, Charisma 1. To justify that low Charisma, Sarah declares Jaziya was scarred in a combat against a demonic monster!*

# Intelligence (INT)

Intelligence measures your character's reasoning, memory, and logical thinking, as well as the sharpness of your senses.

| WHAT YOUR INTELLIGENCE MEANS... | |
|---|---|
| SCORE | DESCRIPTION |
| 1 | You can follow the storytellers' tales, but you don't really see what they're getting at. |
| 2 | You're average. Bright enough to be a wandering adventurer, but you'll never be a great sorcerer. |
| 3 | You're attentive and have good powers of deduction. |
| 4 | You enjoy memorising stories and rearranging them as you see fit. |
| 5 | You're refined and sensitive, and no doubt a great writer! |
| 6 | They say great thinkers are often distracted—but you can read a mathematics treatise with one eye, learn a theatre play off by heart with the other, and still have your hands free to write a letter home to your mother. |

## Charisma (CHA)

Charisma measures your character's personal magnetism, charm, and beauty, but also how well you express yourself to those in front of you.

| WHAT YOUR CHARISMA MEANS… | |
|---|---|
| SCORE | DESCRIPTION |
| 1 | You're not the kind of person people would turn to in the street. |
| 2 | You're average, attractive enough to seduce a few people and maybe even marry someday. |
| 3 | Most of your one night stands will never forget your name. |
| 4 | Whenever you open your mouth, people just hang onto your words. Most never pass you by without turning to give you a look. |
| 5 | You're no stranger to fleeing from villages with a horde of jealous husbands or wives at your heels. |
| 6 | When they're not its creator, the gods are offended by such beauty! |

### Jaziya the Demon Huntress! Step 4(a): Jaziya's Archetype

*Sarah notes down her default skill points. Added to the skill points gained in Step 1, this gives her Endurance 1, Unctuous Bargaining 1, and Willpower 1, and a very good Prayer 3!*

*Next, Sarah ranks Jaziya's archetypes. Above all, Jaziya is a warrior (Warrior +3) and an adventurer (Adventurer +2), but in her demon-hunting work she also uses sorcery (Sorcerer +1). She often uses craft and even farming skills to survive (Labourer +1), and it's not rare for her to need to steal things, break into places she shouldn't, and even kill if she has to (Rogue +1). She's no woman of letters (Poet +0 and Sage +0), and while she kind of belongs to the Saabi nobility, she's more at home in the desert than in a palace (Prince +0).*

# STEP 4: ARCHETYPES AND SKILLS

As well as deciding on a path, which gives you social status (such as a mujahid, macchabah, al-kimyat, myrmidon, Templar or campeador), your character is also defined by his **archetype**. An archetype is a loose grouping of learned abilities known as **skills**. There are several archetypes, and your character's proficiency in the skills of each establishes a "portfolio" of the things you can do.

The archetypes are: the Adventurer, the Labourer, the Poet, the Prince, the Rogue, the Sage, the Sorcerer, and the Warrior. Each archetype grants access to four skills, and it's by choosing archetypes that your character gains proficiency in those skills.

Before selecting archetypes, every character automatically receives 1 point in each of the following skills: Endurance, Prayer, Unctuous Bargaining, and Willpower.

It's assumed that every character can count to 10 (more or less…), but that doesn't mean they know how to read and write! For most characters, counting beyond 10, calculating accurate accounts, and reading and writing are all actions measured by the character's lowest score in his skills of the Sage archetype. Characters for whom the Poet is the most important archetype aren't necessarily skilled in reading; they too must use their lowest Sage skill for reading, writing, and counting. However, characters for whom the Sage is their main archetype instead use their highest Sage skill for reading, writing, and counting.

When you create a character, you assign a number of points to the skills of certain archetypes. Start off by ranking all eight archetypes in descending order of how closely they match your character concept. For example, if you see your character as a noble warrior,

### Skill Scores

The score your character has in a skill corresponds to the following levels of proficiency.

- ❖ 0: You've no idea what you're doing.
- ❖ 1: You're a beginner.
- ❖ 2: You're an average professional (a labourer, soldier, university lecturer).
- ❖ 3: You're a qualified professional (a foreman, captain, professor).
- ❖ 4: You're the village champion in your skill.
- ❖ 5: You're exceptionally skilled.
- ❖ 6: You're a living legend, a founding master! Maybe you'll set up your own school and revolutionise the skill's use forever.

maybe rank the Prince archetype first, and the Warrior second. Do this for all eight archetypes, even those which aren't relevant to your character concept at all.

Then, increase the score in all the skills of your most important archetype by +3. In most cases, that just means the skill gets a score of 3; but if it already had a score of 1, it's now 4, and so on. Your skills in your next most important archetype are increased by +2, and the next **three** archetypes after that all increase their skills by +1. Finally, the skills of the final three archetypes gain no additional skill points at all, either remaining at 0, or perhaps higher if they received skill points from elsewhere. Note that at this stage none of your skill scores may exceed 5, even if you've already received skill points in Step 1 or elsewhere.

Note that if at this stage you end up with enough bonuses to take a skill score above 5, you can put those excess points to one side, and add them to the **freely distributed points** you may spend in Step 5 (page 35).

## Summary of Step 4

a. To begin with, increase the following skills by +1: Endurance, Prayer, Unctuous Bargaining, and Willpower.
b. Then, rank the eight archetypes in descending order of relevance to your character. Increase the skills belonging to those archetypes by +3, +2, +1, +1, +1, and then +0, +0, +0 respectively.
c. Total the scores in each of your skills, including any bonuses acquired in Step 1 (page 8). If any skill score exceeds 5 at this point, reduce it to 5 and set aside the excess points to use as **freely distributed points** in Step 5 (page 35).

## Archetypes and Skills

The skills associated with the eight archetypes are shown in Table 1-1: Archetype Skills, and are described below. Skills marked with an asterisk have special uses which are described in "Special Uses of Skills" on page 75.

| TABLE 1-1: ARCHETYPE SKILLS | |
|---|---|
| **ARCHETYPE** | **SKILLS** |
| The Adventurer | Athletics, Riding, Storytelling*, Survival. |
| The Labourer | Agriculture, Craft, Endurance*, Solidarity. |
| The Poet | Acting, Music, Oratory*, Poetry. |
| The Prince | Elegance, Flattery*, Save Face, Unctuous Bargaining. |
| The Rogue | Assassination*, Intrusion, Stealth, Thievery. |
| The Sage | History & Peoples, Instruction*, Notice, Science. |
| The Sorceror | Prayer, Sacred Word, Sacrifice, Willpower*. |
| The Warrior | Combat Training, Command, Fighting, Intimidate*. |

These skills and their uses are described below, together with suggestions for how they may be used in **dice rolls** together with certain attributes (see "Action Resolution" on page 45 and "Skill Rolls" on page 47), as well as suggested **specialisations** (see "Specialisation and Expertise" on page 74).

## Acting

The dramatic arts and their major forms, comedy and tragedy, were born in the lands of Agalanthia long ago, in sacrificial religious processions. Now there are a thousand forms of theatre throughout the world, from Agalanthian tragedies and comedies recounting stories of the gods and the problems of men and women, to the Quarterian mystery plays played in churches and public squares. Theatre is a very important part of society and culture.

Those mastering the arts of Acting can perform in public, play a role, and pass themselves off as someone else without ever showing their true personality.

- ❖ **CHA + Acting:** Used for seducing and manipulating others, or making them sad or happy.
- ❖ **DEX + Acting:** Used for disguising or applying make-up to yourself or another.
- ❖ **INT + Acting:** Used for lying, quoting theatrical texts, setting up a show and taking care of its staging and direction.
- ❖ **Specialisations:** Disguise, Dramaturgy, Fast Talk, Lying.

## Agriculture

Agriculture is a generic set of abilities allowing you to work the land as well as breed cattle and process associated products (dairy products, wines, vegetables, dried fruits).

- ❖ **CON + Agriculture:** Used for any long-term agricultural work, performed whether it rains or shines, the sands rise or the earth shakes.
- ❖ **DEX or STR + Agriculture:** Used for all manual labour requiring deftness or strength.
- ❖ **INT + Agriculture:** Used for helping a beast give birth, organising your planting, designing irrigation systems, distilling alcohol.
- ❖ **Specialisations:** Cattle Breeding, Fruit Plantations, Grains, Irrigation.

## Assassination*

Assassination is a vast domain which includes many areas of activity and knowledge, and is used for surreptitiously killing people in a variety of ways. It's also used to devise poisons (page 68), find their ingredients, and come up with the best ways for administering them to victims.

- ❖ **DEX + Assassination:** When your victim can't see you coming (see "Combat", page 50), you may use Assassination in the place of any weapon skill to make an attack. See also page 75.
- ❖ **INT + Assassination:** Used when learning or remembering a poison recipe, recognising and finding the plants or ingredients needed for a poison, and finally making that poison. A magnanimous Al-Rawi may let players use this skill to brew

a poison antidote or medicine at an increased **difficulty** (see **Chapter Two: Thalia – Word and Deed**, page 68).
- ❖ **Specialisations:** Poisoning, Strangling, Throat Cutting.

## Athletics

Athletics is the skill used when you push yourself to excel in your physical abilities, jumping from one rooftop to another, tumbling down a staircase without hurting yourself, dropping from a window right onto the back of your horse, breaking down a door and throwing a tree trunk while balancing on a clothesline, and any one of a number of other acrobatic tours de force. Note that for swimming you should use the Endurance skill instead.

- ❖ **CON + Athletics:** Used for long-distance running, and so on.
- ❖ **DEX + Athletics:** Used for acrobatics, jumps, and other body rolls.
- ❖ **STR + Athletics:** Used for ripping things up, lifting, breaking things down and smashing them apart, as well as short-distance sprints (covering a distance equal to DEX x 2 + STR x magnitude in paces per action).
- ❖ **Specialisations:** Acrobatics, Climbing, Games and Feats of Strength.

## Combat Training

A warrior—whether a simple guard at the city gates, a passionate mujahid, or a gladiator—only survives if he seeks excellence through constant training. The many warriors who rest on their laurels and neglect their training and self-improvement don't last long. The Combat Training skill represents a character's level of fitness and combat training; a trained character fights better, is more effective, and can adapt better to combat situations.

Whenever you first determine initiative during a combat (page 51), a character with the Combat Training skill may make a difficulty 6 CON + Combat Training roll. Each point of magnitude provides a bonus die for a single use at any point in the conflict. The die may be used in any physical action at any moment in the fight: to attack, defend, run away, perform acrobatic feats, and so on.

The player is free to choose when and how many of his bonus dice he uses: there are no restrictions. If the combat ends without all the bonus dice being used, they're lost. If a character later begins a new combat, he may make another Combat Training roll.

- ❖ **CON + Combat Training:** All Combat Training actions are made with Constitution.
- ❖ **Specialisations:** Axes, Blades, Bludgeons, Exotic Weapons, Flails, Missile Weapons, Polearms, Thrown Weapons, Unarmed.

## Command

The art of command is everything in times of war. It lets you command the obedience of your men, elaborate a battle strategy, recognise an army's heraldry, evaluate enemy forces, analyse their movements, and more.

- ❖ **CHA + Command:** Used for talking to the troops to issue commands, give instructions, explain a strategy.
- ❖ **INT + Command:** Used to elaborate a strategy, recognise military units, analyse a war situation.
- ❖ **Specialisation:** Heraldry, Orders, Strategy.

## Craft

Like Agriculture, Craft is a generic suite of abilities for working metal, stone, clay, or even glass, cloth, and so on.

- ❖ **CON + Craft:** Used for long-term work performed come rain or shine, whether the sands rise or the earth shakes.
- ❖ **DEX or STR + Craft:** Used for manual labour requiring deftness or muscle power when building something.
- ❖ **INT + Craft:** Used to design new processes, repair weakness in items, evaluate the time required for a job.
- ❖ **Specialisations:** Armouring, Carpentry, Glass-Blowing, Masonry, Mosaics, Pottery.

## Elegance

Although for a peasant, a slave, or bedouin, being well-dressed matters little, the opposite is true for courtiers, merchants, and even artists. The Elegance skill lets you choose a perfume, dress well, and know how to behave properly in society.

- ❖ **CHA + Elegance:** Used to show refinement, speak in elegant language, display discernment and distinguished manners.
- ❖ **INT + Elegance:** Used to choose the right outfit, perfume, jewels, and other apparel for a specific situation.
- ❖ **Specialisations:** Dances, Fashion, Politeness.

## Endurance*

Whether you're a nomad or sedentary, a labourer or an adventurer, you're often faced with long ordeals of harsh weather, the biting sun, hunger and thirst. Resisting heat, marching come rain or shine, swimming through storms—all the challenges where the world conspires to drive you beyond the limits of your body and mind—are handled using the Endurance skill. It's also the skill to use if you're exposed to a disease or poison (see page 68) or if you need to heal more rapidly (see page 75).

Note that in general people don't swim for pleasure or sport, but to survive. That's why you use Endurance for swimming rather than Athletics.

## Languages

*In addition to his native tongue, any **Capharnaum** character automatically knows enough Saabi to survive in Jazirat. On top of that, he also speaks as many languages as his History & Peoples skill score. Choose your languages from Table 1-2: Languages.*

| TABLE 1-2: LANGUAGES | |
|---|---|
| **LANGUAGE** | **COMMENTS** |
| Agalanthian | Spoken by the Agalanthians. |
| Al-Fariqani | Spoken in Al-Fariq'n and by the Walad Badiya. |
| Asijawi | Spoken in far Asijawi and the lands of the farmost East. |
| Krekk | Spoken in the desolation of the Krek'kaos. |
| Manavi | Spoken in the dreaming kingdoms of Nir Manel. |
| Quarterian | Spoken in Aragon, Occidentia, and Orkadia, the Kingdoms of the West. |
| Saabi | Spoken by the Saabi; a common tongue for Jazirat. |
| Shiradi | Spoken by the Shiradim. |

- ❖ **CON + Endurance:** Used to test your resistance and toughness.
- ❖ **Specialisations:** Enduring Hunger and Thirst, Resisting Cold and Heat, Swimming.

## Fighting

The Fighting skill covers your ability to attack or defend yourself, whether it's using weapons or fighting unarmed. Anyone knowing how to fight even a little can use a sword, spear or bow, or even just his fists.

- ❖ **DEX + Fighting:** Most combat actions are performed with Dexterity (Strength contributes to the damage you do—page 56—and Constitution contributes to your hit points—page 42). See "Combat" on page 50 for more.
- ❖ **Specialisations:** Axes, Blades, Bludgeons, Exotic Weapons, Flails, Missile Weapons, Polearms, Thrown Weapons, Unarmed.

## Flattery*

Flattery is an art found everywhere in the world. It plays its part in the courtly games of princes, the haggling of merchants, the begging of slaves trying to avoid the lash. It's even part of the arts of love—see page 75. Flattery means saying what someone wants to hear to rub them up just the right way. Make a Flattery roll against a difficulty equal to your target's INT x 3, +6: success means you mollify them with a classy turn of phrase, a verbal dodge, an amusing or tender word. A jealous husband out for your blood will change his mind, the city guard will let you pass, and so on.

A target of a Flattery roll will almost always realise they've been duped, in the end. A clever prince who also plays the game may wait until the next opportunity to get his revenge, but a jealous husband may seek you out straight away and the guards may hunt you down. A **Normal Success** (magnitude 1—see page 46) lets you get away by the skin of your teeth, giving you a few minutes' head start, while a **Critical Success** (magnitude 6+) mollifies everyone involved until you make your next mistake—whenever that is.

Note that flattering someone to escape a bad situation is viewed as proof of cleverness. Using it to avoid combat isn't considered cowardice, and never entails the loss of Bravery points.

❖ **CHA + Flattery:** Used for seduction.
❖ **INT + Flattery:** Used to get out of tough situations by dint of fair language and well-placed word.
❖ **Specialisations:** Pleasant Language, Seduction.

*For example: Rashi Bar Pharat has been provoked into a duel with a Quarterian knight who is, by reputation, much more skilled than he is. He knows full well the combat is likely to go against him, so he decides to distract his opponent's attention with a trick. "It's very hot, sirrah, for a fight," he says, "and I must confess it would be impossible to defeat you without taking a refreshing herbal bath. And of course my weapon is much shorter than yours! I presume it won't displease you if a man in my condition has a last bath and buys a blade worthy to meet your own? Even assuming I can find one so far from your lands!"*

*The Quarterian knight has an INT of 4, so the difficulty is 18, not an easy target! But Rashi rolls a result of 19, gaining a reprieve from the knight, who is persuaded that our friend only wants to prepare himself so he can die with dignity. Rashi departs, with only a few minutes to leave the city (or hide in a hole no-one will come looking in) before the knight realises he's been duped and sends his men to hunt Rashi down!*

## History & Peoples

The history of the world, its peoples and lands, is so full of nooks and crannies that it will take many human lives to understand it all. A Dragon-Marked with the History & Peoples skill can hope to know some things, but never all the events related to an era, country, or person. This is a skill learned in universities and libraries, at the feet of pedagogues and philosophers.

❖ **INT + History & Peoples:** All History & Peoples rolls are made using Intelligence.
❖ **Specialisations:** Agalanthian Myths, Agalanthian Philosophers, Aragon, Carrassine, the Desert of Fire, Etrusia, Fragrance, Jergath the Great, Occidentia, Orkadia, the Saabi poets, Sagrada, the Shiradi Religion, Therema.

## Instruction*

Educating, transmitting, teaching, building a body of knowledge: the Instruction skill measures what a character knows of pedagogy and general didactics. Practically speaking, it lets you construct a rhetorical argument to convince someone. It's not about getting nervous, shouting or lying, but manipulating dialectical and cognitive mechanisms to lead an audience to a specific truth. An Instruction roll versus a difficulty determined by Al-Rawi (taking into account an audience's stubbornness or opposition) lets you convince that audience, change its mind, calm it down, get it on your side. You can also use it to open someone's mind to new realisations—see page 76.

❖ **INT + Instruction:** The Instruction skill only works with Intelligence.
❖ **Specialisation:** History, Philosophy, Politics, Science.

## Intimidate*

Sometimes you only have to play with appearances and fool someone's idea of you to get what you want. The Intimidate skill lets you calm the ardour of an overly-enthusiastic opponent, make an arrogant blackguard eat his words, even make honourless brigands flee. A STR + Intimidate roll against a difficulty equal to your target's INT x 3, +6, lets you put him in his place, making him less dangerous than a child, even as submissive as a slave. This may even be effective in combat—see page 76. At Al-Rawi's discretion, an NPC target may adopt one of the following attitudes:

❖ **Normal Success (Magnitude 1+):** An unimportant character will change his mind and depart, or even offer to help in return for forgiveness. An important character, enemy or not, will recognise the character's bravery and will confess with dignity that he is impressed. He may propose a debate, or may give the character a few minutes to escape, and so on.
❖ **Critical Success (Magnitude 6+):** An unimportant character will kneel, beg for forgiveness, and readily enter the character's service. A more important character will recognise the character as an equal and treat him as such.
❖ **STR + Intimidate:** Whatever action you take, it's the power of that action that counts, which is why Strength always intimidates.
❖ **Specialisations:** None. Intimidating someone is a primal, simple action.

- ❖ **INT + Music:** Used to compose music, or assess the quality of a composition or performance.
- ❖ **Specialisations:** Agalanthian Music, Quarterian Music, Saabi Music, Shiradi Music.

## Notice

*"The idiot can see, the sage can observe.*
*Everyone can hear—but who can listen?"*
This old Saabi saying well illustrates this skill. It's the ability to notice the tiny detail at the scene of a crime that lets you catch the murderer; to eavesdrop on a conspirators' conversation through a closed door; to find a secret door by feeling your way along a rugged wall; even to smell out a poison hidden in a dish of food.

- ❖ **INT + Notice:** All Notice rolls are made with Intelligence.
- ❖ **Specialisations:** One of the five senses, Spotting Ambushes, Spotting Architectural Faults, Spotting Clues, Spotting Traps.

## Oratory*

Speaking to an audience is one thing—inspiring it is another. A poet, actor, or other individual wanting to convey a powerful, lasting emotion to an audience uses this skill. It lets you inflame crowds, raise morale, give courage, and so on. See page 76 for special uses of this skill in combat.

- ❖ **CHA + Oratory:** Used to move, trouble, or excite an audience with poetry or beautiful tirades.
- ❖ **STR or CON + Oratory:** Used to give a speech in a powerful, imposing voice.
- ❖ **Specialisations:** Artistic Speaking, Military Speaking, Political Speaking.

## Poetry

Poetry is an art practiced by all peoples. Whether Agalanthian, Jazirati, Quarterian, or Shiradi, poetry is never considered a luxury, the preserve only of intellectuals: it's a living means of expression, written or oral, a noble and worthy activity regardless of your social class. Being able to speak poetically lets you infuse your words with philosophy and spirituality. It's the art of speaking well—and of being listened to well. The Poetry skill isn't a question of simply making up rhymes: it's knowing how to choose and deploy the most pertinent words and images for your situation. It includes the activities of writing poetry, novels, and plays.

- ❖ **CHA + Poetry:** Used to conduct a skillful debate, recite poetry, read a text aloud.
- ❖ **INT + Poetry:** Used to compose, appreciate, or fully understand the import of a work.
- ❖ **Specialisations:** Composition, Debate, Interpretation.

## Intrusion

A complement to the Stealth skill (page 33), Intrusion is the miraculous ability of the thief, assassin, and spy. It lets you quickly determine the best ways to penetrate or escape a building; actually break into that building; pick all sorts of locks; detect traps (even outdoors); and even fabricate, in just a few minutes, the basic tools to pick a locking mechanism. With this skill, your stylus becomes a skeleton key!

- ❖ **DEX + Intrusion:** Used to climb every rampart or wall built by man (finding cracks and faults), to slip into a gap only a cat could get through, bounce on a canopy, pick a lock.
- ❖ **INT + Intrusion:** Used to study a map of a building, detect a trap, fabricate a makeshift lockpick.
- ❖ **Specialisations:** Breaking and Entering, Contortion, Escape, Lockpicking.

## Music

Music is present in every culture, whether sung, instrumental, or both. This skill lets you perform as well as assess the quality of a composition or performance.

- ❖ **CHA + Music:** Used to sing or play an instrument.

## Prayer

Invoking and paying homage to the gods is an everyday act, perhaps even one of every moment. Depending on your culture, the smallest gesture, the most modest meal can be consecrated to the gods. None of this requires the Prayer skill: in truth, the gods care little for ritual, only faith.

Using the Prayer skill lets you perform the rituals of contrition, meditation, or devotion which permit your character to regain lost Faith points. You must spend at least half a day or night in prayer. The difficulty is generally 9, although it may be lower if you pray before icons, while burning incense, or if you do so in a temple or on holy ground. On a Normal Success (magnitude 1+), you recover all Faith points lost or spent during the current session; on a Critical Success (magnitude 6+), you recover all Faith points lost or spent during the current session, plus 1!

Note that:

❖ You can't regain Faith points you lost in a previous session.
❖ Prayer takes time, except when it's associated with certain path abilities (page 18), in which case the time required is mentioned in the ability description.
❖ **CON + Prayer:** Prayer is a time-consuming and physically draining activity, and is performed using Constitution.
❖ **Specialisations:** Agalanthian Faith, Quarterian Faith, and so on.

## Riding

In such a vast and varied world, there are numerous creatures you can ride. Use the Riding skill to ride and control any mount, whether it's a horse, camel, pegasus, or even abzul, and whether it runs, swims or flies. The Riding skill is also used for driving a chariot.

❖ **CON + Riding:** On long rides, Al-Rawi may decide Constitution should be rolled instead of Dexterity.
❖ **DEX + Riding:** The standard roll for riding a beast, galloping, and so on.
❖ **Specialisations:** Specific species of mount (Abzul, Camel, Horse), or a specific environment (Desert, Town) or vehicle (Chariot, Flying Carpet).

## Sacred Word

The Sacred Word skill is used by magicians and sorcerers of all cultures, to utter or write the magical terms required when casting spells (page 117).

❖ **INT + Sacred Word:** Used to cast a spell, improvise a spell, or memorise a formula.
❖ **Sub-spells:** Create, Destroy, Transform (see page 118).

## Playing a Sorcerer?

*Playing a sorcerer in* **Capharnaum – The Tales of the Dragon-Marked** *is simple. No one is ever either a "magic-user" or a "non-magic-user", but rather magic can—in principle—be used by anyone. Maybe you learned a recipe to heal minor ailments from your grandmother, or one or two tricks from your fencing master that help you in combat, without having had to devote your life to alchemy or sorcery.*

*Anyone with a Sacred Word skill of 1 or higher can cast a spell (lower than that and you're limited to magical-sounding babble). With a Sacred Word skill of 4 or higher, you're considered an accomplished professional.*

*If you're a Quarterian, Saabi, or Shiradi character, here's what your Sacred Word skill represents:*

❖ *If your Sacred Word skill is at least 1, you know one of the three sacred words (Create, Destroy, or Transform—see page 117). At a skill of 3, you learn a second word; and at a skill of 6, you learn the third.*
❖ *You know a number of* **magical elements** *(page 119) equal to twice your Sacred Word skill. For example: if you have a Sacred Word skill of 4, you know 2 words and 8 magical elements.*

❖ *The sacred words and magical elements you know must be chosen from those linked to your character's blood (see page 122).*
❖ *Your magic works by combining sacred words and magical elements. For lots more on this, see* **Chapter Four: Terpsichore – Magic and Sorcery** *(page 112).*

*If you're an Agalanthian character, here's what your Sacred Word skill represents:*

❖ *If your Sacred Word skill is 1 or 2, you may choose three chiromancy spells of difficulty 9 or less, and two spells of difficulty 12 or less (a total of five spells). See page 141.*
❖ *If your Sacred Word skill is 3 or 4, you may choose four chiromancy spells of difficulty 9 or less, and three spells of difficulty 12 or less (a total of seven spells).*
❖ *If your Sacred Word skill is 5 or 6, you may choose four chiromancy spells of difficulty 9 or less, two spells of difficulty 12 or less, and one spell of difficulty 15 or less (a total of seven spells).*
❖ *Note that if you prefer to select specific spells as a Quarterian, Saabi, or Shiradim character, instead of using the default Tarmel Haja "combination magic" system for these bloods, you may also calculate the number of spells you know in this way. See page 128 for more on this possibility.*

## Sacrifice

All *Capharnaum's* religions use the idea of "sacrifice" in some way, to represent the offerings they make to their gods to appease them or win their support. Often a sacrifice involves a precise ritual during which an animal is slaughtered (or even a person, among some Agalanthians!). You need a Sacrifice skill of at least 1 to know these basic rites. You may attempt a Sacrifice roll no more than once per week.

Make a Sacrifice roll when you want to gain a blessing from a god affecting one or more targets. The difficulty of the roll depends on the number of targets to be affected, as shown on Table 1-3: Sacrifice Difficulties.

| TABLE 1-3: SACRIFICE DIFFICULTIES | |
| --- | --- |
| NUMBER OF PERSONS AFFECTED | DIFFICULTY |
| 1 | 9 |
| 5 | 12 |
| 10 | 15 |
| 20 | 18 |
| 40 | 21 |
| 80 | 24 |
| 160 | 30 |

On a Normal Success on the Sacrifice roll, the very next time the target (or targets) rolls a Critical Failure (whatever the roll), the result will instead be a Normal Failure. On a Critical Success, the very next time the target rolls a Critical Failure, the result will be a Normal Success instead.

The Sacrifice difficulty may be reduced by describing the complex rituals and the inclusion of specific ingredients or components such as icons, incense, henna, drugs, virgins, rare animals, and so on. Performing a Sacrifice in a temple or on holy ground may also reduce the difficulty. In any case, the difficulty may never be reduced by more than 2 steps on Table 1-3: Sacrifice Difficulties.

Note that if the target you want to "bless" with a Sacrifice roll belongs to a different religion than that of the god you're sacrificing to, the difficulty is increased by 2 steps.

❖ **CON + Sacrifice:** Like Prayer, Sacrifice is a time-consuming and physically demanding ritual, and so is performed using Constitution.

❖ **Specialisations:** Agalanthian Faith, Quarterian Faith, and so on.

## Save Face

Whether a simple peasant or a philosopher, a slave or a knight, no one takes a duel lightly. For everyone, a one-on-one fight is a question of honour and the nobility of one's soul (which is why this skill is linked to the Prince archetype). When two people face off, whether in a ritual or in an improvised combat, and whether strict rules are followed or not, the important thing is not winning, but not losing face.

The Save Face skill gives you the panache to ensure that the confrontation you've just failed in will nevertheless show you in a positive light in the history books. Whether it's a warrior's duel (using Fighting), a sporting event (using Athletics), or even a verbal joust between poets (using Poetry or Acting), if you fail in that combat or confrontation, you may follow up with a CHA + Save Face roll against a difficulty determined by Al-Rawi (and depending on how badly you failed, with a minimum of 6). If your Save Face roll succeeds, your character manages to turn the situation to his advantage: everyone witnessing the bout will be convinced you let your opponent win (for whatever reason), and will have no doubt you won the duel. You also gain 1 point of Bravery for each swagger die you take on the Save Face roll.

Sometimes failure makes you stronger: it's all a question of philosophy and class.

❖ **CHA + Save Face:** All Save Face rolls are made with Charisma.

❖ **Specialisations:** Armed duel, athletic duel, verbal joust, and so on.

## Science

As vast as it is exciting, science never ceases to move forward, asking questions, making discoveries always as surprising as they are terrifying. Although sometimes seemingly advanced (surgery, mathematics, astronomy), the science of the peoples of *Capharnaum* is nevertheless in its infancy, and the boundaries between its fields are not always clear.

❖ **DEX + Science:** Used to operate on the wounded, make a practical application of a specific field of science, or administer a healing potion.

❖ **INT + Science:** Used to diagnose a disease, recognise a plant, know the life cycle of a species of animal, the names of the constellations, the anatomy of a supernatural creature; to analyse the ecosystem of a mirage.

❖ **Specialisations:** Life Sciences (botany, geology, medicine, surgery, zoology), Physical Sciences (astrology, chemistry, cosmic eggs (page 272), mathematics, physical phenomena), Spiritual Sciences (demonology, life after death, mirages, psychology).

## Solidarity

Even if you don't have a penny to your name or are completely powerless, you still have friendship and contact with other people, their recognition and trust. The workers of the world live according to an unspoken code of mutual assistance. There are no written rules, no organisations; just a shared feeling of reciprocal duty and obligation.

## General knowledge or not?

Sometimes you'll need to choose between *Storytelling* and *History & Peoples* to determine what a character knows.

*Storytelling* is about travels, the common folk, trivial knowledge. When you make camp, the *Storytelling* skill tells you a prince that once stopped here fell in love with the most beautiful woman he'd ever seen. He followed her into the desert in the middle of the night, and three days later they found his sunburned body: the woman was an evil mirage, and she continues to seduce weak and lustful men to this day. However, using the *History & Peoples* skill tells you that this permanent camp was set up by order of Raiss Sulem Ibn Assali in the year 2037, to provide a base for his caravans crossing the desert.

Anything to do with daily life and trivia, things you can learn by word of mouth on the street, in a tavern or oasis, falls under the *Storytelling* skill. Anything requiring reading, study, enrolling in an academy or university—that's *History & Peoples*.

Wherever he is, a Labourer character may attempt a difficulty 9 Solidarity roll to find temporary lodgings, a roof for the night, a meal, even a job. This skill also allows you to perceive the relationships and tensions which exist in a group of labourers. When you create your character, you also total your Solidarity skill and Heroism score, and use those points to select **contacts** (page 42).

- ❖ **CHA + Solidarity:** Used to find shelter, quickly obtain work, or receive a meal in return for a service.
- ❖ **INT + Solidarity:** Used to recognise the leader of a group, to study a mafia-like network among a group of workers.
- ❖ **Specialisations:** A type of craft, workers of the land, and so on.

## Stealth

Whether you're a thief, spy, or simple slave, sometimes you need to know how to make yourself scarce. To hide in the shadows or behind the drapes, to approach someone noiselessly or attack someone from behind without the victim having any chance to react; these are all uses of the Stealth skill. Stealth also includes interpersonal discretion: knowing when and how to hold your tongue, to release information parsimoniously, to avoid committing indiscretions and to know how to turn an interrogation to your favour.

- ❖ **CHA + Stealth:** Used to redirect someone's attention or change the direction of a conversation.
- ❖ **DEX + Stealth:** Used to hide, sneak, and so on.

- ❖ **INT + Stealth:** Used to analyse an area to find a place to hide, to control your breathing, to know just how much or how little information to give someone, to find a hidden person or item.
- ❖ **Specialisations:** Camouflage, Concealment, Interrogation, Sneaking.

For example: After stealing a magnificent scimitar from a market of the Al-Dhumma medina in Carrassine, the young thief Oda Ibn Aziz Abd-al-Salif has been arrested by militiamen of the VII Legion. Having already disposed of the weapon (sold to a travelling merchant, who paid her well for it), Oda can't reveal where the item is without betraying her oath of sale. So, she has to be discreet. Al-Rawi states the militia have no eyewitnesses and can't formally arrest her, but they suspect her, and their questions become increasingly insistent. She sets the difficulty at 15. Oda's player decides the thief tries to mislead her interrogators by using Intelligence, but she prefers to rely on her Charisma to mollify them. Al-Rawi grants a Stealth roll based on CHA, and Oda's player rolls a result of 19: Oda's feigned candour convinces the militia without resorting to violence! They won't bother her about this theft again.

## Storytelling*

Tales are a traveller's friends. They gather people by the fire, trading stories which mix personal experience, popular culture, and waking dreams. Storytellers are found in all cultures, representing the common knowledge of those who have travelled, spoken, and listened. Al-Rawi may ask for Storytelling rolls to test a character's general knowledge; she'll never give them precise historical details (they'll need a History & Peoples roll for that), but she can reveal rumours about a prince, a caravan, a legend of the sands.

The Storytelling skill isn't an exact science, but a measure of popular cultural knowledge, representing legends as much as facts.

- ❖ **CHA + Storytelling:** Used to tell stories to entertain an audience. See page 76 for using this skill to boost morale.
- ❖ **INT + Storytelling:** Used to test general knowledge, to remember local stories and folklore.
- ❖ **Specialisations:** Local Customs, Rumours, Tales and Legends.

## Survival

In a world filled with wild beasts and frightening creatures, dark princes and malevolent sorcerers, adventure is at every corner, behind every dune, lying in wait in the shade of every oasis. The Survival skill lets you survive and find your bearings in all these environments. You can recognise the roots and spices that heal minor ailments, as well as the plants you can eat; you can track and hunt an animal, catch it in a trap and build a fire to cook it. Survival lets

*Having ranked her archetypes, Sarah now figures Jaziya's skills. These are as follows:*

- **Adventurer (+2):** *Athletics 3 (1+2), Riding 2, Storytelling 2, Survival 4 (1+1+2).*
- **Labourer (+1):** *Agriculture 1, Craft 1, Endurance 2 (1+1), Solidarity 1.*
- **Poet (+0):** *Acting 0, Music 0, Oratory 0, Poetry 0.*
- **Prince (+0):** *Elegance 0, Flattery 0, Save Face 0, Unctuous Bargaining 1 (1+0).*
- **Rogue (+1):** *Assassination 1, Intrusion 1, Stealth 1, Thievery 1.*
- **Sage (+0):** *History & Peoples 0, Instruction 0, Notice 0, Science 0.*
- **Sorcerer (+1):** *Prayer 4 (1+1+1+1), Sacred Word 2 (1+1), Sacrifice 1, Willpower 2 (1+1).*
- **Warrior (+3):** *Combat Training 3, Command 3, Fighting 3, Intimidate 3.*

*Al-Rawi notes that Jaziya's Sacred Word skill is above 0, which means she knows at least a little sorcery. As her skill score is 2, this means she needs to select a single Sacred Word, and a number of elements (page 119) equal to twice her Sacred Word skill (so, 4 in this case). As Jaziya is a demon hunter, Sarah chooses the Sacred Word "Create" and the elements "Courage", "Demon", and "Jahannam" in the Phantasmal World and "Flames" in the Mundane World (see page 123 for much more on these terms). Sarah already sees herself using sorcery to resist the fear caused by demons (Create + Courage) and to banish them back to hell using driving sheets of flame (Create + Flames + Demons + Jahannam). There are lots of other combinations she can come up with, too, but for now these two will doubtless come in useful.*

you find water, predict storms, navigate by the stars, treat fractures and staunch wounds (see "Health and Wounds" on page 67).

- **INT + Survival:** All Survival actions are informed by common sense, prudence and vigilance, so are made using Intelligence.
- **Specialisations:** First Aid, Herbalism, Hunting, Navigation & Orienteering.

## Thievery

All acts that can be considered thieving are grouped under this skill. From simple shoplifting and pickpocketing, to an ambush

*Sarah adds 2 points to each of Athletics and Fighting, raising them to 5. She spends her final points on Notice, increasing it to 1—this can prevent many an unpleasant surprise!*

with a gang, or cheating at gambling, this skill covers a wide field of activity.

- **DEX + Thievery:** Used to cut purses, pick pockets.
- **INT + Thievery:** Used to know about gangs and organised crime, to plan an ambush, organise a protection racket, spot a well-filled purse.
- **Specialisations:** Armed Robbery, Knowing Gangs, Pickpocketing.

## Unctuous Bargaining

Without a doubt, trade is the one field of human endeavour which truly unites the peoples of the world and causes them to forget their warlike concerns. One people always needs the foods produced by another and, since before there was ever any such thing as war, such needs drove people to communicate.

The Unctuous Bargaining skill lets you evaluate the fair value of an item (even gems and works of art), and haggle over their prices with other merchants. It also lets you communicate in a "trade tongue" of words and signs cobbled together from every culture in the world. With this skill, an Agalanthian who doesn't speak a word of Shiradi can communicate with companions belonging to that group, and a Quarterian lost in the desert can ask the way and trade with Saabi nomads.

- **INT + Unctuous Bargaining:** All Unctuous Bargaining rolls are made with Intelligence.
- **Specialisations:** Evaluating Artworks, Evaluating Common Items, Evaluating Gems, Selling.

## Willpower*

Whether viewed as an act of faith or the simple force of one's will, this skill represents the raw inner strength a character draws upon to combat supernatural attacks. It is used by sorcerers to perceive and resist magic, by priests to perform exorcisms, and by common mortals to survive supernatural attacks. Willpower is a mental, spiritual, inner ability, the metaphysical equivalent of the Endurance and Notice skills. See page 76 for using it to defend yourself against magic.

For more details on how to use Willpower, see **Chapter Four: Terpsichore – Magic and Sorcery** (page 118).

- ❖ **INT + Willpower:** All Willpower rolls are made with Intelligence.
- ❖ **Specialisation:** Perceiving (Quarterian, Shiradi, etc) Magic, Resisting (Quarterian, Shiradi, etc) Magic.

# STEP 5: FINISHING TOUCHES

In this last step, you have the chance to give your character some final touches. You may determine his wealth and possessions, calculate his Hit Points and his Maximum Initiative, and roll one or more events to highlight his destiny.

## Freely Distributed Points

The world is vast and its paths winding; two characters born in the same place and following the same teachings will never end up exactly the same. You may now freely distribute 5 points among your character's skills, as long as you don't allocate more than 2 points to the same skill and no skill is ever raised above 5.

If you set aside any skill points in previous steps, add those to your freely distributed points now.

## Your Legend

Now it's time to fill in some colourful details of your Dragon-Marked character's past life. Use the **Legend Tables** below to generate dramatic snippets for your character's story—things he or she did or which happened before you start play. These snippets shouldn't contradict or distort how you imagine your character, so feel free to adapt them to your character concept. If in doubt, talk it over with Al-Rawi.

Roll on the Legend Tables four times:

- ❖ **Roll 1:** Roll the dice twice on the table for your character's blood (Saabi, Quarterian, etc—see page 36) and incorporate the results into your story. If you follow a path which isn't of your blood, roll once on the table for your blood, and once on the table for the blood matching the path you follow.

*For example: If your Saabi character follows the teachings of a Quarterian Academy, roll once on the Saabi table and once on the Quarterian table.*

- ❖ **Roll 2:** Roll the dice once on the table for your character's main archetype (page 38) and incorporate the results into your story.
- ❖ **Roll 3:** Roll the dice twice on Table 1-16: Legendary Archetypes. Each roll will indicate which table to roll on next. Incorporate the results of those rolls into your story.
- ❖ **Roll 4:** Roll the dice once on Table 1-17: Legends of the Dragon Mark.
- ❖ Note that if the result of a Legend roll would take one of your skills above 5, or one of your attributes above 4, and the text of the legend doesn't explicitly say you can do so, you should roll again.
- ❖ Note also that increases in Heroism or heroic virtues refer to complete levels of that virtue, instead of stars.

Some Legend roll results are marked with an asterisk (*). One asterisk (*) means that you also gain one **level 1 contact**; two asterisks (**) means you gain one **level 2 contact** (page 42).

## Roll 1: The Legend of Your Blood

Roll the dice twice on the table for your character's blood (Saabi, Quarterian, etc—see page 13) and incorporate the results into your story. If you follow a path which isn't of your blood, roll once on the table for your blood, and once on the table for the blood matching the path (page 17) you follow.

| TABLE 1-4: LEGENDS OF AGALANTHIAN BLOOD | |
|---|---|
| 2D6 | YOUR LEGEND |
| 2 | You went on pilgrimage to the place where Agalanth was spared by the gods. Increase your Faith by +1. |
| 3 | You spent part of your childhood serving as an apprentice and servant in a temple. Increase Prayer or Sacrifice by +1.* |
| 4 | Your parents were slain by Orkadian pirates and you were raised by an important representative of your school (see page 17). Increase your Loyalty by +1.** |
| 5 | Your spent part of your childhood as an official servant to a master of your school. Gain an intimate and unfailing bond to that master, and increase one of the skills your school favours by +1.** |
| 6 | You fought in the arena to save the innocent. Increase your Bravery by +1.* |
| 7 | In your youth you took part in chariot races. Increase your Riding skill by +1. |
| 8 | You have a distant Thereman origin. Increase your Fighting skill by +1. If your blood is already Thereman, roll again. |
| 9 | For a few weeks, months, or years, you belonged to a theatre troupe. Increase your Acting, Poetry, or Music by +1.* |
| 10 | You have a distant Fragrantine origin. Increase your Elegance skill by +1. If your blood is already Fragrantine, roll again. |
| 11 | For a few weeks, months, or years, you worked as a horse groom in a charioteer stable (increase your Agriculture skill by +1), or as a masseur / perfumer for the racers (increase your Flattery skill by +1).* |
| 12 | You have a distant Etrusian origin. Increase your Riding or Survival skill by +1. If your blood is already Etrusian, roll again. |

| TABLE 1-5: LEGENDS OF QUARTERIAN BLOOD | |
|---|---|
| 2D6 | YOUR LEGEND |
| 2 | You made a pilgrimage to the Magisterium. Increase your Faith by +1. |
| 3 | You spent part of your childhood performing in a church choir. Increase your Prayer skill by +1.* |
| 4 | Your family was ravaged by the plague, and you were raised by an important member of your academy. Increase your Loyalty by +1.** |
| 5 | You spent part of your childhood as an official servant to a master of your academy (see page 17). Gain a +1 bonus to one of the skills your academy favours.** |
| 6 | You led an expedition in hostile territory to save your family from starvation. Increase your Bravery by +1.* |
| 7 | In your youth, you took part in a Quarterian purge (a massacre of unconverted pagans, a Shiradim hunt, a witch hunt, etc). Increase your Sacrifice skill by +1. |
| 8 | You have a distant Aragonian origin. Increase your Riding skill by +1. If your blood is already Aragonian, roll again. |
| 9 | During a voyage to Al-Ragon, you distinguished yourself in a battle against the Saabi. Increase your Command skill by +1.** |
| 10 | You have a distant Orkadian origin. Increase your Athletics skill by +1. If your blood is already Orkadian, roll again. |
| 11 | During a voyage to Orkadia, you took part in a long voyage (trading, military, exploratory) in the icy and hostile northern lands. Increase your Survival skill by +1.* |
| 12 | You have a distant Occidentian origin. Increase your Elegance skill by +1. If your blood is already Occidentian, roll again. |

| TABLE 1-6: LEGENDS OF SAABI BLOOD | |
|---|---|
| **3D6** | **YOUR LEGEND** |
| 3 | You made a pilgrimage to the ruins of the Village of the Prophets (page 181). Increase your Faith by +1. |
| 4 | You were the personal servant of a *kahini* for most of your childhood. Increase your Prayer skill by +1.** |
| 5 | Your parents were slain by raiders. You were raised by an important member of your path. Increase your Loyalty by +1.** |
| 6 | In the name of your path, you took part in a reconciliation or conflict mission between Jergath the Great and one of the Caravan Kingdoms. Increase one of the skills favoured by your path by +1.** |
| 7 | You crossed the lands of a djinn unarmed to prove your love to another. Increase your Bravery by +1. |
| 8 | Whether by obligation or choice, you travelled for a time with the *Califah-al-Sahla* (the "Caravan of Purification" of the Tarekids—see page 254). Increase your Sacrifice skill by +1.* |
| 9 | You have a distant Hassanid origin. Increase your Combat Training skill by +1. If your blood is already Abd-al-Hassan, roll again. |
| 10 | You worked for a time at a military school in Jergath. Increase your Fighting or Command skill by +1.* |
| 11 | You have a distant Salifah origin. Increase your Elegance skill by +1. If your blood is already Abd-al-Salif, roll again. |
| 12 | You once lived in Jergath or another large Saabi city. Increase your Unctuous Bargaining skill by +1.* |
| 13 | You have a distant Tarekid origin. Increase your Assassination skill by +1. If your blood is already Abd-al-Tarek, roll again. |
| 14 | You lived a nomadic life among the bedouins for a time. Increase your Survival skill by +1.* |
| 15 | You lived in a Saabi enclave in Aragon (or "Al-Ragon"—see page 286) for a time. Increase your Agriculture, History & Peoples, or Storytelling skill by +1.* |
| 16-18 | You fought against the Holy Crusade during the Quarterian invasion. Increase your Endurance skill by +1. |

| TABLE 1-7: LEGENDS OF SHIRADI BLOOD | |
|---|---|
| **2D6** | **YOUR LEGEND** |
| 2 | You made a pilgrimage to the Temple of Sagrada. Increase your Faith by +1. |
| 3 | You spent part of your childhood as a servant of a *kahan*. Increase your Prayer skill by +1.** |
| 4 | Your parents were slain by Abd-al-Tarek raiders, and you were taken in by your path brothers and sisters. Increase your Loyalty by +1.* |
| 5 | You spent part of your childhood as an official servant of a sage of your path (see page 17). Gain a +1 bonus in one of the skills favoured by your path.** |
| 6 | You crossed the territory of a djinn unarmed to prove your love to another. Increase your Bravery by +1. |
| 7 | You were persecuted by Quarterian or Saabi zealots. Increase your Endurance skill by +1. |
| 8 | You have a distant Pharati origin. Increase your Instruction skill by +1. If your blood is already Pharati, roll again. |
| 9 | You took part in the defence of Sagrada during the Holy Crusade of the Quarterians. Increase your Fighting skill by +1. |
| 10 | You have a distant Ashkeni origin. Increase your Save Face skill by +1. If your blood is already Ashkeni, roll again. |
| 11 | You lived in a Shiradi enclave in the West. Increase your Flattery skill by +1.** |
| 12 | You have a distant Saloni origin. Increase your Assassination skill by +1. If your blood is already Saloni, roll again. |

## Roll 2: The Legend of Your Archetype

Roll once on the table for your character's main archetype (page 25) and incorporate the results into your story.

| TABLE 1-8: ADVENTURER LEGENDS | |
|---|---|
| **2D6** | **YOUR LEGEND** |
| 2 | You own a rare and mysterious item (a flying carpet, magic lamp, etc). Discuss this with Al-Rawi and select an item from **Chapter Nine: Melpomene – Gamemastering Capharnaum**). |
| 3-4 | You competed in athletics contests in a large city. Increase your Athletics skill by +1. |
| 5-6 | You took part in a famous riding contest or race (across the desert, a chariot race). Increase your Riding skill by +1.* |
| 7-8 | You survived a dangerous voyage. Increase your Survival skill by +1. |
| 9-10 | You crossed the desert with strangers, who became friends. Increase your Storytelling skill by +1.* |
| 11-12 | You made a fabulous voyage around the known world. Increase your Storytelling and Survival skills by +1. |

| TABLE 1-9: LABOURER LEGENDS | |
|---|---|
| **2D6** | **YOUR LEGEND** |
| 2 | You were a slave, but were freed for your devotion and determination. Increase your CON by +1. |
| 3-4 | You worked in the Hanging Gardens of Carrassine (or some other structure of the same magnitude). Increase your Agriculture skill by +1. |
| 5-6 | You served with one of the greatest craftsmen in Fragrance. Increase your Craft skill by +1.* |
| 7-8 | You were in the service of a lord of Sagrada, and travelled a lot and held many jobs. Increase your Solidarity skill by +1.** |
| 9-10 | You were forced to work in a water mill, a galley, or mine. Increase your Endurance skill by+1. |
| 11-12 | You own a workshop or a small manufactory. Increase your **Wealth Level** (page 42) by +1.* |

| TABLE 1-10: POET LEGENDS | |
|---|---|
| **2D6** | **YOUR LEGEND** |
| 2 | You have read the Agalanthiad (or some other fundamental work), in the form of a very old manuscript, perhaps dating from the time of its original writing, which was owned by an old thespian (now deceased). The text disappeared with him. Increase your Charm skill by +1. |
| 3-4 | You performed in the play of a great writer, or took part in poetry duels, during a very important festival. Increase your Oratory skill by +1. |
| 5-6 | You saved a whole village from being massacred, thanks to your fast talking. Increase your Acting skill by +1.* |
| 7-8 | You wrote a theatre play or epic poem which had a measure of success. Increase your Poetry skill by +1. |
| 9-10 | You were part of a famous troupe of wandering artists. Increase your Music skill by +1.* |
| 11-12 | You own a musical instrument whose sound puts to sleep animals of a specific species in 1D6 seconds. Work out which species with Al-Rawi: it could be cats, canines, reptiles, etc—anything except for abzulim! |

| TABLE 1-11: PRINCE LEGENDS | |
|---|---|
| **2D6** | **YOUR LEGEND** |
| 2 | You own a trading guild or another company or association which brings you money without you having to lift a finger. Increase your **Wealth Level** (page 42) by +2.* |
| 3-4 | You were a courtier in one of the great cities of your country. Increase your Save Face skill by+1.* |
| 5-6 | You were an ambassador, consul, or another representative of your lord or king, in a foreign land. Increase your Elegance skill by +1.* |
| 7-8 | You were one of the favourites of your prince or princess. Increase your Flattery skill by +1.* |
| 9-10 | You protected and administered a large amount of wealth for your tribe or kingdom. Increase your Unctuous Bargaining skill by +1.* Your **Wealth Level** (page 42) is now 4! |
| 11-12 | You are—or were—the lord of a region, master of a palace, or chieftain of a lesser clan. Increase your Flattery and Unctuous Bargaining skills by +1.** Increase your **Wealth Level** (page 42) by +1, or raise it to 5, whichever is higher! |

## Table 1-12: Rogue Legends

| 2D6 | Your Legend |
|---|---|
| 2 | You found a treasure, robbed a rich trader, or set up a prostitution and protection ring that brings you money without you having to lift a finger. Increase your **Wealth Level** (page 42) by +1.* |
| 3-4 | You assassinated a rich and famous individual. Increase your Assassination skill by +1. |
| 5-6 | You organised the hijacking of a large caravan. Increase your Thievery skill by +1. |
| 7-8 | You were a spy for a lord or a rich merchant. Increase your Stealth skill by +1.** |
| 9-10 | You escaped from a terrible prison, such as a Quarterian dungeon or Agalanthian labyrinth. Increase your Intrusion skill by +1. |
| 11-12 | You served the interests of a criminal network while infiltrating a lord's household. Increase both your Intrusion and Stealth skills by +1.** |

## Table 1-13: Sage Legends

| 2D6 | Your Legend |
|---|---|
| 2 | You've read a manuscript from the Time of the Prophets (or from the time of Jason for the Quarterians, or the Republic for Agalanthians), which was owned by a now-dead sage. The text disappeared with him. Increase your INT by +1. |
| 3-4 | You travelled in the company of a famous Shiradi physician. Increase your Science skill by +1.* |
| 5-6 | You studied in an Agalanthian university. Increase your Instruction skill by +1. |
| 7-8 | You assisted a historian in the composition of an encyclopaedic treatise. Increase your History & Peoples skill by +1.* |
| 9-10 | You were the physician and/or confidant of a prince or princess. Increase both your Flattery and Poetry skills by +1.** |
| 11-12 | You were the physician and/or lover of a prince or princess. Increase both your Elegance and Flattery skills by +1.** |

## Jaziya the Demon Huntress! Step 5(b): Jaziya's Legend

*Sarah rolls 3D6 twice on Table 1-6: Legends of Saabi Blood, and gets the following results:*

❖ *You were the personal servant of a kahini for most of your childhood. Increase your Prayer skill by +1.***
❖ *You have a distant Hassanid origin. Increase your Combat Training skill by +1. If your blood is already Abd-al-Hassan, roll again.*

*This gives her Prayer 5 and Combat Training 4.*

*Rolling 2D6 on Table 1-15: Warrior Legends, Sarah gets:*

❖ *Whenever you're in danger, you emit a faint purple aura, coming from your Dragon Mark. Increase your Intimidate skill by +1.*

*This gives her Intimidate 4.*

*Sarah rolls 1D8 twice on Table 1-16: Legendary Archetypes, and gets 3 (Poet) and 5 (Rogue). Rolling 2D6 each on Table 1-10: Poet Legends and Table 1-12: Rogue Legends, she gets:*

❖ *You were part of a famous troupe of wandering artists. Increase your Music skill by +1*.*
❖ *You escaped from a terrible prison, such as a Quarterian dungeon or Agalanthian labyrinth. Increase your Intrusion skill by +1.*

*This gives Sarah's character Music 1 and Intrusion 2.*

*Finally, Sarah rolls 3D6 on Table 1-17: Legends of the Dragon Mark and gets a 9:*

❖ *A mysterious figure follows you everywhere: a desert-dweller, dressed in black with a face hidden by a silvered veil. You only catch glimpses of this elusive figure—at the turn of a street, on the top of a dune—but you feel a strange bond. Increase one Adventure or Labourer skill of your choice by +1, which may exceed the usual maximum of 5.*

*Wishing to optimise a little, Sarah increases her Athletics to 6!*

*Sarah now links all these legends to Jaziya's back story as a wandering demon hunter. As the daughter of a kahini, Jaziya seemed destined to become a temple servitor. However, she was also the bastard great-granddaughter of a famed Hassanid mujahid, whose family had no male heir, and so by royal decree she was sent to a Hassanid military academy. Insubordinate and rebellious, she was flogged and sentenced to death by starvation in a hellhole prison cell buried twenty feet underground, but managed to escape. Using an assumed identity, she hid for a year in a troupe of wandering artists until, one day, a mysterious silver-veiled figure appeared to her. Since then, the Dragon Mark on her back has lit up with a strange aura whenever danger has approached. It was thanks to this aura that Jaziya was alerted when a demonic horde attacked her wandering troupe. Terrified by the aura, Jaziya fled, only to find later, when she returned, that all her friends had been killed. She swore to find the demons which had done this foul deed and destroy them all!*

| TABLE 1-14: SORCERER LEGENDS | |
|---|---|
| **2D6** | **YOUR LEGEND** |
| 2 | You own a relic representing one of the gods of your people. As long as it remains in your possession, increase the magnitude of all your Sacred Word rolls by +1! |
| 3-4 | You went through a mystical experience, a sort of astral voyage—crossing the hells, engaging in spiritual combat with a demonic creature, and so on. Increase your Willpower skill by +1. |
| 5-6 | You served as spiritual guide for an important person from your people. Increase your Prayer skill by +1.** |
| 7-8 | You worked in a temple. Increase your Sacrifice skill by +1. |
| 9-10 | You were disciple to a famous sorcerer. Increase your Sacred Word skill by +1.** |
| 11-12 | You were member of a powerful cult (good or evil). Increase both your Sacred Word and Sacrifice skills by +1.** |

| TABLE 1-15: WARRIOR LEGENDS | |
|---|---|
| **2D6** | **YOUR LEGEND** |
| 2 | You own a suit of armour or a weapon of exceptional quality: increase the weapon's damage or armour's Armour Value (page 63) by +2. |
| 3-4 | You fought in a famous battle. Increase your Fighting skill by +1. |
| 5-6 | You led a group of civilians (peasants, slaves, caravaneers) defending themselves during a siege. Increase your Command skill by +1.* |
| 7-8 | Your friend or master was a famous warrior from an elite army. Increase your Combat Training skill by +1.* |
| 9-10 | Whenever you're in danger, you emit a faint purple aura, coming from your Dragon Mark. Increase your Intimidate skill by +1. |
| 11-12 | Even if you're young, you're a veteran, with a solid experience of battle and warfare which makes you difficult to ignore. Increase both your Intimidate and Combat Training skills by +1. |

## Roll 3: The Legends of Your Other Archetypes

Roll twice on Table 1-16: Legendary Archetypes. Each roll indicates which table to roll on next. Incorporate the results into your story.

| TABLE 1-16: LEGENDARY ARCHETYPES | |
|---|---|
| **1D8 (OR CHOOSE)** | **YOUR ARCHETYPE** |
| 1 | Adventurer |
| 2 | Labourer |
| 3 | Poet |
| 4 | Prince |
| 5 | Rogue |
| 6 | Sage |
| 7 | Sorcerer |
| 8 | Warrior |

## The Dragon Mark

Roll once on Table 1-17: Legends of the Dragon Mark.

## Your Past

Your character has a name, family and friends, a life. We've developed some elements, but now it's up to you to fill out the rest. Do you have a goal in life? A code of conduct? How do you view Jazirat's other peoples? Have you travelled? How far did you go? What does your Dragon Mark mean to you? What about your loved ones?

### Jaziya the Demon Huntress! Step 5(c): Jaziya's Contacts

*Sarah's Legend rolls got Jaziya one level 2 contact and one level 1 contact (see page 42). Sarah decides the first is Jaziya's father, a* kahini, *and the second is a rich caravaneer who once sponsored the wandering artist troupe Jaziya belonged to. Sarah also adds Jaziya's Loyalty (2) and Solidarity (1) scores for a total of 3. She can use these points to define additional contacts: 1 point gives a level 1 contact, 3 points gives a level 2 contact. Sarah decides Jaziya's uncle Jibril, her father's brother, was the man who made her a* mujahid *of the Sand Preachers. Jibril will always be there to help Jaziya advance on her path (and access its higher abilities!). She spends all 3 points to make Jibril a level 2 contact.*

| 3D6 | YOUR LEGEND | 3D6 | YOUR LEGEND |
|---|---|---|---|
| | **TABLE 1-17: LEGENDS OF THE DRAGON MARK** | | |
| 3-5 | You come from a Dragon-Marked lineage. Although there hasn't been one for centuries, your family traditions speak of many flamboyant heroes among your distant ancestors. Gain 2 points to divide among the skills of your main archetype, which may exceed the usual maximum of 5. | 12 | Whenever you compose a piece of music, a poem, or a theatre play, or whenever your perform a piece before an audience, you hear the Muses whispering advice. Increase one Poet skill of your choice by +1, which may exceed the usual maximum of 5. |
| 6 | You come from a Dragon-Marked lineage. One of your distant ancestors, at least six centuries ago, faced a lord of hell in single combat and won. Increase your Bravery by +1. | 13 | You experience strange and intuitive insights whenever you commit certain crimes. Perhaps you sense danger, or understand how locks work with incredible ease. Increase one Rogue skill of your choice by +1, which may exceed the usual maximum of 5. |
| 7 | You come from a Dragon-Marked lineage. One of your distant ancestors was and still is considered a minor deity, nature spirit, djinn, etc (you choose) by the locals. Increase your Faith by +1. | 14 | Demons, djinn, and other creatures of the otherworlds constantly whisper to you. You don't know what forces they represent—whether gods or devils—but you feel powerful magic course within you. Increase one Sorcerer skill of your choice by +1, which may exceed the usual maximum of 5. You also acquire 1D6 Adventure Points towards your *shaytan* (see page 340). |
| 8 | You come from a Dragon-Marked lineage. One of your distant ancestors, at least six centuries ago, founded his own school or academy or spread his own teaching of the path he followed (which is recognised by the official path). Increase your Loyalty by +1. | 15 | You have a recurring dream: an Agalanthian man armed with a Saabi scimitar walks towards a throne of gold and gems in a vast and sumptuous palace. He sits in the throne and contemplates the spectacle of a thousand and one corpses he has himself slain. You then wake up in a sweat, feeling you're capable of the same, and reigning over the world! Increase one Prince skill of your choice by +1, which may exceed the usual maximum of 5. |
| 9 | A mysterious figure follows you everywhere: a desert-dweller, dressed in black with a face hidden by a silvered veil. You only catch glimpses of this elusive figure—at the turn of a street, on the top of a dune—but you feel a strange bond. Increase one Adventure or Labourer skill of your choice by +1, which may exceed the usual maximum of 5. | 16 | You sometimes wake up several miles from where you fell asleep, with the strange feeling of having walked all night. Sometimes you have blood on your hands, and a strange joyous feeling of triumph you can't explain. Increase your DEX or STR by +1, which may exceed the usual maximum of 4. |
| 10 | Twice in your life, when you were just about to be slain in combat, you've been saved by an arrow that came out of nowhere and struck your adversary in the throat, killing him outright. Each time, you never saw who shot the arrow, but you feel it might happen again, and that some strange force ties you to the archer. Increase one Warrior skill of your choice by +1, which may exceed the usual maximum of 5. | 17 | You have a recurring dream: a man (or woman), who doesn't seem to be you, is making tender love to a goddess (or god). Increase your CHA, CON, or INT by +1, which may exceed the usual maximum of 4. |
| 11 | Your Dragon Mark glows with a light bluish aura. Increase one Sage skill of your choice by +1, which may exceed the usual maximum of 5. | 18 | Your Dragon Mark glows with a flame-coloured aura. Whenever you fight during the daytime (and only during the daytime), you're particularly affected by the Dragon's Breath (page 48). Reroll your Dragon Die whenever you roll a 5 as well as a 6! Note that this doesn't apply to Dragon Dice you acquire after this point. |

## Jaziya the Demon Huntress!
## Step 5(d): Jaziya's Soak, Hit Points, Max Init, & Passive Defence

*Jaziya's beginning Soak (CON + Heroism) is 6. Her HP (CON x10) are 30, her Max Init (1 + average of CON, DEX and INT) is 4, and her Passive Defence (DEX + Athletics + 6) is 16.*

## Equipment Quality

*Managing the quality of equipment and other items is a matter for Al-Rawi's judgement. Here are a few suggestions.*

* **Poor quality** *items don't reduce a character's abilities, but rather become unusable on the first Critical Failure. A weapon breaks, clothing tears, a building collapses in a storm.*
* **Average, good** or **very good quality** *items don't affect a character's abilities, but can be advantageous in social interactions.*
* **Very good quality** *items are always recognisable as such, even when damaged or broken.*
* **Superior quality** *items can provide rules mechanical advantages. For example, a weapon's damage or the Armour Value of armour may be increased by +1, or a horse may increase the magnitude of all Riding rolls by +1.*
* **Exceptional quality** *items provide greater advantages. Weapon damage or Armour Value increases by +2, a horse increases the magnitude of all Riding rolls by +2, etc.*

Finally, what did you do during the Holy Crusade, when the Quarterians invaded Capharnaum to retrieve the *Mirabilis Calva Reliquiae* and seized the sacred Sword of Hammad from the Saabi, taking it back to the distant Western Kingdoms (page 177)? It's an important question: those recent events shook the world, and no-one in Capharnaum was unaffected. Most Quarterian characters are former soldiers or military chaplains who have remained behind in Jazirat to rebuild their lives. Agalanthians may be here for similar reasons, but maybe they've always lived in one of Capharnaum's great cities? As for the Saabi and Shiradim, it couldn't be simpler: Capharnaum is their home!

### Friends and Acquaintances

In the life you've led so far, your Dragon-Marked character has made many friends and acquaintances. Each starred result (*) you rolled on the Legend Tables means you can now (if you want) define a **level 1 contact**. Each double-starred result (**) means you can define a **level 2 contact**. See page 348 for more on these terms.

Your character may also have additional contacts linked to your blood, path, or main archetype—mentors, masters, best friends. Total your Loyalty score and Solidarity skill, and use those points to select contacts. For 1 point, select a level 1 contact; for 3 points, select a level 2 contact.

## Survival and Initiative

Your character's health will often be brutally tested. You'll face combat situations where it's important to know your Maximum Initiative score (page 51).

Your character's health is defined by your **Hit Points** (HP) and your **Soak**.

**Hit Points** represent your real health. They're equal to your Constitution score multiplied by ten (CON x 10). If your Hit Points ever drop to zero, your character falls unconscious and may die if untreated (see page 67).

**Soak** is re-calculated at the start of each session (at the same time as Heroism, page 23), and remains the same as long as your Heroism score doesn't change (sometimes you'll spend Heroism points dur-

ing play—see page 72). Soak is equal to your Constitution plus your Heroism (CON + Heroism). Note that the **Armour Value** of any armour you're wearing is usually added to your Soak when determining the damage you take—see page 56.

Your **Maximum Initiative** is equal to the *average* of your Constitution, Dexterity, and Intelligence, plus one: ((CON + DEX + INT)/3) +1.

Your **Passive Defence** is a score used when your character is defenceless in combat, or when you've decided not to use an action to actively defend yourself by parrying or dodging (page 55). It's equal to your Dexterity plus your Athletics skill plus 6 (DEX + Athletics + 6).

$$HP = CON \times 10$$
$$Soak = CON + Heroism$$
$$Max\ Init = ((CON + DEX + INT)/3) + 1$$
$$Passive\ Defence = DEX + Athletics + 6$$

## Wealth and Possessions

Now your Dragon-Marked character is ready to adventure, let's not let him go empty-handed! It's time to determine your wealth and possessions.

Firstly, your main archetype grants you a certain amount of equipment and other possessions.

* **The Adventurer:** You have a weapon of your choice; a *jambiya*; a short bow and fifteen arrows or a javelin; an outfit of city clothes; an outfit for desert travel; shoes or sandals; a tent; a camel or horse; 50 feet of rope; 3 large leather sacks; 5 torches; and a portable incense burner.

## Jaziya the Demon Huntress! Step 5(e): Jaziya's Wealth Level and Equipment

*Jaziya's Wealth Level (determined by the Prince Archetype) is 0 (an Impoverished character). This means Jaziya owns: a scimitar, a jambiya, a javelin, a set of urban clothing, a desert travel outfit, comfortable shoes, a tent, a camel, 50 feet of rope, 3 large leather sacks, 5 torches, and a portable incense burner, all poor quality. She has 10 ounces of cumin to buy extra gear; she spends 8 ounces of it on some light armour (AV: 3).*

- ❖ **The Labourer:** You have a workman's outfit; an outfit of city clothes; a tool kit or other work gear; and one of the following, depending on your secondary archetype: a travelling outfit (Adventurer); your choice of weapon (Prince or Warrior); a calligraphy kit (Sage); art supplies or musical instrument (Poet); a lockpick set (Rogue); ceremonial clothes (Sorcerer).
- ❖ **The Poet:** You have 3 performance outfits; an outfit of city clothes; a painting or juggling kit or musical instrument, or 3 books or scrolls of poetry or theatre.
- ❖ **The Prince:** You have lands and real estate (a castle, city villa, etc, appropriate to your Wealth Level—see below); 5 weapons of your choice (with 1D6 x 10 arrows for archers); light or heavy armour (your choice); a harem of 3D6 concubines and 1D6 wives (for male characters) or 1D6 besotted lovers and 2D6 camels (for female characters); and 1D6 slaves.
- ❖ **The Rogue:** You have 3 outfits of city clothing; a lockpick set; a *khanjar*; and a weapon of your choice (plus 1D6 x 10 arrows if it's a bow).
- ❖ **The Sage:** You have 3 outfits of city clothing; a *khanjar*; 3D6 books or scrolls (your choice of subject); a calligraphy kit; an astronomy kit; a hermit's cave, university room, or house (appropriate to your Wealth Level).
- ❖ **The Sorcerer:** You have an outfit of ceremonial clothes; an outfit of city clothes; 1D6 scrolls or grimoires, each containing 3 spells or magical elements you haven't learned yet.
- ❖ **The Warrior:** You have a suit of light armour; 3 weapons of your choice (plus 1D6 x 10 arrows for archers); an outfit of city clothing; and a camel or horse.

## Wealth Levels

A character's **Wealth Level** is equal to the skill bonus you received from the Prince archetype, a score between 0 (the lowest) and 3 (the highest). If you ranked the Prince archetype first, gaining a +3 skill bonus on Prince skills, then your Wealth Level is 3, and so on. Your Wealth Level may end up higher than 3 due to bonuses gained when

| TABLE 1-18: WEALTH LEVELS | | | |
|---|---|---|---|
| **WEALTH LEVEL** | **LABEL** | **DESCRIPTION** | **STARTING MONEY (OZ OF CUMIN)** |
| 0 | Impoverished | An impoverished character with poor quality equipment. | Unctuous Bargaining x 10 |
| 1 | Struggling | A struggling character with average quality equipment. | Unctuous Bargaining x 50 |
| 2 | Well-to-Do | A well-to-do character with good quality equipment. | Unctuous Bargaining x 100 |
| 3 | Rich | A rich character with very good quality equipment. | Unctuous Bargaining x 500 |
| 4 | Filthy Rich | A filthy rich character with superior quality equipment. | Unctuous Bargaining x 1000 |
| 5 | Extraordinarily Rich | An extraordinarily rich character with exceptional quality equipment. | Unctuous Bargaining x 5000 |

## Summary of Step 5

a. Freely distribute 5 points among your skills, adding no more than 2 points to any one skill, and with no skill exceeding 5.

b. Roll for your Legend, rolling twice on the Legend table for your blood, once on the Legend table for your main archetype, twice on Table 1-16: Legendary Archetypes, and once on Table 1-17: Legends of the Dragon Mark.

c. Create a back story for your character, incorporating your Legend roll results.

d. Determine your contacts and acquaintances.

e. Calculate your Soak, Hit Points, Max Init and Passive Defence.

f. Determine your equipment and your Wealth Level.

# CHAPTER TWO
# THALIA – WORD AND DEED

## The Fighter and His Blade

Luther realised the crowds weren't cheering him. He pulled his pilum from the body he'd just impaled, moments after smashing another opponent to the ground with a flurry of mace blows, then snatched a turban from the corpse of a warrior who no longer needed it. He wiped his forehead, dripping with sweat—his own—and the blood of others, then saw his face in a shield's reflection. Not even his wife, sweet Ingrid, left behind in distant Orkadia, would have recognised him now. His beard was gone, his torso shaven, his body oiled. His hair was a golden mane, for which his companions in misfortune now called him "the Lion of the North". His skin, usually pale, had turned to copper beneath the Capharnaum sun. Today it was darker still, stained with the blood of foes, a smell which hung heavy in the air.

On this ill-fated day Luther had already killed more men than he had ever done. The Orkadian had quickly been picked out as a potential champion. His first bouts had been easy: they had pitted him against poor fighters. He had tried to avoid the senseless slaughter, had tried to parley—his opponents weren't his enemies, after all—but had quickly faced facts: slaughter was why they were there. The families of the fighters stood to make money, and with luck they'd escape with only minor wounds. So Luther had started slow, trying not to kill. But the longer he took to dispatch a foe, the more opponents appeared. He gave way, succumbing to the battle rage that was the pride of his ancestors, and savagely butchered all who stood before him. Animals, first, then warriors; the survivors got rid of the beasts together. Then came duels, from which Luther emerged the grand victor. He had watched with pity as a friend—for a time—from Al-Fariq'n had fallen to a nomad from the north, whom he had slaughtered next. With a light wound to the thigh, he'd hoped the fighting was over, but then six new warriors charged from the corners of the arena—a formation the herald had announced as "the star of the valiant". More like "the killing of the champion", Luther thought. It cost him a slash across the arm, but he passed even that ordeal, and had believed it the last.

But, no, the crowds weren't cheering him. There, on the central dais, the reigning champion had just appeared, fresh and ready for the final combat against the winner of the afternoon's games. Against him, Luther Magnusson, knight of Grunwald, stood in miserable slavery.

He would have preferred a long, straight sword against such a warrior. But since he had started fighting in the arena, every sword Luther had seen had been a short or curved blade. How in Ragnarok could the Jazirati fight with such unbalanced weapons? Still, he snatched up a gladius and lodged it behind his shield: he'd start by staking everything on his pilum and the new combat technique he'd devised. For that, though, he would need to force his opponent to descend onto the sand of the arena floor. He climbed onto the dais, took a position close to the edge. Opening his guard wide, he let the champion charge. At the last moment he blocked with his shield and pulled his opponent over the rail.

Luther was unused to the pilum, but the shield held no secrets for him. He approached his opponent without cover, inviting him to strike, parrying without stopping his advance, taking advantage of his larger size. And he kept advancing—faster and faster, only parrying, never striking. Then, when he felt his opponent weaken, he leaped and brought down his pilum with all his size and strength. Blood spurted. Luther kicked his opponent to the ground. He drew his gladius and thrust it through his foe's throat.

Resolute, he stalked towards the prince's booth, where the master of the games sat clean and pampered beneath a canopy protected from the sun, a heathen dog with a new wife—forty years his junior if she was a day—at his side. The Orkadian expected nothing: favour was rarely granted on a champion's first victory. Instead he stared into the prince's onyx eyes. A turbaned silhouette leaned in to whisper in the prince's ear. Against all expectations, the prince stood, and pointed his finger to the sky. The sign of freedom!

This time, Luther realised, the crowd was cheering for him.

*I am wildfire.*

*I spread among you like a rumour of plague.*

*You ignore me, yet already I tear at your flesh and the wombs of your women.*

*I am the sand in the eyes and ears of Quarterian pilgrims seeking holy places.*

*I am the despair in the hearts of Agalanthian heroes who find only ruins of past glory.*

*I am Fauzi Ibn Tufiq Abd-al-Tarek, the scourge of Hubal. Even death feels cold in my presence, and fear knows fear before me, because at him I smile...*

—Poem set down by Oda Bat Pharat, 12-Second-04-5994, during a poetry contest at the court of Sagrada. Survivors still wonder if Fauzi, official poet of the Sagrada court, was a traitor to his own blood trying to warn Queen Helicandra, or a traitor to his queen announcing her imminent death.

*Capharnaum: The Tales of the Dragon-Marked* is a bright and heroic game, with rules that aim to be as cinematic and as fun as possible. It's a simple system which encourages player description, eloquence and invention.

# ACTION RESOLUTION

Most of the actions your characters attempt in the game work automatically: speaking, eating, walking, and so on. But, when the result of an action is uncertain, both Al-Rawi and players rely on chance and the roll of six-sided dice (also called D6). The success or failure of an action is most often resolved by rolling between 2 and 15 dice. This is called a **dice roll.**

The number of dice used in a dice roll depends on several factors, including the kind of action you're trying to resolve. Mostly, you roll a number of dice equal to your score in one of your **attributes** (page 23)—Strength (STR), Constitution (CON), Dexterity (DEX), Intelligence (INT), or Charisma (CHA)—and sometimes add a number of dice equal to your score in one of your **skills** (page 25)—such as Fighting, Flattery, or Unctuous Bargaining. There are 32 skills in *Capharnaum*, representing the things your character knows how to do—see page 26.

Scores in attributes and skills are usually between 1 and 5, so you'll usually end up rolling between 1 and 10 dice. For example, you may make a roll of your DEX 5 attribute and your Riding 3 skill, in which you'll roll 8 dice. There are several types of dice roll, including **attribute rolls, skill rolls, unskilled rolls,** and **opposed rolls** (see page 47).

When you make a dice roll, you add up some of those dice, called your **result dice,** to make a total, called a **result.** The number of result dice is always equal to the attribute you're using in the roll. In the above example, you'd roll 8 dice and total 5 of them. Sometimes this is written using the notation:

**Number of Dice Rolled / Result Dice**

In the above example, the Riding skill roll could be written DEX + Riding 8/5, or just Riding 8/5.

## Difficulties

In an action, your result is compared to a number called a **difficulty** to see whether you succeed in your action or not. The difficulty is determined by Al-Rawi according to the descriptions given in Table 2-1: Difficulties. It's up to Al-Rawi whether or not she announces the difficulty of a roll to the players: sometimes it's more exciting to keep it secret, but sometimes it raises the tension to let the players know.

**If the result of a dice roll is equal to or higher than the difficulty, the action succeeds.**

Dice rolls often have the following notation:

**Difficulty n Component 1 + Component 2 roll**

A roll of Strength and Athletics with a difficulty of 9 is written: difficulty 9 STR + Athletics. It means you roll a number of dice equal to your scores in your Strength attribute and your Athletics skill, and add up a number of them equal to your Strength attribute. If the result is equal to or greater than 9, you've succeeded.

| TABLE 2-1: DIFFICULTIES | | |
|---|---|---|
| **DIFFICULTY** | **DESCRIPTION** | **EXAMPLES** |
| 6 | Simple | The default difficulty for most easy tasks. You may not even need to roll for this. *Reciting verses you know well, kicking open a rickety door, urging a Saabi horse to gallop down an empty road, picking the pockets of a distracted chatterbox.* |
| 9 | Average | The default difficulty of a professional-level task, and hence for most dice rolls. *Repairing your own armour, lifting more than your own weight, writing a long letter, evaluating a precious stone at first sight, stealing from a market stall on a quiet street.* |
| 12 | Difficult | An action worthy of a specialist. *Forging a weapon of quality, succeeding in a feat of athletics, organising a festival for an entire city quarter.* |
| 15 | Heroic | Now we sort the wheat out from the chaff! *Crossing a street by jumping from one roof to another, winning a running race against a dog, juggling with sabres, riding back to front and shooting arrows from the back of your horse, dropping 30 feet onto a shop awning.* |
| 18 | Insanely Heroic | These actions are recklessly heroic, and have serious consequences! *Sleeping with the king's wife while the king is sleeping next to you, winning a running race against a horse, dropping 60 feet onto a shop awning.* |
| 21 | Fabulous | People will be talking about you in a hundred years' time! *Persuading the king who's just woken up next to you and his wife to let you carry on, winning a running race with an abzul, diving from a clifftop into a rocky river.* |
| 30+ | Legendary | Actions beyond the reach of ordinary mortals! *Pole-vaulting over a 60-foot high rampart, juggling excitable snakes while blindfolded, stopping a bolting horse on a slippery surface using only one hand.* |

## Magnitudes

In some cases (like combat), it's useful to know and quantify the **magnitude** of a success or a failure—how well or how badly you've succeeded or failed. Magnitude is a numerical score equal to the number of dice not kept when calculating your result, also known as your **magnitude dice**. Any magnitude die roll of 1 is not counted towards your magnitude; any roll of 6 is counted twice. This gives the following calculation:

| TABLE 2-2: FIGURING MAGNITUDE | |
|---|---|
| **RESULT ON MAGNITUDE DIE** | **ADDITION TO MAGNITUDE** |
| 1 | +0 |
| 2 | +1 |
| 3 | +1 |
| 4 | +1 |
| 5 | +1 |
| 6 | +2 |

Your magnitude gives you an idea of how great the success (or failure!) of your dice roll is, as follows:

| TABLE 2-3: DESCRIBING MAGNITUDE | | |
|---|---|---|
| **MAGNITUDE** | **SUCCESS** | **FAILURE** |
| 0 | Marginal Success | Marginal Failure |
| 1 | Normal Success | Normal Failure |
| 2 | Good Success | Stinging Failure |
| 3 | Very Good Success | Painful Failure |
| 4 | Memorable Success | Memorable Failure |
| 5 | Exceptional Success | Catastrophic Failure |
| 6+ | Critical Success | Critical Failure |

**Note:** You can end up with magnitudes higher than 6. These are always Critical Successes or Failures, and represent increasingly superhuman results. We often call these Legendary Successes and Failures.

*For example: While chasing a traitor, Amin Ibn Malik tries to gallop across a street on his camel. Al-Rawi sets the difficulty at 6 (the street is pretty empty), and Amin's DEX is 4 and his Riding is 3. He rolls 7 dice, getting 1, 2, 3, 3, 4, 5, 5. He keeps the 4 best (equal to his DEX), giving him a result of 17 (5+5+4+3)! The action succeeds, because 17 is (way!) higher than the difficulty of 6. The three dice which don't contribute to the total are his magnitude dice: with results of 1, 2, and 3, they contribute +0, +1, and +1 to his magnitude, for a total magnitude of 2. It's a Good Success.*

## Critical Successes and Failures

You'll find that the points of magnitude you generate on a roll get used in a variety of ways in these rules. Often, though, we consider there to be a qualitative difference in your success or failure when you achieve a magnitude of 6 or more, and some special rules kick in. One of the most obvious is that if you score a Critical Success on an attack roll in combat, the damage you do ignores your opponent's **Soak** (page 42), inflicting terrible wounds.

In other cases, it's up to Al-Rawi and the players to decide what a Critical Success or Failure means. Here are some ideas.

- ❖ **Describing a Critical Success:** Someone miraculously passes by with a cart full of hay just at the moment you make a daredevil leap; the woman of your dreams immediately falls in love with you; the bandit leader befriends you against all expectations.
- ❖ **Describing a Critical Failure:** Your weapon breaks or shatters in your hands; you stumble and fall over; you believe everything you're told; you fumble in a way which gives your opponent a **bonus die** (page 49) on his next attack.

# Types of Dice Roll

Almost all dice rolls fall into one of the following four categories.

## Skill Rolls

Most of the time when you want your character to attempt an action with an uncertain result, you roll a number of dice equal to the sum of an attribute and a skill score, from which you only count a number of dice equal to your attribute as your **result dice**. You must always keep the best dice in your result dice. Note, however, that this doesn't apply to your dragon dice (page 48): you have the choice to include them in your result dice or not, regardless of the numbers rolled.

## Unskilled Rolls

If you have a score of 0 (zero) in the skill required in a skill roll, then you must make an **unskilled roll**. In this case, you only roll a number of dice equal to your relevant attribute; you have no additional dice from your skill score. Even if you succeed on an unskilled roll, your magnitude will always be zero (unless you're **swaggering**—see page 49), and therefore your action, even if it does succeed, will do so only with a Marginal Success.

*For example: Having seen the men he chased enter a shop, Amin dismounts his camel and tries to sneak up to the building. His Stealth skill is 0, so Al-Rawi ask him to make a difficulty 9 unskilled DEX roll. Amin rolls four dice, for his DEX 4, all of which are result dice:*

*he gets 2, 2, 3, 5, for a result of 12. Although this is a success, Amin has no magnitude dice, so he has only just succeeded in his attempt (magnitude 0, a Marginal Success).*

## Attribute Rolls

Sometimes, no obvious skill is relevant to the action you're attempting. In this case, Al-Rawi may call for an **attribute roll** of a specific attribute. In an attribute roll, you roll a number of dice equal to the sum of that specific attribute + your current Heroism score (page 23), from which you only count a number of dice equal to your attribute as your **result dice**. The result is then compared to the difficulty and magnitude is calculated as usual.

## Opposed Rolls and Ranking Rolls

Sometimes, when you attempt an action, that action may be opposed by another character instead of an inanimate force or object. This may be someone actively opposing you to stop you doing what you're doing (such as someone trying to find you when you're trying to hide); or it may be another person trying to perform the same action as you, only better (such as a running race or arm-wrestling match). These are called **opposed rolls** and **ranking rolls** respectively.

In an **opposed roll**, one participant is opposing the action of another. Two different rolls are made, and the higher result prevails. For example, if you're trying to sneak past the Palace Guard, your ability to use your Stealth skill is pitted directly against the guard's Notice skill; the result of the guard's INT + Notice roll effectively becomes the difficulty you must **equal or exceed** in order to successfully sneak past. Sometimes this is also called an **active difficulty** (see also the Active Defence action on page 54).

In a **ranking roll**, all the participants are attempting the same action to determine a winner (such as a running race, an arm-wrestling match, or other such contest). All participants make the same roll (such as STR + Athletics for a short-distance sprint), and the highest result wins the contest. Magnitudes are calculated normally. In the case of a tie on a ranking roll, the higher magnitude wins.

*For example: Amin is arm-wrestling a vigorous Orkadian knight. Al-Rawi asks for a ranking roll of STR + Athletics, and rolls the same for the Orkadian. Amin rolls 6/3 and gets 1, 2, 3, 5, 5 and 5, for a result of 15. The Orkadian rolls 8/4 and gets 1, 2, 2, 3, 4, 5, 5, 6, for a result of 20. The Orkadian wins the bout. His magnitude is 3, or a Very Good Success. Amin didn't last long in the face of the northerner's might!*

## Summary of Dice Rolls

❖ *Skill Roll:* Roll as many dice as attribute + skill.
❖ *Unskilled Roll:* Roll as many dice as attribute. You have no magnitude dice.
❖ *Attribute Roll:* Roll as many dice as attribute + Heroism.
❖ *Opposed Roll:* One character rolls, and his result becomes the difficulty another character must equal or exceed.
❖ *Ranking Roll:* Both you and your opponent make rolls, and compare the two (or more) results. The higher result wins.
❖ *Result:* The sum of the kept dice, called the result dice (which must be the best ones, except for your Dragon Dice—see page 48), to equal or exceed the difficulty.
❖ *Magnitude:* The number of dice not kept, called the magnitude dice. Dice which roll "1" don't count; those which roll "6" count twice.

# The Whims of the Dice

## Dragon Dice—The Dragon's Breath

The dragons are the servants of the gods. They watch over the Dragon-Marked as they pursue their destinies. In game terms, each player has at least one **dragon die**, which should be a different colour from the other dice, which you roll whenever you make a dice roll. For example, if you have 1 dragon die and have to roll 8 dice in a dice roll, you roll 7 normal-coloured dice, and 1 die that's specially coloured to mark it out as a dragon die.

Only the Dragon-Marked have dragon dice; normal humans and monsters don't.

If you roll a 6 on a dragon die, your action is said to be "carried by the dragon's breath". You keep the 6 you rolled as part of your result, and roll the dragon die again! And, if you roll a 6 again, you keep going! Note that even when you total up all these multiple rolls of your dragon die, that total is still considered to be a single die as far as your result dice are concerned.

*For example: Amin rolls 5 dice and has to add the 2 best results (usually written 5/2). He rolls 1, 2, 2, and 5, and 6 on his dragon die. So, he rerolls his dragon die and gets a 5. He then adds that 6 and that 5 together, which gives him a result on his dragon die of 11! His final dice roll result (the 2 dice out of 5 that he keeps) is therefore 16: the 5 he rolled on one of his normal dice, plus the 11 he rolled on his dragon die (6+5).*

As long as the dragons breathe, the dragon die is rerolled! So, if you reroll a dragon die and get another 6, you roll a third time, and so on. The dragon's breath can let you achieve some amazing results!

*For example: Amin's player rolls 3 dice and gets 2 and 4, and 6 on his dragon die. He re-rolls his dragon die, and gets another 6! The dragons are with him! He rolls the dragon die yet again—a third*

time—and gets yet another 6! He re-rolls a fourth time, and this time the dragon die comes up a 2. Amin's player totals up all these results— that's 6+6+6+2—which means his dragon die gives him 20 points towards his result. Adding that to the 2 and 4 on the other two dice, his final result is 26!

Note that, unlike normal dice, you can choose whether or not to include your dragon die in your result, regardless of the total rolled. Instead, you can treat your dragon die as a magnitude die. In this case, each re-roll of a dragon die is treated as an additional magnitude die.

*For example: Amin is making a roll of 4/2 on a difficulty 9 roll, and gets 4, 4, and 5, and 6 on his dragon die. He re-rolls his dragon die, and gets a 2. Because that 6+2 was rolled on a dragon die, Amin's player doesn't have to include it in his result if he doesn't want to. Instead, he decides to keep the 4 and the 5 in his result, as that's enough to succeed against a difficulty of 9.*

*That leaves him with the 4 he rolled on his ordinary die, and the 6+2 he rolled on his dragon die. He can treat the two rolls of the dragon die as two separate magnitude dice, meaning his magnitude dice are 2, 4, and 6. This gives him a magnitude of 4, which is a Memorable Success!*

Don't neglect to describe the awesomeness of the dragon's breath! It's your schtick, it's what sets your character apart from normal mortals. You're inspired by the mystic power of the dragons and the heroic destiny which awaits you, you succeed at an amazing stunt or manoeuvre, leaving everyone speechless and impressed. The greater the bonus on the dragon dice, the more superhuman your effort appears. Any additional points your dragon dice give you make you look special, but if you get more than 10, then something uncanny, even supernatural, is happening; and if you get more than 20, even the gods themselves start to take note!

## Constellations

Rolling the same number on three or more dice in a dice roll is called **lighting up a constellation**. Constellations can do miraculous things.

If your dice roll is a success, a constellation can activate special abilities your character has because of the **path** (page 17) he follows.

*For example: Amin Ibn Malik is facing three brigands, and must fight to survive. While attempting a riposte, Amin rolls 9/5 for his attack, getting 1, 2, 2, 2, 3, 4, 4, 5 and 5. The three 2s light up a constellation, letting him activate the Path of the Fire Scimitars (the path he chose to follow) until the end of the fight... No doubt the brigands are going to regret attacking a Dragon-Marked!*

Note that you don't have to keep the constellation dice as result dice or even magnitude dice for them to be effective: rolling three 1s will still light up a constellation.

Note also that re-rolls on your dragon die don't count towards constellations: only the first roll counts.

For example: Amin keeps the 5 best dice as his result dice: 3, 4, 4, 5 and 5, for a result of 21. Even though he's not keeping any of his constellation dice in his result, his path ability is still activated.

You can even light up a constellation to activate a path ability when you haven't rolled enough constellation dice. To do so, you must spend one star of the **replacement heroic virtue** of your path for each missing constellation die (see page 73). So, if you've already rolled a double, you must spend 1 star to light up a constellation; if you haven't rolled even a double, you must spend 2 stars.

In the example above, let's imagine that Amin rolled 1, 2, 2, 3, 3, 4, 4, 5 and 5 on his dice. As he didn't roll a triple or above, he hasn't lit up a constellation. However, he still wants to activate his path ability. To do so, he has to spend 1 star of Bravery (the replacement heroic virtue for the path he follows—see page 73) to make the constellation light up and activate his path ability.

It's said that when the nights are clear and a follower of a path lights up a constellation, you can actually see the stars of the constellation belonging to the founder of that path shine brighter for a few seconds...

## Bonus Dice and Penalty Dice

There are two types of modifier in *Capharnaum*: numerical modifiers to the **difficulty** of a roll (or, rarely, the result); and an increase or decrease in the number of dice rolled. These modifiers are quite different.

In *Capharnaum*, the number of dice you roll directly affects how great your success or failure will be. Changing the difficulty of a roll won't affect that very much; it'll be harder to succeed at the roll in the first place, but once you succeed you'll have almost the same chance of a great success as you would have had without the difficulty being modified. Sometimes this is exactly the effect you're looking for.

However, if you want to directly modify the magnitude of success or failure of a roll, you need to change the number of dice rolled. This is where **bonus dice** and **penalty dice** come in.

For example: Amin Ibn Malik is in a duel with a distant cousin who he thinks is responsible for his father's murder. Burning with the desire for vengeance, Amin hurls himself headlong into a fight to the death. Taking Amin's past history and reckless determination into account, Al-Rawi decides that he should receive a bonus die on all his offensive actions in the duel. Amin makes his first attack with a roll of 8/5 instead of his usual 7/5.

## Swaggering

Characters in *Capharnaum* are swashbuckling, heroic types who like nothing better than to cut a dash and look cool while accomplishing great feats, apparently effortlessly!

**Swaggering** involves taking risks when you attempt an action, in order to look cool, shine more brightly, and achieve greater mag-

nitudes of success. But—be careful!—you also risk failing much more catastrophically on a bad roll!

When you choose to swagger, you hold back one or more dice from your result dice, and instead add them to your magnitude dice. These are often called **swagger dice**. You must specify the number of swagger dice **before** you make your dice roll. You can never roll more swagger dice than your Heroism score (page 23).

Note that this means that, when you swagger, you actually **lower** your chance of success! But, if you do succeed, your chance of getting a greater magnitude of success is much higher. However, if you fail on your dice roll, your magnitude of failure will be that much worse!

For example: Frank's character, Don Felix Belmonte de Valladon, is climbing down the outside of a tower in Jergath in a daring escape attempt, attempting a difficulty 15 action, for which he's rolling 7/5 (rolling 7 dice, keeping 5). He decides to swagger, increasing the stakes so that he can impress the women in the street below that are following his actions with interest. Frank says to Al-Rawi: "These three storeys are but small steps when compared to my escape from the dungeon of Lord Al-Shamin! I'll take 2 swagger dice, grinning and waving at the lard-arsed eunuchs trying to catch me and showing them what a real escape is all about!"

His Heroism score is 3, meaning Frank could have taken up to 3 swagger dice, but that looked too risky even for him. His 2 swagger dice mean his climbing roll goes from 7/5 to 7/3! He rolls against the difficulty of 15, getting 2, 3, 3, 5, 6, 6, and 6. He keeps the highest

## Dice Roll Sequence

❖ **Step 1: Difficulty.** Al-Rawi determines the difficulty of the dice roll.
❖ **Step 2: Swaggering (optional).** Before you roll the dice, you may move dice from your result dice to your magnitude dice, in an attempt to get a more impressive success. You must describe how you swagger ostentatiously, exposing yourself to greater risk!
❖ **Step 3: Roll the Dice.** Roll all the dice, and total up your result dice. Compare the result to the difficulty. If the result is equal to or higher than the difficulty, you succeed at your action. If the result is lower, you fail.
❖ **Step 4: Magnitude (optional).** If the magnitude of your success or failure is important, count up the number of magnitude dice. A magnitude dice roll of "1" doesn't count towards your magnitude; a roll of "6" counts twice.

*three dice, a total of 18; his climb action is successful! The remaining 4 dice are now his magnitude dice (without the swagger, he would only have had 2), for a final magnitude of 4—a Memorable Success!*

All intelligent creatures may swagger, not just the Dragon-Marked.

# Helping and Hindering

Sometimes you may want to take an action which helps someone else do something, or which tries to stop them doing something. These actions are called **Help actions** and **Hinder actions**. You must describe Help actions and Hinder actions in a way which makes logical sense for your situation; Al-Rawi is the final arbiter of whether a Help or Hinder action is possible.

A **Help action** is an action (see "Actions and Rounds", page 50). If you succeed, you give a number of bonus dice to the person you're helping equal to the magnitude of your success, up to a maximum of that person's own skill score, plus one (skill +1). If you fail, however, you inflict a number of penalty dice on the person you're "helping" equal to the magnitude of your failure—and there's no limit!

A **Hinder action** is an action. If you succeed, you inflict a number of penalty dice on the person you're hindering equal to the magnitude of your success. If you fail, nothing happens unless you roll a Critical Failure; in that case, you actually *give* one bonus die to the target for every point of magnitude above 5.

If you want to stop someone performing a Help or Hinder action, you can do so with an Active Defence action (page 54).

# COMBAT

***Capharnaum: The Tales of the Dragon-Marked*** is a heroic game. Action scenes and combats are a frequent occurrence, and even an average Dragon-Marked fighter has their chance to shine, emulating Sinbad the Sailor, Ala'ad-Din, or the great names in the epic poems and chivalric romances (like Saladin, Lancelot, or El Cid) or Mediterranean legends (like Achilles, Gilgamesh, Hector, or Herakles). Strength, honour, cleverness and luck drive your Dragon-Marked character in his quest to defeat evil djinn and demons, steal treasures and gem-studded idols, or even a kiss when they rescue the prince or princess!

## Actions and Rounds

A combat is divided into **rounds** of about twelve seconds each. During one round all sorts of **actions** take place, the fighters run, attack, dodge, shout, jump, take cover, wound or are wounded. In each round, your character may do the following:

❖ **Take any number of the following free actions:** speak, drop an object, look at something, make a small gesture.
❖ **Take 2 of the following standard actions:** defend; parry; make an alert, cautious, defensive move of your DEX in paces (1 pace = 5 feet); jump; manipulate something, break a chiromancy tablet.
❖ **Take 1 attack action or cast 1 spell,** plus any other standard action.
❖ **Take a Brutal Attack action,** which takes up all of the current round, and which does +6 damage if it succeeds.
❖ **Take a Charge Attack action,** which takes up all of the current round and an attack action in the following round, and which does +10 damage if it succeeds.

See "Combat Actions" below (page 51) for more.

## Get Creative!

*The **Capharnaum** system provides a flexible framework of rules with a lot of permutations in play. Try and get creative when describing your characters' actions: start by describing what your character is trying to do, and then use the rules to work out how to model it. Your characters should attempt amazing swaggers and stunts, help one another and hinder their foes, create bonuses, and improvise awesome magical effects with their spells. Not only will you get rules mechanical and descriptive advantages (as well as looking thoroughly cool!), you'll also get rewarded with extra Adventure Points (page 78) for making creative use of the rules during play! Throughout this book, we give you hints and tips about some of the cool things you can do with these rules.*

## Initiative

When a round starts, each player rolls 1D6. The result indicates the order in which each character acts in a round, a higher result acting before a lower. This is known as **rolling for initiative**. Initiative is rolled at the beginning of every round.

### Maximum Initiative

There's a limit to how quickly a character can act in a round, known as your **Maximum Initiative** score, or simply **Max Init**. To determine your character's Max Init, average your DEX, CON, and INT and add 1 to the result. (Generally you'll calculate Max Init when you create your character: it only changes when one of the attributes involved changes.)

$$\text{Max Init} = 1 + (\text{DEX} + \text{CON} + \text{INT})/3$$

When you roll for initiative, if the die result is equal to or higher than your Max Init, then you act at an Initiative score equal to your Max Init. If the result is lower than your Max Init, then your Initiative score is equal to the number shown on the die.

*For example: Ralph's character has a Max Init of 4. At the start of the round he rolls 1D6 for initiative and gets a 5. His Initiative score for the round is 4.*

Note that if you have a Max Init greater than 6, **you roll 2D6 for initiative**.

### Acting in Initiative Order

Once everyone has rolled for initiative, Al-Rawi calls the highest Initiative score at the table. Any character with that Initiative score can then take his actions for that round. Once all actions for every character acting at that Initiative score are resolved, Al-Rawi calls the next lower Initiative score, and so on, continuing her countdown until 1. At Initiative score 1, any character who hasn't yet taken his actions does so, or loses their chance for that round. Al-Rawi then announces the end of the round and the beginning of the next one (assuming the protagonists want to continue to act), and everyone rolls for initiative again.

Note that if your character is performing an action that takes a number of actions to perform (such as a Brutal Attack), you roll for the action at your Initiative score as normal, but you may only take that action in that round. If you're rolling for an action which requires more than a round to complete (such as a Charge Attack action), you act at your Initiative score (having rolled for initiative again) on the **following** round.

*For example: Ralph's character has an Initiative score of 4 this round. He decides to charge, letting him do more damage (see "Combat Actions", below). However, a Charge Attack takes place as an at-*tack action in the following round. Therefore, Ralph takes no action in the current round (he can't even defend, as he's charging), and in the following round he rolls 3 for initiative. He acts at Initiative score 3 in that second round, completing his charge and making his attack.

### Who Acts First in a Tie?

During a round, characters act in descending order of Initiative score. However, if more than one character acts at the same Initiative score, the character with the highest DEX goes first. If that also results in a tie, make a ranking roll (page 47) of DEX to see who goes first. It's often a good idea to jot down Initiative scores in descending order so you can visualise things more easily (Al-Rawi will often be the one to do this).

### Delaying Your Action

If it's your turn to act, you can always **delay your action** to a later point in the initiative order and let other people go first if you wish. This can be very useful if, for example, you plan to make a Brutal Attack action, but want to retain the option of changing your mind and making an Active Defence and Normal Attack instead if you're attacked, or if you can see an opponent approaching (perhaps making a Charge Attack) and want to wait until he passes by and make an opportunistic attack.

If you don't act in a given round, your action is lost: it doesn't carry over into the next round.

# COMBAT ACTIONS

A character may attempt all kinds of actions in a round. Talking is free, can be done at any point in the Initiative order, and doesn't require a dice roll. On the other hand, attacks, parries, and other feats take a certain amount of time and a certain number of actions. For example, although a simple sword strike only takes 1 action, charging an opponent by running, weapon in hand, to strike a violent blow takes 3 actions (and is called a **Charge Attack**).

### Combat Training

*Don't forget that characters with the Combat Training skill (page 27) can, at the beginning of any combat, make a difficulty 6 CON + Combat Training roll, and gain 1 single-use bonus die per point of magnitude for use at any point during the current combat.*

## Table 2-4: Duration of Combat Actions

| Name | Duration | Description |
| --- | --- | --- |
| Talk | 0 actions | |
| **Attack Actions** | | |
| Normal Attack | 1 action[1] | DEX + Fighting. |
| Brutal Attack | 2 actions | STR + Fighting, +6 damage. |
| Charge Attack | 3 actions[2] | STR or DEX + Fighting, +10 damage; -6 Passive Defence. |
| Ranged Attack (Bow) | 2 actions | DEX + Fighting. |
| Ranged Attack (Thrown) | 1 action | DEX + Fighting. |
| **Defend Actions** | | |
| Active Defence | 1 action | DEX + Athletics or Fighting; a skill roll. |
| Passive Defence | 0 actions | DEX + Athletics + 6; a static value, no dice roll. |
| **Magic Actions** | | |
| Cast a Spell | 1 action[1] | INT + Sacred Word. |
| Break a Tablet | 1 action | No dice roll required. |
| **Move Actions** | | |
| Combat Move | 1 action | DEX in paces (5 ft). |
| Unengaged Move | 1 action | DEX x 2 in paces; -6 Passive Defence. |
| **Other Actions** | | |
| Aiming | 1 action | +1 bonus die. |
| Disengage | 2 actions | DEX + Athletics or Stealth. |
| Draw a Weapon | 1 action | No dice roll required. |
| Help or Hinder | 1 action | See description. |

*1: You may only take one of these actions per round.*

*2: Your Charge Attack takes place at your Initiative order in the following round.*

# Attack Actions

## Normal Attack

To physically attack an opponent, make a DEX + Fighting roll and compare your result to your opponent's Passive Defence, or the result of the latter's Active Defence roll if he takes an action to defend himself. A Normal Attack only requires one action, but you may only make one such Normal Attack action (or a Cast a Spell action) per round. Usually you must be no more than 1 pace from your opponent to make a Normal Attack.

## Brutal Attack

A Brutal Attack is an attack where you use brute force and unforgiving violence to inflict as much damage as you can on your opponent. It works exactly like a Normal Attack action, except that it takes two actions (ie a full combat round). If a Brutal Attack is successful, you inflict +6 additional points of damage on your opponent (see page 56).

While you're making a Brutal Attack, you may take no other actions. You're considered to be engaged in combat for the duration, and must rely only on your Passive Defence against any attacks against you. However, you may decide to cancel your Brutal Attack action at any point during the round before you make it, for example in order to take an Active Defence action. The Active Defence requires one action as usual, leaving you with an action still to take that round, which may be a Normal Attack. For this reason, you may want to **delay your action** until the end of the round when making a Brutal Attack (page 51), to keep the option of making an Active Defence roll if you need to.

*For example: Amin and Thufir are in combat against a giant who's trying to eat them for supper. Amin has the initiative, and wants to make a Brutal Attack with his two-handed scimitar. However, he doesn't think even a Brutal Attack will take the giant out in a single blow, and he's not sure whether the giant will then attack him or*

## Defence Modifiers

*Whenever a character attacks a target, conditions such as cover, posture, light, and mobility may affect the chance of successfully hitting. The following defence modifiers are applied to the Passive Defence score or Active Defence roll of the target.*

### Table 2-5: Defence Modifiers

| Condition | Defence Modifiers |
| --- | --- |
| Target in partial cover | +3 |
| Target in near-full cover | +6 |
| Target prone | -6 |
| Target with back turned | -3 |
| Target on lower ground, inferior position | -3 |
| Target on higher ground, superior position | +3 |
| Target dodging and weaving | +3 |
| Target making a headlong dash | -6 |
| Attacker attacking in darkness | +3 |

*Thufir—if it attacks him, he's going to want to make an Active Defence! Consequently Amin decides to delay his Brutal Attack action until after the giant has attacked. If the giant attacks him, he'll cancel his Brutal Attack and make an Active Defence and Normal Attack instead.*

## Charge Attack

A Charge Attack is an action where you run full tilt at your opponent and strike him hard, using your built-up momentum to deal massive extra damage. It works exactly like a Normal Attack action, except that it takes longer to complete, requiring three actions. This means that you must begin a Charge Attack action in one round, and complete it in the next.

If a Charge Attack is successful, you inflict +10 additional points of damage on your opponent (see page 56).

A Charge Attack may only be made if you and your target are at least 2 paces apart. You must also not be engaged in melee at the moment you begin your charge. You spend two of the three actions of the Charge Attack moving; in each action you may move up to your DEX x 2 in paces, but must move at least 1 pace. In any action where you move more than your DEX in paces, your Passive Defence suffers a -6 penalty.

During a Charge Attack action, you may not take any other actions, including Active Defence actions. However, you can cancel your Charge Attack at any point before you roll your attack, perhaps to make an Active Defence.

## Ranged Attack

A Ranged Attack is any attack made at range with a missile weapon (such as a bow) or a thrown weapon (such as a spear or throwing knife). It works like a Normal Attack action, with the following differences.

Firstly, as shown on Table 2-9: Ranged Weapons, Ranged Attack weapons can be used at four possible ranges: Short, Medium, Long, and Extreme. The precise distances of each of these ranges for any given weapon are shown on the table. Ranged Attacks are not possible beyond these ranges.

Secondly, Ranged Attacks with missile weapons require 2 actions: the first is to assume a viable attack position while still being able to use your Passive Defence; the second is to notch an arrow, take aim, and loose it. Ranged Attacks with thrown weapons only require 1 action.

Thirdly, Ranged Attack rolls become more difficult the greater the range. Any attack roll for a ranged weapon at greater than Short range incurs a penalty to the result: an attack at Medium range incurs a -3 result penalty; at Long range, a -6 penalty; and, at Extreme range, a -12 penalty. This is summarised on Table 2-6: Ranged Attack Penalties.

| TABLE 2-6: RANGED ATTACK PENALTIES | |
|---|---|
| **RANGE** | **PENALTY TO THE RESULT** |
| Short | No change; attack at your full ability. |
| Medium | -3 result penalty. |
| Long | -6 result penalty. |
| Extreme | -12 result penalty. |

Finally, note that Ranged Attacks have a **minimum range**. For thrown weapons, this is 2 paces; for missile weapons this depends upon the weapon and the attacker's DEX, but is usually greater. See Table 2-9: Ranged Weapons (page 62) for more.

## Free Attack

Some path abilities (page 17) or other events permit you to make an immediate additional attack as a free action. These attacks may be Normal (melee) Attacks or Ranged Attacks; they may not be Brutal Attacks or Charge Attacks. They take place immediately after the action you just took, and require no additional action (in

## Using Miniatures in Combat

*It's absolutely not necessary to use miniatures, pawns, or tokens when running a combat in* **Capharnaüm**—*in fact, it's basically assumed you won't be doing. However, if you do decide to use them, then it can be fun to map out the relative positions of combatants to determine who can move where and attack whom. This tactical movement becomes particularly interesting when characters start making Combat Move, Unengaged Move, Brutal Attack, and Charge Attack actions, where either they're moving a considerable distance, or are completely unable to move at all, and therefore may be subject to passing or delayed action attacks, or may be out of range of melee.*

fact you can consider them part of that first action for timing and book-keeping purposes). Note that under no circumstances may you take more than one Free Attack in a given action.

# Defend Actions

## Active Defence

When attacked, you may attempt an Active Defence. This takes 1 action, and represents parrying, dodging, or a combination of the two, to avoid an attack. An unarmed character making an Active Defence rolls DEX + Athletics; an armed character may choose to make an Active Defence using either DEX + Athletics or DEX + Fighting. Most animals and monsters attack only using natural weapons and will usually make Active Defence dodges using DEX + Athletics.

The result on your Active Defence roll becomes the difficulty which an attacker must equal or exceed in order to successfully hit you.

Note that you can take an Active Defence action at any point during a round, even before your turn in the Initiative order or at a higher Initiative score than your own Max Init, as long as you still have actions left to take. If you've already used up all your actions for a round, you may not take an Active Defence action, and must instead rely upon your Passive Defence (see below) to protect you. Additionally, you may only take one Active Defence action at a particular step in the Initiative order; if two characters attack you at the same step in the Initiative order (say, at Initiative 3), you may only actively defend against one of them, even if you have actions to spare.

**Active Defence = DEX + Athletics or Fighting**

## Fighting With Two Weapons

*If you have a score of at least 4 in DEX, INT, and Fighting, you can choose to fight with one weapon in each hand. The weapon you're wielding in your dominant hand is your* main weapon; *the weapon in your off-hand is your* secondary weapon.

*Fighting with two weapons has two advantages:*

❖ *Firstly, you gain a +3 bonus to your Passive Defence score or the result of your Active Defence roll.*

❖ *Secondly, if you get a Critical Success (magnitude 6+) on a Normal Attack, Brutal Attack, Charge Attack, or Active Defence with your main weapon, you may immediately make a Free Attack with your secondary weapon. This Free Attack does not cost you an action.*

For example: Micah Bar Bethlaim, a reputed duellist from Sagrada, has DEX 5, INT 4, and Fighting 4. His Passive Defence of 16 (DEX 5 + Athletics 5 + 6) increases to 19 when he wields two weapons.

In a fight against a fierce Al-Fariqani warrior, Micah wields two *suyuf* scimitars. He attacks first at Initiative 5 and succeeds with a magnitude of 6—a Critical Success. This does damage, and also means he can immediately make a second attack at Initiative 5, this time with his secondary weapon. The second attack is also a success, ripping through the armour of the Al-Fariqani, doing even more damage.

## Double Attacks

*When fighting with two weapons, you may choose to attack with them simultaneously, in a* Double Attack *action. This works just like a Normal Attack, except you add a bonus to your result equal to your skill level in your secondary weapon (this is usually your Fighting skill, but may include any bonus for specialisation or expertise (page 74)). If the Double Attack succeeds, you add your Heroism score to the damage done by your main weapon to find the total damage done.*

The fight continues! In the next round, Micah chooses to make a Double Attack action, attacking simultaneously with both scimitars. This is a DEX + Fighting roll. Micah rolls 9/5 for a result of 17, and adds his Fighting 4 score as a bonus, for a final result of 21. Micah's magnitude dice come up with a magnitude of 2.

The fierce Al-Fariqani warrior rolls an Active Defence of 9, so Micah's attack succeeds. The damage is STR 3 + *suyuf* 8 + 2 magnitude, plus the Double Attack damage bonus of +3 Heroism, for a total damage of 16.

For example: Ralph's character rolled 3 for Initiative, but is attacked by a desert bandit at Initiative order 4. Because you can make an Active Defence at any point in a round, Ralph opts to take an Active Defence action against the attack on Initiative 4. He successfully dodges the attack, and still has one action remaining, which he uses to take a Normal Attack action at Initiative 3. Note that if a second desert bandit also attacks Ralph's character at Initiative order 4, he won't be able to make an Active Defence, even though he still has an action to spare, because you may only make 1 Active Defence at a given step in the Initiative order.

## Passive Defence

If you're attacked and don't have any actions to spend on an Active Defence, you must rely on your **Passive Defence**. You may also choose to use a Passive Defence if you prefer to use your actions for attacking, moving, and so on.

Your Passive Defence is a fixed score representing the difficulty an attacker must equal or exceed to hit you. It's equal to the sum of your DEX + Athletics, plus 6.

**Passive Defence = DEX + Athletics + 6**

# Magic Actions

## Cast a Spell

Casting a spell or otherwise using magic in combat takes 1 action. It's usually a roll of INT + Sacred Word (see page 31). You may only take 1 Cast a Spell or attack action per round.

## Break a Tablet

Breaking a chiromancy tablet (page 135) and releasing the magic contained within it takes 1 action. You may break more than one tablet per round.

# Move Actions

## Combat Move

If you're on foot and engaged in combat, you can move a number of 5-foot paces equal to your DEX score in a single action. This isn't a sprint or even a brisk walk, but a cautious and considered shift in position while maintaining your stance and guard. Normally a Combat Move requires no roll. Note however that if you enter combat with someone with a long weapon or equivalent, you do

so at a distance of 2 paces instead of 1. Your opponent may make Active Defence rolls against your DEX + Athletics or Fighting to prevent you from making a Combat Move to close. You may only attempt to close this way once per round.

## Unengaged Move

Characters who aren't engaged in melee combat may move more rapidly. Doing this anywhere near an active combat, however, exposes you to increased danger: it's assumed you're making a headlong dash as fast as you can, paying no heed to other people, incoming attacks, the need to dodge and weave, etc. A character making an unengaged movement action may cover a distance up to his DEX x 2 in paces every action; running faster than that requires a STR + Athletics skill roll (see page 27).

If you're making a headlong dash like this, your Passive Defence is reduced by -6.

# Other Actions

## Aiming

Aiming is an action that is used to improve the accuracy of Ranged Attacks, both thrown and missile. It takes 1 action to aim, and provides 1 bonus die.

## Disengage

If you wish to leave an active melee combat, whether to escape or for any other reason, you must take two successive Combat Move actions to get out of range. Depending on the situation, Al-Rawi may ask you for Athletics or Stealth skill rolls to represent disengaging from melee, particularly if you're opponent doesn't want to let you disengage.

## Draw a Weapon

If you're not currently holding your weapon, you must take an action to draw it from its scabbard, grab it from the floor, etc. If you're trying to retrieve a thrown weapon which has landed at a distance equal to or less than your Combat Move (DEX in paces) from you, then you can move and pick up the weapon in a single action.

## Help or Hinder

You may take a Help action or a Hinder action during combat. Each takes 1 action, and lets you give bonus or penalty dice to the target you're helping or hindering. See "Helping and Hindering" on page 50 for more.

## Mounted Combat

Mounted combat—on horseback, camel, or abzul—brings several advantages.

Firstly, a mounted attacker benefits from a higher, advantageous position when attacking targets on foot (see "Target on Lower Ground" in Table 2-5: Defence Modifiers, page 52) and when being attacked (see "Target on Higher Ground").

Secondly, a mounted Charge Attack may be made at a minimum distance of 4 paces, and gains an additional damage bonus equal to the Riding skill of the attacker. This bonus is cumulative with those gained from certain path abilities, for example such as the first path of the Walad Badiya (which adds the abzul's STR to damage done) or the second path of the Fragrantine Charioteers (which adds the attacker's Riding skill to damage, therefore adding the Riding skill twice).

**Mounted Charge Damage = Damage + 10 + Riding skill score (+ other bonuses)**

# Combat Effects

## Damage

**Damage** is the most common effect of a successful attack. You inflict wounds on your opponent equal to your STR + your weapon's damage + the magnitude of your successful attack roll. Attacks such as Brutal Attacks and Charge Attacks may provide additional bonuses to the damage you inflict.

The damage you inflict on an opponent is subtracted from his Hit Points. Before this happens, though, the damage may be reduced by two factors:

❖ First, the opponent's Soak score is subtracted from the damage done (but see "Critical Success and Critical Failure" below).

❖ Second, the Armour Value of any natural armour or armour worn (including a shield carried) by the opponent is subtracted from the damage done.

Whatever damage is left (if any) is then subtracted from the opponent's Hit Points—see page 67 for more.

**Damage = STR + weapon damage + magnitude – Soak (– Armour Value)**

## Non-lethal Damage

Damage inflicted by punches, kicks, or even sticks, clubs and chair legs is considered **non-lethal damage**. These attacks may knock opponents out, but will never kill unless the victor decides to finish off his opponent (see page 57).

Additionally, half of any non-lethal damage sustained by a character is recovered in the five minutes following. The remainder is considered to be long-term damage and must be treated normally (page 71).

For example: Amin has been ambushed by a gang of rogues. The first blow knocks him silly, and the thugs jump on him and beat him black and blue, inflicting 44 points of damage. As he had 30 HP, this leaves him at -14 HP, out cold on the ground. Five minutes later, Amin recovers 22 HP (half of the 44 points of damage), giving him 8 HP. He regains consciousness alone, stripped of everything of value he had.

## Chariot Combat

Chariot Combat is a variant on Mounted Combat, and uses the same rules, with the following modifications.

Chariots are highly mobile weapons platforms, capable of depositing fighters right into the midst of raging battles, as well as allowing missile weapons fire to be conducted from a moving position. Chariots may also be used as weapons in their own right. Some chariots are small, with about 80 HP and only enough room for a single charioteer, who may be armed with one or more javelins; others are larger, with about 160 HP, big enough for a charioteer and one or two additional combatants, who may fire short or recurved bows. Chariots are usually only damaged by smashing weapons and fire.

Charioteers use their Riding skill to manoeuvre their chariots. You may make a Charge Attack on a chariot as if it was a mount, adding your Riding skill (or the Riding skill of the charioteer, as appropriate) as a damage bonus to any attacks, including missile attacks. Combatants riding a chariot enjoy Partial Cover and a superior position in combat.

If someone else is driving, you may also make Active Defence rolls when fighting from a chariot. The charioteer may attack with the chariot by making a Riding roll; the base damage is equal to the mount's (or mounts') STR score; blades may be fitted to the chariot wheels for +6 damage. Critical Failures on a chariot usually mean you fall off, taking 2 dice falling damage. If you're making a Charge Attack at the time, you must add your mount's STR to the damage you sustain.

## Critical Success and Critical Failure

In combat, magnitudes of 6 or better (Critical Success or Critical Failure) on attack and defence rolls have special effects, as shown on Table 2-7: Critical Success and Critical Failure Effects in Combat.

| TABLE 2-7: CRITICAL SUCCESS AND CRITICAL FAILURE EFFECTS IN COMBAT | |
| --- | --- |
| **CRITICAL RESULT** | **EFFECT** |
| Critical Success on Attack | The damage the attacker does ignores the defender's Soak. |
| Critical Failure on Attack | The defender acts before the attacker on the next round, and gains 1 bonus die. |
| Critical Success on Active Defence | The defender acts before the attacker on the next round, and gains 1 bonus die. |
| Critical Failure on Active Defence | The damage the attacker does ignores the defender's Soak. |
| Critical Success on Attack vs Critical Failure on Active Defence | The damage the attacker does ignores the defender's Soak. The defender is disarmed, knocked to the ground, and at the attacker's mercy. |
| Critical Failure on Attack vs Critical Success on Active Defence | The defender turns the attacker's attack back on him, causing the attacker to suffer the damage he would have inflicted on the defender. The defender acts before the attacker on the next round, and gains 1 bonus die. |

## Death Does Not Become You...

Killing is no fun, and heroes never kill gratuitously. The reason is simple: honour, bravery, and loyalty dictate that any enemy who surrenders or loses consciousness is considered "taken out" of combat and deserving of mercy. It's common to see a defeated enemy become the best friend of the one who defeated him: Quarterian chivalric romances and Jazirati epic poetry are filled with such stories.

In game terms, when a character falls unconscious, he doesn't automatically die (although he might if there's no one to treat him—see "Health and Wounds" on page 67). For a character to be killed, the attacker must, at the moment of attack, announce that he's striking a lethal blow and intends to kill. If the target is below 0 HP (and therefore unconscious), he's unable to defend himself, and Al-Rawi can simply decide any subsequent blow is a *coup de grace* and the victim is slain.

## Optional Rule: The Epitaph

To reinforce the heroic and dramatic nature of **Capharnaum**, we recommend the **Epitaph Rule**.

According to this rule, when a character wants to summarily dispatch a foe that is already out of action, he must come up with an exemplary, panache-filled phrase like: "You were an admirable opponent. I have killed one thousand before finding one like you...!" or even "It is over for you, blackguard! Now go present your miserable self before your pitiful ancestors!" And so on.

Al-Rawi is the judge of the Epitaph's validity. If she doesn't find the phrase sufficiently dramatic, funny, sad or incisive, she can declare the victim wasn't dispatched. The character is assumed not to have had the guts to finish the job.

For example: Amin has just beaten a *myrmidon* hired killer an old enemy sent after him. Dropping to -3 HP, the hired killer loses consciousness and is about to fall, when Amin's player announces he wants to behead him before the body hits the floor. Amin cries "Run to hell and prepare a bed for the cowardly scum who sent you!"

Al-Rawi accepts the Epitaph. Amin twirls around while pronouncing these incisive words, and at the end of the twirl his scimitar detaches the head of the *myrmidon* from his body, which collapses to the sand!

# WEAPONS

There are many weapons available in Jazirat and the wider world beyond. This section presents just some of them. Weights are given in **pounds** (lb) for use with the Encumbrance rules (page 78), and costs are given in **ounces of cumin** (OC, also equal to 1 silver talent or ST) for average quality items. See the weapons descriptions for more on their special attacks or bonuses. See page 356 for a much more extensive list of equipment.

| | | TABLE 2-8: MELEE WEAPONS | | |
|---|---|---|---|---|
| **WEAPON** | **DAMAGE** | **DESCRIPTION** | **WT (LB)** | **COST (OC)** |
| **SHORT AND NON-LETHAL WEAPONS** | | | | |
| Aragonian Whip | DEX +3 | 3-pace reach, non-lethal damage. | 4 | 6 |
| Choora | STR +4 | Triangular-bladed dagger, easy to conceal. | 4 | 6 |
| Jambiya | DEX +3 | Curved dagger, parry bonus. | 4 | 8 |
| Khanjar | STR +3 | Wavy-bladed dagger, -3 AV. | 4 | 10 |
| Kick | (STR x2) +3 | Non-lethal damage. | n/a | n/a |
| Punch | STR x2 | Non-lethal damage. | n/a | n/a |
| **LONG WEAPONS (-3 attack / Active Defence in restricted spaces; Normal Attack at 1 or 2 paces)** | | | | |
| Agalanthian Trident | STR +8 | Break weapon / disarm. | 10 | 40 |
| Hoplite Spear | STR +10 | +1 bonus die vs Charge. | 10 | 24 |
| Quarterian Lance | STR +8 | +12 mounted charge damage bonus. | 10 | 20 |
| Rumh | STR +8 | Poleaxe; "whip" attack: +1 bonus die vs Babouche-Draggers. | 10 | 6 |
| **ONE-HANDED WEAPONS** | | | | |
| Agalanthian Gladius | STR +8 | +6 Passive Defence with 2 weapons; +1 bonus die to attacks or Active Defences. | 4 | 10 |
| Common Axe | STR +8 | -3 Active Defence penalty. | 4 | 0.9 |
| Crusader Sword | STR +8 | Two-edged hvy longsword; +1 bonus die vs Babouche-Draggers. | 4 | 30 |
| Espada Valladena | STR +6 | Longsword with basket guard; knockout attack. | 4 | 40 |
| Falkata (Aragon), Khedama (Kh'saaba) or Yatagan (Capharnaum), Kopis (Agalanthia) | STR +6 | Two-edged straight sabre; +3 damage on Brutal and Charge Attacks. | 4 | 20/26/ 20/22 |
| Military Flail | STR +8 | -3 Active Defence; +1 bonus die vs Babouche-Draggers. | 4 | 20 |
| Orkadian Axe | STR +10 | Double-bladed war axe; -6 Active Defence. | 4 | 40 |
| Sayf | STR +4 | Short scimitar; possible Free Attack on failed attack roll. | 4 | 12 |
| Spatha (Agalanthia), Kaskara (Jazirat) | STR +8 | Longsword; -3 Active Defence unless STR & CON 4+. | 4 | 20/20 |
| Suyuf (Capharnaum), Shimshir (Kh'saaba) | STR +8 | Long scimitar | 4 | 30/30 |
| War Hammer | STR +10 | On Critical Success, break weapon or -3 penalty bruising. | 4 | 10 |
| **BASTARD WEAPONS** | | +2 damage if used two-handed. | +2 | +10% |
| **TWO-HANDED WEAPONS** | | +4 damage. | +4 | +30% |

## Short and Non-lethal Weapons

### Aragonian Whip

An assembly of dried and woven leather straps, a whip is principally a tool for cattle breeders. It's by adding lead beads at its ends that it becomes a weapon of war.

*Special: Although not the most formidable of weapons, a whip nevertheless lets you inflict non-lethal damage (page 56) at a range of up to 3 paces (15 feet) without running the risk of being disarmed (as would happen with a throwing knife, for example).*

### Choora

A straight stiletto with a triangular blade, the *choora* is often used by women because of its lightness and small size. It's easily concealable.

*Special: When you try to conceal a choora, you gain a bonus die on your Stealth roll.*

### Jambiya

A recurved dagger, the *jambiya* is more a survival tool than a weapon, and is proudly worn at the belt of every self-respecting caravaneer. However, it can also be used in combat, and some use its curvature to deflect or even block their opponents' blades.

*Special: When you use the jambiya as a parrying weapon, you gain a bonus die on your Active Defence rolls against daggers, swords and sabres.*

### Khanjar

The *khanjar* is a dagger with a wavy blade. It's designed for penetrating between the chinks of armour.

*Special: Against an attack by a khanjar, reduce an armour's Armour Value by -3.*

### Kick / Punch

Fighting unarmed, whether with fists or feet, you inflict non-lethal damage (page 56) based on your physical strength.

## Long Weapons

Long weapons are extremely effective on the battlefield, where they make Normal Attacks at a 1 or 2 pace distance, but less so in confined spaces. Al-Rawi may impose a -3 result penalty to attack and Active Defence rolls with long weapons in marketplaces, crowded places, narrow buildings, caves and tunnels, and so on.

### Agalanthian Trident

A light and handy weapon, the trident is mostly used by gladiators and charioteers. Although it does less damage than a typical spear, it's still a formidable weapon, and often used more to disarm opponents than wound them.

*Special: On a Critical Success Active Defence roll with a trident, you may break your opponent's weapon or disarm him.*

### Hoplite Spear

Hoplites, the footsoldiers of Agalanthian armies, are most of all spearmen. This weapon is their most faithful companion, and it's even worshipped in their cult of the Benevolent Sister.

*Special: Hoplite spears provide a bonus die when attacking a charging opponent.*

## Quarterian Lance

Also called a cavalry lance, this weapon is prized by the Occidentian nobility, who have turned its use into sport and spectacle.

**Special:** *When using a Quarterian lance in a Charge Attack on horseback, you gain a +12 damage bonus instead of +10.*

## Rumh

A spear with a long bamboo haft, the *rumh* has a wide blade like that of a halberd. It's used by footsoldiers and horsemen, is renowned for its lightness, and is as common as a scimitar.

**Special:** *With a slightly flexible haft, the* rumh *can make "whip" attacks against adjacent opponents without necessitating Combat Move actions. It grants a bonus die in combat against Babouche-Draggers (page 65).*

# One-handed Weapons

## Agalanthian Gladius

Shorter than the spatha, the gladius's blade is no longer than 2 feet. It's a handy, fast weapon, adapted to two-weapon fighting.

**Special:** *When fighting with two Agalanthian gladiuses (see page 54), your Passive Defence increases by +6 rather than +3, and your Active Defence and all attacks gain a bonus die.*

## Common Axe

The axe is probably one of the oldest weapons in the world, forged many centuries before the sword. Although relatively poor for defence, attacks with an axe, when done properly, inflict more damage than a common sword.

**Special:** *Any Active Defence rolls made with a common axe suffer a -3 result penalty.*

## Crusader Sword

A double-edged sword with a 3-foot blade, this Quarterian weapon is heavy and effective.

**Special:** *Balanced for mass combat, the Crusader Sword provides a bonus die to any attacks against Babouche-Draggers (page 65).*

## Espada Valladena

A longsword with a basket hilt, the *espada* is the emblem of Aragon. Solid and light, it nevertheless deals heavy blows with impressive damage. It's most often forged from good steel from Sarajon, the centre of Aragonian weaponsmithing. It's said that thinner and lighter weapons have been turned out under the hammers of the city's master smiths in recent years. These **rapiers**, as they're known, might soon replace the proud *espada Valladena*.

**Special:** *On a Brutal Attack, if the damage sustained equals or exceeds twice the target's Soak (damage >= Soak x 2), the target must make a difficulty 18 CON roll or fall unconscious for magnitude x 1 minutes.*

## Falcata (Aragon) / Khedama (Kh'saaba) / Yatagan (Capharnaum) / Kopis (Agalanthia)

A single-edged sabre convex towards the hilt and convex towards the tip, this weapon can deliver a blow with the momentum of an axe, while retaining many of the advantageous characteristics of a sword (such as the longer cutting edge and the ability to thrust). It's extremely common among troops of all nations.

*Special: This weapon is highly effective in Brutal Attacks and Charge Attacks, each of which have their damage bonus increased by +3 points.*

## Military Flail

A steel ball at the end of a chain (with or without a haft), the military flail is a formidable weapon in mass combat since its blows are generally not stopped by one obstacle.

*Special: Military flails provide a bonus die to any attacks against Babouche-Draggers. However, its cumbersome nature makes it harder to parry and dodge: subtract -3 from the result of any Active Defence roll made by the wielder.*

## Orkadian Axe

Longer and heavier than a common axe, the Orkadian axe needs more strength to wield. It has a correspondingly greater destructive force.

*Special: Subtract -6 from the result of any Active Defence roll.*

## Sayf

Also called a short scimitar, the *sayf* is often preferred by city guards as it is easier to wield in confined spaces. It's the most commonly encountered weapon among Jazirati or Shiradim in Capharnaum. Its thin, curved blade doesn't exceed 18 inches, and never gets snagged on uneven wall surfaces or pieces of armour. It's particularly effective against heavy armour.

*Special: If an attack with a sayf against heavy armour misses with a magnitude of less than 2, the attacker may make an immediate, second, free attack with a -3 result penalty. Only one such free attack may be made by a given sayf in a given round.*

## Spatha (Agalanthia) / Kaskara (Jazirat)

A long gladius (its blade measures two-and-a-half feet) generally used from horseback, the *spatha* is a formidable weapon. Even if used on foot, it's advisable to also carry a shield for parrying, as the *spatha* is very heavy and difficult to employ for defence.

*Special: Although it does more damage than a simple one-handed sword, the spatha requires STR and CON of at least 4 to be used for defence, otherwise any Active Defence rolls made with it suffer a -3 result penalty.*

## Suyuf (Capharnaum) / Shimshir (Kh'saaba)

Also called a long scimitar, this sword has a two-and-a-half foot blade, and is the pride of the Saabi or Shiradim warrior. Traditionalists such as the Tarekids and Hassanids believe that wielding a long scimitar means you consider yourself a descendant of the Prophets, and it's not uncommon to find simple warriors challenged to duels to prove they have the right to wield the weapon.

*Special: Light and handy for its size, the long scimitar offers speed and penetrative power not usually available to weapons of this category (hence the higher damage).*

## War Hammer

Whether metal- or wooden-hafted, the war hammer is widely-used. Rarely exceeding 2 feet 8 inches in length, it's relatively handy, and permits inexperienced fighters to hold their own without too much technical know-how.

*Special:* On any Critical Success attack, the wielder of a war hammer may, in addition to dealing damage, choose either to break his opponent's weapon or inflict bruising causing a cumulative -3 result penalty to all physical action rolls until he recovers the lost HP.

## Ammunition

*In general, you can usually assume you have the arrows necessary to use your bow—unless you're in a battle which is going on a very long time and you're using a lot of ammunition, Al-Rawi will usually assume you're looking after your arrows, recovering them after combat, and so on; every now and then she may require you to spend a few ounces of cumin when you're in a souk to replenish your supply.*

*Sometimes, though, ammunition can become really important to play. For example, if you're adventuring underground beneath an ancient ruin out in the trackless desert, weeks away from the nearest habitation, running out of ammunition can be a matter for tension and excitement during play! At such times, Al-Rawi may require you to account for every arrow you have with you, and roll Urim and Turim, the Stones of Fate (page 77), to see whether you're able to recover arrows shot during combat. Figure a quiver of arrows costs 1 ounce of cumin and weighs 4lbs. If you run out, your bow is going to be useless—unless you can figure out some way to fletch your own arrows!*

*With thrown weapons such as javelins, axes, and knives, we recommend you keep track of these as individual weapons, rather than treating them as ammunition.*

| TABLE 2-9: RANGED WEAPONS | | | | | |
|---|---|---|---|---|---|
| WEAPON | DAMAGE | MINIMUM RANGE[1] | SHORT / MEDIUM (-3) / LONG (-6) / EXTREME (-12) RANGE (5-FOOT PACES) | WEIGHT (LBS) | COST (OC) |
| THROWN WEAPONS | | | | | |
| Javelin / Throwing Axe | STR +8 | 2 | <12 / na / 12-24 / 24+ (Max = STR x 6) | 2 | 4 / 5 |
| Knife | STR +6 | 2 | <12 / na / 12-24 / 24+ (Max = STR x 6) | 2 | 1 |
| Sling | STR +1 | 2 | <12 / na / 12-24 / 24+ (Max = STR x 6) | 2 | 0.8 |
| MISSILE WEAPONS | | | | | |
| Jazirati Recurved Bow | STR +7 | 7 – DEX | <36 / 36-72 / 72-120 / 120-150 | 8 | 15 |
| Long Bow[2] | STR +9 | 9 – DEX | <36 / 36-72 / 72-120 / 120-150 | 9 | 9 |
| Short Bow | STR +6 | 5 – DEX | <18 / 18-36 / 36-72 / 72-90 | 6 | 5 |

1: Range is in 5-foot paces. Minimum range is 2 paces.
2: +2 bonus dice when aiming.

# Bastard and Two-handed Weapons

Many of the weapons introduced in "One-handed Weapons" above also come in hand-and-a-half ("bastard") and two-handed versions. These have the following characteristics.

## Hand-and-a-Half (Bastard) Weapons

The hand-and-a-half version of a weapon is +2lbs heavier and +10% more expensive. The wielder gains a +3 damage bonus when making an attack two-handed.

## Two-handed Weapons

The two-handed version of a weapon is +4lbs heavier and +30% more expensive. The wielder gains a +6 bonus to damage. Obviously a character using a two-handed weapon may not use a shield, nor fight with two weapons, although a character with STR 5 or higher may wield a two-handed weapon in one-hand without losing the damage bonus.

# Thrown Weapons

## Knife / Javelin / Throwing Axe

Used to keep both foes and wild animals at bay, these ubiquitous thrown weapons form part of the kit of any self-respecting adventurer.

*Special: Because of their weight and balance, these weapons can be thrown at melee distance and while engaged in combat. If thrown at a distance equal to or lower than your Combat Move (DEX in paces), you can quickly retrieve* a knife, javelin, or throwing axe by spending a single action. It's assumed you're already committed to retrieving the weapon the moment it's thrown.

## Sling

A weapon prized by the Saabi and Shiradim, a sling is a simple strap of leather or fabric which is spun round to project a bullet-like projectile (often a rounded stone). It's most often used for hunting, but many warriors like to use it as a deterrent.

*Special: Anything small and heavy enough can be a projectile for a sling. Unless you're in a very unusual environment, it's almost impossible to run out of ammunition.*

# Missile Weapons

## Jazirati Recurved Bow

A good trade-off between power and speed of use, the Jazirati recurved bow can be used both at range and close-up.

*Special: You can attack with a Jazirati recurved bow from a distance of (7 – DEX, minimum 2) paces.*

## Long Bow

The epitome of the war bow, the long bow has an impressive range and a greater accuracy than other ranged weapons.

*Special: If you take an Aiming action (page 55), you gain 2 bonus dice instead of 1. As aiming and shooting a bow requires 3 actions (ie more than 1 round), it's advisable to do so from cover or a position safe from attack.*

## Short Bow

Used for hunting as well as war, the short bow is a common weapon in Jazirat.

*Special: Less accurate and with a shorter range than the long bow, the short bow can sometimes be used close-up.*

# ARMOUR

There are many types of armour. All peoples have their own, and it's generally easy to recognise a warrior's origin from the armour he wears.

Armour in *Capharnaum* doesn't detail every piece and type, but rather defines four broad categories: Shield, Partial Armour, Light Armour, and Heavy Armour. Each category provides an Armour Value which is combined with the wearer's Soak when reducing damage sustained in combat. In addition, Heavy armour, due to its weight and encumbrance, makes some of its wearer's skill rolls more difficult.

| TABLE 2-10: ARMOUR | | | | |
|---|---|---|---|---|
| ARMOUR TYPE | ARMOUR VALUE[1] | WEIGHT (LB) | COST (OC) | DESCRIPTION |
| Shield, Buckler or Targe | +1 | 10 / 20 | 5 / 10 | +1 bonus die to Active Defence rolls. |
| Partial Armour | 1 (2) | 4 | 2 | A helm, pieces of mail, leather doublet, epaulettes, etc. |
| Light Armour | 3 (4) | 20 | 8 | A helm, plus leather armour (may be studded), or ring or plate mail. |
| Heavy[2] or Myrmidon[3] Armour | 6 (7) | 60 | 30 / 100[3] | A helm, plus solid plate armour over mail. |

*1: AV in brackets are if a shield is also carried.*

*2: All rolls of Assassination, Athletics, Intrusion, Riding, Stealth, and Thievery are one step harder (+3 difficulty).*

*3: Myrmidon armour (page 65) costs 100 OC. It does not suffer the skill penalty of other forms of Heavy armour.*

*Partial Armour*

*Light Armour*

## Swimming in Armour

*It's impossible to swim while wearing Light, Heavy, or Myrmidon armour. If you fall into water while wearing Light or Myrmidon armour, you must make a difficulty 6 DEX + Heroism roll to remove enough of the armour to be able to make swim rolls (see page 28). If you're wearing Heavy armour, the roll is difficulty 15.*

*If you fail this roll, you start to drown (page 68). Each round you drown, you may make another roll to remove the armour, but the difficulty is one step harder (+3 difficulty).*

## Shield

Whatever its size and shape, a shield provides 1 point of protection. Its Armour Value is cumulative with all other armour types, so you can wear Partial, Light or Heavy armour with a shield and benefit from its protection.

A shield also provides 1 bonus die to Active Defence rolls.

## Partial Armour

Whether a simple helmet, pieces of mail, a simple breastplate, leather doublet, or simply epaulettes, Partial armour has an Armour Value of 1. Elements aren't cumulative: wearing a helmet and a few pieces of mail doesn't give you AV: 2. Al-Rawi should decide when you're wearing a sufficient amount of Partial armour for it

to constitute Light armour (as a rule of thumb, four pieces or so should do it).

## Light Armour

Bulkier than Partial armour, Light armour is often made up of a helmet, leather pieces (studded or not), mail or ringed pieces, and plate.

## Heavy Armour

More common among Quarterians than other peoples, Heavy armour is made up of metal plates, mail pieces, and a helmet. It's very

*Heavy Armour*

cumbersome and heavy, and increases the difficulty of Assassination, Athletics, Intrusion, Riding, Stealth and Thievery rolls by one step (+3). Myrmidon armour, however, while much more expensive, is specifically created so as not to incur this penalty.

# CHAMPIONS, VALIANT CAPTAINS, AND BABOUCHE-DRAGGERS

*Capharnaum* distinguishes three categories of combatant: Champions, Valiant Captains, and Babouche-Draggers.

## Champions

Champions are exceptional individuals who play an important part in your adventures. They're evil geniuses, town champions, famous knights, Princes of Thieves, or even other Dragon-Marked. They're tough, clever, dangerous opponents, far from easy to defeat.

In combat, Champions use the default rules for combat presented above. Dragon-Marked are always considered to be Champions, regardless of how good they are at fighting.

## Valiant Captains

Valiant Captains are the principal henchmen of your main villains, the chief of the guards of a castle or city, a village champion, and so on. They're hardy and pugnacious, but ultimately are second-rate opponents, less formidable and less cunning than Champions.

When a Dragon-Marked obtains a Critical Success on an attack against a Valiant Captain (a magnitude 6 or greater), the Valiant Captain is automatically considered to be **taken out** (dead, knocked-out, etc—see page 57).

## Babouche-Draggers

Babouche-Draggers don't even have Hit Points! They're the common soldiery, the hordes of guards or bandits that rush up, their *babouche* slippers flapping and dragging along the floor, only to fly out of windows when hit by the weakest punch. You face six of them at a time in tavern brawls, a half-dozen city guards cornering you in an alleyway, and they act as a **group**, rolling just once for initiative and making just one attack roll representing the accumulated attacks of all six Babouche-Draggers (or however many are left in the group). When you provide stats for Babouche-Draggers,

you do so as a group of 6. Instead of Hit Points, you just need to list their number.

*For example: Dalila Bint Mimun Abd-al-Tarek, a Saabi courtesan-rogue, has been taken prisoner by a band of fearsome pirates who wish to sell her in a slave market somewhere on an island south of Kh'saaba. Having managed to untie her bonds and climb from the hold of the pirate ship, she now confronts the pirates on deck. Al-Rawi announces that all the pirates except for the captain and the second-in-command are Babouche-Draggers. There are 12 of them, in 2 groups of 6. With CON 2, DEX 3, and INT 1, their Max Init is 3.*

*Al-Rawi rolls for initiative. She rolls once for the captain, once for the second-in-command, and once each for the two groups of 6 Babouche-Draggers, which get Initiative scores of 2 and 1 respectively.*

When a Dragon-Marked or Champion succeeds on an attack roll against a Babouche-Dragger group, he takes out a number of them equal to the magnitude of his success. If you're confident, you can even swagger against Babouche-Draggers, taking out still more—these flailing minions should go down like cut grain before your sword!

*Dalila throws herself into the melee: "I'm currently unarmed, so I'm going to take one swagger die to get myself a weapon. I run at the first Babouche-Dragger and grab the sword he has at his belt. When I draw it, my elbow violently hits the rascal's jaw!"*

*Rolling 6/3 for her attack (DEX 4 + Fighting 2, with one swagger die), she gets 2, 2, 2, 5, 5, and 5. She keeps three dice for a result of 15. The Babouche-Dragger group's Active Defence roll is 14, so Dalila's attack is a success, despite her swagger. She succeeds with a magnitude of 3, so Al-Rawi declares that, first, the unsavoury individual Dalila stole the sword from is beaten and taken out of combat. Moreover, two other pirates are also out of the fight: dragged back by the momentum of the pirate that was hit, they crash down the steps to the hold and are knocked out...*

Babouche-Draggers are rarely paragons of courage. If half or more of a Babouche-Dragger group is taken out (so a minimum of three), the rest turn and flee!

*The three other pirates from that first group of Babouche-Draggers quail as their fellows tumble down the steps. Dalila snarls at them, and then yells a war-cry in their face. As half of their group has been taken out, the remaining members panic and flee!*

Babouche-Draggers also attack the same way, with a single attack roll for each group of 6 or less; the group gets 1 bonus die for every member in the group after the first. Al-Rawi can describe a group's attack however she likes—perhaps only one of the six Babouche-Draggers lands a blow on a successful attack, or perhaps all six do, but the result is the same: a single attack roll and a single amount of damage done.

With the captain and second-in-command still holding back, Dalila is now attacked by the second group of 6 Babouche-Draggers, who draw their scimitars and rush towards her.

*Al-Rawi rolls 10/3 (DEX 3 + Fighting 2 + 5 Babouche-Draggers above 1) for the group of 6 Babouche-Draggers, rolling 6, 6, 6, 5, 5, 4, 3, 3, 3, and 1, for a result of 18! This exceeds Dalila's Passive Defence, so Al-Rawi announces she was hit several times: the edge of one blade struck her right shoulder, while the tips of three others perforated her entrails. It all looks wildly spectacular, but Dalila only suffers damage once, losing 12 Hit Points minus her Soak.*

| TABLE 2-11: OPPONENTS | |
|---|---|
| Champions | Use the normal combat rules. |
| Valiant Captains | On a Critical Success, a Valiant Captain is dead, knocked out, taken out of the fight, etc. |
| Babouche-Draggers | No HP. Attack in groups of 6. 1 bonus die for each Babouche-Dragger after the first. One Babouche-Dragger is taken out for each point of magnitude on a successful attack. If half or more of a Babouche-Dragger group is taken out, the rest run away. |

| TABLE 2-12: EXAMPLES OF MAJOR WOUNDS | | | |
|---|---|---|---|
| ROLL 1D6 OR CHOOSE | MAJOR WOUND | EFFECTS | MAJOR WOUND TYPE[2] |
| 1 | Partially or Fully Severed Limb[1] | Lose 1-3 points of DEX. | Open Wound. |
| 2 | Maimed Limb | Lose 1-3 points of DEX. | Broken Bones. |
| 3 | Damaged Muscles | Lose 1-3 points of STR. | Open Wound and / or Bludgeoning. |
| 4 | Head Trauma | Lose 1-3 points of INT. | Open Wound and / or Bludgeoning. |
| 5 | Disfigurement | Lose 1-3 points of CHA. | Open Wound. |
| 6 | Perforated Organ | Lose 1-3 points of CON. | Open Wound and / or Bludgeoning. |

1: Attribute loss from a fully severed limb is always permanent. Attribute loss from a partially severed limb becomes permanent if it is not successfully stitched (page 71)—the limb is amputated.

2: The most common major wound type associated with this major wound. See "Healing, Medicine, and Surgery" on page 70 for how to treat it.

# Health and Wounds

## Hit Points

**Hit Points (HP)** quantify your character's health and your ability to remain on your feet and continue to adventure. A human in good health generally has 10 – 60 Hit Points. This is a reserve that drops when your character is wounded or sick; when it drops to 0 or below, your character falls unconscious.

An unconscious character cannot act, and must be treated to regain consciousness and start to heal (but see "Non-lethal Damage" on page 56). If you lose more than half your Hit Points in a single combat (or especially in a single blow!), you may, at Al-Rawi's discretion, suffer a **major wound**. A Dragon-Marked character may always spend a point of Heroism at that instant to avoid that major wound.

In addition to causing Hit Point damage, a major wound immediately causes a reduction of 1-3 points (roll 1 die and halve the result, rounding up) in one of your attribute scores, as shown on Table 2-12: Examples of Major Wounds. The attribute in question depends on the nature of the wound: for example, whether it was caused by a blade, a bludgeoning weapon, teeth and claws, fire, falling, and so on. Al-Rawi is the final arbiter of the nature of the major wound; you can roll 1D6 for a random major wound.

Suffering a major wound is a big deal, and the attribute reductions caused can even be permanent if not treated. See page 71 for how to do that.

Even if he has fewer than 0 HP through illness or wounds, a character only dies in *Capharnaum* when he is dispatched (see the Epitaph Rule, page 57), or if Al-Rawi decides.

There are no other penalties associated with a character's health status or Hit Points. *Capharnaum* is a heroic game; a character fights hard until he drops.

### Avoiding Hazard and Environmental Damage

By spending 1 point of Heroism, Dragon-Marked characters can stave off the damage and other penalties you'd suffer from hazards and environmental damage such as hunger, thirst, exposure, and fatigue for an entire day. Note this doesn't apply to things like drowning, asphyxiation, and poisoning; at Al-Rawi's discretion, it may apply to diseases. The expenditure also lets you avoid encumbrance penalties during the same period (page 78).

## Soak

Each character also has a **Soak** score. Soak represents your combativeness, your resistance to damage, and also the natural toughness of your skin, hide, carapace, and so on. Soak is equal to the sum of your character's CON and Heroism scores (page 23). Since Heroism is recalculated at the beginning of each game session, Soak is, too.

When your character takes damage, the damage points are reduced by your Soak score, as well as the Armour Value of any armour you're wearing.

*For example: After falling from a horse, Marina's character takes 9 points of damage. As her Soak is 6, she only loses 3 HP.*

## Hazards and Environmental Damage

Combat isn't the only way your character can take damage. The world of *Capharnaum* is a dangerous place, and there are many deadly hazards out there. Here are some of them.

### Hunger and Thirst

Your character can go a number of days without food equal to your Soak score, and a number of hours without water equal to your Soak score x 6. Beyond that, you incur a -1 result penalty to all rolls for each additional day without food or each additional hour without water.

Your character will die after a number of weeks without food equal to your Soak score, or a number of days without water equal to half your Soak score.

*For example: Jibril is a valiant* mujahid *with a Soak of 9. This means he can go 9 days without eating and 2 ¼ days (54 hours) without water, without incurring any penalty. If he goes 15 days without eating (but drinks regularly), he'll incur a result penalty of -6 on all his rolls. He'll die from thirst after 4 ½ days without water, and from hunger after 9 weeks without food.*

### Storms, Sunstroke, and Frostbite

Your character can withstand a number of hours under a burning sun, in intense heat, or in freezing temperatures, equal to your Soak score x 2, without taking any damage or incurring any penalties. After that, you lose 1 HP for every subsequent 2-hour period spent under those conditions.

*For example: Jibril can withstand 18 hours of intense heat without suffering any damage. After that, he'll lose 1 HP at the end of hour 20, and every 2 hours thereafter.*

## Fatigue

Your character may stay awake for a number of hours equal to your Soak score x 6 without incurring any penalty. Thereafter, you suffer a -1 result penalty to all your rolls for every 2 hour period you remain awake. Your character will fall unconscious from fatigue after a number of hours equal to your Soak score x 12.

*For example: Jibril can stay awake for 54 hours in a row without penalty. After that, he suffers a -1 result penalty to all his dice rolls at the end of hour 56, and every 2 hours after that. He'll fall unconscious from fatigue after 108 hours awake.*

## Falls

When your character falls a distance at least equal to his own height, he suffers 1D6+1 damage for each 2 paces fallen, rounded down. Both Soak and your armour's AV should be subtracted from this. If the distance fallen is less than or equal to your Soak score in paces, you may attempt a DEX + Athletics roll with a difficulty equal to the distance fallen in paces x 6 to land correctly and cushion your fall. On a success, any damage taken is halved; otherwise full damage is taken.

*For example: This time, instead of escaping through the top floor window of a harem, Amin has been hurled bodily through it! He's facing a fall of 15 paces. As this is way above his Soak score of 6 in paces, there's no way he can land correctly and cushion his fall. He slams into the ground.*

*Al-Rawi rolls 7D6+7 to determine the damage (15 divided by 2, rounded down), with a result of 30 points of damage. Amin subtracts his 6 points of Soak, taking 24 points of damage and reducing his Hit Points to 6!*

## Burns and Frostbite

You may suffer damage from direct exposure to fire or intense, freezing cold. The damage you take is proportional to the size of the source of heat or cold, and the duration of your exposure. Each round you spend exposed to the heat or cold source increases the damage you suffer by a like amount (for a camp fire, for example, that's 10 damage on the first round, 20 on the second, 30 on the third, and so on). Your character's Soak score reduces the damage taken each round as usual.

| TABLE 2-13: BURNS AND FROSTBITE DAMAGE | |
| --- | --- |
| **DAMAGE SOURCE** | **CUMULATIVE DAMAGE PER ROUND** |
| Small Flame / Hoar Frost | 1 x rd |
| Torch / Clothes on Fire | 5 x rd |
| Camp Fire / Ice Storm | 10 x rd |

| Brazier | 15 x rd |
| --- | --- |
| Raging Fire / Plunging into Freezing Water | 20 x rd |
| Dragon Breath | 30 x rd |
| Molten Lava / Absolute Zero | 50 x rd |

*For example: Jibril has 50 HP and a Soak score of 9. He spends 3 rounds in contact with a burning torch. The damage caused by the torch is 5 on the first round, 10 on the second, and 15 on the third, from each of which Jibril can subtract his Soak. This means he takes 0 damage on the first round, 1 damage on the second, and 6 on the third. At the end of round 3, Jibril has 43 HP left.*

## Drowning and Asphyxiation

Characters who fail a swimming roll (usually CON + Endurance) immediately start to drown, as do characters who find themselves trapped under water. Similarly, characters who find themselves in an area without breathable air (a smoke-filled room, a cloud of poison gas, even a vacuum, etc) immediately start to asphyxiate.

In order to avoid taking damage from drowning or asphyxiation, your character may try to hold his breath. This is a CON + Endurance roll, and must be made every round. The initial difficulty is usually difficulty 6, although it may be higher if conditions make it more difficult. However, each round your character holds his breath, the difficulty of the roll increases by one step (+3 difficulty).

Once you fail the roll, you can no longer hold your breath. A drowning or asphyxiating character immediately takes 10 points of damage every round thereafter until he dies or can breathe again. If you were holding your breath to resist the effects, say, of a poison or narcotic gas, you begin to suffer those effects instead.

Note that your Soak score does **not** reduce damage suffered from drowning or asphyxiation.

## Poisons and Disease

Venomous snakes, poisonous plants, and human poisoners are all frequent hazards in *Capharnaum*. Your character may also easily catch various unpleasant diseases when drinking dodgy water, living in unhygienic places, or coming into contact with diseased individuals or even animals. A good sword is no protection against infection or carelessness, and if you want to live a long life you should keep your eyes open!

Diseases, poisons, and venoms are all handled the same way. Each has three attributes: **Deadliness**, **Incapacitation**, and **Rapidity**. Each attribute has a score of 1-6, and the total of all three for a given hazard (referred to as the hazard's **Potency**) may not exceed 12.

This means that, when creating a disease, poison, or venom, Al-Rawi should divide no more than 12 points between these three attributes, with no one attribute exceeding a score of 6. For a less potent hazard, she may allocate less than 12 points.

| TABLE 2-14: POTENCY OF DISEASE, POISON, OR VENOM | |
|---|---|
| **ATTRIBUTE TOTAL** | **POTENCY** |
| 6 | Common, low Potency. |
| 8 | Average Potency. |
| 10 | Rare and potent. |
| 12 | Extremely rare and highly potent. |

## Deadliness

**Deadliness** determines how lethal the disease, poison, or venom is. Once contracted, ingested or injected into the blood (depending on the method of administration), the hazard inflicts damage equal to the result rolled on a number of dice equal to the Deadliness. Soak is subtracted from this damage as usual. For hazards with a high Rapidity, Deadliness damage may be inflicted more than once—see below.

## Incapacitation

**Incapacitation** determines how great a result penalty the victim of a disease, poison, or venom suffers on his dice rolls for physical actions, mental actions, or both. Some hazards don't necessarily kill, but instead cause massive incapacitation. A character suffering from a hazard suffers a result penalty to appropriate dice rolls equal to the Incapacitation score x 3. This penalty lasts for a number of days equal to the Incapacitation score, or until the disease is cured or the poison treated (see page 72).

## Rapidity

A poison or venom affects a subject in a number of minutes equal to his Soak score, minus the poison or venom's Rapidity. If the result is zero or negative, it takes effect instantly. In the case of a disease, the period is measured in days rather than minutes.

The Rapidity score also determines how many times the Deadliness damage is done to the victim. For a Rapidity greater than 1, the Deadliness damage is applied again after a period equal to the victim's Soak in minutes (or days in the case of a disease).

## Some Poisons and Venoms

### The Penitent's Mint

This potent poison has a strong odour usually masked with mint liqueur; added to food or tea, it may go completely unnoticed. Originally from the Magisterium, it's also called Cardinal Death, as it's often used in the political assassinations all too common in the City of Priests.

- ❖ **Deadliness:** 6
- ❖ **Incapacitation:** 1
- ❖ **Rapidity:** 4

### The Rakshasa

This poison was imported centuries ago by a Shiradi adventurer who made his fortune prospecting copper mines far to the east of Jazirat. The mines were haunted by the demonic half-tiger, half-reptile rakshasas. Thanks to their relentless cunning, the Shiradi adventurer and his followers defeated and enslaved the rakshasas, gaining access to a potent and fast-acting paralysing venom. Rare and expensive, and prized for use on sword blade and arrow heads, this venom can sometimes be found for sale in market alcoves away from prying eyes.

- ❖ **Deadliness:** 1
- ❖ **Incapacitation:** 6
- ❖ **Rapidity:** 6

### The Poor Man's Spice

Not all poisons are killers—fortunately! Poor Man's Spice is a mixture of common herbs and the gall of a toad easily found by the Gulf of Oxyrhynchus. It's a powder strongly resembling cumin, although its odour is similar to laurel. It's difficult to spot if you're not familiar with it, but equally its effects are fairly trivial: a mild paralysing effect, and stomach pains that can nevertheless provoke some impressive vomiting.

- ❖ **Deadliness:** 1
- ❖ **Incapacitation:** 2
- ❖ **Rapidity:** 1

For example: Amin has been stung by a scorpion with a venom with the attributes Deadliness 2, Incapacitation 5, Rapidity 5. That's a Potency 12 venom, extremely dangerous.

Amin's Soak is 6, meaning the scorpion venom takes effect only 1 minute after Amin is stung. At that point, Al-Rawi rolls 2/2 for Deadliness and gets a result of 6. Amin's Soak is subtracted from this, so initially the venom does no damage. However, Amin begins to feel the creeping paralysis the venom causes: it has an Incapacitation of 5, which means Amin suffers an immediate -15 result penalty to all his physical actions for 5 days!

After another minute, the Rapidity 5 means the venom does its Deadliness damage again. This time the roll is 7 damage, which after Soak means Amin suffers 1 HP damage. Another minute later, the third damage roll (there will be five of these...) is a 9, meaning 3 HP damage. Amin was only at 6 HP at the point he was stung (he took a terrific fall earlier), so now he has only 2 HP. Unconsciousness isn't far off!

Finally, diseases, poisons, and venoms often have all kinds of fun side effects—although often more annoying and spectacular than truly dangerous. Al-Rawi may have her own ideas, or may roll on Table 2-15: Side Effects a number of times equal to the Rapidity score.

| TABLE 2-15: SIDE EFFECTS | |
|---|---|
| ROLL 2D6 OR CHOOSE | SIDE EFFECT |
| 2-3 | Vomiting |
| 4-5 | Itching |
| 6-7 | Skin discolouration |
| 8-9 | Pustules |
| 10-11 | Fever |
| 12 | Temporary blindness |

# Healing, Medicine and Surgery

When your character loses Hit Points, for whatever reason, he'll usually get them back—eventually. In between adventures, you may want to say this happens automatically; but often, and especially during an adventure, when deadly danger is still all around, whether or not your character can be treated or healed, or whether he succumbs to his wounds, can be exciting moments of tension and drama. Here's how to handle that in play.

## Minor Wounds

Most wounds are **minor wounds**—damage caused by non-lethal weapons, brawls, or minor falls, or even wounds dealt by slashing, crushing, or piercing weapons which are mostly blocked by armour and only end up doing a few points of damage. They often represent little more than serious bruising or cuts and scratches. If you like (okay, it's a good idea…), you can apply **first aid** to minor wounds using bandages, poultices, and ingestible medicines. This is a difficulty 9 INT + Science or Survival roll, and success restores HP equal to twice the magnitude in the 12 hours following treatment.

Thereafter, even if the first aid roll fails, the character recovers HP equal to his Soak score every 12 hours.

## Major Wounds: Open Wounds

**Major wounds** (see page 67) resulting from bladed weapons, animal teeth and claws, falls onto sharp rocks or stakes, etc, represent bloody, messy, and extremely painful **open wounds**. Open wounds must be disinfected by a healer and then stitched, or must be cauterised.

A healer may automatically apply a dose of a disinfecting agent he's bought or acquired previously (for example in a Physician's Kit—see page 359), or he may concoct one on the spot by making a difficulty 9 INT + Science roll or a difficulty 15 INT + Survival roll. If this roll is failed, or the disinfecting agent is not applied, the major wound becomes infected.

---

### No Instant Healing?

*As you'll have noticed, getting wounded is a serious business in* **Capharnaum***! Even physicians can do little more than patch you up and then wait for nature to take its course. There are sorcerous spells of healing, using the* Tarmel Haja *(page 116), such as Create Health, but sorcerers are often reluctant to use their powers for such apparently trivial ends…*

#### Simple Healing

*These rules for healing, medicine, and surgery are intended to highlight the real danger and drama associated with combat and wounding—many warriors succumb to their wounds days and even weeks after battle! That might not always be appropriate for your game, however—sometimes you just might want to forge ahead with combat, and assume healing just takes care of itself.*

*In such a case, simply assume that all characters are capable of giving first aid when others are wounded, and that characters who have lost Hit Points will automatically regain them at a rate equal to their Soak score every week. You can halve that amount for characters who persist in fighting, leaping, climbing, and vaulting from horseback if you want to.*

---

An infected major wound causes 1 HP damage per day, ignoring Soak. The victim may overcome the infection by making a difficulty 15 CON + Endurance roll; the roll may be attempted each day. An attending healer may make a difficulty 6 INT + Science or Survival roll as a Help action (see page 55). A major wound that is infected may not be closed (well, you can, but it won't help).

Once a major wound has been disinfected, a further INT + Science or Survival roll is required to stitch it using a Surgical Kit (page 359). The difficulty of this roll is 6, plus one step (+3 difficulty) per point of attribute loss caused by the major wound (page 67). Alternatively, a healer may attempt to disinfect and close the wound at the same time, by cauterising it. Cauterising is a difficulty 9 INT + Science or Survival roll, and does 2D6 damage, minus the target's Soak. If the roll to cauterise fails, the wound is automatically infected and remains open.

If any roll to stitch a major open wound fails, then 1 point of attribute loss caused by the major wound becomes permanent. If a major open wound is cauterised, all the current attribute loss becomes permanent. In the case of a partially severed limb resulting from a major wound, permanent attribute loss usually indicates the limb has been amputated.

The magnitude of a successful roll to close or cauterise a wound indicates the number of HP recovered in the next 24 hours. Thereafter, the wounded person recovers HP equal to his Soak score for each day of rest. If the patient doesn't rest, the HP regained are halved.

## Major Wounds: Broken Bones

Major wounds resulting from heavy falls, impact weapons, or animal stampedes often indicate broken bones. Firstly, the broken bone must be set using a difficulty 15 INT + Survival roll or a difficulty 9 INT + Science roll; the magnitude indicates the number of HP recovered over the following week. A failure on this roll may indicate the break heals badly, inflicting a temporary result penalty on physical rolls (Athletics, Fighting, Stealth, etc, as appropriate) equal to the magnitude of failure until the damage is healed; on a Critical Failure, this result penalty may be permanent.

Thereafter, the patient recovers HP equal to his Soak for each week of rest. If the patient doesn't rest, the HP regained are halved.

If the broken bone is associated with an open wound, that wound must also be treated (see above).

## Major Wounds: Bludgeoning

Major wounds to the head, torso, or abdomen can result in concussion, internal bleeding, and other conditions which may not be immediately visible but which are nevertheless significant and hard to treat. A character with a bludgeoning major wound must rest completely, recovering 1 lost attribute point (see page 66) and HP equal to his Soak for each week of rest. If he resumes normal activities for more than a few minutes during that period, he immediately takes 1 die of damage, and no healing occurs that week. Additionally, if the character is still suffering from any attribute damage, he must make a difficulty 12 CON + Endurance roll or take 1-3 additional points of attribute damage. On a Critical Failure, the character suffers 1 die additional HP of damage, and any current attribute loss becomes permanent!

## Disease, Poison and Venom

To treat disease or counter poisons or venoms, someone must concoct a medicine or antidote. This requires an INT + Science roll against a difficulty equal to twice the highest attribute of the hazard (page 68). An INT + Survival roll may be made instead at a +6 difficulty. Assuming access to herbs or other ingredients, it takes 12 hours to concoct this medicine, minus 1 hour per point of magnitude. On a failed roll, the full 12 hours is spent to no avail.

Taking the medicine reduces the Potency of any currently active disease, poison, or venom by the magnitude of the roll. You may choose which attributes are reduced. Each attribute is reduced by 1 point at a time, in the order Rapidity, Deadliness, Incapacitation. The medicine then restores HP equal to the magnitude of the roll over the course of the next 12 hours. Each day of rest after

that, HP equal to the victim's Soak will be recovered. If the victim doesn't rest (insisting on travelling, adventuring, or working), the HP regained are halved.

# USING HEROIC VIRTUES

Every Dragon-Marked has a "Heroic Virtues" section on his character sheet, for the three heroic virtues of Bravery, Faith, and Loyalty. Each virtue has a numerical score, and is surrounded on the character sheet by five stars. When you create your character, each point allocated to a given heroic virtue increases its score by one. However, in play, things work differently: the stars around each virtue are instead filled in one by one; when all five are filled in, the sixth star gained increases the virtue score by one, and all the stars are set back to zero.

When writing down a heroic virtue and its score, we usually put the virtue score first, and the number of stars in brackets after, thus: Bravery 4 (+3 stars) or Bravery 4 (3).

| TABLE 2-16: HEROIC VIRTUE GAINS AND LOSSES | | |
|---|---|---|
| **HEROIC VIRTUE** | **GAINS (STARS)** | **LOSSES (STARS)** |
| Bravery | ❖ Saving a life: +1<br>❖ Saving a stranger's life: +2<br>❖ Disregarding your own safety to save a stranger's life: +3<br>❖ Facing certain death in a disinterested way and living: +4 | ❖ Lying to save your skin: -1<br>❖ Leaving someone in danger: -2<br>❖ Placing someone else in danger to save your skin: -3<br>❖ Surrendering for fear of dying, begging or asking for mercy: -4 |
| Faith | ❖ Making a ritual sacrifice: +1<br>❖ Talking about your faith or gods in an important speech or debate: +2<br>❖ Dedicating a poem, song, mosaic, etc, to your gods: +3 to +4, depending on duration and quality of work<br>❖ Converting a village, neighbourhood, caravan, troupe, etc, to your faith: +4 | ❖ Letting someone disparage your gods (either through words, deeds, artworks, etc) without trying to make them repent: -1<br>❖ Letting someone preach another faith without contradicting them, however gently: -2<br>❖ Disrespecting a precept of your faith: -3<br>❖ Refusing to die for your faith: -4 |
| Loyalty | ❖ Proudly displaying your people's colours in an enemy land: +1<br>❖ Turning against your peers to defend your own people or other Dragon-Marked: +2<br>❖ Dropping everything to go and support one of your people several days from here: +3<br>❖ Killing a loved one (not a PC!) for the sake of your own people: +4 | ❖ Hiding your allegiance in an enemy land: -1<br>❖ Preferring a foreigner to your own people (unless it's one of your Dragon-Marked companions): -2<br>❖ Refusing to help one of your people for any reason at all: -3<br>❖ Refusing to give your own life for your people: -4 |

*Chapter 2 - Thalia*

*For example: Amin has Bravery 4 and three stars filled. After a brilliant performance in an encounter, Al-Rawi rewards Amin with two stars of Bravery. This takes his score to Bravery 4 (+5 stars). If he gets one more star, his Bravery score will increase by 1, taking him to Bravery 5 (+0 stars).*

# Spending Heroic Virtue Stars

During play, you can choose to spend stars of your heroic virtues. If you were hoping to roll a constellation to activate one of your path abilities (page 48) and didn't, you may spend one star of an appropriate heroic virtue to make up every die missing from the constellation. The heroic virtue you spend depends on the path in question, and you can also indicate it on your character sheet: it's often referred to as your **replacement heroic virtue**, as each star spent replaces a constellation die. Whenever an action requires you to spend a heroic virtue, it's these stars that are spent, not the raw scores themselves.

*For example: Amin faces a gang of Babouche-Draggers (page 65), and decides the Path of the Fire Scimitars he is following will be of great use. Unfortunately, the dice don't fall in his favour and he doesn't light up a constellation—in fact, he doesn't even roll a double on his dice. He decides to spend two stars of Bravery to make up the missing dice and activate the path. His Bravery score, which was previously 4 (+5 stars), is reduced to 4 (+3 stars).*

# Gaining and Losing Heroic Virtue Stars

Dragon-Marked heroes will also see their heroic virtue scores rise and fall based on their actions. We encourage you to use this system as much as possible, as it's a great way of playing according to your character's personality and getting rewarded for it.

Whenever you act in an intense and meaningful way that matches one of your heroic virtues—when you're especially brave, faithful, or loyal—Al-Rawi can award you one star (or even more) in that virtue, effective immediately. However, if you act in an intense and meaningful way that runs counter to your heroic virtues—if you're especially cowardly, faithless, or disloyal—Al-Rawi may **remove** one of your stars in that virtue instead!

You'll find examples of gains and losses in Table 2-16: Heroic Virtue Gains and Losses. The numbers are indicative—it's up to Al-Rawi to judge the number of points gained or lost.

Note that, as a general rule, we don't advise increasing or decreasing a heroic virtue score by more than two full points in a given session—it really does represent a huge swing. In moments of high adventure, however, even this may occur!

Note also that these rules aren't intended to generate friction between player characters at the table! A party of Dragon-Marked

are assumed to be acting in concert and putting their group's solidarity above personal concerns. So, Al-Rawi isn't going to be handing out virtue points if one player character kills another because he spoke ill of his gods! That doesn't mean there won't sometimes be tension within a Dragon-Marked party—maybe even a duel to the first blood if things get too heated—but rather that these rules are intended to manage the relationship of your Dragon-Marked heroes with the world around them.

## Heroism

The average of your three heroic virtues, rounded down, provides your Heroism score. It gets recalculated at the beginning of every session of play, which means you get back any Heroism points lost or spent during the previous session, to account for possible changes in individual virtue scores (this means that minute-by-minute changes in heroic virtue scores don't affect your Heroism score). Note that Heroism is based only on the heroic virtue *scores*; the number of *stars* you have in a given virtue have no effect.

*For example: a character with Bravery 3 (+2 stars), Faith 3 (+2 stars) and Loyalty 3 (+1 star) has a score of 3 in Heroism. Another character with Bravery 3 (+5 stars), Faith 3 (+5 stars) and Loyalty 3 (+4 stars) also has 3 in Heroism.*

Heroism is a single score; it doesn't have stars like the heroic virtues. So, if you lose (or spend) a point of Heroism for any reason, it's the whole point which is subtracted. Note that your **Soak**, which is calculated based on your Heroism (page 23), is re-calculated at the same time your Heroism is recalculated.

Also note that losing points of Heroism for any reason doesn't affect your scores in Bravery, Faith, and Loyalty.

*For example: Amin has a Heroism score of 3 (Bravery 3, Faith 3, and Loyalty 3). He spends 1 point of Heroism to consult Urim and Turim, the Stones of Fate (see page 77). His Heroism score drops to 2, but his Bravery, Faith, and Loyalty still remain at 3.*

## What Do You Use Heroism For?

To summarise, you use Heroism for the following:

❖ **To calculate your character's Soak.** Soak = Constitution + maximum Heroism.
❖ **To consult Urim and Turim, the Stones of Fate.** See page 77.
❖ **To determine the maximum number of swagger dice you may take in a single dice roll.** Maximum number of swagger dice = current Heroism.
❖ Some paths also use Heroism.
❖ **To make an attribute roll.** Roll = attribute + current Heroism.
❖ **To make a Double Attack.** Your current Heroism score is a damage bonus in a Double Attack (page 54).
❖ **To avoid a major wound.** See page 67.
❖ **To avoid environmental and encumbrance penalties.** Costs 1 point of Heroism, lasts an entire day. See pages 67 and 78.

# ADVANCED RULES

The following optional rules are expansions of those already given above. You don't have to use them, but they'll add more detail, depth, and richness to your game.

## Specialisation and Expertise

So far we've treated skills simply: you have a skill, and you have a score in that skill. Skills, however, are often very broad, and there are fields within that broad coverage which characters may be more skilful in than others. For example, one character with the Athletics skill may be especially good at climbing, while another with the same Athletics skill may be good at acrobatics. These fields within a broad skill are called **specialisations**.

When you create your character, or later during play, you may declare that your character is a **specialist** in one area of a skill. You may even opt for a still higher degree of concentration in a skill area, and declare your character to be an **expert**. Your character may be better with a scimitar than a gladius, more gifted in astronomy than philosophy, more at ease on the back of a camel than a horse.

Being a specialist or an expert in a skill doesn't cost you any points during character creation or in play, although in play you must wait until an **advancement milestone**—see page 79. However, it's a double-edged sword. Here's how it works.

### Specialist

**Prerequisite:** You must have a score of 3 or higher in the skill.

Your Dragon-Marked character can decide to be a **specialist** in a skill area (examples are given in the skill write-ups on page 27) for a skill in which he has a score of 3 or higher. He gets +2 bonus dice on all his skill rolls pertaining to that area of specialisation. However, **for all other skill rolls with that skill**, he suffers 1 penalty die: he rolls **one fewer die**.

### Expert

**Prerequisite:** You must have a score of 4 or higher in the skill.

Your Dragon-Marked character can decide to be an **expert** in a skill area for a skill in which he has a score of 4 or higher. He gets +3 bonus dice on all his skill rolls pertaining to that area of specialisation. However, **for all other skill rolls with that skill**, he suffers 2 penalty dice: he rolls 2 fewer dice.

## Annotating Specialisation and Expertise on Your Character Sheet

When you specialise in a skill, indicate your specialisation in parentheses after the skill name. Next, note down the reduced skill for general use, and then in parentheses note down the specialised skill score.

*For example: Frank decides that Majid, his faithful* mujahid, *should specialise in the use of bladed weapons in his Fighting skill. He has Fighting 4. When he attacks with a bladed weapon (such as a scimitar), he'll get 2 bonus dice, attacking at Fighting 6; with all other attacks, he'll incur 1 penalty die, attacking at Fighting 3. On Majid's character sheet, Frank notes the skill as Fighting (Blades) 3 (6).*

## Multiple Specialisations in a Skill

Characters may choose to have multiple specialisations and even expertise in the same skill. This isn't easy, and requires skill, patience, and dedication.

If your character is already a **specialist** in a skill, and you want to take an additional specialisation in that skill during character generation, you must spend 2 skill points. To do this during play, you must spend the number of Adventure Points it would normally cost you to increase your skill score by 2 points (see page 80). Note that in both cases your skill score doesn't actually increase; you just gain the additional specialisation. Obviously this is very expensive—it takes a lot of time and dedication to maintain multiple specialisations.

*For example: Frank wants Majid to also specialise in the javelin (the Thrown Weapons specialisation). Currently he attacks with a javelin with a single penalty die, at Fighting 3. In order to also specialise in the javelin during character creation, Majid could spend 2 additional skill points. To acquire the additional specialisation during play would cost him the number of Adventure Points he'd normally spend to increase his Fighting skill from 4 (its current level) to 6. As shown on page 80, this would cost (5 x 10) + (6 x 10) or 110 AP—extremely expensive! Majid would then attack with Fighting 6 with both blades and thrown weapons (including the javelin), and Fighting 3 with all other weapons. Note that he could instead opt to spend those AP to increase his Fighting skill, from its base 4 to 6. If he did that, he'd attack with Fighting 8 with blades, and Fighting 5 with everything else.*

*If Majid took the additional specialisation, Frank would note this on Majid's character sheet as Fighting (Blades, Thrown Weapons) 3 (6).*

If your character is already an **expert** in a skill, and you want to take a specialisation or additional expertise in that skill during character creation, you must spend a number of skill points equal to the difference between the reduced skill score and the specialist or expert skill score.

For example, Majid is already an expert in acrobatics. His base Athletics skill is 3, so this is noted on his character sheet as Athletics (Acrobatics) 1 (6).

Frank decides he also wants Majid to specialise in climbing. If he does this during character creation, it'll cost him 4 skill points—the difference between the reduced Athletics skill score of 1 and the specialist skill score of (base 3 + 2) 5.

For an expert to take a specialisation or expertise in the same skill during play, you must spend the same number of AP it would cost you to increase your skill from its reduced score by either 4 points (for a specialisation) or 5 points (for an expertise).

For example, if Frank wants Majid to take the climbing specialisation during play, he'll have to pay 140 (20 + 30 + 40 + 50) AP! He'd then annotate this: Athletics (Acrobatics)(Climbing) 1 (6)(5).

# Special Uses of Skills

Now that we've introduced the core rules of *Capharnaüm*, you've probably begun to see that there are lots of cool ways you can use the skills presented in **Chapter One: Polymnia—Creating Characters** (see page 26). In this section, we're going to discuss some of these. Note, though, that they're not exhaustive: you can use skills in many ways, and you should come up with other special uses for your skills using the examples below.

For ease of reference, skills which have special uses described below are marked with an asterisk (*) on the character sheet and elsewhere in these rules.

## Assassination

Besides poisoning, Assassination is also the skill of killing by slitting throats, breaking necks, garrotting, backstabbing, and so on. It lets you identify a target's weak points to kill them more easily.

When you try to assassinate a target, you can make an opposed roll (page 47) of your Stealth against the target's Notice skill to approach them unawares. If you succeed, you may then attack your target using your Assassination skill instead of Fighting skill against his Passive Defence. However, if you take **at least one swagger die** on your Stealth roll, you also gain an additional damage bonus on your Assassination attack equal to three times your Assassination skill score (Assassination x 3).

*For example: Aziz, the "Cobra of Makhra", has decided to assassinate his master, Sheik El Yakubi, after a disastrous falling out. He creeps in through his window by night.*

*First, Aziz has to make an opposed roll of DEX + Stealth against El Yakubi's INT + Notice, with at least one swagger die. He gets a result of 19, against El Yakubi's 13, meaning Aziz manages to sneak up on his victim unawares. Now he makes his assassination attempt: a roll of DEX + Assassination 4 with his* choora *dagger. El Yakubi is*

*asleep, so Al-Rawi halves his usual Passive Defence 12 to just 6! Aziz rolls a result of 19, with a magnitude of 3. He gets a damage bonus of +12 (Assassination 4 x 3) to his 11 points of damage, for a total of 23.*

You can also use your Assassination skill to exploit your opponent's weak spots in normal combat, too, although this is often considered cowardly and ignoble. If you do so, you automatically gain a number of bonus dice on your attack equal to your Assassination skill score, but you must lose one star of Bravery.

## Endurance

When wounded, poisoned or sick, you may make a difficulty 6 CON + Endurance roll **with at least one swagger die** to recover more rapidly. On a success, add +1 HP per magnitude to the 12-hour, daily or weekly amount of HP you recover after receiving initial medical treatment (see "Healing, Medicine, and Surgery" on page 70). You may continue to make this CON + Endurance roll every period thereafter; a failure on the roll simply means you only recover the base amount of HP.

*For example: Mektirion has been bedridden with a raging fever for several days. A healer friend administers a medical draft that, on the first day, lets him get back on his feet, restoring 6 HP. Each day thereafter, Mektirion is due to recover 7 HP (equal to his Soak score).*

*Mektirion's player decides he's going to use his Endurance to try and heal faster. He describes how, for three days, Mektirion will climb onto the roof of his house and shout out the name of the god Kalos to grant him healing (this represents the swagger die he has to take on the roll). So, on the second day Mektirion makes a difficulty 6 CON + Endurance roll, succeeding with 2 magnitude. That day, he regains 9 HP rather than 7. On the third day, Mektirion tries the roll again but fails; on that day, he just regains 7 HP.*

## Flattery

Flattery is also the art of love. The best lovers in the world master it: it's the games of seduction, the knowledge of what pleases your partner, the best way of building a reputation as a masterly paramour.

When a character makes love to someone, he or she may make a difficulty 9 CHA + Flattery roll **with at least one swagger die**. On a success, he emerges with a reputation as a fantastic lover which will last 6 months per point of magnitude—unless undone by a subsequent disastrous bout of lovemaking! The effect of this reputation is to grant the character one or more bonus dice or a lowered difficulty on interpersonal rolls with potential partners. Potential partners should be those similar to the partner in the original lovemaking roll: a character who sleeps with prostitutes or gigolos will have a reputation with other prostitutes or gigolos, whereas one who seduces the son or daughter of a sheik will have other sheiks agog and their offspring breathless with anticipation!

Jazirat is a land where being expert in the games of love is considered a virtue, even an art. Success in lovemaking rolls will never work against the character's reputation: he or she won't end up being considered a menace or a person of easy virtue, but rather a seducer or seductress of skill and passion. However, a Critical Failure or worse on a lovemaking roll may land the character with the reputation for being a boor or a man-eater...

*For example: Dona Gabriella, the formidable duellist, is a peerless lover—although she chooses her partners very carefully. Travelling on a diplomatic mission with a Quarterian military company across the desert to Kh'saaba, she finds herself treated with less respect than she considers her due. Realising that before long she's going to end up in a duel, she decides to seduce a handsome Orkadian captain, well-behaved and well-placed in the company, and make him her ally.*

*Dona Gabriela invites the captain to her tent. She is making a CHA + Flattery roll to seduce him, and takes two swagger dice. She gets a result of 18 with 2 magnitude, succeeding with flying colours. The next day the captain has shining eyes and a besotted grin and is constantly singing Dona Gabriela's praises, and rumour spreads that she is a great seductress and fabulous lover. Henceforth—indeed, for the next 12 months—she gains at least 1 bonus die on interpersonal rolls with everyone in the company. Everyone treats her respectfully—and never once does her sword have to be drawn!*

## Instruction

Instruction isn't just about conveying knowledge—it's about opening a student's mind to new ideas and information. If you spend at least two hours a day for a week discussing and debating "wisdom" with a student, you may make an INT + Instruction roll **with at least one swagger die** against a difficulty equal to 20 minus the student's INT score. On a success, the student gains a bonus die on all his subsequent INT-related rolls for a number of days equal to the magnitude.

## Intimidate

When you first confront an opponent in combat, you may make a STR + Intimidate roll **with at least 1 swagger die** to put your opponent on his back foot. The difficulty is equal to your opponent's INT x 6. On a success, you gain a result bonus on all your attack rolls against that opponent during this combat equal to your magnitude.

## Oratory

When you use Oratory to fire up a group of warriors before battle, you may make a difficulty 9 roll **with at least one swagger die**. On a success, you grant a result bonus to all the combatants' skill rolls in the subsequent battle equal to the magnitude. This bonus doesn't affect the character making the roll.

You can use this with a party of Dragon-Marked. One party member—usually the one with the highest STR or CON—makes a speech motivating his comrades. It's even possible to do this before a duel, with one character giving a pep talk to another. Only one character may make this Oratory roll to a group of warriors before any given combat, so it's not possible to aggregate bonuses by having multiple characters make speeches.

*For example: After being attacked by bloodthirsty Tarekid warriors, the Quarterian military company has taken refuge at an oasis where they're now under siege. Exhausted and fearful, the soldiers are facing the decisive battle like a one-way passage to hell. Dona Gabriela decides to raise morale, making a fiery speech from the back of her camel just before the battle begins. She only just succeeds with her STR + Oratory roll, but manages a magnitude of 3. The soldiers will get a +3 result bonus to all their actions in the battle.*

*After Dona Gabriela's speech, knight-commander Gislan de Mermonte makes his own speech to the troops. However, it has no game mechanical effect, as the soldiers are already benefitting from the bonus provided by Dona Gabriela.*

## Storytelling

You can use Storytelling to tell stories which reassure the listener and boost their morale and courage. To do so, you must be telling stories around a fire or similar location, with an attentive audience. Make a CHA + Storytelling roll **with at least one swagger die**. The difficulty depends on the audience's morale: a low morale is difficulty 12, whereas a tipsy and buoyant audience may only be difficulty 6. Al-Rawi may even drop the difficulty a step if the player tells a good story. For every point of magnitude, 10 people in the audience gain 1 bonus die to all their Athletics or Endurance skill rolls for the next 24 hours. On a Critical Success, these bonuses are valid for a week!

## Willpower

Willpower can also refer to a sensitivity to the supernatural or a state of enlightened or heightened awareness. If you have a hunch that "there's something uncanny going on", maybe that there's some magic being used somewhere, or even that you're looking at a mirage or an illusion, you can make a difficulty 9 INT + Willpower roll **with at least one swagger die** to be sure.

If you can also use Sacred Word to defend yourself against magic you've detected, either by fighting the sorcerer with sorcery, dispelling a mirage, exorcising a possessed individual, etc, the roll also grants you a result bonus on such rolls equal to its magnitude.

# Urim and Turim — the Stones of Fate

Legend says that, before their disappearance, the Prophets carved two small stones the size of walnuts, and asked the gods to bless them to ease the fates of men in their absence.

The stones were called **Urim and Turim**—the Stones of Fate. They allowed those who consulted them to augur whether a given course of action was auspicious or inauspicious in the eyes of the gods. All people were able to consult the Stones; today, not only the Jazirati, but the Shiradim, Quarterians, and Agalanthians alike consult the Stones to glimpse their fate.

## Al-Rawi and the Stones of Fate

At critical moments in your game, your characters can consult Urim and Turim during play. Al-Rawi places a small pouch on the table containing two "stones" (dice, marbles, pebbles, tokens, or other similar objects) of identical size but different colours (ideally black and white). The player of the character consulting the Stones of Fate formulates a yes / no question, and then, without looking, draws one of the stones. If the black stone is drawn, the Stones of Fate have answered "yes" to the question; if white, they have answered "no".

Al-Rawi may also ask a player to consult the Stones of Fate to simulate the workings of chance. She may even turn to the Stones to determine the workings of chance instead of deciding for herself.

*For example: Amin's player asks Al-Rawi if his character recognises anyone in the crowd before him. Al-Rawi asks Amin to consult the Stones of Fate. His player draws the black stone. Yes, says Al-Rawi, there's a person in the crowd you recognise!*

## Players and the Stones of Fate

If you want your character to consult the Stones of Fate yourself, you can do so by spending 1 point of Heroism. This can have two effects.

Firstly, if you've failed a roll (any roll at all), you can consult the Stones of Fate for a Heroism point. If you draw the black stone, your roll is considered to be a Normal Success, even though the result you rolled indicated it was a failure. If you draw the white stone, the roll remains a failure as rolled. It must have been at least physically possible to succeed on the roll to be able to consult the Stones in this way.

*For example: Dona Gabriela looses an arrow at a wild goat, intending to feed her companions in their time of misfortune. She rolls badly, indicating her arrow is going to miss. Given the risk of starvation she and her companions face, Dona Gabriela throws herself upon the mercies of chance, begging the gods for their favour. Marina, her player, consults Urim and Turim: she marks off one point of Heroism on Dona Gabriela's character sheet, and plunges her hand into the pouch of the Stones of Fate. She draws the black stone: the gods have been merciful! Miraculously, the arrow strikes the goat, which gives up the ghost...*

Secondly, you can consult the Stones of Fate to try and modify one of Al-Rawi's descriptions, complementing but never totally contradicting it. If you draw the black stone, the gods take your modification of reality into account; otherwise things remain just as Al-Rawi has described them.

*For example: the player characters are cornered in a blind alley, their exit blocked by a band of brigands, armed to the teeth. One player spends 1 point of Heroism and consults the Stones of Fate, saying "By Urim and Turim, could there be a hidden door at the end of this alley?" The player draws the black stone and, miraculously, stumbles upon a hidden door!*

## The Limits of the Stones of Fate

Spending Heroism to consult the Stones of Fate is a significant power only the Dragon-Marked enjoy. However, there are some limits to their use.

The Stones of Fate let you modify your immediate surroundings (you chance upon an oasis when you're dying of thirst, a hospital when you're wounded, a path when you're lost), add objects to that environment (a chandelier you can hold on to jump from, a weapon suddenly to hand when you're unarmed, a tool you need on a table, shelf, or stall), or encounter a minor character amongst those around you (a good guide in a caravanserai, the best blacksmith in the street, a good weaponsmaster or sorcerer willing to teach). However, these modifications can never be so great that they directly change the plot of your adventure or do your job for you: the Stones of Fate won't tell you who the murderer is, or let you find the ultimate warrior who'll kill the bad guy and save you the job, and certainly won't turn mountains into volcanoes!

## Encumbrance

So far we haven't really paid attention to the amount of equipment, treasure, or other belongings your character may carry. Generally speaking, you can assume that, within reason, your character is carrying various items with him in appropriate ways—swords may be in a scabbard, coins or cumin in a pouch or box, whips are coiled and hooked over a belt, bedrolls, tents, and rations are slung over shoulder in a sack or carried in a backpack or even in saddle bags on camel or horse.

You may want more detail than this, particularly if your character is adventuring in some remote area where the gear he's carrying (or, probably, not carrying!) is going to be an important factor in his survival. For such times, we offer these rules for **encumbrance**.

Broadly speaking, your character may carry around on his person a load of gear equal in weight to his Constitution + Strength multiplied by 10, in pounds ((CON + STR) x 10lb), without suffering any penalty or inconvenience. For every 2 lbs he carries **over** that amount, he suffers a -1 result penalty to all of his physical action dice rolls (those made with CON, DEX, or STR).

*For example, Jibril has CON 5 and STR 4. He can carry up to 90lb of equipment without penalty. If he has to carry 100lb of gear, he suffers a -5 result penalty to all of his physical action dice rolls.*

## Using Heroism

By spending 1 point of Heroism, you can cancel the effects of encumbrance penalties on your character (within reason!) for an entire day. Note that this also lets you avoid certain types of hazard and environmental damage (see page 67).

## How Much Do Things Weigh?

For the most part we haven't provided detailed weights for absolutely every item of equipment described in this book, assuming you'll want to gauge encumbrance by rule of thumb. However, if you do want to calculate how much weight your character is carrying, Table 2-17: Sample Equipment Weights provides approximate weights (in pounds) for broad categories of equipment. We've also reproduced some of these as appropriate on the weapons and armour tables on pages 58, 62, and 64.

| TABLE 2-17: SAMPLE EQUIPMENT WEIGHTS | |
|---|---|
| ITEM | WEIGHT (LB) |
| Leather boots | 3 |
| Backpack | 2 |
| Tent | 9 |
| 50ft rope | 9 |
| Set of clothing | 3 |
| Torch (burns for ½ hour) | 2 |
| Bowl, goblet, and spoon (wooden) | 2 |
| Writing materials | 2 |
| Cooking materials | 6 |
| Toiletry materials | 4 |
| Musical instrument (medium) | 2 |
| Musical instrument (large) | 10 |
| One week's rations | 6 |
| Two-handed weapon | 8 |
| One-handed weapon | 4 |
| Thrown weapon | 2 |
| Missile weapon and 20 arrows | 8 |
| Long weapon | 10 |
| Short weapon | 4 |
| Light armour | 20 |
| Heavy armour | 60 |
| Partial armour | 4 |
| Shield | 10 / 20 |

# THE ADVENTURE CONTINUES!

As your characters tread the trails of Jazirat, they learn from their adventures, becoming more skilful, more influential, stronger, better, more capable. This process of improvement is handled in *Capharnaum* by the use of **Adventure Points** or **AP**, which you can spend to improve your skills and attributes, and even acquire new skills, known as **advancements**. AP are awarded by Al-Rawi at **advancement milestones** (or just **milestones**), usually the end of an adventure.

# Calculating Adventure Points

The Adventure Points your character is awarded, and the speed at which you're awarded them, depends on how well you succeed in your adventures, how well you roleplay your character, and how large scale the adventure you've just played is (usually measured in terms of its duration).

When you reach an advancement milestone (usually the end of an adventure), Al-Rawi calculates the Adventure Points to be awarded using the following steps.

## The Victory Step

Your character automatically receives 1 AP for completing the adventure.

## The Virtue Step

Your character also receives AP equal to your highest Heroic Virtue. If that's 0 (even if only temporarily), then you don't gain any AP in this step.

## The Game Step

Depending on how well or how inventively you've used the game rules (swaggers, Heroic Virtues, Urim and Turim, etc), Al-Rawi may award you up to 5 AP.

## The Roleplaying Step

Depending on how well you've roleplayed your character (immersing yourself in the story, society, and setting, and generally making the game fun and dynamic), Al-Rawi may award you up to 5 AP.

## The Adventure Scale Step

Total up all the AP awarded above, and then multiply that total as indicated below, based on the scale of the adventure.

- ❖ **A Challenge:** A small scenario of one or two sessions, or less than 2 hours total; a single session of challenging play in between adventures. Award the AP as calculated above (AP x 1).
- ❖ **A Tale:** A scenario of three or four sessions, or less than 24 hours total. Double the AP award (AP x 2).
- ❖ **An Epic:** A large scenario of five or six sessions, or more than 24 hours total. Treble the AP award (AP x 3).

## What If We're Not Currently Playing an Adventure?

*Sometimes you may be playing through events which aren't formally part of a single adventure. Maybe you've finished an adventure and are travelling through a desert to another city, or maybe you're in the city and searching for a contact or some information to lead you to greater adventures. What should you do about Adventure Points in these cases?*

*Generally, unless you're very obviously sat at home (or in an inn, caravanserai, or palace) just resting up and doing absolutely nothing, being actively out and about leading an adventurous and perilous life in* **Capharnaum** *counts as "an adventure", and Al-Rawi should consider a single session of play to be a Challenge milestone for the purposes of awarding AP—perhaps with a smaller number of awards if the events you're playing through are less perilous or significant than usual. Travelling through the Aramla El-Nar, even if you're just travelling between two locations, can be as dangerous as any trap-filled ruin or djinn-haunted lair!*

| TABLE 2-18: SUMMARY OF ADVENTURE POINT AWARDS | |
| --- | --- |
| **EVENT** | **AP AWARD** |
| Completing an adventure | 1 |
| For being virtuous | 1 x your highest heroic virtue |
| Creative use of the rules | 0-5 |
| Immersive roleplaying | 0-5 |
| After a Challenge (1-2 session adventure, <2 hrs) | AP total x 1. |
| After a Tale (3-4 session adventure, <24 hrs) | AP total x 2. |
| After an Epic (5-6 session adventure, >24 hrs) | AP total x 3. |

# Spending Adventure Points

After an advancement milestone (usually when there's enough time to take several days rest, catch your breath, and contemplate the amazing experiences you've just been through), you may spend your accumulated AP to improve your character's abilities. You don't have to spend your AP when you're awarded them; you can keep accumulating them until you reach the amount needed to spend on a given advancement. This is particularly true the more

TABLE 2-19: ADVANCEMENTS

| ADVANCEMENT | AP COST | COMMENTS |
|---|---|---|
| Increase a skill by +1 | New skill score x 10. | |
| Increase an attribute by +1 | New attribute score x 20. | |
| Acquire your second path ability | 40 | You must have a score of at least 2 in all your path skills.[1] |
| Acquire your third path ability | 50 | You must have a score of at least 3 in all your path skills, and a Loyalty score of at least 3.[1] |
| Acquire your fourth path ability | 60 | You must have a score of at least 4 in all your path skills, and a Loyalty score of at least 4.[1] |
| Acquire your fifth path ability | 70 | You must have a score of at least 5 in all your path skills, and a Loyalty score of at least 5.[1] |
| Acquire your sixth path ability | 80 | You must have a score of at least 6 in all your path skills, and a Loyalty score of at least 6.[1] |
| Acquire a second dragon die | 50 | You must have a Heroism score of at least 5.[2] |
| Acquire a third dragon die | 100 | You must have a Heroism score of at least 6.[2] |
| First specialisation or expertise in a skill | 0 | During play, you must wait until an advancement milestone. |
| Second specialisation | AP to increase skill score by 2. | The skill score doesn't increase; you gain the specialisation instead. |
| Second expertise | AP to increase skill score from reduced level by 5 points. | See page 74. |

*1: You must also be accepted by a master of your path. See below.*

*2: You must take a truly heroic action to activate the new dragon die. Your Heroism must remain equal to or above this threshold. See below.*

powerful you get, as the higher-power advancements have increasingly high AP costs.

The advancements you can spend AP on, and their AP costs, are given in Table 2-19: Advancements. Note that in some cases you must have a certain score or higher in a specific skill before you can take an advancement: this is known as a **prerequisite**.

Note also that acquiring a new path ability (see page 81) is never automatic: your character must approach a master in your chosen path and ask him to teach you the new ability. Whether or not the master accepts you as a student is at Al-Rawi's discretion, based upon your character's behaviour and past history. Characters who act ignobly or in ways which bring disgrace to their path will find it very difficult to gain training in its path abilities!

Note also that activating a second or third dragon die is never automatic either: your character must make a truly heroic action in play before the new dragon die becomes usable. Also, as a Heroism score of 5 or 6 is a prerequisite for the second or third dragon die, if your Heroism drops below that level (even temporarily), your corresponding dragon die also becomes temporarily unusable until your Heroism score has risen back above that threshold again.

*For example: At a Challenge advancement milestone at the end of a single session of play, Al-Rawi awards AP to Amin. She begins by awarding 3 AP for his lowest heroic virtue, Faith. Then she decides that Amin's player made inventive use of swaggers during the adventure, and also made an effort to come up with exciting, fun, and original uses of the game rules, so awards 2 AP for the Game Step. Finally, Al-Rawi decides that, as Amin's player mostly focussed on combat, didn't really follow the plot, and made no effort to play the social side of Amin's character, she won't award any AP for the Roleplaying Step. Al-Rawi therefore awards Amin 5 AP.*

*Amin has already accumulated 19 AP from previous milestone awards, so now has 24 AP. As Amin only has Survival 1 and has used the skill a lot in his adventures, Amin's player decides he wants to improve it by 1 point. Going from a score of 1 to 2 in a skill costs 20 AP (new skill score x 10). Amin is left with 4 AP, but his Survival skill score is now 2!*

# OF PATHS AND PEOPLES

For the Saabi, paths represent the mystical ways of power which were once explored by the Prophets, their companions, or their descendants. They allowed those who subsequently led the Saabi people to continue to use those ways of power, taught in forms matching particular conceptions of the cosmic order and the ties between people and gods. The Shiradim turned the paths of the Prophets into secular traditions: social castes or classes, the mundane human expression of divine powers, handed to them by the dragons. Among the Quarterians, the opposite occurred: popular figures such as Gerda or San Llorente emerged and, in their final sacrifice, left their own mark on history, which the civilisations of the West enshrined in **academies** of many kinds. Finally, the Agalanthians, with the protean nature which characterises the vast Agalanthian world, encapsulated these teachings into **schools**—military, religious, philosophical, and others—to guide to godlike power practitioners of arts which humankind had made its own over the centuries: swordsmanship, chariot-racing, chiromancy, and more.

## So What Is a Path?

*"The paths are professional philosophies, military tactics, spiritual disciplines. Their goal is to breathe into human endeavours a spark of divine wisdom and power."*

Such is the description you'll find in any university which values freedom of thought. Whatever their roots, the many paths, schools, and academies of the world present their followers with hardships and challenges to lead exceptional individuals to the very gates of the celestial kingdom.

### Nobility of Heart and Soul

In Saabi lands, you sometimes come across peasants or simple caravaneers who claim to follow some unknown path, one whose name reeks with superstition and fairy tale. Nevertheless, everyone knows that the true paths to power are the preserve of those who share the blood of the Prophets. Even a street child, a scion of thief and prostitute, a descendant of twenty generations of ne'er-do-wells, can become the follower of a path if he can prove his noble blood.

The world "noble", though, is misleading. Everything depends on definitions. For most people, being noble means you're rich, with land, slaves, and camels. But, to the Saabi, nothing could be more relative: great deeds of heart and soul, pushing people to sacrifice themselves for justice, love, or honour, prove a nobility of spirit to which not even the most level-headed *kahini* are immune. There are countless rumours of peasants ennobled by passing lords

who witnessed their heroism, of street urchins lifted out of squalor by sages who saw their deeds. While it may seem that following a path is reserved for the nobility, in reality access to their mystical teachings is more flexible than most people believe.

### The Dragon-Marked

It's impossible to discuss how people rise to follow the paths without talking about the Dragon-Marked. Not all followers of a path are Dragon-Marked, and not all Dragon-Marked are followers of a path. Far from it; it's estimated that only one in a hundred people following a path today bear the Dragon Mark. However, any sage will tell you that both conditions must be met to become a Hero and walk the path to godhood. It's therefore not unusual to see a Dragon-Marked child automatically ennobled so they can join a path. Even if they renounce their titles, the lands, wives or husbands that may be their due, even if they refuse the advantages which nobility bestows, the heart and soul of a Dragon-Marked are often believed to be noble in themselves.

## Following a Path

Noble or not, Dragon-Marked or ordinary mortal, there are countless adventurers who are princes-of-this, or archons-of-that, gifted with superhuman talents and capable of wicked deeds as much as they are of good. So it is with the paths, too. Their rules are many and varied, often changing. Some are sacred, royal, or secret; others are taught to whoever wants to learn and can pay; others still are transmitted freely by generous wandering masters.

Wherever you travel, you find people who put the search for excellence and personal accomplishment above all else. Often it's with just such people that you find a path, school, or academy—or perhaps a place where a new one is being born.

# Paths of the Blood

There are many paths in *Capharnaum*. Depending on your people and land, they may be schools, academies, cults, institutions, or even criminal gangs. Each tribe, clan, or city has seen dozens of paths come into existence over the centuries. In this section and the next, we present two types of path. Firstly, in this section, we present a typical path for each of the eighteen bloods described in **Chapter One: Polymnia – Creating Characters** (see page 13). You can choose these **paths of the blood** for your characters, but they also act as examples for the types of path followed by those of your blood, and you can use them to devise your own. Secondly, in the next section (page 98), we're presenting a number of **common paths** which can be followed by characters from any blood. If you choose one of these, you should customise it and add detail and colour as you see fit to make it consistent with your view of your character and his blood.

Note that it's possible for characters to follow a path different from that of their blood. This is a way of making your character unique, and enriching your back story. For example, while you can always play an Aragonian character who received his education in an Aragonian academy (such as that of San Llorente de Valladon presented below), it can be fun to decide his fate was far different, and that he was brought up following the path of one of the Saabi Prophets!

Also, while we recommend (for story reasons) that most Dragon-Marked characters should follow a path, you don't actually have to do so (more on that on page 11).

# Paths of the Saabi

## The Fire Scimitars

### Path of Malik, Servant of Hassan

- ❖ **Members:** 900.
- ❖ **Replacement Heroic Virtue:** Bravery.

## A Constellation is a Constellation

Some path abilities can only be activated when you light up a constellation. If you have multiple paths of this type, then when you light up a constellation it's up to you to choose which path is activated. Note that the dice roll in question must be a success in order for the path ability to be activated; lighting up a constellation on a failed dice roll has no effect.

## Constellation or No Constellation?

Some path abilities don't require a constellation to be lit up. Usually that's because the path ability represents some form of know-how, specific training, or is the result of a certain way of life. Such path abilities are acquired permanently, and require neither concentration, trance, nor the attention of the gods to be activated.

## When a Constellation Lights up Another Constellation

Lighting up a constellation can never activate two path abilities at once. However, lighting up a constellation can activate a path ability whose effects stack with those of a permanent path ability.

For example: A member of the Order of the Thereman Myrmidons (page 20) who has learned the fourth path in his school now benefits from a riposte if he lights up a constellation on an Active Defence roll. On top of that, if he's also wielding gladius and shield, he benefits from the advantages of two-weapon fighting and also gets a damage bonus equal to his Combat Training skill score. These latter are permanent benefits he gets from the second path ability of the Thereman Myrmidon school.

Sometimes, lighting up a constellation activates a path ability which provides you with an immediate free action, such as the fourth path ability of Saint Gerda Dragonslayer (page 97). In this case, if the dice roll for that additional free action also lights up a constellation, you can activate another path ability. For Saint Gerda, for example, your character could activate the first or third path abilities.

The *mujahidin* following the path of the Fire Scimitars are the greatest swordsmen and strategists in all Jazirat. They lead armies, inspiring their troops with their courage. Some are even initiated into the secrets of sorcery (page 115).

The Fire Scimitars were born the night Hubal destroyed Agalanthian Jergath to rebuild it as the city known today. Malik, leading a band of 100 rebels, aided the dragon in cleansing the city, before resisting the 10,000 troops of the Agalanthian army in a counterattack which lasted several weeks. Fighting against incredible odds to ensure Kh'saaba's greatness and preserve Hubal's honour, regardless of the cost, is the core philosophy of the Fire Scimitars.

In the kingdom of Kh'saaba, the path of the Fire Scimitars is the one most followed by the martial classes. Hundreds of Saabi are members, most occupying key positions in the army or at court (captains, wazirs, diplomats, ambassadors to Capharnaum, swordmasters, and so on).

## Initiation

Most young noble soldiers become disciples of the Fire Scimitars because a parent or relative followed the path. Sometimes, though, a member notices a child with potential and decides to initiate them, regardless of their social status.

## Training

The path of the Fire Scimitars is taught in military schools in special buildings reserved for disciples. Lone masters, local lords, war chiefs, or wandering mercenaries may also take on students. Its teachings focus on putting a disciple in constant danger: he must rise before dawn each day and train in running, acrobatics, and climbing until noon, the first meal of the day. After noon and until nightfall, the disciple studies swordplay and strategy. The period after dark, up until midnight, is given over to the study of sorcery.

## First Path Ability

The Fire Scimitar *mujahid* is a war dancer, a combat fury capable of whirling into melee as fast as a flame, dealing wounds without ever being touched. If you're in combat against more than two Babouche-Draggers or Valiant Captains (page 65) and you light up a constellation on an attack action where you take out at least one opponent, you automatically take out an additional number of opponents equal to your Bravery score. Note that this does not apply to the powerful opponents called Champions.

## Second Path Ability

Facing a Fire Scimitar mujahid is extremely intimidating for those not prepared. You may add your Heroism score to your score in the Intimidate skill.

## Third Path Ability

On the battlefield, the mujahid is the scourge of the heroes of the opposing army. Whenever you light up a constellation on an attack roll against an enemy Champion, you get a damage bonus equal to your Bravery score.

## Fourth Path Ability

As a war leader, the mujahid can get the best out of his troops in battle. Whenever you light up a constellation when using your Oratory skill to fire up your troops before battle (see page 76), you add your Heroism score to the bonus granted to your troops.

## Fifth Path Ability

Whenever you make a Sacred Word roll relating to battle, combat, or war, you roll a number of bonus dice equal to half your Bravery score (round down).

## Sixth Path Ability

The mujahid is one with the path of Malik, understanding the secrets of the Fire Scimitars to the core of his soul. If you light up a constellation on a Combat Training roll, you gain a number of bonus dice equal to your Bravery score, in addition to those gained normally.

# The Alchemists of Men

## Path of Mussah, Servant of Hassan

- ❖ **Members:** 300.
- ❖ **Replacement Heroic Virtue:** Loyalty.

If the prince is strong, then the one who advises his decisions is stronger, for he does not expose himself to danger. Such is the motto of the Alchemists of Men, the powers behind the throne, wazirs and powerful mages, court astrologers and personal physicians of princes. The followers of this path never seek the spotlight, never make themselves targets; they remain always in the shadows, playing second fiddle, ensuring that their actions and thoughts are attributed to others. While they may never enjoy the glory of victory, nor do they suffer the shame of defeat: they are never congratulated, but nor are they assassinated. Is that not the greatest of freedoms? Power without being the enemy of your enemies? The Alchemists of Men truly rule the world.

The Alchemists of Men are the faithful confidants of Saabi dignitaries, masters in the arts of diplomacy and deceit. Most people only see their expertise in science and the arts of healing, but their honeyed tongues are paired with a bite as deadly as a sand viper.

## Initiation

Most Alchemists of Men are noticed during childhood by a family member already following the path. Some may come from universities where they were initiated by other disciples.

## Training

Although the goal of the Alchemists of Men is unchanging, their teachings vary from mentor to mentor. There are no schools or dogma, only lone disciples who may one day choose a successor. Many mentors choose two students, hiding their existence from one another; when they reach maturity and have learned the first path ability, they face off in a sorcerous duel of the mentor's choosing. The first to resort to easy, direct and damaging sorcery is declared the loser and sacrificed to Hubal.

## First Path Ability

You're an *al-kimyat* magician, plying your trade in classrooms, universities, gardens and palaces. Whenever you light up a constellation when using magic for social purposes (helping, healing, reconciling, persuading, etc), you gain a result bonus on your dice roll (page 45) equal to your CHA score.

## Second Path Ability

The al-kimyat can use his elegance and honeyed voice to attract the attention of the powerful. You gain bonus dice on any Flattery roll equal to half your Elegance skill score (round down).

## Third Path Ability

Lying is second nature to the Alchemist of Men. If you light up a constellation on an INT + Acting roll when talking to someone, you instantly know if your interlocutor is lying. The difficulty of the roll is equal to the interlocutor's INT x 6.

## Fourth Path Ability

The al-kimyat can extract information just by talking to someone. If you light up a constellation on a CHA + Acting roll when talking to someone, you obtain a number of pieces of information equal to the magnitude + 1. The difficulty of the roll is equal to the interlocutor's INT x 6, and a roll may only be attempted if none of the answers places the interlocutor's life in danger, even indirectly.

## Fifth Path Ability

Living at court, the al-kimyat knows everything is only appearance. If you light up a constellation on an INT + Notice roll, you can see through any disguise or even magical illusion employed by a given perpetrator. The difficulty of the roll is equal to twice the perpetrator's Acting or Sacred Word skill, as appropriate, plus 6 (Acting or Sacred Word x 2, + 6).

## Sixth Path Ability

When using sorcery to deceive or influence someone, you roll a number of bonus dice on your Sacred Word rolls equal to half your Loyalty score (round down).

## *The Suspicion of Traitors*

### *Path of Rashid, Servant of Hassan*

- ❖ **Members:** 200.
- ❖ **Replacement Heroic Virtue:** Loyalty.

The *mujahidin* of the Suspicion of Traitors are the bodyguards of Jazirat's greatest dignitaries. Although they mostly act as human shields, some become daggers striking from the shadows. It's said they're so fearsome because they prefer death to the dishonour of failure. This isn't true, however, for only Hubal is worth dying for.

The truth is darker and more cynical. For the disciples of the Suspicion of Traitors, death is a science requiring experimentation, a fire in which one must be burned to experience its heat. A fire to which they offer their own selves.

Paradoxically, despite this darkness, the disciples of the Suspicion of Traitors often come to admire those they're protecting, loving them like parents or lovers, even identifying with them.

### Initiation

Disciples are often selected from the children of the Ibn Rashid for their selflessness or even nihilism. Sometimes, a child from another clan or people may be abducted into the path by the assassin of his parents after witnessing their deaths, usually when the child's courage or toughness has impressed the one that becomes their mentor.

### Training

The training of a young disciple is harsh. They must witness a murder, sometimes even of a loved one, experiencing terror and pain. This traumatic experience forms the basis of their future identity as a protector and killer. Thereafter, under the tutelage of a master, the disciple learns to protect, to frustrate the plans and subterfuges of assassins, to remain one step ahead. He learns to kill, but is also taught the skills of the court, to let him mingle in palaces as a courtier like any other.

### First Path Ability

A *mujahid* of the Suspicion of Traitors can detect traitors and assassins. Whenever you suspect a target, you may make an INT + Assassination roll with a difficulty equal to 3 times the Assassination skill score of the target, plus 6 (Assassination x 3, + 6). On a success, you confirm your suspicions about the target. If you roll a constellation, you also gain a result bonus equal to your Loyalty score on any defensive rolls (including your Passive Defence) in combat against that target **at any point in time thereafter.**

Note that this ability only works when you suspect a **possible** traitor or assassin; it's not possible to make this roll against a target you already know full well to be an assassin or traitor. Moreover, this path ability requires great concentration, and may only be attempted once against a given target per game session.

### Second Path Ability

The immediate environment may hold a myriad dangers for the dignitary the mujahid is protecting. Whenever you must make an INT + Notice roll when protecting a target in a situation of clear and present danger, you gain bonus dice on this roll equal to half your Loyalty score (round down). Additionally, your Soak increases by your Loyalty score for the duration of the danger.

### Third Path Ability

The mujahid's selflessness leads him to put himself right in front of attacks aimed at the dignitary he's protecting. Whenever the dignitary you are protecting is attacked, if the attacker is fewer than CON x 2 paces from you, you may attempt an Active Defence roll as a free action to protect the dignitary. Drawing a weapon, moving, and performing the Active Defence are all included in the free action. However, the Active Defence is only successful if you light up a constellation on the roll.

### Fourth Path Ability

The mujahid is the personification of death striking from shadows. On any DEX + Stealth roll, you gain bonus dice equal to half your Heroism score (round down).

### Fifth Path Ability

Life as a bodyguard teaches the mujahid to be one with the shadows. If you light up a constellation on a DEX + Stealth roll, you gain an additional damage bonus equal to the magnitude of that roll on any roll to assassinate a target (see page 27). Note that this damage bonus stacks with the damage bonus gained from the special use of the Assassination skill described on page 75.

### Sixth Path Ability

If you light up a constellation on an attack roll and knock your opponent out, you may choose not to inflict any damage which would take the target below 0 HP. For each point of damage not used for this purpose, you receive one bonus die which you may use against any other opponent in the same combat (not just that round).

## The Saffron Dunes

### Path of Yussef, Servant of Salif

- ❖ **Members:** 300.
- ❖ **Replacement Heroic Virtue:** Faith.

The *al-kimyati* of the Saffron Dunes live only for profit, keenly aware of the most profitable transactions. To consider them merely greedy negotiators would be a mistake, however, for they are far more cunning. Good-natured and wise, they're often optimists with a reputation for bringing luck to their travelling companions.

### Initiation

If any path can be called a family path, this is it. Where knowledge, science, and swordplay can be passed on to others, wealth tends to remain within the family. Because of this, a follower of the Saffron Dunes mentors only family members: his child, son- or daughter-in-law, niece, nephew, or grandchild. There are exceptions, but they are rare.

### Training

Mentors of the Saffron Dunes expose their disciples to real-life situations. The path has no theoretical classes, no doctrine or dogma, nothing but the know-how that comes from negotiating, bargaining, even swindling others. Some mentors hire out their students for months as pages or clerks to a lord, at whose court they learn the arts of flattery and lying.

### First Path Ability

If you light up a constellation on an opposed Unctuous Bargaining roll to sell something (food, jewels, palaces…), the price you receive is increased by +50%. If you light up a constellation on an Unctuous Bargaining roll to buy something, the price you pay is reduced by -50%.

### Second Path Ability

The al-kimyat knows the commodities which are more valuable to his seller or buyer. You gain a pool of bonus dice equal to half your Survival skill (round down) to divide between your Unctuous Bargaining rolls with a buyer or seller.

### Third Path Ability

The al-kimyat instinctively knows what route his caravan must take to avoid disadvantageous encounters. To do this, you must light up a constellation on an INT + Survival roll against a difficulty of 6 (or 12 for a long journey). The roll must be made every morning, or every week in the case of a long journey. On a success with a constellation, your caravan avoids getting lost, or having to negotiate damaged bridges, places infested with brigands, and so on.

### Fourth Path Ability

Even in the worst circumstances, the al-kimyat can force an opposing party to remain at the negotiating table. To do this, you must light up a constellation on an INT + Flattery roll against a difficulty equal to 3 times your opponent's INT (INT x 3).

### Fifth Path Ability

The al-kimyat has the gift of "the Golden Sight", and can appraise the exact, real-world price of an item, and also the personal value it has for a specific individual. To do this, you must light up a constellation on an INT + Unctuous Bargaining roll, against a difficulty of 6 to appraise the real value, and against a difficulty of twice the target's INT score (INT x 2) to determine the personal sentimental value.

If you succeed on this roll with a Critical Success, you gain a vision showing you the most important event associated with the item. This may be the birth of a prince (for a building), the sacrifice of a human to a powerful god (for a weapon), a person surviving a mythical battle (for a suit of armour), and so on. The importance and accuracy of this vision is at Al-Rawi's discretion.

### Sixth Path Ability

Whenever you try to deceive or manipulate someone using sorcery, you gain a pool of bonus dice to use on your Sacred Word skill rolls equal to your Flattery skill.

## The Children of the Souk

### Path of Aziz, Servant of Salif

- ❖ **Members:** 2000 throughout the known world.
- ❖ **Replacement Heroic Virtue:** Loyalty.

In ancient times, Aziz sacrificed his nobility for the good of Kh'saaba. He joined the shadows and became the first Prince of Thieves, dooming his loved ones and their descendants to become the Lost Tribe. Embracing the criminal underworld, he composed an epic poem whose seven chapters were dedicated to murder, prostitution, torture, banditry, lying, sacrilege, and theft. The final chapter gave rise to the "Seventh Path"—the Children of the Souk. Its followers are found throughout Jazirat and even beyond, always growing and multiplying, as their area of activity is the most important in the world. Stealing, trafficking, turning a profit; all these things are their specialties, all carried out in an atmosphere of belonging, of boundless fraternity, with a sense of honour worthy of the greatest mujahidin.

Behind the activities of the Children of the Souk lie both talent and crime: they're the greatest crooks in Jazirat, unequalled in cunning and dexterity. When a spectacular theft happens someplace, people whisper it's the work of the Children. Some say no theft happens anywhere in Jazirat without their say-so.

### Initiation

The Children of the Souk only admit those who are prepared to risk everything to join. Most become members by asking to join a gang or begging an infamous thief to train them. The whole thing is a set-up, though: prospective members are manipulated so that they think they're asking to join the gang or requesting training of their own free will. That way, they think themselves indebted, joining up gratefully, never knowing it's they who've been chosen rather than choosing to join.

### Training

New members, or "little brothers" and "little sisters" as they're known, are placed in groups of ten or so under the authority of a "big brother" or "big sister" who oversees their apprenticeship in the craft, its organisation, and its rules of solidarity. When a little brother or sister reaches adulthood, or when they have proven themselves an equal of their big brother or sister, they may decide to become a "cousin". At that moment, they're free to found their own gang and take apprentices—although in doing so they give up all chance of continuing their own progress on the path. For that reason, it's rare to find Children of the Souk who know more than the first three path abilities. Those who stay in the gang may continue to advance, remaining little brothers and sisters until their deaths if need be—assuming they're not automatically appointed big brother or sister by their city's Prince of Thieves. They may continue to climb the criminal hierarchy, initiating into the higher path abilities.

### First Path Ability

As a Child of the Souk, if you light up a constellation on a difficulty 9 INT + Thievery roll when attempting to set up a robbery, ambush or any other risky, secret, but not necessarily illegal operation (freeing a hostage, relieving a Prince of Thieves of his goods, etc.) in urban territory, you may recruit in half a day a number of Babouche-Dragger henchmen equal to your CHA score multiplied by your Loyalty (CHA x Loyalty). The henchmen will be reliable, working for your cause and only asking for a share of the take (Al-Rawi's discretion).

### Second Path Ability

In combat, the Child of the Souk knows how to strike best in order to guarantee his escape. If you light up a constellation on an attack roll, you may disengage from combat as a free action (page 55).

### Third Path Ability

The Child of the Souk will never betray his people, even if captured and tortured. You gain a pool of bonus dice equal to half your Loyalty score (round down) to spend on Endurance rolls to resist torture.

### Fourth Path Ability

The Child of the Souk is an elusive shadow, a slithering serpent. When attacked, you add your Stealth skill score to your Passive Defence, or to the result of any Active Defence roll.

### Fifth Path Ability

The Child of the Souk knows how to extract information by means of even a casual conversation. If you light up a constellation on a CHA + Acting roll against a difficulty of 6 times your interlocutor's INT score (INT x 6), you may uncover a number of items of information equal to the magnitude +1. This only works if none of these items of information puts the life of the interlocutor at risk, even indirectly.

### Sixth Path Ability

The Child of the Souk knows even the smallest theft should be executed with style and panache. If you light up a constellation on an Intrusion, Stealth or Thievery roll, you get a result bonus equal to your Heroism score.

# The Walad Badiya

## Path of Khalil, Servant of Salif

- ❖ **Members:** 600.
- ❖ **Replacement Heroic Virtue:** Bravery.

Many surprising things have been born from the meeting of Saabi, Al-Fariqani, and saurian, including the paths of Khalil, Servant of Salif. The Walad Badiya, also called the Path of the Al-Fariqani Lancers, is an example of the empathy between human and beast, and of human solidarity. It has produced some of the most impressive and formidable warriors ever known.

Travellers with honour and courage beyond the comprehension of ordinary people, the Walad Badiya elicit curiosity wherever they go. Whether solitary or in groups, they seem to some like warrior gods riding mystical dragons. To others, though, they are little more than degenerate demons, monsters half-lizard, half-man, come to sow destruction. Their ways can be shocking, their customs disturbing, incomprehensible even to their Saabi peers. They are adventurers, warriors, and philosophers, ill at ease (and unwelcome) in cities, at home (and always welcoming) in the great outdoors.

The Al-Fariqani mujahidin of the Walad Badiya are the fiercest fighters in the Salifah tribe. Their bond with their abzulim mounts makes them strange in the eyes of other Saabi. They make excellent soldiers once you gain their loyalty. Their skill with the spear is beyond compare.

### Initiation

No-one understands what pushes a child to become one of the Walad Badiya. One day, he or she succumbs to a fever, and an instinctive urge drives them to seek out and find the egg of a young abzul and then bury it. Later, when the egg hatches, the dragon bites the child's hand, thus sealing their union. Thenceforth, a life of adventure begins.

### Training

The Walad Badiya have no schools, nor are there mentors to teach the ways once followed by Khalil. Older Walad Badiya guide the young in their wisdom, but their role ends there: it is from the communion of rider and abzul that the knowledge of the first path ability comes. Later, when they are ready, they become aware of the second ability, then the third, and so on.

### First Path Ability

In combat, the mujahid and his abzul act as a single entity: the Walad Badiya. Whenever you light up a constellation when attacking or defending, you may:

- ❖ Add the STR of your abzul to your damage (if attacking); against Babouche-Draggers, double your magnitude.
- ❖ Subtract the abzul's DEX from the damage you suffer, as long as you're performing an Active Defence (see page 54).

### Second Path Ability

The bond between you and your abzul is so strong that your HP are increased by your steed's Soak score. Also, the result of all rolls involving the beast's INT gain a bonus equal to your own INT. The distance between you and your abzul must be less than the total of your Heroism score and the abzul's **Legend** score (page 307) in paces.

### Third Path Ability

The mujahid's travelling life gives him deep practical knowledge of his environment. If you light up a constellation on an INT + Storytelling roll, you gain a pool of bonus dice equal to the magnitude to use on any Survival rolls made the same day.

### Fourth Path Ability

The mujahid draws strength from his loyalty towards his travelling companions. When you light up a constellation on an attack roll, you get a damage bonus equal to your Loyalty score plus the number of players around the table (excluding you).

### Fifth Path Ability

The charge of a skilled abzul and rider is brutal and sudden. Your Charge Attack action (page 53) now only requires one action instead of three!

### Sixth Path Ability

The mujahid and his abzul can perform amazing feats. Whenever you light up a constellation on a Riding roll, you gain a pool of bonus dice equal to your Heroism score, to be used on any rolls involving CON, DEX, or STR made that same day, even if you're no longer riding your abzul. This path may only be activated a number of times per day equal to your Bravery score.

## The Walkers on Bloodied Feet

### Path of Tufiq, Servant of Tarek

- ❖ **Members:** 900.
- ❖ **Replacement Heroic Virtue:** Faith.

The Walkers on Bloodied Feet are the most fanatical and violent mujahidin in Jazirat. They fall upon the ungodly like a cleansing sandstorm, erasing everything in their path. They are the desert's wrath.

Born from the vengeful anger of Tufiq, this is one of the most violent paths known. Followed by many bedouins of the Tarekids, for many it represents the death that waits at the end of the road. The Walkers on Bloodied Feet were born during the Agalanthian occupation, thousands of years ago, when, outnumbered a hundred to one, they attacked the Empire's caravans, dying for the glory of Hubal and each taking ten Agalanthians with them to the tomb. Since then they have never stopped growing in hatred and destructiveness, and would have long since disrupted the balance of power among the Saabi had not the king of Kh'saaba himself intervened to request the "pacification" of their Caravan of Purification (see page 254).

Recently, the elite of the clan of Tufiq have found a new quest: to recover the Holy Sword of Hammad and seize control of Aragon. Far away in the lands of the West, many of the Walkers on Bloodied Feet have found positions of importance in the Saabi legions.

### Initiation
In any caravan, children with souls tough enough to become mujahidin are soon noticed. From a young age they are raised as *taali*, squires who look after the weapons and animals of the mujahid they will serve.

### Training
A mujahid who has *taali* squires must see to their martial and religious training. Although this may vary from one individual to another, it always includes long desert marches, days spent praying on the burning sands, mystical quests into Tiamat's entrails, desperate combats outnumbered ten-to-one, and insane sacrifices to Hubal.

### First Path Ability
In combat, you may use your Prayer skill instead of Fighting for all your attack and defence actions. If you light up a constellation when doing so, you gain a damage bonus to any damage you do on your attack, or a result bonus on your Active Defence roll, equal to your Faith score.

The main disadvantage of this path is that, by using your Prayer skill in combat, you may not specialise in a weapon (see "Specialisation and Expertise", page 74), unlike when you use the Fighting skill.

### Second Path Ability
When you use a *shimshir*—the weapon of the Prophets—you gain bonus dice equal to half your Faith score (round down) for use on your attack and defence rolls each round.

### Third Path Ability
The mujahid is the fighting arm of his religion. When you light up a constellation on an attack roll, you may make an immediate second attack as a free action. This second attack uses your Faith score to attack instead of your Fighting skill.

### Fourth Path Ability
The mujahid's face blazes with fanatical devotion. When you light up a constellation on an Intimidate roll, you gain a result bonus equal to your Faith score on all dice rolls against the target of the intimidation.

### Fifth Path Ability
The mujahid's faith shields him from harm. You gain a permanent bonus to your Soak score equal to your Faith score.

### Sixth Path Ability
If you light up a constellation on an attack roll against an opponent with a Faith score lower than your own, you gain a damage bonus equal to double the difference between the two Faith scores (Faith – Faith, x 2).

## The Beloved of Agushaya

### Path of Mimun, Servant of Tarek

- ❖ **Members:** 700 Paper Virgins throughout the world, with as many protectors.
- ❖ **Replacement Heroic Virtue:** Faith.

The *al-kimyati* of the Beloved of Agushaya are part of the order of Paper Virgins (page 254), the sacred prostitutes of Kh'saaba and the greatest experts in the arts of sensual pleasure in Jazirat. They are also the most implacable foes of the decadence and corruption which gnaws at the heart of the Saabi faith, the fire which fights fire, wielding evil to fight evil. Found in cities and palaces, they are magnificent houris, sublime consorts, sensual dancers. They have ruled the sex trade in Jazirat and beyond since time immemorial.

The Beloved of Agushaya is one of the most important Saabi paths, if only because it's the most ubiquitous. Although the houris of the Ibn Aziz are highly organised, they can't compete with the sheer power—individual and collective—of the Paper Virgins. At their heart operate the disciples of the Beloved, who are said to rule the world from their boudoirs. For the good of Kh'saaba and the glory of the Thousand and One Gods, the Paper Virgins manipulate clients from all walks of life, at all levels of influence, without them ever realising who holds the power. From famous merchant to mighty lord, from head of the guard to greedy wazir, many of the mighty of Jazirat rarely act without a Paper Virgin having had a say in their decisions. And, with the Beloved, the Paper Virgins go even further, dealing death when the good of Kh'saaba demands it. For the Beloved of Agushaya, sex is a weapon as deadly as any other.

## Initiation

Initiation to the Beloved of Agushaya follows the process described for the Paper Virgins (see page 255). Beginning characters are considered members of the **Tawl**—the Virginal Host.

## Training

The training of the Beloved of Agushaya is identical to that of other Paper Virgins (page 255), except that it also includes assassination by carnal means. Each Beloved spends a year in Naratmajah Fortress in Nir Manel (page 228), learning the ancient arts of seduction, pleasure, and the distilling of the Rukh Essences (page 256).

## First Path Ability

As an artist, courtesan, lover and killer of the Beloved of Agushaya, you worship the Goddess of Love and War, source of your power. During lovemaking, if you light up a constellation on a CHA + Flattery roll against a difficulty equal to 3 times your partner's INT (INT x 3), you gain 1 point of temporary Heroism (to a maximum of 6) which must be spent in the current session.

## Second Path Ability

The Beloved of Agushaya can turn lovemaking into an agonising experience. On a roll of CHA + Flattery against a difficulty equal to 3 times your partner's CON (CON x 3), your partner suffers damage equal to the magnitude of your roll plus your Faith score, times 2 (magnitude + Faith, x 2).

## Third Path Ability

The Beloved of Agushaya use their voices to charm, whispering a thousand and one promises of voluptuous pleasures. If you light up a constellation on a CHA + Flattery roll, you gain a pool of bonus dice equal to your Faith score to be used on interpersonal rolls with the target.

## Fourth Path Ability

If you light up a constellation on an Assassination or Flattery roll when trying to assassinate a target during lovemaking, you leave little or no trace which may lead back to you as the assassin. The difficulty of any attempts to track you is increased by the magnitude of your roll, plus your Faith score (magnitude + Faith).

## Fifth Path Ability

You attain the status of **Beloved Sister** (or **Beloved Brother**)—see page 255—mastering the mystical techniques of the *abat ittijah* (page 255) which allow you to retain mental control during lovemaking. You gain bonus dice equal to your Faith score on any rolls to resist seduction, temptation, or corruption.

## Sixth Path Ability

By the merest touch—a stroke across the back, a brush of a hand, even a sensual gaze—the Beloved can drive a target of either sex to distraction. Any opponent who tries to act against you in any way must first succeed at an INT attribute roll against a difficulty equal to 4 times your CHA score (CHA x 4). On a failure, your opponent loses his cool and becomes unable to concentrate on anything other than your body, incurring a result penalty on all rolls equal to your CHA + Faith for the rest of the encounter.

# The Sand Preachers

## Path of Yazid, Servant of Tarik

- ❖ **Members:** 150.
- ❖ **Replacement Heroic Virtue:** Faith.

The Sand Preachers are wandering desert pilgrims who carry the words of Yazid wherever they go. Everything they do is guided by their unshakeable belief in their righteousness; they are the honour-guard of the self-proclaimed prophet, the elite of his first followers. Preaching a monotheistic form of Hubal worship, they are everywhere in Jazirat, spreading their faith by voice and sword.

This is a new path, and its disciples are almost all converts from the Tufiq or Mimun clans. Members of the path make up fully a third of the new Ibn Yazid clan.

## Initiation

Most Sand Preachers begin by following Yazid, who has declared himself the prophet of Hubal. One day, Yazid takes the initiate aside and asks them what they would be willing to die for. Those who answer "for you" are immediately slain; those who answer "for your words" or "for the glory of Hubal" are initiated into the first path ability. Those who answer something else may continue to live in the clan, even as a mujahid if they wish, but they will never again get the chance to become a Sand Preacher.

## Training

Only Yazid can pass along the abilities of his path, and he demands devotion and patience. Renouncing one's former life, becoming a firebrand preacher in a Quarterian district, challenging a chieftain of the Ibn Tufiq in the name of your faith, crossing the domain of a djinn without weapons or clothes—surviving all these trials and more is what the prophet demands in return for his teaching.

sequently increases, you also gain knowledge of another element. These additional elements must all be related to the desert.

### Sixth Path Ability

The Sand Preacher can foresee fateful events to come the next day. If you light up a constellation after spending an hour meditating on a difficulty 12 CON + Prayer roll, you experience a blurred vision of a number of events to come in the next day equal to the magnitude +1. At Al-Rawi's discretion, you may exchange one or more points of magnitude for greater precision in your vision.

# Paths of the Shiradim

## The Red Lions of Shirad

### Ashkenim Sect

- ❖ **Members:** 900.
- ❖ **Replacement Heroic Virtue:** Faith.

The Law of the Body, one of Shirad's commandments to help the soul enter the Land of the Righteous, says the people of Shirad shall not kill. However, the strongest of his tribes, the Ashkenim, is home to the mightiest of his sects—the Red Lions of Shirad—whose very purpose is the meteing out of death. This paradox hinges upon ancient sacrificial rites, considered heresy today except when practised by the followers of this path. When a Red Lion kills, he offers his opponent as a sacrifice to Shirad.

The *macchabim* are the sword and shield of Shirad, the defenders of his faith. Their style of combat comprises graceful movements more reminiscent of dance than martial attacks—a dance of death. In peacetime they are found in palaces, honouring their lords with their dance, sacrificing unseen enemies to the glory of Shirad as if they were declaiming heavenly verse. Besides offering their dances, they spend hours in prayer in their Temple. Most Red Lions are stationed in Carrassine, a city they migrated to at the side of Sarah Bat Caleb (page 174).

### Initiation

Divine grace imbues every movement of the *macchabah*, and is the first thing the sect's masters look for when selecting initiates. They regularly visit Shiradi schools, organising sports and martial competitions, recruiting not the winners but those with the leonine sleekness, elegance and nobility they seek, even if they did not win. The Shiradim have often had to bend to better survive; for the Red Lions, there is no dishonour in defeat, as long as one maintains one's dignity and one's faith in the greatness of Shirad. Each master of the sect chooses a dozen disciples every five years, and ensures their training with a mother's love and a father's strictness.

### First Path Ability

When you commit a "hands-on" assassination (stabbing, garrotting, slitting the throat, etc, but not poisoning), you may use your Prayer skill instead of Assassination. If you light up a constellation, you gain a damage bonus equal to twice your Faith score (Faith x 2). The main disadvantage of this path is that, because you attack with your Prayer skill instead of Assassination, you may not specialise (see "Specialisation and Expertise" on page 74).

### Second Path Ability

The Sand Preacher lives in harmony with the desert. Whenever you use sorcery relating to the desert (its sands, winds, creatures, etc), you roll bonus dice equal to half your Survival skill (round down).

### Third Path Ability

By meditating for an hour at the start of each day, the Sand Preacher toughens his body against the rigours of his environment. If you light up a constellation on a difficulty 15 CON + Prayer roll, you gain a bonus to your Soak equal to your Faith score for the next 24 hours. This path can only be activated once every 24 hours.

### Fourth Path Ability

The Sand Preacher's ascetic discipline allows him to go without sleep, food, or drink for several days. If you light up a constellation on a difficulty 6 CON + Endurance roll, you may go without these things for a number of days equal to the number rolled on the constellation die; after that you are subject to hunger, thirst, and fatigue as normal (see page 67). You must eat at least one meal before attempting this path ability again.

### Fifth Path Ability

Living in the deep desert brings an understanding of its secrets. You gain knowledge of an additional number of **magical elements** (page 119) equal to your Survival skill. If your Survival skill sub-

## Training

The training of the Red Lions is among the harshest known. To better train in elegance, from a very young age students confront and overcome their arrogance in spectacular exhibition duels which frequently end in death. Once they have learned humility, they spend three years serving the poor of all peoples and religions, during which they renounce all weapons, even in self-defence. At the end of this period, the student is considered a *macchabah*. Death and poverty no longer scare him, and he shines with divine light, and fights that he may continue to do so. He is initiated into the secrets of Shiradi sword fighting and its connection with dance and prayer. This takes three long years of intensive training, night and day, when his body and mind are repeatedly tested and broken. Once he reaches his majority, the *macchabah* is named a Red Lion of Shirad.

### First Path Ability

By means of a quick prayer at the beginning of combat (a free action—see page 50), you may enter a mystical trance making your combat actions (even magical ones) more effective. If you light up a constellation on a difficulty 9 CON + Prayer roll, you gain a result bonus on all your combat actions, whether for attack, defence, movement, casting spells, and so on, equal to your Faith score.

### Second Path Ability

The Red Lion fights like a one-man army. If you light up a constellation on an attack roll in combat against more than one opponent, you use the Babouche-Dragger rules (page 65) and add your Bravery score to the number of opponents you take out. Note that this works against both Babouche-Draggers and Valiant Captains, but not against Champions (page 65).

### Third Path Ability

You add your Faith score to the result of all your Prince archetype skill rolls (page 26). Additionally, if you light up a constellation on a Combat Training roll, you gain extra bonus dice equal to your Heroism score.

### Fourth Path Ability

The Red Lion knows he is the righteous hand of god. You may use your Prayer skill instead of Intimidate against non-Shiradim targets. Additionally, if you light up a constellation on a Prayer roll to intimidate, you roll bonus dice equal to your Faith score.

### Fifth Path Ability

The Red Lion knows his weapon is an instrument of Shirad's divine will. You gain a damage bonus equal to your Faith score.

### Sixth Path Ability

The maccabah's dance is an unstoppable whirl of blades. If you light up a constellation on an attack roll, you may immediately make a second attack as a free action.

## The Heavenly Voice of Shirad

### Pharatim Sect

❖ **Members:** 900 throughout the known world.
❖ **Replacement Heroic Virtue:** Faith.

The Shiradim have always depended upon the Pharatim tribe for their religious guidance and salvation. The sect of the Heavenly Voice of Shirad has been the organising force of the Pharatim, and has allowed the tribe to spread throughout the known world. Today there is no city without a Shiradi presence, no Shiradi community without at least a disciple of the Heavenly Voice. Philosophers, politicians, guardians of knowledge and spiritual advisors, the sect underpins the administration of Shiradi groups and guarantees their stability and longevity. Members can be found holding important positions in universities and advising powerful public figures like artists and rich merchants. People say they're the greatest scholars in Jazirat.

### Initiation

The Heavenly Voice of Shirad operates centres of learning known as "Universities of Light" in all the world's great cities. Sometimes they're secret and hidden in catacombs (as in Occidentia), sometimes they advertise openly and are official establishments, as in Carrassine or Sagrada. After passing moral and intellectual tests put to them by their clan's *kahan* (page 263), young Shiradim enrol at the Universities of Light for a year of probation, after which they either matriculate as permanent students of the Heavenly Voice or are asked to leave (the *kahanim* sometimes get it wrong).

### Training

A sorcery school as much as an academic university, the Heavenly Voice of Shirad offers a rich and varied curriculum to all its students. Enhanced with study trips and meetings with luminaries, it offers an education in diversity. Upon reaching majority, a student is awakened to the first path ability—but ever after he will always remain a student, as each new revelation brings its own questions.

### First Path Ability

You can extract a fact or anecdote from the accumulated knowledge of centuries at your disposal, to help you answer a question or solve a problem. If you light up a constellation on a roll of INT + History & Peoples or INT + Science, you gain a result bonus equal to your Faith score on any dice rolls made that day to solve the problem, which may relate to military strategy (Command), diplomacy (any of the Prince archetype skills), survival (Survival, Endurance), medical treatment (Science), and so on. In rare cases these may even be combat or sorcery rolls, but Al-Rawi should take care that this path doesn't become systematically abused in this way: it's about a flash of insight to solve a major problem, not a trick to be used to enhance your attacks.

If the problem isn't solved the same day, you must make a new roll the next day if you want to benefit from the bonus again.

### Second Path Ability

The sage of the Heavenly Voice becomes the receptacle for part of the wisdom of Shirad. Your maximum History & Peoples or Science skill score (whichever you selected at character creation) is raised from 6 to 7.

### Third Path Ability

By praying while raising your left hand palm forward, you cause the light of Shirad to shine forth from your hand. If you light up a constellation on a difficulty 9 CON + Prayer roll (taking one action in combat), you dazzle your enemies for a number of actions equal to your Faith score, +1 per swagger die. Dazzled enemies suffer a result penalty to any physical actions equal to your Faith score.

### Fourth Path Ability

If you light up a constellation on a Sacred Word roll to cast an improvised spell (page 119), you may reduce the difficulty increase from improvising elements by as many steps (page 46) as your Faith score divided by 2 (Faith / 2).

### Fifth Path Ability

Shirad himself speaks through the words of the sage of the Heavenly Voice. You gain knowledge of an additional number of **magical elements** (page 119) equal to your Faith score. If your Faith score increases, you gain knowledge of an additional element. You don't lose knowledge of an element if your Faith drops, although it must rise above its previous maximum for you to learn more additional elements. The additional elements must relate to wisdom, knowledge, or religion.

### Sixth Path Ability

The sage's faith in Shirad is his holy shield and protection. If you light up a constellation on a Willpower roll to resist a magical effect (page 120), you gain a pool of bonus dice equal to twice your Faith score (Faith x 2), to be spent to destroy or remove the cause or origin of that magical effect (a sorcerer, djinn, artefact, etc). The bonus dice must be used in the next 24 hours.

## The Sacred Heart of Shirad

### Salonim Sect

- ❖ **Members:** 800 throughout the world.
- ❖ **Replacement Heroic Virtue:** Loyalty.

The Shiradim have the felicitous trait of indispensability, and none more so than the tribe of the Salonim. When a powerful individual anywhere succumbs to a life-threatening disease or wound, it's the children of Salone he calls upon.

Shiradi healers are the most renowned and skilful in Jazirat, and perhaps in the whole world. Their custom of sharing knowledge means a given healer can treat almost any ailment his fellows have already encountered. But even the purest, most altruistic souls have a dark side: the followers of the Sacred Heart of Shirad also know how to bring death, as one who masters life also masters how to destroy it.

### Initiation

Chosen from among the best Salonim teachers or physicians found in dispensaries or universities, the followers of the Sacred Heart of Shirad often join the sect quite late in their careers. The elite high council of this Shiradi sect of physicians rarely chooses young candidates, no matter how promising they may appear, instead preferring those with experience.

### Training

When initiated to the Sacred Heart, the physician is already a gifted sage of considerable skill. The sect fills out his knowledge by presenting him with difficult cases, often exacerbated magically for the purposes of study. Working from his own initiatives or the mistakes he makes, the physician is led to develop his own understanding until he makes break-throughs in knowledge and science himself. Only rarely is knowledge directly imparted.

### First Path Ability

If you light up a constellation when making a Science roll to operate on a wounded person, diagnose a disease, or heal anyone (page 70), you gain a magnitude bonus equal to your Loyalty score.

### Second Path Ability

By dint of being around the sick, the physician develops a great resistance to disease. You add your Loyalty score to your Soak when resisting poisons or disease.

### Third Path Ability

The physician is unequalled when treating wounds. If you light up a constellation on a Science roll to treat minor or major wounds (page 71), you increase the number of Hit Points recovered in the first day by a number of points equal to your Loyalty score. At each subsequent recovery check under your care after the initial treatment, you increase the HP recovered by half your Loyalty score (round down).

### Fourth Path Ability

The physician knows how to kill without leaving any trace, or while making the death look like an accident. If you try to kill a target in this way and you light up a constellation on your attack roll, you get a damage bonus equal to twice your Science skill score (Science x 2). All tests to discover that the accident was really a murder are made at a difficulty increased by the magnitude of your roll plus your Loyalty score (magnitude + Loyalty).

### Fifth Path Ability

Through rigorous training and the consumption of medicinal concoctions rendering his body more flexible, the physician can fit his body into places that would normally be impossible for someone of his size (Al-Rawi's discretion). All your Intrusion and Athletics rolls related to contortion or squeezing through spaces gain a result bonus equal to twice your Loyalty score (Loyalty x 2). You have a lean and slender physique.

### Sixth Path Ability

The physician knows how to inflict massive and incapacitating pain on his victim. Whenever you light up a constellation on an attack roll, you inflict a result penalty equal to the roll's magnitude on all of your victim's dice rolls for a number of actions equal to your Science skill score.

# Paths of the Agalanthians

## The Thereman Myrmidons

### Agalanthian School of the City-State of Therema

- ❖ **Members:** 1500 (800 make up the Thereman elite guard, 300 are elite soldiers in various Agalanthian armies, 200 work as freelance mercenaries or in *myrmidon* corps elsewhere in the known world).
- ❖ **Replacement Heroic Virtue:** Loyalty.

In an age before Agalanth united the peoples of the land under his name, Hades rose up to try and conquer the mortal world. Cthonos, God of the Earth, guarantor of peace in the Underworld, was forced to contain the invasion erupting from his own realm. His role as Guardian of the Infernal Portals, Gaoler of Shaytan the Black and his Legions, was put rudely to the test.

To fight against the terrifying demon hordes, Cthonos required the fiercest yet most disciplined army ever created. Thus, he decided to shape soldier ants into human form, creating the first **myrmidons**. The insectoid monsters perished long ago, but their heritage survives to this day.

The Thereman Myrmidons are the fiercest and most disciplined warriors of the Agalanthians. The Praetorian Guard of the city of Therema, they preserve the martial expertise which once vanquished the very legions of Hades. Although no one has been troubled by invasions from the Underworld for millennia, the warriors of Cthonos have never stopped preparing for a new attack. If the demons strike again, they will be welcomed appropriately.

### Initiation

Only one school exists for the Thereman Myrmidons. It trains the greatest Agalanthian warriors and *strategoi* (page 270) at their families' request. Enrolment is expensive—hundreds of gold talents—although it may be reduced (and even waived) by signing up as a legionary for a term of five or ten years. However long one serves, one never stops being a myrmidon, and every graduate remains on the reserves for life. In the case of a major Agalanthian crisis, all myrmidon veterans become available for call-up.

### Training

Following a harsh military training regime, the school of the Thereman Myrmidons puts discipline and physical preparedness above all. Most exercises are aimed at striking fast and often, denying one's opponent the slightest respite. Additionally, full-scale strategic exercises, live-action reconstructions of battles from the Agalanthiad, and terms of service with different armies across the world, all form part of a myrmidon's training.

### First Path Ability

You're a *myrmidon*, a member of an elite unit founded during the ages of Agalanthian glory and a terrifyingly effective warrior. If you light up a constellation on a CON + Combat Training roll with the intention of obtaining bonus dice (page 27) for a round, you gain additional bonus dice equal to half your Heroism score (round down).

### Second Path Ability

When fighting with gladius and shield, you may use the "Fighting With Two Weapons" rules (page 54), treating the shield as a weapon. You don't need to fulfil the usual prerequisites for two-weapon fighting (DEX 4, INT 4, Fighting 4). Your shield does STR + 5 points of damage, and you gain an additional damage bonus when fighting with these two weapons equal to your Combat Training skill score.

### Third Path Ability

The myrmidon can exceed his body's physical limits to accomplish great feats. If you light up a constellation on a Combat Training roll made at the start of combat, you gain additional bonus dice equal to your full Heroism score (ie not half your Heroism score, as with the first path ability).

### Fourth Path Ability

The myrmidon's riposte is lightning fast. If you light up a constellation on an Active Defence roll, you may make an immediate attack against the same target as a free action (page 50). Note that, if you're fighting with two weapons, this may be in addition to the additional Normal Attack you may make on a Critical Success (page 54).

### Fifth Path Ability

The myrmidon's training renders his skin as hard as the chitin of the insectoid warriors he is reputedly descended from. Your Soak gains a bonus equal to your Combat Training skill score.

### Sixth Path Ability

You gain a damage bonus when attacking with thrown weapons such as javelins equal to your Heroism score. If you light up a constellation on your attack roll with such a thrown weapon, you may double the weapon's range. Additionally, ranges of 12-24 paces are treated as Medium range (-3 penalty), and ranges of 24 to STR x 12 paces (instead of STR x 6 paces) are treated as Long range (-6 penalty). Attacks beyond STR x 12 paces are not possible.

## The Fragrantine Charioteers

### Agalanthian School of the City-State of Fragrance

- ❖ **Members:** 400 members world-wide (150 in Fragrance).
- ❖ **Replacement Heroic Virtue:** Bravery.

Charioteer, gladiator and athletics schools aren't rare in Agalanthian lands, but none equals in prestige the great school of the city of Fragrance. The Fragrantine Charioteers are glorious heroes on both race track and battlefield, magnificent in their gleaming chariots when they charge the lines of opposing armies. Merciless, they only live to write their names in history. Their vanity is their biggest flaw, a self-worship they would extend to everyone around them.

Popularity is the abiding concern of charioteers everywhere, more even than wealth or victory, but among the Fragrantine Charioteers it borders on obsession. In Fragrance, being the best charioteer lets you hobnob with princes and bed their wives, own villas you'll never pay for, and ride shoulder-high in triumph through the city streets.

### Initiation

The school of the Fragrantine Charioteers is a powerhouse. It produces chariots, trains craftsmen to build and repair them, breeds horses, maintains race tracks, and more. It presides over all the races that take place in the city. Consequently, there are numerous ways to join; the school will even provide you with a free licence to compete in one race, let you take tests, get the chance to be scouted by a merchant or stable wanting to invest in your training. Once you've been discovered, a full license can be bought from the school, where you'll then embark upon its legendary training program.

### Training

In reality, training charioteers is only one percent of the school's activities. But what little it does, it does masterfully! Its students—only 20 per year—are initiated into the arts of Agalanthian life as well as combat and racing. At the end of the three-year training period, the charioteers graduate to racing wearing the colours of a private stable. Even then, they still share the bonds of brotherhood, always ready to help one another even when they face off on the race track.

### First Path Ability

If you light up a constellation when performing a Charge Attack when driving your chariot (page 56), it takes you only 2 actions instead of 3!

### Second Path Ability

The charioteer knows how to exploit the strength of his mount or mounts (camels, horses, etc) in combat. If you light up a constellation on an attack roll when you're actively moving in mounted or chariot combat, you gain a damage bonus equal to your Riding skill score.

### Third Path Ability

The charioteer's charge through enemy lines is devastating. If you light up a constellation on an attack roll, you get a bonus equal to your Bravery score to apply to damage or the number of Babouche-Draggers you take out.

### Fourth Path Ability

Growing up with camels and horses since early childhood, the charioteer develops a bond of trust with these noble beasts. Your steed will never be skittish, always letting you approach, mount, and ride, as long as you aren't aggressive in your treatment. Additionally, because of your status as a popular hero and renowned athlete, you gain a result bonus to any Flattery rolls equal to your Riding skill score.

### Fifth Path Ability

The charioteer is one with his chariot. As long as you're at the reins, you gain a bonus to your Soak equal to your Riding skill score.

### Sixth Path Ability

The charioteer is a role model for young people, a popular hero, a subject of envy and desire for the powerful. You gain a result bonus equal to your Bravery score to all skill rolls from the Prince archetype.

## The Etrusian Bacchantes

### Agalanthian School of the City-State of Etrusia

- ❖ **Members:** 300.
- ❖ **Replacement Heroic Virtue:** Faith.

People imagine Agalanthian sorcerers as gaunt, bearded types living in caves, malnourished and devoting their lives to sacrificial cults. Although this is sometimes true, it's certainly not the case for the Etrusian Bacchantes, a group of mystical philosophers who celebrate the creative power of the gods through the pleasures of the flesh. They exalt vice and pleasure in all their forms. The school's founder, Archores Menetrias Bacchoris, claimed to be the son of

Bacchoros, God of Pleasure and the Vine, allegedly born from the union of the god with an alcoholic old witch that had managed to summon him for a night by accident when they'd both had more than their fair share of drink. After sobering up and realising what he'd done, the shamefaced god bought the witch's silence by promising a great destiny to the son he had planted in her womb. Thus was Archores Menetrias Bacchoris born—destined from the start to found his own school of magic.

Even today, the Bacchantes have little in the way of organisation. They're as much winemakers as sorcerers, as much drunkards as seducers.

## Initiation

Most initiate to the Bacchantes after working in vineyards, or meeting one of their sorcerers or sorceresses and becoming their lover then student.

## Training

Properly speaking there's no overall "school" of the Etrusian Bacchantes. Instead, each follower of the path commits to founding his own Bacchantian *scolarium* after attaining the fourth path ability. At that point, he surrounds himself with up to fifteen disciples, to whom he imparts his knowledge while strolling around, engaging in bookish studies, and indulging in wild and drunken mystical experiences.

## First Path Ability

As a Bacchant, debauchery, alcohol and the decadent arts are your main concerns. Transcending mere ecstasy, your devotion to these activities lets you draw upon an energy which simplifies your practice of magic. If you light up a constellation on a CHA + Flattery roll during an orgy or drunken extravaganza, or on a CON + Endurance roll to withstand drunkenness at the same, you receive a result bonus equal to your Faith score to all subsequent Sacred Word rolls. This bonus lasts a number of hours equal to the constellation die (so if you roll three 2s, the bonus lasts 2 hours).

## Second Path Ability

Noise and excitement are part and parcel of the Bacchant's life. Any action you attempt in such an environment (a souk, drunken party, battle, etc) receives a result bonus equal to your Faith score.

## Third Path Ability

The Bacchant is accustomed to seducing and flattering people to get what he wants. Whenever you light up a constellation on a Flattery roll against a target, you gain bonus dice equal to your Faith score on any relationship roll you make against that target in the next 24 hours. This ability may only be used once every 24 hours.

## Fourth Path Ability

The Bacchant knows how to attract the attention of the gods to his cause. Whenever you spend a Heroism point to consult Urim and Turim (page 77), or whenever Al-Rawi asks you to consult Urim and Turim to check your luck, you may redraw the stone if you don't like the result of the first draw.

## Fifth Path Ability

In homage to the gods, the Bacchant has transformed his very body into a source of life. The bodily fluids—whatever they may be—you produce in a single day may be mixed and boiled into a magical nectar, the consumption of which can replace food and drink for one person for a number of days equal to your Faith score.

## Sixth Path Ability

The Bacchant's magic is imbued with the fruits of his dissolute escapades. Whenever you inscribe a chiromancy tablet (page 138), you subtract your Faith score from the inscription difficulty, as long as the spell in question relates to pleasure, vice, or licentiousness.

# Paths of the Quarterians

## The Duellists of San Llorente de Valladon

### Aragonian Academy

- ❖ **Members:** 400.
- ❖ **Replacement Heroic Virtue:** Loyalty.

The origins of this academy are lost in the early centuries of the Quarterianisation of Aragon. Most of the country was still under the Agalanthian yoke when Don Constantino Arranz y Garcia, a *campeador* returning from Sagrada, decided to liberate his country in the name of the new faith. A charismatic individual leading an army of warriors and peasants, he liberated the cities of Valladon, Pamblosa and Barcajoyosa, and was probably instrumental in the mass conversion of

Aragon to the Quarterian faith and its emergence as a kingdom that lasted until the recent arrival of the Saabi. A popular hero, the campeador exalted the values of the pure and fearless knight devoted to justice, freedom and faith. It's said that whenever he slew a foe, he knelt and wept, praying to Aether for his soul. Recently canonised, Don Constantino Arranz y Garcia is now known as San Llorente de Valladon, the Weeping Saint of Valladon.

Although we use the term "academy" in keeping with the Quarterian convention, no specific institution exists to promote the philosophy and swordsmanship techniques of the Weeping Saint. Instead, across Aragon, Don Constantino's companions made his thoughts and practices their own, imparting them to their children, who did the same. The term these campeadors use to refer to these informal establishments is "hacienda"—a family stable and farm.

### Initiation

Most members of a hacienda learn its secrets from a family member. It's not uncommon, however, for a particularly spirited and skilful hacienda worker to be initiated and become a family member.

### Training

Although training in the techniques of swordsmanship and the use of the whip is arduous and strict, the hacienda of San Llorente de Valladon is more a way of life than a formal academy. Throughout their lives, the young cattle farmers improve their riding skills and learn to live on horseback.

### First Path Ability

If you light up a constellation when attacking with a whip, you may immediately make a second attack against the same target with another weapon (a sword, axe, spear, fist, etc.) as a Free Attack (page 53). This second weapon need not have been readied: drawing the weapon is part of the free action. The attack is resolved as part of the same action as the whip attack. If you aren't in range for this second attack (for example, a whip is longer than a dagger or a sword), then the move to close range is also free and takes place in the same phase. If your target is out of range of the whip attack (about 3 paces), then this ability may not be used.

### Second Path Ability

A peerless horse rider, you gain a result bonus on all Athletics, Endurance, Fighting, and Survival skill rolls equal to your Loyalty score when on horseback.

### Third Path Ability

The duellist of San Llorente wields his whip as if it were an extension of his own arm. You gain an additional damage bonus with the whip equal to your DEX score. Moreover, on a successful DEX + Fighting roll against a difficulty set by Al-Rawi, you can use your whip to grab things at a distance of up to 3 paces (catching a flying item, picking up a weapon, snatching a weapon from an opponent's scabbard, and so on).

### Fourth Path Ability

Horses, regardless of their origin, instinctively trust your expert horse-handling skills and the affection you feel for them, and are docile in your hands. You gain a result bonus equal to twice your Loyalty score (Loyalty x 2) to any rolls of Athletics, Endurance, Fighting, or Survival made while on horseback.

### Fifth Path Ability

Although Aragonians are a sedentary rather than nomadic people, their horsemen nevertheless spend long hours in the saddle each day travelling their lands. The open trail is your life, nature your domain. You get a result bonus on any Agriculture or Riding rolls equal to your INT score.

### Sixth Path Ability

Friends of the winds, the duellists of San Llorente de Valladon are able to defend themselves effortlessly. You may make an Active Defence as a free action during any action you take.

## The Order of Saint Gerda Dragonslayer

### Orkadian Academy

- ❖ **Members:** 500.
- ❖ **Replacement Heroic Virtue:** Bravery.

In ancient times, the warrior-woman Gerda unified the barbarians of the Agalanthian frontier to found Gerdenheim, the Realm of a Thousand Fortresses. It's said she personified brutality and womanly rebelliousness, to the extent that when she found out she was one of the Dragon-Marked, she spent five whole years looking for the dragon who had chosen her. When she finally found it, she challenged the dragon and killed it. As it died, she told it: "No-one decides for me what my life shall be. Now I have slain you, I will take your place and serve your gods." To the end of her life Gerda fought against the Agalanthians, and it was only after her death of extreme old age that her enemies were able to march on Gerdenheim. This is the reason for Gerda's canonisation by the Quarterians, despite the fact that she was a pagan.

The members of this academy, known as *Slayers*, are the strongest and toughest warriors in the West. They advance relentlessly in battle, slaying without mercy, driven by the Wrath Within.

### Initiation

Any squire wanting to devote himself to the art of war, any young Quarterian passionate about faith and justice, can attempt to join the Order of Saint Gerda Dragonslayer. The order does not recruit: it awaits the bravest volunteers. Each year it organises a great tournament of many combats; the hundred strongest candidates must, in groups of ten, best monstrous creatures, usually from the Krek'kaos steppe. The survivors join the order.

## Training

Combat, and nothing but combat, fills every day in the elite order headquarters in Gerdenheim. Twice a year, long journeys through the Eastern Steppe offer young knights the chance to prepare themselves for a life of travel and battle in a hostile environment.

### First Path Ability

You can draw upon Saint Gerda's strength to promote justice. If you light up a constellation in combat, you gain a damage bonus equal to your STR score (this is in addition to your usual STR damage bonus, ie you add STR twice).

### Second Path Ability

The Slayer's defensive ability is as intimidating and impenetrable as dragon scales. You add your Intimidate skill score to your Passive Defence. For Active Defence rolls, you roll bonus dice equal to half your Intimidate score (round down) for the duration of combat, regardless of the number of opponents.

### Third Path Ability

The Slayer is possessed by the Wrath of Saint Gerda. If you light up a constellation on an attack roll, you gain bonus dice equal to your Bravery score for use in the current round.

### Fourth Path Ability

If you light up a constellation on a roll that reduces your opponent's HP to zero or below, you get an immediate additional attack as a free action against any other opponent within range. Note that you may only make one Free Attack in a given action (page 53).

### Fifth Path Ability

The Slayer partakes of the speed of Saint Gerda. Your Brutal Attacks only require 1 action instead of 2.

### Sixth Path Ability

The Slayer's endurance is a gift from Saint Gerda. If you light up a constellation on a Combat Training roll, you gain additional bonus dice equal to your Bravery score.

## The Order of the Temple of Sagrada

### Occidentian Academy

❖ **Members:** 2000, few of whom go beyond the Second Path Ability (fewer than 50 know the Fourth, Fifth, or Sixth Path Abilities, created by the Grand Master of the order, Albermond de Dorbagne).
❖ **Replacement Heroic Virtue:** Faith.

The *Templars* of Sagrada have sworn on the *Mirabilis Calva Reliquiae* (page 177) to protect Quarterian pilgrims and interests in Jazirat. They are warriors as strong as the Orkadian Slayers and as devout as the Magister himself.

The order was founded in 5990, seven years ago, when Sagrada fell into Quarterian hands and the last Shiradim defenders were hanged from the walls of their temple. Kneeling before the hanged men, Duke Albermond de Dorbagne swore before Aether that the city would never be taken from him. He then chose his ten finest companions, each of whom chose ten of their own, and so on, until a thousand knights of the Holy Crusade were gathered. Together they descended to the sea and were re-baptised by the chaplains of the army. Finally, de Dorbagne knighted each of the companions by naming them Templars of Sagrada, guardians of the Quarterian faith in Capharnaum. Since then, those who have not returned home to squander their looted fortunes or to join some religious-political conspiracy have become the ultimate strike troops of the Occidentian forces in Jazirat.

### Initiation

Entry into the order is possible in two ways: by recruitment or enrolment. The former is informal, when a soldier with a gift for sorcery comes to the attention of his superiors, who recommend him to the masters of the order. The latter is more spontaneous, when a knight with sorcerous gifts presents himself before the order and requests the Second Baptism. In both cases the knight is required to fight five duels with blunted weapons against other Templars, and to still be standing after the fifth (even if he doesn't win). The applicant must then spend three days and nights kneeling in vigil, eating only once each day.

### Training

Once admitted to the order, the knight is immediately given the title of Templar. However, he will only be initiated to the first path ability at the end of his first year, and only if he has shown exemplary behaviour and skills. His daily life is made up of prayer and military training, patrols and pious readings. Once per week during that first year, the young Templars undertake a penitential progress, hobbling on their knees along the cobbled road from Jason's Wall to the palace courtyard where he lived through the ordeal of quartering. There they are flogged, to the rhythmic chanting of monks who have been blinded so that the dignity of the penitent Templars is preserved.

### First Path Ability

As comfortable with matters of war as with the magical uses of the Holy Scriptures, if you light up a constellation on either a combat roll (whether an attack or a defence) or on a Sacred Word roll, you gain a magnitude bonus equal to your Faith score.

### Second Path Ability

The Templar's duty requires him to wear heavy armour in all circumstances. Armour penalties (page 64) to Assassination, Athletics, Intrusion, Riding, Stealth, and Thievery skill rolls no longer affect you.

### Third Path Ability

Whenever you utter a short prayer as a free action and light up a constellation on a difficulty 6 CON + Prayer roll at the start of a round, you get a pool of bonus dice equal to the number on the constellation die which can be used on any of your actions that round.

### Fourth Path Ability

The Templar is filled with the divine power of Aether. If you light up a constellation on an attack roll, you may make an immediate second attack as a free action against the same opponent, but instead rolling your Faith score instead of your Fighting skill.

### Fifth Path Ability

Religious fervour and devoted study of Holy Scripture bestows upon the Templar a deep affinity with one of the Sacred Words (choose one). You gain a result bonus equal to your Faith score on any roll you make with this Sacred Word.

### Sixth Path Ability

The Templar's fervour and devotion is inspiring. If you light up a constellation on an Oratory roll, you increase the bonuses granted to your companions by your Faith score (see page 22).

# COMMON PATHS

Over the millennia, the peoples of the world have met, fallen in love, betrayed one another, fought, and in doing so have exchanged and shared many things. The paths people follow have sometimes undergone the same: it's possible to find, in any land, individuals who claim to belong to different cultural traditions, but who use the same swordsmanship techniques, the same sorcerous rituals, the same tricks to shine in society.

This means that some paths are in effect common to all the peoples of the known world. No one can really say when or where they originated. Obviously, everyone claims their own version is the original one, and only true way.

But why should you devote yourself to a path, with all its rigours and restrictions, when your neighbour is teaching just the same thing and claims it's from a different master or even a different god? Ultimately the only answer that matters is the pragmatic one: it's the benefits you receive, and the level of expertise you can attain.

To give you a better idea of the nature of these **common paths,** we've organised them according to the **archetypes** (page 25) they most correspond to. In the end, though, all common paths are intentionally generic. They provide a structured yet flexible foundation for characters to break out of their cultural norms. If you find them too formulaic, feel free to modify and customise them to your needs.

# Paths of the Adventurer

The following path abilities are found in the common paths of the Adventurer.

### First Path Ability

If you light up a constellation on any Adventurer archetype skill, increase your magnitude by a number of points equal to the value on the constellation die.

### Second Path Ability

Luck is the friend of all Adventurers. When your opponent rolls a Critical Success on an attack against you, that attack is considered only a Normal Success.

### Third Path Ability

You're as tough as leather. Double your Soak score when calculating your resistance to hunger, fatigue, encumbrance, etc (see pages 67 and 78).

### Fourth Path Ability

You're an animal friend. You may gain a result or magnitude bonus (your choice, before you roll the dice) on any dice roll when interacting with animals (to train them, calm them down, fight them, etc) equal to your replacement heroic virtue (see the "Rules Considerations" text box).

## Fifth Path Ability

You have nine lives. All your Athletics skill rolls automatically succeed, with at least a magnitude of 0.

## Sixth Path Ability

You gain a result or magnitude bonus (your choice, before you roll the dice) on any Adventurer archetype skill roll equal to your Heroism score.

# The Dark Rain Healers

## Shiradi Sect

❖ **Replacement Heroic Virtue:** Bravery.

A Salonim military order of combat medics. Always on the alert, the Dark Rain Healers are often the last chance of those who fall in combat. More adventurer than physician, they tend the fallen under a constant hail of arrows and often seem heedless of death. They love strong sensations and death-defying wagers.

**Note:** The second path ability is modified as follows: Any rolls you make to treat wounds not caused by Critical Successes receive a magnitude bonus equal to your Bravery score.

# The Phalanx of the Rangers of Septra

## Agalanthian School

❖ **Replacement Heroic Virtue:** Loyalty.

Wandering guardians on the northern frontier, travelling from outpost to outpost all year round, the Rangers of Septra are disciplined adventurers, whose mettle and sobriety is unrelenting except for their one day of leave every month, determined at random at the end of the previous month. This day permits the Rangers to get some much needed rest and recuperation and return to the field refreshed.

**Note:** The fifth path ability applies to your Notice skill.

# Paths of the Labourer

The following path abilities are found in the common paths of the Labourer.

## First Path Ability

If you light up a constellation on any Labourer archetype skill roll, you gain a magnitude bonus equal to the value of the constellation die.

## Rules Considerations

### What Heroic Virtue should I use?

Common paths are generic, so it's up to you to specify their feel and nature, based on what you want for your character. When customising a common path, work with Al-Rawi to decide whether your version of the path will be based on Bravery, Faith, or Loyalty. The examples given in this section indicate which replacement heroic virtue they use.

### Spending Heroic Virtue Stars

Some path abilities let you spend stars of heroic virtue scores to get a result or magnitude bonus. The amount of stars you can spend is limited by your Heroism score and the number of stars your character has. So, if your character has a Heroism score of 4 and at least 4 stars in a given heroic virtue, you may spend up to 4 stars of your replacement heroic virtue to get a +4 bonus.

### Result Bonus or Magnitude Bonus?

Some path abilities provide a result bonus, others provide a magnitude bonus. A result bonus is a way of improving your success chance with an action. A magnitude bonus doesn't affect your chance of success, but does affect how well you succeed if you do.

### Spending Points for a Bonus or not?

Sometimes you have to spend Heroism points or heroic virtue stars to get a bonus. Sometimes, though, no such expenditure is mentioned, as in "Gain a magnitude bonus on all Sorcerer archetype skill rolls equal to your Heroism score". In such a case, the bonus is fixed, but doesn't require any expenditure of points.

If it's necessary to spend Heroism points or heroic virtue stars to get a bonus, you must declare how many points you're going to spend before you roll the dice.

## Second Path Ability

Perseverance is the friend of the Labourer. You may re-roll any failed Labourer archetype skill roll which was not a Critical Failure. You gain a +1 result bonus on the re-roll.

## Third Path Ability

You're as tough as leather! Your Soak score is doubled for the purposes of calculating resistances (hunger, fatigue, encumbrance, etc). See pages 67 and 78.

### Fourth Path Ability

You're a jack of all trades. You can repair or even cobble together any item you need, as long as you have the necessary raw materials. You may spend stars of your replacement heroic virtue to gain an equivalent result or magnitude bonus (your choice, before you roll the dice) on your next Craft skill roll.

### Fifth Path Ability

You can turn difficult situations to your advantage. You may use your Endurance skill instead of one specific Adventurer archetype skill, chosen when you acquire this path ability.

### Sixth Path Ability

You gain a result or magnitude bonus (your choice, before you roll the dice) on all your Labourer archetype skill rolls equal to your Heroism score.

## The Wandering Smiths of Hubal Shamin

### Saabi Path (particularly the clan of Malik)

❖ **Replacement Heroic Virtue:** Faith.

Revering Hubal Shamin, god of lightning, the smiths of this path learn how to imbue the weapons they forge with the anger of their god. Rare today, they are bearers of a knowledge divinely inherited, considered great sages by the Saabi despite their vagabond lifestyle.

Solitary and mysterious, the Wandering Smiths devote their lives to the search for truth and justice. Thus it is that they encounter those their path calls "the Just", individuals who sacrifice themselves for the sake of others, proving their honour and their bravery. The Wandering Smiths forge a "Lightning Weapon" for them as a reward.

**Note:** The fourth path ability is replaced as follows. You may spend 1 point of Heroism whenever you light up a constellation on a Craft skill roll to create or modify a weapon, and in so doing you may bestow upon that weapon a power linked with lightning. The magical item thus created has the ability to strike its target (by a bolt of lightning or a shock wave, etc, at the wielder's choice and in keeping with the type of weapon). Whenever the wielder lights up a constellation on an attack roll with the weapon, he gains a damage bonus equal to the value of the constellation die.

## The Wood Soul Sect

### Any Blood

❖ **Replacement Heroic Virtue:** Faith.

Essentially a religion in its own right, the Wood Soul Sect has existed for centuries among all peoples and all denominations. It's a belief that the root systems of all the world's ancient trees are knitted together in a single network covering all the world's lands and even continents. The sect requires that its members protect ancient trees, for, according to their beliefs, when a person dies, their soul discharges its emotions—love, hate, anger—before joining the afterlife appropriate to its religion; but the feelings it has shed remain within the ancient trees, strengthening their root network into a protective barrier preventing the forces of the Underworld from invading the surface world. Members of the Wood Soul Sect may hail from any of the world's peoples, and their mission is the protection of its ancient trees. Often foresters or mountain rangers, they survive for the most part as crafters.

Members of the Wood Soul Sect are frequently considered to be heretics. For this reason they conduct their rites, in which all members are considered priests, in the greatest secrecy, contenting themselves with watching over the ancestral trees and protecting them at any cost. Even if they may not admit it for fear of persecution, they believe they are protecting the world from demonic invasion.

**Note:** The fifth path ability refers to Sorcerer archetype skills.

## Paths of the Poet

The following path abilities are found in the common paths of the Poet.

### First Path Ability

If you light up a constellation on a Poet archetype skill roll, you gain a magnitude bonus equal to the value of the constellation die.

### Second Path Ability

You are conversant with the Language of Art! If you light up a constellation on a skill roll to create a work of art (taking at least one day), you may hide within it a message for its intended recipient. This message may contain information (several sentences) as well as a result bonus equal to your replacement heroic virtue score, to be used on the next roll made by the recipient of a skill chosen by the artist (based on the theme or atmosphere of the work).

### Third Path Ability

The Divine Word speaks through you! By spending stars of your replacement heroic virtue, you may gain a corresponding result or magnitude bonus (your choice, before you roll the dice) on your next Oratory skill roll.

### Fourth Path Ability

You are never deceived. By spending 1 star of your replacement heroic virtue, you may immediately detect if someone is lying to you.

## Fifth Path Ability

You know how to turn difficult situations to your advantage. You may use your Acting skill in place of any one Prince archetype skill (chosen when you acquire this path ability).

## Sixth Path Ability

You gain a result or magnitude bonus (your choice, made before you roll the dice) on all your Poet archetype skill rolls equal to your Heroism score.

# The Troubadours of Dorbagne

## Quarterian Academy

❖ **Replacement Heroic Virtue:** Loyalty.

This academy of the arts traces its origins to well before the emergence of the Quarterian faith, and may even date from an era when the frontiers between nations were very different from today. There are even those who claim that the itinerant artistry of the Troubadours comes from Aragon, or even the northern reaches of Al-Fariq'n. In reality the origins matter little: the only thing that counts is its evocative and communicative power. A travelling theatre or circus, a lively and active grouping of highway artists, the academy of the Troubadours comprises no more than sixty or so tumblers, poets, actors, acrobats, and sword-swallowers, who travel the world sharing their stories, talents, and dreams. Teaching their skills, holding balls and parties, staging spectacles and contests, they refuse all payment except in kind: food, clothing, and other essentials.

Generous of heart and spirit, Troubadours may still belong to their troupe, or may have left it, or may simply have joined it for a season to exchange their skills, creations, and emotions. Fond of games and communal living, Troubadours generally develop an aversion for political and economic matters, to the extent that they frequently end up leading lives on the fringes of the law.

# Paths of the Prince

The following path abilities are found in the common paths of the Prince.

## First Path Ability

If you light up a constellation on any Prince archetype skill roll, you gain a magnitude bonus equal to the value of the constellation die.

## Second Path Ability

The Gifts of the Prince! Once per session, you may benefit from a gift from a rich ally, a windfall, or a particularly lucrative business endeavour. You may make an immediate expenditure of up to 1000 gold talents in value.

## Third Path Ability

You dress to kill. By spending stars of your replacement heroic virtue, you gain a corresponding result or magnitude bonus (your choice, before you roll the dice) on your next Elegance skill roll.

## Fourth Path Ability

Bluffing is a prince's saving grace. Once per session, you may re-roll a failed Prince archetype skill roll.

## Fifth Path Ability

You know how to profit from others' weaknesses. If you succeed on a roll of INT + Save Face against a difficulty equal to three times the INT of the target (INT x 3) in a verbal exchange of at least 2 minutes in length, you may identify one of your interlocutor's psychological weak points (determined by Al-Rawi). If this weak point is so much as mentioned, your interlocutor will lose his cool and suffer 1 penalty die on any actions he's taking or about to take.

## Sixth Path Ability

You gain a result or magnitude bonus (your choice, before you roll the dice) on your Prince archetype skill rolls equal to your Heroism score.

# The Guides of the Three Tribes

## Shiradi Sect

❖ **Replacement Heroic Virtue:** Faith.

It's said that, when Pharat, Ashken, and Salone led their people to the Chosen Land, men and women joined to study the movements of the stars before taking actions and making choices. United in a single body devoted to religious and scientific study, these men and women called themselves "the Guides of the Three Tribes". Their path, which still exists today, studies the relationship between politics (the art of ruling over people) and the stars (the movements of the dragons in the heavens). Counselors, astrologers, teachers, and even clan chieftains, the Guides of the Three Tribes belong to all strata of Shiradi society, and work constantly to keep human life in balance with celestial laws.

Bookworms or wandering astronomers, the Guides of the Three Tribes are men and women of science before they are courtiers. They are more attached to the forces which link facts, choices, and star charts than to individuals, which differentiates them very clearly from the Pharatim. Sometimes, Guides prefer to sacrifice lives rather than oppose a political-astronomical theory, since by its very nature science must always be right.

**Note:** The third path ability is replaced as follows. If you light up a constellation on a difficulty 9 INT + Science roll, spending at least one hour to study the celestial charts for a given moment, you gain a result or magnitude bonus (your choice, before you roll the dice) equal to the value of the constellation die on all Prince archetype skill rolls for the next 24 hours.

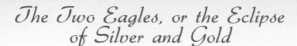

## The Two Eagles, or the Eclipse of Silver and Gold

### Saabi Path

❖ **Replacement Heroic Virtue:** Faith.

Cutting across all Saabi tribes, this is the path of the diplomat. For centuries, its members have sought to help differing parties understand one another and resolve their conflicts. It's not uncommon to see members of this path accompany Saabi lords abroad, or indeed to accompany foreign lords, having sold their services at a high price.

First and foremost, the followers of the Two Eagles (the gods Sayyin and Almaqah—see page 238) are adept at dissimulation. They seem to always want to help, but always have something to gain. Yes, they are diplomats, but above all they are merchants, and never do anything without being sure of a return. Thus, the adepts of the Eclipse of Silver and Gold never act with an open acknowledgement of their motives, and they alone are the true beneficiaries of their interventions. Obviously, this fact is only known to themselves, and is not part of their public reputation.

**Note:** The fifth path ability roll is made against a difficulty of INT x 2. The sixth path ability only benefits two skills: one from the Prince archetype, and one from the Rogue archetype, chosen when you acquire the ability.

# Paths of the Rogue

The following path abilities are found in the common paths of the Rogue.

### First Path Ability

If you light up a constellation on a Rogue archetype skill roll, you gain a magnitude bonus equal to the value of the constellation die.

### Second Path Ability

Daring is the rogue's best friend! Every swagger die you take on a Rogue archetype skill roll gives you a +2 magnitude bonus.

### Third Path Ability

Shadowspawn! By spending stars of your replacement heroic virtue, you gain a corresponding result or magnitude bonus (your choice, before you roll the dice) on your next Stealth skill roll.

### Fourth Path Ability

You're hard to catch. Once per session, you may automatically succeed on an Intrusion skill roll. The attempt must have at least a remote chance of success.

### Fifth Path Ability

You're an expert at distracting other people's attention. You may use your best Rogue archetype skill instead of one specific Prince archetype skill, chosen when you acquire this ability.

### Sixth Path Ability

You gain a result or magnitude bonus (your choice, before you roll the dice) on all your Rogue archetype skill rolls equal to your Heroism score. This does not apply to your use of the fifth path ability above.

## The Pipers of Carrassine

### Saabi Path

❖ **Replacement Heroic Virtue:** Faith.

A fellowship of beggars and street artists, the Pipers of Carrassine were first a mystical order of Carrassine snake-charmers. Over centuries the path spread throughout Capharnaum to all the "street occupations". The Pipers aren't a single organisation, but rather individuals who work solo or at the heart of criminal groups following precepts laid down long ago. The Pipers steal, embezzle, and deceive, with the ultimate aim of finding a single object: the Flute of Nabu. An ancient legend says that Nabu, god of music, once offered his sacred flute to a princess he had fallen in love with, but who was killed out of revenge by a villainous prince to whom she had been offered in marriage. Finding the flute, which Nabu had invested with a part of his knowledge, strength, and love, is the only way to restore the god to his former power.

Faith is a powerful motivator, and most of the followers of this path believe with a fervour bordering on fanaticism. Their piety manifests itself as a kind of blind romanticism, each believer convinced that the flute might literally be in the next purse or pack he filches. Although for the most part street artists or even beggars, they are no less smitten with a love of poetry and knowledge, curious about everything and permanently enthused about what the cosmos may be about to teach them next.

**Note:** The first path ability also affects one Poet archetype skill, chosen when you acquire this ability.

## The Will-o-Wisps of the Storm Coast

### All peoples (but especially Quarterians)

❖ **Replacement Heroic Virtue:** Bravery.

This fellowship of ship-wreckers has been active along the Occidentian coasts for centuries. Founded by nobles seeking to avoid onerous royal taxes, the Will-o-Wisps lure lone ships and convoys into treacherous waters and onto reefs and rocks. The cargoes of the resulting wrecks are garnered without the Crown taking its share. The fellowship still exists today, but even if one finds small

### Third Path Ability

Heightened awareness. By spending stars of your replacement heroic virtue, you gain a corresponding result or magnitude bonus (your choice, before you roll the dice) on your next Notice roll.

### Fourth Path Ability

You're never deceived. By spending 1 star of your replacement heroic virtue, you can detect if someone is lying to you.

### Fifth Path Ability

You know how to charm others to resolve interpersonal problems. You may use your Instruction skill in place of a single Prince archetype skill of your choice, to be selected when you acquire this ability.

### Sixth Path Ability

You gain a result or magnitude bonus (your choice, before you roll the dice) on all your Sage archetype skill rolls equal to your Heroism score. This does not apply to your use of the fifth path ability above.

## The Drinkers of Dust

### Shiradi Sect

❖ **Replacement Heroic Virtue:** Faith.

No one remembers the exact name which was once given to this path by Elbekh, nephew of Salone, so much so that today even its followers use its most famous nickname, "the Drinkers of Dust". The name derives from the fact that, every seven years, on the date of the regular appearance of a comet, its followers must make a pilgrimage to the depths of Limherk Plateau, to a valley covered in volcanic dust. During this rite, they retrieve samples of volcanic ash which the passage of the comet is said to imbue with exceptional curative virtues. The followers of the path mix this ash with a strong wine which is drunk during subsequent religious ceremonies in the city of Sagrada.

Contrary to popular belief, the Drinkers of Dust are not healers. They are seers who gain great personal insights by helping the poor and sick using their ancient rituals. Beyond this stricture, they are free to conduct themselves as they see fit, whether that means teaching, studying, or practicing any other activity.

## The Sapientists of Senegarthia

### Agalanthian School

❖ **Replacement Heroic Virtue:** Loyalty.

From the passage of the stars across the sky, from the celestial games of the dragons against the dark vault of the night, the Sapientists of Senegarthia have learned to read the truth of the world. Or at least that's what people say about this ancient Agalanthian school. In reality, the Sapientists read nothing in the stars; they realised long ago that there

---

groups of Will-o-Wisps along shorelines close to every major shipping lane, ready to lure vessels ashore using misleading signals from their torches and lanterns, rare are those who still teach the techniques originally created by Sir Erwenn Lekorr, Duke of Kertigane. With the passage of time, the fellowship has extended its activities into all forms of embezzlement, with the aim of enabling everyone to profit from their own labours.

The solidarity and sense of belonging typical of many paths is noticeably absent from the Will-o-Wisps of the Storm Coast, whose members ultimately share little other than a common origin. Thus, even if the wreckers are tight-knit in their own groups, there is no higher level of organisation. The thing that most characterises the Will-o-Wisps today is a permanent desire for revolt and liberty, whatever the foe or the designated prey.

**Note:** The fourth path ability applies to Athletics skill rolls made at sea.

## Paths of the Sage

The following path abilities are found in the common paths of the Sage.

### First Path Ability

If you light up a constellation on any Sage archetype skill roll, you gain a magnitude bonus equal to the value of your constellation die.

### Second Path Ability

Contemplation is the friend of the Sage! Whenever you spend twice as long as normal on an action (including in combat), you gain a +2 magnitude bonus.

was a fundamental difference between science and divine truth. In their heart of hearts, many Sapientists have retreated from faith and fear of the gods, and now believe in only the mundanity of the world. Past masters in the scientific understanding of their surroundings, the Sapientists are effective and pragmatic teachers, but also—and perhaps most of all—they are people who cannot be deceived, so much so that they excel in the art of apprehending the deep truth of things in every sign, every clue they perceive. It isn't uncommon for an archon (page 270) to call on a simple Sapientist preceptor to conduct an investigation, explain a mystery, or invent a puzzle to entertain his guests. Note also that, although this school was founded in Senegarthia, philosophers following its precepts are found throughout Agalanthian lands.

Curious by nature, Sapientists are open to the world and to their fellow man or woman. However, their ability to analyse the world to get at its inner truth means that some become distrustful, even paranoid, obsessed with signs, symbols, and mysteries, almost to the point of madness.

**Note:** The first path ability is replaced as follows. The difficulty of dice rolls made to deceive you, lie to you, or lure you into a trap, is increased by your Heroism score.

# Paths of the Sorcerer

The following path abilities are found in the common paths of the Sorcerer.

## First Path Ability

If you light up a constellation on a Sorcerer archetype skill roll, you gain a magnitude bonus equal to the value of the constellation die.

## Second Path Ability

You have incredible strength of will. You may spend stars of your replacement heroic virtue to gain a result or magnitude bonus (your choice, before you roll the dice) on your next Willpower skill roll equal to the stars expended.

## Third Path Ability

The gods are with you. You may spend stars of your replacement heroic virtue to gain a result or magnitude bonus (your choice, before you roll the dice) on all your Sacrifice skill rolls that day equal to the stars expended.

## Fourth Path Ability

Determination is the sorcerer's friend. Once per session, you may reduce your *shaytan* total (page 340) by a number of points equal to your replacement heroic virtue score, down to the beginning of the current threshold (page 343).

## Fifth Path Ability

You can steal sorcerous knowledge! By succeeding on an opposed roll of INT + Sacred Word against another sorcerer's INT + Willpower roll, you may temporarily steal a number of **magical elements** (page 119) equal to the magnitude of your roll. The elements are chosen by Al-Rawi, and the theft lasts a number of minutes equal to your replacement heroic virtue score. During this period, you may use these elements as if you knew them yourself, while the sorcerer from whom they were stolen may not.

## Sixth Path Ability

You gain a result or magnitude bonus (your choice, before you roll the dice) on your Sorcerer archetype skill rolls equal to your Heroism.

# The Last Breath of Kings

## Saabi Path

❖ **Replacement Heroic Virtue:** Faith

A legend of the Ibn Malik says that whenever a prince or king dies, his last breath enchants the life of a poor unfortunate somewhere. The followers of this path believe that they may find this enchanted individual, who will appear to them in the guise of an unknown friend or mysterious ally, a kindred soul who is otherwise unaware of their existence, yet who alone can open the portals of the Kingdom of Heaven.

Profoundly altruistic, the sorcerers who follow the Last Breath of Kings are mystics who have renounced their titles of nobility and who visit the courts of the world in a state of ascetic self-denial, offering their services to whoever needs them, hoping to one day find the kindred soul who, unknowingly, is awaiting their arrival.

**Note:** The fifth path ability is replaced as follows. You can loan sorcerous knowledge! You may temporarily provide (for as many minutes as your replacement heroic virtue score), to one person of your choice, and who knows at least one Sacred Word, 1D6 of the magical elements you know. During the period of this loan, you may not make use of those magical elements yourself.

# The Mother Earth Magic School

## Quarterian Academy

❖ **Replacement Heroic Virtue:** Loyalty.

Vaguely pagan, this magical tradition tries as best it can to fit its ancient cult practices to the tenets of the Quarterian faith. Its adepts today worship the earth as personified by Jason Quartered. The academy devotes itself to the education of the rural peasantry. Its members are not monks, but scholars and nobles for the most part, almost always seeking to share knowledge or to teach their techniques.

Between faith, the search for knowledge, and the desire to teach people to improve their lot, the sorcerers of the Mother Earth Magic School are open-minded, often far removed from academic or religious disputes. It's not uncommon to see them act as mediators in conflicts which otherwise do not concern them.

**Note:** The second path ability is replaced as follows. By spending 1 point of replacement heroic virtue, you may gain a +1 result or magnitude bonus (your choice, before you roll the dice) on your next Instruction skill roll.

## Paths of the Warrior

The following path abilities are found in the common paths of the Warrior.

### First Path Ability

If you light up a constellation on any Warrior archetype skill roll, you gain a magnitude bonus equal to the value of the constellation die.

### Second Path Ability

Courage is the warrior's friend. Every swagger die you take in combat gives you a +2 magnitude bonus.

### Third Path Ability

Your virtue protects you! For every star of your replacement heroic virtue you spend at the start of a combat, you may increase your Armour Value by +1 for the duration of that combat.

### Fourth Path Ability

In your face! For every star of your replacement heroic virtue you spend, you may increase the damage you do to a target by +1.

### Fifth Path Ability

Backs to the wall! You can make the best of a desperate situation to harass your opponents. If you're outnumbered by 2-to-1 or more, you gain a bonus to your Passive or Active Defence equal to your replacement heroic virtue score.

### Sixth Path Ability

You gain a result or magnitude bonus (your choice, before you roll the dice) on your Warrior archetype skill rolls equal to your Heroism score.

## The Kh'saaba White Lancers

### Saabi Path

❖ **Replacement Heroic Virtue:** Bravery.
A fellowship of lancers claiming to be followers of Mozhair Ibn Dhama, once the chief of a now defunct minor clan, the White Lancers protect the frontiers of the Kingdom of Kh'saaba and travel alongside noble or merchant caravans. They paint their faces with white stripes when on military expeditions; the more numerous the stripes, the higher the rank of the Lancer.

Gregarious by nature, the White Lancers enjoy taking part in caravan life, looking after animals, and teaching children the rudiments of weapon handling.

**Note:** On the second path ability, the bonus is +3 when the weapon used is a lance.

## Master Gorgonte's Fencing Academy

### Quarterian Academy

❖ **Replacement Heroic Virtue:** Loyalty.
Originally from Marrzech-Lorin, a small fishing village in the province of Kertigane, Master Gorgonte spent many long years codifying the fighting techniques used by sailors. Although he died centuries ago, there are still numerous academies throughout Occidentia which teach his techniques.

The students of Master Gorgonte's Fencing Academy are usually men and women from the lower middle class, or even the urban working class. They feel themselves to be more soldiers than knights, and enjoy a powerful solidarity, helping one another and sharing their belongings.

**Note:** The first path ability is replaced as follows. If you light up a constellation on a Solidarity skill roll in combat, you may provide moral support to your fellow combatants. You may distribute a number of bonus dice equal to your Bravery score, which may be used as bonus result dice for the rest of the combat.

# CHANGING PATHS

A character may decide to change paths for many reasons: too great a divergence with his clan or its path, changes in himself, to discover new knowledge, and so on.

A character who changes paths does not lose his previous path abilities. However, he may only use them under certain conditions, as shown below.

❖ Whenever you use one of your old path abilities, you lose:
> 1 star in the replacement heroic virtue of the old path.
> 1 star of Loyalty, reflecting the fact that you're using a path other than your own. Note that this doesn't apply to those without a path.
❖ In addition, **the difficulty of all rolls when using an old path ability are increased by +3.**

Once your character has left his path, his Loyalty score drops by 1 point (not 1 star!) and he becomes **pathless** until he finds a new master who will initiate him to a new path. Being accepted as an initiate into a new path can be difficult, and may lead to many adventures while the character attempts to persuade the masters of the new path of his worthiness to join. Some paths may even be impossible to join except as a result of extraordinary campaign events (joining the Walad Badiya, for example).

The following prerequisites must be met (stipulated, for example, by the future initiator to the new path) before the character may join:

- ❖ You must have a minimum score of 3 in the attribute and skills of the new path, as well as its replacement heroic virtue. Your Heroism score must also be at least 3.
- ❖ You must submit to whatever initiation rites exist for the path, and fulfil any other requirements (such as possessing a certain level of wealth, etc).
- ❖ Once you have met the above prerequisites, you learn the first path ability of the new path. Note that you do **not** gain the attribute or skill bonuses which you would get if you were creating a character belonging to the new path from scratch.

Joining a new path may have other limitations, similar to those mentioned in "Rebels, Dissidents, Mixed-Bloods, Cousins, and Traitors" on page 11. However, the limitations mentioned there are principally to be used in character creation. Dragon-Marked characters who are playing long-term campaigns (such as *The Kingdom of Heaven*) may, at Al-Rawi's discretion, change path with fewer restrictions, as follows:

- ❖ **Changing path within the same clan, kingdom, or city-state** (from an Ibn Rashid path to another Ibn Rashid path, or from an Occidentian path to another Occidentian path) **or changing from a path of your own blood to a common path** (unaffiliated with any clan, kingdom, tribe, or city-state): Your Loyalty may not exceed 6.
- ❖ **Changing from a clan path to another clan path within the same Saabi tribe** (from an Ibn Mussah path to an Ibn Malik path, for example): Your Loyalty may not exceed 6.
- ❖ **Changing from a Shiradi tribal path to another Shiradi tribal path** (from a Salonim path to a Pharatim path, for example): Your Loyalty may not exceed 6. Note that requirements for joining any of the three great Shiradi tribes are very strict.
- ❖ **Changing from a Quarterian kingdom path to another** (from an Aragonian path to an Orkadian path, for example): Your Loyalty may not exceed 4 if you do this during character creation, or 5 or 6 (Al-Rawi's discretion) if you do so during play.

- ❖ **Changing from an Agalanthian city-state to another** (from a Thereman path to a Fragrantine path, for example): Your Loyalty may not exceed 4 if you do this during character creation, or 5 or 6 (Al-Rawi's discretion) if you do so during play.
- ❖ **Changing from a path of one people to another** (from a Saabi path to a Quarterian path, or from a Shiradi path to an Agalanthian path): Your Loyalty may not exceed 2 if you do this during character creation, or 3 or 4 (Al-Rawi's discretion) if you do so during play.

# Two Paths

After many adventures, and under exceptional circumstances, with the full agreement of Al-Rawi, it's possible for you to reconcile your character to following two paths, simultaneously and without penalty. Doing so requires you to respect your allegiances (and all associated requirements) to both paths in their entirety. Your Loyalty score is not modified. For example, an aging member of the Fire Scimitars of the Ibn Malik may gain a new lease of life as an advisor of the Alchemists of Men of the Ibn Mussah. In no case may the two paths be in opposition or conflict, otherwise Al-Rawi may impose the penalties listed above (and you don't get back any Adventure Points already spent on acquiring the new path).

To follow two paths simultaneously in this way, you must first have found a master willing to initiate you to the second path while you remain a member of the first, and then:

- ❖ Meet the attribute, skill, and replacement heroic virtue prerequisites indicated above (but without the limitations to Loyalty).
- ❖ Spend 50 AP.
- ❖ Finally, choose which of your two paths will be your **main path** and which will be your **secondary path**. You will advance in your main path normally, but acquiring new path abilities in your secondary path will cost an additional 10 AP each time (so 50 AP for the second path ability, 60 AP for the third, and so on).

# Chapter Three
# Urania – Science and Knowledge

## Swirls of Steam

Luther felt the gentle hands leave his relaxed body. He sat up, issued a command in an approximation of Agalanthian, forgetting that the masseuses didn't even speak the language. He didn't know enough Jazirati to ask why they were suddenly leaving in such a hurry. The women vanished into the swirling steam, peals of crystal laughter echoing against the tiles of the hammam walls.

He had been brought here after his victory, washed clean and left in the expert hands of the three delectable creatures he had cavorted with, fully expecting to bed each of them before leaving. First, though, he had surrendered to the magical succession of ablution chambers, sumptuously decorated, glowing in the lamplight. Steam baths of all temperatures, pools of all manner of scents. He had even bathed in milk. But what was he doing there? What did they expect of him? That was when the girls left.

He was about to follow, when a man appeared from the arch through which they'd scampered. Smaller than Luther—like most Jazirati—but no less tight and muscular, he stood before him naked as the day he was born. Luther had kept his loincloth. The man addressed him in impeccable Orkadian.

"An excellent morning to you, champion. I'm delighted to make your acquaintance."

"Who are you?"

"For the moment my name is not important. But you'll be curious as to what I am…"

"Go on!"

"I'm your new master! And you can thank me for it! You'll no longer have to fight in the arena—that isn't my pleasure. I'm offering you an escape from the fate of all gladiators—disgrace, by death or injury."

"What do you want of me, heathen?"

"Now then, now then, let me think… Well, you'd make a good bodyguard, wouldn't you? Or even a perfect eunuch to watch the harem of the girls you were enjoying so much just now. Unless you're a good lover yourself…?"

The stranger had drawn closer, and regarded Luther with green eyes outlined with kohl, a lustful gaze. He held his hand out to Luther's chest. The knight grabbed it, pulled the light body to him, turned the man round, twisted his arm up his back and caught his throat in the crux of his muscled arm. He squeezed a little.

"I have no master!" he growled, "and I'm not one of your catamites! Give me a reason not to kill you!"

"Stranger, I'll give you two," the Jazirati hissed, his teeth bared. "The first is that pressure you're feeling against your groin. Yes? It's the spike of my poisoned ring. If I die, so will you. And the second reason—look at my shoulder blade…"

Slowly, Luther released the man who clearly thought himself cleverer than him. He was indeed wearing a ring of substantial size, which glinted with a threatening needle. And there, on the back of his shoulder…

What? How could that be?

The neat image of the heraldric mark of his own family—the Dragon of the White Mountains. And it was no tattoo. How could a godforsaken heathen be graced with such a thing?

"How is it you're bearing our mark?"

"There are things you don't know, young foreigner. But I'll tell you this: I'm the same breed as you. That's why I asked Prince Achim to spare you today."

"And why did he agree?"

"Tsk… that's none of your business. Let's just say the Prince is… indebted to me. And that a fresh champion is worth his weight in gold."

"I don't like you, heathen. What's your name, so I can pray to all the saints to damn you to hell?"

The man smiled. "Hafiz Thufir Jamil Ibn Rashid Abd-al-Hassan." He bowed. "At your service."

# THE MANY WAYS OF KNOWING

## Agalanthian Science

Throughout the centuries, the ways of science and knowledge have been charted by all the peoples of *Capharnaum*. Historically, the Agalanthians have had the greatest influence, but they are now a people in decline. Agalanthian science is an affair of philosophers, of great individuals: they make no distinction between mathematicians, physicians, and politicians. For them, science is merely a part of the greater art of philosophy, and the philosopher must approach "Knowledge", or *cognos*, through its many facets. Agalanthians remember how Claudius Tetramegas Silemnos applied his observations of the social organisation of ants to a treatise about the political structure of the city, or his geometrical study of the organised movement of bodies to the military manoeuvres which allowed the Agalanthian myrmidons to be victorious on the bat-tlefields of Kh'saaba or Krek'kaos even when outnumbered ten-to-one. Agalanthian science holds that a discovery cannot be considered true until it has three different proofs. It's empirical, aiming to gradually uncover the deep metaphysical truths beneath reality; it even aims to discover the principles of physics which govern the gods, to find out just what makes them immortal and gives them their awesome powers (obviously, the distinct lack of test subjects makes this field highly theoretical...).

Alas, since the fall of Therema, Agalanthian science has suffered the brunt of the increasing disinterest affecting the Agalanthian people. Why try to protect truth, when the Golden Age is no more? This people, once passionate about rational discourse and the pursuit of knowledge, now wallows in superstition, preferring the counsel of chiromancers to that of philosophers.

## Saabi Science

The Saabi are a curious people, passionate about the sciences. However, the study of science is not seen as a "serious" activity in Saabi society: a Saabi scholar is usually a rich individual, person-

ally interested in knowledge and wishing to devote himself to its pursuit. Indeed, only those with the time and money can afford to indulge themselves in abstract speculation; for, among the Saabi, scientific study has no concrete application. The knowledge and techniques developed by one's ancestors are sacred, and trying to improve upon them is a sin. Can you improve on the creations of the gods? Mortals know their place, and submit to the gods, even if their curiosity sometimes impels them to question.

This means that Saabi science is, by necessity, theoretical, based on mathematical and geometrical abstraction. Discoveries are rare, and rarely shared. Even when they are, it's usually with the aim of creating beautiful artworks. Collections of mathematical formulae, complex equations, and the like, are often finely calligraphed, commissioned by rich dilettantes who love to have their contents declaimed to them like fine verse.

## Shiradi Science

Shiradi science is in flux. Once orally transmitted from master to disciple, the invention of the Shiradi alphabet in Occidentia has revolutionised its propagation, and it's now possible for anyone with enough wealth to acquire works containing the knowledge of the greatest Shiradi physicians or rhetoricians. This revolution has the Shiradi elders worried. They know that the morality which is indissociable from knowledge cannot be learned from the written word. How can the essence of Shirad be contained within a mere book? How do you debate with a tome and grasp the hidden teachings between its lines, the thousand nuances that enrich human understanding?

The alphabet revolution has caused a schism among Shiradi scholars. Two schools have arisen: the traditionalists, who dislike writing and argue that knowledge without morality can only lead to the ruination of the soul; and the innovators, who believe that the thousand numerical declinations of the Shiradi alphabet will reveal greater truths and elucidate more mysteries to the scholar who studies them than anyone relying solely on the fixed legacy of the ancients.

## Quarterian Science

Finally, for the Quarterians, all knowledge is religious, and the Church is its sole repository. Secular sages are discouraged, often subtly—at first by their neighbours, then by discreet persecution and even pogroms if they persist. Only by finding influential protectors can scholars attempt to explore the mysteries of the universe. Quarterian science venerates the Agalanthian legacy: the Empire's philosophers are, for them, models of excellence that can never be equalled, to the point that any theory contradicting them can never be taken seriously.

Torn between scientific objectivity and religious faith, Quarterian science tries to save face, attempting to justify Aether's role as prime mover and secret engine of the cosmos. The vast majority of scholars are low-ranking priests, isolated in the countryside and driven by their faith. A veritable epistolary network allows them to communicate their discoveries and doubts, even if, close to the Quarterian Magister (page 289), the cardinals conspire to have scientific pursuits declared blasphemy.

# THE SCIENCES IN DETAIL

## Astronomy

Astronomy and astrology are inseparable. All peoples understand that the sky merely reflects the phenomena that happen in the material world. By understanding the heavens, it becomes possible to divine what is going to happen in the world. The Shiradim and the Saabi have the best astronomers, and the *kahan* Isaac Bar Mirdon has even predicted eclipses by comparing the cycles of the sun and moon.

The constellations were mapped out by explorers in the earliest days of the Agalanthian Empire, and are now landmarks for travellers everywhere. The Empire itself, however, has turned its back on astronomy as a science, and now accepts the model of a flat Earth, above which the sun, moon, and stars tirelessly turn. Even the unexplained appearance of comets in Capharnaum's skies have not managed to attract the attention of philosophers, although they seem to excite chiromancers beyond measure.

The Saabi proved long ago that the Earth is a sphere floating in a liquid—dubbed *phlogiston*—out of which Hubal rises each day, and into which he descends to recover his energy every night. The nature of phlogiston eludes Saabi astronomers, who perceive in it a fiery principle similar to that of the dark oil of the desert. They have never been able to analyse a sample to be sure.

Among the Quarterians, the country priest, Father Alberto Eberrias, joined the inner circle of cardinals at only 32 years of age by proving, with the use of clever calculations, that the Earth revolved around the sun, and not the opposite. The Quarterian clergy sees in this discovery major evidence of Aether's superiority over the pagan gods.

## Mathematics and Geometry

To the Saabi, the most beautiful of abstractions; to the Agalanthians, the ultimate language of creation: mathematics is the noblest science of all. A universal language, it allows scholars from around the world to understand one another and share theories. In this way, the Agalanthians learned from the Saabi and borrowed their base-ten numeric system, far more practical for calculation than the alphabetical system of notation they had used until then.

Among Agalanthians, mathematics is the basis of all knowledge. It permitted the advances in architecture and shipbuilding that contributed to their domination of the world, despite them having lost all knowledge of the science of the dragons (see page 272). It has influenced, analysed, and improved Agalanthian society, from its politics through its military tactics right through to its rhetorical techniques. Music is seen as its purest expression, its ultimate language, speaking directly to the soul; its laws of harmony are of such incredible complexity that Agalanthian philosophers laugh politely at the naïvity of other peoples who would see it as just another form of entertainment.

The Saabi are considerably more advanced in geometry and algebra than other peoples. Some scholars have developed complex equations for measuring the dimensions of the Earth, allowing them to correct inaccuracies in their sea and land maps.

Finally, the Shiradim are on the cusp of revolutionising the ancient mathematics of the Agalanthians and Saabi. Their alphabet, which gives a numerical value to each letter, drives them to seek meaning in numbers and values. The measurements of a single individual, his height, weight, and various proportions, can reveal secrets about his behaviour; and the number of children a couple has in their family can shed light on the nature of their faith. Even reducing a person's name to its numerical value can indicate their nature, their fate, perhaps their importance to the world. Shiradi mathematicians follow mystical and hermetic principles, leading them away from Agalanthian ideals of mathematical purity and bringing them closer to the divination practiced by the chiromancers and other mystics.

## Medicine and Anatomy

To the Shiradim, medicine is the Queen of the Sciences. They have always practiced it as a discipline where knowledge of the body meets that of the mind. For a Shiradi physician, any affliction of the body is caused by an illness of the mind—or eventually creates one in its turn. Diagnosis is made by observing the patient's urine, examining his eyes, and measuring his pulse. If an illness requires no surgical intervention—one of the greatest and most feared risks of any malady—herbal concoctions and massage are prescribed, as well as support activities such as passing time in the company of a parent or friend, visiting a temple to speak with a *kahan*, and so on. Surgery is always dangerous, for the Shiradim know nothing of the principles of infection and sterilisation. However, their knowledge of anatomy and the treatment of wounds is the best in the world; they are the only people to permit the practice of dissection.

The Saabi, although they don't share the knowledge and insights of the Shiradim, are just as skilful physicians. Their signal discovery is that certain desert winds can penetrate into wounds and cause infection. These "ill winds" are sent by the djinn and enemy gods, and can only be avoided by blessing surgical tools in the purifying flame of an appropriate altar. Like the Agalanthians, the Saabi believe the body is regulated by four humours: blood, black bile, yellow bile, and phlegm, whose unbalances explain mood swings and diseases. Many treatments aim to re-balance those humours, using leeches or pressure on the organs that are believed to generate them (the heart, spleen, gall bladder, and brain respectively). The Quarterians prefer to use herbal concoctions for this purpose, using plants whose effects have been documented for generations.

## Geography

Although the Saabi have the most accurate maps, thanks to the skill of their mathematicians, no people has maps as comprehensive as the Agalanthians. The Empire's conquests gave it an unequalled view of the world, enabling it to contact more cultures than any other. Contact with distant civilisations like Asijawi and Nir Manel was lost ages ago. Nevertheless, the great chamber of the Agalanthian Senate is said to have a mosaic of the world beneath its dome that Saabi merchants and Quarterian sailors would kill to see.

## History

With the exception of the Shiradim, most consider history to be little more than a footnote to the study of literature rather than a noble science in its own right. The Agalanthians jumble up their founding myths in an agreeable mix with the annals of their cities, and like to fictionalise their victories with interventions by mythological creatures and divine beings. The Saabi love storytelling, with an oral culture that renders the transmission of precise dates a delicate endeavour. Add to that the fact that each tribe is neck-deep in hereditary feuds and tends to dress up its histories to make its enemies seem even more hateful, and the end result is a wealth of exciting but barely credible annals. Finally, for the Quarterians, history has another name: genealogy. Battles are well documented, as are births and deaths of the nobility, but the sole purpose of such documentation is to make the transmission of power easier, and to facilitate primogeniture and the inheritance of wealth and land.

The Shiradim have suffered so much that history comforts them. It gives them proof that their people will survive every ordeal Shirad sends to test their faith—and of his endless compassion for their suffering. Shiradi historians are impartial realists, and the true chroniclers of Capharnaum. The invention of the Shiradi alphabet has permitted the written word to replace the work of some of the Shiradi "rememberers", those *kahanim* who once memorised and bore within their memories whole swathes of the world's history. Alas, if some tribal feuds were ended by the clarity and neutrality of these new written records, many others have broken out. Some members of the Agalanthian bureaucracy have even advocated confiscating these books from the Shiradim communities in their cities to limit these violent consequences.

## The Law and Social Sciences

In all the realms of *Capharnaum*, laws are based on custom and religion. Every people has its sacred texts recounting the prohibitions of their gods. Interpretations were added to these often arbitrary prohibitions, which today have become codes of laws and ways of ruling.

Without a doubt, Quarterian governments are the simplest. They are based on absolute power wielded by a nobility which is judge, jury, and often executioner. Within the Quarterian kingdoms, the clergy follows its own rules and laws, and serves as counsel and caution to the nobility, exhorting those to wield authority to justify their acts in the eyes of the people.

Saabi law is based on an interpretation of their holy texts. Often it differs slightly from city to city, depending on precedent. The Saabi view their laws as mutable, evolving with each judgement. This view has given birth to a professional class of lawyers, half-priests, half-diplomats; prosecuting or defending a person requires a deep knowledge of a city's customs, as well as great proficiency in oratory, to prove what the intentions of the gods were when they transmitted the holy texts.

The same art of oratory can be found among the Agalanthians. However, there it has assumed such an importance that today it supersedes the content of the sacred texts themselves. Agalanthian civilisation debates ideas, and the success of a trial or the passing of a law owes more to performance and rhetorical finesse than any underlying substance. *Logos*—the Agalanthian term for "word"—has become a synonym for *cognos*, "the truth", that ideal of absolute knowledge possessed by the gods.

Finally, to the Shiradim, laws and words mean nothing without morality. The sacred texts can be interpreted in a thousand ways—interpretations which matter little to the *kahanim*, who seek what is just. That's why the kahanim are priests, scholars, **and** judges in Shiradi society: only by combining these three disciplines can they make good decisions before God.

## Natural Sciences

Of all the civilisations there have been, the Agalanthians were the closest to dominating the natural world, and doubtless those who best understood it. Of course, the Quarterians may have a deeper knowledge of plants and their qualities, and the Saabi developed

the foundations of optics before their invasion by the Imperial legions; but the genius of the Agalanthians lay in integrating the discoveries of each people they encountered, and comparing and extrapolating from them. The irrigation systems which allowed the Empire to triple the harvest in desert cities would have never been possible without combining a knowledge of the physics of river flooding with the techniques of Imperial engineering; and countless naval battles would never have been won without the Empire hanging from their flagship masts the lenses used by desert tribes to observe their enemies and setting fire to their enemy's sails.

# Chapter Four
# Terpsichore – Magic and Sorcery

## The Gates of the Diplomat

*T*hufir saw the white of the caravanserai outlined against the red of the Aramla El-Nar—the Desert of Fire. He spurred his thoroughbred and galloped towards the inn, that crossroads of trade, last bastion of civilisation before the endless expanse. He hoped the barbarian had reached safe harbour and had found the information they sought.

Passing through the gate under the watchful gaze of the turbaned guards, he saw the two different moods that faced off in the compound. On his left glared tense and worried people, as anyone would be before departing into the burning sands. On his right rang out laughter and song, people drinking without restraint, eternal signs of relaxation after weeks spent under the murderous sun. Houris danced and swayed for the money the travellers brought with them, triumphant, from the ends of the world. Although Thufir was preparing to leave for the desert, he hoped his companion had lodged with the merrymakers.

Praise Hubal! There was the Orkadian, at the back of the room, a girl on his knees. He tumbled her off his lap and onto the floor as he caught sight of Thufir. He looked annoyed. And drunk.

"So there you are, you damned heathen! I've been having the devil's job standing the company of these degenerates while I waited for you to arrive."

"Beg pardon, o pig among pigs. I was detained by the women of the Bint Mimun Abd-al-Tarek..."

"I hope you at least found us a crew, you saucy dog!"

"In that, your efforts clearly exceed mine..." Thufir eyed the girl approvingly as she stood and claimed her due from the knight. "But don't worry yourself—the greatest caravan guide in the whole of Jazirat is en route. He'll meet us at the next oasis, with food, mounts, and guards. But what about you? Have you found the place where your ancestor disappeared?"

"I have. A village called Calamar-Grand-Tour. Or something like it."

"Khal-Ahmar Ban'Thur, I suppose. And the thing your ancestor was looking for?"

"I met a priest of Hubal who had talked with Ingmar Björnson, my father's father, knight of Grunwald—blessed be his name. Apparently the runes my grandfather had found in our own lands spoke of the same mysteries as are found in the stories of your prophets. My grandfather and the priest even thought your three wise men had visited my northern homeland..."

"Interesting—but unlikely. You said your runes were a thousand years old, at most? Our prophets disappeared from the world more than three thousand years ago..."

The Orkadian looked exasperated. Thufir couldn't tell if it was because of him, or the doxy badgering him for money. The knight slipped a gold talent into her bodice and she withdrew. He continued:

"I've spoken with all manner of people while I've been waiting. Nomads from the desert tribes. Not all of them agree with your version of history. Some even say the prophets are still alive..."

"Nonsense! But never mind that—we'll see for ourselves. Did you find out any more about the place described in the runes?"

"No, unfortunately. It looks like my grandfather deciphered part of it, and that led him to this village. Apparently it was the last place anyone saw him. The treasures of the prophets and all those jewels the runes talk about can't be far away..."

"Permit me to doubt that until we have them before our eyes..."

*Thufir produced a map of Jazirat, inked in detail, and ran his finger along the eastern coast. He stopped at some tiny dots: Khal-Ahmar Ban'Thur. Immediately, he regretted having already paid master Said Ibn Salah. Although far from being the best guide in Jazirat, he still knew his business, and was therefore expensive. There was a way of reaching the village by following the desert to the north: not too much risk, and no need to dive into the burning depths. But in any case the risk mattered little: the stakes were worth it. Whatever the Orkadian's venerable grandfather had found, if it was true his ancestor had born the Dragon Mark, despite his great age, the game was worth his attention. He, Hafiz Thufir Jamil Ibn Rashid Abd-al-Hassan. As he lost himself in contemplation of shining treasures, powerful relics, magical creatures, precious gems, and sorcerous scrolls—Hubal only knew what waited at the end of this path—the Orkadian's powerful voice dragged him back to the reality of the caravanserai.*

*"Can you play Dhamet? I've been learning while I waited."*

*"Of course I can! All Jazirati can. I'm the best player in Prince Achim's court. Let it not pass your lips but I beat him in private."*

*"Agreed. If you beat me, I promise to hold my tongue..."*

# AN INTRODUCTION TO SORCERY

The cosmos is filled with **magic**. The practices which mortal beings learn to manipulate these magical forces are known as **sorcery**. This chapter reveals the secrets and wonders of sorcery in the lands of *Capharnaum*, with special reference to Jazirat.

## The History and Role of Sorcery

There are many forms of sorcery. Inspired by legends, gods, and dragons, there are as many ways of manipulating the magic inherent in the world as there are peoples, tribes and regions.

### Sorcery Through the Ages

Magic has existed forever, and the world has always had those who would manipulate it: its diviners, sorcerers, healers, and magicians. No records exist of its earliest use: writing came long after. But, in the shelter of courtyards, in the shade of temples, even under the burning desert sun, certain powerful sorcerers whisper that magic was born before even the gods themselves. Created by the dragons when even they were young, they say magic was a gift to mortals to permit them to draw closer to the gods, by sharing a tiny fraction of their power. To most scholars, how-

ever, this story does not ring true. How could the dragons, despite their ancestral wisdom, control and dispose of the power of their masters and creators in this way? And, if magic had really been born before the gods, how could it have been made by the dragons? Almost all the world's peoples agree that the gods are the creators of all things, the dragons merely their servants and messengers. How could they have gained control of the gods' essences to create magic, especially if the gods had not yet been born?

Thus the myths are unclear. However, this has never prevented people from interpreting them their own way, and today the world's peoples have many ways of explaining the origins, presence, and purpose of magic in their lives.

### The Agalanthians

According to the historians and storytellers of the Agalanthian Empire, the world we know today was created by the first dragon, Utaax, who also created the gods, the plant and animal world, and ultimately mortal men and women. Other dragons, far less powerful, came later, created by the gods themselves. Utaax had sacrificed himself to create our world, having contemplated the degenerate world of Kryptos; and, so that the mistakes of Kryptos were not repeated, he had used his last breath to command the young gods to fashion the dragons who would be his successors, to watch over the new world so that the flaws of previous civilisations would never happen again. The soul of Utaax then rose into the highest firmament, where it exploded into an infinity of fragments that showered the new world, impregnating everything with his essence. Thus was magic born, a legacy of the world's creator, and the principle connecting every thing and every being and giving the world its cohesion.

### The Saabi

Saabi legends claim that the gods created the world before embarking upon a merciless war. The children of the two primordial gods, Apsu and Tiamat, jealous of their parents' powers, attacked them

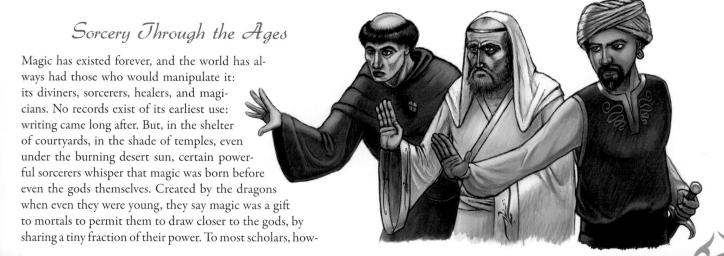

to usurp their places. Apsu died in his sleep: his magical dreams continued interrupted, and continue even today as the mysterious **mirages** (see page 298). Then it was Tiamat's turn; to defend herself, she created a monstrous horde. However, despite her powerful protectors, Tiamat was defeated, and slain by the god Marduk, her son; the djinn were born from her final breath.

In the aftermath of these murders, Marduk created men and women from his mother's flesh and blood. This is why all mortals have, deep inside, a sliver of the Primal Goddess enabling them to work magic—although their power no longer has any connection to Tiamat, in either its nature or effects. Once men and women had been created, Tiamat's body turned to salt water, and washed all around the world, encircling the land. This is why deep water navigation is considered unholy and accursed by the Saabi, although their proscriptions have not prevented certain pirates and explorers from making a name for themselves on the high seas.

## The Shiradim

Shirad, the One Almighty God, created the world. In order that his children did not disappear into oblivion after death, he decreed that each should be reborn into its cycle of years and days, if they had died without having the time or opportunity to distinguish themselves. Each person so reborn would begin again, but with a new family and new body, with their memories wiped clean to avoid repeating the errors of their past lives. And, during all their days, Shirad, in his infinite goodness, allowed mortals to call upon his power to manipulate the world. Thus, the Shiradim believe that magic is not part of the world, but a power granted by Shirad in answer to their prayers.

But the new-born humans lacked maturity, and the prayers they addressed to Shirad to work magic were beyond number, measure, and reason. In response, the One God created the dragons—creatures of infinite wisdom—to guide mortals in their lives, to moderate their use of magic, to help them use it best. Even today, when night falls, the stars of the dragons light up the sky, so the Shiradim never forget that their spells must always be hymns to life and wisdom.

## The Quarterians

Quarterian cosmology resembles that of the Shiradim. Despite this, their conception of magic is very different. Quarterian myths relate the birth of magic thus: "In the beginning, there was Aether, king of the universe, master of all things. After creating a perfect world, he filled it with life, and bore men and women of his divine will. But humans were disorganised and weak, wandering through the chaos of their lives. Thus Aether taught to nascent mortals the Grand Design. More than a path, the Design is a vast road, with many intersections, on which a man may move as he might wish. Once Aether completed the Road of a Thousand Ways, he fashioned new creatures whose minds went far beyond those of humans, whose role was to bring back to the path of righteousness

any sheep that wandered too far from the road their Creator had made for them.

In his magnanimity, Aether bethought himself that men and women deserved more than simple punishment if they deviated from his path. And so he gave them the power of miracles, to help them achieve the Grand Design and, thus, complete their lives".

Because of this gift, Quarterians believe they are serving Aether when they use sorcery; this is the main difference from the Shiradi conception of magic. For the Shiradi, magic is God answering their requests: for the Quarterians, such an idea is blasphemous. Who would claim to command Aether? No, the truth lies elsewhere: every time a mortal practices sorcery, he unknowingly takes one more step along the path of light, answering Aether's call which guides him out from the darkness of sin. Sorcery contributes to the fulfilment of the Grand Design, a small but significant step towards one of the destinies Aether offers his faithful. But, even then, the sorcery may do little more than scratch the surface of this Grand Design—the minds of mortals being far too weak for the contemplation of its true magnificence and glory.

### El-Seghir Iliah

*A small and unique group, as yet with little influence, El-Seghir Iliah has disproportionate ambitions as far as sorcery is concerned. Its members, all powerful sorcerers, come from different regions, peoples, and creeds. Fate has brought them together and, over time, they have exchanged points of view and spent much time philosophising, to conclude that magic has been put to poor use by mortals, and that the gods are no longer fulfilling their promised roles in providing it. For the moment, their views are restricted to their own arts, but it's only a matter of time before they extend their theories to the whole world, convincing themselves that the gods have become redundant in all areas of life.*

*The current leader of the El-Seghir Iliah is Wasil Ibn Yazid Abd-al-Tarek. Following the way of his master (page 258), Wasil leads the El-Seghir Iliah with an iron fist, intending to do whatever he has to in order to reach his goals. For the moment, the group is travelling down the Halawui River seeking a powerful magical item, the Mirror of Heaven, which, if turned towards the night sky, is said to show Night's True Face—an overview of the domain of the gods. They believe the artefact will show to the world that the gods have fallen, forcing sorcerers everywhere to rally to their cause.*

## Magic Around the World

Magic is deeply rooted in the minds of mortals; sometimes venerated, sometimes hated, but always there. However, not all mortals may use it; far from it. Whether it brings dreams or nightmares, everyone knows magic is a reality, part of the universe everyone must deal with, one way or another.

The world has no great organisation of sorcerers, no official guild bringing sorcerers together, whatever the country or people. Everyone agrees—in their own way—that magic comes from the gods, by whom it is ruled and ordered. Because of this there is no need to watch over or control those who practice this art, as it is by nature divine. This doesn't preclude the existence of sorcerous groups or associations, but none of them have pretensions to large-scale hegemony.

Some schools, paths, sects, and academies are deeply interested in sorcery. Although they don't provide their own magic, they do have special teachings, interpretations, and ways of approaching it. A path dedicated to an **Ancient Art** (page 125) may not have its own spells, but will concentrate on spells which correspond to its philosophy, as well as methods to teach, use, and even modify them.

Magic is powerful and spectacular, with many applications, and often attracts the attention of the envious and ambitious. Nevertheless, the number of sorcerers remains relatively constant, the practice of this art requiring a commitment and rigour few can achieve. The way the peoples of the world imagine sorcery depends on the social status of those who practise it.

## Chiromancers

In Agalanthian cities, chiromancers (page 135) are usually in the service of their rulers, either as advisors or physicians. In wartime, their services are required on the battlefield, whether to lead offensives or to treat wounded soldiers. However, no law obliges chiromancers to enter the service of a city-state's government, and even those who do are free to leave whenever they want, as long as they have completed their **conscriptorium**, a form of magical conscription similar to a military term of service. For two years, a chiromancer binds himself by oath to an **archon** (page 270), who he must serve to the best of his abilities. At the end of this period, if the chiromancer has distinguished himself, he may be offered a permanent position in the service of a city-state, often his city-state of origin. Otherwise, he may enlist in a mercenary company. This obligatory two-year period of service discourages most candidates, and the conscriptorium's harshness usually manages to separate true chiromancers from quitters unworthy of the art. As a result, magic is considered hard and character-building by Agalanthians, and consequently inaccessible, reserved for the most persevering and enduring. Anyone who survives the ordeal of sorcerous study enjoys a certain prestige and indeed admiration in Agalanthian society; chiromancers are among the legendary heroes who have the power to call on the gods and to write history according to their will. Nevertheless, this does not prevent some people from learning sorcerous tricks without completing the conscriptorium, practising their unauthorised magic in the souk or the shade of a diviner's tent.

## Al-Kimyati

In Saabi tribes and cities, **al-kimyati** are poets, musicians, artists, who summon the divine spark hidden deep within their souls to create an empathic bond with the world, manipulating their environment according to their will. The Saabi opinion of these sorcerers depends on whether they are nomads or city folk. Among the nomads, al-kimyati consider themselves no better than anyone else, practising their art humbly and going where they are required. They're regarded by their neighbours as simple people worthy of respect. In the cities, things are very different. At court, al-kimyati are also courtiers and diplomats, who the Saabi regard as untrustworthy, ever involved in intrigue, the subjects of suspicion and rumour. Cityfolk always visit an al-kimyat with some slight apprehension, and are careful never to vex them.

Al-kimyati are few in number. On the one hand, working sorcery entails a life of austerity, dedication, and abnegation; on the other, being an al-kimyat means being versed in diplomacy, etiquette, and lying. This duality only attracts those Saabi who are already gifted in traditional arts.

## Sephirim

During their long centuries of bondage, the Shiradim were forbidden to practice magic. Of course, this did not prevent some from learning it in secret. Because of the ban, the **sephirim** developed a purely oral form of sorcery, so nothing might betray their transgression of Agalanthian laws. Now the Shiradim are free, sorcery is widespread, even more so than among other peoples, precisely because of the ban that long prevented them from developing their art.

The sephirim have maintained their oral traditions as a lesson from their painful past. They are humble, at least among their own, and none consider themselves superior to any other. Thus, among the Shiradim, sorcerers have no privileged status. As a consequence of their oral traditions, sephirim are storytellers, messengers, even poets; some non-sephirim sorcerers have also become scribes and historians, although few in number, responsible for setting down on paper the adventures and legends of their people. Sorcerers are respected for what they are and what they do. However, a rivalry tinged with contempt exists between the sephirim and the handful of sorcerers who have turned to writing.

## Thaumaturgists

As the Quarterian religion is relatively young, one might think **thaumaturgists** would be weak sorcerers. Nothing could be further from the truth. In just a few centuries, Jason's faithful have teemed with geniuses and enlightened individuals, and today their magic is as powerful as that of any other people. The Quarterians have also had the time to form a solid opinion of their own sorcerous powers and those of their neighbours: in Quarterian society, sorcery is accepted and respected, and thaumaturgists are believed to be chosen by Aether and Jason to work miracles towards the achievement of the Grand Design. Sorcery is never a choice, but a calling and a duty: children with strong sorcerous potential are noticed from a young age by religious authorities, who take them under their wing and ensure their education.

Those Quarterians called to a sorcerous life are few in number, and even fewer are those who successfully complete their apprenticeships. Quarterians consider all sorcery other than thaumaturgy—in other words, sorcery as used by foreigners—to be evil and heretical. Magic was given to mortals to work miracles and help Aether in his task, not to use and abuse according to one's own selfish whims. The authorities are clear: Quarterians must abstain from contact with any sorcerer other than thaumaturgists; and thaumaturgists themselves must fight against the infidels who would betray the trust of Aether and Jason his son.

# Tarmel Haja: The Divine Combinations

Sorcery is flexible and profound, with many applications and permutations. Its principle form is an improvisational magic known as the **Tarmel Haja**. This term means "the divine combinations" in Saabi, and is used throughout Capharnaum to refer to magic in general, with the exception of Agalanthian magic or **chiromancy** (see page 135). Indeed, the magics used by the Saabi, Shiradim, and Quarterians share a common foundation: the combination of **elements**, specific to each people, to obtain desired effects. The Quarterians in Jazirat have reluctantly adopted the term Tarmel Haja to refer, not without disgust, to the infidel heresies; the Orkadians insist on referring to **combination magic** in their own tongue, refusing to lump their magical practices to those of the other peoples.

Whenever a sorcerer uses his power to work a magical effect, he always does so in the same way, regardless of his origin: he combines one of three actions—Create, Destroy, or Transform—with one or several **elements** specific to the type of sorcery used by his people, which may be physical things like sand, food, people, weapons, fire, or trees; or emotions such as fear, happiness, peace, or anger; or even more abstract concepts like health, beauty, speed, or dreams. In this way he affects his own environment, or himself, or even other people.

In game terms, this means that you have a lot of freedom describing what you do with your magical powers. This chapter provides you with the underlying rules for magic, but be aware that very often, you'll be making up your magical effects on the fly, improvising what you do. This is different from many roleplaying games which present you with rigidly defined lists of magical spells; *Capharnaum's* Tarmel Haja is versatile magic, simple at base but

with almost limitless flexibility. We'll be providing lots of examples and guidance to show you just what you can do with it below.

Here's an overview of the ways in which the Saabi, Shiradim, and Quarterians use sorcery. For Agalanthian sorcery, see page 135.

## Saabi Workings

The Saabi term **tamasheq** means "inspiration". It refers to the techniques Saabi *al-kimyati* sorcerers use to undertake magical actions, also known as **workings**. First, an al-kimyat draws upon his divine nature to Create, Transform or Destroy one or more **elements** belonging to the "Three Magical Worlds" which make up the Saabi universe. These magical worlds are the **Mundane World**, referring to the material world; the **Philosophical World**, referring to the world of the mind (and maybe super-ego); and the **Phantasmal World**, referring to the world of the soul, spirit, and of dreams (and maybe the Id).

The techniques of tamasheq require the al-kimyat to express their magical working in the form of one of the **Ancient Arts**—epic poetry, music, astronomy, and so on (see page 125). In game terms, this most often affects how you describe your magical working; some ancient arts are easier to use in some situations than others. Additionally, Saabi clans prefer ancient arts whose governing muses they are used to calling upon.

*For example: By creating a dream using the ancient art of Music, an al-kimyat will not control the visions created by that dream, but will control the moods the dream gives rise to, based on the success of his action. The result in terms of the game rules will generally be the same, but the effect of the magical working described (and the way you can describe it) will differ.*

You can find out more about tamasheq workings on page 127.

## Shiradi Covenants

The Shiradim were slaves for much of their history, and developed a form of magic based exclusively on spoken utterances. This magic is known as the **tasannu**. Using the tasannu, a Shiradi sephir combines one of the three Sacred Words with one or more **names** (magical elements—see page 119) into short phrases or sentences known as **covenants**, each of which expresses a desired effect.

*For example, a sephir who knows the Sacred Word "Create" and the elements "Dream" and "Peace" may utter a covenant such as "I create a dream of peace", causing the target of the covenant to have a dream which calms them down and makes them peaceful, at least for the dream's duration. If the sephir also knows the element "Sailing", he may refine the covenant further, for example by saying "I create a dream in which you are sailing peacefully".*

See page 129 for much more on covenants and the tasannu.

# SORCERY IN THE GAME

This section describes the core rules for using the Tarmel Haja "combination magic" introduced above. It's followed by more detail on the forms of the Tarmel Haja used by the Saabi, the Shiradim, and the Quarterians. Agalanthian magic or **chiromancy** is described on page 135.

Sorcery uses the Sacred Word skill, representing a sorcerer's ability to call on the gods to obtain a magical effect. The sorceries of the Saabi, Shiradim, and Quarterians are based on three verbs, each of which is a "sub-skill" (**not** a specialisation!) of the Sacred Word skill:

❖ **Sacred Word (Create)**
❖ **Sacred Word (Destroy)**
❖ **Sacred Word (Transform)**

The number of Sacred Words which a sorcerer knows depends upon his Sacred Word skill score, and is described on page 31. Additionally, if a sorcerer knows only Sacred Word (Create) or Sacred Word (Destroy), the next Sacred Word he learns must be Sacred Word (Transform): for mystical reasons, it's not possible for a sorcerer to know the Create and Destroy Sacred Words without also knowing Transform. Note that you learn a new Sacred Word automatically when your skill score increases appropriately, although it takes a week of study and meditation to do so.

## Quarterian Miracles

Quarterian magic takes the form of **miracles.** To obtain a magical effect, a Quarterian thaumaturgist combines one of the three Sacred Words (Create, Transform, or Destroy), with an element associated with the **Three Domains** of mortal being. These domains are: the **Ephemeral Domain**, associated with the human body; the **Eternal Domain**, associated with the human mind; and the **Receptacle Domain**, associated with the human soul. The thaumaturgist formulates these elements together into a **prayer** expressing an effect which he requests Aether to grant as he attempts to further his god's Great Work. This effect is called a **miracle**. A prayer for a miracle will also contain at least one **homage** to one of the Quarterian divinities—Aether, Jason, or Mira (see page 284).

*For example: "All powerful Aether, allow me, in Thy holy generosity, to create a dream in the mind of this man to appease him, that in this way Thy will may be done on Earth. Blessed be Thy Son, our guide, for ever and ever. Amen".*

See page 131 for more on Quarterian miracles.

## Magic and Roleplaying

*We strongly encourage you to embrace the free-form nature of magic in* **Capharnaum**. *Improvise the descriptions of your spells, the way you cast them, even their effects. Al-Rawi is there to guide you, but ultimately these rules provide clear indications of the rules mechanical effects of magic, while leaving a lot of the external description up to your own creativity. If your sorcerous character is transforming another person into a camel, enjoy yourself describing that slow magical transformation, the growth of the hump, the voice of the victim changing into low-pitched braying. This way you'll feel like you're really controlling the magic you're working, creating your own spells, deciding the form they take and how they work.*

*Equally, if you ever roll a Critical Failure (or worse!) when casting a spell, don't be afraid to jump in and describe those effects, too. Try and do so in keeping with the way you're envisaging sorcery working for your character—yes, it'll be a disadvantage to you, and it may even harm your character, but you get to describe the type of disadvantage and the nature of the harm, and establish the parameters of what Al-Rawi then gets to work with. That's some powerful juju!*

# The Philosophy of the Sacred Words

The definitions of the Sacred Words Create, Destroy, and Transform are not those you'll find in a dictionary. Rather, they're philosophical terms, fundamental forces of the cosmos which the Tarmel Haja allows your sorcerous character to invoke.

The Sacred Word **Create** represents the positive, creative force of the universe, that power broadly called "good". It creates wholesomeness and health, warmth and light, life, stability, law, and integrity. It can be used to oppose and counter manifestations of the Sacred Word Destroy, even those which haven't been created by sorcery. Thus, Create Health can be used to heal wounds, whether those wounds have been caused by weapons, injury, or magics such as Destroy Flesh.

The Sacred Word **Destroy** represents the negative, destructive force of the universe, that power broadly called "evil". It destroys wholesomeness and health, life and light, leaving instead sickness and wounds, darkness and chaos in its wake. Thus, if you want to "create" wounds, or fear, what you're actually doing, in philosophical, Tarmel Haja terms, is using the Sacred Word Destroy to destroy flesh, calm, peace, and so on.

That's why, when you learn certain elements (see page 119), you automatically learn their opposites. If you know the element "Light", for example, you automatically know "Darkness". You can even write down "Light / Darkness" on your character sheet. In terms of the Tarmel Haja, you use Create + Light to cause light, and Destroy + Light to cause darkness.

The Sacred Word **Transform** represents the force of transformation in the world. It works to change one element into another, unrelated, and completely different element. Note that the first element must already exist, and that, instead of being destroyed (which is the province of the Sacred Word Destroy), it must actually be transformed into another element. Thus, Sacred Word Transform may transform sand into water, or a person into a camel. The sand or person must already exist, even if they have been created by Sacred Word Create. Note that Sacred Word transform always requires two elements, even if those elements may sometimes be improvised (page 119).

# The Effects of Magic

Casting a spell is a single action: see page 55. To cast a spell in *Capharnaum*, first declare the Sacred Word and elements that you're using, then describe the effect you're trying to achieve. Then make a roll of INT + Sacred Word: the difficulty is 15, unless your target is a living thing, in which case the difficulty is equal to 9, or a roll of its INT + Willpower (called a **resistance roll**—see page 120), whichever is higher. If you succeed, you get to "spend" the magnitude of your roll on Table 4-1: Magical Effect Parameters to determine your spell's exact effect in terms of the game rules.

*For example: Nazir is trying to set fire to the robes worn by Hakim, his rival, to show off to his peers. He succeeds with a magnitude of 2. He chooses to allocate the magnitude as follows:*

❖ *Target: 1 (0 magnitude). It's just Hakim that Nazir is aiming at.*

| MAG | DURATION | RANGE (PACES) | TARGETS | AREA / VOLUME[1] | HP | ATT | VIRTUE | SKILL | DMG / AV[2] |
|---|---|---|---|---|---|---|---|---|---|
| 0 | 1 action | 1 | 1 | 1 | 5 | +0 | +0 | +0 | +/-1 |
| 1 | 1 round | 5 | 2 | 2 | 10 | +/-1 | +0 | +/-1 | +/-2 |
| 2 | 1 minute | 10 | 5 | 5 | 20 | +/-1 | +/-1 | +/-2 | +/-3 |
| 3 | 15 minutes | 50 | 10 | 10 | 30 | +/-2 | +/-1 | +/-3 | +/-4 |
| 4 | 1 hour | 100 | 20 | 20 | 40 | +/-2 | +/-1 | +/-4 | +/-5 |
| 5 | 4 hours | 500 | 50 | 50 | 50 | +/-3 | +/-2 | +/-5 | +/-6 |
| 6 | 1 day | 1000 | 100 | 100 | 60 | +/-3 | +/-2 | +/-6 | +/-7 |
| 7 | 1 week | 1 league | 200 | 200 | 70 | +/-4 | +/-2 | +/-7 | +/-8 |
| 8 | 1 month | 2 leagues | 500 | 500 | 80 | +/-4 | +/-3 | +/-8 | +/-9 |
| 9 | 1 year | 10 leagues | 1000 | 1000 | 90 | +/-5 | +/-3 | +/-9 | +/-10 |
| 10 | 1 lifetime | 20 leagues | 2000 | 2000 | 100 | +/-5 | +/-3 | +/-10 | +/-11 |

*1: The area unit is the square pace, the volume unit is the waterskin (2 pints), except for rare or precious materials, in which case the unit of measurement is the ounce.*

*2: Applies to increases or decreases in weapon damage or armour value.*

*Al-Rawi may modify the difficulty of the Sacred Word roll for any effects which are not represented in the above table.*

- *Duration: 1 round (1 magnitude). Nazir wants to make Hakim look ridiculous, so he wants the fire to burn for at least one round.*
- *Range: 5 paces (1 magnitude). Hakim isn't right next to Nazir.*
- *Damage: 5 HP (0 magnitude). This is a small amount of damage, pretty much a side effect of the greater goal of making Hakim look ridiculous. If Nazir had just wanted to harm Hakim, he could have reduced the duration to 1 action (0 magnitude) and put 1 magnitude into damage, doing 10 HP.*

*The robe catches fire, doing 5 HP damage to Hakim, who departs, his tail between his legs.*

## Describing a Spell Effect

When you describe a spell effect, you combine one of the three Sacred Words (you'll usually only know one or maybe two to begin with) with one or more **elements** (you'll usually know several to begin with). Elements are always **nouns** (never adjectives, adverbs, pronouns, etc), such as "Sun", "Weather", Body", "Sand". When you learn them, it's usually in the singular, but you can always use them in the plural, too (so the element "Body" also includes "Bodies"—you don't need to learn a second element). Note also that some elements automatically include their opposite, such as "Light / Darkness"—see "The Philosophy of the Sacred Words" on page 118 for more.

Some elements may be **broadly-defined** or **narrowly-defined**. This is often a subjective decision, and may depend on the actual spell being cast—if in doubt, discuss it with Al-Rawi. Broadly-defined elements are more widely applicable, but increase the casting difficulty by +3. Narrowly-defined elements are more restricted in their approach and applicability, but reduce the casting difficulty by -3. Elements which are neither broad nor narrow are referred to as **normally-defined**. This means that spells using narrowly-defined elements are much easier to cast.

*For example: Assabi is travelling with his caravan in the deep desert, and has got lost, unable to find the oasis which is his destination. With supplies running low, he tries to cast a spell to transform sand into water (very useful in the desert!). He knows the Sacred Word Transform and both elements, and faces a difficulty of only 12 rather than 15 because the element "Sand" is narrowly-defined.*

There's no limit to the number of elements which may be combined in a spell. If you don't know a specific element, you may **improvise** it, but each element improvised increases the difficulty of the spell-casting by +6.

*Next, Assabi decides to try and transform a handful of sand into jerked meat. This time, he doesn't know a "Jerked Meat" element, or any related element, and so must improvise it. He now faces a difficulty of 18: a -3 for "Sand" (as above), and a +6 for improvising "Jerked Meat".*

Note that you can never improvise a Sacred Word, only elements. You must learn a Sacred Word by having the requisite Sacred Word skill score before you can use it.

## Targeting a Spell

Some elements, such as emotions, by definition must affect a person, so it isn't necessary to include a target as an element in a spell creating, transforming, or destroying emotions. If you Create Joy, Create Dreams, etc, then a target is automatically affected; you just have to specify which.

However, physical objects or substances created by magic don't automatically have targets. Create Fire simply creates a fire right in front of you. In order to set a person on fire, or to fill their lungs with water, you must include a target element in your spell which explicitly references that person. If you don't, you're improvising the target as an element, which increases the difficulty by +6 (see above).

*For example, if Assabi wants to transform the water in his enemy's tears into sand (ouch!), then he needs a target element, such as "Person". He doesn't have one, so must improvise, automatically increasing his difficulty by +6: the target makes a resistance roll (page 120), and adds +6 to the result. If Assabi succeeds, he allocates his magnitude on Table 4-1: Magical Effect Parameters to determine what the spell does.*

*On average, Assabi will have a magnitude of 2. He could choose to inflict 10 points of damage (costing 1 magnitude) to 1 target (costing 0 magnitude) within 5 paces (1 magnitude); or he could inflict 5 damage (0 magnitude) on 2 targets (1 magnitude) within 5 paces (1 magnitude). Alternatively, if his target is within 1 pace (0 magnitude), he could choose to inflict a -1 penalty on the target's skill rolls (1 magnitude) for 1 combat round (1 magnitude).*

The more powerful your spell is (the higher the magnitude), the more you can do!

## Supplementary Elements

Sometimes your character may know a magical element which isn't strictly necessary for the spell, but which could clearly play a supporting role. Each of these **supplementary elements** reduces the casting difficulty of your spell by -3.

## Handling Duration

Generally speaking, the direct effects caused by magic have a duration, which you can spend magnitude on; with enough magnitude, a duration can be extended to be long enough as to be virtually permanent. Otherwise, once the duration of a spell ends, its direct effects end, too.

This means that if you use the Tarmel Haja to "Transform a Person to Sand", a success against that person's resistance roll (page

## Magical Elements

Table 4-2: Magical Elements lists some example elements: there are many more. Elements may change from being **broadly, normally,** or **narrowly defined** based on the context of the spell. Generally, however, they fall into the categories below.

(Note that elements used by Saabi al-kimyati and Quarterian thaumaturgists may also be categorised by Magical World or Domain. These categories don't have any direct rules mechanical effect—indeed, you don't have to use them at all—but instead give you background detail you can use them when describing your tamasheq workings or thaumaturgical prayers. We've provided examples of such categorisations on pages 125 and 133.)

| TABLE 4-2: MAGICAL ELEMENTS | | |
|---|---|---|
| **BROADLY-DEFINED ELEMENTS (+3 DIFF)** | **NORMALLY-DEFINED ELEMENTS** | **NARROWLY-DEFINED ELEMENTS (-3 DIFF)** |
| Animal | Feline | Cat |
| The Elements (air, etc) | Fire | Flame |
| The Elements (air, etc) | Earth | Sand |
| The Elements (air, etc) | Water | Ice |
| Plant | Tree | Palm Tree |
| Food | Meat | Beef |
| Sense | Sight | Night Vision |
| Weapon | Bladed Weapon | Scimitar |
| Living Being | Human Body | Heart |
| Person | Man / Woman | You / Me / Amir |
| Person | Adult / Child | You / Me / Amir |
| Treasure | Jewel | Ruby |
| Truth / Falsehood | Telling the Truth / Lying | A Lie |
| Attribute | Strength | Lifting ability |
| Health / Unhealthiness | Recovery / Injury | Healing / Wound |
| Cloth | Clothing | Boots |

## Sorcery Difficulties and Resistance Rolls

As described above, the difficulty to cast a spell depends upon the nature of the target:

❖ If your target is **not a sentient being** (so it's an object, building, natural element, or even a tree or plant, etc), or if there is no obvious target, then you must make a roll against a difficulty of 15.

❖ If your target is a **sentient being** (it's a person, animal, etc, or even a demon or ghost), then you must make an opposed roll against your target's INT + Willpower, or a difficulty of 9, whichever is higher. This is called a **resistance roll**.

There are several modifiers which may be made to the difficulty of your roll to cast a spell. Note that if you're casting a spell against a sentient target, these modifiers apply to the target's resistance roll instead. Table 4-3: Spell Difficulty Modifiers lists some example modifiers; we encourage Al-Rawi to come up with others during play.

| TABLE 4-3: SPELL DIFFICULTY MODIFIERS | |
|---|---|
| **SITUATION** | **DIFFICULTY MODIFIER** |
| Noisy environment: Tavern | +1 |
| Noisy environment: Crowd | +2 |
| Noisy environment: Battlefield | +3 |
| Caster's Faith at 0 | +3 |
| Narrowly-defined element | -3 per element |
| Broadly-defined element | +3 per element |
| Improvising an element | +6 per element |
| Supplementary element | -3 per element |
| Per step of duration concentrating* | -1 |
| Complete silence | -1 |
| Place of worship | -1 |
| Burning incense (al-kimyati) | -1 |
| Wearing ritual apparel (sephirim) | -1 |
| Burning a candle (thaumaturgists) | -1 |
| Performing an act of faith (fasting, etc) | -1 |
| Sacred ground | -2 |

*Uses the steps of duration on Table 4-1: Magical Effect Parameters, ie 1 action is -1 difficulty, 1 round is -2, 1 minute is -3, etc.

120) will turn them into sand. They're not dead, strictly speaking, but in that state there's probably not much they can do! However, once the duration of the spell ends, then the sand will transform back into the original person.

This also means, for example, that if you "Transform Sand to Water" (handy in the desert!), then the resulting water will only remain as long as the spell duration lasts. Once it's over, the water turns straight back to sand.

There's one exception to this: if you use magic to cause an indirect effect, then that indirect effect remains after the magic ends. For example, if you drink the water you've just turned the sand into, then your thirst is quenched and remains quenched after the spell ends. Likewise, if you Create Fire in a person's hair and use your magnitude to cause HP damage, that HP damage remains after the fire has gone out. The same goes for healing; once the healing power ends, the HP healed remain healed.

This has some interesting consequences. In theory, you can use "Transform Life to Death" to kill a person outright. However, as soon as the spell ends, the life that was transformed to death will be restored, reducing the spell's effectiveness unless you've got a lot of magnitude to spend on duration (or a sharp axe and a decent amount of time to chop the currently dead body into small pieces...). However, if you use something like "Destroy Flesh" instead, and cause HP damage, then once again the damage caused will remain after the spell has ended.

This means that powerful sorcerers are truly scary; but even lowly beginning spell-casters may create some impressive effects, with some imagination and judicious spending of magnitude.

# Learning New Elements

Throughout your adventures, your sorcerer characters will have the opportunity of improving their art and learning new elements for their spells. When you create a sorcerer character, you start by

## Detecting Magic

*Any character is capable of detecting magic, whether a sorcerer or not. It's a roll of INT + Willpower against a difficulty set by Al-Rawi, based on the proximity and power of the magic in question (figure a base difficulty of 15 for a non-sorcerer, maybe 9 for a sorcerer). The magnitude of the result determines how much the character perceives about the magic detected (see Table 4-4: Detecting Magic).*

| TABLE 4-4: DETECTING MAGIC | |
|---|---|
| **MAGNITUDE** | **DETECTION** |
| 1 | The character detects the presence of magic, and is able to determine whether its source is a spell, or the presence of a sorcerer or magical creature. |
| 2-3 | As above, and the character may determine which people's magic he is detecting (Saabi tamasheq, Shiradi tasannu, Quarterian prayers, etc), whether or not the magic is being used by a human being, and whether the magic is benevolent, malevolent, or neutral. |
| 4-5 | As above, and the character may accurately locate the source of the magic in relation to himself. He also gains a vague impression of the magic's nature and effects (heat if it's connected to fire, suffocation if connected to death, and so on). |
| 6+ | As above, and the character knows the target's location, the effects of the spell or exact nature of the creature, and how powerful the magic is. |

knowing a number of elements equal to your Sacred Word skill times 2 (Sacred Word x 2).

When your Sacred Word skill score increases by +1, you may immediately learn two new magical elements. See the appropriate sections below for how to choose these elements for al-kimyati (page 122), sephirim (page 129), or thaumaturgists (page 131). For chiromancers, see page 135.

You may also learn new elements through experience, at the rate of 15 AP per element: see page 80 for more.

Finally, whenever you get a Critical Success (magnitude 6+) on your Sacred Word skill roll to cast a spell, **you may immediately learn a new element**. The element must be related to the effect or description of the spell you're casting; it may also be an element you've just improvised.

## Exorcism

Characters who are possessed by demons or djinn must be **exorcised** to be freed from that possession. You may do this yourself, if you're possessed and have control over yourself; or someone else may perform an exorcism upon you.

Exorcising a djinn or demon usually takes at least several minutes, and is an INT + Prayer skill roll against a difficulty equal to the djinn or demon's INT score, times 5 (INT x 5). Note that the possessing demon will resist the exorcism, often violently—thrashing around, straining, even dashing themselves against walls or other objects. In such a case, you can treat the magnitude of failure of an exorcism roll as damage done to the possessing character.

For example: Ralph is playing an al-kimyat called Felihs Ibn Tufiq Abd-al-Tarek, who wants to cast a spell at a Saabi guard using the Sacred Word Destroy and the elements "Tooth" and "Tongue". However, Felihs doesn't know the element "Tongue", and so must improvise it. This means that the Saabi guard's resistance roll against Felihs's spell gets a +6 bonus (for the improvised element—see page 119).

Ralph rolls the dice and succeeds with a magnitude of 6—a Critical Success! The inside of the guard's mouth disintegrates in a messy and spectacular fashion. On top of that, Felihs may immediately learn a new element: Ralph may note down "Tongue", "Mouth", or even "Guard" on his character sheet as a new element and henceforth use it without penalty.

# Workings, Covenants, and Miracles

## The Saabi and Tamasheq

### The Practice of Tamasheq

**Tamasheq** is the name given to the Tarmel Haja combination magic practiced by the Jazirati. It refers to the flash of artistic genius which operates through the al-kimyati when he casts a **working** (the Saabi term for a sorcerous spell). In practice, casting a working comprises several steps: first, the sorcerer concentrates to connect with his divine spark; then he draws on one or more elements from

## Grimoires

There's another way for sorcerers to learn new magical elements: **grimoires**. These rare and precious items are written works containing scraps of magical and ancestral wisdom. When a sorcerer finds a grimoire, he must read it and then spend time meditating upon its contents. If he does so correctly, he may learn one or more magical elements.

Learning a magical element from a grimoire requires a week's study, followed by an INT + Willpower roll vs a difficulty of 9, plus the grimoire's Power score (INT + Willpower vs 9 + Power). Table 4-5: Grimoires provides details for sample grimoires, showing their rarity, number of elements, and Power.

| TABLE 4-5: GRIMOIRES | | |
|---|---|---|
| **ELEMENTS** | **POWER** | **RARITY** |
| 1 | 3 | **Common:** the grimoire can be found in the possession of a professional sorcerer, or even by a careful search of the *souks*. |
| 2 | 6 | **Fairly Common:** the grimoire can be found in the profession of a great and accomplished sorcerer, or on the black market. |
| 4 | 9 | **Uncommon:** the grimoire can be found in a prestigious private collection, or deep in ruins or lost archives, buried by time and nature. |
| 8 | 12 | **Extremely Rare:** impossible to find without a lifetime of searching. |

Elements found in grimoires are usually presented in the form of technical discussions, or as workings, covenants, or prayers used by other sorcerers. If you're using **pregenerated spells** in your game (page 127), then grimoires are a great way of introducing new ones—including lost magics with astounding effects!

### The Writings of Dabir Ibn Aziz, the Lion of Azrak

❖ *Uncommon Grimoire*
❖ *Power: 9*
❖ *Elements: Leaping, Lion, Rending, Roar.*

Written on forty sheets of lion-skin vellum and bound in a lion's tail, this grimoire has been forbidden several times during Kh'saaba's history because of the bloody murders which generally follow its use. Several copies are known to exist.

the Three Magical Worlds (see below) to interact with his environment; finally, he focusses these energies through the medium of an ancient art (page 125), giving them form and further refining the magical effect.

*For example: the al-kimyat Maha Wadia Bint Daoud wants the opinion of her tribal chieftain to prevail in negotiations for control of an oasis. She spends an action concentrating to connect with the divine spark in her soul, then fixes on the elements she needs for her working, which she determines to be "Truth / Falsehood" (from the Philosophical World) and "Word" (from the Mundane World). She then recites a brief epic poem (in this case, a brief poem in the epic style—the ancient art she has chosen to use), which she skilfully introduces into the debate, and makes a Sacred Word (Create) roll to cast the spell on the chieftain of the opposing tribe, in order to make him think that he's hearing an undisputable truth in her chieftain's words, thereby making things easier for her own chieftain to take control of the oasis. If the working succeeds, the opposing chieftain will be swayed by the epic vision and grandeur in the words of Maha's chieftain.*

*Note that Maha could have used tragedy instead of epic poetry as the ancient art for the form of her working. In this case, the opposing chieftain would still have accepted his rival's words as truth, but would have interpreted them with tragic gravity, feeling the urgent, desperate necessity for Maha's tribe to take control of the oasis.*

## The Dark Side of Magic

*Sorcery as presented in this chapter may seem to be almost unlimited in power, with no downside or disadvantage to its use. This is not the case. All magic use by mortals has a dark side, which becomes increasingly evident the more a sorcerer gains in power. To enable Al-Rawi to make full use of this element in play, we've separated the rules for the darker aspects of sorcery use into their own section: see "The Dark Side of Magic" on page 339 for more.*

Note that, in rules terms, a Saabi al-kimyat performing a working operates essentially like any attempt to cast a spell. The process takes a single action (page 55). First, choose which Sacred Word you're going to use (Create, Transform, or Destroy), and then select which elements you'll be combining with it. The Magical Worlds which the elements belong to provide you with additional descriptive hooks for narrating just what your spell looks like and how it works. Depending on the elements you select (specifically, whether they're broadly-defined, narrowly-defined, improvised, etc), Al-Rawi may assign bonuses or penalties to the difficulty of your roll.

*For example: Mary is playing Labiba Bint Zafir, a Saabi sorceress who is performing a working to give life to a tree in the middle of the desert. She selects the elements "Tree" and "Life", as well as "Miracle" and "Alchemy". As the working isn't facing any active resistance from a sentient living target, the difficulty is 15, which Al-Rawi lowers by two steps each of -3, since she declares that only the two elements "Tree" and "Life" are essential to the working, and the two elements "Miracle" and "Alchemy" each provide supplementary element bonuses (page 119). The final difficulty for the working is 9.*

Next, optionally, you may choose the ancient art (page 125) which you use to express the form of the working (music, epic poetry, dance, and so on). You don't have to do this: however, it's a great way of adding colour to your tamasheq working and helping you describe the form your magic takes. Also, if you use the ancient art favoured by your clan (this won't always be possible—see page 126), you **gain a bonus die** on your Sacred Word skill roll.

Finally, make your INT + Sacred Word skill roll against the difficulty to perform the working. On a success, the working succeeds and the spell takes effect. Describe those effects, incorporating the ancient art used if appropriate (see page 126). On a failure, the working fails and the spell does not take effect. On a Critical Failure, the working fails disastrously and the spell effect rebounds against the al-kimyat in the worst way possible.

## Elements and the Magical Worlds

When performing tamasheq workings, al-kimyati manipulate their surroundings using the divine spark in their souls. They draw on ancient Saabi lore, including that of the Three Magical Worlds which they believe make up the cosmos: the Mundane World, the Philosophical World, and the Phantasmal World. Al-kimyati use elements from these worlds in their workings. Here is a description of each.

### The Mundane World

The Mundane World encompasses all that is physical, all that is perceptible by the five senses, and all that answers to the laws of nature. It includes objects, living beings, sounds, smells, tastes, pain, the four elements, the sun and the moon, wood, stone and metal, the human body, sand, and more.

## Tamasheq Summary

- ❖ **Step 1:** *Choose which Sacred Word to use.*
- ❖ **Step 2:** *Choose the elements needed for your working. Al-Rawi may adjust the difficulty as required.*
- ❖ **Step 3:** *Choose the ancient art which will be used in the working. You may gain a bonus die.*
- ❖ **Step 4:** *Make an INT + Sacred Word skill roll to perform the working.*

## The Philosophical World

The Philosophical World is the world of ideas. It contains everything that relates to the mind and mentality: thoughts and human concepts, judgements and opinions, and the fruits of the imagination. It includes the concepts of truth, equality, justice, and forgiveness; human interpretation; betrayal, naivity, and gentleness.

## The Phantasmal World

The Phantasmal World is made up of all things pertaining to emotions and urges, and the strange and inexplicable forces of the cosmos. It includes intuitions, flashes of genius, the arts, dreams and nightmares, fantasies; unreasonable fears such as phobias; universal concepts like life, death and time; the djinn, the dragons, the gods; and emotions like joy, sadness, wrath, love, hatred, happiness, and friendship.

Some elements may be found in more than one of the Magical Worlds, although when they do so they have different uses, interpretations, and applications. For example, one may perform a working to Cause Fear by using the Sacred Word Destroy to manipulate the Philosophical World element "Calm / Fear". In this case, the fear which results is justified and rational—perhaps it's the fear of being ridiculed or of being killed. However, if you do the same with the Phantasmal World element "Love / Fear", then the fear which results is more instinctive—perhaps a fear of veiled women, darkness, shadows.

## Magical Healing

*You can use magic such as Create Health to heal wounded targets. For major wounds (page 71), you must restore enough HP in a single casting to remove that wound entirely, otherwise the spell has no effect. For minor wounds (page 71), you may restore HP based on your magnitude. Usually, a given sorcerer may only attempt to heal a given wound once.*

## Learning New Tamasheq Elements

As an al-kimyat, learning your first magical elements is straightforward. Simply choose an element, and assign it to one of the Three Magical Worlds. It can be any element: the Magical Worlds are vast and unlimited. What matters most is to choose an element that will be useful in play. An element can be something broad, like a living being; or something more precisely defined, like the heart, or even a specific bone in the body. Knowing all the elements which themselves belong to another, broader element does not preclude you from also knowing the broader element; you may use the broadly-defined Mundane World element "Living Being" to target a person physically without using any of its component elements.

Learning elements during play, such as when your Sacred Word skill increases, is handled a little differently. The element which you pick to learn next must be related to the last element you learned. If you haven't learned any new elements yet (ie, this is the first time you're choosing a new element in play), then simply pick one of your starting elements as the "most recent" element you learned.

*For example: when your Sacred Word skill score increases by +1, you may learn two new elements. If the last element you learned was "Tree" from the Mundane World, then you must choose an element related in some way to trees. This is fairly broad: you could choose "Leaf" or "Wood", of course, but also you could choose "Life", "Light", or even "Earth". Let's say you choose "Light". If you then choose your second new element, it should in turn be related to "Light", and not "Tree". This time, let's say you choose "Sun". If your Sacred Word skill later increases again, you might then learn the elements "Moon" (related to "Sun") and then "Tide" (related to "Moon").*

The idea is to create a chain of linked elements. It's up to you to make and justify the links between the elements; Al-Rawi may disallow elements which are not clearly or logically linked, but once again there's a lot of room for leeway here, and any reasonable link should be allowed. This gradually extending chain of elements represents your al-kimyat character's own spiritual journey through the Magical Worlds.

Note that you don't have to stay within the same Magical World when you link a new element (although sometimes it may be obvious to). Once again, moving between the Magical Worlds is part of your al-kimyati character's exploration, and you can use such movements to create cool descriptions for your inner magical journey.

## Table 4-6: Example Tamasheq Elements

| Mundane World | Philosophical World | Phantasmal World |
|---|---|---|
| **BROADLY-DEFINED (+3 difficulty)** | | |
| The Elements | Human | Art |
| Heavenly Bodies | Interpretation | Demons |
| Living Beings | Judgement | Djinn |
| Physical Objects | Mental State | Dragons |
| Physical Sensation | Mind | Emotion |
| Sights | Opinion | Fantasies |
| Smells | Thought | Gods |
| Sounds | Truth | The Inexplicable |
| Tastes | | Intuition |
| Weapons | | Life / Death |
| | | Time |
| | | Undead |
| | | Urges |
| **NORMALLY-DEFINED** | | |
| Agility | Calm / Fear | The Arts |
| Air | Equality | Calm / Wrath |
| Bow | Fruits of the | Craving |
| Dexterity / | Imagination | Dream / Nightmare |
| Clumsiness | Ideal | Envy |
| Earth | Justice / Injustice | Love / Fear |
| Fire | Logic | Flash of Genius |
| Food | Openmindedness / | Happiness / Sadness |
| Health / Illness | Prejudice | Longing |
| Human Body | Perfection / | Love / Hate |
| Light / Darkness | Imperfection | Lust |
| Litheness | Proof / Refutation | Phobia |
| Metal | Sense / Nonsense | Sexual Desire |
| Moon | Will | Year |
| Pain | | |
| People | | |
| Person | | |
| Stone | | |
| Strength / | | |
| Weakness | | |
| Sun | | |
| Travel | | |
| Tree | | |
| Water | | |
| Wood | | |

| NARROWLY-DEFINED (-3 difficulty) | | |
|---|---|---|
| Corpse | Betrayal | Animated Skeleton |
| Granite | Complexity / | Claustrophobia |
| Hands | Simplicity | Enervation / |
| Heart | Forgiveness | Indolence |
| Ice | Gentleness | Friendship / Enmity |
| Iron | Maturity / | Joy / Misery |
| Jerky | Immaturity | Murder |
| Long Bow | Naivity | Sculpture |
| Man | Politeness / | This Year |
| Moonbeam | Rudeness | |
| Oak | Rationality / | |
| Quarter-Size | Irrationality | |
| Sand | Sophistication / | |
| Sandstone | Crudeness | |
| Semolina | Thought | |
| Sunlight | Thoughtfulness / | |
| Toothache | Thoughlessness | |
| Woman | | |

There are nine ancient arts, each linked to one of the nine **muses** of Agalanthian myth. Correspondingly, the nine Saabi clans have each developed a particular talent and preference for one Ancient Art. This doesn't prevent them from using the other arts, but, in game terms, an al-kimyat using his clan's preferred ancient art in a tamasheq working gains a bonus die on appropriate Sacred Word skill rolls.

Ancient Arts determine what tamasheq workings look like and how they work. Each Ancient Art also corresponds to one of *Capharnaum's* skills: the ancient art of Astronomy, for example, corresponds to the Science skill. You don't have to make an Ancient Arts dice roll when you use an ancient art in a working, but if you do have the skill and the time, you may spend an action to make a **Help action** (page 55) using the corresponding skill (see Table 4-7: Ancient Arts Skill Correspondences).

When you use an ancient art in a working, remember that it doesn't just represent the way the spell works, but also the way your character is casting it. This means that some situations will be unsuitable for the use of some ancient arts. An al-kimyati riding a horse at full gallop will have trouble writing something down, for example. Also, it's a rare working that can be used with all nine of the Ancient Arts: some arts are simply inappropriate for certain workings. You should talk this through with Al-Rawi if you think a given ancient art may or may not be particularly appropriate, with the proviso that the use of the Ancient Arts is meant to add colour to al-kimyati magic, not to restrict the fun you have in your game!

Here's a list of the nine Ancient Arts and their muses, together with some suggested effects they may have on spells. You're encouraged to explore the nature of the arts and their muses more deeply to expand upon these effects.

## The Ancient Arts

The Ancient Arts are the outward forms by which tamasheq workings manifest in the world. Workings often derive their names from them.

The Ancient Arts themselves are not of Saabi origin. They were inherited centuries ago from the Agalanthians when the Empire still ruled over Jazirat. Today, the Ancient Arts are part of Saabi culture, used not only by al-kimyati but by tribal artists of all kinds.

## Ancient Arts Skills

There are no Ancient Arts skills on the **Capharnaum** skill list (see **Chapter One: Polymnia – Character Creation**, page 26). Instead, each Ancient Art corresponds to a particular skill. If a situation ever requires an Ancient Arts skill roll, you can use the corresponding skill as shown on Table 4-7: Ancient Arts Skill Correspondences.

| TABLE 4-7: ANCIENT ARTS SKILL CORRESPONDENCES | | | |
|---|---|---|---|
| ANCIENT ART | CORRE-SPONDING SKILL | MUSE | PREFERRED BY CLAN… |
| Astronomy | Science | Urania | Ibn Yussef Abd-al-Salif |
| Comedy | Acting | Thalia | Ibn Mussah Abd-al-Has-san |
| Dance | Elegance | Terpsichore | Ibn Khalil Abd-al-Salif |
| Writing & Mime | Acting | Polymnia | Ibn Yazid Abd-al-Tarek |
| History | History & Peoples | Clio | Ibn Rashid Abd-al-Has-san |
| Music | Music | Euterpe | Ibn Malik Abd-al-Has-san |
| Epic Poetry | Poetry | Calliope | Ibn Tufiq Abd-al-Tarek |
| Lyric Poetry | Poetry | Erato | Ibn Mimun Abd-al-Tarek |
| Tragedy | Acting | Melpomene | Ibn Aziz Abd-al-Salif |

### Astronomy and Urania

To cast a work using Astronomy or Astrology, you must trace a constellation with your fingertips in the air before you and in the direction of your target. Urania's tamasheq is filled with notions of orientation, travelling, destiny, and divination, and is associated with the desert and the sea and everything within them; with the night, stars, and moon; with cycles, material or spiritual paths, wishes and omens.

*Example Workings: The target is convinced he has accomplished his destiny; he is disoriented and lost; he feels the need for renewal.*

### Comedy and Thalia

To perform a working using Comedy, you must cup your mouth with your hands and recite a brief comic tirade, which must be heard by the target (but not necessarily understood). Thalia's tamasheq is filled with feelings of happiness, joy, peacefulness, relief, and of course laughter and smiling, and is connected to misunderstandings, equivocal situations, lying, staging, deceit, diplomacy, false pretences and deceptive appearances, the ephemeral, and twists and revelations.

*Example Workings: The target is fooled by the sorcerer; takes him for something he isn't; feels hugely well; thinks he is having a revelation.*

### Dance and Terpsichore

To perform a working using Dance, you must perform a brief dance with steps and rhythm based on the effects you desire. The dance need not be seen by your target. Terpsichore's tamasheq is filled with grace, beauty, elegance, lightness, movement, and change, and is associated with rhythm, freedom, unpredictability, flexibility, effort, perseverance, and couples.

*Example Workings: The target enters a state of grace, and feels untouchable; he yearns to be more flexible, in touch with his surroundings; he feels a need for change.*

### Writing, Mime, and Polymnia

To perform a working using Writing or Mime, you must either write a brief text (which need not be read to or by your target) or mime an action. Polymnia's tamasheq is imbued with thoughtfulness, calmness and silence, with poise, accuracy, concentration, creativity, and creation, and is associated with narration, inspiration, persuasion, philosophy, adventure, wonders, manipulation, imitation, and even derision.

*Example Workings: The target has writer's block or another form of creative or mental blockage; feels the urge to be a storyteller; no longer feels like talking at all.*

### History and Clio

To perform a working using History, you must close your eyes and visualise a past historical scene. The type of scene—battle, a meeting, someone's death—depends on the effects you desire. Clio's tamasheq grants wisdom, erudition, greatness and decadence, memory, amnesia and forgetfulness, uncertainty and doubt, red

herrings, lessons, experience, old age, and death. It is associated with extrapolation, synthesis, errors, incomprehension, legends, anticipation, and immersion.

*Example Workings: The target feels like he knows a people's customs; has trouble searching and untangling his memories; feels like there's a lesson to be learned from the situation.*

## Music and Euterpe

To perform a working using Music, you must play or hum a melody or rhythm, either using an instrument or simply by singing or whistling. The target of the working must hear the music. Euterpe's tamasheq inspires creativity, beauty, play, spiritual journeys, improvisation, the sensation of being part of a greater whole, sensitivity, nobility of soul, generosity, union, listening and attention. It's associated with bewitchment, charm and charisma, admiration, morals, subtlety and daintiness.

*Example Workings: The target feels much more sensitive and vulnerable; pays full attention to whatever the sorcerer chooses; appears more charismatic.*

## Epic Poetry and Calliope

To perform a working using Epic Poetry, you must fervently recite an epic poem that must be heard by the target of the spell. Calliope's tamasheq exhorts to eloquence, the spectacular, violence, strength, subjugation, crowds, enthusiasm, youth, morale, carelessness, courage, confrontation, rebellion, ordeals, physical fitness, and moral behaviour. It often affects crowds, and is associated with fantasy and the unbelievable, sagas and odysseys, nobility of heart and grandiose sentiments.

*Example Workings: The target feels subjugated by the situation or by a specific person; is completely demoralised; is easily impressed; feels he has the soul of a hero.*

## Lyric Poetry and Erato

To perform a working using Lyric Poetry, you must recite a few verses that must be heard by the target of the spell. Erato's tamasheq whispers of the pleasures of physical charms, power, spiritual and physical enjoyment, flights of fancy, finesse, attraction, self-overcoming, and carnal pleasure, and is associated with love and betrayal, revenge, exceptionalism, perfection, rest and prayer, and the whirl of intoxicating emotion.

*Example Workings: The target feels above everything; is overwhelmed by a flood of troubling emotions; is physically attracted to someone; wants to go beyond his own limitations.*

## Tragedy and Melpomene

To perform a working using Tragedy, you must recite a tragic speech that must be heard by the target of the spell. Melpomene's tamasheq is filled with unhappy emotions, sadness, sorrow, despair, melancholy, nostalgia, fear, anguish, the fear of being in public, the loss of well-being, malaise, apprehension, and bitterness. It's associated with the accoutrements of drama, emphatic and declamatory speech and behaviour, morbid fascination, terror, pity, torture, abandonment, treachery, cowardice, suicide, stubborn fury, jealousy, the weight of years and decisions, renunciation, pain, mourning, madness and suffering.

*Example Workings: The target feels stricken, as if a terrible drama has just happened; no longer has the courage to keep fighting; feels unfounded jealousy; is overcome with bitterness.*

# Tamasheq Workings

Saabi magic is intensely personal. Each of the Sacred Words is linked to one of their gods: Creation is the province of Hubal the All-Powerful, uncontested master of the Saabi pantheon; Transformation is the purview of Al-Uzza, mother of the world, goddess of love; and Destruction comes from Manat, daughter and mother of Hubal, goddess of death.

The Tarmel Haja of the Saabi tamasheq and the other peoples of Capharnaum as presented here is intended to be a very flexible form of magic which you can use creatively, improvising magical effects on the fly. Over time, though, you may find that you come to use some magical effects more than others; effectively these become "favourite spells", which you may even want to jot down and give names to.

Similarly—and especially when you first start playing *Capharnaum*—you may sometimes find the freeform nature of the Tarmel Haja to leave you with option paralysis. There are *a lot* of things you can do with sorcery, and sometimes it may be hard to work out how to do what.

For both of the above reasons, we're going to present in this section and in the two sections below (see page 130 and page 133) a number of **pregenerated spells** which are intended to showcase just what you can do with the Tarmel Haja. These spells have been formulated using the rules above, so they're the type of things you could come up with yourself. If you like, you can use these during play, or use them as examples and templates for improvising your own spell effects or even defining more pregenerated spells. *Capharnaum* isn't intended to be the type of game with pages and pages of strictly defined spells, but we figured an example selection would be a useful reference.

## Starting Characters With Pregenerated Spells

*You can pick pregenerated spells for your beginning sorcerer characters. For each point of Sacred Word skill, pick two spells. Make sure that you follow the rules for Sacred Words given on page 31: if you have a Sacred Word skill of 1 or 2, you may only have spells with the same Sacred Word (Create, Transform, or Destroy, etc), and so on.*

*Note that, if you do this, the elements you begin play knowing will be determined by the spells you know. This may actually be more or less than the number of elements you'd normally know using the rules on page 31. Don't worry too much about this; you can use these elements, and the Sacred Words you know, to create spell effects using the Tarmel Haja as usual.*

*Likewise, you can use AP as normal to buy new Sacred Words and elements. If you want to buy a pregenerated spell, then simply multiply the number of new elements in that spell by 15 AP. Note that you must buy the Sacred Word skill (Create, Transform, or Destroy) separately, following the rules on page 80.*

### Body Excellence

❖ **Preferred Art:** Dance.
❖ **Sacred Word:** Transform.
❖ **Elements:** Body, Agility, Strength, Litheness, and Me / You / A Person (Mundane World)
❖ **Difficulty:** 9 or 6.

This working is usually cast by an al-kimyat on himself before going through a physical challenge; the difficulty is 9, or 6 if the sorcerer has himself as a narrowly-defined element. Using the magnitude gained on the Sacred Word roll, the al-kimyat gains attribute bonuses on DEX, STR, and / or CON for the spell duration. Note that a magnitude of 2 is the minimum magnitude required for this spell to be successful.

### Freezebrittle

❖ **Preferred Art:** Epic Poetry.
❖ **Sacred Word:** Transform.
❖ **Elements:** Ice, Metal (Mundane World); Thought / Will (Philosophical World).
❖ **Difficulty:** 15.

This working gives the target the ability to destroy metal he is touching by cooling it in an extreme way with the power of his thoughts. If you're casting this spell on yourself, you only need the Metal and Ice elements, and may cast the spell at range by spending magnitude (see Table 4-1: Magical Effect Parameters on page 118). By default, the spell affects one weapon-sized object; you may spend magnitude to affect larger objects. Any metal object affected

will shatter if struck hard immediately (or within the duration if you spend magnitude). On a Critical Success, the object explodes, doing damage based on the unspent magnitude to anyone within 5 feet or so (or more if you spend magnitude).

### Infatuation

❖ **Preferred Art:** Lyric Poetry.
❖ **Sacred Word:** Create.
❖ **Elements:** Man / Woman (Mundane World); Sexual Desire (Phantasmal World).
❖ **Difficulty:** Resistance roll (-3 penalty).

This working causes a target within range (page 118) to feel overwhelming sexual desire for another person, man or woman. He'll do anything to please that person, seduce them, protect them, and of course take them to his bed. The effect lasts as long as the spell duration.

### Murderous Urge

❖ **Preferred Art:** Tragedy.
❖ **Sacred Word:** Create.
❖ **Elements:** Murder (Mundane World); Mind (Philosophical World); Craving (Phantasmal World).
❖ **Difficulty:** Resistance roll.

The working creates an irresistible homicidal urge in the target's mind, which can only be exorcised by committing a murder. If an element representing an intended murder victim isn't included in the working, the target attempts to kill the first person he sees, or himself if alone.

### Naturalisation

❖ **Preferred Art:** Comedy.
❖ **Sacred Word:** Transform.
❖ **Elements:** A Person, A People, Body (Mundane World).
❖ **Difficulty:** 15 or resistance roll.

This working causes the target to assume the physical traits of the Blood or people specified by the al-kimyat, and for the duration of the spell he may pass as a member of that people. He doesn't gain any knowledge of the people in question (including language, history, folklore, etc), but he will be able to move about unnoticed in a city or a camp, or deceive a person who isn't expert in the ways of that people.

### Openmind

❖ **Preferred Art:** History.
❖ **Sacred Word:** Create.
❖ **Elements:** Openmindedness / Prejudice (Philosophical World); a target prejudice.
❖ **Difficulty:** Resistance roll (-3 penalty).

This working makes a target less narrow-minded. Specifically, the spell removes all prejudices the target has concerning a specific subject, chosen as an element when you learn this spell, which reduces the spell difficulty by -3 (a narrowly-defined element: see page

119). You may remove a prejudice for which you don't know the element by improvising that element, but the difficulty of the spell is increased by +6 (see page 119).

## Politeness
- ❖ **Preferred Art:** Music.
- ❖ **Sacred Word:** Create.
- ❖ **Elements:** Politeness (Philosophical World).
- ❖ **Difficulty:** Resistance roll (-3 penalty) or 6.

The target (or targets) of this spell becomes extremely polite and will do anything to make everybody happy and, most of all, to ruffle no feathers. This isn't ridiculously exaggerated politeness, but rather the art of being diplomatic and presenting things in acceptable ways. The working helps smooth the way through difficult negotiations or towards a reconciliation with your partner.

## Restore Life
- ❖ **Preferred Art:** Astrology.
- ❖ **Sacred Word:** Transform.
- ❖ **Elements:** Corpse (Mundane World); Life / Death (Phantasmal World).
- ❖ **Difficulty:** 15.

This work restores life in a dead body whose time has not yet come. If the target is already old or has otherwise died of natural causes, the working will have no effect. Otherwise, the target is restored to life for the duration of the spell. Sacred Word Transform is used because the working does not create new life, but restores the life that was there before (transforming death into life). Note that this working does not heal wounds; if the target had died of wounds, his body is alive with the HP at which he died (which may mean he is unconscious). If the target has not been sufficiently healed by the time the spell duration is up, it dies again.

## Sand to Jerky
- ❖ **Preferred Art:** Writing & Mime.
- ❖ **Sacred Word:** Transform.
- ❖ **Elements:** Sand, Jerky (Mundane World).
- ❖ **Difficulty:** 9.

This working transforms sand into jerked meat. It's a common spell among the al-kimyati who travel the desert, and has saved the life of more than one starving Saabi. The jerky created will remain edible for the duration of the spell (depending on the magnitude—see page 118), after which it will turn back into sand.

## Shrink
- ❖ **Preferred Art:** Writing & Mime.
- ❖ **Sacred Word:** Transform.
- ❖ **Elements:** Quarter Size (Mundane World); target is any Mundane World element.
- ❖ **Difficulty:** Resistance roll (-3 penalty or +6 bonus); or 12 or 21.

This working reduces the size of a target element to exactly one quarter of its original size; it has a -3 difficulty modifier. You may also reduce the target to a different size by incurring a +6 difficulty penalty. If the spell duration ends and the target doesn't have room to return to its original size, it will break through any confinements or be destroyed, depending on its nature.

## Wanderlust
- ❖ **Preferred Art:** Astronomy.
- ❖ **Sacred Word:** Create.
- ❖ **Elements:** A Person, Travel (Mundane World); Longing (Phantasmal World).
- ❖ **Difficulty:** Resistance roll.

This working fills the target with an irresistible longing for a change of scenery, to leave everything behind and just go. He will continue to be obsessed with this idea for as long as the spell's duration, or until such time as he actually makes a voyage to some truly exotic location, and will be unable to start new projects or undertake actions requiring his full concentration.

# The Shiradim and Tasannu

**Tasannu** is a Shiradi word referring to the flourish, panache, or energy used in the effective enunciation of a speech. Those with tasannu speak in a grandiloquent tone, constructing beautiful and sophisticated sentences, filling their words with conviction. By extension, **tasannu** has also come to refer to Shiradi sorcery, which itself is based on specific forms of speech.

Using tasannu, Shiradi sephirim construct sentences, calling upon Shirad to transform their sentences into reality. It's a procedure similar to a prayer, but the Shiradim prefer the term **covenant** to refer to their particular form of magic: a sephir formulates a covenant using his tasannu, and Shirad fulfils it.

To formulate a covenant, a sephir selects which Sacred Word he will use (Create, Transform, or Destroy), and then chooses the "**names**" (elements—see page 119) he will combine with it to address Shirad. Once the covenant is constructed, the sephir enunciates it, chants it, whispers it, or even shouts it, depending upon its contents and the desired effect.

*For example: Madih Bar Saad, sephir and poet at the court of Jergath, has vowed to refrain from wine for thirty days and nights as an act of faith. In a banquet with foreign dignitaries where he is negotiating a trade treaty, Madih is offered an exotic wine he can't refuse without offending his guest. However, he still needs to keep his vow. He decides to formulate a covenant to change the wine into water. He selects the Sacred Word Transform, which he combines with the names "Wine" and "Water". He then whispers the covenant: "I transform this wine into water" in such a way that no one can hear him. He can then drink the contents of the glass without causing a diplomatic incident, and while keeping his vow.*

## Covenant Names

The Shiradim, during their enslavement, developed an oral form of sorcery drawing upon the power of their god. Today their practices have evolved, but are still based on the enunciation of formulated names for Shirad to hear and make real. Covenant names have nothing intrinsically magical about them: they're words spoken daily by anyone. The important thing is for the convenant to be understood by Shirad; that is where the magic lies.

Unlike the Saabi and Quarterians, the Shiradim don't categorise their covenant names in Magical Worlds or Domains. In fact, there are only two categories: **Sacred Words** (Create, Transform, and Destroy) and **covenant names**, which are magical elements (see page 119). These names are numerous, not to say infinite: they can be proper nouns (the names of people and places), or general nouns referring to things. A sephir wanting to manipulate bees may know the name "Bee" (a narrowly-defined element) or "Insect" (a normally-defined element).

Sephirim have no restrictions on learning new names; they need not be linked, and sorcerers may choose them as they see fit.

## Tasannu Covenants

A covenant is a temporary agreement between a sephir and Shirad. According to this improbable association, the god listens to the wish formulated by the sorcerer, and fulfils it if the sorcerer proves worthy.

The Shiradim associate each Sacred Word with a Face of Shirad (see page 263). Creation is associated with **Innpa**, the female Face of Shirad representing birth, apparitions and miracles; Destruction is associated with **Caiya**, the male Face representing endings, death, and renewal; and Transformation is associated with **Assiel**, the androgynous Face representing evolution, change, and time.

Each Shiradi tribe specialises in a certain type of covenant, for which their sephirim gain a bonus die. The Ashkenim, peerless fighters, are gifted with names relating to battles and physical conflicts, including agility, strength, and reflexes; the Pharatim have a gift for names relating to thought, memory, reflection, and philosophy; and the Salonim have a gift for names relating to life and death, birth, care, healing, pain, and even torture.

Here's a selection of sample covenants. You can use these as templates, or you can choose them for your characters using the guidelines on page 128.

### Amnesia
- ❖ **Sacred Word:** Destroy.
- ❖ **Covenant Names:** A Person, Memories, A Word.
- ❖ **Difficulty:** Resistance roll (-3 penalty) or 6.

This powerful and dangerous covenant destroys all of a target's memories related to a specific theme or word. This may be as trivial as forgetting a meeting, right up to turning the target into a mindless vegetable. When the duration ends, the memories return.

### Artistic Talent
- ❖ **Sacred Word:** Create.
- ❖ **Covenant Names:** An Art, Person.
- ❖ **Difficulty:** Resistance roll (-3 penalty) or 6.

This covenant bestows an artistic talent upon the target: the ability to declaim a poem to a court, to play a melody in a tavern, to paint a canvas, to perform an artistic dance, and so on. The covenant bestows the desired artistic skill on the target at a skill score based on the magnitude spent (page 118). When the duration ends, the skill is lost.

### The Call of the Djinn
- ❖ **Sacred Word:** Create.
- ❖ **Covenant Names:** Person, Call or Voice.
- ❖ **Difficulty:** Resistance roll.

This covenant allows the sephir to summon a person to him. The only prerequisite is that he must have seen the target at least once; it doesn't matter if the target knows the sorcerer or not. The target will hear the Call of the Djinn wherever he is, and will feel compelled to immediately begin to move towards the sephir. The effects of the covenant fade once the duration has ended, or as soon as the target is in sight of the sephir. Until then, he will do everything necessary short of risking his life to get to the sephir.

### Combust Organ
- ❖ **Sacred Word:** Create or Destroy.
- ❖ **Covenant Names:** Fire, An Organ, Person.
- ❖ **Difficulty:** Resistance roll (-3 penalty).

This covenant causes one of the target's organs, specified by the sephir, to catch fire and be consumed inside his body. The intolerable pain makes him scream; after a few seconds, he loses consciousness, and dies in the following hour unless he can get medical or magical care. If the targeted organ isn't a vital one, the target may survive (at Al-Rawi's discretion, and possibly requiring a CON attribute roll).

### Desiccation
- ❖ **Sacred Word:** Destroy.
- ❖ **Covenant Names:** Water, a living being or object.
- ❖ **Difficulty:** Resistance roll or 15.

This covenant eliminates any trace of water in the body of a living being or an object. In the course of a few seconds, the target dries up and possibly even turns to dust. The covenant does HP damage to a living target, based on the spell's magnitude (see page 118), but will also empty a waterskin in the desert or even dry wood to make a fire.

### Galvanise
- ❖ **Sacred Word:** Create.
- ❖ **Covenant Names:** Person or Crowd, Enthusiasm.
- ❖ **Difficulty:** Resistance roll or 9.

This covenant galvanises one or more persons (depending on the magnitude) to action. A covenant such as "I fill the people with the fervour of Shirad!" is pronounced; if the Sacred Word roll is successful, the target or targets will follow the sephir's instructions with an appropriate degree of enthusiasm. A galvanised target won't do anything to directly risk their own life, but they may support a fiery speech, become enraged and attack a building, block streets, and so on. Once the spell duration ends, the targets will disperse naturally, without asking questions.

### Immaculate Conception
- ❖ **Sacred Word:** Create.
- ❖ **Covenant Names:** Life, Woman, Womb / Loins.
- ❖ **Difficulty:** Resistance roll or 9.

This covenant impregnates a female target. Nine months later, she gives birth to a child. The covenant works even if the target is sterile, although she must be of childbearing age.

### Incandescent Light
- ❖ **Sacred Word:** Transform.
- ❖ **Covenant Names:** Fire, Light.
- ❖ **Difficulty:** 15.

The covenant works two ways. First, it allows the sephir to transform a fire into a cold source of light. This illuminates like daylight, in a radius not exceeding that of the original fire. The light will go out when the fire would have otherwise been extinguished naturally. Second, this covenant allows the sephir to turn light into fire. A house in the sunlight may thus burst into flames (note that you'll need a target element or an improvisation penalty in this case). Critical Failures with this covenant are especially dangerous, especially if the sephir is himself bathed in light!

### Rose-Tinted Vision
- ❖ **Sacred Word:** Transform.
- ❖ **Covenant Names:** Person or Animal, Vision or Eye.
- ❖ **Difficulty:** Resistance roll (-3 penalty) or 6.

This covenant can sometimes work miracles, but can also make a situation much worse. It causes the target to see what he wants to see. This doesn't create an illusion, but rather modifies the target's perception of his environment based on his preconceptions. This means he'll see a woman as beautiful if he's positively inclined, or ugly if he's suspicious or hateful by nature. The sephir can tell his target that he's going to the king's palace: if that's something that would delight or flatter him, he'll be enchanted by the next hovel he's shown; but if he sees the king as wicked and evil, the most beautiful dwelling will appear to him like a terrifying dungeon.

### Water of Death, Water of Life
- ❖ **Sacred Word:** Transform.
- ❖ **Covenant Names:** Poison, Water.
- ❖ **Difficulty:** 15.

This covenant transforms any poisoned liquid into clear, pure water. It's used to counter possible assassination attempts, or when refusing an alcoholic drink would cause a diplomatic incident.

# The Quarterians and Miracles

**Miracles** is the name for Quarterian sorcery. To pray for a miracle, a Quarterian thaumaturgist formulates a request to Aether, combining a Sacred Word with one or more magical elements from the three magical **Domains**, and including a certain number of **homages** aiming to please the god and attract his blessing. Holding his rosary, he speaks the prayer either silently in his head, in a whisper, or out loud.

*For example: Wido Carem, an Occidentian thaumaturgist, wants to pray for a miracle to open a blocked door. He chooses the Sacred Word "Create" and the elements "Door" and "Rot" from the Ephemeral Domain, and "Time" from the Receptacle Domain. He adds the homages "Aether almighty", "thy will be done", and "glory to thee, o lord". Wido then whispers: "Glory to thee, o lord, Aether almighty, create rot in this door so thy will be done". His prayer is heard, and the miracle is granted: Wido breaks the now weakened wood the door is made of to discover what lies beyond.*

## Thaumaturgical Elements and Spiritual Domains

Thaumaturgists work miracles by prayer, unconsciously obeying Aether's will to take them one step further in the Almighty's "Grand Design". To formulate these prayers, they draw elements from the Three Spiritual Domains (Ephemeral, Eternal, and Receptacle) taught by the Holy Quarterian Church. These Domains encompass the whole of Creation, by means of sacred correspondences with the human form from which the thaumaturgists draw their inspiration. Here is a brief description of each Domain, with example elements for each.

### The Ephemeral Domain

The Ephemeral Domain corresponds to the human body. It encompasses everything in nature that is physical and perceptible to the senses. It includes the elements, living beings, the stars, buildings, physical sensations like pleasure or pain, wind, clouds, or the air you breathe.

### The Eternal Domain

The Eternal Domain corresponds to the human mind. It includes all things pertaining to spirituality and thought, including opinions, ideas, prejudices, wisdom, cogitation and meditation, intellectual endurance, attention and concentration, psychoses and mental illnesses, philosophy, stupidity, and openness of mind.

### The Receptacle Domain

The Receptacle Domain corresponds to the human soul. It encompasses dreams, art and the phantasmal, and includes nightmares, delirium, love at first sight, genius, emotions, gods and dragons, the Dragon-Marked, life and death, mystery, the unexplained, and the impossible.

As a thaumaturgist, you may be unsure which Domain a given element belongs to, because many seem to apply. Some elements may even belong to several Domains. In any case, choose a specific Domain for the element you learn to belong to. Unlike the al-kimyati of the Saabi, but like the Shiradi sephirim, Quarterian thaumaturgists have no restrictions when learning new elements, and may choose whichever ones they want.

### Homages

Thaumaturgists claim to have no personal magical power, and that their miracles come from Almighty Aether. However, addressing Aether is an act reserved for the most faithful and devoted of his servants, since it requires formulating very specific and codified prayers, requesting the attention of the god.

Specifically, when a thaumaturgist prays for a miracle, he formulates the effect he wants as a request. This request may be simple and direct, although the Quarterians have developed elaborate forms of politeness and servility towards Aether which they hope will grant them additional blessings.

These forms of politeness and servility are called **homages**. They are short formulae that, when included in a prayer, make the granting of the miracle more likely. Each homage included in a prayer reduces the difficulty of the Sacred Word skill roll by -1, and increases the time taken for the prayer by one action. Table 4-8: Example Homages includes several popular homages; you're encouraged to come up with your own.

*For example: "Lord Almighty, I am not worthy of Thy wisdom, but I pray to Thee, heal the body of this woman, and my body will be Thine until thou callest me to Thy side. May Thy kingdom last forever, amen." In this prayer you can find five homages; praying for the miracle will therefore take six actions (three rounds), and the difficulty will be reduced by -5.*

| Table 4-8: Example Homages |
| --- |
| Lord Almighty |
| Thy Kingdom Come |
| Glory to Thee |
| Praised Be |
| Father of the Righteous |
| Protector of the Faithful |
| Creator of All Things |
| Blessed Be |
| I will serve Thee unto Death |
| In thy Great Wisdom |
| I am not worthy |

## Quarterian Miracles

Quarterian miracles depend upon communion with Aether. However, unlike the Shiradim, when a thaumaturgist prays for a miracle, he does not believe it is his own choice, but rather Aether who is inspiring him to request divine aid. When a miracle is granted, it is Aether bestowing upon the thaumaturgist the honour of participating in His Grand Design, granting him the miracle's desired magical effect.

The Quarterians associate each Sacred Word with one of their divinities. Creation is the purview of Aether, the Almighty God;

| TABLE 4-9: THAUMATURGICAL ELEMENTS | | |
|---|---|---|
| **EPHEMERAL DOMAIN** | **ETERNAL DOMAIN** | **RECEPTACLE DOMAIN** |
| BROADLY-DEFINED (+3 difficulty) | | |
| Cloth<br>The Five Senses<br>The Four Elements<br>Heavenly Bodies<br>Living Beings<br>Physical Sensations<br>Place | The Human Mind<br>Ideas<br>Spirituality<br>Thoughts | Art<br>Atmosphere<br>Demons<br>Dragons<br>Emotions<br>Gods<br>The Human Soul<br>Life / Death<br>The Phantasmal |
| NORMALLY-DEFINED | | |
| Air<br>Animal<br>Armour<br>Beauty / Ugliness<br>Buildings<br>Clothing<br>Fertility / Infertility<br>Fire<br>Flesh<br>Food<br>Health / Illness<br>Heat / Cold<br>Hole / Patch<br>The Human Body<br>Large Size / Small Size<br>Light / Darkness<br>Lightness / Heaviness<br>Metal<br>Pain<br>People<br>Person<br>Pleasure<br>Poison<br>Sight<br>Sound<br>Speed / Slowness<br>The Stars | Coherence<br>Growth / Dying<br>Intelligence / Stupidity<br>Mental Illnesses<br>Openmindedness / Prejudice<br>Philanthropy / Misanthropy<br>Philosophy<br>Politeness | The Arts<br>Calm / Anger<br>Dragon-Marked<br>Dreams<br>Genius<br>Ghosts<br>The Impossible<br>Mystery<br>The Unexplained |

| NARROWLY-DEFINED (-3 difficulty) | | |
|---|---|---|
| Bat<br>Beer<br>Body Part<br>Boots<br>Bread<br>Breath<br>Clouds<br>Dog<br>Flame<br>Growth / Dying<br>Hands<br>Magnet<br>Pregnancy / Barrenness<br>Scimitar<br>Sirius<br>Vision<br>Voice<br>Wind | Attention<br>Cogitation<br>Concentration<br>Confession<br>Intellectual<br>Endurance<br>Meditation<br>Megalomania<br>Racism<br>Wisdom / Foolishness | Aether<br>Artistic Genius<br>Delirium<br>Dream / Nightmare<br>Epic Poetry<br>Faith / Loss of Faith<br>Happiness / Sadness<br>Jason Quartered<br>Love at First Sight<br>Mental Robustness<br>Musicality<br>Optimism / Pessimism<br>Peaceability / Aggressiveness<br>Writing |

In game terms, a thaumaturgist gains one bonus die on his Sacred Word skill rolls to pray for miracles which include one or more elements from his preferred Domain. This bonus is not cumulative.

There are many ways to pray for a miracle. The prayer may be silent or whispered, chanted or shouted. Most thaumaturgists use rosaries, each bead calling on a spiritual element.

Here is a list of pregenerated miracles, for use as templates or as spells for your thaumaturgist characters according to the rules on page 128. Naturally, you may use the Tarmel Haja combination magic to pray for freeform miracles instead.

### Call Clouds
- ❖ **Sacred Word:** Create.
- ❖ **Elements:** Clouds (Ephemeral Domain).
- ❖ **Difficulty:** 12.

This miracle allows the thaumaturgist to pray for clouds to form in the sky directly above him. The prayer is much appreciated in hot, dry areas, as it provides a few hours' shade and maybe even rain. It can also be very useful for impressing non-sorcerers: the clouds form with astonishing speed.

### Confession
- ❖ **Sacred Word:** Create.
- ❖ **Elements:** A Place (Ephemeral Domain); Confession (Eternal Domain); Atmosphere (Receptacle Domain).
- ❖ **Difficulty:** Resistance roll (+3 penalty).

With this miracle, the thaumaturgist imbues his current location with an atmosphere conductive to confession. Targets will reveal secrets they know, relieve their consciences, feel guilty, share their pains and burdens. Some unscrupulous thaumaturgists use this miracle to quickly become rich, powerful, and influential; others use it to justly punish hardened sinners and criminals.

Transformation is the gift of the goddess Mira / Nerea; and Destruction is the purview of Jason the Rebel, Son of Aether.

The Quarterians are divided among themselves, and rule over three great nations, whose worship specialises in one of the three spiritual Domains. The Aragonians, peerless mounted warriors, specialise in prayers including elements of the Ephemeral Domain; the Orkadians, hard, cold fighters, favour prayers with elements from the Eternal Domain; and the Occidentians, seasoned priests, lean towards prayers involving elements from the Receptacle Domain.

## Crisis of Faith

- ❖ **Sacred Word:** Destroy.
- ❖ **Elements:** A Person (Ephemeral Domain); Faith (Receptacle Domain)
- ❖ **Difficulty:** Resistance roll (-3 penalty).

The target of this miracle undergoes a crisis of faith. He doubts the existence of his god or gods, and stops listening to his priests. His Faith score is reduced based on the magnitude spend (see page 118) for the miracle's duration. If this reduces the target's Faith to 0, then even when the miracle ends, the target loses one point of Faith permanently (AP may restore this).

## Draconic Inspiration

- ❖ **Sacred Word:** Create.
- ❖ **Elements:** Breath (Ephemeral Domain), Dragons (Receptacle Domain)
- ❖ **Difficulty:** 15.

This uncommon prayer is known only to a few thaumaturgists. It calls upon Aether to inspire the caster with the breath of the holy dragons. For the duration of the miracle, the whites of the thaumaturgist's eyes blaze like the sunset, while his irises turn night-blue, speckled with stars. Filled with dragon power, he becomes stronger, faster, more enduring, and may treat all the dice used in dice rolls as dragon dice!

## Fuse

- ❖ **Sacred Word:** Transform.
- ❖ **Elements:** Two objects (Ephemeral Domain).
- ❖ **Difficulty:** 15, or a resistance roll.

This miracle welds two objects together for the duration of the spell. They may be separated by force, weapons, or magic, but risk being damaged or becoming unusable. Some thaumaturgists use this on living beings, which requires a resistance roll if the targets are unwilling. If you ever meet conjoined strangers, consider that they may have fallen foul of a thaumaturgist... In time of war, this prayer is a crude form of healing, used to fuse the wounds of soldiers injured in battle; the process leaves impressive scars. Finally, some priests use it to wound and then heal themselves in impressive ceremonies, showing the world Aether's power of healing the faithful.

## Lay On Hands

- ❖ **Sacred Word:** Create.
- ❖ **Elements:** The Human Body, Health / Illness (Ephemeral Domain).
- ❖ **Difficulty:** Resistance roll or 9.

This miracle heals wounds represented by HP damage; it restores HP based on the magnitude spend (see page 118). If the miracle fails, it may not be tried again on the same wound. It is usually done by laying on hands, and on a single target, to permit the greatest amount of magnitude to be devoted towards healing; although powerful thaumaturgists may heal multiple targets, and at range.

## Living Magnet

- ❖ **Sacred Word:** Transform.
- ❖ **Elements:** Hands, Magnet, A Person (Ephemeral Domain)
- ❖ **Difficulty:** Resistance roll (-6 penalty) or 6.

This miracle transforms the target's hands into powerful magnets. Their appearance remains the same, but they will attract any metal object (or metal-containing object), as long as that object's weight is less than the target's Strength score in pounds multiplied by twenty (STR x 20lb). You can rip a door off its hinges, relieve a soldier of his weapon (make an opposed STR roll), make knives fly out of your hands and across a room (causing HP damage), or knock a target in heavy armour to the floor (STR vs DEX).

## Nerea's Breath

- ❖ **Sacred Word:** Transform.
- ❖ **Elements:** Air (Ephemeral Domain), one element, Person.
- ❖ **Difficulty:** Resistance roll or 9.

This powerful miracle allows the thaumaturgist to control what enters the lungs of his chosen target (usually a person). The thaumaturgist chooses a magical element in addition to the element "Air" from the Ephemeral Domain; he may then transform the air entering or leaving a target's lungs into that element, or transform that element into air if it is entering the target's lungs.

*For example: By praying for Nerea's Breath using the elements "Air" and "Water", the thaumaturgist can bestow upon the target the ability to breathe underwater, or to spit water when breathing out. With the elements "Air" and "Sulphur", Nerea's Breath allows the target, with the aid of a naked flame, to spit jets of fire—at the risk of burning their lungs!*

## Nightmare

- ❖ **Sacred Word:** Create, Transform, or Destroy.
- ❖ **Elements:** A Person (Ephemeral Domain); Nightmare (Receptacle Domain); any other element (or two elements for Transform or maybe Destroy).
- ❖ **Difficulty:** Resistance roll (-3 penalty).

This miracle is generally used against non-believers or enemies of the Quarterian Church (these definitions get stretched sometimes...). It involves manipulating a target's dreams to form a terrifying nightmare. The nature of the manipulation depends on the Sacred Word used: Create permits the thaumaturgist to add a holy avenging element into the target's dreams; Transform lets him change one element in the dream into a holy avenging element; and Destroy lets him remove comforting elements from a dream, resulting in a nightmare. This miracle may be used at range, but the thaumaturgist must have a mental or physical connection with the target (usually this means he must be able to see him, or must know him well, or have touched him recently, or have an item important to the target in his possession). The target must be asleep when the miracle is prayed for.

Nightmare may be used to physically exhaust the target, reducing his attributes, heroic virtues, or skills, for a period of time equal to the duration once he wakes.

## Voices of Babel

- ❖ **Sacred Word:** Transform.
- ❖ **Elements:** Noises or Sounds, Voice, Person (Ephemeral Domain)
- ❖ **Difficulty:** Resistance roll (-3 penalty) or 6.

Prized by thaumaturgists at war with heretics, this miracle works two ways. It causes whatever sounds reach the ears of the target to turn into incomprehensible whispering; for the duration of the spell, that's all the target can hear. The target's reaction to this is personal: some feel threatened, surrounded by tempting demons, and may even go mad; treat this as a reduction in INT based on the magnitude spent. Others feel themselves touched by grace, and are inspired to become prophets; treat this as an increase in Faith, as long as the target belongs to the Quarterian religion.

## Withering

- ❖ **Sacred Word:** Destroy.
- ❖ **Elements:** A Body Part (Ephemeral Domain); Coherence (Eternal Domain).
- ❖ **Difficulty:** Resistance roll (-3 penalty).

This miracle withers part of the human or animal body—a limb, organ, etc. It may do HP damage based upon the magnitude, or impose an attribute or skill penalty for the duration of the effect. Withering wounds can be treated with traditional healing, or by sorcery that reverses the effect, including Lay On Hands.

# THE AGALANTHIANS AND CHIROMANCY

*Listen to me, young people! Truly you have undergone hard trials to study at my scolarium. Do not expect to rest on your laurels! For chiromancy is one of the most delicate magics, the noblest of all, requiring the greatest attention. If I see your mind wandering even once, expect to be expelled! The inattentive have no place here.*

*So, now that you're listening, let me begin...*

## What Is Chiromancy?

*What are you doing here? Is it just that you want to become rich, pursuing the art of chiromancy? Forget all that—to work our magic well, you must understand it, and how it is perceived!*

*Many call chiromancy "Fate Magic", because by it we call on the gods to intervene in the fates of men, women, even animals and things. How do we do that? By the ancient and mystical power which dwells within the writing of words. We take our sacred tablets of clay, and inscribe them with enchantments. Then, once the tablets are fired and hard, they may be broken, to release the magic within. This is the most ancient of magics—and, although only we know the ways of enchantment, any person may break the tablets we make. And that has allowed us to become rich indeed!*

*Strangers call it Money Magic, but strangers know nothing. Their sorceries are wild and uncontrolled, and they regard our carefully prepared, traditional enchantments as a perversion. Let them! For the people of Agalanth, chiromancy is a blessing, for it brings magic within anyone's reach. No need to study for years to learn magic—buy an enchanted tablet from us, and you have its power at hand for when you need it!*

*Chiromancy tablets are common in our Agalanthian lands. In our city states, people give them as gifts. Tablets against disease are often given as a birth gift, so a mother can heal her child from the most common illnesses. A young woman at her initiation into adulthood is offered a tablet to break on her wedding day, to guarantee the most beautiful consummation possible. A young student receives a tablet giving him concentration during his exams. Travellers buy tablets for fair winds on their voyages, or to calm the waters.*

*The most popular are those which bestow good or bad luck, broken on the days before the greatest chariot races to induce fate to favour one's preferred faction. Ultimately, such tablets end up having little influence, as their overall effects tend to cancel out.*

*All these uses of chiromancy tablets make us, the chiromancers, rich. What other magic does that?*

## In the Beginning

When Great Utaax was dying, spreading his divine essence over the earth, at a time when even the gods were but children and civilisation was only just beginning, the magic of the Agalanthians was immature and unformed.

Even then, people understood the power that lay in the enchantment of clay tablets. Indeed, that is a discovery so ancient that it has left no trace. Perhaps it is to be found in Agalanthian myths of Utaax's death, as only that permitted the discovery of chiromancy.

The first form of chiromancy was the magic of the lines of the hand. The first chiromancers were mostly women, who pressed an imprint of a person's palm in clay, and then changed its lines to manipulate the forces of destiny. Then, when the clay tablet was broken, the lines of the original hand were redrawn and the person's fate changed. Even today, this magic still exists, and remains just as hard to control, as it has always been easier to change a person's fate for ill than good, especially by mistake.

This means that hand magic is ancient and deeply-rooted in Agalanthian culture, but also feared by all. There are few practitioners who'll admit to using it, and they're always portrayed in the tales as dirty and wrinkled old harridans living up in the mountains surrounded by stinking animals, responsible for everything that goes wrong. The reality of course is different; yes, hand magic today is more often practised by women, but it is a magic of small things, with many precautions, to alter the fates of those close to them in tiny ways.

## Writing, the Two-Edged Blessing of the Gods

Writing was the discovery which allowed people to progress to civilisation—to retain their knowledge and to communicate. It also allowed the ancient chiromancers to refine the way they made clay tablets, so that rather than calling on the essence of Utaax to change people's fates by manipulating the lines in their palms, today they call upon his divine children in a much more reliable way.

According to legend, it was Erius the Old who first tried to codify the old ways of chiromancy into a science. He never achieved it, and even lost an eye trying. However, he perfected his study of clays, determining those best suited for magical manipulation. Chiromancers still make tablets today according to his rules, and his writings are fundamental to the art.

Erius began to experiment with his "new" chiromancy, leaving the erratic forms of hand magic and replacing it with writing. His son and apprentice, Erius the Young, first created the form of chiromancy tablet known today.

It's said this first tablet was a prayer to Nerea for his wife to give birth. Before then, she'd lost all her children before her third month of pregnancy. The tablet worked so well that she had eighteen children in less than five years, and all of them boys (Erius had requested a son...). All in turn became chiromancers, apprentices of Erius the Young, and established the precepts of chiromancy.

There are those today who still believe that chiromancy tablets change the lines in your palm—but in such a tiny way it's impossible to see.

### The Importance of Clay

Clay is known by all people as being a good receptacle for magical power. However, only the Agalanthians have made a school of sorcery out of it.

Clay is vital to the practice of chiromancy. It is impregnated with Utaax's divine nature, and when chiromancers create tablets, they call on his children—the gods, heroes, muses, and dragons. Breaking a tablet reminds Utaax's children of their duties towards their father, and asks them to intercede in their worshippers' favour.

It's always better to prepare your clays yourself. You know where they come from, how they were made, which helps you gauge the essence of Utaax when inscribing your enchantment. Some chiromancers even choose and prepare their clays according to the nature of the enchantment they're inscribing. They choose clay from

a field for Demeter's blessing at harvest time, or they knead their clays with seawater for an enchantment to bring good fortune to a seafaring expedition. Some even paint the clay with colours appropriate to their enchantment—green for harvest, red for love, black for disease, and more.

It's never been proven that these elements affect the enchantments in a chiromancy tablet, but people are superstitious. Perhaps the gods and heroes appreciate these small attentions!

## What You Learn at Your Scolarium

Let's look next at what all students learn in their time at the scolaria. The scolaria are not numerous, and getting in is hard; students are hand-picked, and must pass difficult tests of their abilites, their memory, and their powers of concentration. From their very first day, every student gains a mentor who will teach them most of

### A Few Clarifications

*Chiromancy is a painstaking body of knowledge which takes years to learn and which is usually imparted in special schools in the Agalanthian city states, known as* **scolaria**. *It uses the Sacred Word Transform; in modern chiromancy, Create and Destroy are not used at all (but see page 137). It's not enough just to know the Sacred Word Transform, though, to enchant a tablet: you need to have attended a chiromancy scolarium to have learned the required techniques.*

*Chiromancy is a form of sorcery which is completely different from the Tarmel Haja combination magic of the Saabi, the Shiradim, and the Quarterians. It uses different rules, outlined here, and, most importantly, it is not affected by the powers of the shaytan (page 340).*

their enchantments: chiromancers guard their knowledge jealously, although there are enchantments which all students learn.

Creating a chiromancy tablet may be relatively quick, or may take a long time, depending on whether the chiromancer is adapting an existing enchantment, or trying to inscribe a new one, requiring him to research who would be the correct god or hero to address, and how. That said, chiromancers who leave the beaten path to create new enchantments are few in number, and most are content adapting common enchantments to their needs.

## How to Incorporate Chiromancy Into Your Game

Now, the tasks described below for creating chiromancy tablets are often things that happen "off-screen", when you're back at your base, or in-between adventures. This isn't always the case: sometimes you may be in the middle of an adventure when you suddenly need to inscribe an enchantment, and start frantically searching for suitable clay! Most of the time, though, you'll be carrying one or more prepared chiromancy tablets with you, ready to break them and release their enchantments in play.

There's an uncertainty about chiromancy tablets. You don't actually know how well you've done until you break that tablet and let the enchantment free. Because of that, and also because it's great fun to play, we recommend you only make the necessary dice rolls for creating a chiromancy tablet **at the moment you break the tablet**. You may ignore this recommendation when it's more fun: sometimes you may really be chewing on the scenery during

## Utaax the Creator, Cthonos the Destroyer

*Chiromancy is unique among the magics of **Capharnaum** in that it cannot create anything, for creation was the sole preserve of the divine Utaax. Thus, chiromancy aims to influence the fates of men, of animals, of all things that exist—an act of **transformation**. Mortals cannot create fate: those that tried paid with their lives.*

*In game terms, this means that a chiromancer must know Sacred Word (Transform). If you then learn Sacred Word (Create), you may not use it for chiromancy.*

*For the most part, chiromancy cannot destroy, either, for destruction is the domain of Cthonos. However, chiromancers who are priests of Cthonos can work chiromancy using Sacred Word (Destroy)—see the enchantments given on page 144. Given the scars and missing limbs typical of Cthonos's priesthood, this is clearly a perilous path, and not one to be explored alone.*

## The Fountain of Chiromantic Knowledge

*Legend relates how Erius the Young died when trying to inscribe an enchantment using the Sacred Word Create. He wanted to create a mirror which would reflect all the tablets created by a given chiromancer, so he could easily research the best formulation for a given enchantment. His creation enchantment called upon the goddess Demetra who, it is said, did not appreciate the request. She acceded by transforming Erius into a mirror-like pool of water capable of reflecting every chiromancy tablet ever created. Even if such a fountain existed, no one alive now knows its location—let alone how to control and exploit it.*

some adventure downtime in that village north of the Aramla El-Nar, preparing your tablets before adventuring into that ancient ruin you've found. Or you may decide to pay the gold talent costs for your clays instead of rolling, or assume that you've successfully created the tablet without needing to roll. Even then, though, we recommend you save the final dice roll—whether or not the inscription of the enchantment was successful—until the moment you break the tablet in play. Keep up that suspense!

## Finding the Clay

All chiromancers learn how and where to **find suitable clay**, how to evaluate how much of it is impregnated with Utaax's essence, how to clean and prepare it into a thin tablet upon which an enchantment may be inscribed; and finally how to bake it so it will shatter into countless shards when struck, so that the gods and heroes may better hear its prayer (and incidentally so other chiromancers may not steal its secrets...).

A chiromancy tablet should be two hand-widths wide, by two hand-lengths long, by two fingers thick. First of all, you must find clay of the right quality for the enchantment. This is usually an INT + Willpower roll against a difficulty as shown below; the quality of the clay found depends on the magnitude of your roll, as shown on Table 4-10: Type of Clay Found. Good clay gives you a bonus on your roll to create a clay tablet (see page 138).

❖ First, all chiromancers have a store of clay in their workshops, whose properties they know well. If you succeed on a difficulty 9 INT + Willpower roll, you can find just the clay you need there.

❖ Failing that, you know several nearby deposits where you can find appropriate clays. A difficulty 12 INT + Willpower roll lets you find the right kind of clay.

❖ Failing that, you can try prospecting for new clay deposits. This is an INT + Survival roll, against a difficulty from 9 to

## The Golden Rules of Chiromancy

The sons of Erius the Young formulated the following precepts for creating chiromancy tablets. They're still in use today.

❖ *Call Upon the God or Hero!* Always choose the appropriate divinity for the favour you're requesting: Nerea for fertility, Cthonos for death or disease, Thalia to make things lively, and so on. (See pages 271 and 275 for more on Agalanthian heroes and gods.)

❖ *Work With Humility!* Never forget that, unlike chiromancers, gods and heroes have nothing to prove. If you want their help, you must approach them humbly.

❖ *Inscribe With Perfection!* Remember that whatever you inscribe will be the literal result you receive if the gods and heroes favour you. Be clear on what you want, how much you want, and who you want to effect. Sometimes you won't be able to specify absolutely every parameter, but in that case the enchantment will be harder to inscribe.

20 or more, depending on your knowledge of your locale, and the likelihood of finding good clays there.

❖ Finally, if you're in a town or city, you can buy clay; the price is as shown on Table 4-10: Type of Clay Found. Note that if you buy clay, you don't need to make an INT + Willpower roll.

| TABLE 4-10: TYPE OF CLAY FOUND | | | |
|---|---|---|---|
| **MAGNITUDE** | **TYPE OF CLAY** | **BONUS DICE**[1] | **COST**[2] |
| Failure | Poor quality clay | 0 | 1 gold talent |
| 0-3 | Average quality clay | +1 | 2 gold talents |
| 4+ | Good quality clay | +3 | 5 gold talents |

*1: Bonus dice for use in the tablet creation roll (below).*

*2: You don't have to make a roll to buy clay. Double prices in large Jazirati cities, and multiply by x4 or x5 in Jazirati trade towns. It's almost impossible to buy chiromancy clays in camps and Jazirati villages, or in cities without direct or indirect contact with Agalanthian culture.*

## Making the Tablet

Once you've acquired clay for your tablet, cleansed it of possible impurities and hydrated it to make it properly malleable, **making the tablet** itself takes about two hours. This requires a difficulty 12 DEX + Craft skill roll, plus possible bonus dice based on the clay quality (see above). Each point of magnitude on this roll grants

a bonus die for inscribing the enchantment, as long as the tablet creator and the enchantment inscriber are the same person.

*For example: Seb decides that his character, Julius, wants to inscribe the chiromancy enchantment "Find the Path" (page 143), a prayer to Urania, the Muse of Astronomy. Julius has enough clay in his store for about ten tablets, so starts by studying the clay he has, its origin and texture. This is a difficulty 9 INT + Willpower roll. He has INT 4 and Willpower 2, so rolls 6/4, getting 5, 5, 4, 4, 2, and 2, for a result of 18 and 2 magnitude. Al-Rawi explains that Julius finds average quality clay in his stock that will grant him +1 bonus die on his tablet creation roll.*

*Julius gets to work immediately, moulding his clay to the right shape. Julius has DEX 3 and Craft 3, so is rolling 6/3 plus the 1 bonus die from the clay, so 7/3, against difficulty 12. He rolls 6, 5, 5, 5, 3, 1, and 1, a result of 16 and a magnitude of 2, providing 2 bonus dice on the roll to inscribe the enchantment. Julius will rest up and inscribe the enchantment that night, the auspicious time for prayers to Urania.*

## Inscribing the Enchantment

Once the clay tablet has been prepared, the next step is to inscribe the enchantment upon it. Students are taught how to write in the scolaria, but the enchantments written on chiromancy tablets need to be perfect: the tiniest mistake may open the wording of the enchantment up to interpretation, with possibly disastrous consequences.

## Learning Under a Mentor

It's not absolutely necessary to attend a chiromancy scolarium, but it's a rare mentor who wants to invest the time to teach a student absolutely everything they need to know from scratch. That said, some mentors do prefer to take very young students and teach them all the basics. Many are wanderers, and their students often become excellent chiromancers, although the scolaria refuse to recognise them. Nevertheless, this doesn't exempt them from the **conscriptorium**, the two-year magical conscription they must serve under the archon of their city-state once their studies are done (see page 141).

Such itinerant chiromancers have been known to take foundlings under their wing, favoured by the gods, and who have a great destiny. This is also the only way for a woman to become a chiromancer, as the known scolaria admit only boys. Even then, women chiromancers encounter many obstacles, as few archons will go against the scolaria and permit women to serve in the conscriptorium. For these reasons and more, women chiromancers often end up turning to the old ways of hand magic to work their enchantments.

Students learn a corpus of basic enchantments at the scolaria, and use those to inscribe their first tablets. Once they master this process, they participate in scolaria-funding work by serving several months in the chiromancy shops in their city state.

It sometimes happens that a chiromancer lacks the necessary information to completely inscribe an enchantment upon a tablet. For example, you may not know the name of a plant you want the enchantment to cause to grow. In such cases, you may make an accurate drawing on the tablet, or even embed a dried flower in the clay. These actions and more contribute to the uncertainty of inscribing an enchantment. Additionally, the more difficult the enchantment in question, the longer it takes to inscribe. A simple enchantment takes an hour or so; more complex magics may take as much as a day, and may even require more than one chiromancer.

Table 4-11: Enchantment Inscription Difficulties summarises the difficulties and difficulty modifiers for Enchantment Inscription rolls.

| Table 4-11: Enchantment Inscription Difficulties | |
| --- | --- |
| Condition | Difficulty (or modifier) |
| Moderately difficult enchantment[1] | 9 |
| Difficult enchantment | 12 |
| Heroic enchantment | 15 |
| Insanely heroic enchantment | 18 |
| Fabulous enchantment[2] | 21 |
| Per unspecified element, declared loudly when the tablet is broken. | +5 |
| Per element replaced by a drawing or paraphrase. | +3 |
| Per extra detail requested | +3 |
| Per additional target | +3 |
| To target a group of ten or so people | +9 |
| Per point of Faith | -1 |

1: See Table 2-1: Difficulties (page 46). Note that chiromancy enchantment difficulties differ from spells of the Tarmel Haja.

2: There are enchantments of greater power and difficulty, but they are usually in the hands of priests of Cthonos (page 144), certain archons (page 270), or the scolaria. Few chiromancers can inscribe enchantments of such power.

**Inscribing an enchantment** is an INT + Sacred Word skill roll, against a difficulty as determined on Table 4-11: Enchantment Inscription Difficulties, and requires a number of minutes to complete equal to the difficulty squared (difficulty x difficulty minutes). If the chiromancer inscribing the enchantment is also the

one who created the clay tablet, you may add bonus dice equal to the magnitude of the tablet creation roll (page 138).

*For example: That night, Julius surrounds himself with candles and prepares to inscribe the enchantment "Find the Path". The enchantment requires him to specify a constellation, and also who will break the tablet and trigger the spell. Julius knows from a nomad the name of the constellation most suited for getting one's bearings in this part of the desert, but he doesn't want to specify who will break the tablet, because, if Julius should fall ill, no-one else would be able to use it. This counts as an element "replaced by a drawing or paraphrase" (Julius won't specify the name of the breaker of the tablet, but will paraphrase that someone unspecified will do the breaking), which increases the base difficulty of 12 by +3, to 15. He then gets a difficulty reduction equal to his Faith score, so -2, which means a final difficulty of 13.*

*Julius inscribes the following enchantment on the clay tablet: "O Urania, help the breaker of this tablet find his way by the stars!" He could also have chosen to write something like: "O Urania, help the person whose name I declare find their way!" This would have been the same difficulty (13), but would have a slightly different effect: the breaker of the tablet would name a separate person at the moment of breaking, who would then be able to "find the path".*

*Julius has INT 4 and Sacred Word 2 and 2 bonus dice. Seb rolls 8/4 against a difficulty of 13, and gets 5, 4, 4, 4, 3, 3, 2 and 1, meaning a result of 17 and 3 magnitude. Julius concentrates intensely for three hours (actually 169 minutes—the difficulty of 13, squared), inscribing the enchantment on the tablet, and then baking it in the correct manner. Then he can admire the result and go to sleep.*

If you fail your INT + Sacred Word skill roll to inscribe an enchantment, then you won't actually know until you break the tablet (see below) and nothing happens: the spell was not cast. On a Critical Failure (magnitude 6+), then the enchantment was botched in some way, draining Utaax's essence from the clay. Not only does the enchantment not take effect, but you also lose a point of your Faith heroic virtue, beset by doubt after this botched attempt to appeal to the gods.

If you roll a Critical Success (magnitude 6+) on your inscription roll, Al-Rawi may declare that you've boosted the enchantment to effectively make a new spell!

*For example: Julius has rolled a Critical Success when inscribing a Blessing of Good Fortune enchantment (see below) for his friend, Hergus, who wants to seduce the woman of his dreams. Al-Rawi declares that Julius has discovered a new enchantment, "Fabulous Fortune", which gives the target a bonus die on his rolls, in addition to the normal effects of the Blessing of Good Fortune enchantment.*

## Breaking a Chiromancy Tablet

Breaking a chiromancy tablet is easy. All you have to do is strike it sharply against a wall, table, or even your knee, or hit it with a hammer, and it will smash into tiny pieces and release the enchantment within.

## Chiromancy and Religion

*The best chiromancers are often fervent believers in the gods, and a chiromancer who loses his faith also loses his ability to practice his art. The Agalanthians believe in many gods, and that they are everywhere, right down to the smallest gods of the local village fountain.*

*Some chiromancers believe it is the act of believing that creates the gods and heroes, and not vice versa, and that all divine beings are nothing more than the manifestations of the fragments of Utaax. This makes them no less real, and even such chiromancers will believe in their reality if they wish to inscribe enchantments.*

*In game terms, if a chiromancer's Faith score ever drops to 0, he may no longer enchant chiromancy tablets.*

No-one ever needs to learn to break a chiromancy tablet, nor do they need any kind of magical aptitude (such as a Sacred Word skill score). With the exception of any possible resistance rolls (see below), no rolls are required to break a tablet, as all the rolls have already been made when the tablet was created. That's why chiromancy tablets command such handsome prices—and are so sought-after.

However, as we mentioned in "How to Incorporate Chiromancy Into Your Game" (page 137), we actually recommend you take this moment to retroactively make the Enchantment Inscription

roll above, unless you've done so already. If you don't know who made the tablet, then Al-Rawi may tell you the dice to roll and the difficulty (we recommend a roll of 7/3 as average), or she may declare the enchantment automatically takes effect with a result equal to the difficulty + 1D6.

This is the moment of truth—you break the tablet, and you get to know if the enchantment was inscribed correctly. If it was, it takes effect!

## Resisting Chiromancy Enchantments

The rules for resisting magic (page 120) also apply to chiromancy, regardless of whether the target is aware of the enchantment or not. The difficulty of the roll to resist a chiromancy enchantment is the result of the chiromancer's roll to inscribe that enchantment. Note that, as per "How to Incorporate Chiromancy Into Your Game" above (page 137), you may well be making this enchantment inscription roll retroactively during the heat of the action.

If you don't know the skill and attribute scores of the chiromancer who created your tablet when you're breaking it (this will probably be the case if you purchased the tablet, or found it somewhere, and so on), then assume it is equal to the difficulty of the enchantment shown in the sections below (page 141, 143, and 144), + 1D6. You may choose not to resist a chiromancy enchantment, in which case it is automatically successful (note that this is different from Tarmel Haja magic—see page 116). However, you must be aware you're the target of an enchantment to lower your resistance like this; otherwise, the same rules apply as for the Tarmel Haja (a resistance roll, with a minimum resistance of 9).

*For example: Julius has been injured in an attack by bandits, and is feverish and incapacitated. With their guide fled, it's down to Hergus, Julius's friend (played by Alex), to find the way as soon as possible—the night is falling, and Julius will probably not live to the morning!*

*Alex decides the stakes are worth it, and Hergus breaks the "Find the Path" tablet. Al-Rawi describes how it breaks into a thousand fragments, mingling with the desert sand. Because he's the one breaking the tablet, Hergus is the target of the enchantment. Alex declares he doesn't resist. Raising his eyes to the night sky, Hergus espies the constellation of Archippus shine for 3 seconds (the magnitude Julius rolled when creating the tablet), and can therefore see the direction they have to go.*

## The Life of the Chiromancer

Eventually the student of a chiromancer learns many enchantments from his mentor, including some which are jealously guarded secrets, and readies himself for his life as a working chiromancer. This is doubtless a difficult time, often filled with harsh discipline and drudgery, since many mentors frown upon their student's curiosity and fear they may steal away their customers. The period may last several years before a student has enough expertise and confidence

*Chapter 4 - Terpsichore*

to embark upon his two-year conscriptorium in the service of the archon of his city state. Only once this has been completed is the student authorised to begin his trade as a chiromancer.

## Creating New Enchantments

To create a new chiromancy enchantment, you must first describe the effect you want to achieve, and specify which god, hero or muse (see pages 271 and 275) is to be called upon for their aid. If you don't have a clear idea of the divine figure to approach, Al-Rawi may require you to make an INT + History & Peoples roll against the difficulty of the enchantment to identify the ideal god to call upon.

Note that if such a divinity isn't obvious, then you can always work with Al-Rawi to invent one! You may even get a bonus on your rolls if you come up with a particularly appropriate legend, hero, or deity—or all of the above. The Agalanthian pantheon is vast, and there are countless divine beings and lesser gods which aren't mentioned in this book. It's even said there are enchantments which call upon Hubal, Shirad, and even Jason Quartered. No self-respecting Agalanthian would risk his faith for a mere enchantment, though, even if it was rare and powerful—surely?

When you first inscribe a tablet for the new enchantment, the inscription difficulty is doubled (including any bonuses or penalties), as is the time taken to inscribe it. If you fail the roll, the magnitude indicates the number of days you must wait before trying again to create that enchantment or a similar one. These increased times and difficulties represent the research, trial and error, erasures and reformulations which are all required in this first draft. Once you succeed on your enchantment inscription roll, you will thenceforth know the enchantment well enough to make future rolls at the original difficulty.

## Learning New Enchantments

You may learn new enchantments from tablets you did not write. This requires a roll of INT + Sacred Word to study the tablet, with a difficulty equal to that of the enchantment. You must obtain a Critical Success or better (magnitude 6+) on this study roll in order to be able to memorise and learn the enchantment; only then can you reproduce it.

# Chiromancy Enchantments

## Common Enchantments

There are certain chiromancy enchantments which are taught in every scolarium; here is a small selection of them. The prices given are for an enchantment with all the information to be inscribed and a magnitude of 1. For each item of information which is to be

## How Many Chiromancy Tablets Should I Carry?

*Chiromancy tablets are heavy and fragile; each weighs 4lbs (see "Encumbrance" on page 78). They're also incredibly bulky; if you try and carry more than, say, 10 on your person at any one time, then you're considered to be fully encumbered, and any additional gear you're carrying should be considered to be in excess of your encumbrance limit. Whenever you start an adventure, you can consider you have up to 10 tablets you've already created on your person: choose which of the enchantments you know they contain (see "How to Incorporate Chiromancy Into Your Game" on page 137 for more).*

*Chiromancy tablets are incredibly useful, but also a bit of a risk: if one breaks accidentally, it may suddenly and uncontrollably release the enchantment within.*

*If you take more than 5HP damage from any physical, bashing source (especially falls—see page 68), then one chiromancy tablet in your possession per additional 5HP damage (rolled randomly) will break. For each broken tablet, consult Urim and Turim, the Stones of Fate: if the answer is "Yes", then the enchantment in that tablet is released, affecting a random target!*

For example: Julius, with a Sacred Word 2, knows 5 enchantments (see page 31). He has inscribed tablets for each of these already, and is carrying them on his person; they weigh a bulky 20lbs. During an adventure, he takes 11 HP damage from a serious fall. This breaks two of his tablets. Al-Rawi randomly determines these to be his Blessing of Good Fortune and Find the Path enchantments. For each of these, Seb consults Urim and Turim.

For the first tablet, Seb draws Turim, the white stone, a result of "No": although the Blessing of Good Fortune tablet is now broken, its enchantment disipates with no effect. For the second table, Seb draws Urim, the black stone, a result of "Yes": suddenly, Julius glimpses a constellation shine brightly in a midday sky, pointing the direction towards the goal of his quest. If only he didn't already know exactly where he was!

*Note that if you're carrying more than a few chiromancy tablets, Al-Rawi is quite within her rights to say it takes time to find the one you want—perhaps 2 tablets per action. If you're carrying 10 tablets, not only will you be groaning under the weight, it'll take you 5 actions to find the one you want. And may the gods help you if you fall off your camel!*

## Creating a Chiromancy Tablet: Summary

❖ **Step 1:** Decide which enchantment you're inscribing.
❖ **Step 2:** Select your clay: INT + Willpower roll, variable difficulty.
❖ **Step 3:** Create the tablet: difficulty 12 DEX + Craft roll.
❖ **Step 4:** Determine the difficulty to inscribe the enchantment.
❖ **Step 5:** Inscribe the enchantment: INT + Sacred Word roll, difficulty as determined in 4.
❖ **Step 6:** Break the tablet: Automatic Success!

left blank, double the price of the tablet; for each additional point of magnitude, increase the price by +20%.

### Against Wind and Tide

*"O Kalos, let your strength and breath help the captain of this ship to find his way through all the trials the sea, winds, and currents will set before him."*

❖ **Sacred Word:** Transform.
❖ **Calls Upon:** Kalos, God of the Sea.
❖ **Difficulty:** 12.
❖ **Information Inscribed:** The name of the captain and vessel; the names of the seas, currents, and winds to be braved.
❖ **Cost:** 2.4 gold talents.

Breaking this tablet provides a difficulty reduction equal to the enchantment's magnitude, to be applied to the difficulty of all dice rolls relating to the sea voyage described for the period of 1 day.

### Blessing of Good Fortune

*"Gracus, o thou whom Fortune so favoured that she made you her blessed son, ask thy mother to gaze but for a moment on this person when they attempt this feat."*

❖ **Sacred Word:** Transform.
❖ **Calls Upon:** Gracus, the proverbial Thereman hero who, according to legend, had no outstanding qualities other than his prodigious good fortune. He went from being a beggar's child to the most important person in the city, through the workings of luck alone.
❖ **Difficulty:** 9.
❖ **Information Inscribed:** Name of the beneficiary; the action or feat that the good fortune should favour.
❖ **Cost:** 1.2 gold talents.

When this tablet is broken, the beneficiary may re-roll a number of dice for the action concerned up to the magnitude of the enchantment.

### Carry Pregnancy to Term

*"O Nerea, grant this woman the most beautiful gift of the gods, and let her bring forth life."*

❖ **Sacred Word:** Transform.
❖ **Calls Upon:** Nerea, Goddess of Fertility.
❖ **Difficulty:** 12.
❖ **Information Inscribed:** The name of the woman or animal; any problems with previous pregnancies.
❖ **Cost:** 2.4 gold talents.

Breaking this tablet increases the chances of carrying a pregnancy to term by the magnitude of the enchantment (chance x magnitude).

### Cure This Disease

*"O Demetra, Queen of the Earth, help this person to recover from the disease that afflicts them! Thou who controlest nature, purge it from their form!"*

❖ **Sacred Word:** Transform.
❖ **Call Upon:** Demetra, Goddess of Nature.
❖ **Difficulty:** 15.
❖ **Information Inscribed:** Name of the target, name of the disease.
❖ **Cost:** 4.8 gold talents.

When the tablet is broken, the progress of the disease the target is suffering from will cease and they will begin to recover rapidly. The usual recovery time should be divided by the magnitude of the enchantment. The enchantment has no effect on incurable diseases, and acts only slowly on serious diseases that were treated late.

### Curse of Misfortune

*"O Cthonos, I crave pardon! This person does not deserve to succeed in his feat. O Cthonos, I beseech you, thwart his attempt!"*

❖ **Sacred Word:** Transform.
❖ **Calls Upon:** Cthonos, God of Death.
❖ **Difficulty:** 9.
❖ **Information Inscribed:** Name of the target; the action to be beset by misfortune.
❖ **Cost:** 1.2 gold talents.

When this tablet is broken, the target must reroll the best-rolling dice for the action in question. The number of dice re-rolled equals the magnitude of the enchantment.

## Buying Ready-Made Chiromancy Tablets

*The nature of chiromancy means that in any city or large settlement where chiromancers are plying their trade, you may buy ready-made chiromancy tablets, which you may then carry with you and break to release their enchantment when needed (see page 55).*

*The base price of a chiromancy tablet is 1 gold talent (1 GT). This represents a difficulty 9 enchantment successfully written with a magnitude of 0.*

*Double the price for each 3-point (1-step) increase in difficulty. A difficulty 12 enchantment costs 2 GT, a difficulty 15 enchantment costs 4 GT, and so on.*

*Increase the price by 20% for each point of magnitude of the enchantment. You can't normally buy enchanted tablets with a magnitude of greater than 6, at least not without going to considerable additional effort (perhaps including providing a favour or even undertaking a minor quest). So, a tablet with a 5-magnitude enchantment will have a +100% cost, ie will cost twice the usual amount; a 5-magnitude difficulty 15 enchantment will cost 8 GT.*

*Note that Al-Rawi may require Unctuous Bargaining or other interpersonal rolls in order to acquire chiromancy tablets in this way.*

### Find the Path

*"O Urania, thou whose gaze doth shine like the stars at night, help this person see this constellation."*

- ❖ **Sacred Word:** Transform.
- ❖ **Calls Upon:** Urania, Muse of Astronomy.
- ❖ **Difficulty:** 12.
- ❖ **Information Inscribed:** Name of the target, name of the constellation.
- ❖ **Cost:** 2.4 gold talents.

When the tablet is broken, the constellation the traveller is seeking suddenly shines brightly in the sky for a number of seconds equal to the magnitude, enabling him to see it and so determine its direction, regardless of weather conditions or time of day.

### O Joy, Light Up His Face

*"O Thalia, thou whose smile doth make others smile, bring joy to the heart of this person!"*

- ❖ **Sacred Word:** Transform.
- ❖ **Calls Upon:** Thalia, Muse of Comedy.
- ❖ **Difficulty:** 12.
- ❖ **Information Inscribed:** Name of the target.
- ❖ **Cost:** 2.4 gold talents.

When the tablet is broken, the target's mood instantly lightens, as if he'd just heard a story that made him smile, or even laugh, depending on the magnitude. Al-Rawi may provide other benefits from this happier mood, such as bonus dice equal to the magnitude for interpersonal rolls with, against, or by the target.

## Special Enchantments

The following chiromancy enchantments may only be learned from the limited number of mentors who know them, or if you research them yourself. These tablets are traded in great secrecy, as their owners wish to keep their secrets intact. Costs are at least +10% to +20% more expensive than common enchantments, and the price of a newly discovered enchantment that can revolutionise the lives of those employing it may reach astronomical sums.

### Blessing of Great Fortune

*"O Demetra, I beseech thee, that the nature that is thine, the elements and winds, the earth and the water of plants, and all that lives and that does not live, may help this person to carry out this deed!"*

- ❖ **Sacred Word:** Transform.
- ❖ **Calls Upon:** Demetra, Goddess of Nature.
- ❖ **Difficulty:** 15.
- ❖ **Information Inscribed:** Name of the beneficiary; the action which the great fortune should affect.

When the tablet is broken, the beneficiary of the blessing rolls bonus dice equal to the magnitude of the enchantment for the action in question.

### Curse of Great Misfortune

*"O Cthonos, God of Death, I am naught but a miserable mortal and will be your humble servant in death. Grant me your favour and cause this person to fail in their deed!*

- ❖ **Sacred Word:** Transform.
- ❖ **Calls Upon:** Cthonos, God of Death.
- ❖ **Difficulty:** 15.
- ❖ **Information Inscribed:** Name of the target; the action which the great misfortune should befall.

When this tablet is broken, the target incurs penalty dice on his dice roll for the action equal to the magnitude of the enchantment.

### Earthquake

*"O Demetra, express thy wrath, let the earth shake with great strength in these places!"*

- ❖ **Sacred Word:** Transform.
- ❖ **Call Upon:** Demetra, Goddess of Nature.
- ❖ **Difficulty:** 18.
- ❖ **Information Inscribed:** Name of the place.

When this tablet is broken, an earthquake strikes the specified location with an intensity equal to the enchantment's magnitude (for example, using the Modified Mercalli Scale for intensity). This enchantment is greatly feared, as it has destroyed many cities during the civil wars which have ravaged the Agalanthian Empire and city states.

## Give Me Strength

*"O Vigus, thou whose might is recognised by the gods, lend me thy strength until nightfall!"*

- ❖ **Sacred Word:** Transform.
- ❖ **Calls Upon:** Vigus the Charioteer, a hero famous for having raced against Cthonos for his very life. Having exhausted his horses, he finished the race before nightfall by carrying the animals and pulling the chariot himself. He tied with Cthonos who, impressed, allowed him to live.
- ❖ **Difficulty:** 15.
- ❖ **Information Inscribed:** Name of the target.

From the moment this tablet is broken until the time of the next sunset, the target gains a number of bonus dice equal to the enchantment's magnitude, plus 2 (magnitude +2) on all dice rolls involving strength (including skill and attribute rolls made with STR, etc).

## Enchantments of Cthonos

There are chiromancers working for all the temples of the Agalanthian pantheon. They inscribe enchantments calling on the gods which are sold or given to the faithful.

The chiromancers of the Temple of Cthonos are exceptional. Only they can inscribe enchantments using the Sacred Word Destroy. The examples below are some of those enchantments. You may only create them if you're a chiromancer who's a priest of Cthonos, and you can only buy them directly from a Temple of Cthonos itself. All of these enchantments use the Sacred Word Destroy, and call upon the god Cthonos. Their price is double that of any other chiromancy tablet; the costs given below are for tablets with a magnitude of 1.

## Destroy Clouds

*"O Mighty Cthonos, heed my prayer! Destroy the clouds which hang over this place!"*

- ❖ **Difficulty:** 12.
- ❖ **Information Inscribed:** Name of the place.
- ❖ **Cost:** 4.8 gold talents.

When this tablet is broken, the enchantment causes part or all (roughly 10% per point of magnitude) of the cloud cover and foul weather affecting the area to dissipate. The enchantment is prized by Agalanthian nobles wanting nothing to disturb their private parties.

## Destroy Life

*"O Cthonos, Lord of Death, heed my prayer! Let this person die!"*

- ❖ **Difficulty:** 15.
- ❖ **Information Inscribed:** Name of the target.
- ❖ **Cost:** Officially, this tablet isn't for sale; it's reserved for those in great suffering who wish to leave this world as gently as possible. Cthonos's priests usually meet the target and gift them with the tablet, which they break themselves, so the priests are not accomplices to murder. Unofficially, however, it's another story...

When this tablet is broken, the target dies. The higher the magnitude, the quicker this happens. The enchantment may be resisted.

## Destroy Wall

*"O Wrathful Cthonos, heed our prayer! Destroy this wall in this building!"*

- ❖ **Difficulty:** 21.
- ❖ **Information Inscribed:** Name of the building and wall.
- ❖ **Cost:** 38.4 gold talents.

When this tablet is broken, the wall specified in the enchantment collapses. The extent of the collapse depends upon the magnitude of the enchantment. If the magnitude is high, it's advisable to take shelter as there's a risk of being wounded by flying rocks! In game terms, assume any magnitude not spent on destroying an area of wall is instead spent on range and HP damage. The Temple of Cthonos does not sell this enchantment to just anyone, especially without specifying the building and wall beforehand.

# Avienus Morcilius Gorgo

**Blood :** Agalanthian (Fragrance)

**Path :** The Etrusian Bacchantes

**Occupation:** Drunken Philosopher (Sorcerer-Thief)

**Status:** Bored playboy son of a petty lord

| | |
|---|---|
| **STR:** 1 | **Max Init:** 4 |
| **CON:** 3 | **HP:** 30 |
| **DEX:** 3 | **Soak:** 6 |
| **INT:** 3 | **Passive Defence:** 11 |
| **CHA:** 3 | **Heroism:** 3 |

- ❖ **Heroic Virtues:** Bravery 3 (0), Faith 6 (0), Loyalty 1 (0).

- ❖ **Skills:** Acting 1, Agriculture 2, Assassination 2, Athletics 2, Combat Training 1, Command 1, Elegance 2, Endurance 2, Fighting 2, Flattery 2, History & Peoples 1, Instruction 1, Intimidate 1, Intrusion 2, Notice 2, Prayer 4, Riding 2, Sacred Word 4, Sacrifice 4, Save Face 1, Science 1, Stealth 2, Thievery 2, Unctuous Bargaining 2, Willpower 5.

- ❖ **Attacks / Active Defences:** Choora stiletto 5/3 +5 damage, Throwing Knife 5/3 +7 damage.

- ❖ **Armour:** Partial Armour (AV: 1).

- ❖ **Magic:** Sacred Word 4 (+1 mag on Destroy, Transform) Face, Light / Darkness, Person, Sobriety / Drunkenness, Sound / Silence, Water, Wine (Mundane World); Concentration (Philosophical World).

- ❖ **Path Ability:** If Avienus lights up a constellation on a CHA + Flattery roll during an orgy or a CON + Endurance roll during an alcoholic debauch, he receives a result bonus equal to his Faith score to Sacred Word rolls for a number of hours equal to the constellation die.

- ❖ **Wealth Level:** 4 (Filthy Rich): 1989 OC.

- ❖ **Equipment:** (Enc: 12lbs)
  - Flasks of strong drink (useful when casting Transform Drunkenness to Concentration).
  - The *Mask of Bacchoros* (+1 mag on Sacred Word rolls).
  - Outfits of ceremonial clothes and city clothes.
  - 2 scrolls and 1 grimoire (The *Liber Ebrietatis*) each containing 3 undiscovered spells or elements.
  - 3 throwing knives, 1 *choora*, partial armour (12lbs).

Avienus is a twenty-something man from Fragrance, son of a Thereman lord and an orgiast of the Etrusian Bacchantes. Seeing the Dragon Mark on his back, his father wrenched him from his mother and educated him in Fragrance with Avunculus, one of the city's sages (a level 1 contact). But Avienus felt drawn to the ecstasy of the Bacchantes, and became a heavy drinker, finding a magical stillness at the bottom of a flask. He sought excitement in thievery, seeking out rare and even magical treasures.

Today Avienus affects the manner of the bored son of a Fragrantine lordling. He's somewhat overweight and always drunk in public. Some years ago, he stole a valuable treasure, the devil-faced *Mask of Bacchoros*. The Mask enabled him to transform his drunkenness into magical stealth. Since then, however, spirits and djinn have whispered to him constantly.

By day Avienus appears to be a bumbling, drunken philosopher, well-dressed and foppish, unimportant beyond being the scion of a wealthy family. But by night he dons the *Mask of Bacchoros* and pierces the veil of drunkenness into a mystical space beyond, and passes unseen.

# Don Alfonso Diago Infanzo de Sarajon

**Blood:** Aragon

**Path:** Duellists of San Llorente de Valladon

**Occupation:** Adventurer

**Status:** Hidalgo

| | |
|---|---|
| **STR:** 2 | **Max Init:** 3 |
| **CON:** 3 | **HP:** 30 |
| **DEX:** 3 | **Soak:** 6 |
| **INT:** 2 | **Passive Defence:** 11 |
| **CHA:** 3 | **Heroism:** 3 |

- ❖ **Heroic Virtues:** Bravery 4 (0), Faith 1 (0), Loyalty 5 (0).
- ❖ **Skills:** Acting 1, Agriculture 2, Athletics 2, Combat Training 2, Command 4, Elegance 4, Endurance 1, Fighting 5, Flattery 3, History & Peoples 1, Instruction 1, Intimidate 2, Music 1, Notice 1, Oratory 1, Poetry 1, Prayer 1, Riding 3, Save Face 4, Science 1, Stealth 1, Storytelling 2, Survival 3, Unctuous Bargaining 4, Willpower 1.
- ❖ **Attacks / Active Defences:** Aragonian Whip 8/3 +5 damage, Espada Valladena 8/5 +10 damage[1], Jazirati recurved bow 8/3 +9 damage.
- ❖ **Armour:** Light Armour (AV: 3).
- ❖ **Path Ability:** If Don Alfonso lights up a constellation on a whip attack, he may immediately make a second Free Attack against the same target with another weapon. He must be within 3 paces of the target.
- ❖ **Wealth Level:** 3 (1000 OC, 200 ST, 80 GT).
- ❖ **Equipment:** (Enc: 47lbs)
  - Superior city clothes (+1 bonus die on Prince skills).
  - Lands and real estate back in Sarajon.
  - Aragonian whip, heirloom *espada valladena*, Jazirati recurved bow + 30 arrows, 2 *choora* daggers (24lbs).
  - Light Armour (20lbs).

Don Alfonso is an elegant and refined Aragonian in his late 20s. Hailing from Sarajon, where he practically grew up on horseback on the extensive lands he has since inherited, he spent years in the royal court at Valladon, coming to the attention of the King as a member of the Duellists of San Llorente, and to Dona Angela, his powerful and influential wife (a level 1 contact), who still lives at court.

Don Alfonso wears traditional Aragonian clothing and a tattoo of a tear below his left eye. He wields a whip together with his masterwork *espada valladona*, a family heirloom, and wears light armour, stripey pirate pants, a head scarf, goatee, and earring—a legacy of his sea voyages since the beginning of the Holy Crusade. He fought in the ill-fated defence of Aragon against the Saabi invader, distinguishing himself in battle when the Dragon Mark spontaneously appeared on his shoulder, surrounding him with an aura of flame on the battlefield[2]! During the intense fighting he came to the attention of General Don Iago Garcia de Olvidad, with whom he came to Sagrada and who he considers a great ally (a level 2 contact). After the defeat at Al-Ragon, he travelled the known world, including an expedition to the frozen north of Orkadia, where he made the acquaintance of Captain Schneewald (a level 1 contact), a regular on the run between Russo and Sagrada. He has developed a reputation for great loyalty, although he has seen things that have challenged his faith.

Since arriving in Sagrada to fight against the Saabi, Don Alfonso has become fascinated by Capharnaum. He has found a lover in Sagrada, a beauty he calls Dona Yamira, who seems to know everyone in the city (a level 2 contact). Although he tells himself he'll soon return home to his lands, wife, and king, he never seems to actually do so...

Don Alfonso is accompanied by two servants: Enrico from Aragon, and Ayman from Sagrada. Both are level 1 contacts.

[1] +2 damage because the sword is an heirloom of exceptional workmanship.

[2] Don Alfonso's Dragon Mark still glows with a flame-coloured aura when he fights during the daytime, making him particularly affected by the Dragon's Breath. At such times, his first Dragon Die explodes on a 5 or 6.

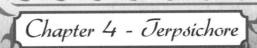

# - Part Two -
# The World Of Capharnaum

## At the Edge of the Aramla El-Nar...

O my master!

My quest is at an end! Here as promised is an account of my last journey, its encounters, and of the state in which the Holy Crusade of the Quarterians has left our land.

I came out of the desert, triumphing over the Aramla El-Nar, and reached civilisation. I have seen Jazirat's cities, I have seen Capharnaum — I have survived the perils of the Jebel Omphir, escaped the assassins of Al-Kasir and the swamps of Limhere. I found Kh'saaba — your Kh'saaba, since it will never be mine again. My mission, o my master, is done. I leave your service and abandon myself to fate. This is my final report — for tomorrow my new life begins...

# THE INNER SEA

**FRAGRANCE**

*Arm of Tiamat*

KAWIMSHA

AL-MAMLAKAH
JABALI

*Samsara
Camel Track*

*Claws
of Cthonos*

*Eastern
Mines*

ALBAGDIR

**CARRASSINE**

*Gulf of
Oxyrhynchus*

Master Eliahu
Bar Nissim's Workshop

*Wall of Emera*

**SAGRADA**

*Lazurine Sea*

*Limherk
Plateau*

*Thieves'
Cave*

*Nejah Plain*

*Jebel
Omphir*

**Village of
the Prophets**

*Tiahm*

AILHU
MUNJI

**MESSARA**

*Genies Lake*

**ZARBETH**

**BELETMEI**

**YASMINABAD**

■■ ■■
**100 LEAGUES**

*Quarterian
Monastery
of St Jude*

**AL-KASIR**

*Ilmenite Oasis*

*Bay of
Dragons*

*Forbidden
Fountain*

*Abandoned
Palace*

**Aramla
El-Nar**

*Kallopni River*

# Capharnaum
*At the heart of the world...*

\*\*\*\*\*\*\*\*\*\*\*\*\*\*\*\*\*\*\*\*\*\*\*\*\*

*Beyond the Jebel Omphir stretch the vast plains of Capharnaum. They were not yet in view, but my senses were already afire
at the thought of Etrusian wine, mutton stew with figs from Messara, peppers fried in olive oil from Beletmei, seasoned with
cumin from Fragrance. Capharnaum has changed, but not much: here and there Quarterian chapels and forts dot the landscape,
whilst elsewhere Agalanthian troops hunker down in the rocks and bide their time. Sometimes you see a wandering mujahid,
looking for illumination, or caravans brimming with joy and victuals, colourful tesserae to enliven the wild mosaic of the desert.
You may find yourself facing one of those contradictions in which Capharnaum seems to abound—perhaps, in some corner of the
endless desolation, a birthplace of fertile hills. In such a place I met Cyprian, the doughty templar.*

# Carrassine

It was approaching Carrassine that I met Hakim N'Gassa, the Dragon Rider. Like me, he was a man shaped by each league he had travelled, each combat he had fought. When we met, the warrior of the Walad Badiya was travelling from Balzahaar, having returned from fearsome Al-Fariqn. He filled my evening with tales of evil jungles and man-eating apes. We entered Carrassine together. I was looking for dancing girls and wine, Hakim for answers. We both found more, for Carrassine is all things at once. Just as the Walad Badiya is both man and dragon, so is the city both rampart and freedom, temple and brothel, tower and terrace. War and peace. Light and dark. Carrassine opened its gates to us to reveal other gates within, like a dancing girl who lowers her veils without ever revealing all. In Carrassine, every medina is a city unto itself, every street a palace, every beggar a prince...

Old Port

Hippodrome
Building Site

Circus Port

Via
Avolonia

TEMPLE
OF MARDUK

Al-Ziggurat Medina

Al-Yassine Medina

Al-Moallaka Medina

Al-Arkan Medina

Al-Wudu Medina

Al-Dhumma Medina

Al-Marduk Medina

Al-Ziyada
Al-Shaytan Medina

Legions

Copper &
Turquoise Road

Sarah's Orchards

# Sagrada

Sagrada remains immutably the city of the dawn. Its walls, temples, and awnings are bathed each hour of the day in a light like that of morning. It is forever being born and reborn. You and I know, o my master, that it is here that the future of the world is being decided. Although the city knows a semblance of peace under the Quarterian administration, you can see in their eyes how the Shiradin yearn to take back what is theirs, how the Quarterian patrols eye everyone with distrust, how the Agalanthians dream of a return to greatness if they could only retake the city. For my part, I spend my time rediscovering the joys of city life in the company of the daughter of my old friend, Nubib. Najah is a woman, now. You would not know her. By her side I am learning about modern medicine. But she has been chosen by the Dragons, her blood is too rich for the effeteness of the city. I have no doubt she will be gone within the year...

Watchtower of
Doroge Murakaba

Gulf of
Oxyrhynchus

Ibttas
Jazira

Sea
Road

Gate of the
Setting Sun

Pleasure Port

Temple of
the Senses

Commercial Port

Fragrance R

O'donta's
Tooth

Gate of the
Rising Sun

Halawui Delta

Old
Palace

Jason's Wall

The
Banks

The Common
Quarter

Migdash
Arishdon

The Terraces

Halawui River

Lips
of Jade

Traditional Shiradi
Quarter

South Gate
(to the Outer Souk

# Fragrance
## City of a Thousand Scents

✳ ✳ ✳ ✳ ✳ ✳ ✳ ✳ ✳ ✳ ✳ ✳ ✳ ✳ ✳ ✳ ✳ ✳ ✳ ✳ ✳ ✳ ✳

*I came to Fragrance for chariot racing, for parties, for women
—and for those things alone. Fragrance is Agalanth's great whore,
wallowing in our lands as if she had collapsed after a night of excess.
To think that the Agalanthians once ruled the world, that we owe them so much!
Please excuse my scattered thoughts, o Jafar my master, but I find myself so affected
by such a demonstration of lost greatness, of opulent decadence, that my mind wanders.
What should one think of Fragrance? Is it nothing but a mum-show of art and politics?
A temple to debauchery? A local hero I met here embodied this duality: half
Dragon-Marked gladiator, half gigolo feeding off the caprices of old patrician
women, he aims to restore to his people their greatness of yore.
Wandering Fragrance's dirty streets and ruins, you can find
yourself thinking that perhaps the Empire never fell.
For surely this city has two faces.*

*Harbour Villages*

The Arena

University

*Agalanthian
Quarter*

Upper
*Pleasure Quarter*

*Pleasure
Quarter*

PALACE OF
THE ASSEMBLY

CATHEDRAL

Min
*Maydan*

*Tenderloin*

*Old
Town*

GREAT
MARKET

*Quarterian
Quarter*

FORUM

*Jazirati
Quarter*

*Shiradi
Quarter*

HOSPITAL

# THE COSMIC ORDER

*Antistia*

## THE BATTLE OF THE TITANS

## THE MIRROR

*Yonka*

*Octavia*

*Shai*

*Ka*

*Archippus*

*Sulpicia*

*Jala*

*Kaha*

*Dunia*

THE MYSTERY

THE RETURN OF THE DRAGONS

*Qayim*

# FREEDOM

# MARDUK

## The Vault of Heaven

### The Fevers of the Eastern Night

\* \* \* \* \* \* \* \* \* \* \* \* \* \* \* \* \* \* \* \* \* \* \* \* \*

I went to the crossroads of the worlds. There, where Jazirat—without touching—marries Nir Manel, in a sweep of luxuriant jungle and cascades which seem to carry all the gold of Tarkibol. Only lost caravans come here, and only a few isolated kingdoms survive. The war never came to these lands, which doubtless explains their atmosphere of unlikely tranquillity. In contrast to the hostility of the countryside, the contemplative calm that bathes these lands makes one think that a dream of Tiamat, most beautiful and sweet, still lingers here. And yet the forests are dangerous—haunted, it is said, by the spirits of those devoured since the beginning of the world by the afreeti hiding in the darkness. Madmen and hermits take refuge here, in search of quietness and magic. I was the guest of the banished ambassador, Oda Bint Mimun, the Drag-on-Marked, whose hospitality kept me more readily than the most powerful mirage...

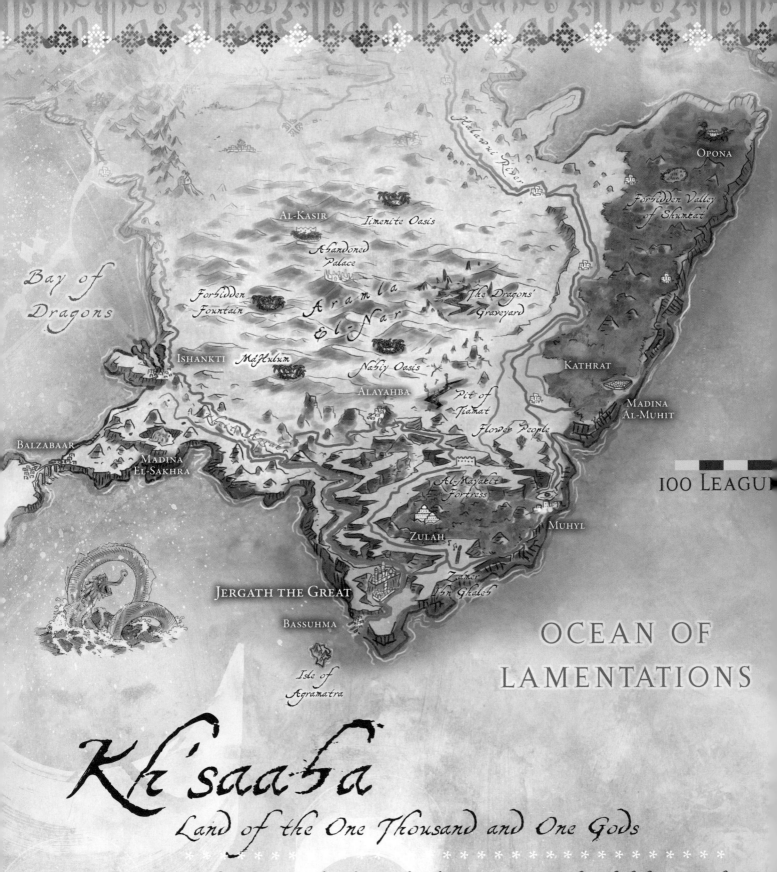

Bay of
Dragons

OCEAN OF
LAMENTATIONS

100 Leagui

Opona

*Forbidden Valley
of Shumeat*

Kathrat

Madina
Al-Muhit

*Atalapui River*

Al-Kasir          *Ilmenite Oasis*

*Abandoned
Palace*

*Forbidden
Fountain*

A r a m l a
E l - N a r

*The Dragons'
Graveyard*

Ishankti    *Majhulum*

*Nafiy Oasis*

Alayahba

*Pit of
Tiamat*

*Flower People*

Balzabaar

Madina
El-Sakhra

*Al-Mayaeit
Fortress*

Zulah

Muhyl

**JERGATH THE GREAT**

*Zamer
Ibn Ghaleb*

Bassuhma

*Isle of
Agramatra*

# Kh'saaba
## Land of the One Thousand and One Gods

✳ ✳ ✳ ✳ ✳ ✳ ✳ ✳ ✳ ✳ ✳ ✳ ✳ ✳ ✳ ✳ ✳ ✳ ✳ ✳ ✳ ✳ ✳ ✳ ✳ ✳ ✳ ✳ ✳ ✳

*Crossing the friendly kingdom of Kathrat, I entered Kh'saaba through its most stunning reaches. The high plateaus, when you
travel the dry wadis below them, look like hanging gardens, and the rich and fertile Kh'saaba is so beautiful that it's said som
visitors perish, overwhelmed, at their first sight. I thought that this, beautiful as it was, would be merely a step on my journ
and did not count on staying long, but on a street corner in a village called Jibin I met Jaina—one of your nieces, I believe. S
painted for me a picture of Kh'saaba's political life that I had never imagined. Far away from her political duties, having brok
with her past since starting the path of the Dragon-Marked, this young al-kimyat opened my eyes...*

Al Kasr
Malaki

Maabad
al Kabir

Temple
Quarter

Muhafid
Caves

Divine
City

The Cliff

Old
City

Barracks

Agalanthian
Ruins

Kheit
Azrak

Farm
lands

Port
Quarter

Ahlen
Raha

Al-Malikah
Alsouk

East Gate

Palm Grove

Bassuhma
Road

# Jergath the Great

## The Fabulous City of the South

✳ ✳ ✳ ✳ ✳ ✳ ✳ ✳ ✳ ✳ ✳ ✳ ✳ ✳ ✳ ✳ ✳ ✳ ✳ ✳ ✳ ✳ ✳ ✳ ✳ ✳ ✳ ✳ ✳ ✳ ✳ ✳ ✳ ✳

I had wandered Jazirat looking for something I found only in Kh'saaba. The world had opened its doors to me, I had
seen cities and deserts, beggars and princes, and yet I had only learned one thing: that the world is holding its breath.
Everything everywhere is waiting—for something. A thousand meetings on my path, a thousand friendships—but now when
I reread what I have written, and listen to my dreams, feeling the knot in my stomach tighten, I feel only one thing:
impatience. At every step my journey had torn me away from fast friendships with an urge to undertake some great feat,
to fulfil my destiny. When I met Jilali at the Gates of Zulah, I knew I would never go back. He was one more Dragon-Marked on my path—one more mirror of my fate.

## Travelling the roads of the world, beneath the stars

O my master, I have travelled the world and I am not coming back. On this, my last journey, I have learned more things than most learn in a lifetime. Now I know—better than anyone—where our world is going, what it is turning into. We stand between two wars. The first saw the arrival of the Quarterians en masse, in the name of a god we didn't even know existed only a thousand years ago.

The second will see the rest of the gods fight back.

My last journey has convinced me: the gods are among us. They walk beside us like the times of yore. The Dragon-Marked are returning, after centuries of absence. Many have only appeared in the past few decades.

Master, I am one of them.

My service to your house ends today. Today I join my own—those for whom adventure awaits, those to whom the gods are calling.

I must accept...

## ...the Dragon Mark

# CHAPTER FIVE
# CLIO – HISTORY

## Drowned by the Tides of Time

Thufir waited patiently beneath the awning protecting him from the merciless sun. He watched Luther pace the bridge of the felucca they had chartered at the coastal village of Khal-Ahmar Ban'Thur. There, everyone had remembered his northman grandfather and his band of drunks, their strange ship with few sails but many long oars. "A drekar," the grandson had explained. "The winds of our fjords are often weak and unpredictable, so we have to row."

The locals' tongues had loosened at the mention of the Orkadians' visit—they had doubtless left behind more than a little gold. But their faces had darkened when Thufir had tried to discover their fate. After several days walking steep and slippery alleys between white houses with colourful shutters, an old fisherman finally approached.

"Lad, I'm eighty, and believe me I'd never seen a storm like that night. A strange storm, right in the middle of the dry season. There I was, at my window, and I saw them as clear as I see you now—dragons! Up in the sky, flying, out to sea over there! The next morning we found the wreckage of the strangers' ship. They gambled with foreign gods, I reckon, and paid the price!"

"Where was the Orkadian ship anchored?"

"Over there. In Janissary Cove."

"Is it deep? Could my ship anchor there? The one over there, with the red sail."

"I'm sure it could—but I wouldn't chance it, the place is cursed. Haunted by the ghosts of those barbarians!"

The old man had clung to the end of Thufir's turban, not wanting to let go. But as surely as there was no red-sailed ship, the old fisherman with salt-burned eyes had added those dragons to his tale of a storm which—however violent—he thought needed embellishment. But when the Jazirati announced the news to the Orkadian, he saw with surprise a tear roll down his cheek.

"If my grandfather drowned, that means he never made it to the warriors' heaven."

"Doesn't Aether have only one heaven?"

"I come from the edge of the civilised world. Aether has only just reached us..."

Then Thufir had mentioned the dragons, too, thinking it good to include the possibility of a glorious death in combat for the ancestor of the man who—he had to admit—was fast becoming his friend.

So now there the knight was, trying to convince the pearl divers he'd hired in the village to dive into the haunted waters of Janissary Cove. Thufir had searched beneath the waves the whole morning, but had given up during the hottest hours of the day for a well-earned rest. His eyes widened with surprise when one of the strapping young Adonises dived into the water. He left the shade of the awning and joined his Orkadian friend.

"How did you talk him into it?" he asked, as the bubbles disappeared from the surface.

"I just dived in myself with the protection of my talisman, and then said I'd lend it to him."

"You have a talisman?"

"Nope. It's just my family's torc. But it's enough for you superstitious heathens."

"Ah. Your knowledge of our language and customs is coming on in leaps and bounds."

Some seconds later, the diver resurfaced.

"The ship is right below us. Twenty fathoms, no more. It's filled with skeletons, drowned by their own armour!"

Luther's huge fists tightened on the rail. Coldly, he ordered that everything that could be brought up should be retrieved.

Hours later, the cabin of the felucca was full: a jumble of lanterns, hooks and grapples, pots, horns and goblets, helms, axes and shields. All gnawed at by bladderwrack and barnacles. Luther turned over in his hands a scroll case he had found in a casket.

"I remember this. My grandfather kept a set of runes in it..."

He broke the seal and emptied it onto the table. Several scrolls slid out. Carefully, Thufir unrolled one that looked very old. Papyrus, covered in writing that—the two companions exchanged a glance—neither of them knew...

# THE BEGINNING OF THE WORLD

## Utaax and Kryptos

"Don't you know the word?" the tutor snorted, with an air of false amazement. "*Cosmogony* is a word of Agalanthian origin that means the 'birth of the universe'. But how should two young lads like you have heard of it? Don't worry, boys!"

The two children didn't look worried. The tutor carried on regardless.

"As I was explaining, his lordship—your father—has asked me to further your education concerning the history of our world. Thus my first lesson is entitled 'Cosmogony'." The tutor waited. "At least write it down."

Raskin Bar Nahmias was an elderly man of the Shiradim. He had travelled many lands, met many people, had fought more often than he had liked, and had known true love. But all that was behind him now. As he spelled out the word to the two young boys, he recalled fleeting moments from his life. He was about to teach history, the stories of great men and women, of great battles and wars. Would he one day be part of it?

"Well," he continued, "first you should know that the beginning of the world is not a straightforward affair. In ancient times, no one knew how to read and write, and people told one another stories out loud."

"Like the desert tribes?" Habib, the older of the two boys, interrupted.

"Yes. Exactly like those Jazirati tribes who continue their oral traditions. But it is complicated, because the different peoples of the world do not tell exactly the same story. Let us review how they differ..."

"For some Agalanthian philosophers, the universe emerged from the void. In the beginning, there was only a vast black sea, always moving, called Kryptos, and Utaax, the great dragon, flying ceaselessly above it. One day, fruit of their mighty wills, a huge egg was born of their unnatural union. Utaax incubated it for three millennia, waiting patiently for the day it would hatch. But Kryptos grew tired of waiting, and gently began to withdraw. That's how the first land appeared. It was bare at first, but plants, animals, and soon men and women took their places. Several civilisations were born. Utaax watched all these events from afar, without ever leaving the egg. He had no time for the men and women and the civilisations Kryptos had created; the people were evil, deceitful, greedy and stupid. So, Utaax decided to rise into the heavens with his egg, and look for a world worthy of his offspring."

Raskin paused, to make sure his audience was following. Habib's quill flew over his parchment, trying not to lose a word of the tale; Jabil, Habib's younger brother, sat with his nose in the air, lost in his thoughts. Raskin pictured the child imagining the gargantuan dragon, traversing the darkness, searching for a welcoming land. The tutor was content; his audience was hooked.

"But, after a millennium, Utaax had still found nothing," Raskin continued in a quieter voice. "Then, the great dragon decided to sacrifice itself, so its body could be used to create a new, untouched land, far from Kryptos's corrupt civilisation. And the new world that was born was our own world. A little later, the egg hatched. First, the gods came out of it, led by Ioptis, Zamul, and Nerea. Then came mortal men and women, followed by animals and plants and everything that makes up our world."

The old man looked Habib and Jabil in the eyes, each in turn. After a few moment, the older boy spoke.

"But, master, what happened to those first people, the ones created by Kryptos's impatience? What happened to that world?"

Capharnaum is an ancient land, with a history going back six thousand years. Here are some of its major events.

### Table 5-1: A Timeline of the Known World

| Year | Event |
|---|---|
| 0 | Founding of Therema by King Agalanth. |
| 315 | Creation of the Agalanthian Republic. |
| 618 | First king of the Jazirati tribes, Aref Ibn Jelul. |
| 804 | Jazirat falls into the hands of the Agalanthians. The land is divided into Exortivus (later Capharnaum) and Kh'saaba, which will become the part favoured by the natives. |
| 862 | Founding of Fragrance. |
| 950 | Founding of Jergath the Great. |
| 1000 | The Agalanthians, using knowledge and science now lost, rule the world. |
| 1225 | Saabi revolt led by Ismet Ibn Sayed. |
| 1506 | End of the Republic, and the beginning of the Agalanthian Empire. |
| 1540 | The Saabi take control of Fragrance and the peninsula of Jazirat. |
| 1984 | The Agalanthian Empire regains control of Jazirat. |
| 2500 | Death of the Saabi prophets. |
| 2600 | The Shiradim return to Jazirat. |
| 2954 | The Shiradim fall under Saabi domination. |
| 3536 | Mogda flees his country. |
| 3588 | Founding of Jergathine. |
| 4200 | Creation of the Jergathine merchant guilds and the beginning of hostilities with the Saabi. |
| 4450 | Founding of Carrassine by General Yassin (Shiradi). |
| 5000 | The first great Agalanthian provinces located far from the centre of the Empire begin rebelling, obtaining greater and greater autonomy. |
| 5050 | Official recognition of the Kingdom of Kh'saaba, with Jergath the Great as its capital. |
| 5100 | The Agalanthian administrative and political system has its first great crisis. Corruption is everywhere, the legal system stymied. From this date on, there are many such crises. |
| 5180 | Siege of Jergathine by the Saabi. |
| 5200 | Arrival of the first Agalanthian mercenaries (from Therema) to defend Jergathine against the Saabi. |
| 5230 | The Agalanthians repel the Saabi. |
| 5280 | The Agalanthians enslave the Shiradim. |
| 5300 | Jergathine becomes the City of the Mercenary Kings. It begins to reign over the known world. |
| 5400 | Jason (the son of a minor Agalanthian king), aged 15, undertakes his military service at Jergathine. |
| 5410 | Jason falls in love with a Shiradi prostitute who falls victim to a raid ordered by one of Jason's captains. Appalled, Jason converts. |
| 5417 | Jason becomes a priest of Mira, one of the lesser incarnations of Shirad, and goddess of peace and love. He proclaims himself the Son of the Goddess and creates a personal pantheon centred on Mira and Aether, an unknown god. Peace and love will be won by force of arms! |
| 5422 | Beginning of six weeks of civil war in Jergathine between the Shiradim slaves and the Agalanthians. Building of Jason's Wall separating the Shiradi and Agalanthian parts of the city. When reinforcements arrive, the Shiradim surrender and betray Jason, who is sentenced to death by quartering. Miraculously, Jason survives quartering and faces King Pelorius in a duel that costs him his life. |
| 5432 | Three Quarterian martyrs arrive in the northern lands and begin to preach a new religion worshipping Jason Quartered, Aether, and Mira. |
| 5450 | The Agalanthians begin mass persecutions of the adherents of the new religion. |
| 5564 | The Agalanthian Empire is dying, victim of attacks from barbarian peoples it can no longer handle. The new emperor is remarkable for his incompetence and madness. |
| 5588 | First appearance of Sarah, the Shiradi hero. |
| 5616 | Sarah marches on Carrassine. |
| 5666 | Therema, ancient capital of the Agalanthian Empire, is levelled by earthquake. The provinces still under the yoke of the Empire take advantage of the chaos to declare independence. |
| 5700 | The West adopts the new Quarterian religion. Jergathine is renamed Sagrada. |
| 5800 | Birth of the Western nations in their modern form (Aragon, Orkadia and Occidentia). |
| 5987 | Quarterian troops disembark in Jazirat on a Holy Crusade to recover the *Mirabilis Calva Reliquiae*, located in Sagrada / Jergathine. |
| 5988 | Quarterian forces of the Holy Crusade take the city of Fragrance, making it into a Quarterian stronghold. |
| 5990 | Carrassine falls to siege, carried out by Simeon IV. Suleiman, seneschal of Carrassine, is nowhere to be found. In the same year, Queen Helicandra of Sagrada refuses to surrender and deliver her city to the Quarterians. |
| 5994 | An alliance between the Quarterians and the Saabi to retake Sagrada. The Quarterians betray the Saabi and sack the Holy City. Simeon gets hold of the *Mirabilis Calva Reliquiae* and also steals the Moonstone Sword of Hammad. |
| 5995 | Departure of the Saabi expeditionary force to the lands of the West to recover the Sword of Hammad. |
| 5997 | The Present Day. In Jazirat, all the forces present keep a wary watch on one another. Many Quarterians remained behind after the Holy Crusade to seek their fortune, begin new lives, and impose Quarterian law. There's a fragile peace, but everyone wonders when the Jazirati will try to retake the Holy City. |

"History does not tell us. But the Agalanthians believe there is another world, beyond the reach of the telescopes of the chiromancers."

Habib nodded, and noted the words on his parchment.

## What the Saabi Believe

Raskin Bar Nahmias stroked his white goatee, collecting his thoughts.

"Now let's now speak of the creation of the world according to your own people, the Saabi. Their tales are different from those of the Agalanthians. For the fierce nomad warriors of the ancient past, almost nothing at the beginning of the world had a name, so almost nothing existed. There were just two things: Apsu, called "Sweet Water", and Tiamat, called "Salt Water", who had the shape of a dragon. From their union were born the One Thousand and One Gods, of whom the most important are Hubal, Anu, Malakbel, Enki, and Marduk the Dragon, Protector of Carrassine. Anu ruled over heaven; Malakbel over the earth; and Enki over the waters. But the young gods, with their passionate and stormy natures, would not let Apsu sleep; so he determined to destroy them. Learning of Apsu's intentions, Enki slew him and took his place, to rule over all the waters in the earth. Anu, King of Heaven, decided in his turn to attack his ancestress, Tiamat. To defend herself, Tiamat begat monsters, against which Enki sent his own son, Marduk. After an eternity of war in heaven, Tiamat was defeated but, before dying, she unleashed a demonic horde—those beings your people call *djinn*—on the world."

"Djinn?" young Jabil asked. "Father told us Marduk was the strongest of all! He fears no djinn, no matter how many there are!"

"That's right!" Habib said. "Marduk fears no-one!"

"His lordship, your father, is right, children. Marduk descended to the earth to hunt down the djinn, but the demons were clever. They spread across the desert and sought refuge in mirages. The tales say Marduk slew a thousand and one of them before his duties called him back to heaven."

In his heart of hearts, the Shiradi believed neither myth. However, at least the Saabi version explained the existence of the djinn. For the creatures were indeed real: he had encountered them himself more than once. Concealing his thoughts, he continued his explanation.

"Now, by the time Marduk returned to heaven, the world had been pacified, and order could finally be created. The Vault of Heaven, the stars, the Earth itself, the Underworld—all these things were formed from the vast corpse of Tiamat. Marduk was given the task of peopling the world, and so he created mortal men and women to serve the gods. The first man was fashioned from clay, dipped in the blood of a sacrificed god which gave him a spark of divine intelligence."

## Shirad, the One God

"Let us now study the last of the tales of creation I know."

In fact, Raskin Bar Nahmias knew other tales. He had travelled to the strange and splendorous lands of the east, and to the icy expanses of the farthest north, and knew those distant peoples too had their own stories of how the world began. Did his own people really possess the one true story, as they believed? Did anyone—could anyone?—really know the truth? Did truth even exist?

Perhaps it was best not to think of such things.

"Indeed," he began, "the Shiradim and Quarterians tell the same story about the beginning of the world. Some small details change, but otherwise the tale is similar. In the beginning, there was one sole and all-powerful god. My people call him Shirad, while the Quarterians worship him by the name Aether. He created the world by separating light from darkness, the heavens from the sea, and the oceans from the land. At that time the land was a vast desert; but Shirad caused a jet of water to spurt forth from the arid ground, irrigating the earth and filling it with life. He made the plants to grow, the trees to become heavy with fruit, and he also made animals. Finally, Shirad created a man and a woman. He made them with such zeal, that they were the most beautiful of his creations. The man and woman knew one another, and begat offspring, who begat others, and so on, until people spread and multiplied across the surface of the world.

"But, perfect as it was, Shirad's creation was not immortal. Indeed, god designed the world in cycles—day and night, seasons and years, birth and death. But when the first humans died, Shirad grew regretful, and determined that men and women should live another life, the first being too short. He created another world, similar to the first, save that there it would be possible for all people to distinguish themselves, and live forever.

"This second world is not accessible to everyone. You must be chosen by Shirad, and only his most fervent servants are. That's why every self-respecting Shiradim and Quarterian strives to lead a virtuous life and be worthy of a second chance. And—who knows, children?—maybe my people are right. Maybe you'll be given a second chance, too."

The tutor grinned widely, radiant with belief, in all things striving to be worthy.

Habib replied fervently:

"Mother explained that, when we die, our spirit rises to heaven to join the gods and be welcomed by Hubal..."

Jabil completed the thought:

"...and if we were to become a proud warrior *mujahid*, we would ride with Marduk and receive virgins by the score!"

"That is indeed what your religion teaches. But, even if your beliefs tend in that direction, it is still important for you to know

what other religions teach. His lordship your father is a great diplomat, who handles important matters for all the peoples of Jazirat, and hopes you will one day follow in his footsteps. For that, children, you must open your minds. I myself am convinced that there is more than one truth. Perhaps we are all right—or all wrong! Remember my words well—they will serve you on many occasions."

## The Rain of Stars

"For example, children, one finds common features among all our beliefs, similar stories that preoccupy all our philosophers and dogmatists."

Raskin stopped, and turned round to face his students, one finger pointed to the sky.

"The Rain of Stars!"

"Yes!" Habib cried. "The Rain of Stars! Mother has told us the story so many times!"

The old tutor smiled and stroked his beard, wondering for a moment if he should joke that the story was indeed an old wives' tale. He thought better of the idea.

"The legend of the Rain of Stars is common among the Saabi and the Shiradim, but is also found in ancient Agalanthian tales. I have even heard mention of it in apocryphal Quarterian scripture…"

"Does apocryphal mean the end of the world?" Jabil asked.

"No, my boy, that's 'apocalypse'. Apocryphal texts are religious writings the Magisterium does not recognise as official. But it's a complex matter, so let's focus on the Rain of Stars before we finish for the day.

"Each of the great religions agrees that, during the primeval battles of the gods, the stars fell to the earth in vast numbers. The Agalanthians believe that when Utaax discovered our world, the celestial forces manifested and welcomed him, and the fall of the stars was a gift to the peoples of Utaax of the precious *orichalcum*. Some Saabi, however, believe the Rain of Stars was the fall of the djinn to earth following the battle in heaven between Marduk and Tiamat. We Shiradim believe that, before our own, there was a first

human civilisation that Shirad punished because of its great sinfulness, and that the stars fell to ravage the world, leaving only a handful of chosen people to rebuild. The Quarterians agree with this, although not officially."

Raskin Bar Nahmias smiled to himself, then continued:

"In any cases, it doesn't matter: the stars once fell, on that we all agree, and traces can even still be found in the orichalcum mines of the Agalanthians. Whichever god was responsible, the sky once fell to the earth.

"That's the end of our first lesson. I hope you appreciate the subtlety of our world a little better. Tomorrow, we'll speak of the greatness of the Agalanthian Empire; I'll tell you tales of heroes, and show you why, years after its fall, the Empire is still important in your lives today."

# AGALANTHIAN GREATNESS

"Good morning, children," Raskin Bar Nahmias said, entering the library that Lord Ketab Ibn Mussah Abd-al-Hassan had made available for teaching his sons. "Today we'll learn about the Agalanthian Empire. As far back in time as the first known writings, it ruled over the world. Even today, even in the desert's furthest reaches, we find remains of their greatness."

## The Foundation of Therema

"Agalanthian legend says everything begins with the founding of the city of Therema, the gathering place of barbarian tribes. There were farmers and cattle breeders, animal tamers and warriors, and those who took their living from the sea, who were then the only ones who ventured far from their shores. Their small world, their town and a few nearby villages, was united under the rule of a single king, who was called Agalanth. His legendary successors would make Therema a great city, with walls, districts, temples and palaces. There it was that the Agalanthian religion developed and expanded."

"But what went before it?" Jabil asked.

"No one can say, my child. You see, history has existed since the gods gave us writing. But before then—well, how are we to know? Writing gave us a calendar, and hence history. But before—all we have are old wives' tales."

# The Agalanthian Republic

"Centuries later, Agalanth XIV, who was called the Proud Tyrant, was the last king of Therema. His people deemed him too author-itarian and incompetent, and brought his rule to an end, exiling him in the year 315, over five thousand years ago. The members of the Agalanthian senate set up a new and innovative system which they called the Republic, according to which power was in the hands of two groups. The first group comprised rich and powerful families; the second was chosen by the people; and together they formed a council called the Senate. It made all the necessary deci-sions for the smooth running of the city."

"Does that mean there was no king? No one to rule?" Habib asked.

"Not really. Someone did indeed head the council, but he did not inherit his title, but rather acquired it through merit, being chosen by the other members of the council. Perhaps you find the idea absurd? I fancy it is an attractive one..."

## The Agalanthian Legacy

The greatness of Agalanthian civilisation has marked all neigh-bouring lands, including Jazirat. Without even knowing it, all Jazirati use things in their daily lives that date from the time of the Agalanthian conquerors.

### Languages

Every people speaks its own language. In the streets of Sagrada, you can hear Quarterian, Saabi, Shiradi, and Agalanthian. In some fields, though, certain languages have emerged as tools. For exam-ple, scientists, theologians, and playwrights usually speak Agalan-thian among themselves, an ancient and noble language that's hard to understand. In contrast, merchants and politicians usu-ally know how to get by in Saabi which, enhanced by gestures and words borrowed from other tongues, is the language of exchange, business, and negotiation.

### The Calendar

The calendar places year 0 as the foundation of the city of Ther-ema by Agalanth. The year is divided into four **seasons** (spring, summer, autumn, winter) each of three **months**, which every peo-ple names differently. Each month is divided into three **tendays** (Primus, Secundus, and Tertius) of ten **days**. Finally, each day is divided into twenty-four **hours**. One month equals one lunar cycle (thirty days) and one year equals a solar cycle (360 days).

For example: the ninth day of the first tenday of the fourth month of the year 5483 is noted: 9-Primus-4-5483.

This calendar is also used throughout Jazirat, except that the days have names instead of numbers. These names derive from the stages of the final voyage of the Saabi prophets, who first camped in a daya, ascended a sebkha to a wadi which led to the foot of a jebel. The next day, the prophets crossed sand dunes in the Aram-la El-Nar, and on the sixth day Hassan tricked the djinn and saved his brothers. On the seventh day, Salif negotiated for food and fed his starving brothers, and on the eighth Tarek, the first to see the end was near, sacrificed himself to give his brothers some respite. On the ninth day, Hubal appeared in the form of a bull, announcing that the prophets' end had come, but that their people would be great. Finally, on the tenth day, the prophets arrived at Kafer Nahum to die.

The ten days of the Jazirati week are therefore named (even by the Shiradim): Aldaya, Alsebkha, Alwadi, Aljebel, Alaramla, Al-hassan, Alsalif, Altarek, AlHubal and Kafer Nahum.

### Money

The monetary system of the Agalanthians was widespread in con-quered lands, stabilising exchanges, promoting trade, and acting as a vehicle for imperial propaganda. Today the heads of the Agalan-thian emperors no longer appear on coins, instead replaced by those of local kings; but their standardised system of two types of coin—**gold talents** and **silver talents**—still prevails.

**1 gold talent = 10 silver talents**

Nevertheless, most Jazirati desert nomads, whether Saabi or Shi-radim, use barter instead of coin. Commodities are evaluated ap-proximately according to a system based on the weights of certain precious spices.

**1 ounce saffron (*za'faram*) = 10 ounces of cumin (*kammun*) = 100 ounces of cardamom (*hal*).**

One ounce of saffron is roughly equivalent to one gold talent, and one ounce of cumin to one silver talent.

**1 ounce of saffron = 1 gold talent**
**1 ounce of cumin = 1 silver talent**

Raskin smiled enigmatically.

"Things were hard to begin with. The young Republic suffered from conflicts between the masses and the influential families, but eventually a balance was reached, and Therema began to expand. The Agalanthians faced off against their neighbours, and their territories grew, becoming more and more effective and advancing in all directions. The shores of neighbouring continents, then their hinterlands, all fell to the Agalanthians. Bold and ambitious, they even spread into the endless East. The Lyoch War, made famous by literature and theatre, is just one among the many adventures making up the Republic's history."

"At that time, the Agalanthians discovered **orichalcum**, a metal which allowed them to develop powerful weapons. It was also during the Republic, and not the Empire as many think, that the Theremans subjugated Jazirat, in the 8th century, over five thousand years ago, making their mark on the world forever.

"You must not think the Republic was a Golden Age. As with any prosperous civilisation, it was beset by greed, lies, and abuse. The elite benefited from looted wealth, while the masses tottered on the edge of crisis. The Republic, which owed its success to balancing these disparate parts, finally collapsed under the pressure of its uncontrolled growth, its institutions, designed as they were for a city, woefully inadequate to the running of what had become an empire in all but name. From the year 1500, tensions multiplied, and ruthless men and women appeared."

"I knew it would never work," Habib said, triumphant.

"Try not to be so adamant. No system is perfect, all of them have flaws. Even the Agalanthian emperors were not always up to their jobs, as you will see..."

## The Advent of the Empire

Raskin Bar Nahmias took a deep breath.

"The Agalanthian Empire was born with the rise to power of Antonicus Pachtius Maximus, who rearranged the organisation of the senate to promote his own personal power. Thanks to the legions, he considerably increased Agalanthian territory and organised it into provinces. Jazirat was divided in two provinces: Exortivus in the north, and Kh'saaba in the south."

"Centuries passed. Antonicus Pachtius Maximus's successors led the Agalanthian Empire to its apogee in the 18th century. Therema, with two million inhabitants, was the largest city in the world. The peace and stability brought by the Empire favoured prosperity; the provinces developed and large cities flourished."

"The Agalanthian Empire was a theocracy. More than a mere king, the Emperor was chief administrator, leader of the armies, first magistrate, and high priest. His mission was to ensure harmony between mortals and heaven, to vouchsafe his people's morals and thus safeguard their eternal life to come."

"I know about the Agalanthian Empire," Jabil said innocently. "It was the largest of all, and lasted longest."

"Quite so. More than four thousand years. Next time, we'll consider how it fell."

## Weights and Measures

### Table 5-2: Distances

| Measure | Distance |
| --- | --- |
| Finger | 1/30 foot (1 cm) |
| Inch | 1/12 foot (2.5 cm) |
| Foot | 12 inches (30 cm) |
| Cubit | 1.5 feet (45 cm) |
| Step | 2.5 feet (75 cm) |
| Pace | 5 feet (150 cm) |
| Arpent[1] | 100 paces (150 m) |
| League[2] | 3 miles (5 km) |
| Area | Areas are all expressed in square cubits, square steps or in acres (1200 m²) |

1: The arpent corresponds to the average range of an arrow.
2: The league corresponds to the average distance travelled in one hour of walking.

### Table 5-3: Volumes

| Measure | Volume |
| --- | --- |
| Spoon | 1 centilitre |
| Cup | 10 centilitres |
| Pint | 50 centilitres |
| Skin | 1 litre |
| Bushel | 26 litres |

### Table 5-4: Weights

| Measure | Weight |
| --- | --- |
| Scruple | 1g |
| Ounce | 27g |
| Pound | 500g |

# THE HISTORY OF THE SAABI

The next day, Raskin Bar Nahmias waited in the library until the two boys arrived.

"Today," he began, "I want to talk about the Saabi. The history of your people, from its very beginnings. The Saabi are the inhabitants of the Kingdom of Kh'saaba, which occupies the southern half of the land of Jazirat. Although Jazirat contains many small Caravan Kingdoms paying homage to Kh'saaba, the Saabi comprise the vast majority of the Jazirati peoples."

"The first known kings of the Jazirati reigned over nomadic herders—not really a kingdom, but rather groups sharing the same faith and respecting the same tribal chief. The first king of Jazirat, the founder of the Saabi, was Aref Ibn Jalul. He and his followers settled a vast high plateau, where they founded a city at the start of the 7th century. It was a fertile land, which allowed the kingdom to develop its economic power."

"This was probably why the Agalanthians set their sights on the emerging kingdom. In about the year 800, Kh'saaba fell to the repeated assaults of the conquering Agalanthian legions. Imperial administrators transformed the settlement on the high plateau, which until then had mostly comprised relatively insubstantial buildings, into a true defensible city."

"According to legend, the year 950 marks the foundation of the city of Jergath the Great, Jewel of the South. The city we know today is therefore very old—some five thousand years—but its location, far from the great centres of politics, has allowed it to retain a certain independence. A very important mercantile centre, merchants from Jergath the Great maintain extended networks permitting profitable exchanges with eastern lands. Do you know Jergath the Great? Have you visited the city?"

Young Jabil shook his head, but his brother answered. "I went there once with mother. I don't remember much—I was very young—but I remember high walls, crowds of people all dressed differently, all kinds of smells. People say that the flavours of the great Orient meet those of the West at Jergath. Is that true, Master?"

"Precisely so, Habib," the old man replied. He had visited the Jewel of the South many times. It was the most captivating city he had ever seen.

## The Saabi Revolt

"Several decades after Jergath's foundation, in the year 1225," Raskin Bar Nahmias continued, "the Agalanthian governor suffered terrible defeats at the hands of the dreaded South Sea Pirates that weakened both his authority and his administration. The native Saabi joined forces with the other Jazirati and rose up against the Agalanthians, massacring their representatives and expelling their families from the city. The new king of Jergath the Great, Ismet Ibn Sayed, declared that the Agalanthian Tribute would no longer be paid."

"History tells that King Ismet's descendants subjugated the rest of the mountainous region, as well as the fertile black soil lands of the west, which had been ravaged by civil strife. King Adad Ibn Nerari and King Salazar Ibn Assad were forced to reassert their claims by force of arms, in order to repel Agalanthian incursions, and a policy of territorial domination and even colonisation was established around Kh'saaba and in the north of Jazirat, which little by little became a Saabi province."

The tutor paused, letting the children register his words. The Saabi revolt against the Agalanthians was proof that the Jazirati would never submit, that they would never stop fighting.

"In 1540," he continued, "when the Agalanthian Republic had given way to Empire, the Saabi kingdom reached its zenith under the rule of King Yusuf Ibn Marek. He crushed the Agalanthian legions deployed in the north of Jazirat and seized the city of Fragrance, successes which made the Kingdom of Kh'saaba the second most powerful realm of its age. But the king's reign ended in chaos after he was assassinated in a conspiracy at court. Kh'saaba emerged from the dynastic crisis weakened, and the new king was defeated and taken captive by envoys of the Agalanthian emperor. Eventually, after much intrigue at court, a new dynasty took the throne of Kh'saaba, but its kings were subdued by the ceaseless Agalanthian attacks which in a few short years robbed them of their northern possessions and cut their communication channels to the west. The Kingdom of Kh'saaba shrank, to the lands around Jergath the Great."

---

## Orichalcum

**Orichalcum** is a mysterious metal that has all but disappeared today. Agalanthian sages describe it as the most precious of metals after gold. Extremely strong and durable, its great malleability meant it could be used to make items of incomparable fineness and beauty. Even its colour varied. Depending on the sun, it could go from the coldest blue to the most intense carmine red. It's said the Emperor's throne was forged from this metal, and that it encrusted the columns and dome of the Temple of Utaax and covered even its pavements and walls. Orichalcum weapons were said to be the best ever made.

Today, rare treasures of orichalcum are sometimes found in perilous Agalanthian ruins (page 300). Their prices are astronomical, and few people alive know the secrets of forging them.

## The Southern Province

"The Kingdom of Kh'saaba suffered greatly under the new dynasty. Saabi control of neighbouring territories was weak, little more than a sworn submission and payment of tribute, and necessitated constant and repeated expeditions to re-assert Saabi power. Indeed, whenever Saabi pressure relaxed, the territories stopped paying tribute.

"The kings of Kh'saaba were unable to curb these problems, and as a result lost authority among the nobility. Having grown rich during Jergath's conquests, these nobles had amassed lands and wealth, giving them power at court. Their families saw the kingdom losing its treasures and holdings, and realised they stood to gain if Kh'saaba returned to the Agalanthian fold. They joined together, refusing to contribute to the war effort, and—worse still—sold strategic information on troop movements and city defences in exchange for favourable trade rights."

"Traitors among our own people?" Habib exclaimed. "How can that be?"

"My dear Habib, you will learn for yourself that people remain people, whatever the circumstances. Whether Saabi, Agalanthian, Shiradim, or even Quarterian, there is good and bad inside us all. Most of us look to our own comfort before others. It is human nature."

Habib scowled. His younger brother looked on, amused.

"In the year 1984, the Agalanthian Empire attacked the Kingdom of Kh'saaba. Once more the land became an imperial province, just as it had been under the Republic. The Agalanthian gov-ernors returned, controlling the Saabi by a series of reforms. They reinforced control of the dominated territories by replacing certain vassal kingdoms with provinces administered directly by Saabi governors, and reformed the army, which they led to great victories."

Raskin stopped, sipped the tea an ebon-skinned Al-Fariqani slave had served him.

"Five centuries passed without any major upheavals. The province consolidated and developed. In the year 2500, a group of spiritual guides—teachers whom your people would come to revere as much as their gods—gathered in northern Jazirat. No one really knows why Hassan, Tarek and Salif chose to travel together. Was it the will of Hubal? A sacred quest? Or were they simply chasing a djinn? History tells us only that a terrifying wind lifted the desert sands against them, forcing them to shelter in an abandoned village, a horde of demonic spirits riding in pursuit! There was a terrible confrontation, in which all three of the spiritual teachers lost their lives. Since then, the place has been known as the Village of Consolation, or *Kafer Nahum*, as people said the deaths of the prophets brought consolation to the gods, saddened by the sins of mortals. Thanks to the sacrifice of the prophets, henceforth any mortal who followed their paths would be blessed by the gods."

"The name of Kafer Nahum was changed over time, until it became the Capharnaum of today. Its meaning expanded to refer to the whole of northern Jazirat, which the Agalanthians had previously referred to by the rather inelegant name of Exortivus."

"This is the origin of the three great noble tribes of the Saabi, around which Saabi society started to reorganise, despite the Agalanthian administration. There was another important event which took place around this time, too. In the year 2900, a small nomadic tribe, which had been a vassal tribe until then, was completely enslaved."

Raskin Bar Nahmias felt a twinge in his heart. But his words were the truth, however painful.

Jabil seemed to realise. "So your people were enslaved by ours?"

"Indeed," Raskin replied.

"So your people are inferior?" Habib interrupted his younger brother.

"Isn't an inferior people the one that falsely believes itself to be superior?" the Shiradi snapped. "I hope my teachings will show you no people is inherently inferior. A people may be inferior in number, or in military or commercial power; but no person is worth more than any another because of his origins."

The tutor waited for the moral of his lesson to sink in.

"The third and the fourth millennia that followed were an age of prosperity, when the province of Kh'saaba reached levels of power and cultural sophistication it had never seen before.

## The Legend of the Prophets

In ancient times, around the 7th century of the Agalanthian age, the earliest tribes to worship Hubal chose a place in the fertile Kh'saaba mountains to gather once a year and perform rites to their gods. Some settled there, and a town sprang up during the reign of Aref Ibn Jalul. The rare records from those days speak of a golden age without economic or political constraints or religious rivalries.

Then came the soldiers and engineers of the Agalanthian Empire. Looking for a place to build their headquarters on the incense and silk routes, they seized the town and enslaved the Jazirati living there. With their science and mathematics, the Agalanthians used their slaves as beasts of burden, placing the first stones of a city at the heart of a conquered paradise. Not without irony, the invaders gave the city a Jazirati name: Jergath the Great.

This perfect city would nevertheless live under a heavy doom, for the land where it stood had been chosen by the Jazirati gods for their people. However, judging his worshippers unworthy, Hubal punished them with twenty centuries of futile wars and subjugation to the Agalanthians. Losing their lands and honour, only to regain and then lose them again—these events are well-known to history.

The time came for Hubal to restore to the Saabi their pride, and his worshippers to the land. Choosing the three mightiest warriors of his people, the most skilled poets, who were also the wisest, and beloved of those closest to them, he created the holy mujahidin: Hassan the Just, Salif the Wanderer, and Tarek the Devourer. Then, inspired by their powers, Hubal himself took form in the mortal world, becoming the dragon, Jergath. With his breath, he annihilated the Agalanthian troops occupying Jergath the Great, and in one night raised on the ruins of the old city a new Jergath of his own, a divine city whose towers reached to heaven, crystallising the faith, bravery, and devotion of those chosen people of god.

The god had not yet finished, however. Having given Jergath a Jazirati face and restoring the pride of his worshippers, Hubal exhorted them to fight for their freedom! Agalanthian forces converged on the city and reinstated their power within the new walls.

Hubal-Jergath entrusted the three prophets with the task of unifying the Jazirati. The divine city would be the symbol of their greatness, and they should strive so that the new Saabi people would be worthy of it.

Kh'saaba was the first of the Caravan Kingdoms. One part was nomadic, strengthening themselves in the harsh desert wastes so that one day they could retake Jergath and free their fellows from the Agalanthian yoke. Hassan offered the throne to his brother, Malik, and asked his friend, Mussah, to be Malik's advisor, and his cousin Rashid to protect them both. Their offspring and loved ones would perpetuate these roles. Salif founded the first royal guild, that would one day formalise trade laws throughout Jazirat; he asked Yussef to run the guild, and Aziz to protect the caravans, and finally asked his youngest nephew, the curious Khalil, to explore the world beyond Jazirat and return with the wisdom of the gods.

Unlike Hassan and Salif, Tarek did not come from the ancient Jazirati nobility, and wanted to prove that his faith, bravery, and devotion were just as strong as the other chosen. He chose the three most notorious bandits of his tribe, lawless raiders, and spoke with them for nine days and nights. He asked them to travel all over the desert of Jazirat and beyond, spreading the word of the gods and cutting the throats of unbelievers. Tufiq, Mimun, and Mustafah acquitted themselves magnificently.

Twenty centuries passed. Jergath was ruled by the Hassanids and their relatives under the Agalanthian aegis, while in the desert, little by little, the worshippers of the One Thousand and One Gods multiplied and gained in strength. All the while, the Empire was weakened. When it began to fall, they would attack.

Hassan, Salif, and Tarek left Kh'saaba, never to return. They travelled Jazirat for years, spreading the peace and wisdom of their gods. They faced a thousand dangers and pursued the demonic enemies of their gods to the borders of damnation. Some parables claim they still live; others, that their holy madness twisted them into djinn. Some think they sleep the mystical sleep of the mujahidin, and will return to unite the tribes anew and expel the unbelievers. Everyone agrees that, in the year 2500, they gave Capharnaum its name before retreating from the mundane world. They sealed the future, not just of Kh'saaba, but of the whole of Jazirat.

Other realms tried to foment revolts within its frontiers, but all were defeated."

"Nevertheless, the province of Kh'saaba itself wasn't stable. The court had problems, including assassinations and civil wars, and numerous revolts broke out and had to be put down by force. Yet Saabi culture, art and religion developed apace. The Agalanthian occupation allowed the Jazirati to establish and manage their own religious administration, and even helped them build temples to the glory of Hubal." Raskin recalled his own visit to the Temple of Hubal. He had been young, and had gone to the sanctuary out of curiosity—the one flaw he readily admitted—and which that day got him beaten with a stick when he inadvertently interrupted the wedding of the eldest daughter of a tribal chief. He would keep that anecdote to himself...

"In 3536," he resumed, "a revolt occurred of the Shiradim, slaves of the Jazirati, under the leadership of Mogda Ibn Yussef, the younger brother of Jergath's governor. They escaped from Kh'saaba province to settle in the north, where some years later they founded the free city of Jergathine, direct competitor to Jergath the Great. From the year 4213, the trading power of Jergathine grew, and the Saabi started to raid the caravans passing through the city."

## Independence!

"At the start of the sixth millennium, the Agalanthian Empire was in decline. Provinces farthest from the centre were in revolt, gaining more and more autonomy. In this way, in the year 5050, the Agalanthian province of Kh'saaba became once again the sovereign Kingdom of Kh'saaba. Pressure mounted on Jergathine; the city was under continuous siege from 5180 to 5230, fifty years of war that ended when the mercenary troops of the Shiradim repelled the Saabi army to the desert's edge."

# THE HISTORY OF THE SHIRADIM

Raskin Bar Nahmias had material aplenty for his fourth lesson. The history of the Shiradim was a subject close to his heart, long, beautiful, often cruel. He sent for Habib and Jalil earlier than usual and started without preamble.

"The Shiradim were originally a Jazirati people, who left for the east to find more fertile lands. In isolation for several generations, they developed their own religion of the One and Only God, Shirad, who promised them the Land of the Just when they died. When the Shiradim returned to Jazirat in the year 2600, they were run out of villages and put to the sword by the Agalanthians, and found themselves mixing with the Saabi in cities like Jergath the Great under the imperial yoke. To start with all went well, but,

little by little, because of their different religion and maybe their insistence that they alone were the chosen of Shirad, the Shiradim encountered intolerance from the Saabi who had hitherto accepted them, even to the extent of accepting Shirad as an aspect of mighty Hubal.

These tensions eventually led to civil war. But the worshippers of Shirad were few in number, and the Agalanthians took the Saabi side. In 2954, the Shiradim were defeated and enslaved."

## Freedom from Slavery

"For five hundred years the Shiradim lived as slaves. During that time, around the year 3530, a man named Mogda lived in the palace of Jergath the Great. He was the youngest brother of the governor, and led great building projects in the kingdom, often in contact with the Shiradim under his command. His detractors say he was ambitious, obsessed with taking his brother's place, but he was too good a politician to become ensnared. People say he came to consider his slaves as his only chance to found his own kingdom. The Shiradim were an industrious and community-oriented people, capable of great deeds, but limited by their enslavement. Little by little, Mogda began to defend them in public, securing numerous freedoms for them, and eventually they accepted him. At the same time, his advocacy alienated his brother's court."

"Eventually Mogda was banished from Kh'saaba. He converted to the religion of Shirad and guided the Shiradim northward, to where in 3536 they would found their own country of the free, on a journey called *Et Gadol Galut*—the Great Exile. Not without irony, they had settled in the land immortalised by the prophets of their persecutors—Capharnaum!"

"And his brother allowed his workers to flee? He didn't forbid it?" Habib asked.

"An excellent point. When the governor learned his slaves were leaving, he ordered his army to bring them back. But when they reached the desert a terrible sandstorm blocked their way, clearing the way for the escapees."

## The Time of Prosperity

"Mogda's great insight was that all the world's gods are different faces of Shirad, and that Shirad is the One But Many God. He led the Shiradim to the north, and founded Jergathine in 3588. The people of Shirad had to work hard to cultivate the northern lands, but after a few decades the city prospered. The Shiradim fell in love with the desert and settled there, creating merchant caravans, occupying important oases, and becoming a major power in the desert of the Aramla El-Nar. Trade flourished, and in the year 4213 the first merchant guilds were founded."

### The Relationship Between the Agalanthians and the Shiradim

*Historians have wondered about the chequered relationship between the Agalanthians and the Shiradim. When the Shiradim were subdued by the Saabi in 2954, the Agalanthian Empire, of which Kh'saaba was a province like any other, supported them. However, six centuries later, they did nothing to oppose the Great Exile, giving the Shiradim, whose inferiority and submission they had previously endorsed, an opportunity to emancipate themselves and become a political force in Jazirat.*

*The truth of the matter is lost to history. Records of the Great Exile are rare in Agalanthian archives, and no one can really say what happened. Did the Agalanthian phalanxes oppose Mogda? Were they defeated? Did Shirad intervene to help his people reach their promised land?*

*Even today, scholars lose themselves in conjecture. Why did the Agalanthians let the Shiradim found Jergathine so close to the lands of Agalanth? How did Jergathine emerge as an economic power when the Empire was at his peak? Did it serve some divine plan?*

"The wealth of the Shiradim attracted the Saabi. Raids were numerous and violent. In 4450, the Shiradi general Yassin Bar Shimon founded his own city, Fort Yassine—pronounced Kar Yassine in my tongue, which became Carrassine, the city we're in now. Our city was originally a military stronghold, protecting Jergathine and the surrounding lands."

"Is that why Carrassine has a star-shaped wall?" Jabil would run on the ramparts whenever he escaped his parents' watchful eye.

"Yes, that's why. Carrassine was designed as a fortress. Admittedly, we're running out of room within the walls, but our city has never been taken by force, as we'll see. But let's return to the year 5180. War broke out with the Kingdom of Kh'saaba, which had just regained its own independence, and Saabi troops besieged Jergathine. Since the Saabi were more numerous and better prepared, the Shiradim were forced to use Agalanthian mercenaries—to their misfortune. Once the Saabi were driven back into the desert in 5280, the Agalanthians re-took Jergathine and once again enslaved Mogda's people!"

## Jason the Saviour

"With the Agalanthian Empire weakened, and the free Shiradi desert tribes exerting pressure on trade, the Shiradim of Jergathine went from slaves to second-class citizens, free but forbidden from holding jobs in politics or the army. Nevertheless, thanks to their desert brethren, they became an economic power. Then, in 5410, came Jason, the soldier who turned against his own when answering the divine call. The Shiradi poor saw in Jason a saviour who would give them back their cities, and the rich and powerful saw in him a means of seizing the reins of power again. But the situation got out of their control, as the new religion preached by Jason threatened their positions. Finally they decided to betray the fiery and arrogant hero of the people by delivering him to the Agalanthians, hoping to ingratiate themselves further with the Empire. Shortly after Jason's death and the Agalanthian repression which followed, the Shiradim asserted themselves once more. Taking advantage of the troubles that Jason's cultists provoked, they negotiated for a return of part of their rights and property. Helped by the desert tribes, they sought to extend their power and retake that powerful symbol: Carrassine, founded by a hero of their people."

"In 5588 came Sarah Bat Caleb, the Shiradi heroine. Sarah was a desert warrior followed by the toughest Shiradi fighters, determined to free her people. She had made a pilgrimage into the desert, where she claimed to have heard the voice of Shirad asking her to liberate Carrassine as a symbol of the covenant between the god and his people. In 5616, at the head of several tribes and the citizens of Sagrada, she marched on the City of Mercenaries that had been founded by the Shiradi general and whose wealth rivalled that of Jergath and Jergathine. Where Jason defended his own interests and give birth to a new religion, Sarah restored the pride of the Shiradi people, and managed to take one of Capharnaum's greatest cities. When her armies camped at the gates of Carrassine, Archemon the Moderate, the city's ruler, decided to parley. Sarah received him in her tent, where they spoke throughout the night. Archemon accepted the Shiradim as the majority rulers of the city, on condition that Sarah marry him to seal the alliance."

"What did she say to make him submit?" the older brother asked.

"No one knows, Habib," replied the tutor. "That is the secret of women, bending men to their will, as life will teach you to your cost. In any event, Sarah Bat Caleb's line has had a seat on the city's ruling council to this day, its vote counting double. She has become an intellectual reference for numerous thinkers, deciphering and modernising the worship of Shirad, insisting on the role of women. She had always wanted a child, and gave birth to a boy when she was 108 years old. She later withdrew to the desert to let her child command. She founded a line of priests, entrusting executive power to her cousin who became King of the City State of Carrassine. Since that day, Carrassine has been administered by my people; there's even a law that stipulates that the first councillor must be Shiradi. It's a diverse city with an eventful history, bending to the whims of trade as well as war. Mercenaries of all sorts come here. In Sagrada, formerly called Jergathine, Shiradi wealth rebuilt most of the city once the Quarterian forces left, and the Shiradim are now considered full citizens. Although several centuries of prejudice are rarely erased that easily..."

# THE HISTORY OF THE QUARTERIANS

"Do you remember Jason? We spoke of him in our previous lesson. Today we'll discuss him in greater detail. Let me tell you the story of the Quarterians."

Habib and Jalil exchanged glances; in the palace of Carrassine, there had been agitation overnight, as a delegation of those very same Knights of the Quarter had arrived for an audience with their father. They would have loved to see them, but their father had been firm: Master Raskin Bar Nahmias's lesson must come first.

"Six centuries ago, in the year 5410," the tutor intoned, "a single man tried to restore Jergathine to the Shiradim. His name was Jason, and he was the son of a minor Agalanthian king. A violent young man with a rebellious streak, he had been sent to Jergathine on military service at the age of 15. Nicknamed 'the Scourge of Shirad' for the military raids he organised in the quarters and villages of the Shiradim, filled with rape and pillage, one day he suddenly became, against all expectation, their guide and protector."

"At that time Jason was 25. He had fallen in love with a Shiradi prostitute, but, when she was killed in a raid ordered by one of his captains, everything changed. Jason's eyes were opened to the evil he had done. Suddenly, he knew all people were equal and should be loved, not despised. He converted to the Shiradi religion in 5417, becoming a priest of Mira, a female Face of Shirad which incarnated the virtues of peace and love."

"The young priest believed that peace and love should be fought for and won. With the force of his voice and his sword, he gained the trust of Shiradi extremists who presented Mira as a conquering goddess. The soldier-turned-priest claimed for himself a divine father—Aether, the All-Powerful, a god whom no one had ever heard of before—who he claimed was the War Face of Shirad. He said he was also the son of the goddess Mira, placing her foremost in his personal pantheon at Aether's side."

"Now, the goddess Mira also exists in the Saabi pantheon and many, including myself, identify her with the Agalanthian goddess Nerea, goddess of the moon, fertility and sea voyages."

The two brothers were listening with half an ear. Outside, in the corridor, the Quarterian delegation could be heard walking by. Raskin raised his voice.

"And so Jason led his group of revolutionary warriors, liberating the Shiradi quarters, burning other parts of the city and putting their inhabitants to the sword. For several weeks, a civil war raged in the capital. Finally a wall was built to separate the city of the Shiradim, the former slaves, from that the Agalanthians. It's still there today, and is known as 'Jason's Wall'. In the year 5422, after six weeks of war, the leaders of the Shiradi community received a messenger with a proposal from Pelorius, King of Jergathine: armed forces were arriving from the continent, and in three days the Agalanthian army would retake the city, with many thousands dead, innocent and guilty alike. Pelorius proposed that the Shiradim should surrender Jason to him, in return for peace and a pardon for all the rebels."

"Three days later, when the time for battle came, Jason's forces withdrew, betraying him in the sight of everyone. Only a handful of faithful, known by posterity as the Martyrs of Jergathine, remained at his side. Jason was taken, and he and his men sentenced to death by quartering the following morning."

"All of the Martyrs died. Except, it is claimed, Jason. With the strength given him by his mother Mira, Jason resisted the power of the four horses that would tear his body apart. For eight hours he pitted his muscle against theirs. The onlookers, expecting to see a bloody and horrific execution, became restless; eventually, even the horses grew tired. Amid the fiasco of a failed execution, King Pelorius decided that Jason should be released. Henceforth he would be known as Jason Quartered."

## A Duel of Destiny

"Pelorius recognised that Jason's survival was the will of the gods, and decided to grant him a favour. Jason could have asked for anything, even the liberation of the enslaved Shiradim—but they had betrayed him. Instead he challenged Pelorius to a duel. If he won, he'd become King of Jergathine and free his people; if he lost, it would prove Shirad and Mira had abandoned him, and that the Shiradim should remain in chains."

"Jason and King Pelorius withdrew into the palace to fight. Pelorius defeated Jason, confirming that in the eyes of Shirad the Shiradim should remain slaves. However, Pelorius died from his wounds shortly after. Jason's headless body was sent to Jergath the Great, and pieces were dispatched to Shiradi leaders with the message *Here is Jason, son of the gods, prince of the Shiradim.* Henceforth freedom would ever be denied to the Shiradim."

"But you are free now..." Jabil said.

"Now, yes. But, at that time, Jason's defeat and death was a great blow for the Shiradim. However, for the rest of the world, Jason had miraculously survived execution by quartering, before dying while slaying a tyrant and symbolically crushing Agalanthian power. The years which followed saw a religious revolution. In 5432, three more martyrs survived execution by quartering and reached the continent—first in the south, then the west, where they began to preach their belief in the message of Jason and his mother Mira. In 5450, this new sect, who called themselves Quarterians, began to organise, acquiring more and more believers. The Agalanthians, already in decline, tried to curb this spread in a wave of persecutions, but the damage was done. In the year 5666, Therema, capital of the Agalanthian Empire, was destroyed by earthquake, and around 5700 the Quarterian religion, with its "Holy Trinity" of Aether, Mira, and Jason, became the official religion of the western provinces. Jergathine, the city that had seen the rise of Jason Quartered, now became a holy city that needed to be won by

the new religion. The Quarterians began to call it by a new name, which has lasted to this day: Sagrada, the Holy City."

"Two hundred years ago, in about 5800, the Quarterian provinces in the west became independent kingdoms: Aragon, Orkadia, and Occidentia. They are allies, sworn to the Quarterian cause, and all obey the Magister, representative of Aether on Earth and head of the Quarterian church."

"Master, are you saying that the god the Quarterians believe in is not the same as yours?" Habib asked.

"That's right. Although they are similar, the Quarterians call their god by a different name, and worship him through different rites. Nor do we Shiradim believe that a single mortal man has been anointed supreme spokesperson on earth for our god. Today, the Quarterians have become a different religion: new, and young, and filled with fervour."

## The Legend of the Fall of Agalanth

*A legend is told in the lands of Capharnaum that a single man caused the fall of the Agalanthian Empire.*

*According to the legend, Marcus Tullius Callico, last of the Agalanthian emperors, gave an audience to a man named Imagus, who was unknown to all his advisors. Imagus, born from the thigh of the goddess Nerea, offered to help the emperor regain the splendour of the past. The mighty of Agalanthia did not deliberate long when he revealed his skill. He showed them how to unlock the power of the Dragon Eggs.*

*This knowledge should have increased Agalanthian strength tenfold, perfecting their armies, creating engines of war beyond imagining, and so much more—but the Agalanthians wielded it without skill. Consumed by overweening ambition, the draconic knowledge was beyond their ability to control. An explosion of power triggered the devastating earthquake that levelled Therema and sent a huge tsunami to sweep clean a great part of the Agalanthian lands. Only a few initiates into the secrets of the Dragon Eggs survived the cataclysm, and so knowledge of draconic science was lost with the rest of the empire. As for Imagus, no one knows what happened to him...*

# THE RECENT HISTORY OF CAPHARNAUM

## The Fall of the Agalanthian Empire

For his last lesson, Raskin Bar Nahmias asked the children to the palace courtyard. He walked with them in the small orchard that grew there.

"I want you to understand why the Agalanthian Empire fell. It was a custom of their sages to give their lessons outside, while walking. Today we're doing the same in their honour."

The Shiradi nodded towards the north, as if seeing through the palace walls. "Far beyond the sea lie the ruins of the Empire. It did not collapse in one day, and the reasons for its fall are many. Since the beginning of the sixth millennium, the Empire had been facing problems. It had become too vast, too difficult to rule, its peoples and cultures too many and different. Its outer provinces were restless, exerting their strength; some rebelled against Agalanthian authority and seized their independence, as happened in Kh'saaba."

"If I were to choose a date for the start of the Agalanthina collapse, it would be the day Jason challenged King Pelorius to their duel. It was the birth of a new religion, strong and energetic, which quickly spread throughout the Empire. In 5450, the Agalanthian religious authorities decided to fight back, and converted Quarterians were massacred in vast numbers, but it was too late. In 5564, taking advantage of the chaos, barbarian peoples from the icy north began to attack the Empire's borders. Weakened on all fronts, the Agalanthians sought to return to their past splendour, but had run out of time. In 5666, a massive earthquake flattened the capital of the oldest empire the world had ever known. The conquered provinces rose up and threw off the Agalanthian yoke. The West became independent and adopted the Quarterian faith."

"Today, Agalanthia still exists, but it's a shadow of its former self, a cluster of city states fighting among themselves for survival. Such is the fate of the greatest empire of all time. History is merciless, and nothing is forever."

## Recent Events

"History does not end, of course, and our world continues to be shaken. Only ten short years ago, in 5987, the Quarterian Magister, grand master of the religious orders of the Quarterians and supreme spiritual authority in the West, besought the three Quarterian kings to retake Sagrada and punish the 'pagans' responsible for the death of Jason. He charged them with recovering the *Mirabilis Calva Reliquiae*, the holy relic of Jason's skull, whose rightful place was at the Magisterium, seat of their religion. Disembarking in Capharnaum, the Quarterian crusaders stormed the northern and eastern coasts, establishing themselves near Carrassine and Fragrance. Fragrance fell to the Quarterians in 5989. Carrassine initially resisted their assaults, but, at the beginning of the year 5990, after months of siege, for the first time ever its stone ramparts were breached."

"The Saabi and Agalanthian royal families which dwelled within the walls of Fragrance had been massacred, their corpses tied to the backs of horses and sent to Sagrada with a message inviting the city to convert and surrender. Shortly after breaching the walls of Carrassine, Simeon IV, King of Occidentia, leader of the Holy Crusade, learned that Suleiman, Prince and Seneschal of the city, had fled the siege. In the hours which followed, the army of Carrassine retook their city from the Quarterians, but their former leader was nowhere to be found."

"Meanwhile, Queen Helicandra of Sagrada replied to King Simeon, declining his invitation to surrender. Elsewhere, Agalanthian troops razed Fragrance, killing three quarters of the Quarterians who had settled there. They sent a new message to King Simeon: '*Kill and burn as many Saabi and Shiradim as you please. One who lives in a tower of gold cares nothing for the rats that swarm in the sewers, whether they worship a city or a slave.*'"

"Helicandra held out in Sagrada for four more years, but, in 5994, an alliance was formed between the Saabi and Quarterians to take the city. Sagrada fell, but at the last moment the treacherous Quarterians turned on their Saabi allies. Simeon IV ordered the final attack, but Queen Helicandra, refusing to abandon her people to chaos, had secretly evacuated Sagrada prior to the assault. The plan had begun months earlier, the city emptying little by little through underground tunnels. Simeon IV found Sagrada devoid of resistance, but he also found what he was looking for: the Skull of the Martyr, Jason Quartered."

"During the looting of Sagrada, Simeon also stole a precious relic: the Sword of Hammad. The Saabi believe the blade of this sword is made of moonstone, and has mystical powers to unite the peoples of Jazirat. For it to leave Capharnaum was a terrible disaster. In the year 5995, an expeditionary force financed by Jergath the Great left Jazirat for the lands of the West to recover the sword."

The tutor frowned, thoughtful. "And that brings us to today. A fragile peace has settled over Capharnaum, tinged with paranoia and strife between our communities. Everyone watches everyone else. The greater part of the Quarterian forces have left, but many remain behind: soldiers, clerics, diplomats, and more. Capharnaum, it would seem, has seduced its invaders, who now hope to see fortune smile!"

"This is the last of my lessons. The future is before you, my children, its history yet to be written. Make it your own."

With these words, Raskin Bar Nahmias walked away, leaving the children in the orchard. Perhaps it was time for him to face the future, too. For ten years he had remained in Carrassine, resisting the call of the open road. Maybe, when he had thought it was all over, it was really just time to begin. Maybe he could be part of history again.

# CHAPTER SIX
# CALLIOPE – THE WORLD

## At the Summit of Faith

O nce again Luther stopped to wait for Thufir. The Jazirati had no staying power, he was good for nothing except lounging around on sofas, smoking a narghile. Yes, he had muscles, but he was built for quick, violent action. When it came to putting his back to the wheel, he sweated blood and complained constantly. Or at least so it had been since they'd begun their ascent of the Hermit's Spire.

The two men had sailed to Jergath the Great by felucca, to spend several weeks asking the priests about the strange scroll they'd found in the Orkadian wreck. Not one of them could decipher the ancient writings, but all agreed it belonged to a long-forgotten civilisation, lost beneath the desert sands. A few of them recalled a Shiradi scholar, a man well-versed in ancestral Saabi cultures—the last they'd heard, the learned personage had taken himself away to meditate at the tomb of the hermit Jaim, at the edge of the desert atop a vertiginous jebel...

Luther could just make out the top now. Unable to wait for his straggling companion another minute, he finished the climb with practised movements, honed in the distant northern mountains during the forced marches of his military training in the order of Saint Gerda. For robbing a man of his strength, the fires of the desert had nothing to match the icy cold of the frozen peaks.

At the summit, he removed his sweat-soaked turban and jellaba, feeling the Breath of Marduk, bracing at this altitude. Hand on the hilt of his gladius, he ventured into the olive grove which grew there, seeing the shine of the golden dome of a white-washed temple.

"Not another step, stranger, or thrice cursed you'll be!"

Luther looked around. From the foot of a twisted olive tree, a stunted old man looked up at him, gnarled like the old roots around him.

"I'll walk where I like, old man!"

The old man shrugged.

"As you will, unbeliever. I just wanted to warn you. You're about to step on the tomb of a holy man I call Jom, and whom the people here call Jaim—but whom you people know as Jehaum."

"What? Saint Jehaum and Jaim are the same?"

"That's right. And his tomb here is marked by this simple stone. Jom was so wise he preached all three religions, and all three called him holy. He alone can bless us... or curse us. But it was not him you came to find?"

Luther stepped back, respectfully.

"No. Are you Ezekiel Bar Itzhak?"

"No one else lives here," the old man replied, getting painfully to his feet.

"Good. Your reputation at Jergath precedes you—they call you a wise historian and a skilled astrologer. The high priest of Almaqah claims you're as fluent in the Language of Creation as that of men."

"Old Moktar must have told you I have a weakness for flattery..." the old man grinned. "It's been a long time since he made the climb to see me, and he doesn't know my meditations have humbled me. Get to the point: what do you want?"

"I want you to examine an ancient document for me."

Luther took his grandfather's scroll case from his bag and carefully removed the precious papyrus.

"Do you know this writing?"

"Yes, I do. But I'm sorry—I won't translate it for you."

"What? Why not? Name your price!"

*"Ah, the eternal greed of men! I won't translate it for you because I've done it once already for your relative. Ingmar is your relative, isn't he? An uncle perhaps? A grandfather?"*

Luther couldn't believe his ears. *"My grandfather..."* he muttered.

*"I was a novice in a desert temple when Ingmar came to see me. He spent a year with us, the time it took for me to decipher this unknown script. Eventually I discovered it was a primitive version of a tongue that is still spoken by some rare desert tribes. Your grandfather and I had become friends. I warned him to abandon his quest. He didn't listen."*

*"Warned him? About what?"*

*"About this curse. Here."*

The old man's gnarled forefinger ran along the last line of the scroll.

*"Whosoever approaches the twice-sacred sanctuary will suffer the wrath of demons and the breath of dragons..."*

*"My grandfather's ship sank after an attack by dragons..."*

*"Then Ingmar failed. Why the devil do you Dragon-Marked feel the need to go on so many insane quests?"*

*"I'm no Dragon-Marked. I'm a knight of Grunwald, and my sign is the Brass Hammer..."*

*"Ingmar used to say the same. Nevertheless, he was one of the first of the new heroes who have begun to appear again. Some day soon, the Dragon-Marked will be legion..."*

*"There are so many of us? Besides my travelling companion—"*

*"What travelling companion?"*

Glancing behind him, Luther grimaced.

*"He shouldn't be long. He's... not a great climber."*

*"Then come and sit beneath this olive tree with me and let us wait for him. I'll tell you what I know when he arrives. We'll see if he steps on the tomb of Jaim."*

# JAZIRAT

Although desert dominates the region, Jazirat offers a great diversity of landscapes, even if it's sometimes only to vary the size, shapes and colours of the dunes covering its expanse. The peninsula is divided into three. In the north lies Capharnaum, a relatively flat region that human hands have rendered fertile. In the centre spreads the Aramla El-Nar, the Desert of Fire, with its endless red sands. Few people live there, but the scattered oases allow nomad tribes to eke out their existences as best they can. Finally, in the south, great highlands loom against the sky and make up the Kingdom of Kh'saaba. Its fertile plateaus provide abundant food and a good life. The peninsula of Jazirat has many bays and inlets, and more than six hundred leagues of coastline. Coastal voyages are common.

# Capharnaum

The northern region of Jazirat is today its most populous part. It wasn't always thus: before Mogda and the arrival of the Shiradim, the plains of Capharnaum were wild and empty. But nature can be made to submit: through irrigation, crop rotation, and hard labour, plants spread across these formerly arid lands. But Capharnaum is more than that; it's the place where history is being written, where destinies are made and unmade. It's where the future of the world will be decided.

## Topography

Capharnaum comprises several regions. The highest part lies in the west, sloping gradually down towards the east. In the west, the coastal plain of Tiahm runs 70 km along the Bay of Dragons, bordered by the mountainous barrier of the Jebel Omphir, which rises from the desert to its highest point in the north near the city of Carrassine. To the east of the Jebel Omphir spreads the Nejah Plain, crossed by wadis during the rainy season. Nejah is bordered to the north by the Gulf of Oxyrhynchus. Access points to the sea are relatively rare, as most of the coastline is made up of low cliffs. However, there are numerous beaches or coves where ships can anchor. The heart of the Nejah Plain is dotted with small villages and fields devoted to farming or cattle breeding. Then comes the mouth of the Halawui River and the magnificent city of Sagrada, once called Jergathine. In the northeast, the Oxyrhynchus coast is flatter and partly irrigated; the shallow waters have deposited layers of sediment permitting abundant farming. Nejah ends at the Arm of Tiamat to the north, a sea channel which reaches deep inland and which is guarded by the Agalanthian stronghold of Fragrance. Finally, Jazirat is joined to the mainland to the east by the Limherk Plateau, an arid and rugged waste whose passage is particularly perilous.

## The Tribes of Jazirat

*Jazirati and Shiradi society are both tribal. The Kingdom of Kh'saaba comprises three major tribes, each with three royal clans, as well as a multitude of minor tribes, extended families with varying degrees of influence and power. Sometimes, the term "tribe" designates just those members of a family that have never left the area where their great-great-grandfather was born; sometimes it refers to groupings of clans whose prosperity has given rise to an entire Caravan Kingdom.*

*Whenever the term "tribe" appears in this book, and if there's no mention of names like Hassan, Salif, or Tarek (for the Jazirati) or Ashkenim, Pharatim, or Salonim (for the Shiradim), this is a general term encompassing both major and minor groupings.*

## Climate

Temperatures in Capharnaum are frequently scorching, but the weather varies according to region. The coasts are dry in winter and humid during the summer; temperatures vary, with highs of 113°F (45°C) during the eight-month hot season and lows of 59°F (15°C) during the cold season. Inland, the weather is very hot and dry during summer and mild (even cold) during winter; average temperatures vary between 113°F (45°C) in summer and 44°F (7°C) in winter; in the mountainous regions of the west, temperatures drop to below freezing. The lack of cloud cover lets the heat dissipate at night, creating huge day-night differentials. Precipitation is rare but violent inland, especially in the north. In general, Capharnaum's climate is healthy inland, painful on the coast, and hardly bearable in summer...

## Farming

In Capharnaum, gardens are enclosed areas for growing useful vegetables, or decorative ones in pleasure gardens. Farming transforms the natural environment to produce vegetables and raise livestock. Locals grow wheat, barley, millet and vegetables, including tubers, olive trees, vineyards, rice, fruit trees, and date palms. Irrigation is necessary for gardens. The plough, draught animals, manure, watermills, and windmills are all used, and irrigation uses waterwheels, canals, and even underground conduits. Most farmers also raise cattle, goats, and sheep, for meat or leather; however, dromedary camels are the most representative of Capharnaum's beasts—although Aragonian horses are increasingly encountered.

## Significant Locations in Capharnaum

### The Anchorite in the Mountains

In a cave in the depths of the Jebel Omphir lives a hermit. He retired from the world over fifty years ago to meditate on the meaning of life by leading an ascetic life. He hasn't left his cave or spoken to another soul since. He lives off food given by villagers and bandits—a loaf a week and perhaps a bit of goat's milk. No one knows who the old hermit was before he came to his cave: some say he was heir to a distant throne, others that he's just a crazy old beggar, and others still that he might even be one of the Prophets, in hiding but still in the world.

### The Eastern Mines

In eastern Capharnaum, at the foot of the Limherk Plateau, lies the greatest concentration of mine workings in Jazirat. The region is rich in all kinds of minerals: iron, silver, gold, and more. There's constant activity here, and reserves are well-guarded.

### The Lake of Genies

In the middle of the Plain of Tiahm at the foot of the Jebel Omphir lies a small lake where camels come to drink. It's said the lake is enchanted, inhabited by djinn. It never dries up, even in the most in-

# Camels

The camel is a nomad's best friend. Usually seven feet tall at the withers, its hump rises another foot. An adult can weigh 1500lbs and live for 60 years. Beloved of Hubal, the camel is a wonder of creation. It has immense stamina; although it's slower than a horse, a camel can nevertheless cover as much as 30 leagues per day. They are great survivors, and can detect underground water sources at a distance of up to 20 leagues. For desert travel, they are beyond compare, with several special adaptations.

Firstly, the dromedary camel's single hump is a reserve of up to 200lbs of fat which the animal can use to go without drinking water for several weeks. It allows them to go without food completely for 8-10 days, and indeed for several months by subsisting on little more than the rare thorny plants growing in the driest areas. Starving riders have also been known to slice strips of this fat from a restrained camel's hump, closing the incision afterwards. A camel can drink more than a hundred skins of water in about ten minutes.

The camel is equipped to face the intense heat of the desert. Its thick soles and the callouses on its leg and chest joints, upon which it rests while kneeling, allow it to withstand contact with the burning sand, and its nostrils and long-lashed eyes can shut tight to avoid flying sand particles.

Camel wool makes good clothing, its meat and milk good food, and even its excrement and urine can be used as fuel and poultices, or hair lotion and disinfecting eye drops respectively.

Camels are used in all manner of tasks: transporting commodities in caravans, pulling ploughs and powering devices such as wells and millstones, carrying riders on journeys and races, and more. Mounting a camel isn't particularly difficult, but the animal is rather tall, so you get in the saddle while the animal is recumbent and have it stand afterwards. It has a famous roll, pitch and yaw movement which gives it its nickname—the "ship of the desert".

Camels calve every two years. The female distances herself from the herd to give birth, after which the calf immediately gets to its feet and is able to rejoin the herd with its mother.

The caravaneers and camel riders of Capharnaum will tell you camels are affectionate creatures, although they're capable of holding a grudge for as much as a year before attacking their tormentors. In such cases, camel breeders customarily hold "trials" to apportion blame between camel and rider!

The recent Saabi expedition to Al-Ragon has been trying, without success, to introduce camels to its new territories there.

tense droughts, and gives its water to whomever needs it. However, it's whispered that, on nights of the full moon, if one pure of heart bathes in its waters, the genies of the lake will emerge to greet them and, in exchange for three good actions, they will fulfil one wish...

## Majid Ibn Sayed

Majid is a simple man, living in an isolated farm with his wife and two daughters in the southern part of the Nejah Plain, not far from the desert. His thatched hut has dried clay brick walls, with only two rooms. Majid lives off his farm's produce, breeding sheep and selling fruit and vegetables. Although his farm is like countless others in the region, Majid is known to travellers for his famous predictions. He uses his gift of the Sight freely, requiring neither money nor other remuneration; he asks only that visitors do not annoy his flock too much.

## Master Eliahu Bar Nissim's Workshop

The small harbour village of Kergassha, located between Fragrance and Sagrada, owes its reputation to Master Eliahu Bar Nissim's workshop. The greatest shipbuilder in Capharnaum, his workshops run at full capacity and his thirty employees are overwhelmed. He designs Carrassine's warships, although they're built in the city's famous circular harbour rather than in Kergassha's workshops, which instead are dedicated to special orders. Master Eliahu is currently working on a new ship with a revolutionary propulsion system; rumour says it uses forbidden secrets from the ancient Agalanthian Empire.

## The Samsara Camel Track

For several days every month, the small and tranquil village of Samsara, on the Gulf of Oxyrhynchus, turns into a bustling, noisy place. A circular camel racing track lies just outside the village, where regular races are organised; frenetic betting is the order of the day when races take place, and countless talents are won and lost in a few moments. Some of the owners of champion camels have made a name for themselves, and live only off their winnings.

## The Thieves' Caves

In the fastnesses of the Jebel Omphir in the west of Capharnaum lives a clan of raiders and highwaymen, kings of the mountains. They inhabit a network of natural caves. Their patriarch is Harami Al-Kabir Aziz Ibn Abdelatif (Aziz, son of Abdelatif, the Great Thief), and he rules his clan with an iron fist. With his thirty-two sons, he spreads his reign of terror over the trade routes and runs circles around the troops Carrassine sends after him. Rumour has it that Harami is the richest man in Capharnaum.

## The Village of the Prophets, the Village of Consolations: Kafer Nahum

A holy place for all Jazirati, the most devout of whom make pilgrimage here every year. These days it's a village in name only: it was in this small field of ruins, according to legend, that Hubal's three prophets, founders of the Saabi tribes, met their end. Following their exploits in Jazirat, they gathered here away from their faithful followers to hold council at Hubal's request. But they were deceived by the great dragons, who laid a trap for them, and the village became their tomb. After a titanic struggle lasting three days and nights, the prophets were defeated, although several dragons perished with them. Today you can sometimes find small smooth stones in the sand here, some black, some white: the famous Stones of Fate. It's said the white stones are the residue of dragons, and the black ones the residue of the prophets. The Jazirati call them Urim and Turim, and use them to tell the future—see page 77 for more.

see page 77 for more.

## A Typical Capharnaum Village

*Villages in Capharnaum look much the same, with minor differences. Houses are dried brick, a clever mix of straw and clay that's been in use for generations. There's no upper floor, and rarely more than three or four rooms. Roofing is a wooden structure supporting woven palm leaves. The houses of rich families are more imposing. Houses may be extended with a henhouse and conical tower dovecote.*

*At the centre of a Caphernian village stands a well, in an open square generally used as a meeting place for councils, weddings, and other significant events in the life of the community. There's usually a large fruit tree planted in the centre providing cool shade. Other trees include fig, almond, apricot, olive, orange and palm. Villagers live mainly by farming: there are small corn and barley fields, and gardens planted with carrots, tomatoes, and peppers.*

*In coastal villages, activity turns towards the sea, and includes fishing, harvesting shellfish, and gathering salt to preserve meat.*

### The Well of Emeralds

Somewhere amidst the steep, inaccessible crags of Limherk lies a legendary and hidden spring that only runs once a year. Its waters are extremely special, green in colour and slightly translucent. When exposed to the sun, the water doesn't evaporate, but rather crystallises into a myriad of small, pure emeralds.

## Towns and Cities of Capharnaum

Although much of its land is under human cultivation, Capharnaum remains largely impassable unless traversed in stages. Over the centuries people have founded villages here which have become towns and small cities. Although they have neither the size nor history of major cities such as Carrassine, Fragrance, and Sagrada, they're still vital settlements, filled with life and intrigue.

### Albagdir, the City of Traitors

Albagdir was founded in the 13th century by Bagdir Ibn Sayed, younger brother of the legendary hero Ismet Ibn Sayed. Jealous of his elder brother's popularity, Bagdir kidnapped Ismet's favourite wife and escaped into the desert to sacrifice her to Fals, god of thieves and fugitives, in return for a great destiny. Fals offered the traitor the fate he deserved, commanding him to travel to the northeast corner of the land which would one day be called Capharnaum, where, on the coasts of the Limherk Plateau, he would find a cedar forest where he should erect a statue to the god and build a city which would become legendary through the ages. Bagdir fulfilled this quest and, in that craggy, swamp-filled wilderness, in the largest cedar forest in the known world, he founded the City of Traitors. Also called the Carrassine of the East, Albagdir is a haven for criminals every other city has driven out, and a market for all types of forbidden commerce. It's not uncommon to see barbarians from the Krek'kaos walking the streets here as if the city was their home.

### Beletmei, or Godslie

According to some, this little village close by the desert is the last place where Jason Quartered was seen alive—six days after his death! Naturally, official Quarterian dogma totally rejects this claim, and any Quarterian espousing it is burned at the stake for heresy. Nevertheless, Beletmei has become a place of pilgrimage, and many from the West come here each year. It's a boomtown, just a stone's throw from the desert. A spring here is said to have miraculous powers; anyone who drinks from it is said to have the power to return from death if slain violently!

### Kawimsha

Located by the sea, this city's main industries are fishing and coral gathering. Traditionally, its men are divers, and its women refine a valuable pigment from the produce of their labour. **Kawimsha Purple** is famous throughout Jazirat, and fetches exorbitant prices as a textile dye. Three merchant guilds have set up shop here, turning the once typical village into a centre for trade. The guilds now wage a secret war for control of the Purple market; so far the main casualties have been the divers, whose "air bottles" (terracotta containers tied to their belts allowing them to "breathe" underwater) have been sabotaged, but the rivalry may soon extend to other areas.

## Messara

The northernmost of the Caravan Kingdoms is located within the borders of Capharnaum. In his early days, Messar Ibn Khalil Abd-al-Salif had wandered the world on the back of his *abzul,* and had always promised he would found a prosperous city at the place where his draconian mount died. This happened in south-eastern Capharnaum, at the foot of the Jebel Omphir, a gift of divine providence, since it lay on the route taken by the mining caravans of the mountains. Within months, Messara had become an indispensable stop for miners and caravaneers alike.

Prosperous and protected by its earthen ramparts, Messara has for centuries been independent of Kh'saaba and divested of any political or military support. The city's independence has only become more marked with time, and it has continued to diverge culturally from the rest of the Ibn Khalil (page 249). A break with the former, and therefore also with the Kingdom of Kh'saaba, was inevitable. The current king is contemplating marrying his son, Prince Abir, to the daughter of Al-Aqrab Khelil Ibn Thu'ban, a tribal chief from the Caravan Kingdom of Kathrat. If this wedding were to become a reality, Messara would perhaps regain the support it needs.

## Zarbeth

Zarbeth lies at the heart of the Nejah Plain, at the junction of two important trade routes from Sagrada and Carrassine. It marks the start of an ancient, antediluvian Agalanthian paved road—the Via Sabina—which once crossed the Aramla El-Nar and stretched as far as Jergath the Great. Today, its cobbles vanish beneath the sand just twenty leagues south of Zarbeth.

Modern Zarbeth is an important trade centre, where peoples from all corners of the known world rub shoulders under the watchful eye of a very capable Shiradi administration. Crime is almost non-existent. Ruins of the old Agalanthian city stand on the outskirts and are used, some claim, for nocturnal meetings of sorcerers seeking its mysterious lost catacombs.

# SAGRADA / JERGATHINE

## The Holy City

Built by Shiradi refugees, Sagrada has always been at the heart of great conflicts, as well as being the subject of many songs and the object of religious adoration. An important trade hub since its earliest days, the city has been besieged, liberated, attacked, burned, and put to the sword; a tumultuous history that has created a cosmopolitan society where often fraught links are forged between different ethnic groups from Jazirat and beyond.

Sagrada, also called Jergathine by the Shiradim, is the largest city in Capharnaum. Its different communities watch each other warily under the eye of their unwelcome Quarterian overlords. Memories of wrongs committed are still raw, and it would not take much for this large merchant port to become a battlefield again.

Beyond that, Sagrada remains the Holy City mentioned in the scriptures of several religions, the Promised Land of the Shiradim, and the place where Jason Quartered revealed himself to the world.

## History is Written by the Victors

The important events which made Sagrada the city it is today are related in **Chapter Five: Clio – History** (page 163). Let's take a look at what those events meant for the city directly.

## Et Gadol Galut and the Founding of the City

When Mogda led his faithful into the desert to escape Saabi oppression, the Shiradim embarked upon what they call the Great Exile, or *Et Gadol Galut* in their tongue. For several decades they travelled the desert towards the north, journeying here and there in groups, stopping in pleasant oases. When they reached the Halawui River, they decided to follow its course to enjoy its benefits and, in 3588, arrived at the river delta where the Halawui plunges into the Gulf of Oxyrhynchus. There, Mogda decided to found the city of his people and, in honour of his origins, named it Jergathine. First it was a simple village, growing up on the more level right bank, built around a temple dedicated to Shirad. Its position on the shore and unobstructed by the cliffs which otherwise make up a good portion of the Capharnaum coast made it a choice harbour for merchandise moving between north and south.

## Table 6-1: A Timeline of Sagrada / Jergathine

| Year | Events |
|------|--------|
| 3588 | Founding of Jergathine. |
| 4200 | Establishment of the Jergathine merchant guilds and the beginning of hostilities with the Saabi. |
| 5180 | The Saabi besiege Jergathine. |
| 5200 | The first Agalanthian mercenaries arrive to defend Jergathine from the Saabi. |
| 5300 | Jergathine becomes the City of the Mercenary Kings, and rules the known world. |
| 5400 | Jason, aged 15, undertakes his military service in Jergathine. |
| 5410 | Jason falls in love with a Shiradi prostitute who falls victim to a raid ordered by one of his captains. Jason converts. |
| 5417 | Jason becomes a priest of Mira. He proclaims himself the son of the goddess, and creates a personal pantheon centred on Mira and an unknown god, Aether. |
| 5422 | Beginning of six weeks of civil war in Jergathine between the Shiradim slaves and the Agalanthians. Building of Jason's Wall. Before reinforcements arrive, the Shiradim surrender and betray Jason. Jason survives execution by quartering, and faces King Pelorius in a duel which costs him his life. |
| 5987 | Quarterian troops arrive in Jazirat to retrieve the *Mirabilis Calva Reliquiae*. |
| 5994 | Alliance between the Quarterians and Saabi to take Sagrada. The Quarterians betray the Saabi and plunder the city. Simeon seizes the *Mirabilis Calva Reliquiae*, and steals the Moonstone Sword of Hammad. |
| 5997 | The Present Day. |

## The Golden Age

The Shiradi talent for trade quickly turned Jergathine into a major trading post. Its inhabitants developed an irrigation system inspired by what had been done in the Kingdom of Kh'saaba, essential for feeding the people in this arid region. As the standard of living increased, the rich and powerful settled, building their dwellings along the slopes of the left bank, constructing terraces in the Saabi style.

The Saabi envied the power of their enemy brethren and, in the year 5180, when the southern province of Jazirat became the sovereign Kingdom of Kh'saaba again, they attacked and besieged Jergathine. The Shiradim were strong, and held out a long time; but their military might and numbers proved inadequate against the fearsome Saabi. As a result, they called on Agalanthian mercenaries to help them. These troops came to break the desert tribes' siege in the year 5230.

## The Agalanthian Occupation

In the year 5280, the Saabi tribes were once again pushed back into the desert, weakened enough to no longer be a threat. The Agalanthians coveted the harbour of Jergathine, commanding as it did the trade of the whole region, and so turned on their erstwhile Shiradi allies and seized the city. Power fell into the hands of foreign princes, and the Shiradi found themselves once more enslaved—this time in their own city. They were forced to live on its eastern edge, around the first temple Mogda had built in Jergathine's early days. The river banks, harbour and more agreeable western parts of the city were occupied by the Agalanthians, who arrived in large numbers, constructing many new buildings and mixing Agalanthian architecture among the typical Shiradi dwellings. Jergathine acquired a new face and identity, its population expanding with the arrival of Agalanthian colonists seeking riches in these mysterious new lands. From this era Jergathine began to be the cosmopolitan metropolis it still is today.

When the Empire fell, so did the Agalanthian population in Jergathine. The Shiradim took advantage of eroded Agalanthian authority to increase their own influence and power base, even forcing imperial administrators to grant them citizen status. Even so, they were still not considered the equal of the Agalanthians, being limited in their choice of professional activities, but at least they were no longer slaves. Helped by their desert brethren who had remained free, Jergathine's Shiradim regained some of their past commercial power, reconnecting with their city and using their newfound wealth to build new homes.

## Jason

In the year 5410, an impetuous young Agalanthian named Jason arrived in Jergathine. On military service, his fiery attitude quickly caused him to rise to a position of responsibility. He was extremely violent towards the city's Shiradim, whom he considered inferior, and raids, pillages, and other acts of violence in the eastern quarters gave him the sobriquet "the Scourge of Shirad". As everyone now knows, an ill-fated love affair opened Jason's eyes to his actions and led him to convert to a Shiradi sect. He took up arms and led the Shiradim to retake what was theirs, embroiling Jergathine in violent outbreaks; Agalanthian forces found themselves facing religious fanatics who fought to the death. This terrible time for the city saw many quarters destroyed or burned to the ground, and it's said the Halawui delta ran red. Many tavern songs still tell stories from those desperate times.

To calm the situation and limit Shiradi exactions, Jergathine's Agalanthian administrators built a wall dividing the city in two, just east of the river. Its goal was to keep the Shiradim from the harbour quarter and the city's decision-making centres. Very soon the edifice became known as Jason's Wall, but it failed to stop Jergathine's civil war, which caused hundreds of deaths. Calm only returned after Jason's death.

Following these events, the Agalanthian Empire weakened, fragmented and eventually fell. The occupation of Jergathine ended, and the Shiradim retook power. The wounds of civil war were healed and the city restored, becoming again a prosperous mercantile harbour. At this time, the Quarterian religion was adopted as the official religion of the Western Kingdoms, who began to call the city by the name it has today—Sagrada, the Holy City—regarding it as the sacred site of the revelation and death of Jason. Jergathine thus became the meeting place of enemy religions.

## The Holy Crusade

During the Holy Crusade of the Quarterians, the city was ruled by Queen Helicandra, widow of the Shiradi lord Ebenazar Bar Shilom and a loved and respected ruler. In the year 5990, she refused to compromise with or surrender to the Quarterians, viewing her city as large, tough and ready to resist. In 5994, the Saabi, still refusing to accept their old slaves as the possessors of such economic power, allied with the Quarterians and attacked Sagrada. Their army massed at the city gates, launching a brutal assault under Simeon IV, only to find the city devoid of resistance.

The reason was simple, and amazing. In the month before the attack, and in view of the violence the Quarterians had inflicted in their initial invasion, Queen Helicandra had decided to spare her people the suffering, and organised her city's evacuation. The Shiradim had developed a sewer system of underground tunnels which permitted them to take shelter underground and even move to oases farther away in the desert where other tribes could welcome the escapees.

During the siege, the Quarterians betrayed their erstwhile Jazirati allies, and launched their own solo assault on the city, which they joyfully plundered. They retrieved the sought-after *Mirabilis Calva Reliquiae*, the skull of Jason, and returned it to their own lands. They also seized the legendary Sword of Hammad. Many Quarterian soldiers returned home, proud of liberating the city that had seen the rise of Jason. Simeon IV appointed Inigo Suarez de Bastavda as Quarterian governor of Sagrada, supported by the Quarterian troops remaining behind in Capharnaum. Little by little, the Shiradim and Saabi have returned to Sagrada, but remain under Quarterian authority.

Today Sagrada is officially in Quarterian hands. Their power rests on the threat of a fresh invasion and return of their armies, but the day-to-day reality is more one of balance and compromise between the city's many factions and peoples.

# Bedouins, Pilgrims, and Caravaneers

Sagrada is accessible from all points of the compass, and a traveller can always find his way here, wherever he comes from: everything pulls you inwards, and its mystical and religious energies attract people in droves. Sagrada's walls are tall and solid, ready to defend against attack—well, at least in normal times. Right now, they still bear the scars of the Quarterian siege, and repairs are not yet complete. Building and construction are important sources of employment.

Most often you arrive at Sagrada from the north, across the sea. A ship arriving from the Gulf of Oxyrhynchus sees the cliffs on his right shrink, and the flatter ground to the east decrease as a ship approaches the delta with its islands of mixed sandbanks and rocks. The west bank boasts a pleasure port with Agalanthian architecture; merchant ships prefer the east bank with its high capacity commercial port. The city stretches out beyond that, rising up to the western slopes. River passage is limited to ships small enough to pass beneath the bridges connecting banks and islands, but also those with flat-enough keels to cross the many shallows.

You arrive at the Gate of the Setting Sun along the sea road which runs atop the cliffs. This busy road of solid cobble has many barriers to prevent accidents such as rock falls, still frequent even today. You must keep your cool when travelling here; more than one caravan driver has lost a panicked camel plunging into the waters below.

The Gate of the Rising Sun opens on to the Fragrance Road, and thence to the Orient. It's also constructed of solid cobble, but is busier because of the flatter terrain.

The South Gate opens onto the Nejah Plain. The city approaches are fertile and cultivated, with superb irrigation works bringing water from the western highlands transforming this arid terrain into arable land. Aqueducts join canals, easily crossed by small rounded bridges, and mills run along the banks to grind grain. Finally, all paths join up again to form a single wide thoroughfare leading into the city.

## Ibttas Jazira

During their invasion, the Agalanthians didn't just kill and pillage; they imprisoned people, too. Since the existing city jails were neither numerous nor secure enough, they built their own. Half a league from the city, in the Gulf of Oxyrhynchus, stands a small inhospitable island with sixty-foot cliffs. A small quay with a guard post leads to a stairway which climbs around the rock to the sober, imposing building at the top. Heavy walls enclose it, a sheer drop on all sides; inside, living conditions are brutal, prisoners crammed into cells dug into the bedrock while the guards live above the surface. Escapes are rare, and punishments harsh.

Today the Quarterian occupiers of Sagrada use the prison; it has about a hundred inmates, mostly Saabi and Shiradim. The Saabi name for the prison means "the isle of suffering", from the terrible screams reported by sailors. No one has ever witnessed what goes on here, but everyone suspects something pretty inhuman.

## The Outer Souk

Sagradan trade is under the iron fist of the Shiradim, although they don't have a monopoly on transactions. During Jergathine's golden age, around the year 4200, Saabi merchants tried to set up shop in Sagrada. Poorly received, they tried a different approach, establishing a *souk* along the wide thoroughfare leading up to the South Gate, in the fertile, settled land a half-hour camel ride from the walls. Although the souk's occupants—members of the nomadic desert tribes—change with time, the souk is permanent, and obviously under the control of the merchant lords of the Ibn Yussef Abd-al-Salif. Anyone looking for Saabi goods will be directed to this colourful and bustling souk and its heady smells.

## The Watchtower of Doroge Murakaba

On the western shore of the Gulf of Oxyrhynchus the land rises steeply, forming high cliffs. Within sight of the city ramparts, at the highest spot, the Shiradim built a large watchtower to keep track of sea and land traffic. It's solid and stone-built, not the usual Saabi mud and straw, and Shiradi guards are on constant duty here, ready to send smoke signals to warn of any large-scale approach.

On top of the tower stands a large beacon, where a huge mirror turns around a brazier kept lit from dusk to dawn, illuminating the environs and letting sailors identify the shore and determine their distance from the port.

# Living in Sagrada

## All the World's Peoples

Sagrada is a city of tension between communities. All Jazirat's peoples are found here, as well as those from afar; its important harbour attracts everyone.

The city's most representative people are the Shiradim. They built Jergathine under Mogda's leadership, and the city is sacred to them, especially its original temple, the *Migdash Arishdon*. While simple and small (due to its great age), this is one of the most important temples in Jazirat. The Shiradim are well-established here; after the Quarterian sack of Sagrada, they quickly regained control of trade, and also gained access to many administrative positions, although the running of Sagrada is still firmly in Quarterian hands. The Shiradim are waiting for the moment the Westerners relax the pressure enough for them to recover what is theirs.

The Shiradim are the most numerous people in Sagrada (which they still call Jergathine), mostly inhabiting the historical centre in the city's eastern half around the temple, as well as the areas around the commercial port. The richest dwell in Saabi-style houses on the terraces of the west bank.

Sagrada is ruled by the Quarterians. They're a heavily-guarded minority; if it wasn't for the threat of a new mass landing of Western troops, the Jazirati would have long since taken back control by force. The Quarterian elite lead separate lives cut off from the rest of the population, in large houses in the western heights. Some try to interact with the locals, but current tensions and past history are huge obstacles to overcome.

There are also Saabi in Sagrada, although the Shiradim haven't forgotten their ill-treatment at their hands in the past. Living together isn't easy, but by and large the two populations manage to coexist relatively peacefully. In Sagrada's streets you'll also rub shoulders with travellers, adventurers, and mercenaries, although foreign traders are poorly received and prefer the Outer Souk (above).

You can also find holdovers from the Agalanthian Empire in Sagrada, those who preferred to stay after their previous lords fell from power. Most are mercenaries, descended from troops stationed in Jazirat; others have become merchants, taking advantage of the contacts they still have in Agalanthian lands.

Sagrada is a melting pot of cultures, and even includes minorities from as far afield as Al-Fariq'n, Asijawi, or the distant Krek'kaos.

## Sword and Word

Power in Sagrada theoretically rests with the Quarterian government put in place by the Holy Crusade. Its governor is a nobleman from the kingdom of Aragon appointed by the Quarterian Magister himself to keep the Holy City true to Jason's faith: his name is **Inigo Suarez de Bastavda**, and he exploits his authority without reservation. His principal strategy consists of threatening the other peoples

*Chapter 6 - Calliope*

with the power of the Quarterian army that has returned to the West, but which would return at his request. At any rate, he commands an armed contingent easily large enough to enforce the law; theoretically, Quarterian troops patrol the whole city, but they tend to concentrate on the wealthier districts in the western terraces where many in the administration dwell and work. Equally, the patrols tend to ignore places such as the Temple of the Senses or the quarters around the Migdash Arishdon in the east. Quarterian forces also hold the main bridges in the city and over the delta.

Despite enjoying the support of the Western Kingdoms, Inigo Suarez de Bastavda prefers to avoid large-scale bloodshed because, even if he were to survive such an event (and even that isn't guaranteed), he would certainly lose his position.

There are several other authorities in the city. Each people relies on community leaders to maintain order, and the city elites meet regularly and often unofficially (except for meetings with the Quarterian government) to settle social, economic and religious affairs. No one wants another civil war: the city has already suffered enough, and now everyone wants a slice of the pie. The goal is to please everyone and offend no one, and the tangle of tensions, requirements, demands, traditions, taboos, and objectives of the various factions are utterly unfathomable to the uninitiated.

All this means that the actual day-to-day running of the city happens in an informal, ad hoc way, and separate from the "supreme authority" of the Quarterians. Decisions are rarely official, and an influential person may just as easily be a religious adviser, rich merchant, leader of a network of beggars, robber prince, venal corporal, or even the mistress of an important nobleman.

Laws may also vary, even from one day to the next, as they follow Saabi and Shiradi norms while integrating those of other populations. Punishments vary, too, depending on who applies them, although there is something approaching a consensus. Serious cases are judged by representatives of the different communities involved, and locals try to avoid calling on the Quarterian authorities, which tend to resolve issues in direct, often violent, and frequently arbitrary ways.

For example, if a small-time Saabi pickpocket is caught stealing fruit from a market stall in a Quarterian district, it's likely he'll end up in prison without trial. If the same happens in the Shiradi quarter, the thief will be discreetly arrested by the local militia, who prefer to avoid Quarterian involvement. In this event, the case will be quickly decided by the wisest Shiradi representative available, usually resulting in a reprimand and a fine. If the Saabi authorities get wind of the case, they'll usually demand the thief be handed over to be punished according to their own law.

## Habits and Customs

In Sagrada, it's customary to respect other people's customs, a necessity arising from the diversity of the city's communities. To prevent general mayhem and bloodshed, people avoid giving casual offense or behaving in provocative ways. On the whole, each people present in Sagrada follows their own rites and celebrates their own festivals.

---

## Sagrada, Crossroads of Travellers

There's a tavern in the port of Sagrada that looks like many another, called **Odonta's Tooth**. At the eastern end of the trade wharfs, where ships with the most questionable cargoes dock, it's the only tavern in the city owned by an Al-Fariqani, a huge, ebon-skinned man named **Massun**. Massun arrived with a Saabi caravan from the kingdom of Kumbra-Umbassai long ago; today, Odonta's Tooth is the gathering place for the whole Al-Fariqani community in Sagrada, whether newly arrived travellers or long-term residents. The tavern is famed for its decor and typical dishes, but non-Al-Fariqani aren't always welcome; some have even ended up at the bottom of the harbour after eavesdropping on conversations not meant for them.

**Mei-Ton-Kwai** is a woman of forty years or so, whose severe personality is only rivalled by the hardness of her physical features. From a land in far-off Asijawi, she arrived in the hold of a Shiradi merchant ship and has since used all her guile to adapt herself to local customs. No one knows for certain who funded her business—some evil whispers even suggest the Paper Virgins were involved—but everyone knows Mei now runs one of the most beautiful brothels in Sagrada, and the most well-known outside the Temple of the Senses: the **Lips of Jade**. Built on the terraces in the west of the city in a style chosen by Mei herself, there you can find pleasant gardens, light sliding doors, soft floors where you walk barefoot, welcoming carpets and cushions, as well as vases and sculptures in hues of red and yellow. Madame Mei's girls come from all over the known world, and live in unparalleled luxury.

Anyone making the rounds of Sagrada's taverns will eventually cross paths with **Sven Rotbeard**, a huge bear of a man with light skin, long red hair, and a thick beard. Bigger, tougher, and a better fighter and drinker that anyone else in these desert lands (in his eyes, at least), Sven arrived on an Agalanthian merchant ship and carved out a place in Sagrada's streets using a natural strength that has left countless opponents sprawling unconscious. He has fought in every alley and backroom in bouts of differing legality, amassing a nest egg that today allows him to live life as he pleases. He goes from inn to tavern, brothel to drug den, boasting of his exploits and triggering torrents of insults and outbreaks of violence and brawling, always leaving behind enough coin to cover the drinks and broken furniture.

There is a festival celebrated throughout the city: the Festival of the First Stone, or **Even Haag**. Its date, 2-Secundus-8, marks the foundation of the city, representing the day Mogda placed the first stone in his temple. At root a Shiradi religious festival, everyone in Sagrada knows that without Mogda the city would not exist, and so the day is a holiday and jubilation fills the streets. Past resentments are forgotten, and everyone is reminded they live within the same walls.

## Resources

Sagrada's economy revolves around trade. Few items are produced locally, as raw materials are scarce. The city's harbour is vast, its port known throughout the world, and ships arrive from everywhere to empty or fill their holds. You can find products from all over the world. Gateway to the desert and to Jazirat as a whole, Sagrada is constantly alive with trade.

In times of economic crisis, Sagrada might just be able to support itself, but it would not be easy. It's already tough to maintain the irrigated farmlands around the city, and the desert always gnaws at their edges. Fishing in the Gulf of Oxyrhynchus, however, is always plentiful. Nevertheless, Sagradans love a certain amount of comfort, and tend to seek out luxuries only travelling merchants can provide.

Sagrada also has certain "sacred" resources. It's a holy city in the eyes of both the Shiradim and Quarterians, and a destination for pilgrims from all over the known world.

# Within Sagrada's Walls

Sagrada straddles the Halawui River. The eastern banks are flat, while the west climbs in a series of terraces and slopes, of varying steepness, towards the rocky country beyond. The Halawui delta itself is dotted with islets, connected by bridges of varying shapes, sizes, and styles. Sagrada is a city of social and architectural contrasts: the peoples that have occupied the city throughout its turbulent history have expanded and rebuilt it according to their own styles and tastes.

## The Banks

In the west of the city, where the land rises in terraces, the houses are built and decorated in Saabi style. Houses of earth mixed with straw appear to almost grow out of the hillsides. A city quarter built by rich Shiradim during Jergathine's golden age, the Banks offer a breath-taking view of the city while retaining their peaceful and agreeable character. Agalanthian nobles have settled higher uphill still, and have built mansions in completely different styles, but the Banks are now often home to members of the Quarterian occupation government, and the quarter is heavily policed.

## The Commercial Port

It's important to give credit where credit's due: Sagrada would not survive without its Commercial Port. It has been here since the city's foundation, occupying the whole eastern shore of the delta. Over time it has evolved, modernised, adapted to larger ships, but its style remains one of Shiradi simplicity. Square, sober, essentially utilitarian, a large paved area extends between the sea and the warehouses of local merchants. Most mercantile activity happens here, among the fishermen's stalls and sea taverns, on quays thronged with Sagradans jostling with ship's crews ashore and on wild spending sprees...

## Migdash Arishdon

The name Migdash Arishdon refers both to the temple of Mogda here as well as the traditional Shiradi district around it. A lot of trade takes place here, too, but also of a more complex nature than that done in the Commercial Port. Families of the Shiradi elite live here in sober dwellings—at least on the outside—whose interiors are rich with luxury, featuring atriums and gardens as complex as the owner is rich.

The quarter is divided from the rest of the city by Jason's Wall, a painful reminder of the ancient enslavement of the Shiradim. The Wall has been kept, so that the suffering of that period may never be forgotten; its top is studded with metal spikes. Many Shiradim come here to meditate. The wall itself no longer separates anything: it has been breached by gates in several places, walkways cross over it here and there, and of course the city has long since expanded around it to the south.

## The Old Palace

On a small plateau amidst rocky terraces stands the "Old Palace" of the ancient Agalanthian nobility. Constructed in a columned style typical of the now-defunct empire, the Palace is an important symbol to all Sagrada's communities: the fate of the Shiradim played out here when Jason faced Pelorius; and the Sword of Hammad and the *Mirabilis Calva Reliquiae* were kept here until the Holy Crusade. The Palace is now used by Queen Helicandra and her court, as well as the Quarterian government, which holds public audiences here.

## The Pleasure Port

Built on the western shore of the delta at the foot of the first terraces by the Agalanthians in their heyday, this port is smaller than the Commercial Port facing it. It's used only by small, privately-owned ships, which come to dock at slender pontoons decorated in styles reminiscent of the empire that dominated the world so long ago. Here, small, low white houses with flat roofs and pastel shutters face the sea, interspersed with alleys and stairways that wind up the sides of the hill. Life is peaceful but well-guarded, and homes in the Pleasure Port are reserved for the most fortunate, often serving as small secondary residences for the rich.

## The Temple of the Senses

The largest islet in the delta, reached by interlocking bridges, is the site of an ancient Agalanthian temple from the imperial age. Proud and majestic, it has always been well-kept; however, its purpose is much changed, and it is now a temple devoted to the pleasures of the senses. Here you can find everything for everyone: luxury inns, spice stalls, smoking dens, brothels, and more—all spread among the above- and belowground levels of this ancient holy place. Those Agalanthians still in Sagrada frown upon the temple's use today; it's operated by several clans, some of a more criminal inclination than others, who organise its activities and prevent conflicts of interest, all under the watchful eye of the Prince of Thieves Jaid Ibn Aziz Abd-al-Salif. The Quarterian government has little sway over the Temple of the Senses, and indeed few Westerners venture here, for fear of ending up at the bottom of the delta.

# Wind and Dust

Sagrada is a city filled with intrigue. At the highest level, the Quarterian envoys compete for position; at their head, Inigo Suarez tries to keep their games under control, but he knows he's equally a potential target for attacks. Many Quarterian nobles dream of usurping his position.

Nor are the heads of other factions inactive. For the moment, Helicandra has free rein among the Shiradim. However, her lack of offspring is going to cause problems when she dies. Assassinations and a settling of scores are likely, so even now the clans try to garner popular support for when that time comes. Local Saabi clans also fight surreptitiously among themselves for authority; Sagrada is part of Jazirat, which the Saabi consider their land, and so they dream of taking control here. After all, the Kingdom of Kh'saaba ruled the whole peninsula, once upon a time.

News arrives at the city, of discoveries in far-off places, of exploratory expeditions missing for years on the verge of arriving in the harbour. Seagoing merchants talk about alliances of pirates raiding the Agalanthian isles to get hold of Capharnian wealth—and especially that of Sagrada. And, recently, some strange rocks were found beneath an Agalanthian ruin on an island in the delta, allegedly impregnated with magical powers. Some people have even mentioned dragons...

# CARRASSINE

## The City of Heaven's Bastards

Founded long ago by the Shiradim when they ruled Capharnaum, Carrassine is a cosmopolitan city of great contrasts. A forbidding city of massive, heavy appearance, surrounded by star-shaped double walls, it's nevertheless also a city of welcome and lightness, gifted with magnificent hanging gardens. A city of war and destruction, with its nine legions, it's also a city of peace and culture with its university, parks and theatre. Finally, a city of siege and resistance, it's also a city of travel and mystery, Gateway to the West. Some still call it *Babilim*—the "Gateway of the Gods".

| TABLE 6-2: A TIMELINE OF CARRASSINE | |
|---|---|
| YEAR | EVENT |
| 4450 | Founding of Carrassine by General Yassine. |
| 5588 | First appearance of Sarah, the Shiradi hero. |
| 5616 | Sarah marches on Carrassine. |
| 5990 | Carrassine's walls are breached during the siege led by King Simeon IV. Suleiman, Seneschal of Carrassine, is nowhere to be found. The Quarterians are forced out of Carrassine a few hours later, and the city is still considered impregnable. |
| 5994 | Carrassine's Council of Princes sells the services of two of its legions to Jergath the Great, which allies with Quarterian troops to retake Sagrada from the Agalanthians. |

The people of Carrassine originally worshipped Shirad, god of the formerly enslaved Shiradim, and Marduk the Dragon. In time, worship of Hubal and the One Thousand and One Gods of his pantheon was introduced. Then followed the Agalanthian gods, and finally Jason Quartered. All this happened apparently without disturbing Carrassine's social fabric. In the city, people's hearts and minds mixed together; in heaven, their gods and cults did likewise. Sheltered behind its ramparts, protected by Marduk the Dragon, patron and guardian of the city, the Carrassinians have become heaven's bastards. There are better names to bear!

# History is Written by the Victors

## The Age of the First Walls

Excellence breeds wealth, wealth breeds covetousness, covetousness breeds enemies. In the year 4450, Capharnaum and the Desert of Fire which separated it from the wealthy lands of the south became the stage for great acts of rape, pillage, and massacre, motivated by hatred and jealousy. "There are princes here that are little more than thieves, and thieves worthy to be called princes," said Jeremiah Bar Ibrahim, a Shiradi war leader forced to face the unceasing attacks of Saabi tribes on his caravans and people. Jeremiah asked a certain Yassine Bar Shimon, a Prince of Thieves from Jergathine and his lifelong enemy, and the cleverest man Shirad had ever placed in his path, to find the best place to build a city that would protect Capharnaum from his enemies' attacks, both now and for all time to come. A sage among sages, the Prince of Thieves assured Jeremiah Bar Ibrahim that Jergathine was not yet threatened, but as it kept getting richer, other threats would come, larger and more numerous, bringing alliances and betrayals. What was needed, Yassine told Jeremiah, was not an outpost to protect Mogda's city from the desert, but a fortress dominating north and west, the desert and the sea.

Yassine the erstwhile thief departed with his men and an army provided by his greatest enemy. They wandered Capharnaum for many months, and finally settled upon the ideal location for a settlement that could dominate both desert and sea, watch west and north: a vast rocky overhang that local Jazirati legend called *Babilim*—the Gateway of the Gods.

In this place was built Babilim the Magnificent, a city with star-shaped double walls to protect it from demons borne on the desert wind, the *Ziyada Al-Shaytan*. Within these walls blew another wind—that of the Shiradi high priestess, Tamara Bat Lazarr, who would not permit the city to bear a Saabi (and therefore polytheistic) name. There was conflict between priestess and general, and battle at the heart of Babilim, ending in nearly six hundred dead, but victory went to Yassine. Before long, however, the general was assassinated. He had never forgotten the pleasures of his youth, and enjoyed the company of young soldiers and prostitutes in the hammams of the city, until one morning his body was found in the street, his private parts shoved in his mouth after the fashion of the Saabi desert assassins. No-one dared suspect the high priestess, Yassine's nemesis, so clear was the Saabi signature; but Salima Bint Aziz Abd-al-Salif, Yassine's advisor and mistress, stood up to Tamara Bar Lazarr and fought to keep the city and its name out of the hands of the religious authorities. In time she succeeded in giving the fortress the name of its founder: Kar Yassine, Yassine's Fort, which would later be known as Carrassine.

## The Reign of the Dragon Riders

The years pass and no two are alike when you stand at the crossroads of the world. One by one, decade by decade, Carrassine suffered upheavals. It fell to battle three times.

## Personalities of Sagrada

### Inigo Suarez de Bastavda

An Aragonian noble appointed governor of Sagrada by the Quarterian Magister himself, Inigi Suarez de Bastavda feels he is on a divine mission to keep Jason's holy city true to its faith. A haughty man and a fanatical Quarterian, he believes his is the best possible path—indeed the only possible path—and considers the Jazirati to be infidels who deserve only subjugation. He was a companion of King Simeon IV throughout the Holy Crusade, and today is the epitome of intransigence. Accompanied by an elite bodyguard, he's convinced everyone is out to get him—a conviction that isn't entirely wrong, what with the locals fighting to rid themselves of the Quarterian "invaders" and the other Western nobles who dream of taking his place.

Inigo Suarez is of average size and rather thin, with a proud and haughty bearing. He wears his black hair in a perfectly smooth ponytail, and is very proud of the thin moustache he combs every morning. He lives in a vast manor house in the western heights with his guards, employees, and servants.

### Yoranan Bar Yosef

Yoranan is the most influential kahan in Jergathine, which he absolutely refuses to call Sagrada. A member of the Pharatim tribe (page 266), he is responsible for the Migdash Arishdon, the small yet most important Shiradi temple in the city, built at Mogda's behest when the Shiradim settled here after the Great Exile. He has great influence in the Shiradi community; the voice of reason, he seeks to calm tensions and to avoid new and deadly confrontations at any price.

Yoranan is about sixty, his skin tanned by years in the sun, his body hardened by fasting and meditation. He holds himself well, despite his age, and prefers to remain discreet, speaking only wise, thoughtful, and balanced words.

## Queen Helicandra

Helicandra is an Agalanthian woman of about fifty years of age, whose beauty is not so much traditional as deriving from her personality and inner strength. She is pretty—nothing more—but is gifted with extraordinary charisma. She reached her current position by marrying Ebenazar Bar Shilom, then the King of Sagrada, who had fallen under her charms. There are many songs about their love affair and subsequent union, which represents a unification of peoples. Much loved by the populace, she continued her husband's work after his death. It was Helicandra who prevented a massacre during the Holy Crusade, by allowing Sagrada's citizens to escape through its underground tunnels, while she remained behind to stand up to Simeon IV during the sack of the city. Forced to submit to the invader, she knows she cannot fully recover her position; however, she is the most recognised authority among the Shiradim, and unofficially rules over them. Helicandra remains proud, believing she will one day have her revenge, although she is under no illusions about who has the upper hand today. She forgets nothing, and always seeks to regain her power.

Helicandra lives in a sumptuous palace, surrounded by faithful followers ready to lay down their lives for her. However, she is alone; the Queen has never found a companion to share her life. She has neither family nor heirs, and the Shiradi clans are already preparing for her succession.

## Farah Bint Sufrat Al-Jamila

Farah Bint Sufrat Al-Jamila is almost thirty years old, and recognised as the most beautiful woman in Sagrada. Countless songs pay homage to her body, that only the most foolish ever dream of holding. She is always found in the entourage of Jazirati chieftains, but her role is less clear: she gives herself to no one, does not sell her body, and has a fiery temper that has quelled the ardour of many a would-be seducer. She operates in the shadows, discussing, listening, arranging. She cools the tempers of belligerent chiefs who would seize power by force. Some consider her to be a traitor serving the Quarterian cause, pointing to the beautiful manor house she lives in and her mysterious source of income as proof. Nevertheless, there is something unearthly, almost ethereal about her, and many whisper she is protected by the divine...

## Raiss Hassun Ibn Khalef Abd-al-Sufien

This tall and solid Saabi leads a clan whose mercenary activities are known throughout Jazirat. His frank views find support among a populace tired of compromise; he's a hard-line traditionalist, making use of the warriors under his command to wage a mini-guerilla war against the Quarterian occupiers, in opposition to the desires of most other Saabi clans.

Hassun is not a discreet man. He parades proudly through the streets, a good head taller than everyone else, wearing traditional clothing and his mighty scimitar that has already severed many heads. The sword is the subject of the wildest rumours: some say it's inhabited by a powerful djinn which grants it magical power. Crowds part before Hassun, and he's always ready to fight a duel.

## Gat Bar Gat Yassin, the Poet

Sagrada boasts countless poets, either itinerant or writing for patrons, but none is as famous as the one called simply "the Poet". A Shiradi about thirty years old, the Poet wanders Sagrada's streets, declaiming magnificent verses often improvised on the spur of the moment. He never speaks clearly or concisely, but always in complex symbols, paraphrases, allusions, metaphors and other images, often only understandable to the initiated. He has a deep knowledge of the Saabi and Shiradi religious doctrine, especially considering his youth; however, he has never frequented any recognised school. No one knows his origins; he wanders from tavern to hammam, sometimes welcomed and accepted, and freely fed. His hosts listen to his predictions and announcements, understanding little, but are always keen for him to move on, as his poems are declaimed at such volume that no one can sleep. The Poet can easily spend three hours describing the waves crashing in Sagrada harbour, before just as easily veering off into a loud and obscure parable about the future of the city.

## The Ounces of Truth, the Currency of Currencies

The first major deed of Sarah and her husband was to rebuild the statue of Marduk which stood at the entrance to the ziggurat of the Council of Princes. Destroyed when the Agalanthians had taken the city, it had never been rebuilt. Legend says Shirad himself exhorted Sarah to restore the statue.

Since then, the statue of Marduk in his draconic form has reigned by the steps of the ziggurat. There, he watches over "The Truth". Anyone sincerely swearing a deep and meaningful oath before his statue is met with a strange phenomenon even today: from the statue's mouth, a red and gold liquid flows that quickly takes the shape of two small marmoset-like creatures. Six inches tall and weighing one ounce, these strange homunculi are known as "Ounces of Truth". Weddings that are love matches are performed before the statue, trials held, and nobles come from all over the world to swear before Marduk and seal their oaths with the creation of Ounces of Truth. The pacts made here are real and sacred, committed to deep in the soul of the oathtaker, sworn by honour, and not simply promises that you'll go home before midnight or some other trivial thing. Marduk only seals oaths that have a minimum of gravity: an ounce of truth.

The Ounces of Truth have no intelligence, and neither breathe nor eat. They're kept in glass vials. When a pact before Marduk has united two people in this way, each keeps a vial containing one of the Ounces. If, one day, the oath is broken, both creatures immediately die.

Needless to say, this is an excellent—indeed, foolproof—way of ensuring an oathtaker's fidelity. The Ounces of Truth only die if the oath is broken or otherwise betrayed; if a contract or engagement ends for other reasons (a specified duration is reached, one of the parties dies, etc), the creatures remain alive. In this way, Ounces of Truth are sometimes used as currency: they hold no one to their oaths anymore, but are worth a thousand gold talents and also have great symbolic value. Ruined spouses can pawn the Ounces of Truth that sealed their marriages, and merchants can even speculate on them. If a common Ounce of Truth is worth 1000 gold talents, then how much is one worth that sealed the marriage of a king? A peace treaty? The trial of a king-slayer?

This system is open to abuse, which is why two eunuch warriors are constantly assigned to guard the statue. Although no one can prevent you from coming here each day to swear dreadful oaths and depart bearing your Ounces of Truth, and indeed selling obsolete Ounces at a later time, it's forbidden to abuse this privilege by swearing oaths for Ounces of Truth you then try and sell immediately after their creation. The eunuchs file regular reports to the Council of Princes, who investigate abuses and punish them harshly. In theory, at least, this stops the truth getting turned into funny money...

The first time was an invasion from the sea. Agalanthian triremes laid bare the city's weak points by attacking its seaward flanks. For twenty years thereafter, Carrassine was under the rule of the tyrant Ianos Caliprax Avolonis, younger son of the King of Therema, a brutal child born for voyaging and war. The tyrant built a new port, Carrassine's circular harbour, now famous throughout the world.

Doubtless the tyrant's eyes were too much turned to the sea and the north to notice the threat from the desert to the south and Al-Fariq'n to the west. The next attack must have been long in the planning, because, in one night, the dragon riders of the Ibn Khalil Abd-al-Salif and their Marduki descendants fell upon and seized Carrassine. For the next forty years, Carrassine was no longer a fort but a caravanserai, a city open to the four winds, to travellers from all peoples and all horizons. No longer a stronghold but a realm of sighs, a souk in stone and sand that some called decadent and depraved. The Ziyada Al-Shaytan had blown open its gates to the demons of the desert.

Then came Sarah, and Carrassine fell for the third time.

## The Reign of the Carrassene Princes

Sarah Bat Caleb, the Shiradi hero, true saviour of her people after Jason's selfish deeds, appeared before the gates of Carrassine at the age of 58, at the end of winter in the year 5616.

Her mission was to retake the city and turn it into the pride of her people, a symbol worthy of her god, Shirad. There was neither battle nor siege: just a simple meeting, a night of debate in the tent of Sheik Archemon Ibn Khalil Abd-al-Salif, called "the Moderate". What was said that night no one knows nor ever will, but from it came a marriage and a political agreement that has endured to this day. As a symbol of the return of the Shiradim to the city, Sarah and her troops marched on Carrassine the next morning, and founded the Council of Princes. Never again would Carrassine be taken by force.

## The Present Day

The political structures established by Archemon the Moderate and Sarah Bat Caleb still hold today. A Seneschal King rules the city, aided by a Council of Princes. The council must have a Saabi majority, but is always presided over by a Shiradi. There may be one or more Agalanthians or Al-Fariqani from the Ungaras tribe (see the Clan of Khalil, page 249). The current Seneschal-King went missing five years ago, when the Quarterian King of Occidentia, Simeon the Proud, breached Carrassine's walls. Although the Carrassenes repelled the assault in a matter of hours, Suleiman Bar Zarai was nowhere to be found. Rumour says he was seen in the company of desert bedouins, or that he's in hiding in Kh'saaba.

Two years later, in 5994, the Council of Princes agreed to sell the services of two of their legions to Jergath the Great, as part of an alliance with the Quarterians to retake Sagrada from their ancient foe, the Agalanthians. The outcome is well-known (see page 185); what concerns us here is that two Quarterians ended up joining the Council of Princes. More than ever, today, Carrassine is the city of east and west, north and south, a place of worship for all the gods.

# Bedouins, Pilgrims, and Caravaneers

Situated in northwest Jazirat, Carrassine holds a particular position in an ancient location known as the Gateway of the Gods. An arid place, swept by sea winds on one side and desert winds on the other, it is often beset by sandstorms. Nevertheless, the wind is welcome, helping its population withstand the summer temperatures which approach 122°F (50°C).

## The Copper and Turquoise Road

The Copper and Turquoise Road runs along the coast of the Bay of Dragons which separates Jazirat from Al-Fariq'n, the longest but safest path linking Carrassine and the Kingdom of Kh'saaba. It takes almost five months for a caravan from Carrassine to reach Jergath the Great this way, unlike the three months it takes to cross the desert. However, this road is far less arid, and dotted with many villages of fisherfolk and herders. The road is especially rugged where it crosses the north of Capharnaum approaching the city, as it passes through the northern tip of the Jebel Omphir, the location of many mines which contribute to Carrassine's wealth. There are frequent Carrassene patrols here, which dissuade bandits and robbers.

## Sarah's Orchards

Less than an hour's walk southeast of Carrassine's walls is a wide agricultural space as fertile as it is rich. Palm, date, and fig trees grow here, as well as many cereals. Goats and horses are also bred in great number. These lands, a gift to Sarah from her husband, today belong to two of the city's princes, Taleb Ibn-Suffih and Don Alejandro-Aranjuez de Olvidad.

## The Circus Port

A veritable city-outside-the-city, the Circus Port of Carrassine is more than a simple city quarter. Unfortified, it stands below Carrassine at the end of a 1500-foot slope. Flanked by private warehouses, stalls, and taverns, this slope is called the Via Avolonia, named for its builder Ianos Caliprax Avolonis. The port itself is set slightly inland from the sea, an extension of the Old Port, and is a circular basin some 1000 feet wide, originally excavated by Avolonis's slaves. At the centre of the basin, at the end of a wide and solid jetty, stands an islet 350 feet across, site of the admiralty and port administration. A traveller arriving by sea first enters the old rectangular harbour where numerous ships still dock, before passing through the gates of the Circus Port, from where Carrassine is reached by climbing the Via Avolonia and passing its many temptations.

## The Carrassine Legions

Carrassine is huge, but not huge enough to house its eight legions of twenty thousand men. More than two hundred thousand soldiers, healers, stable hands, and military craftsmen make permanent camp in this gigantic caravanserai, a second city-outside-the-city (after the Circus Port) which encircles Carrassine-Within-the-Walls. Needless to say, there are frequent brawls here between opposing bands from rival legions. The caravanserai also provides rich pickings for gamblers, thieves, and prostitutes.

| TABLE 6-3: THE LEGIONS OF CARRASSINE | | |
|---|---|---|
| **LEGION** | **MISSION** | **COMMANDING PRINCE** |
| I Legion | Security of the Princes' Quarter | Bakar Mani n'Bassal |
| II Legion | Infantry | Yehoshua Bar Ezra |
| III Legion | Cavalry / Wall Defence | Alejandro-Aranjuez de Olvidad |
| IV Legion | Militia / Naval Fleet | Nabil Ibn Aziz Abd-al-Salif |
| V Legion | Military Engineering | Mamud Ibn Yussef Adb-al-Salif |
| VI Legion | Infantry | Javier Jimenez Espoza de Madre-Salud |
| VII Legion | Infantry | Taleb Ibn Suffih |
| VIII Legion | Cavalry / Walad Badiya | Zaina Bint Khalil Abd-al-Salif |

The higher ranks of the legions are lodged in buildings within the walls, but the cleverest prefer to stay outside, officially or secretly, to keep an eye on their men. There are eight legions, each commanded by one of the city princes.

## The Merchant of Dreams

In the warrens of the Carrassine's Al-Ziyada Al-Shaytan medina, the souk heaves constantly, a babble of shouting and people. One day, though, there's a stall of crazy jumble no one has ever seen before. Run by a fat old man in a voluminous jellaba that stretches down to the ground, he's covered in tattoos and bald except for a plaited queue of hair on the back of his head.

And he claims to be selling dreams.

Cross his palm with gold or saffron—nothing else will do—and he'll look you in the eye and present you with an item from his stall. Sometimes it's a lamp, sometimes it's a scrap of paper, sometimes it's a rusty dagger or a cracked mirror. He tells you to place it under your head at night at follow the dreams you have.

He's appeared three days in a row, and people are starting to say the old man is a djinn, and should be driven out of the souk. This is probably the last time he'll be allowed to appear. Now—do you feel lucky? Do you want to know your dreams? And will you follow them?

Chapter 6 - Calliope

## Living in Carrassine

### All the World's Peoples

Carrassine is a cosmopolitan city, open to anyone with a talent to offer. It's a city of stonemasons, potters, soldiers, merchants, princes, and prostitutes. No one here is legitimised by their blood or beliefs, only their merits. Any craftsman capable of displaying their talents may one day become a Carrassene prince.

Of course, there are enclaves, but isn't that the way of people, to seek like-minded fellows? And of course there are intrigues and power struggles, political assassinations and wars between city quarters, trade rivalries and crimes of passion; but aren't they a part of city life? No one can legally prevent you from entering a shop or running a stall because of the colour of your skin, nowhere will ban you because of your religion, no one will kill you for praying to one god instead of another. In Carrassine there are black-skinned Quarterians, priests of Cthonos preaching in Saabi, and polytheistic Shiradim. Behind the Ziyada Al-Shaytan, only one cult really counts—and it's not that of a god, properly speaking, but rather of Marduk, the Protector Dragon of Carrassine. It is he who is said to strengthen the city walls, make the orchards fertile and the mines productive, and give warriors a strong arm and thieves a lucky hand. He carries the word of each prince to their legion.

### Sword and Word

Carrassine's system of government has been tried and tested. A Seneschal King, supreme leader of the city's mercenary legions, is aided in his rule by eight Princes who hail from the nobility as well as from the wealthy merchant and commoner classes. As a mercantile city, Carrassine has no specific political allegiance, and any people may be represented on the Council of Princes. The only restriction is that at least four Princes must be Saabi, and the High Consul—the council leader—must be Shiradi. Princes are selected by majority vote by the other Princes and the Seneschal King, whose vote counts twice, as does that of the High Consul. Candidates are also selected by the Council and Seneschal King, but spontaneous candidates have been known to present themselves, as happened in the case of the two Aragonian Princes currently on the Council.

### Habits and Customs

Carrassine has no specific rites or customs: its cosmopolitanism means that Saabi, Shiradi, Quarterian, Agalanthian, and even Al-Fariqani customs mingle, and it's true that any new arrival will be a little off-balance to begin with, but will rapidly blend in if he plays by Carrassine's rules.

### Resources

First and foremost, Carrassine prospers off the back of trade goods passing through the city. Next come the mercenaries. Copper and turquoise mining is also an important resource, as is animal rearing (goats and particularly horses, following the Holy Crusade). Finally, some farming is done around the city, in patches of greenery maintained by intensive irrigation.

## Within Carrassine's Walls

Carrassine is a dusty city of low, flat-roofed buildings, rarely more than two stories high. Its streets swarm with vendors, artists, animals, beggars and merchants, adventurers and thieves. Built on cliffs overlooking the Gulf of Oxyrhynchus, it offers breathtaking views.

The city is built on eighteen terraces and is divided into eighteen star-shaped quarters or **medinas**, each separated by an inner wall. In the lowest part of the city, behind the Al-Ziyada Al-Shaytan medina, you can find Carrassine's poorest quarters; and in its highest part, the zoo and hanging gardens, overlooking the Al-Ziggurat medina, seat of the Council of Princes and the nobility.

### Al-Ziyada Al-Shaytan Medina

The "Wall of Demons", as it's popularly known, actually comprises two large walls each seventy-two feet high. Shaped like an eight-pointed star, these walls give their shape to the whole city, each subsequent terrace adopting exactly the same form.

These two protecting walls are ninety feet thick and house the barracks of the III Legion. Open to civilians in peace time, a large part of these ramparts are a continuation of the Al-Marduk medina *souk*, making them buzz with trade, prostitution, and carousing. Some of the best shops and taverns in the city are to be found here. In time of war, civilians are restricted to the souks of the Al-Dhumma medina.

The Al-Ziyada Al-Shaytan medina occupies a single terrace.

### Al-Marduk Medina

Between the first and the second walls of the Al-Ziyada Al-Shaytan medina lies a one-hundred-foot wide stretch free of construction. This is Carrassine's great souk, home of the poor and needy, where thousands of tents house thousands of families. The poor, escaped slaves, deposed princes, petty criminals and street gladiators, lepers and plague-stricken, all can be found here. It's a den of thieves where you can find the most varied commodities and the most sordid ways to die.

The Al-Marduk medina occupies a single terrace, the same as that of the Al-Ziyada Al-Shaytan medina.

## Personalities of Carrassine

In the absence of the Seneschal King, Carrassine is ruled by a Council of Princes, headed by the High Consul. Here are those who rule Carrassine; far from being inaccessible regents, all participate in Carrassene life according to their responsibilities.

### Prince Bakar Mani n'Bassal, Legate of the First Legion

This tall man with skin like beautiful ebony hails from the jungles of Al-Fariq'n. He is legate (leader) of the First Legion of Carrassine and Lord of the Al-Ziggurat medina. This means he heads the most powerful legion in Carrassine, and also ensures security in the princes' quarters. A smiling athletic man, he enjoys debating philosophy and poetry with other nobles, students, sacred prostitutes and, most often, with Hassan, his eunuch bodyguard and long-time friend. A formidable warrior, Bakar Mani n'Bassal is also the founder and trainer of the sect of elite bodyguards of the Gateway of the Gods. These are all handsomely-paid eunuchs willing to give their lives for any employer who purchases their services from Bakar.

Fair and much-loved, Prince Bakar was the closest friend of the Seneschal King of Carrassine, and allegedly helped him escape. Some believe he knows where he is hiding.

### Prince Yehoshua Bar Ezra, Legate of the Second Legion

High Consul of the Council of Princes, Yehoshua found himself with enormous responsibilities after the disappearance of the Seneschal King. It was he who agreed, in spite of Quarterian sacrilege and under pressure from Jergath the Great, to hire out the Carrassine Legions to besiege Sagrada. It was he, too, who gave his support to two Quarterian captains to accede to the leadership of the Third and Sixth Legions after their legates were betrayed and killed in battle by Simeon IV's men.

Lord of the Al-Moallaka medina, Yehoshua Bar Ezra is more an intellectual than a politician, more a poet than a warrior. This old Shiradi dreamer and idealist often relies on his three most trusted supporters for important decisions: Bakar Mani n'Bassal, Alejandro-Aranjuez de Olvidad, and Nabil Ibn Aziz Abd-al-Salif.

### Prince Nabil Ibn Aziz Abd-al-Salif, Legate of the Fourth Legion

Lord of the Al-Marduk medina, Nabil is responsible for the people and commercial exchanges within the city. He watches over taxes, smuggling, organised crime, and is the only man the admiral reports to, and is therefore also responsible for the Carrassene harbour and fleet.

These responsibilities leave little time for play. A direct descendant of Salima Bin Aziz Abd-al-Salif, adviser and mistress of General Yassine, Nabil is a dry and severe forty-year-old, feared from one end of Capharnaum to the other.

### Prince Alejandro-Aranjuez de Olvidad, Legate of the Third Legion

Don Alejandro-Aranjuez was captain of one of the most numerous Quarterian orders, the Knights of Aragon. After Simeon IV's betrayal, he could not remain under the banner of the Quartered God and follow the orders of a king who behaved so dishonourably. Considering himself without homeland, he presented himself at Carrassine and offered his life in exchange for that of Prince Marzuk Ibn Malik Abd-al-Hassan, slain in battle by the treachery of the Quarterian king. As Prince of the Al-Ziyada Al-Shaytan medina, Don Alejandro-Aranjuez is now responsible for the city's ramparts. His legion is therefore charged with the defence, maintenance, and expansion of the city walls.

A renowned horse breeder, he has organised the import of Aragonian horses and is breeding them in Sarah's Orchards before selling them throughout Jazirat. These stallions, sold for exorbitant prices, are known as Aranjuez Thoroughbreds. Note that when Don Alejandro-Aranjuez arrived at Carrassine, he brought with him almost a thousand elite Knights of Aragon.

## Prince Mamud Ibn Yussef Abd-al-Salif, Legate of the Fifth Legion

If Carrassine had a minister for trade, it would be Prince Mamud. This elderly caravaneer has always had a good head for business, as well as the eyes of a hawk and the intuition of a thief. As he says himself: "You don't do business by wanting the other man to get rich".

Mamud is also a great traveller, who has not hesitated to voyage to the four corners of the world to negotiate the services of Carrassine (he recently visited the Magisterium). Lord of the Al-Wudu medina, Mamud has long understood that it is through people's weaknesses that you come to own them.

Disliked by his peers, Mamud runs a network of spies and assassins which criss-crosses the known world. It's said he's playing a chess-game by human proxy with an obscure Agalanthian king who loves manipulation and power.

## Prince Javier Jimenez Espoza de Madre-Salud, Legate of the Sixth Legion

In his homeland, Father Javier was a parish priest. All his life he had been a faithful friend of Don Alejandro-Aranjuez. When the captain left for war, he followed, and became his chaplain. When the captain deserted, he also followed, and that's why—to his great surprise—this chubby, little, and already aged priest has become Lord of the Al-Arkan medina, Chancellor of Carrassine university, and Legate of the Sixth legion. He has nothing of the war hero or politician about him, but he's an expert academic, learned in the teachings of the greatest Quarterian and especially Agalanthian philosophers. One of his more famous deeds has been to create street schools, obliging tutors to go several times a week to the Al-Marduk and Al-Dhumma medinas to impart their knowledge to the common people.

## Prince Taleb Ibn-Suffih, Legate of the Seventh Legion

Taleb Ibn-Suffih was once a slave in Jergath the Great. He received his freedom after saving his master's child from drowning. Legend has it that he crossed the desert with nothing but a donkey, a thin nanny goat, and a sickly billy goat. Settling in an uninhabited oasis south of Capharnaum, he managed to get his starving nanny goat and sickly billy goat to give him a family of several kids. Selling a bit of meat and milk to passing bedouins, Taleb saved enough to buy another goat, then another, and his old billy goat tupped them again and again.

And so it was that one day he arrived at Carrassine with a herd of sixty animals. He made the city his home and became an important businessman, then a politician, and, finally, a prince.

An altruistic man, never forgetting where he came from, the Legate of the Eighth Legion and Lord of the Al-Dhumma medina regularly negotiates lower taxes for the less fortunate and an increase in the donations the city gives all sorts of doctors and healers.

## Princess Zaina Bint Khalil Abd-al-Salif, Legate of the Eighth Legion

A great traveller, superb warrior, and clever adventurer, Princess Zaina is rarely found in Carrassine. Although she attaches great importance to her role as Lord of the Al-Yassine medina, she prefers to leave the maintenance of the hanging gardens to Shiradi master botanists and instead do what she does best, exploring the world to bring to the medina the strangest and most exotic animals. A free woman, she is coveted by many of Jazirat's powerful; her love, however, is for Shirad alone, whose religion she converted to not long ago. Although considered a heretic by the Saabi, she has retained the loyalty of many members of her tribe, meaning many Walad Badiya form the elite of Carrassine's cavalry, the Eighth Legion.

Princess Zaina loves challenging Prince Alejandro-Aranjuez de Olvidad to tournaments, raids, and chariot races. The games attract crowds and enrich the city, which pleases Prince Mamud. Although part of him sees Zaina as an infidel trampling the memory of the Prophets, he also sees a sublime young woman, and the only one who ever dared say no to him.

## Al-Dhumma Medina

The greater part of Carrassine spans the five terraces of the Al-Dhumma medina. Here you can find the craft districts organised according to guilds—there are streets of tanners, potters, tea merchants, blacksmiths, and so on. You can also find most inns here, as well as legion recruitment offices and headquarters of the merchant guilds. The first terrace of the Al-Dhumma medina houses eight merchant plazas: the spice market, slave market, exotic market (animals, perfumes, foreign products), horse market, two cattle markets, and two mercenary markets. In the latter two, officers from the V and VII Legions sell the skills Carrassine's mercenaries are famous for: fighters, scouts, healers, and even artists and private teachers.

The fifth terrace has the richest merchant villas in the city, rivalling those of the Al-Yassine and the palaces of the Al-Ziggurat.

## Al-Wudu Medina

When Ianos Caliprax Avolonis took Carrassine, the city stopped at the Al-Dhumma medina. From there, a path climbed to the Ziggurat, the Temple of Marduk. It's in this space that the tyrant created this quarter of thermal baths and relaxation, which is also that of exotic sexual practices.

Here, the Agalanthians diverted hot water springs to supply dozens of bathhouses, giving rise to a culture of relaxation, grooming, and, ultimately, sensual pleasure. As the centuries passed and the city was ruled by every culture, the Ablutions Quarter (the Al-Wudu medina) maintained its importance and was even enhanced. Today, whether you come to Al-Wudu to relax at the hammam while talking politics, or to abandon yourself to the pleasures of the flesh, or even simply to enjoy its massages and sweet medicines, you must always present your credentials to be allowed in. Indeed, although the medina is open to all comers, the establishments you find there—even the free ones—are committed to providing their customers with a calm, sophisticated, hygienic, and secure environment. This means they take steps to exclude those with doubtful reputations. In addition to the V Legion assigned to the medina's security, Prince Bakar Mani n'Bassal offers each establishment the services of an alumnus of his school of eunuch bodyguards. Every member of the Brotherhood of the Guardians of the Gateway of the Gods considers such an assignment a profession of faith and a learning experience testing their willpower, senses, and determination. The medina comprises two terraces, the first housing establishments accessible to common folk (soldiers, craftsmen, petty merchants), the second (far less busy) catering to services only the wealthiest merchants, nobles, and ranking military officers can afford.

## Al-Arkan Medina

Divided into two terraces, the university medina is a place of exquisite architecture, mixing Saabi onion domes with Agalanthian columns. The science libraries give way to academic salons, the university of medicine and its lecture gardens to the *Gymnasium*, an esplanade dedicated to the students' physical training. From marble stairs to flowery passageways, colonnaded forecourts to patios for studying, this quietest place in Carrassine finally opens up onto the Philosophers' Walk, a vantage point overlooking the sea. At the spring celebration every year, the Al-Arkan medina organises one of the most famous carnivals, and the Philosophers' Walk holds balls where the masks are as eccentric as the feverish bodies are bare.

The children of lords from across the known world come to study here.

## Al-Moallaka Medina

Architecturally similar to the Al-Arkan medina, the Al-Moallaka medina is dedicated to epic poetry. Although you can go from one medina to another in Carrassine without really noticing (except perhaps when passing through the arches in the walls), here you can tell almost immediately that you're somewhere different, just by watching the weird individuals wandering the streets. Even with the schools of divinatory arts and those of the muses (such as painting, mosaic, dancing and singing), the duels of epic poetry still stand out the most. Savage conflicts of improvised verse, in turns stylistic, structural and inspirational, with themes of love, religion, politics and history, these bouts, because of their intensity and sometimes length, have already led to deaths by exhaustion of some of their most fanatical devotees.

## Al-Yassine Medina

The Hanging Gardens of Carrassine are spread over three terraces, running along roofs and stairs, columns and pediments, with plants from lands as varied as their forms, and animals from all across the world. Apes and great cats, camels and serpents, saurians and multi-coloured birds, all tamed at the hands of eunuchs, come and go as they will. The medina is sacred, and to enter here requires the permission of the High Consul before you can walk its gardens to relax, philosophise, and seduce. The medina also houses the harem of the Seneschal King.

Because of its sacred nature, wide stairways were built to bypass the Al-Yassine medina, allowing people to walk directly from the Al-Moallaka to the Al-Ziggurat.

### Al-Ziggurat Medina

Finally, the villas and private gardens of the richest of Carrassine's residents span four terraces. The medina is livelier than might be expected, as many of the rich—too out of shape or indolent—demand the city comes to them. In the Al-Ziggurat medina, you may cross paths with street merchants and theatre troupes, military patrols, physicians engaged in vigorous debate, merchants, slaves, and exquisite men and women for sale.

The final terrace is the location of the Ziggurat itself: the Temple of Marduk, palace of the Seneschal King, and seat of the Council of Princes.

## Wind and Dust

### The Elephants' Graveyard

In recent weeks there's been a rumour flying round Carrassine that a wealthy merchant has discovered the location of the legendary Elephants' Graveyard. This paradise for ivory merchants is said to be hidden deep in the Al-Fariqani jungles, and apparently is soon to be the destination for a secret expedition. The first person to reach this place will become wealthy beyond measure—as will everyone he hires to accompany him.

Note that this isn't the first time this rumour has done the rounds in Carrassine. In fact it's several centuries old, and reappears almost regularly. Is it true this time?

### Hippodrome Building Site

What with all the challenges Princess Zaina and Prince Alejandro-Aranjuez made to one another, to horse and abzul races, to contests of strength and expertise between their troops and favourites, the two Princes finally agreed to finance a hippodrome outside the city walls, near the Circus Port. Building work had just begun when three of the hippodrome's architects died under strange circumstances, and several dozen slaves lost their lives in scaffolding collapses. Is it sabotage, or is the project cursed? Rumours are rife.

### The Sabre of Salima

In the poor quarters of Carrassine there's a game called "Street Gladiators". Warriors issue improvised challenges to one another when they cross paths in the streets. Witnesses form a circle and bet on the results. When one combatant is defeated, the crowd decides if he lives or dies. Needless to say, losing a hefty bet can turn the sweetest person into a howling murderer...

Recently, a masked woman has been challenging, one by one, all the greatest street gladiators, almost as if she's been tracking them down. Seven have died in the past two months, and people are getting worried about where it'll all lead. One particular rumour states that two students attending one of her fights recognised the weapon she wielded as the legendary "Scimitar of Salima Bint Aziz Abd-al-Salif", chief adviser and mistress of General Yassine, fabled founder of Carrassine 1500 years ago, frequently represented in city mosaics.

# FRAGRANCE

## The City of a Thousand Scents

Fragrance is the oldest city in Capharnaum, founded by the Agalanthians during their conquest of the world. Initially a military outpost, it became the link between Jazirat and the Empire, between the lands of the West and the mysterious East. It's a mercantile city, connecting peoples, cultures, and nations, who all mix in the Great Market at its heart. The city's magnificence, almost unchanged despite recent conflicts, is impressive even in comparison with Jergath or Sagrada; it mixes Agalanthian, Jazirati, and, more recently, Quarterian styles, giving it an intriguing, strangely attractive quality. Fragrance is a city where all countries collide, although it has never become a cosmopolitan centre like Carrassine, almost its twin; in the City of a Thousand Scents, communities live apart, in their own enclaves, in an atmosphere of mutual distrust. Fragrance's triumvirate tries to ensure a balance of power, but each faction waits warily for the conflagration that is sure to come...

## History is Written by the Victors

### In the Beginning

During the 8th century, the Agalanthian Republic turned its attentions towards Jazirat. In a military campaign masterfully led by its **strategoi** (page 270), the Jazirati tribes were defeated and forced to submit to an Agalanthian domination which was to last many centuries. The military campaigns did not last long, and during them the Agalanthian invader never built a solid fortress from which to rule this region so far from their Republic's heartlands. Some forts and garrison-villages later sprang up along the roads and coasts, but none worthy of being called the capital of Agalanthian Jazirat.

In the end, the Agalanthian Senate decided to construct a mighty fortress that would be the keystone of the Agalanthian domination of the tribes. Its eventual location was the result of long debate: many wanted to build it in southern Jazirat, but the Strategoi objected, saying that, in case of revolt, it would be impossible for reinforcements to come to the aid of the besieged. The decision was therefore taken to site the city at the head of the peninsula in northeastern Jazirat, where it would house a large garrison which could launch attacks in the south and northwest, and also be reinforced rapidly from the Republic heartlands.

Construction took the better part of a year, culminating in a proud and powerful fort with numerous neighbouring anchorages and disembarkation sites. Soon, Jazirati and Agalanthian civilians settled around the military facility, and several suburbs sprawled anarchically, housing a motley population. The fortress was never formally named, but was soon known as the bastion of Agalanth, or simply Bastion.

| TABLE 6-4: A TIMELINE OF FRAGRANCE | |
|---|---|
| YEAR | EVENT |
| 862 | The Agalanthians found Fragrance. |
| 1540 | The Saabi take control of Fragrance and the Jazirat peninsula. |
| 1984 | The Agalanthian empire retakes control of Jazirat. |
| 5988 | The Quarterians seize the city of Fragrance. |
| | The Agalanthians retake Fragrance from the Quarterians. |

## The Birth of Fragrance

Bastion fulfilled its role as an outpost of the mighty Agalanthian Republic for several centuries. Its highly mobile armies kept the peace and, although the Jazirati never really accepted Agalanthian domination, their tribes remained peaceable, and the city became more a place of cultural and commercial exchange than a fortress.

During this time, other cities appeared across Jazirat, often satellites of Bastion. Even Jergath, ruled by a governor from the Republic, was enfeoffed to the proud northern city.

This golden age had to end. In southern Jazirat the tribes eventually rebelled, taking advantage of the weakening of Agalanthian power in Jergath. Ismet Ibn Sayed became King of Kh'saaba, declaring its independence from the declining Republic. It still took several centuries for the Jazirati to become masters in their own lands. While Antonicus Pachtius Maximus proclaimed the birth of the Agalanthian Empire to a Senate ground under his heel, the tribes of Kh'saaba attacked the north. Bastion fell, and the Jazirati razed the fortress. They left the surrounding city intact, since many of their own lived there with their families.

The Saabi victory was short-lived. Asserting his power, the new Agalanthian Emperor retook lost territories, and soon northern Jazirat was once again an Agalanthian province, this time named **Exortivus**. Rather than rebuild Bastion, the Empire decided to make it a trading centre, whose wealth would fund an army capable of subjugating rebellious Kh'saaba.

Over time, the market of the city formerly known as Bastion attracted more and more caravans from all over Jazirat, as well as Agalanthian merchants and even barbarian traders from the north or east. Silk, spices, incense, and myrrh were sold on stalls weighed down with exotic goods, and everywhere the city was filled with their intoxicating scents. Little by little, the city became known as Fragrance. It was as such that the city became the capital of the Agalanthian province of Exortivus.

## The Time of Troubles

The Agalanthian Empire could not last forever. Even after retaking Jazirat and conquering Kh'saaba, a succession of crises weakened and finally destroyed its institutions, and provinces and city-states started to grant themselves independence.

It began with the Saabi revolt led by the Three Prophets (page 171). Southern Jazirat, although still under the Agalanthian yoke, had managed to assert its authority to the extent there seemed little to fear from the Agalanthians. The Shiradim gained their freedom from the Saabi and settled in the north, founding Jergathine, a stronghold and economic power which strongly influenced Fragrance's affairs. More accessible and dynamic, and supported by Carrassine, Jergathine overtook Fragrance for a time, until the Jazirati brought war to its gates. Jergathine was forced to call on the Empire to preserve its existence. Mercenaries from Therema and Fragrance drove off the Saabi, but took possession of Jergathine and from there began to rule over the world.

By this point, Fragrance had sunk to a city of little importance. Its market still attracted merchants, but its influence could not compare with Jergathine or Carrassine. Capharnaum was no longer the Agalanthian province of Exortivus, and Fragrance seemed an irrelevance, a relic of a dying imperial power. Withdrawing into itself, the city-state was hardly touched by the rise and revolt of Jason Quartered and the events which followed. The rulers of Fragrance had bet everything on trade, and politics had ceased to interest them.

## Fragrance's Double Sacrifice

In the end, Fragrance became a simple city-state, ruled by Agalanthian power but peopled by Jazirati and Shiradim, so that it looked little different from Capharnaum's other cities.

It was in this capacity that, like its sister-cities, Fragrance fell prey to the Quarterian invaders. It was unprepared for the fighting of the Holy Crusade and, in 5988, when the Quarterians arrived before its walls, the Archons wished only to negotiate. However, the besiegers' bloodlust outweighed their reason: Fragrance was plundered, and the Agalanthian and Jazirati nobili-

...ty massacred. The Quarterians occupied the city and raided all along the northern Capharnaum coasts.

Although the Agalanthian Empire was fractured, its city states could not let this affront go unanswered. The feud between the Quarterians and Jazirati did not concern the Agalanthians, so why had the western barbarians attacked them? A fleet was gathered, and the Quarterians learned why Agalanthia had once ruled the world. Fragrance was retaken and the Quarterians slain.

No city escapes from such exactions unscathed. Fragrance was in ruins, its population bled dry, its decimated and terrorised communities at one another's throats.

## The Present Day

The Strategos that had reconquered Fragrance knew it would be impossible to rule the city without the assent of all its communities. Taking for himself the title of First Archon, he invited the surviving Jazirati and Quarterians to each name a leader from their number. These leaders would rule at his side, to rebuild the city and restore its splendour, welcoming all comers. The Triumvirate was born from this decision to heal a city traumatised by senseless massacres. The balance of power it established has held ever since.

Hector Caius Sulos, the First Archon, rules Fragrance and its surrounding lands, together with Duke Charles d'Estang and Amir Nusri Ibn Malik Abd-al-Hassan. Despite this three-headed government and the rebuilding of the city, the situation in Fragrance remains tense: Agalanthians, Saabi, and Quarterians refuse to forgive past offenses, and the Shiradim in the middle play their cards as best they can.

# Bedouins, Pilgrims, and Caravaneers

Fragrance is sometimes called the Gateway to the East. Fertilised by Agalanthian irrigation works, the surrounding lands are dotted with farms and villages, peasants growing crops and grazing several breeds of cattle on rich pasture. Although the east becomes arid steppe as its rises towards the Limherk Plateau, the lands where Fragrance rules are rich and generous.

## The Claws of Cthonos

Where the fertile plain gives way to desolate steppe, where the wind wails like a tormented wraith, there have stood for centuries the dozen towers of the Claws of Cthonos. Built from black stone, capable of housing a garrison of twenty fighters, and separated by only a few hours' ride, the Claws are watchtowers to warn of any invasion from the east.

Life in the towers is an ordeal. Blasted by a constant and burning wind by day, and a freezing one by night, the solitude and the wild beasts that roam the wastes may break even the healthiest mind. Only soldiers and officers in disgrace are assigned here.

## The Harbour Villages

Although located virtually by the sea, Fragrance is not a port city. Its founders built the city inland, so it could not be attacked by a fleet. However, fifteen or so coastal villages provide port and harbour facilities: with docks and garrisons, they serve both commercial freight and the city's navy. None of these villages is located more than a day's ride from Fragrance, to which they're connected by wide, paved and well-maintained highways. The recent battles have left their mark on these harbour villages: three or four are in ruins, and Fragrance's authorities must drive away the pirates and bandits before they can be rebuilt.

# Living in Fragrance

## All the World's Peoples

Fragrance is a densely populated city covering a large area. All Jazirat's peoples, and those from elsewhere, come to visit, and sometimes settle permanently, charmed by its greatness and weight of history.

Over the centuries, Fragrance has principally been inhabited by Agalanthians and Jazirati. More recently, Shiradi and Quarterian communities have settled here. Immigration hasn't always been peaceful: the Shiradim were deported from Jergathine to Fragrance as slaves, and regained their freedom through blood and steel. The Quarterians arrived as bloodthirsty conquerors, and their battles against the Agalanthians spared neither the city nor its inhabitants.

Although Fragrance has been rebuilt by combining the influences and styles of these four communities, their past history continues to prejudice their relations. While Carrassine is a cosmopolitan melting pot, Fragrance divides its peoples into separate enclaves, and mistrust, if not outright hatred, is the rule. The Jazirati despise the Shiradim, the Agalanthians believe themselves superior to everyone, and the Quarterians damn everyone else to hell as heretics.

The atmosphere in Fragrance is hardly one of détente and co-existence, and there's little to give hope that it'll change one day.

## Sword and Word

Because of its separate community enclaves, Fragrance's government is unique. Each community lives in its own quarter, and has complete autonomy over its internal affairs, such as justice, taxes, and trade. A crime involving just one people and occurring within that people's quarter will be dealt with "in-house". Each community rules itself in ways which differ little from its people's customs. The Shiradim are headed by a council of nobles, the Saabi and Quarterians are ruled by noblemen, and so on.

Fragrance is governed by a Triumvirate comprising First Archon Hector Caius Sulos; Amir Nusri Ibn Malik Abd-al-Hassan; and Duke Charles d'Estang. Many whisper that the Triumvirate is in fact a four-headed dragon, and that the last and unofficial member is the Merchant Prince Salomon Bar Yonath. Whatever the case, each triumvir has a small court of advisors, and when a problem concerning the whole city turns up, the triumvirs and advisors form an Assembly to decide the steps to take. The Assembly also runs the city's common quarters, shared by all its peoples. Since this system was established, and despite a few clashes, Fragrance has been ruled well, each triumvir aware that only a political union will maintain the city's status among its rivals in Capharnaum.

Similarly, when a crime occurs between communities, a court whose judges are chosen from the peoples concerned arbitrates the case. A common peacekeeping militia of squads provided by each community is charged with keeping order and investigating crimes. Cooperation isn't always easy, but on the whole the system works.

According to tradition, the city's defence is the purview of the Agalanthians. Strategos Akileos Prospero Aerius is the general of the Fragrance armed forces, three quarters of whom are Agalanthian warriors. The other communities are expected to contribute by sending officers and men to make up the fourth quarter, but volunteers must accept Agalanthian predominance in military matters.

## Habits and Customs

Fractured into separate communities, Fragrance has few customs shared by the whole city. In each quarter, people follow their own customs, celebrating their own religious festivals and cultural rites. However, the communities try to show openness, and anyone may participate in celebrations, regardless of their origins or beliefs. The idea is to build bridges between Fragrance's disparate peoples, promoting tolerance in a population more inclined to shut itself away.

There is one celebration common to the whole city: the Summer Carnival. At sunset on the summer solstice, the gates of all Fragrance's quarters are opened, and costumed crowds take to the streets. The costumes, sometimes taking a year to make, are extravagant and colourful, representing almost anything: animals, objects, fantastic creatures, gods, and more. They allow anonymity, permitting individuals to enter any city quarter, talk to members of any community, seduce beautiful strangers, and so on. The Carnival lasts until the morning, and is a vital catharsis, reminding Fragrantines that they live together, and that racial and religious barriers should not prevent them from living in harmony. Only during the Summer Carnival can you see a Shiradi priest debating philosophy with a Jazirati poet, a bell-dancer tinkling to the rhythms of an Occidentian troubadour, an Agalanthian hoplite arm-wrestling an ebon-skinned warrior from the West, and more. The curious from all over Jazirat come to Fragrance to immerse themselves in this atmosphere of relaxation and communion during the Carnival and, despite the merrymaking and excess, the city militia has surprisingly few incidents to deal with.

## Resources

Like almost all big cities in Capharnaum, Fragrance gets most of its resources from trade and taxes. The Great Market, located at the heart of the old Bastion fortress, has a large enough turnover to finance the city, attracting merchants from everywhere, ready to pay through the nose for a trade permit, so sure are they to turn a profit with wagons filled with luxuries they'll sell at exorbitant prices elsewhere in Jazirat.

Although each community in Fragrance rules itself and collects its own fees and taxes, the Triumvirate charges a transaction tax to fund services and administration, including city defence, the militia, and the bureaucracy.

Finally, Fragrance's environs provide resources to the city, lands fertilised by canals and wells built during the heyday of the Agalanthian Empire and still intensively farmed today. This allows Fragrance to export grain, fruit, and livestock throughout Capharnaum and even beyond the sea.

## Charioteers

*Chariot races are the most popular sport in the city of Fragrance, and travellers come in great numbers and often from great distances to see them. Pulled by one to four horses, the chariots are driven by charioteers who are popular heroes, enjoying wealth and status commensurate with their success and popularity.*

# Within Fragrance's Walls

The outlines and contours of Fragrance betray its Agalanthian origins, but today the city has its own identity, its own unique blend of architecture and peoples. Its centre looks indisputably Agalanthian: wide paved streets, square buildings with immense colonnades, sparkling fountains. However, the other quarters resemble separate towns, built according to the rules of the community living there. Each has its own shops, craftsmen, schools, and bureaucracy, and visitors are amazed to leave a typically Agalanthian street and find themselves amidst buildings straight from a city of the West, while in the distance shine the golden domes of a Saabi temple.

Such is Fragrance: a jigsaw city, made of pieces ripped from all over the world. Only the iron will of the Triumvirate stops these disparate forces and populations from flying apart.

## The Old City

The Old City is the heart of Fragrance, what's left of the original fortress of Bastion. It's typical of Agalanthian cities: tall square buildings of white marble reflecting the sunlight. It's surrounded by a wall with eight gates which, in time, has become more decorative than defensive. From the hill on which it stands, visitors to Fragrance see the whole city and, to the north, the sea.

It's in the Old City that Fragrance's official buildings are located, including the Palace of the Assembly, a vast edifice with countless rooms where the Triumvirate and their advisers decide Fragrance's future. The Palace also serves as courtroom and headquarters of the city militia. Other palaces in the Old City serve as embassies, residences for dignitaries, and libraries or archives.

### The Forum

The theatre here, slightly separate from the Old City, is one of Fragrance's curiosities. It's available for anyone to use for half-day periods, upon request to the city authorities. Wandering scholars use it for conferences and espousing their theories, artists perform or exhibit their works, theatre plays are staged, and so on. Access for spectators is free, and a good audience is assured, whatever you have to show.

### The Great Market

The place once occupied by the fortress that gave Bastion its name is now the location of the most famous market in Capharnaum. It's a huge building several stories high with many underground levels, and every day attracts thousands of merchants and customers, some from far away. It's laid out so crowds can move between the countless stalls easily, and stories are connected by frequent stairways and ramps often wide enough for two chariots to pass abreast. Aisles are spacious, dotted with seats and fountains so people can rest, so vast is the market area. Merchants and sellers operate stalls of all sizes to sell their wares—and you can find anything here! Saabi weapons, Agalanthian art, Quarterian clothing, Shiradi books, spices, silks from the mysterious Orient, incense from Kh'saaba, jewels, toys with ingenious mechanisms, tools, maps to vanished cities, and so much more. If you can't find it here, you may not even be able to find it in the realm of the gods!

The most astonishing feature of the Great Market is the wealth of scents and perfumes that waft from the stalls. Far from mixing into a noxious mess, they exude subtle and pleasant fragrances through the market and into the streets beyond, gradually spreading through the whole city and giving it its name.

## The Agalanthian Quarter

So near to the Old City that it seems part of it, the Agalanthian Quarter looks like it's been transported lock, stock, and barrel from a city-state of the fragmented Empire. Paved and well-maintained streets, villas with impressive colonnades, fountains and ponds, decorate the quarter. Here you can find the entire Agalanthian population of Fragrance, with all they need to thrive without ever having to rub shoulders with the barbarians with whom they share the city.

### The Arena

If there's one place in Fragrance the whole population frequents with pleasure, it's the arena, the great amphitheatre where all kinds of shows—often very violent and spectacular—take place almost constantly. Almost every week, you can watch gladiator fights, horse or chariot races, fights between or with wild animals, and even particularly cruel executions.

### The University

Another place patronised by the whole Fragrantine population, the city university welcomes students from all peoples as long as they can pay for tuition.

The current dean of the university, Alexius Mercurios, is an open-minded old man who has established many chairs for teachers from other peoples, often against the opinion of his peers. You can now attend classes in Shiradi philosophy, Jazirati poetry or Quarterian theology in chambers in the several buildings that make up the university.

## The Jazirati Quarter

The villas of the Jazirati quarter have been transformed over the centuries into typical Saabi dwellings, with shining onion domes and pink marble floors. Little by little, this part of Fragrance has become a reflection of the cities of the Kingdom of Kh'saaba, and the Saabi living here feel close to their origins.

The Jazirati quarter has the greatest number of temples, and its population is very pious, encouraged by the priests of the *kahini* Omar Ibn Tufiq Abd-al-Tarek, whose growing influence and anti-Shiradi diatribes are starting to worry Amir Nusri the Triumvir. The quarter also houses many Jazirati from the Caravan Kingdoms (page 225).

## The Shiradi Quarter

A nomadic people in constant exile, the Shiradim have adapted to many environments, and often feel little need to change them. As a result, the Shiradi Quarter of Fragrance closely resembles the Agalanthian Quarter: the original architecture has remained unchanged, and the Shiradim have simply taken possession of the buildings and moved in.

The only noteworthy part of the quarter is its wide, tall wall, built by the Shiradim after they freed themselves from Agalanthian slavery. It symbolises the mistrust that the People of the One God hold towards the other peoples, and their will to defend themselves from aggression. Patrolled by elite Ashkenim warriors, the wall saved the Shiradi Quarter from fire during the two recent battles, which left the Shiradim relatively unscathed.

### The Hospital

The sole Shiradi building located outside the Shiradi Wall, this vast hospital is managed by the tribe of the Salonim. Run by Noam Bar Ezra, it seeks to be a place of peace and concord in Fragrance, and all who suffer have the right to be treated there without consideration of race, religion, or social class. Twice every tenday, the poor are treated for free. For reasons of public health, the hospital also receives a grant from the city (another gift from Amir Nusri to his friend Salomon Bar Yonath).

## The Quarterian Quarter

When the First Archon welcomed the Quarterians to Fragrance as a fully-fledged community, there were many protests. To quell them, Duke Charles d'Estang accepted that the part of the city allocated to them should be the one that had suffered the most from their exactions. Consequently, the Quarterians settled a quarter of ruins, where all the buildings had been destroyed by battle or fire.

Within a decade, the Quarterians had built a miniature Western city within the walls of Fragrance. Here you can find narrow earthen streets winding between wooden, multi-storey houses, large paved avenues leading to grey stone palaces, a church at the centre of a circular layout of streets. It's a striking contrast with other parts of the city, and anyone wandering the warrens of the Quarterian Quarter could be forgiven for thinking that they'd been transported to the distant lands of the west.

## Personalities of Fragrance

### Hector Caius Sulos, First Archon

*Hector Caius Sulos was Strategos in charge of defending Fragrance when the Quarterians attacked the city nine years ago. At the time, his troops were insufficient to repel the Western horde, and his warriors fell to the last defending the walls, and allowing a generally ineffective civilian evacuation. The Quarterians breached the walls and massacred the city's inhabitants, but Hector escaped to Etrusia, where he organised a counterattack. It was he who led the reunified Agalanthian army to retake Fragrance.*

*Hector quickly understood it would be impossible to rule Fragrance without the assent of all its communities. He came up with the idea of the Triumvirate, and as a result the Agalanthians, Jazirati and Quarterians found themselves represented among the city's rulers. The First Archon made a single mistake: he left out the Shiradim, who have held a grudge against him ever since.*

*Now approaching sixty, Hector Caius Sulos is a handsome man whose bearing recalls his Strategos past. A fine politician, his only fault is that, ultimately, he sincerely believes in the superiority of the Agalanthian people over all others, making him sometimes ignore the advice or recommendations of the assembly members.*

### Nusri Ibn Malik Abd-al-Hassan, Amir Loyal to Kh'saaba

*Unlike his clan brothers, Nusri Ibn Malik Abd-al-Hassan is more politician than general, more courtier than soldier. Luxuriously dressed and wearing rich jewellery, his intelligence and culture make him an effective ruler, and Fragrance's Saabi community is well led by such a man. Although he has many advisors from the Clan of Mussah, Nusri knows perfectly well how to defend his people's interests in the Assembly, and needs no one else to disentangle its intrigues and conspiracies.*

Nevertheless, this mighty nobleman counts among his closest friends the merchant-prince Salomon Bar Yonath. The two men have known each other since childhood and, despite the barriers separating them, their friendship has only grown with time. During the Quarterian attack, Salomon organised the escape of Nusri's family to a Shiradi-held oasis; Nusri paid his blood debt in part by naming Salomon as master of the Great Market of Fragrance. With the Saabi in the political arena and the Shiradi in the economic, these two men wield significant influence in Fragrance at the First Archon's expense.

Nusri is a handsome man, despite his forty years. His level voice puts his colocutors at ease, and his faultless manners are highly persuasive. Although a Fragrantine at heart, Nusri's soul belongs to Kh'saaba, towards which he displays faultless loyalty.

## Salomon Bar Yonath, Merchant-Prince

A childhood friend of Amir Nusri, Salomon Bar Yonath unofficially represents the Shiradi community in the Assembly and, for many, he's the fourth member of the Fragrance triumvirate, his influence exceeding that of Duke Charles d'Estang.

A rich merchant running caravans crisscrossing the whole of the Desert of Fire and reaching all corners of Jazirat, Salomon lacked only political power to become one of Capharnaum's leading lights. His friendship with Nusri has let him rise to become master of Fragrance's Great Market, allowing him at last onto Capharnaum's political chessboard. His position has let him improve the conditions of his fellow Shiradim, so that now they are considered full citizens of the city. A man who always pays his debts, Salomon has placed his fortune and power at the service of his Jazirati friend to one day expel both Agalanthians and Quarterians from their city. Both men spend their evenings drinking and planning an alliance of the two native Jazirati peoples to drive the invaders from their land.

The resemblance between Salomon Bar Yonath and Nusri Ibn Malik Abd-al-Hassan is remarkable, and many whisper they were brothers in a former life. One of the few ways of telling them apart is their clothing: the merchant-prince wears simple robes and no outer sign of wealth, unlike his friend, whose lavish outfits brighten up every Assembly meeting.

## Charles d'Estang, Duke of Occidentia

Charles d'Estang was in his teens when he disembarked with his father in Capharnaum, on a mission to chastise its heretics and retrieve Jason's holy relics. He became a man wielding fire and sword; his warrior talents were considerable, but his leadership was lacking, and he failed to organise his troops to prevent the Agalanthians from retaking Fragrance. However, Hector Caius Sulos spared him, and even offered him a place in the Triumvirate to rule the city.

Still young, Charles lacks experience in the games of politics played in Jazirat. His advisers seem unable to adapt their political vision to Jazirat's reality. His priests still urge him to lead an uprising to drive the heretics from Fragrance, despite the Quarterian contingent inside the walls being woefully insufficient to face the Agalanthian troops. Charles has gradually come to understand that, instead of honouring him by offering him a place on the Triumvirate, the First Archon has instead laid a subtle trap, in which the whole of the Quarterian population of Fragrance risks being caught.

Less than thirty years old, Charles d'Estang has aged prematurely. His once black mane and beard are tinged with grey, and his shoulders sag. He remains an accomplished knight, and there are few who can rival his sword.

## The Pleasure Quarter

As well as the Old City, there's another part of Fragrance that's frequented by all peoples—sometimes openly, and sometimes in secret: the Pleasure Quarter. It's divided into two parts: the Upper Quarter, and the Lower, sometimes called the Tenderloin.

The Upper Pleasure Quarter is an agreeable neighbourhood with well-maintained streets and illuminated buildings. It's the location of hammams and public baths where locals come to relax, get clean, and get a massage. There are establishments for all purses, and it's not rare for the communities to mix, wishing to try pleasures usually beyond their ken.

The Tenderloin is less salubrious, a hive of narrow alleys and cutthroat-haunted cul-de-sacs, thick with shabby brothels, gambling dens, and taverns. A large criminal element lives here, extorting the owners of whorehouses and mugging unlucky passers-by. The militia rarely sets foot here, believing that, if there must be a den of thieves in Fragrance, it's better that it's clearly marked and identified.

## The Crossroads Quarter

At the edge of the Old City and Pleasure Quarter there's a unique little district known as the Crossroads—**Min Maydan** in Saabi—where perhaps the only people that can be called truly "Fragrantine" live. It's an anomaly in the otherwise divided city; in Fragrance's earliest years, it was a precinct sacred to Merut, a local Agalanthian goddess of love. A large shrine was dedicated to her and, according to legend, the goddess gave her protection to all comers who loved one another, regardless of their origins or beliefs. Young lovers whose unions were forbidden by their families found sanctuary here and, thanks to the shrine's farm holdings and

workshops, those who claimed sanctuary could later reintegrate themselves into the economic life of the city.

To thank Merut, such lovers would usually consecrate their eldest child to the goddess, who would then go on to join her clergy. Her shrine still exists today, but the few couples who gave it its beginning have since become a multitude. Everyone who feels persecuted in Jazirat because of their choices in love can find a haven of peace in Min Maydan, where everyone is free to love whomever they will.

### Yoelle Bint Miriam

The orphan Yoelle, with as much Jazirati heritage as Shiradi and Quarterian, understood from a young age that her body would be her only weapon as she fought to protect herself from life's wickedness. As a child she sought refuge in a brothel, and eventually became its main attraction, enthralling her clients with her talents as a bell-dancer as well as her arts of love. Soon she earned enough to buy her freedom—and indeed the whole brothel. But this was just the beginning of her rise. Collecting lovers among the leaders of the local underworld, she set them at one another's throats, then stood back while they killed each other. Ever since she has been the uncontested mistress of organised crime in Fragrance, over which she reigns from luxurious apartments in the Tenderloin.

Now still only thirty years old and at the peak of her beauty, Yoelle Bint Miriam is one of the most powerful people in Fragrance, and the authorities prefer to negotiate rather than confront her directly. She runs her organisation with an iron fist, merciless towards any who cross her, and everyone fears her cruelty. And yet, in her heart, part of Yoelle Bint Miriam remains the child who grew up too fast, and who hides behind a shell of ruthlessness to survive.

## Wind and Dust

### The Night of the Daggers

In the depths of his temple in the Jazirati Quarter, Omar Ibn Tufiq Abd-al-Tarek, with the help of his clan brothers, is preparing to wage a religious war that could destroy Fragrance. Preaching against the city's heretics, the *kahini* has won over many Jazirati frustrated with living under Agalanthian rule, who are now ready to avenge themselves on the Quarterians who butchered so many of their own people. When the time comes, this priest of Hubal expects them to rise up, and for him to lead them in an assault on the other city quarters, an irresistible wave of the faithful of the One Thousand and One Gods of Kh'saaba. They will sacrifice every heretic in the city—Quarterian, Shiradi, any Jazirati who has sold his soul (such as Amir Nusri, who shows benevolence towards the Shiradim instead of caring for his own).

Supported and financed by a faction of the clan of Mussah (page 241), Omar senses the day is near where he will launch the faithful on a Night of Daggers to cleanse Fragrance of the impure.

### The Duke's Challenge

Duke Charles d'Estang knows he has little influence in Fragrance, despite being in the Triumvirate. Aware that his gifts as a politician are limited, he has decided to emphasise his strong points to prop up his power.

For that reason, the Duke is organising jousting tournaments in the arena of Fragrance, where warriors from over the known world can come to show off their prowess. To those who distinguish themselves, the Duke is offering a place at his side, whether they're Shiradi, Jazirati, or any other people. In this way, Charles d'Estang hopes to shore up his military power and increase his strategic options by incorporating foreign expertise. If he can't rule by word, he'll do so with steel.

During the tournaments, the Duke plans to enter the arena himself and shake the rust off his sword arm. His advisers are trying to dissuade him, but the young noble is set on demonstrating his swordsmanship, which he hopes will silence once and for all those who call him a weakling.

# ARAMLA EL-NAR, THE DESERT OF FIRE

The Aramla El-Nar desert stretches as far as the eye can see. The children of Mogda say it is like Shirad, both one and many. One, because its ruddy sands are everywhere; many, because it is never the same, always changing. There are regions of shifting dunes, others of fiery plains. The Aramla El-Nar is a land of nomads, mysteries, and djinn, a permanent struggle between fire and water, life and death.

## Sand As Far As the Eye Can See

The Desert of Fire extends from the farmlands of Capharnaum to the fertile valleys of the Kingdom of Kh'saaba, stretching the length of Jazirat. Sand covers three quarters of the peninsula, and every Jazirati has the desert carved deep in their heart. Not everyone has crossed the desert—far from it—but everyone lives with it as part of their daily lives, and all know its dangers. Even ignoring its terrible conditions, the Aramla El-Nar amuses itself by swallowing those with the temerity to cross its depths.

The sands of the Aramla El-Nar vary according to location. Sometimes they are fine, flowing like water; other times they resemble small pebbles. Colour varies from off-white to pale ochre, but all reflect red beneath the midday sun. The Halawui runs along its eastern edge, the presumptuous river that mocks the desert's constraints, and brings its benefits to those who know how to take advantage of them.

### Landscape

Dunes are the ephemeral mountains of the desert, huge masses of sand placed by the breath of the gods, travelling slowly. The winds of the desert, and so the divine will, are behind this miracle, tirelessly pushing the sand over crests that seem to spray golden smoke.

There are several kinds of dunes. The most frequent are the **sand seas** that comprise small dunes like ripples or sometimes large waves. **Serpentines** are long accumulations of sand separated by corridors of naked rock. They can reach 150 feet high, 500 paces wide, and up to 100 leagues long. They run perpendicular to the wind, gently undulating, but are sometimes also crescent-shaped. The most majestic dunes, monarchs of the desert, reach 600 feet high and a hundred leagues round. Desert areas invaded by dunes are called **ergs**.

The **serir** are flat, pebbly expanses, the most common landscape in the centre-west of the Aramla El-Nar. They are particularly inhospitable because water sources are almost non-existent.

**Dayas** are basins with clay bottoms, where water can accumulate. They're areas of persistent vegetation, the delight of nomadic tribes and their herds. They're found mostly in the north of the desert, not far from the last farmlands of Capharnaum.

**Sebhkas** are temporary saltmarshes. Their water may come from watercourses or seasonal springs. Some may be used for salt panning.

**Wadis** are temporary watercourses. Most of the time they are dry, although water pockets may persist below the surface. Violent floods sometimes occur, especially in mountains. Outside of the oases, the wadis support the only living trees in the Aramla El-Nar.

Finally, **jebels** are small rocky hills, heaps of stones, and even mountains. They're numerous throughout the desert. They provide travellers with shade, shelter from storms, and vantage points for getting bearings.

## Oases

In the presence of water, the desert gives way to **oases**, places blessed by the gods. Sedentary peoples live here, selling grain, vegetables, and fruit to nomadic tribes, buying their protection with tribute. Oases are often found in river beds disappearing in the sands, or at the foot of mountain ranges, or even over shallow or emerging aquifers. Watered gardens between the mountain ranges and desert expanses of the Aramla El-Nar, oases are havens of peace, places of exchange and mutual aid, resting places for travellers. Cultures with rich traditions have developed amidst their date palms, with rigid rules for the distribution of precious water. Oases may astonish travellers, teeming with an almost city-like community often of up to several thousand inhabitants, in places where one might have expected to find only a few trees, a lake, a couple of goats. They're wonders of nature, perfect illustrations of the struggle for life in this sea of sand and desolation, splashes of the bright green of palm trees against the burning ochre sand.

Not all oases are equal. They're differentiated by their ease of access to water and its abundance; some need a permanent workforce, while others seem protected by one of the One Thousand and One Gods.

Oases in the deep desert are smaller, but often control vast territories. They're situated in strategic locations for trade and military activity. They're able to keep the desert at bay thanks to complex arrangements. They face huge constraints; water is rare and they need a large workforce to extract it from aquifers often deep underground. Land is divided among numerous small farmers. Oases at the foot of jebels are larger, drawing directly on water from mountain rivers. To maximise the irrigation, naturally restricted to the wet season, dams are constructed along the wadis to redistribute water during the dry season. Finally, the most common oases along the course of the Halawui are the lowland oases, irrigated by dams storing river water, again to redistribute during the dry period.

In general, oases cover a limited area and practice intensive terrace farming of date palms, fruit trees, grain, and vegetables. They have little room for dwellings, which are often situated outside the oasis proper, in a location sheltered from flooding.

## Climate

The climate of the Aramla El-Nar is very dry and very hot. The lack of cloud cover means the sunlight heats and dries the desert constantly. At night, the temperature plummets, sometimes going from 167°F (75°C) to 14°F (-10°C). A slight frost forms, resulting, in the early morning, in a small amount of dew vital to some plants and animals. Precipitation is rare (less than 5cm/year) and almost unknown in some regions, where it may rain as little as once every twenty-five years.

Although the ground temperature may reach 167°F (75°C) when the sun is at its zenith, the air temperature is more merciful, although even then it exceeds 104°F (40°C) in the middle of the day and drops to around 32°F (0°C) in the middle of the night.

The wind blows constantly in the desert. There are two main air currents; in the west, the Breath of Jergath blows from south to north, and in the east, the Breath of Marduk blows north to south. This latter blows counter to the direction of flow of the River Halawui, making river travel dangerous due to numerous stretches of rapids. The area between the two winds is usually avoided, as whirlwinds and sandstorms are frequent there.

## The Animal Kingdom

Life does not have the upper hand in these desolate wastes; only the lethal sun reigns. During the scorching heat of the day, little more than caravans move; fauna and flora seem mysteriously absent. When the sun sets, animals become active during the cool night; insects and beetles—ants, scarabs, scorpions, and more—emerge from their hiding places, as do lizards, snakes, iguanas, gerbils, and fennecs. Plants open up, stretching every pore to retrieve the smallest drop of moisture the dew can grant them. They close with the dawn, ready to face another day in the inferno.

## Living In the Desert

*The caravan brings, takes away, loads and unloads.*
*It departs, stops, departs again, always moving.*
*It makes camp, and is followed by the call to break camp.*
*You live it more than you follow it,*
*Following the rhythm of the desert,*
*On foot or on camel-back,*
*The rhythm of scimitars,*
*Your guides and desert friends.*

—*Traditional Bedouin song*

The desert people travel to find water, nomads in endless motion. When water and game reserves dwindle, they move. Hunting and gathering are impossible in the deep desert, and the nomads are herders. They protect themselves from the heat by wearing voluminous clothing and sleeping in tents. Sometimes they use caves for temporary shelter. They have great humility; in the face of nature's elements, you realise you are nothing. If humility is not your path, then aggression may be your weapon of choice.

To the desert tribes, water is "the blood of Tiamat", just as the desert itself is her body. Ancient legends say the dunes are her breasts. The Mother of Monsters is everywhere, the Aramla El-Nar deadly to those who do not know its ways. The Jazirati know these ways: the rules are simple, but must be learned.

First, you must conserve water. Drink in small quantities but regularly, and do not eat too much. Cover your body, as much as possible, so your clothing absorbs your perspiration: uncovered skin is an offering to the murderous sun. Breathe through your nose, and avoid speaking. Never sit on the burning sand, and always seek the shade. If you must stop during the day, bury yourself in the sand. If you find someone in trouble, do not let them drink freely, but give them only a drop at a time, or they will not recover. Finally, and most important of all: always obey the caravan master. His injunctions may seem absurd, but he is probably right.

## The Nomadic Life

The endless wandering of the nomads through the desert is dictated by the need to find new pastures for their herds. They drive them from one oasis to the next. Camels, goats, and sheep make up most of the nomad's herds. They feed on their milk, eating their meat only rarely. The skins have many uses, sewn to make clothes, waterskins, and other items of equipment or attire. The harsh desert lifestyle has forged a people for whom communal ties are important. Organised in small tribes of a few families, they are very self-sufficient.

The Saabi of the Aramla El-Nar celebrate a tenday of festivities every year, to gather together the desert tribes and allow young people to meet. The event is essential to the coexistence of the nomad tribes; it's at this time that young men make their requests for marriage, inviting their chosen partner to leave her tribe and join that of her husband-to-be. Marriages are not usually arranged, except for the families of tribal dignitaries, whose unions seal alliances. Young people are only considered fully adult once a marriage has been consummated; a young Saabi man must not only win his chosen partner's affections, but must also compensate her tribe before she can join him.

Many young men, perhaps too poor or ill-favoured, or perhaps disinclined, never attain this adult status. After their twenty-fifth birthday, they are exiled from the tribe, and may only return with a woman by their side. Most join bands of desert raiders, the only ones to offer them a life.

### Tea

*The tea ceremony is a way of showing hospitality, and a pretext for conversation with a passing visitor. It's impolite to refuse an offer of tea, and to not drink the "Three Teas". The same leaves of green tea are used to brew three servings, drunk one after another: the first is as bitter as life, the second as strong as love, and the last as sweet as death.*

The Shiradi tribes also organise mass gatherings, but their communal social structure means they do so more often. Marriages may be contracted throughout the year, with fewer constraints than in Saabi tribes, although the custom of compensating the wife's family for their loss is still observed—if often merely symbolically.

Despite the fact that both Saabi and Shiradi tribes take pains to maintain their strong differences, it isn't rare to see Saabi invited to Shiradi festivities and vice-versa. Fellowship and mutual aid in the face of the common adversity of the Desert of Fire sometimes erases feuds even millennia-old. And, although rare, there are even marriages between the communities, although it usually involves the religious conversion of one of the spouses.

## Caravans

As well as breeding animals, many nomads follow another traditional occupation, that of transporting goods across the desert. Sometimes these goods come from the desert itself, but more often they are made in Kh'saaba and Capharnaum. Large numbers of people and camels, sometimes several hundred strong, gather in **caravans** to transport great quantities of such goods. Camels are the only beasts of burden, together with the **abzulim** (page 307), that can withstand the Desert of Fire. Caravan routes usually follow the shortest distance between oases or water sources, which makes some oases into vital trade centres. When the distance between two natural water sources is too great, wells are often dug to reach the water deep beneath the desert's surface.

In a strange way, a caravan is like a ship, setting out for a long voyage. It gathers passengers, sailors, a helmsman, a physician, even a master cook, all relying on the grace of the gods.

A caravan is always led by its guide. He is the only one who knows the trade routes, who holds the maps showing the locations of wells and oases and the favourite ambush spots for desert raiders. Merchants and passengers crossing the desert must raise enough money to pay for his services as well as those of his team, to procure enough food and water for the whole caravan, and—most importantly—to hire enough mercenaries to defend it during the journey.

A caravan guide is assisted by two or three lieutenants, with specific caravan duties: looking after passengers, livestock, mercenaries, logistics, and so on. Each guide has his own way of running his caravan. If he doesn't already have them on his team, the guide also hires a healer and cook; since caravans can comprise several hundred individuals, these positions are never filled lightly, as they must be relied upon for the whole trip.

Mercenary guards are often the largest expense for a caravan. They're paid a retainer in the city of departure, and the balance on arrival. They're indispensable, the only protection against raiders. For, as the best guides of the Desert of Fire say, it's not a question of whether or not your caravan will be attacked, but when. Have you hired enough guards to defend yourselves?

Caravans are slow, often painfully so. They take hours to come to a halt, and just as long to raise camp again. It's partly a factor of their size; because of the expense of hiring guides and guards, caravans crossing the Aramla El-Nar are as large as possible, as it requires a certain number of passengers to properly fund an expedition. Caravans rarely number fewer than fifty people with twice as many livestock. Out of the fifty members, thirty are passengers, a little less than half of the rest are mercenaries, and the rest are the guide's team.

A caravan moves between six and ten leagues a day. Indeed, with the time it takes to raise camp in the morning and make camp again for the night, as well as taking shelter from the midday sun, a caravan may only spend about half a dozen hours per day on the trail. Caravans travel by day despite the heat, as the dangers are fewer than by night. Between raiders who would more easily attack under cover of darkness, and the risk of people and livestock getting lost, guides prefer to avoid travelling by night.

You can find example travel times for caravans on page 353.

## Desert Raiders

The desert raiders are not a tribe, properly speaking. Spread throughout the Aramla El-Nar, they are constantly on the move, looking for fresh pickings to relieve of their gold and, more importantly, of the food and water they're carrying. Although they prefer to attack caravans, they will not hesitate to descend upon isolated oases, choice targets for raids.

There are many tribes in the desert, usually Saabi, that live entirely by raiding. They comprise mostly men, exiles from their home tribes, who have found no other way of surviving. New arrivals must pass through the ordeal of the **Am Tal** before being allowed to join a raider tribe and be considered full adults (as most exiles are not yet considered adults—see page 209 above). This ordeal is simple yet terrible: a potential raider must travel back to his tribe and return with his father's head. If he fails, or if he refuses the horror of patricide, he must live alone in the desert; few are able to survive such an existence for long.

### Dhamet

*Bedouins, gregarious by nature, love games. The most popular is* **Dhamet**. *Considered a men's game, it's a board game combining tactics and strategy in a way that loosely resembles a combination of checkers and Go. Sometimes, feuds between families are settled by a game of Dhamet; together with hand-to-hand combat and camel-racing, it's considered one of the acceptable ways of honourably resolving disputes. Women have a similar game,* **Crur**, *played with small marble-like pieces, where the victor wins all the pieces from her opponent.*

The life of a desert raider is not far different from any other desert tribesman. Although they do not practice herding, they are still nomadic; however, instead of seeking new pastures, they pursue their human prey, mostly following the trade routes the caravans take. Raiders know the desert well; it's a rare caravan guide who can boast of knowing as many water sources, lost oases, abandoned trade routes, and forgotten ruins...

Desert raiders are bound to one another by their terrible crimes—and in particular the blood price of the Am Tal. They live by and for blood; when they die, their bodies are left for the desert. Deserters from the desert raiders are hunted down and slain without compunction; this is one family you can never leave.

## Mercenaries

Like the desert raiders, the mercenary guards of caravans have chosen a life of violence in the desert. Although most people don't see it that way, there's actually little to distinguish a raider from a caravan guard. And it's true that a mercenary probably won't hesitate long between going thirsty and attacking an unprotected caravan...

However, most mercenaries only leave the cities bordering the Desert of Fire to guard caravans on their perilous journeys. Their task is simple: to do anything and everything necessary to make sure their charge arrives safely at its destination. They usually make a round trip, protecting the same caravan in both directions. After returning to their starting point, they then spend their hard-earned pay on wine, women, and song, before leaving on a fresh expedition.

A mercenary's only other expense is the maintenance of weapons and armour and, of course, a steed. Many mercenaries prefer the endurance of a camel to the comfort of a horse. Some mercenaries save their gold, and pay attention to everything they see on their journeys. Often, these are the ones you see years later, working as guides themselves, rich after a life spent fighting the desert. Many fortunes are built from the rigours of the desert.

Some rumours hint at a band of desert raiders who pass themselves off as caravan mercenaries. They hire themselves out in Capharnaum's cities, and lead the caravan they're supposed to be guarding into an ambush set up by their comrades. At the last moment, they turn on their hapless employers, and what follows is a barely imaginable massacre.

## Out Among the Dunes

The Desert of Fire is vast, so much more than an expanse of lifeless sand dunes. Here are some of the things you might find.

### The Abandoned Palace

In the heart of the desert lie ruins of an ancient city built by a long-vanished civilisation. From time to time, at the whims of the sandstorms which sweep the desert, the city reveals itself to passing caravans. Many expeditions have been sent in search of it, but few have returned triumphant, and those that have speak in hushed voices of strange and ancient forces haunting those desolate stones, perhaps the long-dead spirits from the civilisation of an earlier age.

The most remarkable place in the ruins is the Great Palace. It's said its domes are pure gold, its walls covered in bas-reliefs of jasper and carnelian, its mosaics studded with jade and ruby covering the floors. Today it's difficult to decide between truth and legend; the palace hasn't been seen for a hunded years, and may have been

totally swallowed by the desert. If it were to reappear, would there even be any treasure left?

## The Blood Thorn

The fauna and flora of the Aramla El-Nar have developed in one of the toughest environments there is. Many animals have evolved to fit this ecological niche; many are nocturnal, and slake their thirst with the blood of their prey. However, animals aren't the only ones to adopt this bloodthirsty strategy; a cactus known as the Blood Thorn survives this way, too. A perfect illustration of the invisible hand that seems to guide the natural world, the Blood Thorn is identical to another cactus from which you can squeeze a thirst-quenching juice, well known to the nomads and desert animals. The Blood Thorn, however, doesn't quench your thirst: instead, its juice causes drinkers to fall unconscious. Only then can the Blood Thorn's prehensile roots snake around its prey to suck the last drop of blood from their veins.

## The City of Tents

An annual event more than a physical place, the City of Tents is a Jazirati nomad tradition. Each year the Jazirati tribes, Saabi or not, choose a meeting place and time which always differ from previous years. For the Saabi, marriages are forbidden within your tribe, so this event is the one occasion where young Jazirati can socialise in a week of festivities and find husbands and wives from other tribes.

The City of Tents also sees the more powerful Jazirati clans and families renew the pacts that unite them and forge the desert tribes into a single community—dispersed over a vast area, but sharing the same soul.

## The Desert Roses

It's said the Desert of Fire was once a sea, and that the Desert Roses are its legacy. They are salt crystals sculpted by the wind; they're considered a treasure, especially when mounted in gold or silver settings. Older nomads resent seeing the desert's treasures around the necks of city-dwelling women who come to the markets of the Gateways to the Desert to feel—however vicariously—the thrill of the Aramla El-Nar. For them, selling the Desert Roses is like selling the desert's soul. Many believe that when the last Desert Rose has gone from the Aramla El-Nar, the desert will show the tribes what true dryness means, and will cease to feed their children.

## The Dragons' Graveyard

A mountain range sculpted by the burning desert wind, the Dragons' Graveyard owes its name to its geology. A succession of canyons, crevices, and jagged escarpments, the Graveyard is a chaos of stone where the wind reigns supreme. Its tortured landscape has inspired countless legends about how the improbable mountain range came into being; the best known, to which the region owes its name, recounts that the peaks are the skeletal remains of colossal dragons that came to die in the desert at the dawn of time.

## Fire Butterflies

A rare species of butterfly lives in the oases of the Aramla El-Nar. Its diaphanous wings span over three feet, and its coloration varies from deep ochre to luminous gold, in harmony with the desert colours. Its appearance—a rare event—is considered a good omen to those who see it. However, encountering a Fire Butterfly coloured uniform yellow, the colour of mourning among the desert tribes, is considered a bad omen.

## The Forbidden Fountain

The Forbidden Fountain is an oasis lost deep in desert. Many legends are told about it, including that priceless treasure is hidden here. The reality, however, is less romantic: the oasis is the secret lair of a large band of desert raiders. Originally abandoned following an epidemic that killed most of its population, the oasis was believed cursed, and was eventually forgotten by guides and omitted from their maps. Eventually, even its name disappeared from memory.

Today, desert raiders stash their loot here. It's an ideal hiding place as well as a foolproof prison—the raiders lock up their hostages here while waiting for ransoms, and imprison the women they keep as slaves. Life here is unpleasant: filth and arbitrary death and suffering reign, the violent raiders usually settling their differences by the sword. For those hapless souls lost in the desert who neither perish nor find safe harbour, ending up here is like falling from Scylla into Charybdis. The raiders' swords kill far more surely than the desert ever could.

## The Gateways to the Desert

This is how the great cities at the desert's edges are referred to. It's here that the expeditions venturing into the Aramla El-Nar are organised, to trade with the oases in the middle of the desert, and maybe to travel all the way through to reach the cities at the other edge. The Gateways to the Desert are devoted almost exclusively to trade; many are also heavily fortified to defend against attacks by overconfident desert raiders. Their populations are diverse; it's not rare to see merchants talking civilly with desert nomads come to sell the fruits of their labours at market. It's a small world, operating in the frenetic whirl around the arrival and departure of the caravans; one is always ready to depart or arrive. The cities are always busy; mercenaries selling their scimitars to the highest bidder, guides striking deals with merchants; laughing, colourful, and busy, they're famed throughout the known world. Strange items for sale in the markets, often surrounded by extravagant claims of magical powers, may be real or fake, but they cry out to onlookers come to taste the thrills and mysteries of the desert.

Finally, many of the desert peoples choose to escape the hard life of the oases and the frantic hubbub of the Gateways to the Desert. Instead, they settle in small villages at the desert's edges, living mainly off farming and livestock, supplying the cities with foodstuffs, wool, and hides. These villages usually lie along a watercourse large enough to permit irrigation and ensure the survival of their livestock. There's little here to provide gainful employment for passing adventurers; these villages are hymns to tranquillity and monotony, rather than the starting stanzas of the great epics.

## The Holy Wind

One of best-known rites of Saint Jude's monastery (see below) is the Holy Wind. A trick to impress the faithful, this rite makes clever use of the cavernous architecture of the ancient monastery. By opening certain panels, the wind rushes into the cave system honeycombing the mountain, producing a bewitching sound the priests announce as the breath of Aether himself, come to purify the monastery. The Holy Wind is proof that God is happy with his faithful.

## The Iimenite Oasis: The Best Dates in Jazirat!

Trade in the Aramla El-Nar isn't only one way: the oases have products to offer to the cities bordering the desert, too. Livestock, of course, with camels and goats most common. The craftsmanship of the desert nomads is also prized by the city folk, the simplest piece of jewellery a valuable luxury due to its delicious exoticness. And the oases also export perishable goods—namely dates.

The dates of the Iimenite Oasis, named after the tribe that has long been settled here, the Iimenes, are the most sought-after in the Gateways to the Desert. Dried, preserved, or fresh, they're appreciated everywhere, and caravans visit the oasis to trade for them. The difficulty of the journey makes this fruit more expensive—and hence more of a luxury item to the city elites.

## The Quarterian Monastery of Saint Jude

Saint Jude's monastery stands amidst arid mountains overlooking the Desert of Fire. Many of its monks have chosen this life of contemplation; for the rest, it's a punishment, a place where the Quarterian church authorities send their most disruptive members. Between the scorching heat, the desperate bleakness of the landscape, and the imposed asceticism, the place resembles the hell their religion talks about so much. Some monks assiduously seek out this isolation, but, for others, being sent to this monastery is the worst punishment imaginable. Suicide, even though condemned by the Quarterian religion, is rife among the novices. And even escaping

## Spiritual Retreat

*The desert is a place of thirst, crying out to be slaked. It is a place of emptiness, yearning for the divine presence. It is a place of death, desperate for life. Present throughout Saabi, Shiradi, and even Quarterian culture, the Aramla El-Nar is where you go to find yourself, under the watchful eye of your god or gods. Spiritual retreats—beyond walking and meditating upon the landscape—speak to your deepest self, calling you to a one-to-one encounter with Hubal, Shirad, or Aether. The life of the spirit is strong in the desert: ceremonies, worship, times for teaching, stillness, debate and sharing. Community life is part of it, too; your personal experience is deepened in the light of others' experiences; and so you learn to love your fellows better.*

*For all these reasons, temples dot the burning sands of the Aramla El-Nar. Built around springs which become oases within their walls, they usually house small communities which will always welcome a traveller in need.*

the monastery and trying to reach one of the Gateways to the Desert—isn't that tantamount to suicide, too?

## Quicksand

Unlike the swamp slime which bears the same name, the quicksand of the desert is much, well, quicker at swallowing you up. It's an accumulation of very loose sand in rocky basins; whoever walks upon its surface will sink into it with alarming rapidity, and even stretching your body over the surface will only slow down the rate of sinking. It's possible to notice certain telltale signs, such as the particularly fragile sides of dunes that usually surround these basins, but unless a victim's companions react extremely quickly, any victim will vanish from sight, with no hope of survival.

## Sand Avalanches

The desert holds many dangers, not least its sands. Dunes move constantly, advancing and changing the landscape. This poses a risk to travellers: on the leeward side of the dunes, the wind causes many avalanches as the windward side collapses. These avalanches are particularly dangerous for travellers unfamiliar with the desert's caprices. Walking along the crest of a dune, or climbing its windward side, may cause avalanches destroying a whole caravan or expedition.

## The Song of the Dunes

Whispering among the dunes, sobbing across the stony wastes, screaming at the edges of oases, the desert wind is something all nomads learn to live with. At times a companion in the desert, at times a caravan's worst enemy, the wind grants life to the desert, making it moving and independent. Sometimes its soft caresses refresh wandering travellers, while at others its cruel bite unleashes sandstorms blasting the Aramla El-Nar from one end to the other, driving enormous walls of sand clouds before them. These storms remodel the Desert of Fire; it's difficult to survive them, as any person caught will be covered in moments, exposed body parts abraded painfully, skin and flesh torn from bones. The sounds the wind makes while whipping among the dunes have given rise to many legends about the screaming spirits of the desert.

# Kh'saaba

Spectacular terraced farms on the flanks of steep mountains, fortress cities, arid plateaus, tropical vegetation, deserts of sand and stone: Kh'saaba offers a multitude of landscapes of breath-taking beauty. For many, Kh'saaba is the land of good living: from the beginning of time, people have fought to control it and profit from its riches.

## A Many-Tiered Land

The Kingdom of Kh'saaba is bordered to the north by the Aramla El-Nar, the Desert of Fire; to the west, by the Bay of Dragons; and to the south by the Al-Muhit El-Mandab, the Ocean of Lamentations. Its coast is dominated by steep terrain, making access to the sea difficult. In the southeast stands Jergath, the millennia-old capital, on its valley floor. In the east rises the Halawui River, which crosses the whole Jazirat peninsula to empty into the distant Inner Sea to the north. Kh'saaba's landscape comprises rocky high plateaus furrowed by luxuriant valleys where a prosperous civilisation thrives. The clay brick towns and villages seem to have grown from the ground, so difficult are they to distinguish from the landscape. Saabi architecture is characterised by simple, homogeneous spaces. Colours vary from grey through ochre to white, with all possible nuances between. Fortified villages perch on rocky ridges with houses built in dry stone.

Because of its altitude, in places the Kingdom of Kh'saaba benefits from exceptional rainfall. This explains why most towns are located in mountains or on the high plateaus, whose plains lend themselves to farming. The highest peaks in Jazirat rise here, the tallest being Jebel Bru'tahyb at 13,878 feet. In contrast, the high plateaus of the north receive less rainfall, as do the arid coastal plains of the Bay of Dragons to the west, and the coast to the south, with its semi-desert vegetation.

## Climate

The climate in the Bay of Dragons is hot and humid, hardly bearable during the summer months when the temperature regularly rises to over 104°F (40°C). The southern coasts are similar, if less

## Incense

*The word "incense" originally referred to the resin produced by a small tree found in the east of the Kingdom of Kh'saaba. Today, other pure resins, such as olibanum, myrrh, or benzoin, are also called incense. It's an aromatic resin whose perfume is released by slow burning; the most common and traditional method involves placing pieces of resin on burning coals or red hot stone. The art of the perfumer, and his knowledge of resins and of the near infinite number of subtle blends, allows him to control the dosage according to its use and purpose, each god having its own preference.*

*What could be more fascinating, more bewitching, than curls of fragrant smoke rising to the sky? An offering of incense is conducive to spiritual elevation, and to the purification of the body. Essential elements of incense burning rites, censers often occupy the central place in temples or on altars.*

*Although the Saabi were the first to use incense in their ceremonies, the other peoples soon followed suit. The Shiradim make regular offerings of a mix dedicated to Shirad, which his people are forbidden to use for their own ends. The Quarterians use incense widely in religious services, processions, and funerals. The Agalanthians enjoy the sweet fragrance of burned perfumes pleasing to the gods, making them more receptive to prayer. All peoples have fought for the privilege of paying Kh'saaba the high price for a few grams of incense every day, a luxury more precious than gold. For the southern kingdom, it's an immense source of wealth on which many depend.*

### The Incense Route

*A good portion of the incense harvested and produced in Kh'saaba is sent north to be sold to Agalanthian, Shiradi and Quarterian merchants in the markets of Capharnaum and beyond. Navigation in the Bay of Dragons is difficult and ships doing so rare, which is why incense is mostly transported by caravan. The trade routes, at least where they connect the plateaus of Kh'saaba, are patrolled by the kingdom's army, but nevertheless bandit attacks are common. Villages and forts serve as caravan stops, before the hardy traveller leaves the fertile Saabi lands to enter the Desert of Fire, emerging— if the gods are with them—some four weeks later in Capharnaum.*

### Dragonblood

**Dragonblood** *is a sacred incense used in the most important Saabi rituals. It's harvested once per year in the petrified forests of the forbidden valley of Shumkat. Indeed, except for the holy Harvest Week, it's forbidden to even enter the valley, an injunction enforced by dedicated mujahidin. According to Saabi teachings, Shumkat is where Hubal-Jergath, in his draconic form, was wounded in the Battle of the Djinn Army. His holy blood flowed into the earth, turning all the vegetation to stone. Today, the magical sap that flows through these uncanny plants is harvested for its incense. Burning Dragonsblood has remarkable properties.*

humid. The mid-altitude plateaus have a temperate climate, humid in summer, dry in winter; temperatures often rise above 86°F (30°C) and rarely drop below 41°F (5°C). Rains are light, but enough for vegetation, and so these are Kh'saaba's most fertile areas. On the high plateaus, the climate is again temperate, but temperatures vary widely between day and night, when it sometimes freezes. The high plateaus in the north are part of the desert, with very high temperatures and parched air; rains are very rare here, and water is lacking everywhere except in the oases or irrigated areas.

## Agriculture

Southern Jazirat is quite humid. It's the only place on the Jazirat peninsula where forests are found. These stretch for leagues, following watercourses, but are never more than 100 feet wide. Kh'saaba is agriculturally very rich, and you can grow grain, vegetables, fruit, coffee, and qat using a four-year crop rotation with one fallow year.

## On the Trade Routes

### Agizul Naji Ibn Bishr Al-Sheik El-Gafla

Naji, son of Bishr, the fearless caravaneer, is one of the best-known travellers of the plateaus and valleys of Kh'saaba. In this difficult land where the terrain is hard to cross and where it's a challenge to even get your bearings, many imprudent adventurers get lost, never reaching their destinations. Naji Ibn Bishr is one of the few who knows these lands, having travelled each valley, rock, and river since his earliest childhood with his father, also a caravaneer. Naji is your best bet if you want to arrive at your destination alive and with your trade goods intact, although of course such insurance comes at a price—and the more Naji's reputation grows, the more exorbitant that price becomes. But, as long as he's paid on time, Naji and his men are pleasant travelling companions; they know songs, legends, and comic tales to make any trek more cheerful and less arduous. Naji is even ready to give you a small refund if you can tell him a joke he's never heard!

### Agramatra

A few miles off the south coast of Kh'saaba, across a strait easily crossed by dhow, lies the island-shrine of Agramatra. This small volcanic island is the home of the Lullibya, magical female creatures that are half-dragonfly, half-human. Their upper half is the head, arms, and torso of a woman; the rest is a strange amalgam, an insectoid thorax / tail and two pairs of wings. The Lullibya are found only in Agramatra, and seem not to want to leave their island paradise home. Once a year a group of men is sent to lie with the dragonfly-women and continue their line; they return a month later, with no memory of their trip except for vague recollections of having lived in a deep cave...

### Alayahba

On a small rocky hill overlooking a wadi that is dry for most of the year, Alayahba, with its population of 6000, is the last city in Kh'saaba before the Desert of Fire. The Gateway to the Desert, as travellers call such places, is therefore the first peaceful haven you reach when approaching Kh'saaba from the north, and the last you leave when departing its fertile lands. Alayahba's activities focus on commerce with the desert tribes; its relatively permissive laws allow visitors to gamble, carouse, indulge in orgies, and more. It's a true caravan hub, and many expeditions are prepared here—it has everything you need to cross the desert.

Alayahba's ruler is Hava Ibn Zarad Al-Galid. The main occupation of this aging man is writing his memoirs: he shuts himself away the whole day with his best scribes to write and re-write his past exploits, from when he was a mujahid free to roam Jazirat. Today, fate has caught up with Hava, and he has had to assume the duties that had been his father's and work for Alayahba's prosperity. Hava prefers to delegate his powers to Tufiq Ibn Zayel, his faithful right-hand man, who he has known since his childhood when he served his father. Hava has three daughters that will soon be of marriageable age; rumours abound that Tufiq has been trying to win the favour of Hava's eldest daughter, so that he can finally gain the official status he believes his due.

### Al-Hurr Haramit Zohra Bint Abbas

Zohra, daughter of Abbas, heads a band of female raiders who plague the roads of Kh'saaba. The story of Zohra is unique: just a few years ago, she was the first wife of the head of her village, until one day a gang of bandits held it to ransom. After a time, with the villagers unable to pay, the bandits slew all the men and ravished the women. In the aftermath, Zohra became the survivors' spokeswoman, and the women followed her and departed to seek their revenge. Once the bandits' throats had been cut, Zohra's women decided to keep the freedom fate had granted them, and have wandered Kh'saaba ever since, holding villages to ransom themselves and recruiting wronged and abused women everywhere. Now they're the ones making men tremble with fear...

## The Al-Mayakit Fortress

Al-Mayakit is a prosperous village, but it's known for its fort, the largest in Kh'saaba. Built over the ruin of an Agalanthian fort thousands of years old, Al-Mayakit houses nearly 4,000 troops, almost all *mujahidin* (page 235). It occupies a strategic location at the exact heart of the kingdom; if needs be, General Khalil Ibn Malik Abd-al-Hassan can quickly intervene from here to any point in Saabi territory.

## The Flower People

The Flower People are a small isolated tribe of 100 or so souls. Theirs is a society dominated by men, and the tribe's women are virtual prisoners within their huts. The Flower People worship a gigantic, multi-coloured, plant which is thousands of years old, and which blossoms only once every seven years. When this "goddess" blooms, the men of the tribe take part in a ceremony of song and dance, and when the plant's petals are fully open to the sun, the oldest and wisest man of the Flower People makes predictions for every member of the tribe, based on the colours of the petals. In their everyday life, the Flower People pay great attention to their appearance: the men sport well-trimmed beards, straightened hair, impeccable clothes, and crowns of flowers. The tribe also cultivates resplendent botanical gardens. Despite their peaceable appearance, travellers should be wary of the Flower People, as they are masters of lethal poisons, which they use to coat their blades (see page 68).

## The Forges of Ishankti

Ishankti is a large city in western Kh'saaba by the Bay of Dragons, renowned for its many forges. It's a city of iron and steel; from afar, you notice a grey smear on the horizon from which coils of smoke rise; as you get closer, your throat chokes at the characteristic stench the poets never fail to mention. Its streets are dark and winding, thievery and corruption ubiquitous, and it's said its people are the sneakiest in all Jazirat. Nevertheless, the city is essential to the Saabi economy, and to the King's armies; it's here that a great portion of the swords, scimitars, spears, helmets, breastplates and items of metalwork used in Kh'saaba's defence are manufactured. Officially, Ishankti has just over 20,000 inhabitants, but that doesn't count the 5000 or so beggars which wander its alleys. Omar Ibn Raman, Ishankti's governor, is a close relative of the King. In recent years, he's been victim of a disease that has left him bedridden, and it's now his first wife, Bettina Bint Harin, who pulls the strings from the shadows, aided by her three sons.

## Madina El-Sakhra

On the Incense Route in north-western Kh'saaba, in an isolated arid valley, rises a great rock housing inside it a small town. The pink sandstone has been hollowed out, producing corridors and galleries leading to alcoves and living chambers. Madina El-Sakhra has just under a thousand permanent inhabitants, and another thousand temporary visitors at any one time. It's a veritable fort, with natural ramparts more than 150 feet high and 30 feet wide. Access points are few, narrow, and well-guarded; reservoirs and rain-catchers are placed on the very top of the rock, ensuring the town's survival. Madina El-Sakhra is governed by Ali Ibn Yussef Abd-al-Salif; his sons and sons-in-law also occupy key positions in the town's administration.

## Muhyl, the Village of Pearls

At first glance, the small coastal village of Muhyl is nothing special, a village like any other. Upon closer inspection, its inhabitants wear the softest silks, the shiniest jewels, and enjoy the finest food. If the fishers of Muhyl are rich, it's because they do not catch only fish: in a secret place off the coast lie the beds of giant pearl oysters. Twice a year, the fishers of Muhyl gather these giant pearls, a harvest which permits the villagers to live lives of happy luxury. Naturally, such wealth attracts covetous eyes, which is why, with their fortune, the villagers also pay a well-equipped militia to watch over their concerns.

## The Outposts of Kh'saaba

Along the natural northern border separating the kingdom's plateaus and fertile valleys from the Desert of Fire, there stand many round dry-stone towers which guard against invaders, the legacy of the many wars between Saabi and Agalanthians for control of the region. All have underground granaries and cisterns and, situated on the highest peaks, communicate among themselves using polished bronze heliographs; in case of invasion, information is relayed back to the kingdom's forts, alerting the garrisons to enemy movements.

## The Pit of Tiamat

In eastern Kh'saaba lies the Pit of Tiamat, a deep and winding chasm that belches reddish, poisonous fumes. It's said to be one of the Gates of Chaos; legend says that it was here that Tiamat burrowed into the earth after losing her battle to Marduk—all in vain. Legend also says that djinn emerge from the Pit at nightfall, and spread all over Jazirat. This wound in the earth's crust extends for over 6 leagues, in terrain where it's hard for travellers to circumvent it. Here and there the chasm is spanned by ancient and rickety rope bridges; some hang down into the abyss, others are just about holding on, but are hardly used for fear of collapse, and some—a few—are sturdy enough to use.

## Zamer Ibn Ghaleb, the Piper of the High Plateaus

If, one day, on your way to Jergath, you hear the sound of bewitching pipes, it means Zamer Ibn Ghaleb is close by. The echoes of his traditional flute playing can be heard for miles around through the deep valleys of south-western Kh'saaba; he plays from sunrise to sunset, in long improvisations lasting many hours. Some claim the sound of his pipes is magical, permitting grain to grow better, men to avoid falling ill, women to be fertile, and sending miscreants mad. However, Zamer is ever-elusive. You may hear him, you may even glimpse him in the distance; but you can never reach him; he always vanishes before anyone gets close.

# JERGATH THE GREAT

## The City of a Thousand and One Gods

Jergath the Great is a religious city, built in a sacred location for the express purpose of worshipping Hubal, the god who later, in the form of a dragon, liberated the city. It's said Hubal even built the city himself. It's the heart of the Saabi religion, with more temples than the rest of Jazirat put together, attracting huge numbers of pilgrims. Jergath is big, colourful, and lively, the most beautiful city in the world according to many, and most of all a city of superlatives.

| TABLE 6-5: A TIMELINE OF JERGATH THE GREAT | |
|---|---|
| YEAR | EVENT |
| 618 | Aref Ibn Jelul lays the foundations of the city. |
| 804 | Invasion by the Agalanthian Republic. |
| 1225 | Under the influence of King Ibn Sayed, the region is freed from the Agalanthians. |
| 1984 | Invasion by the Agalanthian Empire. |
| 2476 | Intervention of the dragon Hubal-Jergath, who founds the great tribes and asks his prophets to guide his worshippers to salvation. |
| 3536 | Exile of the Shiradim. |

## History is Written by the Victors

### The Birth of Jergath

In the beginning of the 7th century, the first Jazirati king, Aref Ibn Jelul, settled down to lay the foundations of a city dedicated to the glory of Hubal. He chose a valley in the Kingdom of Kh'saaba, where the meanders of a river had dug out a vast open space. It was a location that was both practical and steeped in mysticism, that

had seen, according to tradition, the defeat of Tiamat and Apsu at the dawn of time. The river—today called the Kheit Azrak—flowed peacefully southwest towards the Ocean of Lamentations, along a course that allowed navigation. A cave-dwelling tribe, the Muhafid, had already lived in the carved walls of the cliffs north of the city for many generations, worshippers of Hubal and the One Thousand and One gods.

King Aref brought his household to these holy lands. To render homage to Hubal, he decided to build a temple and a city to house, as well as his family and court, his priests, pilgrims and anyone else wanting to settle there. The buildings covered the northern bank, while, inside the meander, on the southern bank, there developed the farming and husbandry necessary to feed this whole small world. Everything went well, and Jergath grew and prospered rapidly.

### The Agalanthian Republic

In the year 804, Agalanthia conquered Jazirat, with particular attention to Kh'saaba. The invaders quickly understood Jergath's strategic importance, and established their own capital there. They refused to mix with the local population, constructing their own city on the high plateau above the cliff against which the original city had been built; its white walls shone in the sun, a rampart against Saabi resistance. Many conflicts between the local population and new arrivals followed. The Agalanthians were more powerful, with skilled and numerous troops, and oppressed the Saabi, restricting their religious practices and customs. The proud desert warriors were forbidden from bearing arms, had no control over their kingdom's policies, and remained confined to their settlement at the foot of the Cliff of Jergath under the Agalanthians' watchful gaze.

All trade south and east passed through the capital, and the Agalanthian city grew quickly. The Agalanthians named it Jergath the Great in 950. A harbour was constructed at the mouth of the Kheit Azrak, catering for ships too big to sail upriver; an annex to the city, it was connected to Jergath by a waterway and land routes. Situated on the Incense Route and trade routes for many commodities from faraway lands, Jergath became a great mercantile hub.

### Liberation

Jergath freed itself from Agalanthian domination at the urging of King Ismet Ibn Sayed. When the Agalanthian governor's influence waned, the King refused to pay the tribute the Republic demanded, and executed its representatives. The Saabi took by force of arms the land that was already theirs, pushing their conquest as far as Capharnaum.

The next two centuries were a period of rapid expansion for the Kingdom of Kh'saaba. Jergath grew, and the first walls at the bottom of the Cliff were built. The Saabi retained the Agalanthian city on the plateau above, using it as fort and barracks.

## Saabi Food

The Saabi eat quickly, dipping bread into a common plate, and don't stay long at the table. They eat mostly vegetables, fresh or dried; fresh fish is only found at the coast and in Jergath. The main staple is khobs, a round bread loaf with several added grains, eaten with soups and stews of vegetables and sometimes mutton. Poultry is also found on Saabi menus and, sometimes (although more rarely), pieces of beef. Spices play an important role. Finally, meals end with honey, almond or dry fruit sweets. The most widespread drink is tea, often perfumed with cardamom or cloves, and highly sweetened.

At the end of the 19th century, when King Yussuf Ibn Marek had just conquered Fragrance and Kh'saaba was an acknowledged commercial power, the kingdom's power was weakened by internal crisis. After its sovereign was assassinated under obscure circumstances, its rulers became ensnared in petty infighting and were un-

able to put pressure on their vassals. In the more distant provinces, local families seized power and freed themselves from Jergath. The kingdom crumbled.

## The Agalanthian Empire

In the year 1984, the Agalanthian Empire was a powerful force, and the weakened Saabi could not resist the second invasion from its shores. In Jergath, the Agalanthians again settled their city on the plateau, enlarging and fortifying it. While oppressing the Saabi again, the Agalanthian governors nevertheless did all they could to expand Jergath's trade, developing contacts with merchants, trade routes, and the city harbour. By reinforcing Jergath's central power, they once again extended the city's domination over the other regions of Jazirat. They brought modern ideas, social (the integration of women in society), military (strategies and combat techniques), and architectural (solid stone construction), which massively influenced the city's development.

## A Typical Village in Kh'saaba

*Most Saabi villages are found in valleys, taking advantage of watercourses and vegetation. Houses are built on both sides of the river, clinging to valley walls so as not to occupy farmland. Land is irrigated, and each family has its plot; fields are therefore in the middle of the village. Most activity takes place here, including festivals and similar events. Houses have their own hierarchy: those on top belong to the richest families, and it's not rare to see some perched on rocky outcrops. Streets are narrow, enough for a small cart to pass. Saabi houses have flat roofs, used for drying food and clothes, stargazing, entertaining, or just watching the world go by.*

### The Time of the Prophets

After centuries of pain and subjugation, Hubal decided it was time for the suffering of the Saabi people to end. In the year 2476, he took the form of a terrible dragon, which appeared in the flaming sky out of a golden twilight. The Agalanthian city of Jergath could not resist his onslaught: the Empire's soldiers, even their formidable myrmidons, were helpless before the destructive wrath of the god. Hubal laid waste to the Agalanthian buildings, massacring their inhabitants and lighting up the city with a thousand fires. Once the city was reduced to ruins, Hubal undertook to raise another, immediately adjacent to the old one, still at the top of the Cliff. Thus he left the smoking ruins, proof of his wrath against the foes of the Saabi people. A new Jergath rose from the rock, and stood proudly, its buildings each seemingly carved from single blocks of stone, perfectly married to the rock beneath. Tall shining towers and solid walls were raised; no mortal could have built thus in a single night.

The rebuilding of Jergath marked the liberation of the Saabi people. The day following the fateful night of destruction, Hubal gathered the Three Prophets and assigned to them their tasks. Of course, centuries of slavery had not made the Saabi great warriors, and they were unable to withstand the inevitable Agalanthian counterattack. As a result, Agalanthian domination of Jergath continued, but everything had changed: Hubal's intervention had restored faith to the people of Jazirat, and had convinced the Agalanthians to err on the side of caution. Rather than enslaving the Saabi, a people who had just been liberated by their god, they permitted them to rule Kh'saaba themselves, as long as it remained an Imperial province.

So began the reign of Hassan and his Hassanid descendants, who restored unity and power to the Saabi people and the Kingdom of Kh'saaba. The Saabi again found their past greatness and dominated Jazirat; Jergath waxed great in power and splendour;

and the divine structures Hubal had bequeathed his people made the city greatly respected, considered as it was to be under the direct protection of a god.

### Saabi Greatness

Thereafter the Kingdom of Kh'saaba only prospered. Consolidating its foundations, it grew and retook lands it had once held but had lost. Jergath followed the same path. It evolved from its two centres. The Old City at the bottom of the Cliff was filled with houses in the purest Saabi style, clinging to the walls, as well as with farmlands and palm tree orchards further down the river meanders. The Divine City at the top of the Cliff became the power centre, site of the largest temples and palaces, residences of great families and important figures.

In time, all power corrupts, and Kh'saaba was no exception. Riots, revolts, assassinations, and anarchic forces damaged royal authority on many occasions. One of the hardest blows was the Exile of the Shiradim, the *Et Gadol Galut*, in 3536. By leaving the city, the Shiradim asserted their independence and proved it was possible to cast off the Saabi yoke. Yet Hassan's bloodline retained its power, through good times and bad, no matter the cost.

After the fall of the Agalanthian Empire, Kh'saaba had little to fear from other powers. The kingdom began to show itself as the greatest power in the world.

## The Present Day

Jergath's political, military and cultural might is now titanic. No one can ignore its armies, artists, universities. Although remote from the rest of the world, Jergath is the Queen of Kh'saaba, the undeniable ruler for two thirds of Jazirat, and may yet expand, in a new age of empire, to the distant western lands should Aragon fall.

## Bedouins, Pilgrims, and Caravaneers

Jergath is located at the heart of Saabi lands, a country of high plateaus and deep valleys, along the Kheit Azrak river, one of its largest valleys. Famous Jazirati proverbs say "all roads lead to Jergath", and "a camel can always find its way to Jergath"; that might be a bit of an exaggeration, but not much. After travelling the high plateaus of Kh'saaba, a traveller will espy on the horizon the majestic Divine City and its tall, elongated towers, crafted in a single block of stone hewn directly from the living rock by the god-dragon Hubal-Jergath. Its ivory walls reflect the sun, attracting the eye without blinding it, pinpointing its location from afar and serving as a landmark for travellers. Its harmonious, ethereal spires rise above solid city walls capable of repelling even the largest armies.

The other approach to Jergath is via the low road which runs alongside the Kheit Azrak on the valley floor. Wide and solid between the city and Bassuhma harbour to the southwest, it's used by merchant caravans and as a towpath for ships having difficulty sailing upriver against the current. In the opposite direction, heading inland, the road becomes a track as it weaves between the plateaus of the Saabi hinterlands.

You can also reach Jergath by water. From Bassuhma to Jergath, the Kheit Azrak is navigable to small- and medium-sized flat-bottomed vessels. Upstream from Jergath, things are more problematic: not only does the watercourse narrow, it becomes more chaotic and agitated.

## Agalanthian Ruins

Next to the Divine City which Hubal raised in one night lie the ruins of the ancient Agalanthian fortification. Hubal's draconic might could have levelled the structure utterly, but the god preferred to leave this debris as a reminder to mortals of his power. Fragments of Agalanthian structures dot the ground, but it's a far cry from the proud citadel which once stood here. The area is inhabited by homeless paupers and used by people looking to settle secret affairs. Shady meetings take place in the shelter of the broken and lonely columns.

## Bassuhma

The "detached" harbour of Jergath, Bassuhma is a religious and trade centre. As a trade hub for the Incense Route, Jergath needed a port, even though it wasn't located on the coast and its river was unnavigable to larger ships. As a result, at the beginning of the second millennium, the Agalanthian occupiers began construction of a harbour at the mouth of the Kheit Azrak. Today, Bassuhma is a settlement dedicated to a single activity: the transloading of commodities between sea and road. You can find huge quays on both banks of the Kheit Azrak surrounded by vast numbers of warehouses, as well as sea taverns, offices, transport companies, and all manner of scoundrels and ne'er-do-wells taking advantage of the constant bustle.

## Farmlands

On the far banks of the Kheit Azrak, farmlands and grazing areas were established to feed the people of Jergath. Now they're woefully inadequate—the city has outgrown these lands—but they're nevertheless still necessary to guarantee some basic staples, with the rest being covered by trade. The farmlands are a grid of small irrigation canals partly diverting the river's course; intricately organised after centuries of use, a network of roads and bridges ferry the harvests to the city.

## The Muhafid Caves

These caves have long been the dwelling-place of the Muhafid tribe, ultra-traditionalist ascetics worshiping Hubal and the One

Thousand and One Gods. They settled here centuries before the construction of the first buildings of what would become Jergath, considering it a holy place of the Saabi religion. The Muhafid live apart from others, rarely communicating with their invader neighbours. They know they have the weaker hand, but refuse to submit. Their caves run deep: although they seem to stand between Old and Divine Cities of Jergath, they connect to neither, and have their own underground thoroughfares. No one knows how many Muhafid there are, but estimates are around four hundred. Few non-Muhafid have ever entered the caves, but rumour talks about fabulous secrets; the rare non-Muhafid to have entered include the Tarekids (except the Ibn Mimun), and eminent members of the Califah-al-Sahla (see page 254). Indeed, the caravan seems to be becoming more fanatical with every visit Malawi makes, as if he's being inspired by whatever he's encountering in these mysterious caves.

## Palm Grove

Located outside the walls of Jergath, this is a cool, calm and peaceful grove further downstream on the far bank of the Kheit Azrak. The shade of the palm trees permits you to stroll its interlacing paths without suffering from the heat, to lounge next to fragrant plants, or to sit and contemplate the irrigation streams flowing from the fields upriver. You can come across thinkers looking for quiet, pairs of lovers, families out for a stroll, poor people thirsty for a taste of happiness, rich people enjoying the beauty.

# Living in Jergath the Great

## All the World's Peoples

Jergath the Great is principally a Jazirati city, and specifically Saabi, as of course it's the capital of their kingdom. It's also a Saabi religious centre. Consequently, the Saabi make up the majority of the population, some two thirds, holding all the reins of power and occupying all the important positions. The Great Tribes (page 237) hold the best. As a religious centre, there are countless temples, from the most enormous worship complex to the tiniest shrine. Life runs its course between these two beating hearts of royal and religious power, which coexist very well, one deriving from the other.

Long ago, the Shiradim left Jergath under the leadership of Mogda. But not all; some families remained, not trusting the new leader. For generations, these Shiradim have formed a community which succeeded in partially emancipating itself from the slavery they once suffered. They're still considered second-class citizens, but are nevertheless influential in Jergath thanks to their trade contacts throughout Capharnaum.

Since the fall of their empire and the loss of their status as potential invaders, the Agalanthians have returned to Jergath in small numbers. Traders, navigators, and mercenaries, they occupy different positions in society, but are still victims of a shadowy past.

Quarterians from the Western Kingdoms are few. The Holy Crusade did not engulf all of Jazirat, but rather Capharnaum, far from Kh'saaba. Nevertheless, the Quarterians have committed a crime in the eyes of all Saabi: the theft of the holy Sword of Hammad. The Western Kingdoms have sent ambassadors to the lands of Jazirat, including Jergath, to try to smooth things over and prevent the situation from escalating, but relations remain tense.

## Sword and Word

Jergath's politics and society are based on the Jazirati way of life. There are three clearly defined social classes: the Nobles, living in splendour in the Divine City; the People, living mostly in the Old City, with the exception of certain rich merchants and priests who can afford homes at the top of the Cliff; and the Slaves, divided among their masters. The city's laws are those of the Saabi tradition.

## Habits and Customs

Many Great Jergathines frequent the Palm Grove in the evenings, between the scorching heat of the day and the biting cold of night, when the sun lengthens the shadows. The city's pace slows, activity drops to a minimum. The palm orchards see waves of strollers arrive from all layers of society, and people mingle who would otherwise never cross paths. This moment has become the traditional time for new alliances and agreements, and the drafting of treaties. Commoners approach nobles for audiences that would never otherwise take place, fearful women gain the protection of great *mujahidin*, and even duels postponed for months are finally settled.

The Great Jergathines are deeply religious. Each morning, the temples fill, as people request blessings from one or another of the One Thousand and One Gods, depending on the activities of the coming day. Prayer in the temples is the first order of the day for most inhabitants.

## Resources

Jergath lives off trade and travel. Many people pass through the city: pilgrims, merchants, traders, mercenaries, simple travellers, diplomats, or Saabi tribesfolk. Whether they're here on business or not, every visitor always ends up leaving at least part of their spices or gold in the city, which consequently waxes rich. Jergath is Kh'saaba's capital and attracts a vast number of important travellers with well-filled purses. Famous throughout the world for its beauty, the Divine City alone lays claim to be the most marvellous architectural ensemble known. Situated on the Incense Route and at the trade crossroads of the world, Jergath is home to countless merchants and transporters. The seat of Saabi religion, a city built for—and partly by—the god Hubal, Jergath sees a steady stream of pilgrims. Gold and spice ebb and flow at a frantic rate inside the city's walls.

## Within Jergath's Walls

Jergath is split into two distinctive parts. First, at the bottom of the Cliff, stands the **Old City**, founded around an ancient temple of Hubal. Its buildings are traditional mud and straw, and cling to the cliff face to give as much room as possible to farming and livestock along the banks of the Kheit Azrak. The Old City has greatly expanded since its foundation, always along the cliff wall, and houses most of Jergath's population.

On top of the Cliff extends the fabulous **Divine City**, created in one night by the god-dragon Hubal-Jergath. This is the city Jergath is famous for: its buildings rear directly out of the living rock, its tall towers connected here and there by majestic bridges. This is where the Saabi nobility and high clergy live, and where you can find the city's centres of power, whether political, religious, commercial, military or other. Most Saabi intrigues and conspiracies are plotted here. When you arrive at Jergath via the plateau roads (not via the roads which flank the Kheit Azrak), the Divine City is all you can see, its soaring towers and gold domes shining in the sun, a vision of heaven no one ever forgets.

## Ahlen Raha

The *Ahlen Raha* is the largest inn in Jergath. Located in the Old City, a stone's throw from the harbour and the East Gate where the Bassuhma Road ends, it's an ensemble of buildings around an inner yard used as a terrace. Dozens of rooms are distributed among several floors, offering differing levels of quality and price. Services are many and varied, the food is good, and the innkeeper is a respectable man, and many travellers stay here, on short or longer stays. It's an important meeting place, ideal for hearing news from the wider world.

## The Sundowners

The Divine City of Jergath was raised by the will of the god Hubal-Jergath, and its magic is visible even today. Every building bears embedded in its wall a *sundowner*—a fist-sized stone which shines with colours that change throughout the day (see page 339). They give off a bright white light during the day, turning dark green at twilight, and becoming increasingly black (and emitting no light) at night, before turning green again before dawn. Jergath's inhabitants are experts at judging the precise hour of day from the nacreous sheen of the sundowner; some even use them for judging the perfect time for a spot of larceny...

## Al Kasr Malaki—the Royal Palace

At the heart of the Divine City, Jergath's great palace is one of the most famous buildings in the world. Fashioned from a single piece of solid rock like those around it, it seems to grow out of the ground, an ensemble of buildings with smooth and rounded forms. The exterior exudes power and might, dominating the surrounding buildings; once you pass the guards at any of the palace gateways, you may relax in the ornamental gardens among rare and exquisitely scented plants, rest in the shade of majestic trees, or walk the footbridges connecting, like arabesques, one building with the next, losing yourself in a maze of passages. The interior comprises the imposing throne room with its rich decorations, lodgings for the many occupants, nobles to slaves, all housed in comfort, extravagantly stocked kitchens, and the most serene of hammams. It's a dreamlike place—yet still a nest of intrigue and the lies of politicians. Alliances, betrayals, diplomatic agreements, and declarations of war all flare up here in rapid succession.

## Al-Malikah Alsouk

What would a Jazirati city be without a souk? Jergath is no exception, its market the most impressive and best supplied in Jazirat. Although the city counts several small souks spread among its quarters, it's the Al-Malikah Alsouk, the Great Market, which everyone thinks of as **the** market of Jergath. Located at the eastern end of the Old City and running the length of the walls from harbour to Cliff, it's impossible to avoid if you approach the city from the Bassuhma Road. Nowhere in the world has so many colours, perfumes, odours, voices, and languages than those tent-filled avenues, alleys, and squares. There are merchants extolling the virtues of improbable and exotic goods, some of whom have been in their brick-built shops for generations running flourishing businesses, while others are just passing through, nomads bringing their produce and goods gathered on long expeditions before leaving once more.

Naturally, the souk is also a source of unlimited revenue for miscreants and scoundrels of all colours. So as not to scare away potential "clients", the Ibn Aziz Abd-al-Salif maintain order with an iron fist, dealing with freelancers in a brutal, effective way. Thalat Ibn Aziz Abd-al-Salif has personally delegated one of his most trusted men, Faruk Ibn Aziz Abd-al-Salif, to keep an eye on crime in the souk. The city militia is also present, but is more discreet.

## The Barracks

As capital of the Kingdom of Kh'saaba and a major military centre, Jergath has an imposing garrison. This isn't the city militia, but the actual Saabi army. A whole quarter of the Divine City is given over to an entire division of the Army of Kh'saaba which is stationed permanently here: there are barracks buildings of varying quality (depending on rank), training grounds, armouries, and more. Young recruits almost always start here, which means the Barracks also see passing through the future elite of the kingdom. The Barracks are effectively managed by the Hassanids.

## The Port Quarter

Although the largest vessels must stop at Bassuhma, Jergath can welcome many ships in its port quarter on the Kheit Azrak, where a large harbour and warehouse complex stands by the Bassuhma Road. This bustling quarter sees huge transfers of money and goods with varying degrees of legality. Since the Port Quarter is part of the Old City, contacts with the locals are easy.

## The Temple Quarter

Next to the Great Palace lies the other quarter for which Jergath is famed, housing the great temples of the Saabi religion. The One Thousand and One Gods don't all have individual temples, but you can find dozens of fanes here dedicated to their worship. The largest, of course, is the Great Temple of Hubal, **Al-Maabad Al-Kabir**, the only building to exceed the Great Palace in height. People visit this temple from all over Jazirat and even beyond: not just the Saabi faithful, but travellers, the curious, art lovers and aesthetes come here, to have seen it at least once in their lives.

The Temple Quarter is in constant ferment, with religious services, processions, prayers, requests for health. Everybody comes here, although the poorest of Jergath often prefer the temples in the Old City at the foot of the Cliff.

# Wind and Dust

The greatest conspiracy currently gripping Jergath is the one taking place in the heights of Kh'saaba's government: the plot by the Ibn Mussah against King Abdallah himself. It has assumed terrifying proportions. Although it's not yet overt, more than one sordid or lethal "accident" can be traced to its conspirators. However, it's not the only game in town: the King's entourage spends an inordinate amount of its time jostling for privilege, influence, position, and responsibility, and it's a breeding ground for threats, thefts, spying, duels and other perilous skullduggery.

There are also many rumours current about the ancient Agalanthian Ruins, even including whispers of the restless dead wandering the earth among the half-toppled columns and walls by night, their spirits unable to find peace after the ancient massacres here. Many brave—or mad!—adventurers enter the ruined city looking for the priceless treasures that must still be hidden here, but few return. After all, this largest of Agalanthian ruins (page 300) has more dangers than anywhere...

## Up and Down the Cliff

There are many ways to move up and down the Cliff of Jergath. The most common is the complex system of rope- and pulley-driven lifts. Ranging from individual chairs, large planks, baskets, hammocks, or carriages, all manner of services take you up and down in as much comfort or with as much alacrity as you can afford. Ascents and descents are rarely done in one go: it's often necessary to change lifts midway, crossing walkways clinging to the cliff wall (unadvisable if you suffer from vertigo!). The safest lifts were established by the city authorities, and are also the fastest and most expensive; access is controlled by the guards who watch them day and night. Members of the Great Tribes are exempt from many lift charges. Some resourceful entrepreneurs have set up their own parallel lift services, with qualities between good and totally disastrous. Squabbles and violent tussles are constant between competitors, and occasional accidents may not be as accidental as all that.

You can also ascend or descend the Cliff on foot. It takes a long time and is exhausting, but it has the advantage of being free. Several zigzagging paths have been dug into the cliff face for this purpose, and there are also stairways inside the rock.

The most fortunate traveller will use sorcery. Certain unambitious sorcerers even live off their near-instantaneous transport services. The most impressive magical option remains flying carpet, tamed by the sound of an al-kimyat flute.

With all the above paraphernalia, the Cliff of Jergath has become almost invisible in places, behind all the joists, pulleys, scaffolding, walkways, bridges and other mechanisms which cling to its surface like insects.

# THE CARAVAN KINGDOMS

The term "caravan kingdom" is used to refer to the myriad of minor Jazirati polities which share the peninsula with Kh'saaba and Capharnaum. All are worshippers of Hubal and the One Thousand and One Gods, but not necessarily followers of the Prophets. There are dozens of these kingdoms, many comprising little more than a few hundred nomads as poor as their goats. But a handful have real political, economic, or cultural clout, and are powers which Kh'saaba and the cities of Capharnaum are forced to reckon with.

## Al-Kasir

❖ **Relationship with Kh'saaba:** Hostile.
❖ **Relationship with Capharnaum:** Hostile. Anything connected to the Shiradim is considered contemptible.
❖ **Relationship with other Caravan Kingdoms:** Mostly hostile, except towards the most violent fanatics.

At the heart of the Desert of Fire, far from civilisation, an oasis kingdom was once built on the plateau of an imposing, monolithic *jebel*. Over time, the oasis became a verdant paradise, an Eden enclosed within stone walls below a massive castle overlooking austere barracks. Today, the magnificent gardens of Al-Kasir are used for peaceful walks and amusement by the one hundred wives of its Master, and roamed by his menagerie of tamed wildcats and birds of prey, all under the watchful eyes of his Al-Fariqani eunuchs. The castle yard, despite the scorching heat, is the training ground of mujahidin fiercely devoted to the Master, and to Hubal-Uqaytsir, Hubal's most violent aspect.

The Master himself, Ali Rabb Al-Kasir, claims to be a direct descendant of Tarek, and to possess a scroll bearing the words of Hubal when he spoke to the Prophets which declare that Tarek, not Hassan, and his descendants should be the true rulers of the Saabi. Master Ali has the support of many nomad tribes, and plots the downfall of the dynasty of the current King of Kh'saaba, declaring that he will succeed through politics and strength. He is currently growing rich by attacking merchant caravans, and is recruiting the most fanatical warriors as his personal *mujahidin*.

In Jergath the Great, Ali Rabb Al-Kasir's claims are paid little heed. However, if his caravan raids should worsen, Kh'saaba would look to hunt his soldiers down, and perhaps even declare war on the caravan kingdom.

## Al-Mamlakah Jabali, the Camel Kingdom

❖ **Relationship with Kh'saaba:** Some trade ties.
❖ **Relationship with Capharnaum:** Some trade ties.

To the northwest of Jazirat, where Capharnaum gives way to steppes and marshes, there is a small kingdom on the edge of the Limherk Plateau. Al-Mamlakah Jabali was founded a thousand years ago by a Saabi camel driver who claimed he was richer than his prince. To punish his arrogance, the prince made him king of a land of mud and scrub, in the farthest north. Settling there with his family and his hundreds of camels, the driver soon began to trade with the wild peoples of the East and the tribes of the distant Krek'kaos.

Today Al-Mamlakah Jabali is a pleasant kingdom peopled with livestock farmers without military or commercial ambitions, a peaceful land where travellers are also philosophers.

## Balzabaar, or the Bridges of Emerald

❖ **Relationship with Kh'saaba:** Ally of the Saabi kingdom, with numerous agreements, mostly commercial and for mutual protection, tying them to the Ibn Khalil and the Ibn Yussef.
❖ **Relationship with Capharnaum:** Excellent, all Capharnians are welcome in this town which is visited by many travellers each day.

After a long journey through the steep canyons of the Al-Fariq'n Road to the west of the Jebel Omphir, the weary merchant will happen upon a sun-drenched plain covered with endless colourful tents and ramshackle buildings. Balzabaar is a city of caravans travelling to and fro to Al-Fariq'n, a place where you can find exotic goods and all the services needed by travellers, the last stop before crossing to the territories of the Walad Badiya and the most important transit point between Jazirat and those lands. Part of the city stands at the cliff edge which drops precipitously to the waters of the Bay of Dragons far below, while over the water you can glimpse Al-Fariq'n's distant troubled shores. From here the traveller has two choices: he can take the ferry at the foot of the escarpment, or cross the immense arches connecting the different *melkets*—those vertiginous pillars of rock which straddle the strait between the two continents, huge outcrops of ochre against the marine blue of the sea. No one, except the One Thousand and One Gods or the dragons, knows the origin and purpose of these weird natural formations, found only here in this

## Personalities of Jergath

### Abdallah Ibn Malik Abd-al-Hassan, High King of Jergath

*Abdallah is the current king of Kh'saaba, and by extension the supreme leader of the Saabi people. A descendant of the line of Malik, he ascended the throne as a young man of sixteen after his father died under suspicious circumstances, choking during a family meal. At that time, despite his youth, Abdallah had already received an advanced education, and took the reins of power readily, albeit without quite knowing where he was going. His late father's counsellors soon discovered the new king was rather naive and malleable, and have since moulded him to their will. Now thirty years old, Abdallah is a pleasant, competent man, even a passable fighter, although there is nothing exceptional about him. He speaks well enough in public, but does not shine; he can negotiate, but is not a great diplomat; he can hold a scimitar, but would be butchered by the first true warrior he fought. Pleasant to look at, his personality is bland when compared to his noble predecessors. These mediocre traits are all too noticeable when a person occupies such an exalted position, and rumours abound that more than one group is already planning to oust him.*

*Nevertheless, Abdallah is an excellent king, in that he thinks only of his people. Since childhood, he has been brought up to inherit the throne. Unfortunately, his father never had the time to educate him in the shade and nuance of politics, and the secrets of the bedchamber, compromise, bargaining,*

*and shady dealings are a mystery to him, even though that's how the greatest decisions are made. For all that, he's not aware of what he's missing, kept in the dark by power hungry raiss, sheiks and wazirs, who fight among themselves for whatever they can grab. Surrounded by intrigue and dirty dealings, Abdallah remains honest, open, pleasant and generous—but completely disconnected from politics.*

### Melik Ibn Mussah Abd-al-Hassan, Grand Kahini

*The closest man to King Abdallah is his most faithful advisor, the trusted man who served his father for so long. He's also the only person in the King's entourage to be truly faithful. He sticks to the King like glue, trying to protect him from manipulators. He's under no illusions, though, and knows that his great age means he isn't far from death. The fact that he soon won't be there to counsel Abdallah any more is what really scares him, since he knows full well what hyenas the other advisors are.*

### Haynah Bint Yussef Abd-al-Salif

*King Abdallah's First Wife, Haynah plays a primary role in Jergath and the whole kingdom. Almost forty, she was born in the Ibn Yussef clan and is therefore an expert in negotiation, dialogue, and bargaining. She spent her child-*

---

part of the Bay of Dragons, but in their heyday the Agalanthians tried to connect them with gargantuan stone arches. Thus was born Balzabaar—once known as *Phoseion Aldriae*, "The Emerald Bridges", in Agalanthian. Today, these titanic structures bear mute witness to Agalanthia's past greatness. New buildings in Saabi and Al-Fariqani style replaced the sophisticated architecture of the Empire, and a new city developed on the *melkets* and old arches. Other, more sedentary, inhabitants hollowed out the cliff faces to settle in cavern homes.

On the far side of the strait stands a similar settlement to that on the Jazirati side. However, its streets are dustier, and the proximity of the Al-Fariqani jungle just beyond the tent city's canopies and the loud roars of its wildlife all conspire to make you feel you're immediately in a foreign land. Such is Al-Fariq'n: a menacing presence, a dark, ancient and mysterious atmosphere.

*hood and adolescence around the court in Jergath, which is where the future king fell in love with her, a pretty girl whose eyes shone blue like the Kheit Azrak. The Ibn Yussef soon arranged a sumptuous wedding. Today, Haynah is one more person to take advantage of Abdallah's naiveté, and although she's not a bad person, she does exploit her position to satisfy her ambitions and those of her clan.*

## Omar Ibn Malik Abd-al-Hassan

*A cousin of the king and general-in-chief of Kh'saaba's armies, Omar is torn between loyalty towards Abdallah and his own desire to seize power to better serve his kingdom; he knows full well that he's superior to his cousin in all areas.*

## Jafar Ibn Mussah Abd-al-Hassan

*A great wazir of the Jergath court, Jafar advises the king and constantly seeks to obtain his ear. He is the principle architect of the faction seeking the royal family's downfall.*

## Tafir Ibn Jamal Abd-al-Muhafid

*Leader of the Muhafid tribe that lives in the caves in the Cliff of Jergath, Tafir defends its traditions, ancient laws, and ancestral customs, opposing modernity in all its forms. He's sometimes seen in Jergath's streets wearing his sober coloured thawb and matching turban. Grumpy and aggressive, he leads the tribe while maintaining its separation from its urban neighbours: the centuries have changed nothing in the Muhafid's defensive attitude, who still regard Jergath as a pit of debauchery and lust. As well as being a spiritual guide, Tafir is also a respectable fighter, and woe betide anyone who gets in his way or attacks his views.*

## Mehdi Ibn Yussef Abd-al-Salif

*An influential member of the clan of Yussef, Mehdi is a peerless negotiator and a great lover of antiques. He's governor of the port of Bassuhma, responsible for the proper functioning of Jergath's distant harbour, for managing the docks, quays, charters, cargos, warehouses, and the flow of all merchandise entering and leaving the port. He runs the town with an expert hand, with rich magnates and small businessmen, legitimate merchants and illegal smugglers alike, all in his pockets. An expert in the art of the deal, Mehdi dreams of a ministerial position leading Kh'saaba's foreign affairs.*

# Kathrat, the Kingdom of Abundance

- ❖ **Relationship with Kh'saaba:** Although independent, the Kingdom of Abundance is an ally of Kh'saaba. It even supplied a contingent of soldiers for the Aragon expedition.
- ❖ **Relationship with Capharnaum:** Mostly commercial, but it's not uncommon to see young Kathrati nobles in Capharnaum's universities and military units.

The largest and most powerful of the Caravan Kingdoms adjoins Kh'saaba directly in south-eastern Jazirat. It's bordered on the west by an abundant watercourse, the Al-Shukran wadi, the River of Gratitude, a tributary of the great Halawui River which separates it from Kh'saaba. To the north lies the Aramla El-Nar, the Desert of Fire, in the east the Gulf of Marduk, and to the southwest the Kingdom of Kh'saaba.

Kathrat's arable lands are as fertile as any of those in Kh'saaba, but smaller in extent, which explains why the kingdom has always remained in the latter's shadow. Another explanation—for the

## Opona, City of the Monkey King

- ❖ **Relationship with Kh'saaba:** Mutual respect.
- ❖ **Relationship with Capharnaum:** Almost non-existent.
- ❖ **Relationship with other Caravan Kingdoms:** Mostly good, except with the gratuitously belligerent tribes.

Legend says that, in a time when the gods had not yet made men and women, Dhus-Sara, God of Vegetation and Orgiastic Pleasure, and Almaqah, God of the Moon, were victims of a malicious prank played by Agushaya, Goddess of Love and War, who both had deceived at some point before. Wishing revenge, the beautiful Agushaya used magic to cause each god to believe the other was the most seductive and desirable creature he had ever met. The two virile gods thus engaged in endless priapic romps, a divine orgy that lasted for three months. Each time exhaustion caught up with them, the gods would lapse into a few hours' slumber, before rising again to continue their frantic coupling.

Legend does not reveal how the story ended, but many say that the dense and resinous jungle which covers the Horn of Jazirat, in the east, was born out of the divine secretions of Dhus-Sara and Almaqah, as the moon lay with the forest, and that the Monkey King is the fruit of their union. Human in appearance, this strange being with great powers has reigned ever since over the city of Opona, where humans and apes rub shoulders, where peacocks are worshipped, and where every woman has terrifying magical powers. Every three years, Opona elects a champion in a great tournament which opposes fighters and athletes from all over the known world and even beyond. This "Champion of Opona" is then given the task of running the fabled **Caravan of the Monkey King**, which wanders Jazirat, righting wrongs wherever it goes. This massive, motley, and primitive caravan, made up of sacred monkey tamers, fire eaters, snake swallowers and all manner of warriors is always a picturesque attraction for whoever encounters it. It's also a source of terror for brigands and other desert marauders such as the disciples of Al-Kasir.

Saabi—is that the Kathrati do not revere the Prophets correctly: here, only Hassan is the chosen of the gods, and the rest are simply his disciples. This means that Kathrati society rests on a tradition claiming direct descent from Hassan; instead of there being several tribes, as in Kh'saaba, there is only one royal family which reigns over the seven **provinces**, also called **sultanates**, which make up the kingdom.

Cut off from the north of Jazirat by the Al-Ardh Al-Shar, the "World of Evil", an extremely dangerous region of the Aramla El-Nar, Kathrat instead looks towards the East. Its economy relies predominantly on trade with its vast neighbour, Nir Manel (myrrh, incense, silk, etc), and the purple dye obtained from the Gulf of Marduk. Some also maintain that those in power in Kathrat have an unusual relationship with the South Sea pirates.

Madina Al-Muhit, the City of the Sea, is the capital of Kathrat. It's a place of wealth and culture, where a Council of Followers aids the king in his decisions. A whimsical man, King Hassan El-Emnir expresses himself only in verse; depending on his mood, or the tone of a debate, he may speak in tetrameter or pentameter, or in Agalanthines (a form of hexameter invented by the author of the Agalanthiad). He will insist that whoever he speaks to replies in the same meter; it's said that those who don't do so—or who are unable to do so—are immediately decapitated. Fortunately, whenever diplomatic meetings take place, the First Vizier, Mumendar the Great, plays the role of interpreter between the King's verse and the prose of his colocutors, avoiding premature termination of negotiations...

# OTHER LANDS, OTHER PEOPLES

Come, traveller, and sit by the fire, and forgive me for having welcomed you with my sword. But in this isolated land, you never know what evils your fire may attract. Unpleasant surprises are more common than pleasant ones. But your timing is good—I have a yen for company this evening.

My name is Kalamhakim Akhbal Ibn Khalil Abd-al-Salif. I was once a master caravaneer, famous all over Kh'saaba. Perhaps you have heard of me? No? How strange...

So you want to explore the world? Perhaps I can discourage you... What? Don't look at me that way—I haven't visited these places, but I can tell you what I know, for a little cold coin. Then you can make up your mind, yes? Whether to go back home—or to leave for an unknown and dangerous destination.

But where should I start? You want me to choose? Why, thank you, my friend. Let me see... I don't want to frighten you too much, not to begin with...

•••

Well, now. To the West lies Al-Fariq'n—no doubt you've heard of the "Dark Continent", dark in people's minds, dark for danger, dark because no one knows what they will find. Some brave travellers once reached a kingdom there called Kumbra-Umbassai, wanting to set up a trade route to the mines of King Tao-Kar, overflowing with gold and precious gems. Do you know it's said that there are titanic beasts there, like the elephants you sometimes see in the Carrassine legions, or owned by some rich Fragrantine? Creatures with two huge tusks made of something they call white gold? Logodonts, they're called. They say they can think like people! Their precious ivory is hard to obtain, which is why it's price is so expensive in the souks.

Apparently, when they feel their time has come, the logodonts journey to a secret place to die. This titans' graveyard is said to be filled with ivory, so much treasure, just lying around for the taking. But things are never so simple, and nothing is without danger in those lands. Do you know they say the heart of the continent is ruled unchallenged by saurians, the bastard offspring of fallen dragons? Well, they also say that the Logodonts' Graveyard is filled with more than just white gold—it holds the memories of all those near-immortal beings which have died there. There's an Al-Fariqani legend that says the logodonts are almost as old as the world, and know all the past and present of Jazirat and that, in their graveyard, you can hear those memories in your mind. But the way there is dangerous! You need to cross arid steppes and impenetrable jungles where the bastard dragons reign, as violent as they're cruel.

I see you're shaking already.

There were some who wanted to explore those lands. Such a challenge, since few have returned from the Kingdom of Kumbra-Umbassai alive, and fewer still went beyond, deeper into the heart of Al-Fariq'n.

Did I tell you Kumbra-Umbassai was ruled by Tao-kar, king and high priest of a god called Ternal? You probably know nothing about that bloodthirsty god who, they say, provoked Hubal a thousand times. After defeating him, Hubal banned Ternal from ever entering the Kingdom of Heaven, and exiled him to this savage place. Since then, he has been one with these hostile lands.

They also say the the King of Kumbra-Umbassai is assisted by seven sorcerers with monstrous faces who take the form of beasts of the jungle at each new moon. The most violent is the Son of the Snake! He slithers about spreading death and desolation, feasting on the unfortunates who cross his path.

After escaping from Kumbra-Umbassai, those reckless adventurers—or should I say insane?—entered the fever-filled jungles which lead to the heart of the continent and which are, so they say, strewn with magnificent treasures that would drive you mad with covetousness if you ever set eyes on them! Tell me, do you know anyone who can look on untold riches and not be driven mad with desire?

Some of them survived the mosquitoes as big as your hand, bearers of terrible diseases, and even the poisonous snakes and bloodsuckers that can drain you of your life in less time than it takes to say it. And yet these dangers were nothing compared to the plants!

Yes—the plants! I can see you're surprised. They stretch from one end of the jungle to the other, and have the power to communicate among themselves to set traps for the unwary. Then there's the n'boko, an ape made of mud and lichen whose bite makes you take root and transform into an n'boko yourself. Then your legs are freed from the ground, and off you go, ready to hunt!

And, last but not least, there's the Virgin Fever. You get it from the bite of a mosquito, so small you can't see it, which attacks in a cloud of thousands. The natives call the Fever the abasso-m'buka m'bkuba-maima hassai, and it fills you with the maddest urge for sex within minutes of being bitten! It's a terrible thing—you throw yourselves upon one another like animals, no distinction of sex or status, even species, only exhausting yourself hours later. I don't need to tell you the effect a mosquito swarm has when it attacks a caravan, or a city!

They say the climate in Al-Fariq'n is so hot and damp that you can stick a pole in the ground and it'll flower within a week! A caravan master I met in Carrassine told me he went there some years ago, travelling in the rainy season. All he had to to was leave a split gourd on the ground for a few minutes and it would fill with drinkable water. Even the dragons there are made of earth and rain, the mud is their blood and the trees their scales. Blind panthers perch in monstrous trees and foretell the future to whoever dares speak to them.

You're laughing! Oh ye of little faith!

Some talk about the Waladiya, formidable warriors who live only for combat and collect the shrunken heads of their foes! They're the cousins—far removed!—of our Walad Badiya, and they say they defend a lost city where a mysterious civilisation pays homage to giant, fur-covered humanoids of terrifying bestiality!

•••

## The Ten Mistresses of Fate

The ten Mistresses of Fate, wives of the Celestial Lover, are the fruits of the unnatural unions of woman and dragon. They have the power to change reality and the weave of destiny. All ten war on one another, to decide which of them will be chosen by the Celestial Lover on Judgement Day.

On that day, the Celestial Lover will assume his true draconic form and will rise into the heavens with his Celestial Concubine to take the place of the sun and the moon and rule over the world.

Have I talked you out of going west?

Let's look to the east, shall we? Beyond the desert, beyond even the Gods' Wall, if you're brave enough and survive, you may arrive at the gates of the Asijawi Empire. You've heard of it? And of the Celestial Lover who rules those lands? No doubt you've heard of the beauty of its capital, Assoko, and of his women? But do you know that his palace has more than a thousand concubines, the most beautiful in the world? It's as big as a city! Terraces filled with exotic trees, the ground paved with tiles of gold and silver.

Forgive an old man his ramblings.

You want to know more about his ten wives? The Celestial Lover has placed each of them at the head of ten tribes. Each wife has her own harem of seven hundred and seventy-seven holy warriors, lovers and knights, nobles and slaves. Each strives to be named the Only Chosen One. For what mysterious reason? So many questions...

Hah! I see your eyes brighten! You're thinking of yourself as one of those holy warriors! Well, no doubt you're right to dream, it's the spice of life! But know that being chosen is hard—only the handsomest and the strongest are selected. Yes, my friend—like cattle! And to get a place in one of the harems, you must first slay one of its warriors...

...

Maybe you'd prefer to go north? Much good may that do you! Beyond the cold desert lies the Krek'kaos, the land of inhuman nomads. Do you want me to tell you about them? Let me see if I can rekindle my memories... a drop of that liquor you have in your gourd might help. Ah! Thank you, my friend!

Let me think... Arkai, Tarkai, Karai, Misai and Gartai, the five tribes. Their warriors bear scarifications, marks of courage and their deeds. To gaze on a warrior of the Krek'kaos is to gaze upon death! Each tribe travels in huge chariots pulled by giant bears, and wages war on the others tirelessly. Luckily for Jazirat! I can't imagine what they'd do if they ever united—what a Krek'kaos horde would do to our lands! Meanwhile, in the Valley of Devouring Winds, where burned walls rear in rocky outcrops from the mist, where the plants are dry and scorched and exude the stench of death, and where whitened skeletons of animals lie sinister on the ground, an immense army is forming.

Don't be so afraid, young man! You've gone quite pale! I'm only whispering rumours, carried on the wind.

Come, sit down, let's talk about more pleasant lands. Although... let me think...

No, I can't think of any! Pass that gourd again, will you? It's good to quench my thirst.

...

Now, what were you saying? You'd maybe like to take to the sea, visit distant lands, avoid those dangers I told you about?

Don't the pirates of the seas of Nir Manel frighten you? You're braver than I thought!

They're bloodthirsty corsairs, you know, fearing neither gods nor men. They lair on a floating island called Anvaros, in a city run by a council of fifty captains. Yes, a council—it's been a long time since they had a king. One lonely evening I heard a tale in a miserable waterfront tavern, about a place at the heart of Anvaros where the widow of the one king ever to rule there sleeps forever. That king—an adventurous sea captain—died after leaving to explore the ocean bottoms in an infernal machine he had designed himself. It's said his widows sleeps there, and will sleep forever, until one as brave as her husband wakes her with a kiss. If that were ever to come to pass, she would make that hero hers, to become the new King of the South Sea Pirates and Lord of Anvaros! Does that tempt you! I can see it does!

I'm not mocking you! Of course not! Who would dare do that to you, eh?

Do you know the pirates mostly attack merchant ships? I wonder if there's a connection between certain dignitaries and the pirates? Now don't put words in my mouth, no matter what my head thinks! Still, it's a fact that the South Sea pirates only attack ships carrying rich cargoes from Nir Manel and Asijawi. I wonder how they know? The silk route is so dangerous!

Just remember this: if your ship is one day boarded, you only have two choices: die, or become their slave.

Hey! Where are you going? Back to your parents? You've forgotten something important at home?

Well, then, goodbye!

But wait! Where are those coins you promised me?

## The Waladiya

The Waladiya are a warrior people who ride giant monitor lizards with massive heads and powerful tails, a set of serrated teeth four inches long, knobbled grey or blackish skin, and huge strong claws. They take the heads of their prisoners and shrink them down to use as ornaments for their huts, and feed their bodies to their lizards.

# Chapter Seven
# Euterpe – Peoples and Societies

## *Within the Walls of Hatred*

As he entered Qsar Jibreen, his senses on edge, Thufir saw the aperture in the ceiling, ostensibly the emplacement for a second portcullis, but really a spy-hole to watch new arrivals and—if necessary—shoot an arrow through their skull. You couldn't get that past a master assassin like him; he let his companion go first, reassured when he passed beneath the deadly opening without mishap. So the Sheikh of Jibreen had agreed to see them...

This was the last human habitation on the road the two adventurers had followed in their search for the treasure dreamed of by Luther's ancestor. The old hermit, Ezekiel, had been right. As strange as it might seem, the runes Ingmar had found on that far northern dolmen had mentioned a tomb of the prophets filled with fabulous treasure. Its location was in code, but the ancient papyrus Luther's grandfather had found—Hubal alone knew where he had found it!—held the key: an occult geography used by a forgotten civilisation. Curiously, even though it should have predated them, the scroll mentioned the dolmen, as well as other secret shrines throughout the world, warning away would-be desecrators of these rune-marked places. The two companions had wasted no time in hurling themselves into the jaws of the dragon. Here was adventure!

The Tomb of the Prophets lay beyond the Kingdom of Jibreen, deep in the hellish wastes of the Aramla El-Nar, beyond the last oasis. Luther's ancestor had wanted to reach it from the east, crossing the Kingdom of Kathrat and the Jebel of the Rocs. In the end, though, he had never even left the sea, his ship sinking in a storm—or sunk by dragons, as Luther still believed. Thufir and Luther had tried the western approach, via Alayahba and the desert. They'd been lucky, until now.

They took the curving ramp, reserved for riders, to reach the upper courtyard. They left their mounts there, continuing on foot by a steep stair which Thufir noticed had two removable steps—a deadly trap for those who might blunder in by night. He memorised their position. At his side, the unsuspecting knight made clumsy conversation with the servant escorting them to his master.

The Sheikh of Jibreen received them in his Sun and Moon Chamber, with its ingenious wall vents set high and low that cooled the air, watching them with eyes like embers. He was accompanied by three women and two eunuchs, but Thufir suspected false panels beneath the cushions in the window casements, narrow spaces between the floor of this chamber and the ceiling of the one below, classic defences from the mind of the great Nurredine architect, Al Zaki, whose work had inspired—if he had not designed it himself—the fortress of Jibreen. It was a surprise to Thufir to see such architecture in the beetle-haunted depths of the desert.

Even more surprising was the Sheikh himself. Refined but cold, with a haughty bearing, a cruel smile. After the usual unctuous greetings, Thufir formulated his request:

"Prince, we have need of a guide, to travel north..."

"You were badly informed, travellers. Were you unaware that my dynasty was founded five centuries ago specifically to kill all unbelievers who dared enter this holy desert? We have never failed in our task! Your escort has already been put to death in the stables."

The Sheikh almost had time to clap his hands. Thufir's blowgun—it had escaped the attention of the guards—spat its dart at the noble's palm. The deadly poison would work in minutes, it mattered little that the Sheikh scuttled into his secret passage. They had to act quickly.

"Luther! There are guards under that trapdoor! Over there!"

The barbarian charged, leapt, landed on the floorboards starting to rise, crushing hands, grabbed a scimitar. Already mamelukes poured in from other passageways. Thufir took one of the concubines as hostage—as long as the Sheikh didn't arrive to dismiss her life as of little value, she'd make a passable safe-conduct. Luther dispatched the two eunuchs—one losing yet another member—and the two companions faced off against the hesitant guards.

Backs to the window, they held them at bay. Somewhere, the Sheikh would be writhing in pain—for that, they'd never be forgiven. This was going to be tough.

The world is vast, its peoples as numberless as their differences are striking. This chapter presents those peoples in detail: their habits and customs, clothing and beliefs. Treat this as an encyclopedia of life in *Capharnaum*: you don't have to read any of this to play, but dipping in and understanding life in the lands of Jazirat and beyond will deepen your enjoyment of the game.

# THE SAABI

## Saabi History

Jazirat has never truly belonged to the Jazirati. Saabi history is their attempt to address that injustice.

Invaded by the Agalanthians early in their history, the Jazirati resigned themselves to living under the yoke of a foreign people robbing them of their lands and freedom. They managed a brief independence, but the Agalanthians soon regained power, although more subtly the second time.

Thereafter, Mogda's Shiradim took northern Jazirat, of which they still control a part, despite the Agalanthians. Then the Quarterians invaded its shores, also claiming a part of Jazirat and its treasures.

Fortunately, the Kingdom of Kh'saaba rose to became the Jazirati power that finally granted the people of the One Thousand and One Gods the prestige and influence that should have always been theirs. Today, it's the Saabi who leave to conquer the world, to avenge themselves on the Westerners for the wrongs wrought on their land, glorious Jazirat.

## Saabi Daily Life

### Saabi Appearance

The Saabi are a relatively homogenous people, similar in appearance to the Shiradim, with whom they share a common origin. They have dark skin, and their eyes and hair are deep black. The only individuals to deviate from this archetype are of mixed race, usually with Agalanthian or Quarterian blood in their veins.

Men have many different hairstyles. They may cut it short, or grow it to their shoulders, either loose or in a ponytail. Most over the age of thirty have beards; younger men are usually clean-shaven, either out of vanity or because they don't yet see themselves as wise enough to wear one.

Women wear their hair medium to very long, loose or in a ponytail or braids. Vainer women turn their hair into works of art, oiling it to make it shinier, coating it with perfumed balms.

Saabi traditional clothing is varied, according to climate and social circumstance. The **thawb** is a long robe covering the ankles, with wide sleeves, worn by men and women. It's the preferred garb of the desert tribes, as it protects the body from the sun.

The **qumbaz** is a large vest, closed by a belt, that men use as an outer garment. It differs from the short, one-piece vest worn beneath the shirt, which is called a **qamis**.

## Unconventional Individuals

Note that this chapter describes life as it's lived by most people, but not all. It describes the norms, customs, beliefs, and traditions of "most people". Life, however, isn't uniform, and there are always individuals who don't follow the paths most people follow. Some may be rebels, dissidents; some may quite naturally fall outside what's regarded as "the life most people lead".

Some societies frown on non-conformist behaviour. **Capharnaum** is a game which refracts historical cultures of our own world, where sometimes frightening levels of prejudice—even violence—have been (and sometimes, woefully, still are) shown to individuals who step outside social norms. While we in no way condone any such behaviour, we acknowledge their reality, and also that very often they've been the driver of some truly great stories, even if often tragic ones.

Players being players, your characters may often find themselves on the outside of the social norms of their people, or at least struggling to fit in—especially as Dragon-Marked. Maybe you'll take arms against this sea of troubles—who knows?—but either way the often harsh realities of prejudice and peer pressure in **Capharnaum's** societies may push you to great and heroic tales!

The **sarwal** are wide trousers, either worn under a thawb, or with qamis or qumbaz. They may go down to the ankles or stop at the knees.

Finally, the **jellaba** is a long hooded cloak covering the whole body. It's what you wear when you want to go outside.

Men and women alike frequently drape their heads with a veil, both to protect themselves from the sun, and out of "modesty" (or the simple desire to remain anonymous). Men may also wear small caps called **taquia**, or the traditional **turban**, preferred in the desert. Women may wear an ornate headband called an **asaba**.

Clothing is traditionally made of wool, cotton, or linen, with silk being reserved for the wealthiest individuals.

For footwear, most Saabi wear the traditional **babouches** slippers, or sandals. Some may instead wear leather boots.

With an eye for beautiful things, the Saabi love jewellery. Men wear chains of precious metals, decorated leather bracelets, and rings, with or without signets or stones. Women adorn themselves with precious necklaces, bracelets, and rings, and may also wear earrings and diadems. Gems set into the navel are a more intimate item for women, usually reserved for the more daring or enterprising.

## Saabi Society

There are actually many Saabi "societies", depending on whether you live in the desert, Jergath the Great, or one of the cities of Capharnaum. There's a certain commonality, though, due to the social hierarchy of Kh'saaba, the motherland of all Saabi wherever they may be found.

Saabi society is feudal. It has three castes, plus a priesthood. At the top there are the **nobles**, born to rule. There are two categories of noble: the **higher nobility**, who belong to one of the three Great Tribes, and the **lesser nobility**, who don't. Next come the **common people**, under the good governance of the nobles and ensuring the smooth running of the land. Finally, on the bottom rung of the social ladder, are the **slaves**, without rights or status.

Nobles have many titles, indicating their relative proximity to the King of Kh'saaba, the most powerful among them. At the bottom comes the **raiss**, a lesser vassal and local noble closest to the common people; in the desert a raiss rules a nomad camp. A **sheik** is an "honourable sage", and is the highest title available to any noble not from the three Great Tribes. Among the nomads, a sheik has several raiss under his command, and rules over a caravan or oasis. An **amir** is a noble with considerable power; Kh'saaba's amirs may rule fiefs containing several cities. Finally, a **wazir** is a noble close to the King, often with a position of counsellor, advisor, or minister. Most wazirs are found at the royal court in Jergath.

There's a certain amount of social mobility among the nobles. A lesser noble, if deemed worthy, may be invited to join one of the clans of the Great Tribes, while a dishonoured higher noble may have his membership of a Great Tribe rescinded—although this latter is rare.

All Saabi nobles are considered subjects of the King of Kh'saaba, whether they live in Jergath the Great, are desert nomads, or live in one of the cities of Capharnaum. This sometimes creates conflicts of allegiance, for example when a noble holds a position of power in a city which Kh'saaba is at loggerheads with. In most cases, the noble in question will renew his allegiance to the one he considers King of all Saabi, but equally he may opt to remain neutral; such neutrality is currently tolerated in Jazirat by all the present powers.

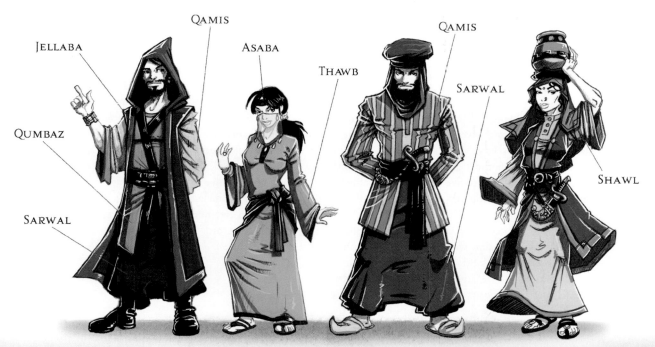

JELLABA · QAMIS · ASABA · THAWB · QUMBAZ · SARWAL · QAMIS · SARWAL · SHAWL

## Saabi or Jazirati?

*Many who consider themselves Jazirati may be called Saabi by others. Strictly speaking, **Jazirati** refers to all natives of the Jazirat peninsula, Saabi as well as Shiradim; or to the Saabi people before Jazirat was invaded by the Agalanthians, when their homeland became confined to the Kingdom of Kh'saaba. In contrast, **Saabi** refers to anyone born in Jazirat who worships the One Thousand and One Gods and follows the ways of the Three Prophets who founded the Kingdom of Kh'saaba, whether they actually live in Kh'saaba or in Capharnaum. So, for example, the people of the Caravan Kingdoms are Jazirati, but not Saabi.*

*These definitions are close to those espoused by certain powerful Saabi, for whom the Shiradim are merely a dissident and monotheistic branch of what was once a single people. Today, however, there's a definite difference in culture and mindset between the people of the south of Jazirat, and the Kingdom of Kh'saaba to which they owe allegiance, and those of the heterogeneous and more multicultural north, the land of Capharnaum.*

The **common people** belong to many different occupations of varying status: peasants, merchants, craftsmen, soldiers, nomads, artists, functionaries, and so on. They're the body and soul of Kh'saaba and of Jazirat.

Finally, **slaves** have no rights and are owned by a master. They may be born that way, or may be individuals stripped of their rights, such as ruined gamblers reduced to slavery to repay their debts, children sold by their parents, prisoners of war, convicted criminals, and so on. The most common slaves include concubines, harem eunuchs, and slave labourers.

## The Saabi Family

Saabi family life is patriarchal, often oppressively so. A Saabi family comprises all individuals living under the authority of the male head of the household, including wives, concubines, and minor children, but also servants and slaves.

Polygamy is the norm among the Saabi. Depending on wealth and social status, a man may take up to five wives. The less affluent (peasants, labourers, shepherds) settle for just one wife, while nobles from prestigious tribes may marry four or five.

The Saabi wedding, celebrated at a temple, is a way to cement alliances between factions, clans, and tribes. This may sometimes leave women as little more than a kind of currency or bargaining chip in subtle diplomatic games. Many Saabi women have little choice as to their marriage, and those who refuse to abide by these rules and live independent lives are the exception rather than the rule. But they exist! Perhaps your character is one of them?

A wife's role in a household is governed by ancient rules. The **First Wife** is the mistress of the household, commanding all the others and delegating responsibilities to them. The **Second Wife** is in charge of raising the household's children (whether hers or those of the other women). The **Third Wife** takes care of general housekeeping: maintenance, expenses, organising receptions, and so on. The **Fourth Wife** is mistress of the kitchens, deciding on the menus and sourcing foodstuffs. Finally, the **Fifth Wife** is in charge of religious matters: she prays to the gods and is the household's spokesperson before the *kahini*. When there are fewer than five wives in a household, these duties are shared.

According to Saabi law, a husband may divorce his wife, but must justify that divorce. Suitable justifications include adultery, the refusal to share a husband's bed, and so on. Saabi law generally protects wives from divorce, as divorced wives have few happy prospects in mainstream Saabi society. A wife may divorce her husband if she can prove he cannot sire children, or if he refuses to fulfil his conjugal duties, or if he is violent towards her. Divorced women who have obtained divorces for these reasons may legally remarry.

Affluent Saabi men often take concubines in addition to wives; some sheiks and amirs may have veritable harems, watched over by eunuch slaves. The concubines themselves are often little more than slaves themselves; some may have been sold by their parents or have previously been prostitutes.

Having a male heir is a major concern for the Saabi. The birth of a boy is cause for rejoicing; that of a girl depends on the parents, but often passes in anonymity. Whatever the sex, the child is presented to the *kahini* a few weeks after coming into the world for blessing by the gods. Adoption is frequent: a man without sons may adopt a male heir who will be considered his own blood.

The hierarchy of the wives determines that of the children. The children of the First Wife take precedence over those of the second, even if younger, and so on. When a Saabi man adopts, he usually designates his First Wife as the mother of the child, to reinforce his status as successor.

Men come of age at fifteen, when they choose a patron god (usually related to their intended occupation) in a temple ceremony, and may thenceforth leave home to found their own household. Women come of age after their first menstruation, after which their father may then arrange her marriage.

When a Saabi dies, the family members gather for a vigil, maintaining a strict silence so as not to disturb the departed soul's journey into the afterlife, and Hubal's judgement. The body is buried after a religious ceremony at the temple, placed in his family tomb in the local graveyard. His next of kin maintain the grave and address him in prayer.

## The Mujahid

*The mujahid, or Saabi holy warrior, is a shining symbol of the devotion which Kh'saaba and its One Thousand and One Gods inspire.*

*A mujahid devotes his life to the protection of the Kingdom of Kh'saaba and his soul to the defence of its gods. Only nobles may become mujahidin, and they must prove their worthiness through physical and spiritual trials: a holy warrior is a swordsman as well as a strategist, a leader as well as a scholar. The rare individuals who succeed in these trials are presented to the King and Grand Kahini and are awarded the title of mujahid and the blessing of the gods. They receive a divinely blessed and richly decorated shimshir, symbol of their rank.*

*Most mujahidin come from the Hassanid tribe; some are Tarekids. Exceptionally, tribeless nobles may become mujahid; technically, women may not, but Saabi legends are filled with tales of heroic female fighters who brought honour to the ranks of Kh'saaba's holy warriors.*

*Most mujahidin serve in Kh'saaba's army as superior officers, but many lead lives of errantry, defending the common people, exploring other cultures, and testing their faith and martial skills. You can find such wandering mujahidin throughout Jazirat; some even serve as mercenaries or bodyguards, or join the armies of Capharnian cities, as long as their positions don't conflict with their Saabi homeland and religion. Capharnaum's leaders know that a mujahidin's loyalty to Kh'saaba is beyond reproach, but their reputation as peerless warriors ensures they can always find work wherever they are.*

## Current Activities of the Saabi

As the majority in Jazirat, the Saabi are present at all levels of society, in all cities, and in the desert. They exercise all trades, from simple shepherd to powerful minister in Capharnaum's cities.

In the fertile lands of Kh'saaba and Capharnaum, most people work in agriculture: they're farmers, herders, livestock breeders, and so on. Most of Jazirat is desert, and only the north and south offer their riches easily.

The Saabi are also cunning traders; there are merchant guilds in every city, and centuries-old rules of commerce are respected everywhere. The guilds compete with Shiradi mercantile organisations, especially in Capharnaum; in places Saabi and Shiradi merchants wage virtual trade wars, fighting to control trade routes and markets in the rich northern cities.

In the desert, these trade wars sometimes turn bloody. The Shiradim tribes have controlled routes linking north and south since the time of Mogda, and their influence is reinforced by Shiradi solidarity. Saabi tribes hungry for more power in the desert wrestle

with the Shiradim for control of oases and trade routes; those less bellicose forge alliances with Shiradi chieftains, declaring that life in the desert is too harsh to waste lives needlessly.

Experts in courtly intrigue, Saabi nobles are good diplomats and courtiers. Their actions have furthered Saabi prestige and influence, so that today Kh'saaba is the equal of the (now faded) Agalanthians and the Quarterians. As ambassadors they excel in obtaining privileges and favours for their homelands or cities; as politicians, they use all the advantages of their positions towards the same ends.

The three Great Tribes, the elite of the Saabi nobility, specialise in trade activities directly linked to their clans: the Ibn Malik Abd-al-Hassan are officers or mercenaries; the Ibn Yussef Abd-al-Salif are tradesmen or caravaneers; and so on.

Saabi leisure activities vary widely, enriched by the many cultural influences which have taken root in Jazirat. Chess, dice, and cards are common games; going to performances, strolling through the souks, visiting the hammam, and enjoying the pleasure districts are all examples of typical Saabi entertainment.

## Saabi Culture

The Saabi language is ancient, deriving from that of the earliest Jazirati tribes. Shiradi is a related tongue. As it evolved, the Saabi language retained its structures and core vocabulary, even upon contact with the language of the Agalanthians: today, it's a rich tongue which has incorporated borrowings from many other languages without losing its character. Although local dialects exist—indeed, often strong ones—anyone speaking Saabi will be understood throughout Jazirat.

Saabi writing is also ancient, originating in the marks used by desert caravaneers to indicate routes, oases, dangers, and so on. Initially limited in scope, it evolved as society grew more complex, and was enriched by contact with the Agalanthian alphabet. The modern Saabi alphabet is a highly modified form of the latter, adapted to the specificities of the Saabi tongue.

Calligraphy is the foremost of all the Saabi arts. It links knowledge and beauty. The prerogative of scholars and poets, its finest works are richly illuminated.

The Saabi love figurative art: anything eye-catching calls to them. Painting, rare on canvas, instead graces ambitious frescoes on palace ceilings, walls separating city quarters, the enclosures of souks. The mosaic art was inherited from the Agalanthians, and today decorates opulent mansions, official buildings, and the central plazas of many cities. As a result, Saabi visual arts are public and civic rather than private and personal; their works aim to touch as many people as possible.

Music plays a dominant role in Saabi society. Percussion, mandolins, flutes and cymbals mark the rhythm of songs ranging from bright and optimistic poems to slow meditative chants. All Saabi own an instrument, and even those who don't know how to play

## Saabi Names

*Saabi names comprise up to five elements. None is mandatory, and there's no fixed order. In these rules we generally give the longest, most complete name possible for a character, but they'll usually use a much shorter version—and your characters probably will, too. Full names are useful for when you want to introduce your character in a formal, impressive way—perhaps with a swagger.*

*For Saabi characters belonging to the Three Great Tribes (if you're making a Saabi character as a beginning character, this will probably be you), you'll only use three elements: your personal name, clan name, and tribe name. The word "Ibn" ("son of") for men and "Bint" ("daughter of") goes before your clan name, and the words "Abd-al-" ("servant of the") before your tribe name.*

*For example: Habib Ibn Mussah Abd-al-Hassan.*

*If you don't belong to one of the Three Great Tribes, then your name may comprise up to five elements, as follows: occupation, name, nickname, father's name, and geographical origin. The word "Ibn" ("son of") for men and "Bint" (daughter of) for women goes before your father's name, and the words "Abd-al-" ("servant of the") or simply "Al-" ("from the land of") go before your geographical origin.*

*For example: Cadi Mimun Kafir Ibn Sifiene Al-Jergathi (Judge Mimun the Unbeliever, Son of Sifiene, From the Land of Jergath).*

horse, and seafood (excluding fish), even if the justifications for these restrictions are medical rather than religious.

The Saabi drink par excellence is mint tea, a cup of which is always offered to guests as a sign of welcome. Alcohol such as wines and fruit liqueurs are reserved for grand occasions.

## Saabi Religious Practices

The Saabi are polytheistic, believing in a pantheon of many gods. Tradition puts their number at one thousand and one, but there are probably more. The Saabi have a god for *everything*, and some are known by different names in different places. The pantheon was established by the spiritual advisor to the first King of Kh'saaba when the kingdom was first founded.

The main deity of the Saabi pantheon, considered the lord of all the gods, is **Hubal, the God of Storm and Rain**. His name has many local variants: Al, Al-lan, El, Ilan, Ilahan, Rahamanan, Ta'lab, and so on. He is both male and female, and the coupling of his two aspects produced other deities as their offspring. The city of Jergath the Great is said to have been founded by an aspect of Hubal, the great dragon Hubal-Jergath.

The **Ancient Gods**, those who took part in the creation of the world, are distant from the realities of mortal life, and little worshipped today. Only **Marduk** and **Enki** have significant followings, the first in Carrassine and the second as God of the Waters among sailors and fishermen.

are invited to join in when the hour of the night comes to fill the air with music.

Saabi dancing is primarily women's business. **Baladi**, or "bell dancing", is named for the wide belt of bells worn by dancers, accentuating the movements of these beautiful, wide-hipped artists. Tattooed with henna, wearing rich jewellery and colourful (and often minimal) clothing, they perform sensuous, languorous dances that celebrate seduction and sexuality. Bell dancers are held in high esteem, and many rich dancers have retinues of amorous fans that may include many prominent citizens.

Culture and scholarship are highly valued. The Saabi are interested in the sciences, and mathematics and astronomy in particular. Poetry is the child of these two sciences: verses structured according to an arithmetic inspired by the stars.

Philosophy and literature are also esteemed. Essays and novels, theological treatises and collections of stories, all have places in Saabi libraries, especially if their calligraphy is of sufficient quality to be worthy of their contents.

The Saabi culinary arts are rich and highly developed, satisfying the palates of the most demanding gourmets. Mutton or beef enhanced with spices, dried fruits and vegetables and cereal wafers are staples. Fish may replace meat on the coasts. Saabi dietary restrictions are similar to those of the Shiradim, and include pork,

Facing the gods of the Saabi pantheon are their enemies. **Tiamat** and **Apsu**, titanic deities who were slain at the dawn of time, begat monsters and demons who torment mortals and pervert their souls to this day. The **djinn** are also never to be trusted: mischievous and sometimes cruel spirits, their tricks often cause great harm.

After death, the Saabi believe that their soul appears before Hubal, who judges whether it led a virtuous existence according to the teachings of the gods. Depending on this judgement, the soul makes a pilgrimage among the stars to learn wisdom and courage from them, after which it returns to earth and is born again in human form, learning from each new life until that man or woman finally proves worthy of joining the One Thousand and One Gods among the stars.

Perhaps paradoxically, the Saabi religion does not impose specific laws or codes of conduct upon its adherents. Each god extols certain virtues and condemns certain sins, and the believer is supposed to live according to the commandments of his patron deity, based on his birth and occupation.

Saabi priests are called **kahini**, and are intermediaries between the Court of Hubal and the mortal world. They perform the many rituals that punctuate an individual's life (his presentation to the gods at birth, his weddings, funeral, and so on), but especially interpret the will of the gods so as to advise nobles and other notables. They are not dedicated to a specific god, but rather venerate them all. A given kahini may have a patron god, as long as his devotion does not distract him from his general functions.

Priests, diviners, and astrologers, the kahini bring the word of the gods to the powerful, and relay the prayers of mortals to heaven. They are helped by **assistants** (young inexperienced kahini, priestesses, or apprentices) who deal with the broader masses of the faithful, the kahini himself usually spending time only with the local elites.

A future kahini enters a temple as a postulant upon reaching majority, as an apprentice to the titular priest. Young girls may become kahini, but often become the temple priest's wives and thereby assistant priests. Kahini are considered a caste apart, neither noble nor commoner, but open to both.

The Grand Kahini is the spiritual advisor to the King of Kh'saaba. He has as much power as the most influential wazirs, and participates in all court decisions in his role as speaker for the gods before the mighty of Jergath. Appointed by the King himself, the Grand Kahini often hails from the highest ranks of the nobility.

Saabi temples are impressive, several storeys high and with extensive pleasure gardens. They are said to be the dwelling places of the gods when they deign to manifest themselves on the Earth, and are thus richly decorated, with walls ornamented with epic frescoes and statues embellishing the rooms and corridors. The main hall of a temple is used for important ceremonies and celebrations; upper floors house libraries, study rooms, and apartments of the priest and his assistants.

Saabi religious life is punctuated by three daily services: one before dawn, a second when the sun reaches its zenith, and a third at twilight. The devout endeavour to attend all three, but most Saabi just go to one at most; the busiest only attend temple services once or twice a week. Even then, whenever the temple bells announce one of these services, every Saabi unconsciously addresses a prayer to the gods.

# THE TRIBE OF THE HASSANIDS

Of the three Jazirati prophets who founded the *mujahidin* and allowed Hubal to take the form of the dragon Jergath to sweep away the Agalanthian forces, Hassan was the proudest and the bravest. Pure of soul, noble of heart, and strong of arm, he was the personification of Hubal's holy warrior, defender of the realm and the Saabi faith.

As the unofficial leader of the prophets, Hassan bequeathed this status to his tribe, bestowing upon his kin major roles in the destiny of the Saabi. The Hassanids are the most influential and powerful nobles in Kh'saaba, the natural leaders of the Saabi people.

# THE CLAN OF MALIK, SERVANT OF HASSAN

## The Ibn Malik Abd-al-Hassan

### History

Malik was Hassan's younger brother, and his most faithful supporter. As a child, he lived in the shadow of an elder brother admired by all and assured by the stars of a brilliant destiny. A less noble soul, resenting his fate, might have become embittered, and plotted from the shadows, but not Malik. Loving his brother more than anyone, he was happy to support him—what did it matter if his name was unknown to History? Only the greatness of the Saabi counted, and Hassan was the only one who could grant the kingdom its independence. Young Malik remained his brother's faithful liegeman and confidant.

Virtuous and disinterested men are blessed by the gods, and Malik was no exception. When the three prophets, in the form of the dragon Jergath, defeated the Agalanthian invaders, Malik was entrusted with the weighty responsibility of ruling the Kingdom of Kh'saaba. Powerful but not autonomous, the Kingdom would remain an Agalanthian province for another twenty centuries, but

# The One Thousand and One Gods

The Saabi pantheon is vast and intricate. Here is an overview of its principle deities—those most worshipped by the Saabi and their neighbours in the Caravan Kingdoms.

## The Identities of Hubal

### Hubal Shamin, Lord of the Heavens

Hubal's main aspect, Hubal-Shamin is God of the Storm and the Fertilising Rains. He's most often called upon using the epithets "Great" and "Merciful".
**Other Names:** *Hubal Athtar (in the east of Jazirat); Hubal Hadad (Carrassine).*

### Hubal-Jergath, City God of Jergath the Great

Legend says the city of Jergath the Great was built by the dragon Jergath, the earthly incarnation of the great god Hubal.

### Hubal-Shirad, God of the Common Folk

An incarnation of Hubal worshipped by the common folk, labourers, and merchants. Some Saabi fanatics believe Hubal-Shirad to be the God of Traitors and Liars, as Shirad is the god of the Shiradi religion, and therefore deemed heretical.

### Hubal-Uqaytsir, God of Sacrifices

Hubal-Uqaytsir is the aspect of Hubal as the God of Sacrifices, worshipped in the northern regions of Jazirat. There, certain isolated tribes sacrifice animals and even people, believing that will secure Hubal's protection. Through these violent rites, this bloody god blesses warriors, families, and harvests. His cult borders on heresy, not just for its savage practises, but also because it recognises none of the other gods in the Saabi pantheon.

### Hubal-Uzza, the Mother Goddess

Hubal-Uzza, also called Al-Uzza, is the Mother Goddess, Hubal's wife and female aspect. Hubal-Uzza gave birth to Allath, and helped Hubal to fashion the Rock of Manat.

## The Servants of Hubal, the Court of Heaven

### Almaqah, the Moon God

Almaqah is the Moon God, Silver Eagle, Night Luminary. He serves the Supreme God.
**Other Names:** *Aglibol (in the east of Jazirat).*

### Malakbel, the Earth God

Malakbel is the true servant of Hubal. He took part in the creation of the physical world as a warrior and craftsman, fashioning the deserts and the mountains alongside Hubal, all the while battling the terrible Tiamat, the Primal Waters. Malakbel is the Earth.

### Sayyin, the Sun God

Sayyin is the Sun God, Golden Eagle, the Day Star in the service of the Supreme God.
**Other Names:** *Iarhibol (in the east of Jazirat).*

## The Children of Hubal, the Gods Born of Gods

### Allath, Goddess of Fertility

Allath is the Daughter of Hubal and the Goddess of Fertility. She's also the Star Goddess who guides caravans at night, and in some northern regions is worshipped as Goddess of War and Conquest. A manifestation of the love of Hubal and Al-Uzza, Allath is both daughter and twin-sister of Al-Uzza.
**Other Names:** *Atargatis.*

---

Malik's reign, and the divine forces that made him king, forced the Agalanthian Empire to consider Kh'saaba an allied province, but never a conquered people.

Malik was a just and wise king, consolidating his country before expanding its lands. Ultimately, Malik, who had so loved his brother that he had been ready to sacrifice his name to serve him, was honoured through the ages as the greatest of all sovereigns, he who made Kh'saaba great, a force to be reckoned with in Jazirat.

The tribal chiefs and warlords that accepted Saabi rule were granted the title "Ibn Malik", and were tasked with giving the kingdom an army, and the command structures that would make foreign powers tremble. For generations, Malik's line gave Kh'saaba its king, and the nobles bearing his name became the backbone of its military power.

The kingdom's early years were not easy. The cities of the north, together with the Agalanthians, who gathered Saabi taxes while letting the kingdom rule itself, took advantage of the instability to foment re-

### Manat, Goddess of Death

Daughter and mother of Hubal, Manat was born of a rock before Hubal and Malakbel made the world as it is today. She gave birth to the God of Gods. In turn, Hubal turned his Rock Mother into a goddess with the body of a woman, thus both his mother and his daughter. Goddess of Death, Manat manipulates the threads of men's fates.

### Nabu, God of Wisdom

Nabu is one of the oldest Saabi gods. Son of Hubal-Jergath, he leads humankind towards its destiny and the accomplishment of those actions decided on at the Gods' Moot which takes place during the New Year Festival every year. He is also patron of scribes, as it is he who writes the fates of mortals. He's considered a saviour god, and is worshipped as the God of Wisdom. He is young, beautiful, with great musical skills. The snake and the scorpion are his symbols.

## The Lesser Gods, Children and Servants of the Gods

These gods are often the children of the aforementioned gods, but some among them are djinn who have been accepted into the Court of Heaven.

### Agushaya, the Warrior in Love

The Warrior in Love, symbol of war and passion. Agushaya rides a lion and is the patron of assassins, bell dancers and prostitutes.

### Azzu and Monimos, the War Brothers

Twin gods of war, Azzu and Monimos symbolise strength, devotion, and brotherhood. Some worshippers consider homosexuality and onanism to be divine offerings and religious practices.

### Dhus-Sara the Plant God

Dhus-Sara the Plant God is god of farming, and also the orgiastic god of pleasure, drunkenness and poetry. He appears either as a bull or an aurochs in his aspect as Protector of Plants, or as a bearded man in a wide pleated tunic bearing a horn of abundance in his aspect as God of Pleasure, Drunkenness, and Poetry.

### Fals of the Red Face

Fals appears as a red face whose mouth is the entrance to a cave. He is protector of fugitives, whether criminals or persecuted, offering them sanctuary and a second chance.

### Harsu, the Protector of Caravans

The servant of Allath, Harsu is a lesser god, although an important one because he is the patron of camel riders, the protector of caravans.

**Other Names:** *Ruda (in the north and east of Capharnaum).*

### Jad Rabb al-Bahkt, Jad the Protector

A protector of humankind, Jad incarnates the wonder of nature and its manifestations in the world. He's protector of villages and families, but also of wells and water sources.

### Ruda Evening Star

Identified with the evening star, Ruda is Allath's twin, born out of a dream of the latter. She appears as a naked woman, and is the protector of royalty and the dispenser of wisdom, joy, and love. She is also the mistress of vengeance, compassion, and healing. Mujahidin frequently call upon her, as she embodies the values of Saabi chivalry.

### Shadrafa the Healer

Shadrafa is the god who heals, the patron of physicians, astrologers, and sages in general.

---

volt among certain tribes and noble houses, undermining the reborn Kh'saaba. Even so, the devotion of the clan of Malik, its bravery in battle, its strategic talent (including its ability to intelligently employ the abilities of the other Hassanid clans), allowed it to suppress popular uprisings and defuse civil wars. The ultimate loser was the Agalanthian Empire, which never regained dominion over the kingdom and finally had to recognise its independence. Thanks to the staunchness of the Ibn Malik, Kh'saaba became a cultural and trading partner of the Empire, inaugurating an era of prosperity.

Traditionally, Kh'saaba's liberation from imperial forces is dated from the fall of the Empire, but in reality its dominion declined gradually, and in its later centuries Kh'saaba was at most a prosperous protectorate.

After the betrayal of Mogda Ibn Yussef, blood brother of the King of Kh'saaba, a new power arose to threaten Saabi supremacy: Jergathine, the city of the Shiradim, in northern Jazirat. The Ibn Malik would not tolerant this affront from their former slaves, and war broke out in the form of raids on merchant caravans, political conspiracies, and secret murders. When the Saabi army besieged Jergathine, the city's rulers employed Agalanthian mercenaries, and the Saabi were forced to withdraw. Shortly after, Capharnaum was plunged into chaos following the arrival of Jason, a chaos the King of Kh'saaba exploited to weaken the cities of the north.

The Quarterian invasion of Jazirat was largely confined to Capharnaum, and Kh'saaba did not suffer directly. However, the Ibn Malik sent troops to help their Jazirati brethren against the heretics. When the Quarterians committed the ultimate insult of stealing the Sword of Hammad, a holy relic sacred to all Saabi, the King of Kh'saaba waxed wrathful and funded a huge military campaign to recover it. Providing equipment and soldiers, the Ibn Malik played an active role in the attack on the Western Kingdoms and the invasion and occupation of Aragon. Since then, the new "Al-Ragon" has been considered a vassal province of Kh'saaba, although rumours whisper that Jalal Ibn Khalil Abd-al-Salif, king of those occupied lands, is aiming at independence.

Malik Abd-al-Hassan, and the right to pass it on to their descendants if they're worthy.

Once trained, young Ibn Malik take up duties in the army of Kh'saaba. Beginning as *aides de camp* to experienced officers, the best climb the ranks quickly, and it's not unusual to see Saabi generals less than forty years old commanding vast companies of troops. Some establish or join mercenary companies, and those hungry for novelty are sent to Al-Ragon to conquer the Western lands. Finally, some serve the Capharnian city states, to demonstrate how Kh'saaba supports all Saabi, wherever they may be.

The council administering the tests to become *mujahid* is made up mostly of Ibn Malik, and malicious tongues insinuate that's why so many of them are found in the ranks of Hubal's holy knights. In fact, because of their military upbringing and leadership ability, the Ibn Malik are inclined to enter this prestigious caste; wasn't Malik himself the very first *mujahid,* knighted by the prophets? Those bearing his name often seem destined to follow in his path and become the most fervent defenders of Kh'saaba and the Saabi faith.

## Organisation

Two reasons explain Ibn Malik domination over the tribe of Hassan and thus the whole kingdom. First, the king descends directly from Malik; and, second and most of all, Kh'saaba is a warrior realm, prizing bravery and martial prowess above all.

The clan of Malik comprises mostly officers; its military traditions run deep. Malik was almost as good a warrior as his brother, Hassan, and legends says he was the first after the three prophets to receive the title of *mujahid*. The first to swear allegiance to Malik were warlords, generals whose legacy has lasted throughout time.

It's expected of every Ibn Malik child that they'll show strength and daring, and from early childhood they receive a thorough training in arms. Each new-born is enrolled from birth in the nearest academy, and rare are those who choose a different path. However, strength is not enough to lead; the military academies founded by the Ibn Malik train well-rounded officers: strategists, fighters, and leaders. The academies aren't limited to the Ibn Malik; members of other tribes and clans may enrol, as may nobles without tribe, if they can afford it. The most deserving may be offered the title Ibn

## Personalities of the Ibn Malik

### Omar Ibn Malik Abd-al-Hassan, General-in-Chief of the Saabi Armies

Cousin of the King of Kh'saaba, Omar was raised to serve the king to the best of his ability. As a child, he heard again and again the story of Malik and Hassan, the younger brother who served the elder from the shadows out of filial love and devotion. The tale became the guiding principle of Omar's life.

Omar joined the prestigious Jergath military academy. Serving his king was his goal, a motivation that made him the greatest student the academy had ever known, a genius swordsman and peerless tactician who was also well-loved by his fellows, who saw in him a model leader for whom they could lay down their lives. Aged only nineteen, Omar scored a decisive victory against an alliance of desert raiders, and his strategic ability protected the border cities while the bulk of his troops went to crush the impudent bandits on their home terrain. This was the first in a long series of triumphs which allowed him to climb the ranks faster than any officer. Today, although not yet thirty-five, Omar is General-in-Chief of the Saabi Armies, a titled granted personally by his cousin the King.

Now at the Jergath court close to his sovereign, Omar has become aware of a terrible truth, namely that he outshines his cousin in almost every area. Whether political finesse, tactical ability, rhetoric, culture, or swordsmanship, the Saabi sovereign is a connoisseur of these skills, but Omar is the better practitioner, a fact which is impossible to ignore now that he's at the heart of Saabi power, Recently, Ibn Mussah courtiers have been seeking his good graces, and their advice has led him to a series of decisions to increase his power.

Deep in his soul, Omar knows his fidelity towards the King cannot be questioned, and that he will serve him his whole life. Nevertheless, a tiny voice within him is growing, whispering that he would be a better sovereign than his cousin, and that the same royal blood flows in his veins...

After all, when Hassan disappeared, didn't Malik become the one and only King of Kh'saaba?

### Yassin Ibn Josef, the "Desert Breath"

Born to a minor noble family, Yassin was brought up on the exploits of the fierce *mujahidin* of Hubal. His grandfather, a former lower-ranking officer, filled his head with tales of his old campaigns, embellishing the feats of the Saabi soldiers and of mujahidin capable of single-handedly defeating dozens of Quarterian knights. The young Yassin decided that one day he'd be one of those legendary warriors.

Every day he trained with a wooden sword. Upon reaching his teens, he joined the local militia, before leaving his father's fief for the capital and the trials to join the ranks of the *mujahidin*. No one in his family thought much of his chances: Yassin was good and loyal, but a poor swordsman and—although no-one had ever dared tell him—a simple-minded soul.

Yassin failed every test, and yet he showed such spirit, naivity, and strength of will that he swayed the judges in his favour. After much stormy deliberation, they accepted the young noble into the ranks of the *mujahidin*, thanks to his unshakeable faith in the mujahid ideal. Yassin received his symbolic shimshir from the King's hands, a moment that will remain engraved on his memory until his dying day.

Now, Yassin wanders the roads of Kh'saaba and Capharnaum, helping the needy and confronting raiders and bandits. His luck and his mujahidin status have permitted him to triumph—often only just—to the point that he has acquired the nickname "The Desert Breath". He's both greatly feared and respected.

### Abdeslam Ibn Malik Abd-al-Hassan

Hailing from a distant branch of the Ibn Malik nobility, Abdeslam used his heritage to claim a place in a military academy. It was a school of little renown, and Abdeslam was not a diligent student. A good fighter and a good leader of men, he rested too much on his laurels to make a name for himself in the army.

Upon finishing his training, Abdeslam packed his bags and took several of his friends with him. They travelled to Carrassine and founded a mercenary company; neither the most brilliant nor the most in demand, it nevertheless lets Abdeslam and his men make enough to live quietly without risking their lives too much. They escort caravans along fairly safe routes, protect warehouses within city walls, and suppress revolts by hungry peasants. They do, however, refuse dubious contracts. It's not that Abdeslam is a paragon of honesty, but he does prefer to avoid entanglements with the city authorities. A long and quiet life is what he's after, and chance to savour all of life's pleasures. And, in a city like Carrassine, those pleasures are legion!

# THE CLAN OF MUSSAH, SERVANT OF HASSAN

## The Ibn Mussah Abd-al-Hassan

### History

Mussah, one of Hassan's three companions, was a wise man and good with people. He was the blood brother of the father of Hassan and Malik, and his advisor and friend. When Hassan was revealed as a prophet, Mussah swore himself to the service of the man he had seen grow from a child, and in whose education he had played a great part. Hassan was wise and brave, but lacked experience, and Mussah played the same role to him as he had to his father, that of faithful advisor, spokesman, and advocate. Many hold that, without Mussah's discreet presence, Hassan would never have realised his glorious destiny.

When Hassan entrusted the Kingdom of Kh'saaba to his younger brother, he ensured Mussah would advise the new monarch as well as he had done him. Mussah swore that he, his descendants, and all the servants of his house would always guide the sovereign in his rule.

Thus it was with Mussah's advice that Malik consolidated his power in Kh'saaba before expanding its borders, seeking to avoid weakening the kingdom and seeing it collapse from within. Mussah and his disciples, skilled politicians and courtiers, spread through the kingdom's fiefs to become the powers behind the throne for the many amirs who had recently sworn allegiance to the crown. Canny middlemen, they negotiated solid agreements to quell the rivalries between warlords that might imperil the kingdom, arranging many marriages to inveigle Kh'saaba's nobles in webs of alliance and reciprocal obligation. They forged trade agreements with the desert tribes, opening the great trade routes to Saabi merchants far more than they were to the Agalanthian occupier.

When conspiracies threatened Kh'saaba, the Ibn Mussah worked tirelessly to stave off revolts and civil conflicts. Ultimately, the Agalanthians grew aware there was no longer any point resisting Kh'saaba's ascendancy in southern Jazirat, and it was the Ibn Mussah ambassadors that negotiated the treaties vital to the continuing good relations between the two powers.

When the traitor Mogda exiled himself to the north of Jazirat with the Shiradim slaves, the Ibn Malik took it upon themselves to destroy the new-born polity. The Ibn Mussah, in contrast, saw the event as an opportunity to forge political and trade links with Jergathine, which would strengthen both sides to the detriment of the Agalanthians. For once, the advice of the Ibn Mussah was ignored; their ambassadors in the north were ordered to foment political and religious chaos in Capharnaum.

The arrival of the Quarterians in Capharnaum made the Ibn Mussah cautious. Not wanting to embroil Kh'saaba in a costly war, they advised the King to provide financial aid to their northern brothers, without committing himself further. However, the theft of the Sword of Hammad overcame reason, and the screams of religious fanatics in the ears of the king drowned out the Ibn Mussah. An expedition was dispatched to wage war in the Western Kingdoms, of which the first to fall was Aragon, a long-time trading partner of Kh'saaba. To minimise the political fallout resulting from the occupation of southern Aragon, Ibn Mussah ambassadors arrived at the courts of King Don Fernando Anduna de Valladon y Aragon and of Jalal Ibn Khalil Abd-al-Salif, leader of the Jazirati legions. To this day, they still work to delay the looming war between northern and southern Aragon.

## Organisation

Within the Hassanid tribe, the clan of Mussah provides advisors to the royal dynasty and high ranking nobles. Politicians, ambassadors, chancellors, powers behind the throne, their role is to analyse situations to take advantage of them not only politically, but also economically, culturally and militarily. Mussah's oath to advise Malik has meant that his descendants do not seek power for themselves, but only in the best interests of their lords, and of the Kingdom of Kh'saaba.

Ibn Mussah children are educated to a high level from an early age. They learn to read when very young, and history and geography form the mainstay of their disciplined studies. A courtier will often take his young children to court with him, so they can see for themselves how the seat of power operates, and the sway that words can have. Foreigners on official visits to Saabi palaces are always surprised to see children running around the banquet tables, the gracious nobles and strict courtiers.

At adolescence, young Ibn Mussah study at university. Many travel to one of the cities of Capharnaum to rub shoulders with the cosmopolitan world they'll be immersed in later in life. There they learn everything a politician must know to defend his interests and those of his lord. After their studies, they are appointed to the court of the noble they'll serve, or sent to a foreign land to serve as ambassador or negotiator. They're not immediately appointed to prestigious positions, but rather serve as assistants to older Ibn Mussah with whom they gain the necessary experience to stand on their own.

## Personalities

### Sayeed Ibn Mussah Abd-al-Hassan

A young and inexperienced ambassador, Sayeed was sent as spokesperson for the King of Kh'saaba to the court of Jalal Ibn Khalil Abd-al-Salif, King of Al-Ragon. His mission is to cool the desert warrior's ardour, whose thirst for conquest and revenge could imperil Saabi interests in the West.

Although the Western lands are pleasant, and he has all the luxury a Saabi noble is entitled to, Sayeed isn't at ease this close to the fanatical Jalal. The King of Al-Ragon is a boor with a touchy temperament, who cares nothing for diplomacy and whose daily bouts of rage jeopardise Kh'saaba's interests. Nothing the young ambassador does—neither reason nor veiled threat—gets through to the King.

Each day, Sayeed wonders why Kh'saaba didn't send an experienced diplomat instead of him. It's as if Jalal's urge for independence isn't taken seriously by the Saabi court. Perhaps they don't care, or don't understand; or perhaps it's in the interests of some in Kh'saaba that the kingdom is weakened by an Al-Ragoni secession. The thought terrifies Sayeed, but it seems increasingly likely, especially since he's begun to feel that he's being spied on even here, at the heart of his palace in Olvidad.

# THE CLAN OF RASHID, SERVANT OF HASSAN

## The Ibn Rashid Abd-al-Hassan

### History

Rashid: the Wall, Shield of the Faith, the Immortal. Rarely has a hero of old been so endowed with epithets, and rarely have a hero's exploits been so ignored as those of Hassan's cousin.

A giant as silent as he was attentive, Rashid did not wait for Hassan to give him his mission. He chose his destiny for himself, making himself the prophet's bodyguard. He fulfilled this role with devotion, almost to his death: he was pierced with arrows, stabbed by daggers, but his resolve never faltered until he got his charge to safety. Rashid slew dozens of assassins sent by the Agalanthians and the chiefs of the desert tribes, and in the end knew their secrets so well that he could foil their plans even before they were set in motion.

Eventually, Hassan asked his cousin to place his steely willpower and boundless loyalty at the service of Malik and his descendants, so that the throne of Kh'saaba might have nothing to fear in those turbulent times. Rashid had more than fifteen sons. He trained them to follow in his footsteps, and thus the clan of Rashid, servant of Hassan, was born.

The Ibn Rashid were kept busy from the beginning of Malik's reign. Foreign powers such as the Agalanthians, the Jazirati cities thirsting for independence, the hostile tribes, did what they could to destabilise the kingdom. Warlords who swore allegiance to Kh'saaba were assassinated, and soon there were no nobles to come and kneel before Malik, and the kingdom weakened more than ever. Malik extended the protection of the Ibn Rashid to all who would swear allegiance to him, granting them a bodyguard from the clan. Thanks to the legend of Rashid the Human Wall, the consolidation of Kh'saaba resumed.

The Saabi decided to fight back against its enemies using the same methods with which it had been attacked. If an enemy used assassins or poisoners, so would they. In this way, Kh'saaba would be feared and respected throughout Jazirat and even beyond. Already trained to counter assassination attempts, the Ibn Rashid established their own shadowy faction of assassins.

When Mogda and his Shiradim departed to found Jergathine and the Ibn Malik resolved to address their affront with blood, the Ibn Rashid were mobilised in their entirety. Assassins were dispatched to the Shiradi city, bringing death to disrupt Mogda's power base before the Saabi armies arrived. The officers of the Saabi armies were themselves protected by the Ibn Rashid, as it was known that the Shiradim were fielding their own caste of assassins.

The Quarterian invasion also necessitated Ibn Rashid involvement. Kh'saaba was reluctant to send troops overtly, but aided the northern Jazirati by sending bodyguards and assassins. The punitive Western expedition to retrieve the Sword of Hammad also took with it many Ibn Rashid. Strangers to the Western Kingdoms, Kh'saaba's generals and diplomats wanted sword and shield ready for any eventuality. The Ibn Rashid were instrumental in Al-Ragon's conquest.

## Organisation

The Ibn Rashid train both bodyguards and assassins, an apparent contradiction which is explained by their history. Officially the protectors of the King of Kh'saaba, his family, and anyone the king honours with their protection, the Ibn Rashid protect the powerful of Kh'saaba and sometimes even those from beyond its borders, such as Jazirati nobles from Capharnaum or the Caravan Kingdoms, or even rich Shiradim or influential Quarterians. Their reputation means that being appointed an Ibn Rashid bodyguard is a mark of great favour, and the sovereigns of Kh'saaba have used that reputation to ensure their subjects' loyalty.

The Ibn Rashid are trained in the same academies as the Ibn Malik, but follow a different regime. Firstly, their senses are trained to the extreme: a good Ibn Rashid can isolate a whisper in a crowd, spot the sun glinting on a dagger in a marketplace, taste the poison in a wine cup and smell the fear in a man's sweat. Only then can he react effectively—and only then may the second part of his training begin. In this stage, the Ibn Rashid trains his body to withstand and transcend the most terrible pain, so they can continue to protect their charge. Using will alone, a wounded Ibn Rashid may exceed normal human limits and still remain effective, as Rashid did often for Hassan.

Once he leaves the academy, a young Ibn Rashid is assigned an individual he must protect. The less experienced become bodyguards to less important individuals, such as ambassadors to minor Capharnian cities; but those demonstrating great talent may join the guard of an influential noble.

The Ibn Rashid learn assassination strategies as part of their training, to better understand their enemy. They receive a killer's basic training: stealthy movement, the use of poison, secret weapons, and so on. In theory, this teaches them how to react when faced with such methods; in fact, this training also singles out those who may themselves make good assassins. The most gifted become the dark agents of the Kingdom of Kh'saaba, those who move in the shadows. These assassins make up fewer than one in a thousand of the Ibn Rashid, but they form an elite whose services are often in demand.

Despite their undeniable martial prowess, few Ibn Rashid ever become mujahidin, due to the obligations their missions impose upon them and the use the king makes of them to ensure the loyalty of his powerful vassals and foreign dignitaries. The life of a holy warrior requires commitments which are ultimately incompatible with those of bodyguards and assassins.

## Personalities

### Makta Ibn Rashid Abd-al-Hassan

For Makta, the world was once simple, his life all mapped out. Kh'saaba was the Kingdom of Hubal, and his task—modest as it might be—was to defend those who contributed to the country's greatness.

The realities of politics upset all that.

Finishing his studies, Makta was assigned to Capharnaum, where he acquired some bodyguard experience, guarding a Shiradi merchant, a Quarterian priest, several Jazirati amirs, and even a narrow-eyed stranger from the farthest East. His experience permitted him to return to Kh'saaba, where he was assigned to powerful nobles in the Jergath court.

His most recent master was the Grand Chancellor Ibrahim Ibn Mussah Abd-al-Hassan. A wise and good man, Makta became his friend as much as his shield. Ibrahim had been on the trail of a conspiracy but, before his investigation could shed much light, an assassin ended his days. Makta had known his master was in danger, and had watched over him night and day, but even so his unswerving loyalty and steely willpower were powerless before the killers. The young bodyguard was disarmed and left for dead by an assassin of supreme skill, who then moved on to Ibrahim…

Against all expectations, Makta survived. A servant of Ibrahim's treated him, and gave him a small strongbox containing documents saved from the fire that had consumed the Grand Chancellor's palace. Makta has pored over reports and correspondence hinting at a conspiracy, whose leads led to Sagrada. Having friends in Capharnaum, he decided to begin his investigation there.

On his way, Makta outwitted several ambushes, and his scimitar put paid to more than one assassin on his trail. His body and will have been tempered in the River of Death, and nothing will stop his quest for the truth—and for revenge for his master and friend.

# THE TRIBE OF THE SALIFAH

Salif the Wanderer, Salif the Lover, Salif the Snake. These were the names of one of the future prophets of Hubal. Wanderer, because he had no attachments, although the mighty sought him out for his legendary wisdom; lover, because he had but one love, his kingdom, Kh'saaba the Fair, Kh'saaba the Mistress of Hubal, so great a love that he would never marry; snake, because he never failed in his solitary travels, winning over raiders and bandits, befriending and travelling with them instead of ending up dead like so many others.

## The Age of Legend

*"The heart perceives what the eye doesn't see."*
—The Sayings of Salif

While still very young, Salif saw a new family of merchants and brigands developing around him. That's why Hassan entrusted him with the Merchants' Guild, to open Kh'saaba's trade routes to the outside world. Salif took to himself two of his nephews who resembled him: Yussef the Silver-Tongued, and Aziz, the Friend of All Men. Together, they travelled the Topaz and Copper Routes, negotiating more fiercely than others wage war, and finished with

their caravans protected by those who had been attacking them the day before.

In the Time of the Prophets, when Hubal called Salif, Hassan, and Tarek, Salif summoned his nephews for the last time, and added to their number their cousin, Khalil the Curious. On that night of farewell, he charged them to serve Kh'saaba the Fair, and that their descendants should continue to protect the beloved kingdom. Yussef would run the Merchants' Guild; Aziz would pacify the deserts and command the brigands to become his faithful warriors; and Khalil would win over foreign realms for the good of Kh'saaba and its King.

Although Salif's words still guide his tribe today, they do so in spirit rather than in letter, because the clans of his descendants have changed from what they once were. But Salif would not have wanted it any other way.

## The First Age

*"Being human is easy, being a man is hard."*
—The Sayings of Salif

Yussef was called the Silver-Tongued, since he was able to articulate the value people gave to things. More than just money, this concerned essential aspects of life, like one's children, or the love of a man or woman. From this insight he developed the Golden Sight which he taught to his firstborn, Kalam, the son who succeeded him as the head of his clan.

At the time Salif's tribe was in crisis. The pacification of the deserts had succeeded beyond all expectation, and competition had sprung up naturally. No longer was the Merchants' Guild the only force that counted.

Aziz had gathered the dregs of society around him. Most worshipped the One Thousand and One Gods, as long as they were allowed to keep on stealing, extorting, murdering, and prostituting themselves. His clan seemed little more than a shameful gang of criminals, and the other tribes were beginning to take a dim view of the direction Salif's tribe was taking—all the more so, because Khalil seemed to have vanished without a trace. The tribe had not heard from the third of its sons for so long that many had been insisting on holding a funeral wake to put his soul to rest—much to the despair of Yussef, who refused to consider his cousin dead.

## The Age of Change

*"The truth cannot be contained within a single dream."*
—The Sayings of Salif

It was in those troubled times that Khalil returned, with his wife, infant son, and a dozen warriors with skin as black as night. Each rode a small wingless dragon, an **abzul**. Khalil had failed in his mission to win over foreign lands, but had found faith and family in Al-Fariq'n, where he had become guardian of the **abzulim** and had founded the Walad Badiya, the "Children of the Desert", as the warriors and saurians called themselves.

Khalil's return restored the Salifah's place among the Saabi nobility, but the failure of his mission made the tribe doubt their beliefs. Yussef, Khalil, and Aziz left for the deep desert, where they faced the djinn for one thousand and one hours, before they heard the voice of Salif (some say it was the voice of Hubal—others say it was Salif-Who-Is-Hubal).

Upon their return, they reorganised the clans of the Salifah. Yussef and his clan were still to be traders, bringing wealth and jewels to adorn Kh'saaba the Fair; but they would also be the guardians of its traditions, satisfying the most ardent defenders of the religion of Hubal and the One Thousand and One Gods, allowing the tribe to retain its influence among the Saabi nobility.

Aziz and his followers were to be the secret financiers of the tribe and the kingdom. Together with Yussef they had understood that organised crime brought much more income than honest business. Moreover, Khalil had called attention to something that Aziz had not previously noticed: that thieves, murderers and mercenaries might not amount to much individually, but bring their information together... After all, what better means was there to know who had ordered an assassination or theft, than to be the one fulfilling the contract? Collating all this information would make the clan the most secret but also the most visible spy network in Jazirat. They were to be the eyes in the shadows for Kh'saaba the Revered.

Khalil himself split his clan between Jazirat and Al-Fariq'n, devoting himself to studying and developing his abzulim and training the Walad Badiya. He would gift his tribe and his kingdom with warriors whose strength and loyalty was entirely devoted to Kh'saaba and its gods.

Henceforth, the three cousins and their clans were to dedicate the traditions, intelligence, and strength of their tribe to the service of the Mother of Kings, the mother of them all, Kh'saaba herself.

### The Present Day

*"To be sad about the future is to have a sick mind."*
—*The Sayings of Salif*

The tribe had found its balance, one which was to last to the present day, in spite of its crises. Today, the Salifah are wherever the kingdom needs them: in Kh'saaba as in the rest of Jazirat and even the neighbouring kingdoms; sometimes in the thick of the action, sometimes preferring to advise with humility the Saabi already there. It's a tribe which serves the Kingdom of Kh'saaba above all, and all its members wait—sometimes without knowing it—for the call.

To everyone else, including other Saabi, the tribe of the Salifah looks like nothing but a motley assortment of men, women and children. The Salifah keep the secret of their unity from prying eyes, as it grants them great freedom.

The Ibn Yussef are the backbone of the Salifah. They ensure its unity and guarantee its integration within the kingdom. They maintain their positions as the most prosperous merchants in Jazirat, thanks to the secret aid of the Ibn Aziz who control organised crime. The Ibn Khalil remain somewhat outside the norm for the kingdom, being half-Jazirati and half-Al-Fariqani. Their ferocity, faith and fidelity has been proven time and again, and all Saabi tribes employ them as guards of tribe, palace or family.

# THE CLAN OF YUSSEF, SERVANT OF SALIF

## The Ibn Yussef Abd-al-Salif

### A History of Unobtrusive Men

*"If Yussef had lived at a time other than that of Salif, the tribe would today certainly be known as the Abd-al-Yussef. Yussef knew that, of course, but was happy with his life of service to the gods, to Kh'saaba, and to his uncle."*
—*Extract from* The People Who Made the World, *by Marteus of Therema*

The Ibn Yussef has always been the public face of the Salifah. They are the main way the tribe interacts with the outside world, including recruiting the Walad Badiya. However, the clan has always been content to serve men and women of power, influencing their actions for the good of Kh'saaba using intelligence gleaned by the Ibn Aziz (page 247). Many Hassanids, especially from the Ibn Mussah, include Ibn Yussef clan members in their retinues serving as advisors and stewards.

This doesn't mean they shrink from important positions. Prince Mamud of the Ibn Yussef is leader of the Carrassine V Legion. Profit and personal success can go hand in hand with service to Kh'saaba; it's up to each Salifah to follow his conscience.

Nor does it mean clan members never go astray in their ambitions. The Ibn Yussef have purged their ranks several times, certain members wanting to found a new Kh'saaba, away from the influence of the other tribes who were unable to appreciate the beauty of the Mother of All. This ambition has always been nipped in the bud.

The Salifah believe it's sometimes necessary to hurt the one you protect to be better able to save them. Whether this Kh'saaba or another, to rule the kingdom is to be its lover, and such a passion invariably obscures the decisions you make.

### Organisation

The Ibn Yussef are travellers, and their only attachment is to Kh'saaba. They're found in every city in Jazirat, and on all trade routes. Part of the clan is sedentary, organising convoys and seeking out cargoes to entrust to the caravans; they are businessmen, stewards, advisors, and even occupy strategic positions in local politics. The other part comprises caravaneers, bound by blood or affection, travelling from city to city.

Adolescent clan members leave their families to go and live with a nomad family for two years. In the depths of the desert, they are initiated, in a rite of passage that reinforces the ties between the tribe's families. Many marriages are decided at this time, and the young adults make contacts they will keep their whole lives.

In return, the more sedentary families of the Ibn Yussef welcome and train all young adults wanting to learn about stewardship and politics. Families are not nomadic or sedentary by heredity—each generation decides the path it wants to take, even if certain families traditionally always make the same choice.

### Unattached Rich Folk?

*Many people view the Ibn Yussef this way. In many respects it's not far from the truth: the clan continues to serve Kh'saaba, but these days the kingdom is so prosperous that they are no longer indispensable, and have begun to feel less useful as a clan—although each individual can still contribute to the life of the kingdom with his own capabilities.*

*If change or disruption were ever to threaten the status quo in Kh'saaba, the Ibn Yussef would launch themselves on the warpath and fight to restore it, even if just to prove to themselves that they still had a role to play serving their motherland. Most would probably never even question if such a change was a good thing or not.*

These two parts are complimentary. The sedentary Ibn Yussef study and decide upon which business is to be done, and are often the first to know what goods will be fashionable in Jazirat's cities, or which cargoes are available at knock-down prices that undercut the competition. The nomadic Ibn Yussef convey these goods throughout Jazirat, whatever they may be.

Historically, the chief of the Ibn Yussef is always succeeded by his firstborn child, whether male or female. The current chief is Farham Ibn Yussef Abd-al-Salif, in the service of the king at Jergath the Great. His daughter, Dahabiya Bint Yussef Abd-al-Salif, will succeed him, and his son Ayman Ibn Yussef Abd-al-Salif will be royal treasurer, a position usually held by a Hassanid. This arrangement isn't to everyone's taste, and Dahabiya's assassination would please those who'd prefer a man to head the clan, as well as those who'd rather avoid a Salifah royal treasurer, as Prince Ayman would be forced to take his father's place.

## Personalities

### Dahabiya Bint Yussef Abd-al-Salif

A young woman with a lively and fierce intelligence, Dahabiya is daughter of the chief of the Ibn Yussef, and a worthy successor. Those close to the family know she is far more suited to rule the clan than her brother: Prince Ayman loves nothing better than to play with numbers, and people, politics, and even Kh'saaba hold no interest for him. Dahabiya's death would be a tragedy for him as well as the clan.

Dahabiya's bodyguard is Warit Ibn Khalil Abd-al-Salif, a Walad Badiya descending directly from Khalil. They are lovers: their marriage may prevent the tribe's looming succession crisis, but Dahabiya has been betrothed from birth to an unambitious cousin who has as little interest in her as she has in him.

### Ikhram Ibn Yussef Abd-al-Salif

Ikhram began life as a street urchin. His lively intelligence was noticed by one of the Ibn Aziz, who took him in. He was eventually adopted by a friend of the latter, Waja Ibn Yussef Abd-al-Salif, who trained him in the Golden Sight. Now a young man of thirty, Ikhram leads a modest but prosperous family which runs two caravans and serves Thalat Ibn Aziz Abd-al-Salif, Prince of Thieves of Jergath the Great. Ikhram has never forgotten where he came from or what he has become, and tries to combine the best parts of both.

### Safara Ibn Yussef Abd-al-Salif

Safara is a fifty-year old former caravaneer now living in Fragrance. He rises every dawn to find out what ships have arrived and, if their cargoes seem interesting, he arranges things so he's the first to bid for them. He does such good business that some suspect he has the Golden Sight, but Safara succeeds through hard work. If he doesn't like the look of the cargoes, he goes home and spends time with his young wife and three children (all under five). He also writes poetry: odes to love, the gods, and the Kh'saaba he misses so much.

# THE CLAN OF AZIZ, SERVANT OF SALIF

## The Ibn Aziz Abd-al-Salif

### A History of the People of the Shadows

*"Faith is not a matter of morals. The most fervent believers aren't always the wisest people, even if the wisest are often great believers."*
—From Salif to Aziz

Aziz was a friend to everyone he met. He always knew what to say, which gifts to give, which silences to respect. When he left Jazirat, the raiders that once plagued the Topaz and Copper Routes had been converted and had joined his tribe, and now protected the caravans they once attacked. Other gangs of raiders would take their place, however, and converting them would not be so easy.

Following Salif's final words of advice, Aziz became the first Prince of Thieves in Jazirat's history, uniting and ruling the dregs of society in every city. He devoted his life to Kh'saaba, and had neither wife nor children (at least, no recognised ones); in the end it was his right-hand man, a former street urchin, who succeeded him at the head of this clan of gangsters. This act was a precedent for the clan's system of meritocratic succession, unlike the hereditary version practiced by other Saabi.

## Organisation

*"If your right hand doesn't know what your left hand is doing, it won't confess under torture."*

—*The Sayings of Salif*

The clan of Aziz is present in practically every city in Jazirat, as well as foreign cities where the clan acts with greater circumspection. In each city, the clan has a "Prince of Thieves" who controls organised crime in his territory, although he never eliminates all his competition so he doesn't lose his edge.

The Ibn Aziz operate in a pyramidal structure. Each individual reports only to his immediate superior, right up to the clan leader or "Prince of Shadows", currently Thalat Ibn Aziz Abd-al-Salif, Prince of Thieves of Jergath the Great.

To climb the clan hierarchy, you must begin at the bottom. Family ties mean nothing; each member is judged by his own actions, contracts, the accuracy of the reports he files, as well as his respect for clan law and loyalty to the One Thousand and One Gods and Kh'saaba.

The Ibn Aziz prefer their members to be as mobile as possible; mobility is a key part of their tests for promotion. Rotations between different clan territories and the transmission of the clan's secret messages are all guaranteed by the caravans of the Ibn Yussef.

The Ibn Aziz conduct a great deal of illegal business: slavery, begging, prostitution, theft, murder, extortion, as well as the hiring of mercenaries. The latter accounts for half of the clan's total activities, and its single most valued: the most honest and readily available mercenaries in Jazirat generally belong to the Ibn Aziz.

### Contracts and Loyalty to Kh'saaba

*The Ibn Aziz are much more than gangsters. Profoundly loyal to Kh'saaba, they're information gatherers beyond compare. They accept all contracts, even those which appear to go against Kh'saaba's interests. For the clan, it's more important to know who ordered a murder than to prevent it.* **Knowing** *is the most powerful weapon the Ibn Aziz possess.*

*This meticulous adherence to contracts never prevents the clan from later killing whoever ordered a murder, or from secretly helping the heirs of the man they killed to re-establish order. But it is all done in the utmost secrecy, so that no one ever suspects the true business of the Ibn Aziz—the clandestine "intelligence service" of Kh'saaba.*

*The clan's apparent venality has always been a disadvantage in their relations with other Saabi. The only ones to have penetrated their secrets are the Horned Vipers of the Tarekids (page 254). They've long mingled in the Salifah whorehouses, and know the Ibn Aziz are far more than they seem.*

### A Few Rules of the Clan

*Always give your loyalty to the gods, to Kh'saaba, to your clan, to your family, and to your people—in that order.*

*If you accept a contract, carry it out to the bitter end, regardless of the consequences, unless doing so would truly threaten your family.*

*Remembering the past is a sacred duty. Relating it to others is a profession of your faith, in the gods and in your clan.*

## Personalities

### Thalat Ibn Aziz Abd-al-Salif

Thalat is thirty years old, exceptional in that he climbed to lead his clan despite having been born on the streets. People claim he can be in several places at once, that he works more than any normal man can, that he can negotiate for days without sleeping, and that he's utterly devoted to Kh'saaba. Even more, he's also the Prince of Thieves of Jergath the Great.

### Tabar Ibn Aziz Abd-al-Salif

Tabar runs a brothel in Jergath the Great, a hammam where magnificent young women and men serve their customers' pleasure. Tabar treats his girls and boys well, and is always on the lookout for that rare pearl that will ensure his establishment's fame—a beautiful houri, divinely handsome gigolo, gifted masseur. He dreams of employing a Paper Virgin (page 254), but all his attempts at corruption, blackmail or seduction have failed. He has even considered kidnapping—an act that would be a death sentence for both concerned.

### Jabhar Ibn Aziz Abd-al-Salif

A mercenary like others in his clan, Jabhar was a violent young man who sought battle in the tavern as much as on the battlefield. His life changed abruptly when he saved the life of an Aragonian nobleman, Javier de la Estrella, ten years ago. Javier was being robbed, and Jabhar saw an opportunity of wading in without ending up in jail. The man hired him as his bodyguard on the spot, and Jabhar followed him to Aragon. Now he's back, still with Javier, who is now assistant to the Aragonian ambassador in Carrassine. Jabhar knows he'll soon have to recontact his clan and once again start informing on the man who has become his friend. He's also hopes to find a wife among the Ibn Aziz, and to start serving Kh'saaba again.

# THE CLAN OF KHALIL, SERVANT OF SALIF

## The Ibn Khalil Abd-al-Salif

### A Tale of a Dark-skinned People

*"The Ibn Khalil are a mystery. Both Jazirati and Al-Fariqani, they're devoted to Kh'saaba!"*
—*Extract from* The Makers of the World *by Marteus of Therema*

Khalil spoke little of his trek before reaching Al-Fariq'n. The peoples he met were at best indifferent to his words, at worst violent. More than once he was imprisoned and scourged for preaching his beliefs, or driven from a city, close to death. His faith in Hubal had deserted him by the time he approached Al-Fariq'n's shores.

It was by saving the son of the king of the Ungara, a large Al-Fariqani tribe, that Khalil found a new family and homeland. He married the Princess Tegest and tried to forget his failure and his faith by adopting the tribe's customs and beliefs.

The death of the Ungara's shaman restored Khalil's faith in Hubal. Before dying, the shaman entrusted him with the secret of his clan. Two sacred stones were in the clan's possession, and an ancient prophesy said they must be forever kept beneath water until the Chosen One should arrive. The shaman believed Khalil to be that Chosen One, and told him to travel into the desert with a bosom friend, to carry the sacred stones and bury them there, and wait until the gods spoke to him as the prophecy foretold.

Out of respect for the shaman, who reminded him of Salif, Khalil left to bury the two stones in the company of Therk, a cousin of his wife's who had become as close as any brother. After several weeks, during which Khalil and Therk kept watch upon the desert where the stones were buried, the stones cracked open, and two wingless dragons emerged from the sand—the **abzulim**. One approached Khalil, the other Therk, and bit his hand—sealing a mental bond between dragon and man.

The abzulim laid more eggs, which in turn gave birth to more abzulim, which bonded with the warriors of the tribe. In this way, the Walad Badiya were born, and Khalil regained his faith in Hubal. He converted the Ungara, who began to worship the One Thousand and One Gods, and to love Kh'saaba as Khalil did. The Saabi may have failed in his mission, but instead had found his clan. Together with his wife, who had also bonded to an abzul, his son, and a dozen warriors (including Therk), Khalil returned to Jazirat.

Today the clan of Khalil is divided between Al-Fariq'n and Jazirat, and the Walad Badiya love both the lands of the Ungaras and Kh'saaba. They travel between both lands freely.

### Organisation

The Ibn Khalil occupy several territories. First are the ancestral lands of the Ungaras, in Al-Fariq'n; second is Ma'Hulum, an oasis on the furthest borders of the Kingdom of Kh'saaba; and third are several more modest oases in the Desert of Fire.

The clan leader of the Ibn Khalil always lives in Ma'Hulum, even if he regularly travels to Al-Fariq'n. He is chosen by the previous chieftain, and is always a member of his family—usually a son or nephew. The Ibn Khalil are idealistic mystics: the original Ungaras adopted the faith of Khalil and his love for Kh'saaba, and so the clan serves the kingdom loyally, going wherever they are needed. They may serve as mercenaries in return for financial or political profit; or they may choose to serve a Saabi noble family if they deem them worthy. The loyalty of the Ibn Khalil cannot be bought: it has to be earned.

Besides the Walad Badiya, the clan is known for breeding goats, donkeys, and camels, as well as more exotic beasts from Al-Fariq'n. Most of this livestock is used for feeding the abzulim, although the clan is also known for its sweet and delicate cuisine mixing Al-Fariqani and Jazirati tastes. Ibn Khalil dishes will keep for several days of desert travel without losing taste or quality.

The Ibn Khalil are led by an elderly Walad Badiya, as they have been since Khalil. Hakim Ibn Khalil Abd-al-Salif is the great uncle of the current King of Ungara. Despite his advanced age (some say he's over 80 years old), Hakim is surprisingly vigorous, and looks to have many years ahead of him.

## Personalities

### Princess Tegest Bint Khalil Abd-al-Salif

A descendant of Khalil and the great-grand niece of Hakim Ibn Khalil Abd-al-Salif, whose name she bears, Princess Tegest Bint Khalil Abd-al-Salif was raised in Al-Fariq'n. A Walad Badiya, she is a black-skinned teenager already initiated to the arts of combat, with the flexibility of body and muscles to prove it. Stubborn and bossy, she decided to return to Jergath the Great and her relations in the local nobility to learn about the land of the other half of her family.

Although her beauty has turned the heads of several young Saabi nobles, Tegest has tired of parties, and now roams the streets with some Ibn Aziz and her abzul.

### Dawaq Ibn Khalil Abd-al-Salif

The poets in the royal court praise Dawaq as the greatest cook of all time. He's an ex-warrior who travelled from Al-Fariq'n to Jazirat for adventure. Encountering Jazirati cuisine was a true surprise, and ever since he's devoted himself to cooking like other artists become poets or painters.

Since becoming chef in the royal kitchens, many have suspected Dawaq of wanting to poison the king. He makes a point of tasting every dish himself, not only to ensure its quality, but to prove nothing is poisoned.

Dawaq's reputation is so great that foreign courts have offered him fortunes to prepare meals for them. His culinary curiosity and the mistrust he experiences from the Saabi might eventually persuade Dawaq to accept their offers. For now, only his love for Kh'saaba stops him.

### Malik Ibn Khalil Abd-al-Salif

Malik is a child of the desert. Upon becoming a Walad Badiya, he was bonded to a sickly abzul which was unable to carry him any great distance. This has never worried him, since he has never particularly liked fighting. He can defend himself, like every desert-dweller, but he prefers a bucolic life at Ma'Hulum, cross-breeding his goats to obtain more milk and tastier meat. His goats now fetch a good price at Jergath's Great Market, where he goes during the great fairs, in search of new stock and new blood for his herd.

## The Walad Badiya

The term **Walad Badiya** refers to the union of human and abzul, and not simply to the human rider, as many think. Abzulim are intelligent creatures, but express themselves through feelings rather than words (see page 307). The bond uniting human and abzul is almost impossible to explain to anyone who is not Walad Badiya.

Not everyone in the Ibn Khalil becomes Walad Badiya. Old warriors recognise the **dragon fever** that drives a child to cleave to an abzul. When a clutch is about to hatch, those who will cleave become nervous, impatient, in a way which is quite unmistakeable to those who have learned the shamanic rituals inherited from the clan's Al-Fariqani side.

There are never more children with the dragon fever than there are eggs in a clutch. If there are fewer, the eggs left over do not hatch, and are kept in water until the day a child feels driven to bury it.

All Walad Badiya, men and women alike, become one with their mounts, and generally take up the profession of warrior. Exceptions are not uncommon, but even those who are not formally warriors remain formidable fighters.

Sometimes the dragon fever affects a stranger to the clan. When this happens, the Ibn Khalil either trust the stranger and allow him to join the clan, or they kill him, condemning one of the eggs in the clutch to bear a stillborn abzul. Abzulim are too sacred to leave in the hands of strangers who do not belong to the clan.

# THE TRIBE OF THE TAREKIDS

## The Legend

Tarek was one of the three prophets that inspired Hubal to take draconic form to raise the city of Jergath the Great. When Tarek was given the mission of spreading the word of the Supreme God, he decided to do so by taking as his disciples merciless raiders from the deep deserts of Jazirat and converting them. Tarek spoke for nine days and nine nights in the desert, in the coldest hours of the night and the most fiery hours of the day. He tested the strength and will of three lawless brigands—Tufiq, Mustafah, and Mimun—who became the founders of the clans of the Tarekids known today.

No one knows what the prophet told the founders. When he had finished, however, the merciless thieves had decided to dedicate themselves to Hubal's hardest precepts, and to spread them throughout the world. Thus was born the tribe of Tarek and the clans of the desert jackal, caracal, and horned viper, dwelling in the deep desert and preaching a return to the nomad life renouncing all earthly temptations. The Tarekids battle the decadence and depravity of the Salifah, often by using their very decadence and depravity as weapons back against them.

## Two Origin Stories

While their clans grew and prospered, the ties between Tufiq, his brother Mustafah, and the beautiful Mimun grew stronger. But how strong, and how close? Those became questions for the ages.

There are two answers. The first, well established in Saabi history, is that told by the "original" Tarekids, the Ibn Tufiq and the Bint Mimun; the second is that told by the much younger clan of the Ibn Yazid.

The official story says that the ties between the three founders were amicable, based on mutual respect and a solid desire for cooperation, focussed on the goals of the tribe as taught by Tarek. It was during an expedition of several moons' duration, inspired by just this spirit, to hunt down a fearsome *afreet*, that the tragic death of Mustafah occurred. For Tufiq and Mimun, the event revealed their weakness, shameful and inadmissible considering the values they had espoused and the example they were supposed to set. Thenceforth they were to be irreproachable in all respects, for this was the only way of assuring the integrity and nobility of the Tarekid tribe.

The Ibn Yazid question this official story. They say that a secret love affair existed between Mustafah and Mimun. In order not to anger Tufiq, whose violent and dominating nature was well known, Mimun had sworn to him that it would be better only for platonic friendship to unite the three founders. Peace was maintained for only a few months, however, as the young woman fell pregnant. She hid her condition, feigning illness, but a servant woman inadvertently gave away her secret. In a fit of rage, Tufiq tried to force his brother to confess to the truth, and slew him. He remained prostrate the whole night in his *mukhayyam*, whilst elsewhere Mimun found out about Mustafah's death. In shock, she gave birth prematurely, and in order to preserve the infant from Tufiq's wrath, she conferred it upon a *raiss* who was close to her. She burned a small animal to make Tufiq believe the child had died.

When Tufiq joined Mimun the next morning, they decided to swear a sacred oath. Mimun had sinned outside the bonds of marriage, while Tufiq had killed a loved and respected chieftain—and a brother. To ensure the future of their clans and their own safety, such a thing must never come to pass again.

## A Pact Written In Blood

Mimun retrieved the half-dried blood of Mustafah (from the claws of the *afreet* or from Tufiq's blade, depending on the version of the story told), and mixed it with her own blood to make a form of ink. This she used to write the pact which was to decide the fate of the clans for centuries to come. In it, she told of everything that had happened, and everything which they swore not to do. If either of them were to break the pact, the other would know immediately, and the one who had broken the pact would die a terrible death within seven days.

# THE DESERT JACKALS: THE CLAN OF TUFIQ, SERVANT OF TAREK

## The Ibn Tufiq Abd-al-Tarek

### History

Tufiq and Mustafah were notorious raiders whose band scoured the villages at the borders of the Aramla El-Nar and, after their depradations, took shelter in the caves of the deep desert.

The day of his brother's tragic death (history tells Mustafah was killed by a wild beast while hunting djinn), Tufiq doubled his ardour in the holy quest Tarek had bestowed upon him. He slew with savagery all the enemies of his religion, and soon his clan became feared by all, even beyond the borders of Jazirat.

---

### The Sacred Dialect

Extremely traditionalist, often opposed to social, technological and economic advances, the Tarekids are hardened conservatives. You can even see this in the way they speak: they use their own dialect, which is still rich with archaisms and is probably the closest modern tongue to that spoken at the time of the Prophets. Although the Tarekids can generally communicate with the Saabi and other Jazirati without much difficulty, there are many terms referring to their ancient traditions which they do not replace with modern terms. There's no way, for example, a Tarekid will refer to their ancestral mukhayyam as "a tent".

Here are a few ancient words from the Tarekid dialect:

A'ila: A gathering of Tarekid nomad families, a political and religious community in itself.

Awwal-Malhud: The true sacred name for the amir of an a'ila.

Kitaba Nader: The "Book of Essences", the true sacred name for the school of sorcery created by Mimun.

Mukhayyam: The traditional Tarekid tent.

Sabil: The territory belonging to a gathering of Tarekid families.

Taalli: A mujahid or kahini apprentice.

Ta'awun: A penitent who submits themselves to ignoble labour for a period, either through his own volition or under the command of a kahini.

---

## Organisation

The Ibn Tufiq have a rigid, hierarchical rigid organisation which is the model for that used by all Tarekid clans. Like the *mukhayyam* they live in, its structure is like a snail shell, its centre the mukhayyam of the Awwal-Malhud.

### The Mukhayyam of the Awwal-Malhud

The leaders of any Tarekid clan are the Awwal-Malhud, amirs descended directly from (in this case) the elder sons of Tufiq. The kahini say Tufiq had twenty-seven children: fourteen boys and thirteen girls. His fourteen sons had their own children; the eldest, called the Awwal-Malhud or *First-born*, had their children in turn, whose eldest sons had the rights of an Awwal-Malhud amir.

An Awwal-Malhud may found his own *a'ila*, exploiting the *sabil* or desert area where the clan may camp, hunt, farm, and exploit its natural resources. He must care for the fragile ecosystem (limiting camping times in more delicate oases, and so on), and also guarantee its security, driving off all those trying to poach there. The Awwal-Malhud should also drive away any foreign nomads trying to settle in the *sabil*.

### The First Circle: the Sheiks

The first circle of the snail-shell after the Awwal-Malhud is occupied by the sheiks. The descendants of Tufiq's younger sons have fewer rights than the Awwal-Malhud, but still have privileges, such as joining higher castes and being served by *ta'awun* and *taalli* (see below). The tents of the sheiks of a given *a'ila* and their families stand in a circle around that of the Awwal-Malhud.

### The Second Circle: the Kahini and Mujahidin

The **kahini** are guardians of the faith, religious scholars and spiritual leaders. They hold supreme authority in the *a'ila*, after the Awwal-Malhud and Rahal Ibn Tufiq Abd-al-Tarek, leader of the Tarekid tribe. They meet once a month, each time at a different kahini's dwelling, and the last month of the year they meet in the oasis of Nabiy. They're protected by devoted *mujahidin*.

The kahini of the Tarekids have a great reputation for religious wisdom, and are often consulted by other tribes, including the Hassanids, to debate complex religious questions. Although these guardians of orthodoxy and law refuse payment, they accept offerings to their temples and "useful" gifts such as animals, food, and slaves. They rule on the thorniest religious questions, including those relating to the Paper Virgins (page 254), who can find themselves in the most delicate situations.

Most of the mujahidin warrior elite left Jazirat on the sacred quest to recover the Sword of Hammad in the West. Others hire themselves out as mercenaries across the world, crusading in their own ways against the corruption which eats away at today's societies. The Tarekid mujahidin do not compromise, and believe Tarek's teachings should be respected by everyone. Some lead the Califah-al-Sahla, the "Caravan of Purification" (page 254). They confiscate the belongings of those who break religious law, aided by *taalli* (below) wanting to join their caste.

## The Third Circle: the Tababi and Taalli

The **tababi** are sages who conduct important rites of passage for the Tarekids, including birth rituals, those for coming of age, weddings, divorces, death rites, and the ritual scarifications associated with important milestones in a person's life—reaching adulthood, having your first child, fighting a duel of honour. The tababi have extensive medical knowledge and treat the wounds and illnesses of clan members. They're effectively the assistants of the kahini.

The **taalli** will one day become mujahidin or kahini. To do so, they must undergo a series of trials, in which each success enables them to progress in the taalli hierarchy. To mark this progress, up to five metal plaques are affixed to a taalli's armour, representing the Five Great Trials.

## The Fourth Circle: Bedouins and Ta'awun

The fourth circle of any Tarekid clan comprises the "common" nomads or **Bedouins** who make up most of the clan. They practice all the essential crafts; blacksmiths take care of horseshoes and hunters' weapons; farmers gather the fruits of their labours from every oasis they pass through; hunters bring meat; tanners make clothing from the skins and maintain the *mukhayyami* tents.

The fourth circle also includes the **ta'awuni**, or "those who help". The ta'awun is "ignoble labour"—any job which a Tarekid would normally consider beneath him. These jobs must nevertheless be done, and individual Tarekids may become ta'awuni for many different reasons. Very often they request these duties for themselves: it's an example of the strength of one's will required of a member of the tribe. A person may

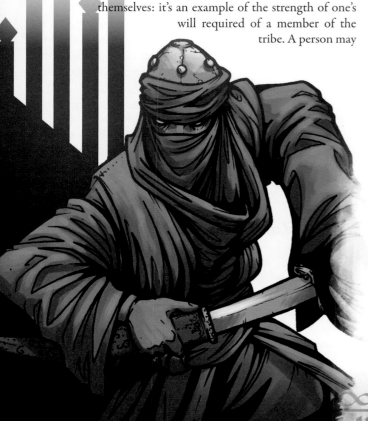

also be declared *ta'awun* on certain occasions: after a duel, the defeated party will ask to perform ta'awun in the service of his victorious opponent, for example. The duration of his ta'awun status is determined by the *tababi* sages. Being ta'awun isn't degrading in any way, but it can be quite humiliating: accepting this with humility is a way of submitting to the truths of Hubal.

## Personalities

### Rahal Ibn Tufiq Abd-al-Tarek

Although the clans include many amirs, only one sits at the table of the King of Kh'saaba. This is Prince Rahal Ibn Tufiq Abd-al-Tarek, leader of the Ibn Tufiq and of the Tarekid tribe, and amir close to the king.

Prince Rahal is now seventy years old. For fifty years, he has ruled the Tarekids with an iron fist. He is a force of nature: six feet six inches tall, weighing two hundred and twenty pounds, his piercing blue stare freezes your blood when he is angry at you. He's also a fierce fighter; right up to the age of sixty he led the Caravan of Purification on a warrior march to bring the word of Tarek to the world by force of arms.

Today, Rahal is tired. Some say it's time for him to retire to the desert and allow his son to take over. Some even think (although they never say it) that it was Rahal's advanced age that Yazid took advantage of when he founded his own clan (see page 258). The truth is more complicated, although it's true that if Yazid had tried to found his clan twenty years ago, it would have ended in a bloodbath.

### Ihul Ibn Tufiq Abd-al-Tarek and Malawi Ibn Tufiq Abd-al-Tarek

Literally the "body and spirit of the Caravan of Purification", Ihul leads the mujahidin and Malawi the kahini in the Califah-al-Sahla. As leaders of the single most powerful religious force in Jazirat, they are powerful and respected. Ihul represents the warrior strength of the soldier of Hubal, handling the Califah's secular affairs, such as troop management, organising the caravan, protecting guests. Despite his shorter than average build—5 feet 7 inches tall and weighing just over 130 lbs—he still exudes a formidable presence. It's said he's as agile as a panther, as fast as a cheetah, as calm as a lion. His hair falls down his shoulder like the mane of a great cat.

Malawi is a much older man (almost 65, against Ihul's 32), representing the spirituality of the Califah and handling all matters divine. He issues the guidelines for the Califah for the year to come, and manages day-to-day communication with religious leaders relating to the Caravan of Purification. He also judges unbelievers and decides upon their punishments when the caravan is in town. He's a cunning and fanatical man, although he appears warm and welcoming at first sight, his grey hair and wrinkled, weathered face making a reassuring impression.

## The Califah-al-Sahla or Caravan of Purification

*This huge procession has its roots in the quest the young Mimun undertook to find her son. The quest gave rise to the Tarekid belief that they should travel to the towns of Jazirat to cleanse their corrupted populations, inciting people to repent, renounce their false gods, and embrace the true faith. This sacred procession became known as the Califah-al-Sahla or "Caravan of Purification". It rapidly acquired the reputation of bringing death in its wake, and yet it was also a trial for* **taalli** *apprentices wishing to prove themselves. The taalli would join the caravan as it left the Oasis of Nabiy and visited the cities of Jazirat, travelling in the company of its mujahidin and kahini for ninety days.*

*Gradually, the Califah's success grew, and the Tarekids received many requests from the common people to join the ranks of the taalli when the caravan passed through their cities. In its best years, the caravan numbered more than six hundred men and women. Many pilgrims and apprentices join its numbers even today.*

*Over time, the governors of the cities the caravan passes through have besought its Tarekid leaders to moderate their members' fervour. Because of the Caravan's increasing popularity, the leaders have agreed. Today, the Califah-al-Sahla is well thought of, although "incidents" are still common, and fanatical individuals, driven half-mad by the extreme hardships of their journey, still attack and even murder individuals they consider to have strayed too far from the path of righteousness.*

*Ultimately, the Califah-al-Sahla is a pretext for the Tarekids to "punish the sinful". Its arrival in a city is often met by professions of faith and scenes of contrition and self-flagellation. However, it's also a bogey-man for the common folk, who threaten their children with the words "if you don't behave, the Califah will come for you!"*

# THE HORNED VIPERS: THE CLAN OF MIMUN, SERVANT OF TAREK

## The Bint Mimun Abd-al-Tarek

### History

Founded by Mimun the Beautiful, one of the desert raiders called to serve Tarek, the clan of the Horned Vipers saw their organisation and goals change upon their founder's death. By developing a unique type of sorcery later called the **Kitaba Nader**, or "Book of Essences", they understood they had in their possession a terrifying weapon, and one that was going to require them to make profound adjustments if they were to employ it effectively.

### Setting Up the Network

To best employ their sorcerous powers, the Horned Vipers realised they would have to go where their particular abilities would be most useful, namely the cities of Jazirat, and specifically those quarters of ill-repute, where violence, thievery, and prostitution were common.

Very soon, the Bint Mimun realised these areas were already controlled by another power: the underworld leaders of the decadent tribe of the Salifah. Never proponents of force, they took discreet action, passing themselves off as common prostitutes from the desert tribes. They infiltrated the brothels of Jazirati cities, establishing secret schools to teach their fellows the arts of the Book of Essences.

### The Foundation of the Paper Virgins

The sorcerous school of the Bint Mimun took the structure of a religious order, and became known as the "Paper Virgins" (see below). From its inception, the order was ruled by a high priestess, the **Umm Kabira**, a direct descendant of Mimun who possessed the power of life and death over the order's members. The Umm Kabira transmits to the Paper Virgins all Mimun's teachings, including the secrets of the Kitaba Nader.

## Organisation

### The Order of the Paper Virgins

Unlike the Ibn Tufiq, who are organised in *a'ilas* and live almost exclusively in the desert, the Bint Mimun are city-dwellers and are organised in orders, and include in their number the Beloved of Agushaya (page 88). Unlike almost every other Saabi clan, they have a matriarchal structure: their name, Bint Mimun, means "Daughters of Mimun", even though half of their members are male. Their residences are often the brothels which serve as their work-places, although the full Paper Virgins, known as **Sisters**, instead reside in the medina temples as sacred prostitutes, where the *kahini* of the Ibn Tufiq provide asylum and protection.

Additionally, several secret palaces are scattered across Jazirati cities, where the order's **Mothers** (below) deploy the *rukh* essences, cunning alchemical preparations of bodily essences, for magical and often political ends (see page 256).

## Abat Ittijah—the Pleasure of the Senses

The term *Abat Ittijah*, or "Pleasure of the Senses", refers to the erotic arts used by the Paper Virgins to overwhelm their sexual partners. At their hands, subjects lose all self-control, becoming malleable, indiscreet, open to suggestion—and perfectly receptive to the manipulations of the Bint Mimun. However, the Paper Virgins themselves need incredible discipline to remain immune to these same sensations—hence the need for the Abat Ittijah art. The restraint they exercise is one explanation of the term "Paper Virgins"; for all their artistry and the pleasure they give, practitioners remain emotionally untouched. Many even say the mysteries of the Abat Ittijah allow the Paper Virgins to remain *physically* untouched, too...

There is a cost to all this restraint and self-denial. Stress, frustration, and even physical pain are all side-effects of the Abat Ittijah, and the Mothers of the order carefully watch over the Paper Virgins who practise it, and ensure they regularly attend confession with the kahini of their temple. Even so, the Paper Virgins are always prey to temptation, corruption, and worse.

### Umm Kabira—the Great Mother

Like the Ibn Tufiq, the Bint Mimun are ruled by a direct descendant of their founder, although, true to their matriarchal structure, this ruler, like their founder, is always a woman—the Umm Kabira, or "Great Mother". However, the clan is less strict about the heritage of its ruler: as long as she can pass the Test of Rulership imposed by the clan's Council of Sisters, it doesn't matter if the chief is Awwal-Malhud or sheik (page 252). The Test of Rulership requires the candidate for Great Mother to read—and triumph over (see page 257)—the **Kitab Tarikh**, the "History Book" that Mimun herself wrote about her final days.

One of the principal duties of the Umm Kabira is to complete the sacred quest conferred upon her by the former Great Mother she is replacing, who herself received it from the one who went before her, all the way back to Mimun herself, who followed visions received during the *Mukhabbat* rite, a voyage alone through the desert to the sacred Oasis of Nabiy.

To complete this quest, the Great Mother maintains a mysterious scroll mapping all the events required for its completion, called the Chart of Sahla, or Chart of Purification. Upon this chart, the Umm Kabira places her acolytes like a chess player, coordinating their activities in a grand plan. Although the Bint Mimun have the same goal as the Ibn Tufiq—the cleansing of society—the means they use are completely different.

The main difficulties facing the Umm Kabira are the fierce competition the Bint Mimun encounter from underworld leaders, and the fortunes the clan is obliged to pay to operate brothels and related businesses across their territories of operations. She employs Mothers to acquire funds from wealthy clients who are "encouraged" to donate to the order (often under the influence of the sorcery of the Kitaba Nader).

The common folk consider the Paper Virgins to be little more than sacred prostitutes, a luxury for the wealthy. Underworld bosses know more, and perhaps guess the rest, aware of the secret order's existence and suspecting complex designs behind the Paper Virgins' activities. The existence of the Guardians (see below) proves the order has considerable resources at its disposal; where a common prostitute would be handled by a pimp in a stable of half a dozen others, a single Paper Virgin has her own Guardian. Underworld kingpins constantly try to kidnap Paper Virgins or their Guardians to gather intelligence on the order's real motivations.

Over the centuries, the Umm Kabira have trained Paper Virgins and Guardians to resist these attempts, even at the price of their own lives. The safety of the order comes before all.

### The Mothers

The Mothers are experienced and senior Paper Virgins who have mastered the Kitaba Nader and the Abat Ittijah. They mostly work alone, distilling the most complex essences, creating powerful charms or painting detailed portraits. Sometimes their endeavours come to the interest of the Umm Kabira in her quest to purify the corrupted civilisation of Jazirat.

The Mothers employ their sorcerous works to manipulate specific individuals, provoking crises, unrest, and even revolts among the common folk. No individual Mother is privy to the Chart of Purification of the Umm Kabira, however, and does not know the role her work plays in the greater scheme.

### The Sisters

The Sisters are **Tawl** (see below) who have mastered the fifth ability of their path (see page 89). They have completed their noviciates in the perilous Salifah fleshpots, and now enter the medina temples where they reside as sacred prostitutes—the legendary "Paper

## The Kitaba Nader Book of Essences

The origin of the Essence Magic of the Bint Mimun is found in the pact sworn by Tufiq and Mimun. By using her lover's blood to inscribe the pact, Mimun employed for the first time the power of the rukh, or "soul essence", to work the spell. It was only later that she became aware of what she had done—and that this magic had existed for aeons in the furthest East. She travelled to Nir Manel, to Naratmajah, and became mistress to the heir of the Maharaja, Prince Sobir. Intending to seduce the Prince, legend says Mimun was bested at her own game and, after nine nights of ecstasy from which she could barely rise, the Prince revealed the secret of his prowess. On their first night, he had stolen some of her bodily essences, and had distilled a magical perfume which gave him complete mastery over all Mimun's emotions. After the nine nights, Prince Sobir recognised Mimun as his equal, and taught her the art of distilling the essences.

Upon her return to Jazirat, Mimun shut herself away for ten moons with a harem of twenty lovers, the most beautiful, handsome, and energetic she could find, and set about creating her own version of the sorcery of Nir Manel. She created the **Kitaba Nader**, or Book of Essences, and Essence Magic was born.

Essence Magic is the use of rukh essences, principally to inscribe parchments, similar to the pact of Tufiq and Mimun, to charm and manipulate others. The effects are more potent if the essences come from the person the magic is intended to affect, but it's sufficient if they're from a person of the same gender (or gender identity).

Essence Magic also allows the creation of literary works and artworks of superb quality, which the magic renders more agreeable to the eye, and also of perfumes, which have a more direct effect. The magic contained within the object is preserved indefinitely, although it may only be used once. The distance between the Paper Virgin and the target of the Essence Magic at the moment it is used is unimportant.

Note that Essence Magic is not a combination magic like the Tarmel Haja (page 116). Instead, it provides bonus dice to the use of certain interpersonal skills and spells, as follows:

❖ A bonus die on interpersonal skills (Acting, Command, Flattery, Poetry, etc) or spells of seduction or manipulation or other interpersonal interaction, used against a target of the same gender (or gender identity) as the rukh essence the al-kimyat perfumes herself (or himself) with.

❖ Two bonus dice on the above rolls, used against a target from whom the al-kimyat has distilled the rukh essences she is perfuming herself (or himself) with.

❖ A bonus die when composing any literary work or artwork using a rukh essence as ink or paint.

All Paper Virgins learn how to distil rukh essences using the Kitaba Nader. They must have at least three separate bodily essences collected from a single subject, usually in quantities of several drops or more. These may be liquids—blood, saliva, sweat, tears, or other more intimate substances—or even hair, eyelashes, scrapings of skin, and so on. Creating the rukh essence is a difficulty 9 INT + Science roll; on a Critical Success (magnitude 6+), the bonus dice obtained are doubled.

---

Virgins". They are charged with categorising distilled rukh essences, including those created by the Tawl Host, and classifying them for possible later use. As well as being Essence Magic adepts, they are also specialists in the Abat Ittijah. They are often tasked with acquiring rukh essences from specific individuals for use in Essence Magic against them.

### The Tawl, the Virginal Host

The **Tawl** comprises those Bint Mimun who will go on to become Paper Virgins once they have mastered the Kitaba Nader and the Abat Ittijah. They are **Novices** of the order, working in the pleasure quarters of Jazirat's cities. It's a dangerous apprenticeship—Tawl Novices are typically inexperienced in the arts of pleasure and the underworld in which they operate, and rely heavily on the protection of the Guardians of the order.

The Sisters keep an eye on the Novices in their charge, sending them regularly to confession with the temple kahini, where they're monitored for weakness, corruption, or breakdowns from stress. The confessionals themselves are often ordeals for the Novices, however, as all of them fear expulsion from the order.

### The Guardians of the Order

The Guardians of the Paper Virgins are warriors of the Bint Mimun faithful to the spirit of its founder. Mostly men, they guard the Tawl Host and the Sisters of the order. They are excellent fighters, experienced in urban combat and experts at preventing "incidents" with unruly clients. They are devoted to the word of Tarek and his descendant Mimun, willing to die for the Novices and Paper Virgins in their charge. Each Novice is assigned a Guardian when she joins the order; when the Novice becomes a Sister, Guardian and Paper Virgin have the right to marry. Until that time, the bond between the two is chaste, although profound.

### The Waladi

The Waladi are servants of the Paper Virgins, usually of the same sex, assisting them in everyday tasks. The relationship between Waladi and Paper Virgin is subtle, one of mutual respect and dependency. Each Waladi is a member of the Bint Mimun, and works towards the sacred objective of the whole clan.

## Personalities of the Bint Mimun

### Aila Bint Mimun Abd-al-Tarek

Aila is the current Umm Kabira of the Bint Mimun. She has recently reached the venerable age of ninety-nine, older even than her august ancestor, Mimun the Fair. She is called the Grey Lady: her hair has always been grey, but the sobriquet also refers to her great wisdom. She is an excellent advisor, and was the power behind the throne for many previous Umm Kabira. During her tenure, she has faced great difficulties associated with the rebirth of the third clan of the Tarekids in the form of the Ibn Yazid (see below), and the turmoil that has caused. She dwells in a hidden palace in a town in southern Jazirat, although rumour says she travels frequently, despite her great age, to avoid problems with agents of the Salifah.

### Ahmel Ikiba Ibn Mimun Abd-al-Tarek, "the Pillar of Mimun"

Master of the Guardians, Ahmel Ikiba is a force of nature. He has occupied his position for almost as long as the current Umm Kabira; he has been her husband for twenty years and, although her junior (he is now close to seventy), they are an exemplary couple. Ahmel commands the Guardians with benevolence, and contin-

## The Test of Rulership—The Kitab Tarikh Ordeal

The **Kitab Tarikh**, or "History Book", is a collection of scrolls written by Mimun as she mastered the Essence Magic of the Kitaba Nader. She experimented on many targets, using their rukh essences to compose strange texts focussing on specific personality aspects. Over the centuries, it's said that the essences contained in the scrolls became mixed, and that fragments of the thousands of personalities they contained somehow combined to form an impossible, hybrid monster. At the heart of this corruption is the very first text—the pact between Tufiq and Mimun.

The Umm Kabira have never understood the nature of the History Book entity, but they have been able to extract information from its constituent personality fragments, despite the hazards involved in untangling its intimate and obscene recollections. Nevertheless, many Sisters have become mentally lost in their readings of the Kitab Tarikh, seduced by its carnal maze, their minds dissolving into the mosaic entity of the Book. As a result, the Mothers forbid any consultation of the scrolls without close and expert surveillance, and even then only for short periods.

It was the same Mothers who designed the Test of Rulership, requiring a candidate for the title of Umm Kabira to read the whole of the Kitab Tarikh and derive precise information from it, without having her mind destroyed by contact with the book's depraved spirit. For centuries, every Umm Kabira has triumphed over the Book. Many more candidates have failed; even now, nightmare fragments of their souls linger within its pages.

ues his sacred duty of protecting the Umm Kabira with great diligence. Although he is based at his wife's side, he often takes to the field, travelling the fleshpots where the Paper Virgins operate, observing events and attempting to nip problems in the bud. He has recently detected friction caused by the preachings of certain **mutlaqi** (see page 258), as well as increased activity from agents of the underworld.

# THE DESERT RATS: THE CLAN OF YAZID, SERVANT OF TAREK

## The Ibn Yazid Abd-al-Tarek

### History

#### From Mustafah to Yazid

The third clan of the Tarekids has its origins with Mustafah, Tufiq's twin brother. Shortly before being killed by Tufiq, Mustafah had a child with Mimun, a son who was entrusted to *tababi* sages loyal to Mimun and—for his safety—raised far from Tarekid lands. He grew up in ignorance of his origins, having been visited by a sad and beautiful woman who told him his parents had been killed by barbarians. As an adult, he fell in love with the daughter of one of the sages who had raised him, and founded a family with her.

In this way, the offspring of Mustafah and Mimun prospered. For generations, the Umm Kabira secretly watched over the bloodline, and those who discovered the truth in the pages of the Kitab Tarikh (page 257) did everything they could to keep it secret.

One day, only five years ago, the last descendant of the bloodline escaped the watchful eyes of the Umm Kabira and vanished into the desert. His name was Yazid.

#### The Revelation of Yazid

Since his earliest days, Yazid had strange dreams leading him into the desert. One day, he decided to follow them. He eluded the attentions of the Paper Virgins and walked alone into the desert—a suicidal step. He walked for many days, not eating or drinking, until he arrived at the sacred oasis of Nabiy, close to death. There he meditated and received four revelations. The first concerned his origins. The second was the truth about his father's death and the identity of his murderer. The third told him the Tarekids' fate if they continued on their current path, which also showed him how they could be saved. And Yazid's fourth revelation? No one knows.

### The (Re)birth of the Third Clan of the Tarekids

When Yazid returned from the desert, he was changed. The first change was physical: his eyes were clouded and he looked blind, although he saw perfectly. The second was psychological: his expression was both haunted and inspired.

Yazid talked with many Tarekids. The Paper Virgins tried to stop him, following instructions from the Umm Kabira. They failed, and many nomads listened to what he had to say. Yazid's words were pleasing to the ear, convincing and impassioned; he hinted that the chiefs of Saabi had gone astray, and that Hubal was displeased.

Yazid's own behaviour was exemplary. This encouraged other Tarekids to listen to his words. Little by little, he found listeners, allies, then finally followers. The Awwal-Malhud who ruled the *a'ila* where Yazid made his speeches grew alarmed at his sudden popularity. He spoke with his fellow Awwal-Malhud and the kahini of the tribe, and decided the troublesome interloper should be banished.

Several Tarekids decided to follow Yazid. The Awwal-Malhud remained firm, and sentenced them to banishment, seizing their lands and goods.

This stern action slowed the departures to a trickle, but did nothing to discourage those who had decided to follow Yazid. These men and women were dubbed **rebels**, or **mutlaqi**. They formed the core of the new Tarekid clan.

In time, nomads from the common folk and some noble Tarekids joined Yazid's new clan. They chose for their totem animal the desert rat, a symbol of intelligence and wisdom in Tarekid culture, and settled in the deep desert. Yazid decreed that all his followers should complete the **Mukhabbat** rite, a journey across the desert towards the oasis of Nabiy, without drinking or eating. Those who succeeded in the Mukhabbat were dispatched by Yazid to the four corners of Jazirat, to plant the seeds of sedition wherever they went.

### Organisation

#### Yazid

Yazid is the central pillar of the "new" clan. He surrounds himself with an honour guard of seven men and seven women, the first to pass the Mukhabbat rite. The guard has allowed Yazid to survive several murder attempts by the Sons of Tufiq, who want to end the rebellion. Rather than being discouraged, Yazid harangues his partisans even further, claiming the attempts on his life prove his word is truly just.

Recently, even some of the Bint Mimun have left their clan to join the Ibn Yazid.

## The Honour Guard

The first *mutlaqi* who followed Yazid during his exile were fanatics from the start. Today they are more than mere warriors, extremists ready to lay down their lives for Yazid. Thanks to the Mukhabbat rite, many have honed their senses and even developed supernatural skills—seeing in the dark, perceiving the immediate future, reacting with superhuman reflexes—that make them exceptional soldiers.

Everyone listens to them; everyone fears them.

## Yazid's Faithful

Increasingly numerous, Yazid's faithful wander Jazirat preaching the word of Hubal, advancing Yazid's vision. They enter cities to seek out the kahini of the medinas and compete with them, but equally penetrate into the nomads' souks where the Ibn Tufiq gather.

Yazid's faithful are not always well-regarded. Many see them as a threat to the stability not only of the tribe, but also of the minor tribes and the entire Saabi people. Once the Tarekids begin openly criticising the Ibn Tufiq kahini, the risk is that everyone will begin to have doubts, perhaps even as far as the Califah-al-Sahla. These worries are well-founded; each year, more and more Jazirati heed the mutlaqis' words. Some listen because they hold a grudge against the traditional kahini—perhaps they were punished by them in the past—, others because they wish to break with a status quo that's no longer satisfying. Many, however, listen to Yazid simply because they think he's right, and that the kahini of the tribes have lost their way.

## Personalities of the Ibn Yazid

### Yazid Ibn Mustafah Abd-al-Tarek, Leader of the Desert Rats

Yazid has the impressive bearing of a holy warrior. Over the course of his pilgrimages, he has acquired a soul-piercing, milky blue stare. He's a peerless fighter and master of bladed weapons; he wears black, with large belts of silver and leather holding several khanjars. He has great physical presence and a deep calmness.

Yazid has recently suffered several assassination attempts. His followers claim he senses the danger before it comes. He spends his time in his mukhayyam with his seven women, all experts in hand-to-hand combat. He often goes alone into the desert, to meditate and listen to the wind, despite the concerns of his honour guard.

---

## The Words of Yazid

*After his trip into the desert, Yazid's worldview changed radically. Hubal had appeared to him, revealing truths which he commanded him to spread throughout Jazirat. Made up of seventy-seven* **teachings,** *also called* **divine commandments,** *the "Words of Yazid" do not yet have a written form, although those close to Yazid have been endeavouring to record them.*

*The most well-known teachings, those that most violently move the disciples of Yazid, are the ones which cause problems for the status quo in Kh'saaba.*

❖ **The First Teaching:** *The true Tufiq, blessed be his name, died beside the three Prophets at the village of Kafer Nahum. The one who lived under his name was an evil djinn whose only purpose was to plunge Kh'saaba into a thousand centuries of darkness.*

❖ **The Twenty-Third Teaching:** *The gods may deceive us, because some are devils. Thou shalt not worship any other god but Hubal the Most Holy, the Most Merciful, who will bring an end to the idolatry offered by the kahini to the demons who pass themselves off as gods.*

❖ **The Forty-Seventh Teaching:** *By death alone are the worst lies ended.*

❖ **The Seventy-Third Teaching:** *Ibn Tufiq, Ibn Aziz, and Ibn Khalil are three names borne by lies, three peoples betrayed by their ancestors, who in the name of false gods led their peoples from the Truth of the One and Only God.*

❖ **The Seventy-Fifth Teaching:** *To the kings of the city of Hubal shalt thou swear allegiance, and offer thy life that their eyes see only the true god.*

*Sliding abruptly into a heretical monotheism, the Ibn Yazid may be destined for a fate similar to that of the Shiradim of yore. However, rather than simply aspiring to the right to exist, the Ibn Yazid hope to impose their Seventy-Seven Teachings on everyone else. That means the annihilation of the Ibn Tufiq, and the purging of those who have strayed from the worship of Hubal, the Ibn Aziz and the Ibn Khalil. The representatives of these clans are the ones most affected by the violent deeds of the Ibn Yazid, and yet, strangely, the new clan of Yazid acquired its noble status directly from the King and Grand Kahini in Jergath. Although he doesn't want his kingdom rocked by open warfare, the King still wishes to grant the descendants of Mustafah the place once offered them by Hubal.*

*In reality, the Ibn Yazid use cunning and politics more than violence to impose their strict religious practises. However, it's becoming increasingly common to see them carrying out the public punishment of a camel driver who made sacrifice to the god Apsu, or of a woman who sacrificed to Shadrafa to heal her sick son. Every week brings tales of terrible confrontations between Ibn Tufiq and Ibn Yazid caravans that leave death and desolation in their wake.*

*Many political leaders are worried about the emergence of this violent clan. Many more blame the king for letting it happen.*

The first wife of the leader of the Desert Rats is a magnificent, slender young woman, with clear eyes which shine even brighter since the Mukhabbat rite. She is called "Wind-Daughter" because of her fleetness of foot—she is noiseless when moving—and her speed with weapons. She can nock and loose an arrow in less than a second, and is a marvel when handling knives. She laughs joyously unless you criticise Yazid in her presence, when she might just slit your throat with her khanjar in less time than it takes you to speak. Yazid finds himself constantly stepping in to stop her doing something irreparable.

# THE SHIRADIM

## Shiradi History

The history of the Shiradim is long and turbulent. Its beginnings are almost lost in the mists of time, with a tale of three mythical figures who led a Jazirati tribe out of the desert to a promised land glimpsed in a dream. The existence of three Shiradim tribes bearing the names of these figures as their founders lends credence to this myth.

The people who named themselves Shiradim in honour of their god, Shirad, had lived for centuries in the east of Jazirat. They left this territory for reasons unclear—tales mention natural disasters and invincible enemies—to return to Jazirat in the midst of the Agalanthian conquest.

Since their return to Jazirat, the history of the Shiradim has been a litany of suffering and thwarted hope. Enslaved by the Saabi, freed by Mogda, enslaved again by the Agalanthians, and finally betrayed by Jason's ambition, the people of Shirad have endured every ordeal with an iron will and an uncommon sense of solidarity.

Recent history seems to have been merciful to the Shiradim. The reconquest of Carrassine by Sarah Bat Caleb has restored their confidence, and the war against the Quarterians has enabled them to rebuild their economic power. At least part of the future history of Capharnaum will be written in the Shiradim tongue.

## Shiradi Daily Life

### Shiradi Appearance

The Shiradim are physically similar to the Saabi and the people of the Caravan Kingdoms; all are representatives of the Jazirati ethnic group. Most have dark complexions, with black hair and eyes, but

### The Mothers' Inquiry

*The Umm Kabira of the Bint Mimun is taking Yazid's mutlaqi very seriously. After consultation with the wazirs, she has decided to infiltrate the Faithful. So far, she hasn't pierced the mystery surrounding Yazid, but perhaps one day the sagacious Mothers will learn the truth. Yazid and his Honour Guard are adept at foiling traps and rooting out lies, so the Mothers are treading carefully.*

as many as one in four have lighter hair and skin. Men are often bearded; few grow their hair below their shoulders unless they belong to certain Ashkenim factions. Women wear their hair long, loose or knotted in a heavy braid.

Shiradi attire is similar to Saabi: in the city people wear jellaba, sarwal, thawb and qamis, and babouches on their feet (page 233). Women wear long gowns, sometimes with sleeves, and often cover their hair with a shawl which can also cover their faces if needs be. Desert Shiradim cover their heads and wear long robes called **talet** to protect themselves from the sun. They wear thick-soled sandals (to protect from the burning sands and scorpion stings), and often wear boots when riding.

A reserved people used to not drawing attention to themselves, the Shiradim wear little jewellery. Women may wear bracelets, rings and necklaces of modest materials, but often do so only in their homes. Some wealthier or more extravagant Shiradim adorn themselves with rich jewellery and eye-catching decoration like the Saabi nobility.

Many Shiradi wear indications of their tribal affiliation: the colour of certain fabrics, a hairstyle or way of wearing a dagger in their woollen belts. They may also use discreet yet distinct greetings: the Ashkenim place two fingers on their dagger guard, the Pharatim do the same to their forehead, and the Salonim to their heart.

## Shiradi Society

Shiradi society has no concept of nobility: in theory, no individual is superior to another by birth, as all are children of Shirad. In practice, of course, wealthy Shiradim or those with political influence rise to become this people's rulers.

A Shiradi community (whether city or desert) is ruled by a council, which includes the *kahan* (or *kahanim* if its population is significant) as well as important local figures (rich merchants, wise old men and women, well-respected physicians). The council's duty is to arbitrate community conflicts too complex for a single *kahan* to deal with alone. It also acts as a court when a crime is committed by a Shiradi against his own people.

## The Shiradi Family

Shiradi families are large, including grandparents, uncles and aunts, their children, and so on. Because of their long and painful history, the Shiradim have a sense of solidarity novel to other peoples; all are brothers and sisters in the eyes of Shirad (even more so for those of the same tribe). The basic traditional family unit comprises two parents and their children, up until the age of majority for boys or marriage for girls.

The Shiradim are monogamists. In ancient times, Shiradi society was polygamous like the Saabi, but since Mogda's exile and the reforms to Shirad's worship, it was decreed that, just as a man should worship only one god, he should likewise only have one wife. Marriage is a serious matter; it is the alliance of two peoples as well as two individuals. Arranged marriages are the norm among high-lineage Shiradim (especially those from the Three Tribes), and they may be formalised even before the birth of the children who will eventually marry. A wedding, celebrated by a *kahan* at a shrine, is a holy and (usually) indissoluble rite. United in the eyes of Shirad, spouses may not separate unless one is barren, or if adultery can be proved.

Among the desert tribes, monogamy is also the rule but, because of harsh living conditions and a lack of men (a great many men perish in raids, or while defending their people against raiders), it's not uncommon for one man to take to his tent one or more concubines in additional to his legitimate wife, ensuring numerous offspring.

The birth of a child is an occasion for rejoicing. One month after birth (or often three months among the desert tribes), when it is certain the child will live, a party is given gathering together the whole family and ending in the Ritual of the Covenant between the child and Shirad, which takes place in the Temple, culminating in a series of ritual scarifications the kahan makes around the child's navel. Adoption follows the same rite, regardless of the age of the adopted child: the Shiradim make little difference between bonds of blood and adoption, since their history is filled with the conversions of foreigners to their faith (Mogda being the most famous example).

A boy attains majority at thirteen, the age when he can marry, have children, and practice a trade (where before he could only claim the title of apprentice to a master). The event is celebrated in a ceremony called "the Presentation to the World". A girl attains majority a year earlier, but is only considered an adult when married.

When a Shiradi dies, the family mourns and conducts a vigil over the body for three days, while praying for Shirad to conduct his soul to the Land of the Just. On the fourth day, the family and friends of the deceased hold a great feast celebrating his life, in which they tell stories about his deeds and adventures. Finally, on the fifth day, the kahan conducts a funeral at the shrine, and the body is buried in a black shroud in a modest cemetery. The burial place is marked only by an engraved stone. Exiled and outcast often during their history, the burial places of the Shiradim dead keep alive the memory of their journeys. Even though funeral sites may be forgotten or abandoned, saying "my ancestor is buried in the valley overlooking Fragrance" is a way of remembering that the Shiradim have been in the city for centuries.

## Current Activities of the Shiradim

The Shiradim are industrious and stubborn, found at every level of society, in cities and in the desert, practicing the most varied trades. Some activities are favoured for historical or traditional reasons. They are most of all a trading people. During Mogda's exodus, many Shiradim settled in the desert, taking control of the oases, establishing caravans regulating the circulation of people and commodities between southern Jazirat and Capharnaum. Throughout their history, both northern and southern Shiradim have at one time or another been slaves, or have at least been relegated to the status of second-class citizens. The only activity in which they were permitted to engage to any great degree was commerce, and as a result they developed a business sense envied by even the wiliest Saabi traders—especially since that skill is accompanied by a scrupulous concern for honesty and commercial equity.

Salone, one of the three mythical Shiradim who guided the people to their promised land and who has given her name to one of the three great Shiradi tribes, is considered the greatest healer in history. Her tribe preserves the tradition, and the Salonim provide the best physicians in Jazirat, their skill and knowledge rivalling those of the Saabi and Agalanthians. Like the Shiradi traders, their physicians enjoy a reputation for professionalism, assuring them of a large clientele.

Pharat the Sage, second of the three founding Shiradim, gives this people its passion for learning and debating ideas. Shiradi

## Tribes or Clans?

*Some refer to the Pharatim, Ashkenim, and Salonim as tribes, while others prefer the term clan. They are enormous groupings, each as vast and influential as any nation in an empire. The confusion stems from the time of the Shiradi return to Jazirat and their enslavement by the Saabi, when the Shiradim were ten times fewer in number than their new masters. At that time, what the Shiradi called tribes were roughly equivalent to Saabi clans. The confusion has remained, woven throughout the ages into many debates, but the term remains erratic. In fact, the Shiradi do indeed have clans, but they rarely exceed the size of a large extended family, and there are hundreds within each tribe. They are only influential because of the legacy of their ancestors; some have political weight, a terrifying military reputation, or enough wealth to make the princes of Kh'saaba quake. Others are as destitute as if they were still slaves.*

scholars are renowned for their breadth of knowledge, ranging from history and strategy, through to the sciences, philosophy, and politics. After the Shiradi return to prominence in Capharnaum, many Pharatim occupy university chairs, are employed as eminent professors, or work as preceptors in Shiradi, but also Saabi and Agalanthian, families.

In addition to their commercial activities, the desert tribes of the Shiradim comprise many fighters claiming descent from the last of the Shiradi founders: Ashken the Mystic Warrior. Their martial skills are essential to desert survival, protecting their herds and defending their camps and oases against raids.

Shiradim leisure activities differ little from those of the places they live: playing games, attending spectacles, and walking in the souks are popular pastimes for city dwellers, and hunting and horse- and camel-racing are favoured among the desert folk.

The Shiradim gather in the evenings with family or friends to share a meal and exchange news. It's a precious time, reminding them that their people is a large family which survives in these troubled times only by virtue of its flawless solidarity.

## Shiradi Culture

Although Shiradi knowledge is traditionally transmitted orally, especially in rural communities, the reconquest of Carrassine and the cultural and religious renewal it sparked led to the development of a Shiradi written language. This was quickly adopted by the *kahanim*, and then by the city and merchant communities. As the Shiradi tongue was similar to that of the Saabi, the Shiradim adopted the Saabi script, whose alphabet had the peculiarity of associating each letter (and even word) to a numerical value, permit-

ting Shiradi scholars to perform numerological analyses of Shirad's holy texts in search of esoteric meaning.

Nonetheless, Shiradi oral traditions persisted: the Shiradim love their evening gatherings, where people give personal touches to their accounts of stories or legends. The storytelling art even becomes ritual during mourning, when people closest to the deceased gather on the fourth day to transform his life into a story.

The Shiradim have long been fearful of the worship of graven images, where worship of Shirad might become corrupted by worshipping statues or images of the god instead. As a result, they have little by little banned all pictorial representation of human and animal figures in their art, instead favouring abstract and mathematical designs. Perhaps to compensate, music has assumed a preponderant role in daily life, and when people sing of the glories of Shirad or the woe in their hearts, they usually do so to the accompaniment of nomad drums and trumpets, or the lyres and harps of the cities. Dances—often complex—are performed, often in groups, during celebrations.

Many Shiradi scholars find themselves attracted by more abstruse pursuits, such as astronomy, mathematics, poetry, philosophy, and literature. Their texts find echoes in those of the scholars of Capharnaum, or even of overseas.

Anyone who wishes it and who approaches without anger or hatred is welcome under a Shiradi tent or at a Shiradi table. There he may partake of cereals, fruits, and fish when the fishing is good. Feasts are an occasion to slaughter a ram and to enjoy honey, mead

## Shiradi Names

*Shiradi names comprise a personal name followed by the father's name, with the particle "Bar" (son of) or "Bat" (daughter of) between the two.*

For example: Shimon Bar Ibrahim

*In theory, a Shiradi can trace his descent back to the pilgrims who accompanied Ashken, Pharat, and Salone in their quest for a homeland.*

*When a Shiradi uses his or her mother's name instead of the father's, it means the father is not known and the child is illegitimate.*

For example: Miriam Bat Shirel.

*Male Shiradi names include: Aaron, Avraham/Ibrahim, Ari, Ariel, Baru'kh, Binyamin, Boaz, Daniel, David, Eli, Ezekiel, Ezra, Ebenazar, Gad, Hillel, Ioranan, Isaac, Isaiah, Levi, Matitiau, Mena'khem, Morde'khai, Mogda, Nathan, Noam, Reuven, Shaul, Shimon, Shiran, Shlomo, Uriel, Yaacov, Yeremiah, Yergad, Yonathan, Yosef.*

*Female Shiradi names include: Ariel, Dara, Devrah, Esther, Hannah, Leah, Maya, Miriam, Naomi, Ophrah, Rachel, Ruth, Sarah, Shayna, Shirel, Susanna, Tamar, Yudith, Zelda.*

and wine. Some food taboos (mostly not eating pork, horse, or shellfish) regulate the composition of meals and avoid food poisoning: enshrined in religious dogma, even guests must follow these proscriptions under the roof of a Shiradi host. Likewise a guest must be modest when meeting women, as women are treasured in Shiradi families. It's unseemly for a Shiradi man to even touch a woman other than his mother, wife, or daughter. Young people soon learn the art of discretion.

## Shiradi Religious Practices

Since their exile, the Shiradim have worshipped one god, named Shirad. Shirad is omniscient and omnipotent: he created the world, and rules over the Land of the Just, the paradise of the virtuous. Shirad's existence was revealed to mortals by Pharat, who claimed it was He that had guided his people to their sanctuary.

Until Mogda's conversion, the Shiradim considered other peoples' deities to be nothing but false gods. Mogda, however, as saviour of their people, received the revelation that all these gods were nothing other than "Faces of Shirad", aspects of his divinity by which he exercises his ubiquity and answers the prayers of the faithful. Those who claim to believe in many gods are merely blind to the reality of the One God of which they are all but aspects. The Quarterians are a notable exception: they recognise Shirad, whom they call Aether, identifying him with the sun, but dissociating him from the moon, who they call Mira, and Jason, the third idol of their trinity.

As a result, even if it is Shirad alone who is worthy of worship, the faithful still pray to his many Faces for guidance or favours in matters concerning their domains. So, a Shiradi general from Carrassine will pray to Marduk, the Face of Shirad who protects the city, on the eve of battle. This approach sometimes leads the Shiradim to refer to Shirad as the "One But Many God", and permits them better relations with polytheistic peoples, as they simply integrate new gods they encounter as new Faces of Shirad, or even associate them with existing Faces.

In addition to Aether, the following Faces of Shirad are the best known. There are many others.

- ❖ **Assiel:** Change, evolution, and time (androgenous Face).
- ❖ **Caiya:** Endings, death, and renewal (masculine Face).
- ❖ **Innpa:** Birth, ghosts, and miracles (feminine Face).
- ❖ **Mira:** Peace and love (feminine Face). Identified with Nerea, the Agalanthian moon goddess.

Shirad imposes on his people a set of commandments the Shiradim must respect if they wish to be reborn in the Land of the Just after death. For them, the night sky reflects this paradise, and its constellations represent the Shiradi ancestors who watch over their descendants with the benevolent approval of the One God.

For centuries, these commandments were transmitted orally, and were often deformed or forgotten. It was Mogda who finally codified them, to give the Shiradim the unity they would need before crossing the desert. He called these commandments "the Laws of Shirad", and they became the pillars of Shiradi society. Of course, since Shiradi scholars never pass up an opportunity for debate, the scope of these laws has since been a matter of intense discussion. Some think they should apply in all circumstances; others believe they only concern the Shiradim, and thus for example cheating an unbeliever does not constitute a transgression of the Law of Property.

Shiradi priests are called **kahanim**. A **kahan** or **kahana** usually discovers their vocation early in life (often from a parent) and, after their Presentation to the World ceremony, embarks upon a programme of study to prove themselves worthy of becoming a spiritual guide for their people. In addition to the Laws of Shirad, studies also include scholarly works interpreting their sense and scope, applying them to the realities of the world and times, and so on.

Ultimately, the kahan's role is less that of a priest and more that of a spiritual leader and counsellor. Although he is supposed to lead prayer and celebrate the many rites of life (the Covenant, the Presentation to the World, wedding, funeral), he tends to spend

## The Laws of Shirad

- ❖ *The Law of the Soul: A Shiradi's faith must be sincere, his love for his god and people unconditional. Scepticism, atheism, or the worship of other gods are considered sins, although secularism is tolerated as long as it doesn't prevent more faithful Shiradim from living according to the commandments of Shirad.*
- ❖ *The Law of the Body: For the Shiradim, causing harm to another is a great sin, and killing even worse. Murder is punished harshly in Shiradim society, although self-defence is tolerated—including, of course, war.*
- ❖ *The Law of the Heart: Lying and cheating are sins condemned by the Law of the Heart. A Shiradi must be sincere and honest, for if one is not honest with others, how can one claim to be so with god? People must respect each other: children their parents, spouses one another, merchants their customers.*
- ❖ *The Law of the Couple: A man may have but one woman, a woman may only know one man. Adultery can lead to separation and opprobrium. Nevertheless, the Law of the Couple permits remarriage in the case of untimely widowhood, or separation in the case of barrenness.*
- ❖ *The Law of Property: Neither theft, fraud, nor dishonesty must stain the people of Shirad. What a person possesses is their own, and taking it from them by whatever means is condemned. Even envying someone else's possessions may be the first step towards breaking this commandment.*

more time counselling the faithful who come to him for comfort and answers. He guides his people by exhorting them to follow the Laws of the One God.

Shiradi worship takes place in a "Temple". The Temple has no fixed shape, but generally has a large common room for ceremonies, a more modest room for prayer groups, and chambers for the kahan. In the desert, the Temple is often simply an assembly of tents.

The Shiradi have no regular worship services. Each goes to Temple when he feels the need, to pray or meditate. When several people gather, they may ask the kahan to preside over their assembly, which becomes as much debating forum as prayer group—the Shiradim love verbal sparring, especially about religion! Finally, anyone may meet with the kahan to request advice, arbitration, and so on.

# THE THREE TRIBES OF THE SHIRADIM

## The Ashkenim

Ashken was an artist and storyteller, a dancer and musician, forced to learn to fight to protect his people during their first exile. He used his expert knowledge of body and rhythm in his fighting techniques; ever since, his warriors have been the most feared of the Shiradim, often considering dance and combat to be two sides of the same coin. But the Ashkenim are so much more than that, and war is not their only specialty.

### History

In ancient times, before the people of Shirad left Jazirat, Ashken was an extraordinary individual, a hedonist beyond compare. An artist, poet, and above all a dancer, the courts of all kingdoms competed for his attentions and men and women threw themselves at him without restraint. Which people he belonged to had as little importance for him as for anyone.

When Pharat, a patriarch of his tribe, prophesied the departure of the Shiradim from Jazirat, Ashken scoffed, pouring scorn on the hopes of his people and the promises of Shirad.

Ashken had achieved great popularity among the worshippers of Hubal, but it did not last. He was eventually stripped of his rights and property when it was discovered that the daughter of one of his patrons, already promised to another man, had been seduced by the words and grace of the Shiradi.

In just a few weeks, the flamboyant Ashken became a penniless outcast, rejected by his former patrons, despised by his own. He wandered aimlessly before joining a nomad camp at the desert's edge, just as Pharat arrived to oversee the preparations for his people's departure.

It was also the moment that a crack squad of soldiers arrived, dispatched by a Jazirati prince to strike down the Shiradi agitator. The soldiers began by plundering the camp.

For the first time in his life, Ashken prayed to Shirad, and made ready to die. However, when the warriors attacked, he began one of his dances, executing every move to perfection. Every gesture became a fatal blow, a grapple, an immobilisation. Deep in his soul Ashken heard chanting urging him deep into the battle where Pharat and his *macchabim* warriors were conducting their desperate defence. Without knowing it, Ashken battled to the rhythm of Pharat's prayers.

Astonishingly, the attackers were driven off. That day, Ashken became a blessed warrior of Shirad, and Pharat took him as a guard and travelling companion. When the Shiradim finally departed into exile, Ashken continued to distinguish himself, becoming the leader of the *macchabim*. He supervised their training, imparting his techniques of movement and dance. His life in the royal courts of Jazirat had turned him into an excellent strategist, and his new faith guided his decisions, bringing him strength and wisdom. By the time of his death, Ashken could be proud that he had ensured his people's survival, teaching his martial arts to their generals, enlightening the people with his choreography, teaching his most sensuous secrets to his numerous wives and concubines. Meanwhile, back in Jazirat, the Shiradim were soon enslaved, and the combat arts of the Ashkenim outlawed. Descendants of famous warriors were particularly persecuted. Yet, in secret, the guardians of Ashken's secrets remained true; some taught dances which were in fact deadly combat techniques; but the keepers of his more sensuous lore found themselves condemned to sex slavery.

When the Shiradi slaves finally revolted, the Ashkenim were Mogda's sword-arm, instrumental in securing the Shiradi escape, at terrible cost. When the Shiradim settled in Capharnaum, the Ashkenim gradually split into urban and rural traditions. The former perpetuated the Ashkenim's artistic and erotic legacy; the latter—often practiced by nomads and those more exposed to danger—their martial teachings. When, during the Agalanthian domination, the shepherd's daughter Sarah Bat Caleb marched on Carrassine, hundreds of Ashkenim marched with her, bringing their greatest *macchabim*.

### Organisation

It's not always easy to see the connection between an old warrior hardened by life, a delicate dancer, and a prostitute sliding into the bed of a prince; but all—at some moment of their lives—have heard the sacred music of Shirad. A prayer chant or a melody carried on the wind, it has settled in the mind of every member of the Ashkenim. And with that music comes grace, precision of move-

discovering and perfecting destructive combat manoeuvres. No ruler, whatever his blood, can force a Red Lion to serve him; they have their own allegiances and enmities, guided by the teachings of Shirad. For any lord of Capharnaum, the arrival of a Red Lion emissary in his court is always a tense moment.

Finally, the sacred prostitutes of the Ashkenim—whatever their gender—keep themselves aloof from the rest of the tribe. No one contests their knowledge of Ashken's legacy, and tribesmembers treat them with respect. However, Shiradi culture has evolved over the centuries, and today sex is the object of far more taboos than during the time of the founders. Those who choose this path often leave their home communities, settling in cities in superb pleasure houses, where a refined clientele pays fortunes for a single night in their beds.

## Personalities of the Ashkenim

### Zvulon Bar Yorai

Like an old wild animal whose fangs have become blunt and his claws soft and broken, Zvulon Bar Yorai watches the children of his tribe play. His tent is open to everyone, and he hosts most of the warriors' meetings. Not all are Ashkenim, but they are children of Shirad, and the old chieftain treats them as if they were his own. Zvulon has been an old man for twenty-five years. His own children have all died, either in battle or by disease; but everyone sees a grandfather figure in the old chief, and maybe his grey eyes enjoy seeing that recognition in the eyes of others. Everyone knows Zvulon's mellifluous tones when he sings for his people, but no one now is old enough to remember his twirling sword dances, a blade in each hand. For years, Zvulon has ensured his tribe lives in peace, in the shade of an oasis, far from the clash of steel and bronze and the metallic taste of blood.

At night, though, when the moon is low, the old beast leaves his tent and heads into the desert. There he offers his god and his desert beasts a martial spectacle of terrifying beauty.

Zvulon knows that danger threatens his loved ones. Shirad has told him. When it comes, he will be ready.

### Mordecai Bar Ilan

In the heart of Carrassine stands an ancient building, perhaps as old as the city itself. No one cares about its old walls, covered with creepers, or the beggar who spends his days and nights on its front porch. However, whoever ventures beyond its dirty verdigris door will be surprised to find a sumptuous interior housing a thousand treasures. A heady music fills the air and, in one of the rooms, men dance in a trance, tirelessly rehearsing the same steps and poses. Overlooking them, on a mezzanine, a priest talks to a huge man with a rough-hewn face, eyes lined with kohl. A thick braid of pearls, gold, and rubies binds the oiled beard cascading down the torso of the scarlet-clad colossus, who chants a prayer in a deep and

ment, elegance—the signs by which the elders notice those worthy of training. All groups affiliated with the Ashkenin begin their programmes of training by teaching ritual dances. Little by little, these dances become more complex, as the Ashkenim master reveals their uses, whether martial, artistic, or (in some cases) sexual.

Ashkenim teachings are imparted in secret schools and circles. This secrecy is justified, at least in part, by the tribe's painful history, but most of all by the fact that Ashken's legacy is to be apprehended as a mystery that each adept must decipher during his own initiatory journey.

Although Ashkenim teachings differ slightly from place to place, there exists a common hierarchy, based on knowledge, the number of "dances" known (the term used is the same, whether it refers to combat, dance, or court), and excellence and mastery. Position in the hierarchy is indicated by the amount and material of jewellery worn, and also by the length of the hair—even (exceptionally for the Shiradim) among male members: Ashkeni masters wear long braids heavy with ornaments. An Ashkenim belongs for life to the school that taught him and—even if he lives outside of the school—he will always answer its call in need, and defend his masters' honour. Rivalries between schools or circles are common, settled in secret tournaments or duels to first blood for the *macchabim*. Sometimes disputes are even resolved through ritual dances.

Among all the Ashkenim groups, there's one whose name and reputation make even the greatest fighters in Capharnaum tremble: the Red Lions of Shirad. These elite warriors, guided by Pharatim scholars, manifest in music and in dance the sacred texts of Shirad, powerful voice which his dancing men answer. When the night deepens, he sends three of his men into the coming battle. They will be more than enough.

### Meriem

*"...First she is a scent, a spellbinding perfume, then an emerald-green eye lined with black over veils. There are hands where henna snakes entwine, and hair that waves to the rhythm of her steps. Those endless copper legs, chains of gold and lapis, a voice clearer than crystal.*

*"Then she is a mystery in the alcove of night, the song of a god and the body of a goddess, a woman who offers a glimpse of heaven in the way she dances, a glimpse that pales in comparison with the ecstasy of her bed. Then a refusal, an unbearable lack. How one misses the caress of her lips!*

*"Finally she is despair, burning, a constant pain, a dark daughter of Shirad. Why didst thou not prefer my wounded heart to their gifts of gold, o my Meriem?"*

—Dark Daughter of Shirad, *the final work of the poet Jibran Al-Wassari, before taking his life.*

# The Pharatim

The Pharatim are the sages of the Shiradim. Whether priests, teachers, sages, or simple scribes, they guard the memory of all the children of Shirad: their history and ordeals, their greatness, past and future.

## History

Pharat was an elder of one of the many desert tribes at the dawn of time, and the first human god ever spoke to. Shirad revealed himself to Pharat, promising to guide his people to a fertile and hospitable land if they took his commandments as their laws.

Having become a prophet, Pharat gathered his tribe, and spoke to them with the holy voice of god. He spoke of the rich land awaiting them, giving them courage to depart Jazirat and seek out the fertile Eden where their descendants would lead happy lives, blessed by the love of Shirad. In just a few months, the small tribe grew, adapting its customs to the laws that Pharat decreed according to the words of Shirad. Finally, it was time for the Shiradim to leave.

During their long and painful exodus, Pharat knew that preaching Shirad's word and reassuring the faithful of their glorious destiny would not be enough. It would neither unite them, nor give them the courage they would need to continue their journey in spite of hardships and ordeals. He decided to abandon his position as guide and become close to his people. He became their advisor, confidant, judge; even friend. Shirad's teachings were not a matter for dry sermons, but were to be lived, demonstrated by example. Thus Pharat became the first *kahan* of the Shiradim. He trained many disciples, and many followed in his footsteps and be-

came priests in their turn. Others embraced the way of knowledge, becoming the oral memory of a people without a written tradition.

According to Shiradi teaching, Pharat never died. In his later years, he strode into the desert, where the One But Many God sought him out in person and guided him to the Land of the Just.

Ultimately, the long and arduous history of the Shiradim has had little influence on the Pharatim. When the people of Shirad returned to Jazirat after twenty centuries of exile, the *kahanim* promised they would find for them another promised land where they would prosper. For a time, the Shiradim believed southern Jazirat might be that land, but were soon disillusioned when the Saabi enslaved them. During that time of humiliation and suffering, the Pharatim tried to rekindle the embers of bravery in their people's hearts, assuring them that their indignity would soon end. When Mogda freed the Shiradim, he used the Pharatim to unite the people and ensure they followed the will of Shirad.

Thereafter, the Shiradim thought northern Jazirat might be their promised land. Once again they were disappointed, as the Agalanthians threw them into slavery. The most serious crisis of the Pharatim, however, occurred when Jason claimed to be the saviour of the Shiradim. He created a new religion, and a large proportion of the *kahanim* converted to the new Quarterian faith. The Pharatim lost many members.

Today, all these torments seem to be behind the Shiradim. They are finally free, and exercise great influence in Capharnaum. Carrassine has been retaken and has been, in many ways, a city under Shiradim domination ever since. An alphabet in harmony with the will of God has been created and, more than ever, the Pharatim think Capharnaum is their promised land, over which the faithful of the One But Many God will soon reign...

## Organisation

To be accepted among the Pharatim, there is no need to have written a scholarly work or to occupy an important university chair; a simple love of knowledge and a desire to see it progress is sufficient to open the tribe's doors. A modest public scribe teaching the rudiments of writing in his community will be accepted as a disciple of Pharat, while a distinguished university professor who inherited his position thanks to his contacts will not. Note that all priests of Shirad are, *de facto*, Pharatim, since they are the heirs of the first *kahan*.

For many centuries, most Pharatim were priests of Shirad. For decades, the predominance of the priesthood has been held in check within the tribe by those members who choose the career of sage or scholar instead. This means that the Pharatim today mostly comprise intellectuals and thinkers. So soon after the Shiradim's return to favour in Capharnaum, it's as tutors (often to non-Shiradi families) or university professors that the Pharatim exercise a much greater political influence than if they had remained confined to the priesthood, a calling which essentially turns its back on the outside world. Their status as teachers allows them to lessen, if not perhaps actually erase, the prejudice against the Shiradim which many other Jazirati hold. Whether sworn instructors, university directors, or simple teachers, the Pharatim now have power over "History", which they can write and present from their favoured point of view.

Pharatim intellectuals also benefit from the increased prestige of the Shiradim. Their philosophers' writings, astrologers' star maps, and mathematicians' theorems are all evidence of this people's intellectual prowess. Many Shiradi works are even considered authoritative in the distant West.

However, although they're less numerous today than they once were, the *kahanim* of the Pharatim are still a force to be reckoned with. Pharat made himself a priest after having been a prophet, a tradition still strong among the Pharatim: even lay sages are fervent believers. Most centres for religious training are run by Pharati priests.

If Pharati teachers and sages are permitting the tribe to increase its political power, its kahanim are guiding it in the way of the One But Many God. They are the keepers of the Sacred Words, ensuring the people respect the Laws of Shirad, providing advice and arbitration of disputes, and occupying important positions on the councils which run local Shiradi communities. Most importantly, the kahanim are the living memory of the Shiradim.

During their early centuries of their existence, the Shiradim had no written language, and their lore was transmitted orally from one generation to the next. Upon their return to Jazirat, they adopted the Saabi alphabet out of necessity, but always considered it something external to their culture, never properly integrated. During the reign of Mogda, scholars laid the groundwork for a true Shiradi writing system to provide cultural independence; but the torments that continually beset them never allowed the work to be completed. The cultural and religious renaissance of the Shiradim today has brought this project back into the light of day, and recently the work of the ancestors has been completed.

Although the Shiradim now have their own writing system, their millennia-long oral traditions remain strong, and many conservatives continue to trust their (supposedly infallible) memories above potentially falsifiable documents. The basic training of the kahanim includes in-depth studies of Shiradi history since the time of Pharat, which every student is expected to be able to recite by heart before being consecrated a priest.

The Shiradi alphabet is designed to represent the words of Shirad as closely as possible. Built on a mathematical foundation, it associates each letter (and thus each word and phrase) to a numerical value. Pharati scholars try to penetrate the secret meanings of the numbers revealed in the Laws of Shirad as they were dictated to Pharat and formalised by Mogda, while Pharati theologians study the esoteric significance of words which might equate to the recurring numeric values which appear in many mathematical theorems. Together, the Pharati numerologists believe that, when the Shiradi alphabet has allowed them to penetrate the secrets of the universe, Shirad's reign will arrive on Earth, preceded by the arrival in the world of his final prophet.

## Personalities of the Pharatim

### Aaron Bar Yonathan

A precocious child with a powerful intellect, Aaron did not embrace the priestly vocation as his father, a kahan, had hoped. Passionate about writing from an early age, he embarked upon linguistic studies, whilst also learning mathematics, which he considered a language in its own right. His work and theories found favour in the linguistics community, and he was quickly accepted among the Pharatim.

Now just beginning his thirties, Aaron has become Chief Numerologist of the Shiradi alphabet. He is one of the most popular sages among the Shiradim, and great hopes rest on him. He commands dozens of linguists, interpreters, kahanim, and mathematicians, whose work he coordinates to reveal the ineffable truths the One But Many God has hidden in His words, to which Shiradi writing holds the key.

### The Preacher

On a high plateau on the desert's edge lives a strange man whom travellers and pilgrims call "the Preacher". Dressed in rags and living in a cave, he's an old man with knotted limbs and long white hair, but in his eyes the light of childhood dances—and a fascinating and unsettling wisdom seen nowhere else. Many Shiradim come to listen to his sermons. Often bordering on heresy, they contain such bold and innovative truths that the Pharatim have more than once invited the Preacher to join their ranks. Every time the old man has just laughed and declined.

Considered a madman by some, a prophet by others, the Preacher seems to have lived in his cave forever. Some even say he is immortal; but the cynical say he is a fraud, and that one mad old man after another replaces the Preacher, perpetuating this joke on the Shiradim.

### Josua Bar Ezra

A young teacher in one of the many villages around Carrassine, Josua is—according to those who meet him—the nicest man they've ever met. He seems dedicated to the children in his care, teaching them history, writing, and legends, and many of his pupils have gone on to study in one of the universities of Capharnaum, a life far different from that of their ancestors. He's much respected for his selflessness, and it was at the villagers' request that the Pharatim asked Josua to join their number.

However, the whole story is a terrifying sham. Josua Bar Ezra is a deranged madman who cavorts with demons. His students who are supposed to go on to university never do any such thing; instead, he sacrifices those in his care to his dark masters in return for untold power. Or does he? Is his diabolic service merely the ravings of a depraved lunatic, or is Josua really one of Capharnaum's greatest demon worshippers?

One thing is sure: no one suspects this pleasant young man. Even when parents come to him, worried about having no word from their offspring at university, Josua reassures them with platitudes about the way young people forget themselves in the big cities and how their studies demand all their time. Doubtless they'll write soon.

After all, who would doubt the word of such a dedicated teacher?

# The Salonim

A tribe of competent and respected physicians, apothecaries, and veterinarians, the Salonim are considered the greatest healers in the known world. They are sworn to protect the Shiradim from harm—whatever the cost.

## History

In ancient times, when the small tribe of the Shiradim left the desert to seek out their promised land to the east of Jazirat, it was guided by three prophets. Of these, Salone was the only woman.

It is said that Salone had learned her midwifery skills from her mother. In any case, she had a great gift; legends says no woman ever died in childbirth in her care, and the children she helped into the world all became great clan leaders. Her intelligence and curiosity led her to take an interest in the craft of healing, and she became indispensable to her people on their painful and deadly exodus. Her gifts saved hundreds of lives, allowing mothers and new-borns to survive in harsh conditions, and curbing unknown epidemics. Salone trained her disciples, but no one was ever as bright, or knew all the areas of medicine, as she. Thus she split her teaching. Each student would study the basic arts of healing, but would then choose a path of medicine which depended on their own affinities and skills. Salone made each swear an oath that remains famous today. The Oath of Salone says that "All disciples of Salone bind themselves to the sacred tasks of tending and healing the people of Shirad, and preserving them from all harm". Salone also encouraged her followers to work as teams, so that each disease, wound or ailment might be examined from several points of view.

The old tales say that Salone died at the great age of two hundred and forty, leaving the Shiradim in the safe hands of her many disciples.

The Salonim have suffered many ordeals during the tumultuous history of the Shiradim. When the Saabi enslaved the Shiradim, the break-up of the tribes forced them to work in secret, visiting the sick after their toil during the day was done, and making do with rudimentary drugs and instruments.

When Mogda re-formed the tribes during the exodus to northern Jazirat, the Salonim once more came to the fore to support their people. At the same time, Mogda made use of the Salonim's knowledge of physiology in secret missions of poisoning and assassination.

The Agalanthians made the Shiradim suffer under their yoke, but this time the tribes continued to exist, and the Salonim exercised their profession without fear of repression. Indeed, the Agalanthian overlords were keen to prevent the Shiradi ghettoes from becoming disease-ridden cesspools spreading epidemics throughout Jergathine and Carrassine.

Since the departure of the Quarterians and the retaking of Carrassine by the heroine Sarah, the Salonim have prospered, taking advantage of the new economic power of the Shiradim to create hospitals and dispensaries in Capharnaum's larger cities, and becoming professors at the great universities to share their knowledge with all the peoples of Jazirat.

## Organisation

Among the Shiradim, the arts of healing may be learned through apprenticeship with a healer, or by following the appropriate curriculum at a university. Only the most gifted and dedicated are invited to join the Salonim, but any Shiradim wishing to practice healing must take the Oath of Salone. Although most Salonim are physicians, some are apothecaries or even veterinarians. Half of their number are women, in homage to Salone; the Shiradim believe that women, as givers of life, have natural gifts for healing.

The Salonim rarely work alone. Most of the time they work in teams of three or four, pooling their knowledge and skills so their patients may be treated in different ways. A typical group might include a surgeon, herbalist, general practitioner, and astrologer, each consulting his fellows about his diagnoses in order to cross-check observations. This way of working is the origin of the Salonim reputation, for it is by bringing to bear all the disciplines of medicine that effective cures are to be found.

In Capharnaum's great cities, such as Sagrada or Fragrance, the wealthiest Shiradim have funded huge hospitals where the Salonim care for many patients. Certain days are given over to the poor and needy who cannot pay, and who are treated for free. In this way, these hospitals have become key tools of political leverage for Shiradim wishing to increase their people's influence in Capharnaum.

Finally, as specialists in the workings of the body, the Salonim are well-versed in poisons and vital spots. Some even use this knowledge to kill.

## Personalities of the Salonim

### Noam Bar Ezra, Dean of the Shiradi hospital in Fragrance

The son of a physician, Noam doesn't remember ever wanting to follow any other profession. As a child, his play room was his father's surgery, his toys his father's medical instruments. By keeping quiet when his father received patients, Noam listened to everything that was said; even if he understood little, he committed it all to memory.

## The Oath of Salone

"All disciples of Salone bind themselves to the sacred tasks of tending and healing the people of Shirad, and preserving them from all harm".

*The Shiradim love to debate, and the interpretation of this oath has been the subject of controversy since the dawn of time. Most people consider that the Salonim are sworn to protect only the Shiradim, and those who have converted to their faith. However, some think the term "the people of Shirad" includes all men and women, since all were created by the One But Many God. This latter interpretation allows (in a rather hypocritical fashion) those wealthy sponsors who fund the Shiradi hospitals in Capharnaum to invite the needy and destitute to come to be treated for free—a gesture that has massively contributed to the increased influence the Shiradim now enjoy.*

When he began his studies of medicine, first as an apprentice in the surgery of his father and associates, then at the university of Carrassine, Noam quickly became the greatest student of his generation. Accepted by the Salonim even before he finished his studies, he promised he would be worthy of the honour.

After his studies, Noam left on a pilgrimage through the desert, travelling from tribe to tribe offering his services and learning as much as he helped. He also took part in a Saloni delegation to Kh'saaba to help curb a deadly epidemic. The chief physician of the delegation died of the mysterious disease, and Noam became the new head. For his dedication, the King of Kh'saaba rewarded him by allowing him to accompany an expedition to Al-Ragon. Once again, Noam took advantage of his travels to increase his knowledge.

Now over fifty, the old physician wishes to rest, and has accepted the post of dean in the hospital of Fragrance. There he works to make his establishment a place of peace and concord between the different peoples of the city.

### Abdelkader

An orphan who never knew his parents, as a boy Abdelkader wandered like a stray animal, trying only to survive the day, find something to eat, a place to sleep. One day he collapsed, exhausted, in a cart. When he awoke, he found himself in a tent in the desert, with an old man watching over him; a Shiradim whose job it was to visit the desert tribes and heal their herds. It was his cart in which Abdelkader had fallen asleep. The man said he had slept for a week, but was out of danger.

It was the first time anyone had ever helped the boy. Not knowing how to thank him, Abdelkader remained with the old man, working as his servant until his debt was paid. The Shiradi accepted, and in time a special bond grew between the two men. Abdelkader remained for weeks, then months, eventually considering the old man an adopted father. The Shiradi taught him everything he knew about treating livestock, explaining that his art was less glorious but no less essential than that of the physician: the herds of the desert tribes are often their only means of sustenance, and must be well cared for.

One day, Abdelkader decided to convert to the faith of his master. In a desert oasis, he celebrated his Covenant with the One But Many God at the same time as his Presentation to the World. He took a wife, the daughter of a clan chief whose herd he had saved from disease, and for which feat he was considered a fully fledged Salonim.

Since that time, with his wife and five children, Abdelkader has followed the profession of his adopted father, and travels the desert as veterinarian to the tribes.

# THE AGALANTHIANS

## Agalanthian History

### Greatness and Decadence

Every Jazirati knows at least a little Agalanthian history. For thousands of years, this northern people has imposed its will on other lands, in particular during the time of its empire which endured for more than four millennia. There are traces of the Agalanthian Empire across the known world, even in the deep desert, witness to the past greatness of this people. Before the Empire, the Agalanthians had laboured under the tyranny of despots and the greatness of their Republic; today the Empire is but a memory, and the people have lost much of their pride. Each city has become independent of its neighbour; some are allied, and some fight one another for primacy.

## Agalanthian Daily Life

For most Agalanthians, all days are alike. Each is an ordeal which the poor and destitute must survive, and in which the powerful must retain their place. Before even this, however, every child must be taught what it means to be Agalanthian, to which end they are enrolled in a **scolarium**, an institution which exists in every Agalanthian city worthy of the name. A scolarium is a public establishment charged with educating young girls and boys between seven and thirteen years old. A master—the *mestre*—fills their little heads with arithmetic, writing, reading, but also literature, and at least an introduction to the great authors of Agalanthian fame. The more gifted pupils—and more often than not the richest, since beyond the age of thirteen scolarium education is at the parents' expense—continue their educations under a *supramestre*. There, students deepen their knowledge of algebra, grammar, and history. One of the fundamental texts recounts the foundation of Therema by the hero-king, Agalanth.

Agalanthians have lighter skin and hair than Jazirati. They are blond or even redheaded, with light green or blue eyes. A very few have brown hair. Agalanthians are generally tall; they claim the greatness of their history has translated into their greatness of stature.

Men have short hair and are clean-shaven; they consider hairiness dirty and degrading. Philosophers are the exception; to them, long hair and beards are marks of wisdom. Either way, all Agalanthians take great care with their appearance and grooming. They wear long tunics held by fibulae and a belt at the waist. In every city, individuals of rank can be recognised by the purple edging of their white tunics, whose thickness denotes their seniority.

Women's apparel is simple. They also wear long tunics, whose colour varies according to fashion from beige to red, even green depending on the season. Indeed, each season has its corresponding colours, a trend set by the richest woman in the city. Women's hairstyles are equally dependent on fashion; they may be loose, or tied in a bun, and the richest may wear elaborate wigs. Few Agalanthians own jewellery, but all care about hygiene and use cosmetics to whiten their skin, redden their cheeks, and colour their hair.

## Agalanthian Society

Agalanthian society has passed through many stages. Today, more than three centuries after the fall of the Empire, its cities have become independent city-states. Each has a slightly different political system, and dominates the surrounding lands and the villages under its protection.

The **archons**—usually a hereditary position, or one acquired gradually—are the leaders of the city states, although not their sovereigns. They are surrounded by a **council** recruited from the aristocracy (the specific means of recruitment depending on the city-state), whose duties include advising and ultimately controlling the archon. Sovereignty rests with the **assembly** of all the citizens of the city state, charged with voting on all decisions important to the community. Public functions are performed by **magistrates**, and command of the armed forces is the purview of the **strategos** (pl. strategoi).

## The Agalanthian Family

After the fall of the Empire, the Agalanthians refocussed on their family lives. Today, several generations of Agalanthians live under the same roof, in a social group known as a **household**, led by the ranking male member; often the mistress of the household has to share a house with her parents-in-law. Girls and boys are raised by their mother and grandmother until age seven. A basic education at the scolarium follows, although men take charge of the practical education of boys until they reach majority at age eighteen, when they are officially enrolled in their father's household. An Agalanthian household is a social structure for regulating an individual's full membership in society. Only well-off families form households; slaves are never considered members of a household.

Daughters are raised as future mothers and mistresses of a household until they marry at around age fifteen. They are then placed under the authority of their mother-in-law. In turn, they'll eventually become powerful mothers-in-law themselves. Widows are well-respected sages and philosophers, but remarriage is frowned upon unless the widow is very young and facing a long life of childless abstinence.

# The Heroes of the Agalanthians

**Heroes** have a special place in the Agalanthian mind. They are great men and women, whose abilities exceed those of other mortals. They have great physical, intellectual, or artistic gifts, and from their earliest childhoods they have an aura marking them out for a great destiny. Perhaps it is the discovery of new lands or a great invention, perhaps it is to bring to an end a merciless war between two peoples that has been going on for generations. Every newborn child is presented to the Dragon Oracle to augur if he or she will be a Hero; if he will, he is raised as such, under the tutelage of a master who teaches him the stories of all the Heroes that have gone before. The master helps his pupil discover the meaning of his Dragon Mark, so that when his time comes he, too, may make his mark on Agalanthian history.

| TABLE 7-1: AGALANTHIAN HEROES | |
|---|---|
| **HERO** | **DESCRIPTION** |
| Agalanth | Founder of Agalanthia, the greatest Hero of all time. |
| Ceraïs | Victim of a terrible injustice at the hands of the god Mercurianus, she spent her life trying to obtain redress until she was proved in the right. The embodiment of perseverance, Ceraïs is invoked by those who fight against adversity. She is also called upon sometimes to resolve injustice. |
| Gracus | Mythical Hero of Therema who only the most bare-faced good fortune permitted to be born the son of a beggar and yet to ascend to one of the city's most important posts. Agalanthians believe that the gladiator Marcus (page 273), who followed a similar path although he was not a Hero, was favoured by Gracus. |
| Nohemia of Therema | Nohemia is known for having saved Therema more than once from raiders, either seducing them or humiliating them in martial jousts. She is said to have created the modern Myrmidons by diving into Lake Therema and begging the sinuous gods of the river to let her take the twenty remaining insectoid Myrmidons to her beds as lovers. Each gave her twelve sons. |
| Plectoi Septimus Imos | Attacked by a kraken during a fishing expedition, this sailor miraculously managed to defeat the monster, which earned him the wrath of the god Kalos. He fled with his family, and spent the next 30 years aboard his boat, between the human realms and the divine, having a thousand adventures before settling once again on terra firma. It's said that he mapped the sea routes of Kalos which links the seas of Agalanthia with those of Olympos the divine. |
| Themis | This Hero diplomat travelled through all the provinces of the Empire to intervene in many delicate situations. Fair and just, she was so gifted that all parties to the disputes she arbitrated bowed to her judgement. The gods themselves have called upon her skills to resolve some of their problems. |
| Vigus | This extraordinary charioteer rode the race of his life against the god Cthonos. He drove his horses to such a degree of exhaustion that he was forced to carry them himself, and pull his own chariot, in order to cross the finish line in a tie. Cthonos, impressed, spared Vigus's life. |

## Birth and Death

During childbirth, widows and midwives assist the mother as she crouches over birthing bricks. Women with magical powers drive away evil demons, playing tambourines and sistra rattles to protect mother and future child. Men are not permitted. When the child first cries out, a priestess of **Nerea** (page 275) gives him his name. The father is informed of the birth and must acknowledge the child by raising it above his head and presenting it to the gods. Without this acknowledgement, the child is abandoned to the orphanage of the temple of Nerea; the mother has no power to prevent this. Cases of abandonment are sadly all too common, especially when the child is a girl. Its fate is then in the hands of the gods, which the child will serve in the temple of Nerea.

When a death is announced, the family gathers before the remains. Women strike their chests and heads, covering their heads with dust; the men stop shaving. Mortuary grooming is performed by the priesthood of Cthonos, God of Death. During the three days and nights of mourning, the family erects a pyre outside the city, near the cemetery. In the funeral procession, women cry and men sing prayers to the dead in deep voices. Once the pyre is reached, the men lift the remains onto the pyre, usually some fifteen feet high. The family is supposed to stay for the entire cremation: at its end, the ashes are placed in a funerary urn and buried in the cemetery. Family tombs are usually the preserve of the elite.

The soul of the dead is believed to travel through the underworld, and eventually to arrive before Tartarus, the son of Cthonos, who asks them a single question. Only those who have lived a virtuous life know the answer to this question, and anyone answering incorrectly is banished forever to the tortures of the Noxeran Hells.

## Current Activities of the Agalanthians

The Agalanthians are merchants, farmers, and sailors. Today they may have lost their arrogance, but their finer qualities remain. Their fertile lands supply all the food they need and more; Agalanth's land is the breadbasket of the Inner Sea.

Fishing is a profitable activity; Agalanthia's many islands offer good places to fish. Agalanthian fisherfolk are highly skilled at preserving their catch; upon opening a box of Agalanthian fish, the catch still seems fresh, as if it was caught just the day before. This is a secret of the Temple of Kalos, God of the Sea, whose priests convey a catch to a sanctum no layperson may enter, where it is left for one day and one night. The fisherfolk then come to retrieve their catch, which is now sealed in a mysterious metal box. Many have tried to fathom the mystery of the Kalos Boxes, but have never succeeded. The fisherfolk themselves are tight-lipped.

Agalanthian boats are easily recognised. The rounded hulls of their largest vessels rise close to thirty feet above sea level, and even simple barges have hulls rising six to twelve feet. Prows of merchantmen and warships alike are decorated with the Eye of Kalos, which guides the ship on its voyages and protects it from the ordeals of the sea.

There are many Agalanthian merchants in the islands of the Inner Sea, and particularly in the free port of Etrusia. There they organise great expeditions across the known world. They have even developed an insurance system for voyages of over a year, which was been adopted by almost all merchants, irrespective of their origin. According to this system, merchants pay a sum equivalent to 5% of the value of their merchandise before setting sail or departing along the overland trade routes; if their ship sinks in a storm, or if their caravan is robbed by thieves or brigands, this insurance policy allows them to recoup their costs. A mercantile family will often work with the same insurers for generations. The system has meant Agalanthian merchants rarely go bankrupt, and for centuries made them the most prosperous in the world.

## Agalanthian Culture

Agalanthian culture is turned towards the past. The Republic and the Empire were a Golden Age, whether for literature, sculpture, or just being alive. Today everyone just copies the great works and deeds of yesteryear; the richest boast of decorating their houses

## Draconic Science

The Agalanthians were always the favourites of the gods—until the fall of their empire. Or so they believe, at least. But was it instead that their gods were more powerful than those of other peoples, and simply bestowed that supremacy on their Agalanthian worshippers? The truth is, no one will ever know how the Pact came to be; but came to be it did.

It was long, long ago. Agalanth himself still reigned, an aging hero-king on a marble throne. One day, three dragons—Arkitektonos, his wife Sapientia, and their child Teknis—appeared before Agalanth's palace and requested an audience with the king. During that audience, Agalanth and the dragons sealed the Pact, which would forever join Agalanthians, gods, and dragons. Legend says the Pact committed the Agalanthians to spread their civilisation and the cults they worshipped across the world, by force if needs be. In exchange, Arkitektonos, Sapientia, and Teknis would provide the Agalanthian despots and their descendants with the mystical secrets of the Builders of Worlds. The lords of every major city were gifted two dragon eggs and a sacred grimoire, required by the mysterious science the dragons taught.

What followed is lost in the mists of time. What is certain is that the intervention of the three dragons changed the destinies of the entire Agalanthian people forever. United under a prophecy, born of the strength and charisma of a single man, the Agalanthians had finally received the gratitude of the gods, in the form of the draconic science of the **Cosmic Eggs**. This science allowed the Agalanthians to construct buildings which defied the imagination and the laws of physics, and to do so in almost no time; it let them create formidable war machines, capable of travelling ten times faster than any army, and of killing enemies by the score. It put the world at the Agalanthians' feet.

Today, all knowledge of the Cosmic Eggs is lost, and no artefact of draconic science has been seen in Agalanthian hands for centuries. No one really knows why, but the Agalanthians appear to have mysteriously lost the ability to understand and use this science somewhere between the years 4500 and 5000. Now, just over a thousand years later, no one remembers the self-propelling chariots, steam galleys, and machines that made the earth shake and fire rain from the sky. People think they're just legends, tales of warriors made of cogwheels, of giant insects made of wood and steel that devoured cities, of three-headed lions and hawks with human minds.

with beautiful copies. Agalanthian art always found its inspiration in nature, and in the deeds and person of the goddess Demetra, daughter of Nerea. Plants and animals are the subjects of frescoes and mosaics in opulent houses in Therema or the sea port of Thalassakala. Mythological subjects are common, especially the life of Bacchoros, god of pleasure and the vine.

Of course, don't believe all Agalanthian homes are like this. Most are simple places without mosaics, statues, and libraries; it's in public places like circuses and bath-houses that you can really see what luxury and art can be.

Circus games are more than mere entertainment. They're religious festivals honouring a city's patron gods, spectacles paid for by the city or wealthy sponsors. One such was Marcus Tullus Severus, who, upon his ascension to the Thereman senate, paid out of his own pocket for games lasting six months. It cost him all his wealth, but the city expressed its eternal gratitude by erecting a statue to him in the Agorarium, the main plaza housing the marketplace, public and administrative buildings, and main temples.

Circus games often begin with scenic set pieces incorporating plays recounting the misadventures of the gods, staged in the middle of the arena. Chariot races follow, where four teams corresponding to the four seasons compete for victory. Gladiatorial bouts and the executions of criminals take place at the end of the festivities and are the most appreciated. You may even see manticores and other fabulous beasts.

Gladiators are prisoners, slaves, or, rarely, free men chosen by the head of a gladiator school. There are many such schools, more than a score in every city, training men and women to fight beasts or monsters or their fellows. They also teach fighters how to die with dignity, without melodrama, accepting their sentence with pride and honour. However, not all gladiators die in the arena: the story of Marcus is an edifying example. A gladiator armed with a simple sword and shield, he defeated more than a hundred opponents in a row. In his last fight, he fell, and the winner requested the sentence: life or death? The people, in the face of Marcus's strength and courage, pardoned him, and he became a free man, buying his freedom with the winnings from his fights. He went on to become a grand magistrate of Therema, dying at the venerable age of 111, according to his epitaph, still to be seen in Therema's cemetery.

## Agalanthian Religious Practices

Agalanthians don't just believe in their gods: they fear them. All religious ceremonies must be performed to perfection, or risk the wrath of the gods falling on the Agalanthian people. That's precisely what the common folk believe caused the collapse of the Empire. It's said that, during a blood sacrifice to Nerea, the officiating priest committed three fatal errors. The first was to neglect his ablutions, presenting himself unclean before the statue of the goddess; the second was not to verify the purity of the lamb to be sacrificed; and the third was not to listen to his acolyte, who had dreamed of the goddess asking him not to perform the sacrifice or the Empire would collapse. As soon as the first drop of blood touched the altar, the sky went black and the elements were unchained. Everywhere through the Empire the armies yielded to barbarian invasions, and pestilence raged.

Since that time, the Agalanthian priesthoods have become fastidious observers of ceremonial proprieties. No longer simple religious magistrates, they are ardent servants of the gods.

Agalanthians are very superstitious. The gods are everywhere, and influence mortal destinies. If a merchant goes to conduct negotiations, he will first make an offering to Mercurianius, god of merchants; if a woman desires a child, she will pray to Nerea, mother-goddess of all. For Agalanthians, offerings and worship are simple guarantees for the future.

## The Theremans

### History

Being a Thereman means living in a dying world. All Theremans know their society—once the centre of the known world—is now little more than a ruin.

The Agalanthiad recounts how Agalanth, sole survivor of the Steppe Wolves, found refuge by a river, in a place where the Noxeran demons didn't dare pursue. Surrounded by enemies and beneath the light of the stars, the young man had a vision of the gods making a pact with him: in exchange for his submission, he would found a city that would last forever. Civilisation would repel the demons and the influence of his people would grow, forcing the demons to hide in the Earth's dark places and finally disappear.

---

### The Agalanthiad

*The great epic of the Agalanthiad is a literary work which recounts the founding of Therema by the Hero-King Agalanth. Written by Maius, the greatest poet of the Agalanthian civilisation, it tells the story of a young man, Agalanth, who, in accordance with the will of the gods, founded the great city of Therema. In more than three thousand verses, we hear how the young Agalanth escaped the massacre of his people by demonic spirits from Noxera. The gods spared his life and gave him a destiny, saying: "Go west until your legs can no longer carry you, and in that place build a shelter. When people come to you, listen to them and bring them together, for this is your destiny". Thus was millennia-old Therema founded, where even today a temple to the glory of Agalanth still stands on the original site of his shelter, that survived the destruction of the city.*

Agalanth accepted the pact of the gods and, upon waking, found at his side a golden measuring rule, a silver compass, and an iron sword with which to conquer the world.

Maius, great poet of the Agalanthiad, reveals how Agalanth single-handedly conquered his first tribe, the Senegarks of the Negra Mountains, slaying their council of elders and forcibly marrying the youngest of their princesses. Thus began the series of Agalanthian victories which would only end with the Cataclysm.

To the leaders of each conquered tribe, Agalanth, and later his successors, granted the status of patrician. The Agalanthians built their roads, settled the new lands, and thus the Empire conquered hills and mountains then descended the Kalixos River to the sea. As it conquered, it spread civilisation, agriculture, law, and philosophy.

The Cataclysm of the year 5666 was the end of the Golden Age. With Therema shattered, the Emperor dead, and the Senate deposed, the cities of the Empire seceded, just as the conquered peoples rebelled.

Theremans today live in the shadow of their past greatness. They are proud of their history, and have no doubt that, with their city's fall, the whole world is facing disaster. They throw themselves into festivities and carnivals, trying to forget the bleakness of a life lived in the ruins of what once was the centre of the world.

## Organisation

Thereman society is an oligarchical meritocracy. Theremans live lives surrounded by statues, frescoes, and other memorials to the legends of the founders. The city reveres those who obtain glory, providing them with comfortable lives of sumptuous parties, men and women of easy virtue, and magnificent palaces. Their feats open doors to wealth, sponsors, investors, even factions hungry to court the favour of heroes. The descendants of the city's heroes are revered, too, as the memory of

their ancestors lives on in them: for a Thereman, the descendant of a Hero is also a Hero, and the old families still control the lion's share of the city's wealth and property.

The downside of this attitude is that the city hates failure. A simple reversal of fortune may cost a craftsman his home, his business, even his wife, while his creditors will pounce on his assets to limit their losses and avoid the contamination of being associated with the infamy of failure.

At the bottom of the social ladder stand the **slaves**. They have no rights; they're simple merchandise, possessions. They may work, but may also be well treated, sometimes like members of the family, more often like pets.

On the next rung up are the **free men**. These people may own businesses and marry freely. Slightly less numerous than the slaves,

## Names

*The Agalanthians employ the* **tria nomina**, *the "three names": a personal name, a family name followed by the suffix -ius or -ia that means "descendant of", and a nickname.*

*For example: Marcus Tullius Callico.*

*This full name is the official name of a citizen; slaves often only have one name, and even citizens rarely use the tria nomina in daily life.*

*Examples of male names:* Aeschylus, Antonius, Charon, Daiemon, Egeus, Egisthus, Hippolytus, Marcellus, Marcus, Paris, Pericles, Zenon.

*Examples of female names:* Antigone, Antonia, Aspasia, Cassandra, Cassiopeia, Charibda, Circe, Dido, Julia, Juno, Nausicaä, Nereida, Penelope.

# The Agalanthian Pantheon

The Agalanthian religion is polytheistic, and inspired by the natural world. People see divinity in every tree, river, and plant. It's therefore impossible to list every single god. However, some some are more important than others: Nerea, goddess of fertility and the sea; Kalos, protector of the seas and rivers, husband to Nerea; Bacchoros, god of pleasure and the vine; Demetra, goddess of the harvest, daughter of Kalos and Nerea; Cthonos, god of death and the Noxeran Hells.

The gods in Table 7-2: The Agalanthian Gods are worshipped in every Agalanthian city; but there are also many others who are only worshipped in one or a few places. Plurality and diversity characterise the Agalanthian religion. Every Agalanthian has his own protector god; every person carries small amulets representing their gods in order to attract their favour.

| TABLE 7-2: THE AGALANTHIAN GODS | |
|---|---|
| **GOD** | **DESCRIPTION** |
| Aeolis | Goddess of the Winds, Storms, and Rains, and also Changing Moods. |
| Atlas | God of Travellers, Explorers, and Cartographers. He provides part of his knowledge to Sollion since the latter helped him find meaning to his divine existence. He was greatly revered during the heyday of the expansion of the Agalanthian Empire. |
| Bacchoros | God of Pleasure and the Vine. |
| The Bavda | The word means "harlot" in Agalanthian. An otherwise nameless goddess who represents luck and the workings of chance. No one worships her in public, for to surrender one's destiny to her is without honour. |
| Cerdus | God of Beggars, Misers, and the Poor. He has a gold coin with only one face which returns instantly to his hand at his command. He is the unloved brother of Mercurianus. |
| Cthonos | God of Death and the Noxeran Hells. One of the first gods to emerge from the Egg of Utaax. |
| Demetra | Goddess of Nature and the Harvest, daughter of Kalos and Nerea and thus sister to Velia. |
| Ioptis | The All Powerful Sun, God of Clear Skies, Father of the Twins Solphea and Sollion, and of Aeolis. One of the first gods to emerge from the Egg of Utaax. |
| Kalos | God of the Sea, Protector of Rivers, husband of Nerea. One of the first gods to emerge from the Egg of Utaax. |
| Mercurianus | God of Merchants. |
| Mnemosyne | Goddess of Memory, Mother of the Muses. |
| The Muses | Calliope, Clio, Erato, Euterpe, Melpomene, Polymnia, Terpsichore, Thalia, and Urania are the Agalanthian muses of the Ancient Arts (see page 125). They are the daughters of Saphios and Mnemosyne. |
| Nerea | Goddess of the Moon, Fertility, and the Sea. The first goddess to emerge from the Egg of Utaax. |
| Noctea | Goddess of Night, Hidden Desires, and Secrets. She embraces Solphea each night so that the goddess may tell her tales of the day just gone. She particularly enjoys hearing of the men who have been dazzled by the latter's worshippers. |
| Noxera | Goddess of the Shades of Hell, the dark and schizophrenic counterpart to Noctea. |
| Saphios | God of Love, Sex, and Political Alliances (including arranged marriages). Father of the Muses and brother of Bacchoros. |
| Sollion | The Benevolent Sun, Sollion brings light, enlightenment, and reason. He is worshipped by philosophers. He is the twin brother of Solphea. |
| Solphea | Goddess of Beauty and the Blinding Sun, the One Who Turns the Heads of Men. She is the great seductress, cunning and manipulative. She is the twin sister of Sollion. |
| Tartarus | Guardian and Judge of the Noxeran Hells. Son of Cthonos. |
| Thalena | Goddess of the Hunt and Cruel Deaths. She is a virginal "barbarian" goddess, the patroness of rootless solitary heroes whom she guides to their inevitable dooms. |
| Urmos | God of Civilised Warfare, the Celestial Strategist. In Agalanthian myth, Urmos and Thalena pursue one another eternally, never able to consummate their mutual desire, so separated are they by many things. |
| Utaax | The First Dragon, present at the beginning of the world and the birth of the gods. He represents the Primal Earth and the magic which flows through it. |
| Velia | Goddess of Women and Wives and their Mysteries. Velia has a highly organised mystical cult with many different levels of initiation and mysteries. Male members are ritually castrated. Velia is the daughter of Kalos and Nerea, and thus sister to Demetra. |
| Zamul | The Primordial God of Time. One of the first gods to emerge from the Egg of Utaax. |
| Zeneus | God of Thunder and Lightning, son of Aeolis. |

free men differ from their counterparts elsewhere in the world because of their education and attitude. They know how lucky they are to live at the heart of the civilised world, and have nothing but pity and contempt for the foreign savages who are unaware of the tragedy that Therema's destruction represents. This pity turns to hatred for the Agalanthian city-states that would attack Therema, and to awe before the Myrmidons that defend it.

Lastly, the **patricians** are the Thereman aristocracy. The law says that all you need to become a patrician is to be head of a household and pay your taxes, but in reality you also have to be accepted by the old Thereman aristocracy—a near-impossibility for anyone not descended from a Hero or covering themselves in glory.

It's worth noting that Thereman women enjoy practically the same rights as men. In ancient times, Queen Sernemis called upon the gods to free the city from the Moon Spirits that had bewitched the men. For a whole month, she was forced to rule a Therema inhabited solely by women and children, a task she accomplished so well that, upon awakening, the men formally recognised the status and abilities of their partners.

In Therema, even beggars, thieves and con men are considered citizens—but it's good manners to pretend they don't exist. But at least they're Theremans, and so more worthy than any foreigner.

Two factions vie for the hearts and minds of Thereman's citizens, both feared and courted by the patricians for their popular power. The **Devout** believe that the earthquake which destroyed Therema was a punishment from the gods for the Empire's hubris. The **Non-Believers**, on the other hand, believe that it was the earthquake which robbed the city of the favour of the gods. The religious basis for this opposition has been long-forgotten, but this doesn't prevent the two factions from roundly despising one another and regularly confronting one another in the Senate or even the arena games.

## On the Edge of the Abyss

Therema stands on the banks of the great River Aestius whose course was disrupted by the earthquake which destroyed the city. Part of the city was lifted up, whilst another was drowned by the waters, creating a lake at its heart.

On the stretch of land between the lake and the foot of the cliff stands the old city and its palaces, the heart of patrician life. Opposite, on the other side of the lake, the marsh and its half-sunken palaces, once the richest dwellings, are today the haunt of criminals and beggars.

Beneath the waters of the lake drowned houses and monuments can still be discerned, of which the old Senate House is the most famous. Miraculously spared by the earthquake and certainly protected by the gods, the Temple of Agalanth—which stands on the site where the Hero-King built his first shelter—rises alone on a small islet in the middle of the lake.

At the top of the cliff stands "New Therema". The city of newcomers is a beautiful city, which houses the middle class quarters, the new Senate House, the Archon's Palace, as well as the Hanging Port. This curious feature is nothing less than the old port, now linked by a system of goods lifts and hoists to the new port which has been built on pilings at the river's edge.

The cliff of Therema is itself sometimes unstable. For the past three years, artists have been painting a vast fresco on it, a league and a half long and one hundred feet high, recounting the events of the Agalanthiad.

Therema is surrounded by beautiful countryside. The fields whose crops support its people stretch for hectares over the hills on the horizon, where great oak forests grow housing the summer villas of the patricians. Once upon a time, the fields gave way to vineyards which once produced one of the finest wines in the world. The climate is mild: not too cold in winter, and rarely unbearable in summer (although it does get hot). The Cataclysm has transformed this into a peaceful yet magnificent landscape, although melancholy: the once regular countryside is now pierced in places with rocky peaks rising out of nowhere, while elsewhere chasms and crevices gape. Fields are still worked, but Therema has fallen back upon riverine imports, depleting even further the already low population of farmers, many of whom perished during the Cataclysm. A traveller can see farmers tilling the land next to ruins of triumphal arches that once straddled the roads. Most farms are ruins, while in the hills patrician houses slumber to the song of cicadas, gradually sinking beneath the tendrils of untended vineyards. Don't even think of plunder, though: these hinterlands are the hunting grounds of Myrmidons and the hounds of the Empire's hunters, who patrol ceaselessly in search of the city's foes.

## Crime and Punishment

The chaos and fatalism that followed the Cataclysm have caused some surprising changes in Thereman behaviour. On the one hand, they no longer really think about "the law"; for them, it drowned beneath the waters with the Senate. On the other, Theremans have idealised Agalanthian civilisation for so long that most of them instinctively defend its rules. Yes, there are criminals. What merchant doesn't hide his profits from the Imperial tax collectors? What assassin doesn't sell his talents in front of the statue of the Death God? What thief doesn't take advantage of market days to pilfer the purses of gullible merchants? If caught, they'll face arrest by the disillusioned and corrupt militia; and citizens waste no time trying criminals who've besmirched the Empire's memory, drowning them in the lake, throwing them to wild beasts for food, or to the gladiators to hack to death during the weekly games. Justice at the hands of Therema's factions is fast and expeditious: a smart criminal knows that the best way of escaping conviction is to flee into the old city. In those swamp-filled ruins, no one cares about your crimes as long as you respect the Rogue's Code.

True Imperial law and justice are now dispensed only by the Myrmidons. The greatest troops in the known world, once present on all the Empire's battlefronts, the Myrmidons have now retreated to Therema to protect their dying city from external attack. They enforce the laws of the Senate and the Archon, and are inflexible and incorruptible; their numbers are steadily dwindling. The prevailing mood of laxness and melancholy prevents most new applicants from acquiring the necessary discipline to train as a myrmidon; the Myrmidons' school is deserted, and troops spend their time guarding the Palace and the Senate, and protecting the city's borders.

Only the Myrmidons are authorised to carry out punishments for the worst crime recognised in these difficult times: treason against the city. Espionage, political agitation or sedition are all punished the same way: crucifixion along a road, face turned away in the direction of the cities of Therema's enemies.

## Personalities of the Theremans

### Julius Nona Selens

Julius is the Archon of Therema, at only 15 years old. The adoptive son of the previous archon, he was born to the Haestes, an extinct Heroic family. He has learned the art of power thanks to his recently deceased adoptive father, as well as to the eunuch Vortis and Nesphes Tremens, the palace chiromancer. Still in mourning following the Archon's death two years ago, he has appeared little in public since. The Theremans are starting to find his absence a trifle long, especially as custom now demands the Archon must take a wife.

### Vortis the Eunuch

Vortis is the devoted servant of the Thereman throne and the adviser to Archon Julius. He's an aged diplomat with failing health, who watches over the city and assures its security the best he can. He has created many ministries and offices to better manage the many tasks in his charge.

### Nesphes Tremens

The Chief Chiromancer of the Palace of Therema is an enigmatic individual of indeterminate age who still seemed old during the reign of the father of the current archon. People say he no longer has all his faculties, but few would dare question his position and his competence for fear of the curses he might pronounce.

# The Etrusians, the People of the Isles

## History

Of Agalanthian origin, the Etrusians live on islands at the heart of the Inner Sea, equidistant between the Agalanthian city states and Carrassine. Since the fall of the Empire, the Etrusians maintain only trade relations with their erstwhile homeland, as there are still many Agalanthian merchants in the isles and the freeport of Etrusia. But if you scratch the surface of their friendly business relationship, you'll uncover many rivalries and points of contention, especially concerning maritime competition.

The proximity of Etrusia to Carrassine and the Agalanthian city states gives the isles an important strategic position which is both a strength and a weakness. The Etrusians have long feared losing their relative independence: even though they're nominally Agalanthians, their relationship with the other city states remains distant, and the Etrusians fear dominance by Therema or Fragrance. That's the reason they have built fortified citadels on every one of their islands, on the flanks of large hills or on the shores, permitting military control of the territory and supposedly preventing invasion. The walls of these citadels are massive unmortared blocks up to thirty feet thick. Over the years, and with the continuing peace, many of these citadels are currently deserted and in disrepair.

## Organisation

Etrusia, although an archipelago of many differently sized islands, is a city state, ruled by an archon with a military, legal and religious role. Each island is governed by a **magistrate** to whom the archon has delegated administrative power. The magistrate is often a member of the archon's family, even if a distant one. Often incompetent, magistrates rely on their underlings to run their islands, instead taking advantage of their wealth and position by throwing endless feasts and orgies, and collecting countless lovers.

## Society

Etrusian society comprises two groups of free people: the **administrators** (who are the entourages of the magistrates), and the **islanders** (the people who live and work on the islands). The Etrusians also own **slaves**, who occupy the bottom rung of the Etrusian social ladder; these aren't usually of Etrusian origin, but are instead bought from slave merchants.

The Etrusians are a happy, seagoing people. Nothing is more important to them than returning home from an exciting sea voyage and getting drunk in the arms of some damsels (or rakehells) of easy virtue, while gorging on smoked meats and cheeses. Etrusian agricultural production is mostly grain (wheat and barley), olives, and wine. Indeed, Etrusian wine is one of the best in the known world. Etrusia is also known for its sausages, hams, and pork bellies, rare products appreciated even in Jergath. Olive oil is not only used for food but also for personal grooming and perfumes.

Etrusians also hanker after products not produced on their islands, one of their main motivations for trade. They maintain good relationships with other peoples, although they usually remain wary, as described above.

Etrusian ships are similar to Agalanthian ones. Their triremes are raised high foreward and aft, with animal head figureheads. They're usually propelled by slave rowers.

## Gods

The Etrusian pantheon includes many deities found among the Agalanthians: Mercurianus, God of Merchants; Nerea, the Mother-Goddess; Demetra, Harvest Goddess; and Cthonos, God of Death and the Noxeran Hells. But you can also encounter the "Mistresses" (or *Potnia* in the Etrusian tongue), spirits linked to places of worship. Examples include the Mistress of the Labyrinth and the Mistress of the Southern Vineyards.

There are few large temples; most worship occurs at home, before small household altars.

## Magic

The Etrusians are a magic-oriented people. They use simple, even primitive, spells, originating in their orgiastic, booze-filled ceremonies. The vast number of vineyards in their islands has no doubt been a major influence.

The core of their magical practices is the enchantment of chiromancy tablets, but the Etrusians also love to wear amulets. These can take many forms: necklaces, gems, ornaments, and scrolls, with different inscriptions, including prayers and incantations. A superstitious people, Etrusians believe wearing amulets brings them good luck, or protects them from accidents, disease, the evil eye, sorcery, or even demons. Amulets are sometimes pierced and worn as pendants; most often, they're shaped like the crescent moon.

## Physical Appearance

The Etrusians show their Agalanthian origins with their light skin and hair. Over the centuries, there has been some mixing with the Jazirati, and they show some of their traits, too. Nevertheless, most Etrusians are blond with light blue or green eyes; unlike the Agalanthians, they sport beards and often have long hair tied in a ponytail. Their clothing is practical—trousers and short tunics—although they retain one Agalanthian tradition: their tunic is bordered with a coloured band which varies according to the individual's social standing. A red border marks a member of the entourage of an archon or magistrate, a blue border marks a free man, and a black border marks a slave.

Women's clothes are simple and once again originally Agalanthian. An Etrusian woman wears a long, coloured tunic held by a fibula, tightened at the waist by a patterned braided belt, which in the richest circles may contain gold or silver threads.

## Personalities of the Etrusians

### The Archon, Antonius Primus

When Antonius Valerius Torvus ascended to the Etrusian throne, he took the name Antonius Valerius Primus. His older brother should have been king, but he had died early. A rumour at the time claimed Antonius had had his brother poisoned, but nothing was ever proved. Today it's an open secret.

Antonius Primus is a large, vigorous man with grey eyes and thick eyebrows, and sporting a small black beard. He's known just as much for his cruelty as his taste in art; he alternates his long sessions of study with races, hunting, and archery, leaving his administration to run his lands. His evenings are spent in drunken orgies where lascivious dancers and courtesans pander to his every whim and those of his guests.

Antonius Primus is thoroughly paranoid, fearing the plots he used to love so much. He has created the Scarlet Guard (referring to the coloured border on the clothing of his entourage) to ensure his security. This comprises a thousand elite fighters who must be of pure Etrusian blood. Over the years, the Guard has become a powerful political force in its own right; although it currently supports Primus, it could overthrow him at any moment—especially since its commanders take a dim view of the fact that the Archon has effectively ceded his power to his administrators.

### Caius Vitellius Minus

This merchant owns the largest fleet of trading ships in Etrusia. He's about forty years old, stocky, average height for an Etrusian, with a dark, expressionless face, and is often dressed in black.

Under this austere exterior lurks a keen mind. Caius has more or less bribed the Etrusian administration and reaps enormous rewards. He's aware of almost all the business transactions that take place, and has become the official supplier for the Archon and his magistrates.

# The Fragrantines

## History

Fragrantines hail from a city which today is an incredible melting pot of ethnic and cultural integration. It wasn't always thus: the citadel which would give birth to the City of a Thousand Scents was originally founded by the Agalanthians. Around the citadel, a settlement grew up housing the families of the Agalanthian soldiers; it attracted shopkeepers, tavern-keepers, and all the traders and craftspeople a military camp requires. It eventually became a truly cosmopolitan city.

Today, Fragrance is unique in the whole of Jazirat. Visitors cannot help but feel a certain longing when their caravan departs: Fragrance leaves no one indifferent, the city belongs to everyone and no one. As the saying goes: "If your eyes have beheld the City of a Thousand Scents once in your life, the djinn may take you to the silent beyond and you will be content".

## Organisation

Characters from Fragrance may belong to any of *Capharnaum*'s peoples; the city has Agalanthian, Jazirati, Quarterian and Shiradi quarters. Each follows its people's customs, both in behaviour and style of buildings. Fragrance touts itself as a city of trade and travel: it asks no tax or tarif of travellers and merchants, who come to sell their wares at the city's many markets.

Characters hailing from the Crossroads Quarter of Min Maydan (page 206) are perhaps the only ones who can be considered truly and uniquely Fragrantine. They partake of the city's great mixing of peoples. This is even seen in their names. If a child of Min Maydan is born of Agalanthian and Shiradi parents, it may take its father's or mother's name, to which will be added the suffix "Min Maydan", indicating the child comes from the Crossroads Quarter of Fragrance. Equally, if the parents wished, the child could have a Shiradi personal name and an Agalanthian family name, or vice versa; the important thing would be that it would still bear the name "Min Maydan" as a suffix.

*For example: a boy born from the union of Titus Hadrianus Maximus and Sarah Bat Barka could be called Julius Hadrianus Maximus Min Maydan, or Ariel Hadrianus Maximus Min Maydan, or even Julius Bar Barka Min Maydan.*

Characters from Min Maydan are ideal candidates for the kind of "dissident" destinies mentioned in "Rebels, Dissidents, Mixed-Bloods, Cousins and Traitors" on page 11. At Al-Rawi's discretion, Min Maydan characters may select from the attribute and skill bonuses and suggested paths of **both** their parent's bloods at character creation.

## Personalities of the Fragrantines

### Tarek Ibn Tarkan Min Maydan, High Priest of Merut

In the Crossroads Quarter of Min Maydan one man enjoys a higher status than all others: the High Priest of the goddess Merut. He's vital to the continued existence of the quarter: without him, star-crossed lovers would not enjoy the protection of the goddess, and the shrine which drives the quarter's economy would fail.

Although the position of High Priest has always been important, its current occupant has taken it to a new level. Any Fragrantine will recognise him immediately: a discreet, reserved man, tall and bald, wearing simple white linen clothing over the caramel skin of a well-travelled Jazirati. What strangers notice are his eyes: their gaze seems to pierce your soul, their unworldly colour amazes, they are the eyes of a god. In turn they seem to reflect the ocean, the dunes, the oases, the sombre lands of the North: no artist has ever succeeded in capturing their colour. They were the reason his parents offered him to the goddess: Tarek was not their eldest, but his eyes showed he could never belong to the world of men.

### Murad Ibn Salif Min Maydan, the Merchant Grandee

As the saying goes: "If you can't find what you're looking for anywhere else, then happiness lies with Murad Ibn Salif". No one has ever discovered Murad's secret, yet in one hour he can find whatever you're after: a complete suit of Agalanthian armour, camel triplets, a mercenary army. Or even just a pair of *babouches*, tunics cut in the latest fashion, some antique fabrics; or even just artists or musicians for hire.

Murad dresses like any other merchant in Jazirat, in a large tunic and long *sarwal*. He's heavy set, with a magnificent red beard (a dye of his own devising). Vain but not effeminate, he sets the fashions for the whole city. When he talks to you, it's like you were the only customer in his vast shop situated just at the entrance to the Min Maydan quarter: a giant palm tree stands by the door. To this day no customer has ever left unsatisfied, in the forty years Murad has been here. He's a Fragrantine institution.

It's said that a man from the desert once came to Murad asking for a bird of a type that had not been seen for two hundred years. He gave Murad a deadline of a single day. In the evening of the same day, he found outside the door of his lodgings a cage, containing not one bird but two, with eggs ready to hatch.

Some say Murad is a great magician; others say he's an influential man with a vast network covering the whole world. A few even think he's a god. Whatever the case, Murad proves that—in Jazirat, and especially in the Crossroads Quarter of the City of Fragrance—*nothing* is impossible.

### Gaius Aphrokes Diocles

Diocles is one of the most famous charioteers in Fragrance. In the twenty-four years of his career, this popular hero has taken part in 4257 races and won 1462. He began his career at the age of 18, and quickly came to the attention of head-hunting scouts for the biggest stables. Now he's been in retirement for the past two years, living comfortably from his winnings, said to be larger than the inheritance of many Jazirati princes. At the end of his brilliant career, he was named the greatest charioteer ever known. Even now, Diocles is still a star throughout the whole of Capharnaum and even beyond.

# Agalanthians of the Other City-States

Although once united, the Agalanthians are no longer. For six centuries, they have been merely neighbours, worshipping the same gods and sharing a common and glorious past. Since the Empire's fall three hundred years ago, the city-states have tried to maintain the political and economic balance between them, but today the world's attention is drawn more towards Capharnaum than the old Agalanthian lands. Decaying Therema is still a buffer between the archons, but it's getting harder and harder to maintain any semblance of Agalanthian unity.

Here's what is left of the Agalanthian Empire.

## Gladiopolis

Gladiopolis has always been Therema's little sister. It was the second city, after Senegarthia, to turn its back on its barbarian gods and join with Agalanth. A major stronghold, it remains to this day one of the proudest Agalanthian fortresses. Its agricultural lands produce a popular wine and olive oil, and its many active fighting schools are loyal to Therema. The ghost of the Empire is everywhere in Gladiopolis—but this has enabled it to remain dignified and strong.

## Melkidonia

Mostly ruined, this fortified town was an Orkadian hellhole for millennia. Before it embraced Agalanth, it had been one of the rare Orkadian urban centres, and even when it became Agalanthian, its warriors never really renounced their mountain axes and kilts for the gladius and tunic. Even today, you could easily mistake these unwashed, unkempt, most barbaric of Agalanthians for Orkadians that never encountered the civilising influence of Jason.

## Nerektonia

Like the fruit of the adultery of Nerea and Cthonos, Nerektonia is a marriage of Earth and Moon before the worried gaze of the Sea. It's a city of cave-dwellers with numerous active orichalcum mines, and one of the largest commercial harbours in the Inner Sea. Its many cliffs house countless dwellings, and from a distance the city looks like an alabaster face pierced with a thousand eyes.

Situated at the mouth of the Kalixos River, Nerektonia is a major river port and the focus of much of Agalanthian trade.

## Senegarthia, City of the Moon Princes

The oldest Agalanthian city and home of the Senegarks mountain and mining folk. Although the moonstone (orichalcum) mines are today almost worked out, Senegarthia's economy still depends on the extraction and working of this metal.

Senegarthia, City of the Moon Princes, is the only city of importance in the Negra Mountains. It rules over and protects a dozen mines and a hundred or so forester settlements.

Cthonos is worshipped here more than anywhere else. Local tradition holds that every orichalcum mine is an opening to the underworld and the Noxeran Hells. Extracting the moonstone without disturbing sleeping demons is only possible thanks to the major weekly ceremonies of propitiation.

## Septra, City of Wolves

To the northeast stands the City of Wolves, last stronghold before the Noxeran Steppe and home city of the Hero-King Agalanth. The city has an icy climate, overlooking steppes and tundra from the top of a rocky peak. In the Agalanthiad, Maius described Septra as "a wolf's eyrie".

In this barren, moonlike landscape, Septra still guards against invasions from the Krek'kaos. It also trades with the lands to its east. Themselves nomadic horsemen, the Septrians travel the steppe and defy the blizzards to battle the creatures of the endless winter.

## Thalassakala

At the mouth of the Tyranos River, Thalassakala has always been the pleasure city for Agalanthian princes. Hot springs feed its many bath houses, highly fashionable during the glory days of the decadent republic. If you've a hankering for it, Thalassakala will cater for your most exotic tastes: gambling dens and casinos, pornographic theatres, arenas with the most decadent spectacles. Just make sure you're not too squeamish! Waxing rich from the kinks and perversions of its fellow citizens and visitors, Thalassakala's magistrates and archon now have a mafia-like influence that is extending its tendrils towards all the other city-states.

## Uranopolis

Although located on the shore, Uranopolis plays only a minor role in maritime trade. Instead, since its foundation, its head turns to the heavens. Once upon a time, its ivory towers served as launching points for creatures tamed by the science of the Cosmic Eggs (page 272), gifts from the gods. Some ancient texts also speak of flying machines used by the Empire to transport its troops: boats with sails like butterfly wings, towing in their wake floating barges held aloft by hot air balloons.

Today, the towers of Uranopolis serve only as the headquarters for the city's decadent government. In the streets, crime is on the rise.

# THE QUARTERIANS

## Quarterian History

The three kingdoms comprising what's now called "the West" or "the Quarterian Kingdoms" were founded in their current form around the year 5800 of the Jazirati calendar. Although their origins are much older, they have been progressively fashioned by wars, unions, and sometimes collapse.

To the south lies **Aragon**, a vast kingdom with a rich and flamboyant history, the oldest of the Western realms. It collapsed due to rivalries between its rich overlords and its decadent landowners. The proud Aragonians are shadows of their former selves: corruption and personal ambition have taken their toll on this kingdom, and these days the king's voice is barely heard.

Aragon's borders have remained steady since the year 5540. The kingdom itself has existed for more than a thousand years. Isolated from the other Quarterian kingdoms by tall mountains, Aragon has never really harboured expansionary ambitions. Huge and sparsely populated, it was self-sufficient. Nevertheless, navigation and maritime trade developed, and Aragon became the most powerful Quarterian naval power. It was Aragonian vessels that carried most of Simeon IV's troops to Jazirat in the year 5987.

Despite having a naval advantage, Aragon was unable to stop the invasion of its southern territories by Jazirati troops coming to recover the Sword of Hammad (page 177); its armies, in disarray at the mercy of disparate interests, could not contain the wave of fierce warriors arriving to avenge the insult they had suffered. Many Aragonian cities fell before the invasion was finally brought to a halt. Today the Jazirati no longer advance, and have entrenched themselves in the captured cities, waging sporadic war against the Aragonian troops. In 5996, King Simeon IV of Occidentia sent his brother Abelard the Fiery with two companies of pikemen, a like number of archers, and about a hundred knights, on the pretext of helping the Aragonian defence. Aragonian distrust of their northern neighbours led to the Occidentian troops being stationed far from the fighting; Abelard is bored to death there, a fact which amuses Simeon IV no end.

**Occidentia** was born in the blood of the tribes that have inhabited its territory and waged ferocious war there since time immemorial. The first unifications took place eight centuries ago, a series of military conquests that led to the emergence of ten realms ruled by self-proclaimed kings. Conflict between the realms was sporadic during the following centuries, until one king rose above the others: Adalbert the First. Energetic, fierce, and merciless,

Adalbert unified at swordpoint what would become Occidentia. In 5704 he was crowned King of Occidentia, reinforcing his position by instituting a rigid feudal system guaranteeing the loyalty of his followers. He founded the line that still occupies the throne of Occidentia today.

Simeon IV ascended the throne at age 16 in the year 5958. Stubborn, machiavellian, an excellent tactician, he has ruled with an iron fist, often forgetting the velvet glove. He has many enemies among the nobility, attached to their privileges, who frown upon the authoritarian positions of the king. Not the least of his opponents is his brother Abelard, six years younger. Simeon's decision to lead the Holy Crusade at the request of the Quarterian Magister surprised many, but the King weakened his opponents by requisitioning their troops, leaving them at the mercy of his own soldiers under his son's command. The King's resounding victory in Jazirat enabled him to re-assert his power upon his return, with many—even the Quarterian Magister—now beholden to him.

A united **Orkadia** has been a reality for about two hundred years. Before the rise of the Orkadian Empire, its constituent states were tribal kingdoms and principalities linked by a common tongue, regular trade, and sporadic warfare. Their unification was the work of one man: Mandernick. This tribal king, of what would become Jarvsberg Province, unified all the other tribes with the help of the unwitting Agalanthians. In the troubled times after Therema's destruction, raiders from fallen Agalanthia devastated the eastern marches of Orkadia, bringing it close to collapse. Mandernick persuaded the tribes to join together to raise a single huge army to drive out the invader. Although able to best one petty king, the Agalanthians could do nothing against ten. From this tribal alliance an empire was born, and Mandernick was its first ruler.

The Orkadian Empire looks strange to outsiders. Comprising ten formerly independent tribal kingdoms sharing common laws, its emperor unifies and organises them into a single whole. The emperor wields real power: no state will refuse his call. For two centuries, the Orkadian Empire has been stable, and trade flourishes.

The current emperor, Jorg the Loyal, watches over the northern and eastern borders of the Western Kingdoms. The Agalanthians no longer seem to be a threat; the Asijawi appear reserved and make no incursions; the tribes of the north are disunited, and Orkadia maintains good trade relations with them all.

# Quarterian Daily Life

## Quarterian Appearance

The peoples of the three Quarterian Kingdoms are physically quite distinct. The Aragonians are generally small (an average of 5ft 5in or 165cm for men and 5ft 2in or 158cm for women) and lean, with skin tanned by the sun of their land. Their hair is black or dark brown, and eyes are dark. Aragonian women are known for their beauty and their sense of family; noblewomen protect themselves from the sun to have as pale a skin as possible—while never being able to compete with blonde Orkadian women.

Occidentians are taller than their Aragonian counterparts, 5ft 7in or 170cm for men and 5ft 5in or 165cm for women. The kingdom's warrior past has forged not only its people's characters, but also their bodies: Occidentians are often solid and tough. Southern Occidentia has a sunny climate, so people there are tanned, whereas they're paler in the rest of the country. Typical hair colours vary from blonde to the darkest black. Eye colour varies also.

The typical Orkadian is big and strapping, blond with pale eyes. These days, though, you can find a bit of everything in the Orkadian Empire, thanks to migrations resulting from its geographical position, political stability, and lively trade. Orkadians used to get called "blond barbarians", but these days people with all colours of skin fight in their armies—although there's very little sun here to keep people tanned. People tend to be tall—5ft 9in or 175cm for men, 5ft 5in or 165cm for women. It's claimed that Gunhilde, first wife of Emperor Jorg, who died not long ago, was the most beautiful woman in the Western Kingdoms.

## Quarterian Clothing

Clothing in the Quarterian Kingdoms depends very much on climate. Garments are broadly similar, and often only cut or colour differentiates Occidentian from Orkadian clothes. Men wear trousers and a long-sleeved tunic, with a thick woollen cloak in winter or, in the north, a bearskin traded with the northern tribes. Aragonians prefer dark clothing (dark blues, blacks), while other Quarterians use the whole panoply of colours except purple, which is reserved for the Quarterian Church.

Belts and hats are essential, or woollen caps in the Orkadian and Occidentian winters. Headgear usually has a wide brim in Aragon, and is a simple cap in other kingdoms.

Women wear long gowns, touching the ground, which reveal nothing of the breasts. Quality varies according to social status. Women do not wear trousers. In winter, a cape is worn; in summer, Aragonian women carry decorated parasols.

Quarterians use soft leather boots with soles of wood or rigid leather. The poorest go shoeless or wear clogs. Boots are usually tall, covering the lower leg; men wear them beneath trousers.

## Jewellery

The goldsmith's craft has become an art in the Quarterian Kingdoms. Magnificent jewellery of gold, silver, or alloys, are unaffordable to commoners, but lords are expected to wear at least one finely crafted signet ring or necklace. Noblewomen wear beautiful jewellery, but wealthy commoners will also pay fortunes for ostentatious displays. Poorer people will wear more rudimentary decoration, often made from wood, dried fruits, or string.

Gemsmithing is the complement of the above, involving crystals and enamels as well as gemstones such as rubies, amethysts, and diamonds. Gems are reserved for the high-born of the Quarteri-

## The Quarterian Calendar

*The Quarterian calendar differs slightly from its Jazirati counterpart. In use for more than four hundred years, it divides the year into 12 months of 30 days. The months are called: Januarius, Februarius, Martius, Aprilis, Maius, Junius, Julius, Augustus, September, October, November, December. The first day of the year is 1 Januarius. The days are named in weeks of seven days (unlike the Jazirati tenday): Dies Dominicus, Prima, Secunda, Tertia, Quadria, Quinta, Sexta. Dies Dominicus is the holy day, the day (at least for the Quarterian Church) of the death of Jason. In one year, there are 51 weeks plus 3 days. These three days are the last in the year and are called Jason, Mira and Aether. The calendar officially begins in the year Jason died, which is also the year 5422 of the Jazirati calendar; each year is suffixed "AJ" or "After Jason". For the years before the death of Jason, the number of the year with the suffix "BQ" or "Before the Quartering" is used (such as "the year 200BQ"). The current year is the year 555AJ.*

an Kingdoms. The crown of Occidentia, for example, is a massive piece of jewellery made up of no less than one hundred good-sized gems and the largest diamond known in the West.

## Quarterian Families

### Marriage

Quarterians are defined by their families. Among the nobility, marriages are arranged, dictated by financial or political needs; this is less true for the rest of the population. A woman may marry at age 15, a man at 16. Brides bring dowries with them. A man may take only one wife before Aether, and vice versa, although this doesn't stop people from having multiple lovers. Female adultery tends to be more poorly tolerated, however, and an adulterous woman may quickly find herself cloistered somewhere far too remote for a viable social life.

The Church controls all marriages, and unions can only be undone by death. Widows may contract new marriages. Repudiation of adulterous partners is possible, but the Church has the final say, and notions of proof and guilt are extremely flexible: totally faultless wives may be repudiated if the husband is influential enough.

### Women in Quarterian Society

Officially, in Quarterian society, a woman has only one role: the raising of a family. This includes bearing and raising children, looking after her husband and home. No other role is open to her: a woman may not be employed, nor may she acquire or sell goods in her name. Upon the death of her husband, a male guardian will be

appointed to manage her affairs until her remarriage or death; she cannot legally manage her property herself.

That's the official story, the product of centuries of abstruse theological debate, mostly by men. Unofficially, things look very different: Quarterian women are hardly shrinking violets, and many wield great influence in Quarterian society—a form of "soft power" which, while unsupported by any legal framework, isn't restricted by one either. Women often manage their husband's activities, and manipulate and guide their household to their advantage. It's a role which requires expert diplomatic skills and the ability to be the "power behind the throne". Among the nobility, it's not uncommon for a guardian to end up totally dependent upon the good offices of the woman he's meant to protect.

### Inheritance

In Quarterian lands, the firstborn son inherits from his father. Everyone else must depend on the firstborn's generosity; morally, he is required to support them. Women may not legally inherit anything. Quarterian history is filled with wives who were repudiated because they did not provide their husbands with a male heir.

Children born outside of marriage may not inherit. Those who have been recognised by their parents, however, may live in their father's household and be raised like his legitimate children. Custom dictates the firstborn son should provide support to his father's illegitimate offspring, too.

## Quarterian Culture

### Music

Unlike the Jazirati, instrumental music occupies no position of importance in Quarterian culture. It's more a matter for the common folk, a break from work, something for festivals and celebrations. It's not written down; transmission is by memory and practice. There are professional musicians who travel between villages and towns, livening up the many festivals with flutes, mandolins, zithers, and drums. Most musicians in a noble household tend to accompany singers; properly speaking, there are no purely instrumental works.

Singing, by contrast, is well developed in the Quarterian Kingdoms. It's also transmitted orally. Any activity may be accompanied by singing: courts have troubadours singing the exploits of famous Quarterians, although such artists are rare, and often famous. The Quarterian Church has large choirs for celebrations; these are usually exclusively male (including choirs of children), and are dedicated to specific churches. The Magisterium has an imposing choir of more than two hundred singers.

### Poetry and Literature

Written texts are very rare except for the Holy Scriptures. Only monastic scribes work to propagate texts, and they focus exclusively on religious writings. Some works exist on scrolls, but there are few copies. It's a rare person who can even read a line.

Poetry and stories are widespread throughout the Quarterian Kingdoms, but they're oral traditions, told by storytellers who often modify and embellish their tales, meaning stories may vary widely from location to location. Travelling storytellers are always eagerly awaited, mixing truth and invention to create unforgettable epics. The wars in Capharnaum provide plentiful material for these wordsmiths, and most people have heard tell of the Holy Crusade, even if the events they hear about may differ widely.

### Figurative Art

Painting is the most developed art in the Quarterian Kingdoms, and many painters create immortal works. Popular themes include war (usually illustrating the victories of one hero or another), religion ("Jason breaking his bonds" is a perennial classic), and portraits of the rich and powerful. Several schools may coexist, depending on regional preferences, but generally you can easily differentiate between the styles of Orkadian portrait painters, Occidentian iconographers, and the Aragonian narrativists who try to immortalise the great events of their time. King Simeon IV took with him to Jazirat ten painters charged with immortalising his victories.

### Food

Quarterian food varies from kingdom to kingdom and based on the foodstuffs available, as well as the wealth of the individual. Ex-cept for periods of famine or want, dishes are rich and varied, and people eat well, even down to the serfs of Occidentia.

The staple foodstuff is wheat bread for commoners and white bread for the nobility, to which are added cheese, roots, fruit, and vegetables such as cabbage, turnip, carrot, chestnut, beans, and peas. Cooking is in olive oil, lard, or suet, and dishes are pleasantly seasoned with cloves, ginger, or aromatic herbs. Meat, fowl, and fish of all kinds are served, sometimes in the form of pies and patés.

The Quarterian Church imposes fast days where meat and animal fats may not be eaten.

### Leisure

Quarterians, whether townsfolk or countryfolk, enjoy ball, board, and card games. They play them during their rest time or at the various festivals which punctuate the yearly calendar. Whether village fete, carnival, or religious festival, these celebrations feature minstrels, bards, and acrobats. Quarterian nobles are fond of tourneys and jousts of all kinds. They enjoy hunting on their lands, either for game or sometimes rarer or even more dangerous beasts. They also celebrate many court festivals, where friendships are made and enmities cemented, and where treaties and alliances are sealed.

## Religious Practices

The precepts of the Quarterian religion and the worship it entails vary in intensity and piety from kingdom to kingdom. Occidentia is the most devout.

The Quarterian religion worships the **Holy Trinity**.

**Aether** is the Almighty God, the Creator of the World. He is associated with the sun.

**Mira** is his wife, and represents peace and love, although she is more than capable of waging war on their behalf. She is associated with the moon.

**Jason Quartered** is their child, he who revealed Aether to the world. He is associated with the earth in its most noble aspect—the Pure Earth.

**The Quarterian Church** is very hierarchical. At the top comes the **Quarterian Magister**, the representative of Aether on Earth.

Next come the **Cardinals**, high dignitaries who serve in the Magisterial Palace, helping the Magister with specific duties (finance, quashing heresy, etc), and various diplomatic and other missions. The **Bishops** come next, who preside over broad geographic regions of a kingdom known as **dioceses** (or **bishoprics** in Orkadia), from their seat in a cathedral in the diocese's main city. The Bishops of Jarvsberg (the Orkadian capital), Valladon (the Aragonian capital), and Theodonis (the Occidentian capital) also represent their respective kingdoms and sometimes report to the Quarterian Magister, in addition to the Cardinals. Also called Archbishops, these three individuals are above the Bishops of other dioceses, but are outranked by the Cardinals.

---

## Quarterian Greetings

*There are no common rules for greeting in the Quarterian Kingdoms, although most people avoid physical contact. In Aragon, men greet others by placing their hand on their heart and moving their arm outwards, palm raised in the sign of peace, to show they're unarmed. Women make a slight bow with the head. A man may also hug a parent, ally, or other person he wants to honour, holding them to his heart in a sign of great esteem.*

*Occidentian men make a pronounced bow of the head, while women make a simple nod. Everyone who isn't a noble must bow their head to nobles. If the noble is high-ranking, you keep your head bowed until the noble gives you permission to raise it again, or until he starts talking or leaves. Before a prince of the royal blood or a king or queen, you must prostrate yourself. Commoners may not even raise their eyes to look at the king without his permission. Nobles are exempt from prostration, but should still adopt an attitude of humility and submission.*

*Orkadian greetings are much less formal. Most people greet one another with a head or hand gesture. Before the Emperor, however, you must stop whatever you're doing, lower your eyes and let your arms fall to your sides, until he is more than ten steps away.*

The dioceses are themselves divided into **parishes**, under the control of a **Father Superior** who has his own church, usually in the largest town. A parish may be divided into **chapelries**, which may in turn be controlled by delegated Fathers Superior or lesser priests such as rural **curates**.

Finally, the local population sometimes assists the Church in its work. The **Children of Aether** help with ceremonies, and **deacons** (who may or may not be members of the clergy) may also be used as secretaries and delegated the management of more mundane affairs.

A Quarterian **church** takes the form of the letter "Y", with each of the three branches representing one god of the Holy Trinity, the main branch being attributed to Jason.

The typical Quarterian is pious. He recites several prayers every day, before meals, or to gain specific favour. A mass is said once a week, every Dies Dominicus, as well as on holy days and during ceremonies dedicated to events such as birth, marriage, death, and so on.

After death, Quarterians believe they will go to **Eden** or **Limbo**. Everyone is concerned to avoid sin, even the most trivial, so as to avoid falling into Limbo. Happily, for those who are unable to adhere fully to the precepts of the Quarterian Magister, the Voice of Aether on Earth (which pretty much means everyone at one time or another in their lives…), there exists an elaborate system of confession and redemption by which the Church can cleanse the individual of sin. Economically the system works very well, and nobles and the middle classes alike make substantial endowments to the Church, particularly as clerics and holy scriptures go to great pains to describe in considerable detail the fate which awaits the recalcitrant sinner. Austere, hierarchical, and implacable, a place of fire, flame, and sulphur, populated by devils, Limbo comprises nine Circles where souls will suffer fates specifically adapted to their sins for all eternity. At the centre of Limbo stands the city of Dis, where reigns the Great Devil himself.

Opposing Limbo, the purest of souls may enter Eden, where they will spend eternity in a heavenly garden of perfect beauty, blessed by the most holy Aether, Mira, and Jason Quartered from their palace of crystal.

# The Aragonians

## History

The Aragonians are cattle breeders and artists, knights and sailors; most inhabitants of this wide dry land of ancient mountains usually combine two vocations. It isn't rare for a sailor to be a musician, a painter or poet to be a valiant duellist, a master farmer to be a fierce reserve captain or even a *hidalgo*.

They have always been this way. Proud, fierce, incapable of founding a homogeneous realm. With strong connections to Occidentia because of its people's piety and common religion, the Aragonian federation of kingdoms is more Quarterian than Western, more believer than pious, more influenced by the South and the East, by the sun and the sea, than by the politics of the countries that make it up. Aragon is a jewel of fire and passion, a hot-blooded barefoot dancing girl, a strong, spicy wine, a campeador with a quick sword.

## Organisation

There isn't really any such thing as an Aragonian kingdom. It's always been divided into nine lands, each with its own "king", with his own laws, named for its main city. The northern part, called La Mancha, comprises six of these lands, while the south, Gitanilla (today known as Al-Ragon), comprises three. One of the nine lands, Valladon, dominates all the others, and their kings owe allegiance to its ruler. The King of Valladon is the King of Aragon. Even if it might differ on paper, it's always been that king who has ruled Aragon and represented the country to the sovereigns of other realms.

## Society

Aragon is as feudal and as Quarterian as it's possible to be. Divided into kingdoms, then provinces, then dukedoms and parishes, it's a land of countless princes, dukes, counts, and knights. The nobility stands at the top of the pile, but even it is split into two: the **hidalgos** and the **campeadores**. The hidalgos are courtly nobles, used to life in castles and cities, gifted in the arts of war and social intrigue. The campeadores are nicknamed "peasant princes" by the court nobles, and are often ennobled workers; whether they're a first generation campeador or whether the title goes back to his ancestors, these nobles love their fields and the hills where the horses they breed roam free. In battle the campeador proudly invokes his god, his king, and his blood, before throwing himself body and soul into the fray.

Below the Aragonian nobility come the commoners: workers and craftsmen, whose world is summarised in three words: Aether, Aragon and *Familia*.

## To the North, La Mancha

Taking up two thirds of Aragonian territory, La Mancha is a succession of fertile valleys, desert plateaus, and hills where horses, pigs and goats are herded unpenned. Olive trees and date palms stretch as far as the eye can see, dotted with occasional villages always announced by the tolling of bells. Sometimes the walls of a majestic city rise above the plain.

Valladon is capital of the kingdom and seat of the Aragonian Council. The kings of Aragon have ruled from here since well before the adoption of the Quarterian faith.

Pamblosa, further north, specialises in crafts and trade. Famous for its merchant fleet, it's one of the main economic centres of the West.

Candruz and Sarajon, at the heart of Aragon, are highland cities. They are mostly farming and cattle breeding centres, although Sarajon is also a university city par excellence. They are the last Quarterian bastions before the lands conquered by the Saabi.

Grande Puerto and Barcajoyosa are Aragon's two military harbours, situated in the northeast and southwest of the country.

## To the South, Al-Ragon

Two years ago, in the year 553AJ (5995 of the Jazirati calendar), in several short weeks, three of Aragon's provinces fell to invading Jazirati fighting for the return of the stolen Sword of Hammad. Even though Aragon is a disunited land, and even though many of its warriors were away fighting in Capharnaum at the time, how was it possible for a few thousand soldiers to overthrow and conquer the entire south of the country?

Contrary to popular belief, the Jazirati didn't only arrive in Aragon in 553AJ. They were here well before: maybe, in a sense, they've always been here. The proximity of the south of Aragon to the northern coasts of Al-Fariq'n, the presence of Jazirati in those lands, the trade ties, cultural exchange, and natural cosmopolitanism of the peoples of the sun, had long led to contacts and mixing between Aragonians and the Ungarans of Al-Fariq'n. It's for that reason that the south of Aragon, with its mix of western and eastern culture, of urban sedentarism and caravan nomadism, has been long called *Gitanilla*, "the land of the walkers".

Today, Olvidad, Gamiz, and Sedunya, the three cities of the south, are under the rule of King Jalal Ibn Khalil Abd-al-Salif (page 287). It was he who twisted the name of his conquered land to give it a Jazirati ring, he who is now King of Al-Ragon, bastion of Kh'saaba.

The situation in Al-Ragon isn't easy. Confined to these lands, the conquering army is recovering its forces before advancing north on their quest for the sacred Sword of Hammad. But already there's talk of softness and complacency among some warlords, of getting bogged down in the decadent rule of Al-Ragoni vassal cities.

The native Aragonians who remained in the conquered lands are confined to their villages or within city walls. Jazirati garrisons are ubiquitous and vigilant, keeping the Aragonians in place and working to enrich their conquerors further. Essentially slaves, they're generally well-treated and rarely try to escape, holding on in the hope that they'll be liberated by the king. Aragonian troops regularly attempt to break through in the north of Al-Ragon, provoking scuffles and regional campaigns, but the situation has hardly changed in half a year.

## Personalities of the Aragonians

### Don Fernando Andunya de Valladon y Aragon, "el Rey Campeador", the Peasant King

The aging King Don Fernando has always been a man of action. He spent his life in the military in the West as in the East, and was known in Kh'saaba long before Simeon IV's attack. Close to the King of Kh'saaba for many years, it took a great deal of persuading to get Don Fernando Andunya de Valladon y Aragon to agree to send troops and ships to Capharnaum. Both the King and his advisers long maintained that the Capharnian War was useless and stupid, even threatening to block the path of the departing Quarterians. Of all Simeon's arguments, one was decisive: that the Jazirati and Shiradim were enemies of Aether, the One True God, and had let his son, Jason, die. They were without souls, and Aether demanded, if not their extermination, then that at least that the city of the Son of God should be liberated. In the face of this argument, the Quarterian Magister decided in favour of Occidentia, and Aragon was forced to decide between joining the campaign or being convicted of heresy. Reluctantly, Don Fernando, the adventurer king who had been raised as a peasant and had won his throne through bravery and wisdom, had to wage his first unjust war.

Today, torn between his friendship for the Jazirati and the need to recover Al-Ragon, Don Fernando dies a little every day, just as much from the wounds in his soul as those the battles of Candruz and Sarajon have left in his flesh.

### Jalal Ibn Khalil Abd-al-Salif

The new king of southern Aragon, Jalal Ibn Khalil is a terrifying warrior and bloodthirsty lord. He knows no other justice than that of Hubal and, despite what Jazirati scholars may say, for him the Quarterians are nothing but worthless and degenerate Shiradim. If Jalal didn't have to obey the King of Kh'saaba, he would have already sallied forth from Al-Ragon and seized the north of Aragon, before razing Occidentia. Now, before he can do all that, he'll have to split with Kh'saaba and proclaim the independence of his Kingdom of Al-Ragon. But how many mujahidin would follow him?

Jalal is no soft nobleman, raised in the luxurious gardens of Jergath the Great. No—he's a man of the desert, a killer of the sands, a beast of war who only lives only for the love of the gods and the greatness of his people. If the Al-Ragoni rulers around him are nodding off on their thrones, overcome by decadence, Jalal has no intention of giving in to the temptations of Olvidad.

# The Occidentians

## History

The Occidentians are cattle breeders, farmers, and soldiers. Their society was born in blood, from the violent union of many tribes which had once been divided into smaller kingdoms.

It's said that Aether created Occidentia as a heaven on earth, its land is so hospitable. The temperate climate has allowed farming to flourish; the forests are filled with game, the rivers rich in fish.

Occidentia's eventful past is everywhere in the landscape, in the form of fortifications dotting its territory. Its population is distributed more or less evenly throughout the countryside; even its largest cities house no more than 25000 inhabitants.

Today the Kingdom of Occidentia is united under the rule of King Simeon, fourth of that name, who is currently riding a wave of popularity since his return from Jazirat bearing the *Calva Mirabilis Reliquiae*. The king relies on the nobility and the Quarterian Church to run his kingdom; each lord is entrusted with a territory he can enjoy, on the condition that he pays an agreed sum to the crown each year. He rules his domain and owes the king military assistance when requested. The king can theoretically confiscate all or part of any domain in his gift, but doing so would be risky

## The Knights Quixotic

*Alonso Quisada, a rich commoner who loved tales of romance, adventure and chivalry, always dreamed of being a knight. However, his blood and upbringing allowed him to only aspire to the position of post-rider. Eventually he was put in charge of a post-route himself, and finally he became the rich overseer of a post-route and money-changing centre. Throughout all this, El Señor Alonso Quisada never lost his love of dressing up like a knight, and would ride out on a lame and emaciated mule while wearing old and rusty armour.*

*Everyone laughed at him. Then the Jazirati invaded, and Alonso Quisada decided his time had come. He adopted a knightly name (a fake one, of course—it's said he asked an innkeeper to dub him), and used his money to arm one thousand peasants. Even though some considered it only a minor military victory, Quisada nevertheless managed to lead his "forces" to retake the city of Sarajon from the Jazirati, preventing them from gaining a symbolic toehold in La Mancha.*

*Thereafter, the one they called "El Quijote" had a seat on the Sarajon military council. A whimsical and dreamy knight, he—somehow!—founded a knightly order based on the virtues of the heart and the imagination. His followers, ignored at best but more often despised by the nobility, are ragtag knights who hail from the common folk of the fields, taverns, and two-penny theatres of the land.*

*Recently Don Quijote died of old age in his sleep. His order has been officially disbanded, but unofficially people are saying that the Knights Quixotic have become Knights Errant, fighting for widows and orphans, sometimes allying to make common cause against the Jazirati invader.*

(although it didn't stop Simeon IV from doing so via the intermediary of his son during the Holy Crusade).

Scholars of the Church are in charge of all the administration outside the cities; the royal bureaucracy only handles the kingdom's most important cities and towns.

## Organisation

Of all the Quarterian Kingdoms, Occidentia is the only one to perpetuate slavery in the form of serfdom. Although they aren't strictly speaking property, **serfs** are attached to a domain and are forbidden from leaving it, and must work for the lord who owns that domain. They don't own the lands they farm, and give all the harvest to the lord. In return, the lord assures their subsistence and must protect them. Serfs may only marry with their lord's permission; it's then he who determines where they'll live.

The serfs occupy the bottom rung of the social ladder. Above them come the **peasants**—free folk who either own their own land or simply rent it. Their lives are often little better than those of serfs, but they're free to come and go as they please, and profit from their labour while paying taxes. The most common inhabitant of a town or city is a **free man** who can come and go at will, but who is still under the thumb of some uncaring boss. **Craftsmen** are better off, especially those with recognised skills. Below the nobility (often called the lords) come the **bourgeoisie**, a vast middle class incorporating merchants, bankers, and even wealthy peasants who have accumulated land and wealth and now have other peasants working for them.

## A Country Blessed by Aether

Occidentia is an enormous kingdom, well protected to the south by a mountain range with well-known passes usable except during winter, a natural border with its Aragonian neighbours. The northeast border with the Orkadian Empire follows watercourses (especially rivers) for more than half its length; the eastern part is marked by rough lands and a range of low mountains.

Occidentia's cities are little developed but relatively numerous, most housing between fifteen to thirty-five thousand souls. Many are fortified. The largest city is Theodonis, Occidentia's capital: once called Facavalle, it was rechristened in honour of Aether and of the conversion of the Occidentian kings to the new faith. It houses two hundred thousand citizens and most of the kingdom's institutions. The king resides here in autumn and winter, while he tours his kingdom in the spring and summer. Theodonis is a fortified city, its yellow stone walls proudly rising more than sixty feet above the ground. Built in extremely good arable country, it produces abundant foodstuffs and its population lacks for nothing. All these factors make it an attractive centre for many renowned artists and craftsmen.

Occidentia is also the location of the spiritual capital of the Quarterian Kingdoms: the Magisterium. Founded on the spot where the first disciples of Aether disembarked at the very start of the Quarterian religion, the city quickly established itself as the centre of the new faith. The Quarterian Magister dwells there in a palace resembling a city in its own right, with its own harbour, many places for prayer, barracks and monasteries. The Quarterian Church rules the city, even if a non-religious authority is supposed to ensure administration and legislation. No decision is made without the agreement of the Magister. A true state within a state, the Magisterium has an army appointed by the Church of one thousand devoted men, and counts about fifteen thousand clerics within the compound of the Magisterial Palace. A total of thirty-two thousand inhabitants live in the city. All Quarterian Kingdoms, including Occidentia, as well as many other lands, have one or more ambassadors in the Holy City.

## Military, Militia and Justice

Every Occidentian lord has the right to maintain an army to ensure the security of his lands; this is a founding principle of the whole kingdom. The king himself has an army, often made up of mercenary troops and often spread over his territory. The kingdom's lords owe financial assistance to the king by supplying troops at his request; most lords use mercenaries, who sometimes become robber bands when their payment fails to arrive.

Maintaining a militia is the responsibility of the lord of a given territory. He is duty bound to ensure the safety of his subjects and their property. The militia is entrusted to **provosts** who organise it according to the needs and means of the land and its people. The brutality of the Occidentian militia is legendary, as is its penchant for corruption. The Theodonis militia is managed the Provost Royal, a specialised corps of the royal army. It's the most effective militia in the kingdom, in particular against political crimes. The Quarterian Church is in charge of the Magisterium militia.

Ten years ago, Simeon IV established a system of common courts. Before then, local lords had been judges of all cases in their jurisdiction (or at least justice had been dispensed by judges who were subjects of those lords). Common justice applies to all crimes committed by non-noble individuals. Each common court (in general there's one common court in each large city, with a jurisdiction extending out to a radius of six to eight leagues) comprises one judge, appointed by the king, and a people's jury of eleven members, designated each year by the drawing of lots among all those men marrying that year. The judge proposes the sentence and submits it to the jury's vote. The defendant has the right to defend himself, either in person or through a third party he designates.

There is another form of justice: that of the Church. In Occidentia, the Quarterian Church has judicial power over all cases concerning religion, its assets, and its representatives. Justice is dispensed by three judges of the **Ordo Inquisitorum**, after interrogation by members of that order. The defendant may defend himself but may not be represented. The trial is never public. In the Magisterium, the Ordo Inquisitorum has full powers over militia and justice.

## Personalities of the Occidentians

### Simeon IV, the Proud

King of Occidentia, Simeon IV is a sturdy fellow of 55, large and well muscled. He has a shrewd analytical mind, capable of calmly planning ahead and undertaking actions whose goals will only appear months, even years down the line. He's a formidable negotiator and strategist, and has attracted the hatred of many Occidentian lords due to his rather disproportionate ego and desire to control absolutely everything. Some claim the king is not mentally sound, and his few attacks of paranoia would suggest they are right.

At the time, his departure on the Holy Crusade looked like madness. But that's to ignore the King's cunning. Not only did he secure the Quarterian Church's support by appointing himself its spokesman on the Jazirat campaign, he also managed, with the collaboration of his son, to weaken his fiercest opponents. His masterly victory in Jazirat led Simeon to gain greater ground than even he had expected.

## Deogratus I, the Quarterian Magister

The Quarterian Magister, Deogratus I, has occupied this powerful position for fifteen years. A former sailor of the islands of the Inner Sea, Helias Mantes arrived at the Magisterium at the age of 20 to begin a highly profitable religious career. He became the Quarterian Magister at age 48, taking the name Deogratus I. Since then, he has ruled the Quarterian clergy and all its faithful, an iron fist in a velvet glove.

Worn down by time, and a disease that gives him a pronounced limp, this gaunt and best figure slowly walks the corridors of the Magisterial Palace, his face wrinkled, his hair sparse and white. He almost never leaves. But this initial impression of weakness is quickly dispelled when you meet him: his is a sky-blue stare with sharp and penetrating eyes, a quick and acerbic wit, a rare intelligence and culture. The Quarterian Magister is not the kind of man to be led by others.

Deogratus hates Simeon IV, but his hatred seems to predate his ascension as Quarterian Magister. He greatly mistrusts the king. Sure of the legitimacy of the Holy Crusade, he was surprised to see the Occidentian king embrace the cause so enthusiastically, while Aragon, which he had taken for a solid ally, joined only reluctantly. Recently, Deogratus sent one of his most trusted advisors to assure Don Fernando, the Aragonian king, of the righteousness of the war waged against the unbelievers, in an attempt to strengthen their strained relations—a strain which can't help but please Simeon IV immensely.

# The Orkadians

## History

The Orkadian Empire was forged by one man, Mandernick, who two centuries ago unified the Ten Kingdoms against the last Agalanthian threat. All the kingdoms of Orkadia shared a common culture and language, which made it easier to unite them under a single flag. Mandernick, King of Jarvsberg, became the first Orkadian Emperor.

Not only was Mandernick a gifted diplomat, he was also brilliantly cunning, and dedicated to ensuring his empire's unity. He created the first bodies of imperial bureaucrats and administrators in charge of the relations with the nine other kings of the Empire. These became the foundation of Mandernick's power; in a few short years, none of the kingdoms could do without their management and accounting skills. Trade with other lands followed, including the Agalanthians, leading to rapid economic development and the beginning of an imperial golden age. The Orkadian Empire expanded, retaking lands the Agalanthians had conquered to the east, and repelling Occidentian troops beyond the Black River to the west.

Mandernick's reign lasted 27 years. Upon his death, the ten Orkadian kings voted that his son should became Emperor, under the name Olaf I. Olaf continued his father's work, and also approached the Quarterian Church, recognising it as the Empire's official religion a little before his death.

Years passed. Today, the Empire has become riven by internal struggles and disagreements between the Ten Kingdoms. For the moment, no one openly questions the power of the current emperor, Jorg the Loyal. He is a wise ruler, who has managed the delicate relationship between the Ten Kingdoms while maintaining flourishing trade with the Empire's neighbours. The threat of invasion has long passed and, in this period of peace, people are growing restless and independence movements are gaining ground—all to the great joy of the Empire's Occidentian neighbour.

## Organisation

Orkadian society is based on a caste system. At the bottom come the **peasants**, rank and file soldiers, employees and labourers, the majority of the Orkadian people. There is no slavery in the Empire, and its people are free to come and go as they please. The peasants are not officially tied to the land which they farm (often for noblemen or rich landowners), but people rarely leave the house where they, their father, and their father's father have grown up. Above the peasants come the **burghers** and **small landowners** who may possess substantial assets and even servants. Some are very rich, and are received with honours among the upper classes of Orkadian society.

The **upper classes** are nobles, military officers, and members of the clergy. The higher you are in this hierarchy, the less you consider other nobles as your equals. Officers of the Orkadian military enjoy great prestige, even if their strategic and tactical skills haven't been tested in years.

At the top of Orkadian society come the kings and princes of the blood. There are ten kings ruling the Empire's royal provinces; one of these is elected by his peers as Emperor. As a result, the position of Emperor is not in principle hereditary (although the rule is that it should always pass to members of the royal bloodlines). However, since the founding of the Empire, the electors have always chosen a direct descendant of Mandernick (and thus the King of Jarvsberg) as Emperor.

The Emperor is above everyone. You can only address him if you're invited to do so, and you're not even permitted to look at him unless you belong to the upper classes.

Orkadians are sometimes considered boorish and uneducated, even barbaric, by the other Quarterians, due to their rather crude customs, their immoderate preference for two-handed weapons, and their propensity to get drunk at the slightest opportunity. However, they prefer trade over war, even if they preserve certain ancestral rites of great violence. An example is the Rite of Passage which every Orkadian must undergo to be considered an adult, in which they must survive three days and nights alone in a forest at the winter solstice, armed with only a dagger. Anyone returning before the third day is considered shameful good-for-nothing and must leave their village. Naturally, the townsfolk of Orkadia see these rites as a confirmation of the backwardness of their rural brethren.

The Church, although officially the state religion, occupies a less dominant position in Orkadia than in the other Quarterian Kingdoms. Its advisors are listened to but not always heeded, and most Orkadians are loath to accept all the Church's rites. Orkadian churches are often half-empty.

## A Harsh Land

While Occidentia benefits from a pleasant climate and geography, Orkadia prides itself on prospering under often harsh conditions. For most of its territory the climate is continental, milder to the south and cold in the north. Snow covers three quarters of the country from the start of winter; only the south, along the Sea of Gorgons, is spared, continuing to supply food through to November.

The western reaches of Orkadia are in contact with Occidentia across the Black River. The coast of the Sea of Gorgons hosts the Empire's largest harbour at Russo, a city of 30,000 inhabitants, allowing trade with the south and, in particular, year-long fishing when the northern seas freeze over and pack ice makes sailing extremely dangerous. To the east, the Empire's frontier is marked by rough, hilly terrain. A long line of defensive structures remains here from the time of the Agalanthian wars, not always well-maintained these days.

The heartlands of Orkadia and its coastal areas comprise well-watered plains and occasional rolling hills, and are home to four-fifths of the Orkadian population. The north is drier, the terrain rougher, with two great expanses of unpopulated marshland where fabulous creatures can still be found.

Orkadian cities are fortified and built on important commercial routes. Kings maintain one or two strongholds capable of stopping an enemy's advance, or at least withstanding a siege. City populations vary between 5000 and 20000 inhabitants, with numerous villages scattered throughout the country. The largest city is Jarvsberg, the current capital of the Empire. It has grown over the past two centuries, and now has a population of 120,000 inhabitants, the cause of not only logistical but also health and sanitation concerns.

## Army, Militia and Justice

The Orkadian Empire is a federal empire, meaning it's made up of states enjoying a certain degree of autonomy, seen in their government, armed forces, militia, and systems of justice.

The Orkadian army is famous for its heavy infantry and cavalry. Its soldiers are proud, and have a tendency to feel invulnerable, despite the fact that they're outdone in both number and quality by the armed forces of Occidentia. Orkadian officers prefer aggressive actions, often ignoring the risks they run when faced with mobile, well-armed opponents.

The Empire's army comprises regiments from several kingdoms, stationed in the most exposed regions. The Emperor has his own armed forces he can deploy in problematic areas to ensure the safety of his lands and people. Each king maintains his own army, in addition to the regiments he provides to the Emperor; however, it may not exceed in size more than one third that of the total imperial army. Usually, the Empire stations troops supplied by one kingdom on the lands of another.

The militia is provided by the Imperial Army. Most often, it comprises soldiers hired by the provincial prefects, officials appointed by the central imperial government. This makes the militia an imperial institution, reporting to the central hierarchy. Nevertheless, militia operations may only be initiated by the king presiding over the region in which they operate; for example, the Emperor may always request for a local noble to be detained or incarcerated by the militia, but the actual decision rests with the local king. As a result, if the common people are protected from the intrigues of the royal courts, the same cannot be said for the nobility (which, when all's said and done, seems to work in the favour of the people). In the most difficult cases, the regional prefect may ask for help from the Imperial Army.

Justice is dispensed through the royal courts; only crimes affecting a royal family or the security of the Empire are judged in the Imperial Court. Judges are appointed and paid for by the kings of the Ten Kingdoms. Punishments are broadly the same across the Empire, but kingdoms may have local laws and differing degrees of permissiveness. The Kingdom of Eckland sentences all poachers to death, whereas they're sentenced only to a few lashes of the whip and the chopping off of the left hand in the other kingdoms. There are no religious courts, and any case regarding the Church is tried in the usual courts.

The Ten Kingdoms of the Orkadian Empire bear the names of the cities where their royal courts sit. They are:

- ❖ Russo, a trading port on the Sea of Gorgons;
- ❖ Jarvsberg, capital of the empire;
- ❖ Eckland, a city in the middle of a magical forest;
- ❖ Albowmnir and Ravenshill, on the shores of the Northern Sea;
- ❖ Neggenstadt, a mountainous kingdom of Northmen;
- ❖ Lothringen, a farming kingdom, breadbasket of the Empire;
- ❖ Gerdenheim, kingdom of a thousand fortresses, founded by Saint Gerda and a part of the Agalanthian border;
- ❖ Grunwald, close by the Krek'kaos;
- ❖ Elwensberg, kingdom of fishermen, on a rock in the violent Northern Sea.

## Personalities of the Orkadians

### Jorg the Loyal, Emperor of Orkadia

Emperor for eight years, Jorg has forged for himself a reputation as a formidable speaker and diplomat, the equal of Mandernick himself. He has kept the Empire together, despite the many disagreements between his royal subjects. His people consider him a good emperor who cares for the weakest among them.

Jorg doesn't trust the Quarterian Church. He wasn't especially prompt with his support of the Holy Crusade, a tardiness which earned him more than one interview with the envoys of the Quarterian Magister. In the end he sent barely four hundred horsemen and as many footsoldiers, paying for their travel to Jazirat.

Nor is Jorg fooled about the intentions of Simeon IV, his bellicose neighbour. His spies report Simeon is fomenting rebellions in the Orkadian kingdoms bordering Occidentia, and Jorg knows the Occidentian army is well-trained and combat-hardened. He also knows he won't get any support from the Quarterian Magister.

Recently widowed, Jorg has turned to the old enemies of the Empire, the Agalanthians, in the hope of forming an alliance that will strengthen Orkadia. Some months ago, his emissaries approached Gracus, Strategos of Therema, whose daughter Naia is now 15 years old and has thus reached marriageable age. The Strategos has approved the union, and soon Jorg is scheduled to make the journey to Therema to meet his young bride.

Jorg is 51 years old, tall, well-proportioned, and attractive. His blond mane reveals greying temples, giving him the appearance of the wisdom of age. He's athletic, a good swordsman, and an excellent horseman. Intelligent and stubborn, he knows how to guard against his enemies and accommodate his allies.

### Edrick Von Mahlersberg, King of Lothringen

Young king Edrick came to the throne five years ago, at the tender age of 17. He quickly displayed the requisite talents for rule by repudiating the regent and then his father's ministers, concentrating power in his hands and only delegating ministries to those he could absolutely trust. Impetuous, enterprising, and ambitious, Edrick is a cause for concern for his neighbours, who worry he'll get carried away and make precipitate decisions.

Lothringen is the closest kingdom to Occidentia, and Edrick maintains good relations with his neighbours. Simeon IV himself came to Lothringen for Edrick's coronation. The Emperor Jorg mistrusts Edrick, assured by his spies that the King of Lothringen openly criticises the Emperor and his handling of affairs of state. The Emperor is convinced Edrick will treacherously ally with Occidentia should war break out between the two realms. In an attempt to muzzle his turbulent vassal, Jorg has placed a garrison of his most loyal troops at Lothringen.

Edrick is a young man whose intense, even violent temperament is expressed in the way he lives, moves, and speaks. He tolerates no opposition. Physically he's rather average, but has a certain charisma, and knows how to inspire his troops. He's very attracted to women, which the Emperor's spies take advantage of.

### Roderick Von Altwald, Archbishop of Jarvsberg

Archbishop Roderick has held the position of Quarterian ambassador to Jarvsberg for ten years. He knows the Emperor well, in addition to the Orkadian kings and the workings of the Empire's politics and diplomacy. He also knows it's impossible to bully an Orkadian, and so found himself in a difficult position during the Holy Crusade when the Emperor's opposition made itself felt. He finally obtained at least a token participation from Jorg, which nevertheless failed to satisfy the Quarterian Magister. Even so, the

Orkadian contingent to the Holy Crusade was bigger than that of Aragon, a thing Roderick has often remarked upon.

Roderick wishes that Orkadia would embrace the Quarterian faith more fully, and take a greater role in spreading the religion throughout the world. He takes things slowly, though, so as not to hurt people's sensitivities. Slow and sensitive isn't the style of the Magisterium, these days, though, and there are rumours that Roderick will shortly be replaced.

Roderick is a small, thin man of about sixty, his face ravaged by smallpox, and with few hairs remaining. His voice has a strange, spellbinding quality, and he knows how to put it to good use.

# – Part Three –
# Al-Rawi's Guide to Capharnaum

# CHAPTER EIGHT
# ERATO – THE MYSTERIOUS WORLD

## At the Heart of the Riddle

Ill at ease on his abzul, Luther felt dwarfed by the vastness of the desert. Despair filled his soul, took his breath away.

They had lost everything at Qasr Jibreen. Their crew, butchered by the Sheikh's men. Their horses, gone. Now they rode these giant lizards that stubbornly ignored their commands. Fortunately, three of the imposing beasts had been waiting in the courtyard, saddled and ready to go, when Thufir and Luther had jumped from the great hall, a three-storey fall cushioned by awnings protecting the ground from the sun. Luther had leapt to his feet like an expert, but Thufir's ankle was sprained. While the Jazirati had struggled painfully into the saddle of the beast at the front, the Orkadian freed the last one and slapped and kicked it until it had lashed out and had begun attacking everything around. Then he'd mounted the last of the three, and quickly followed his companion through the tunnel leading to the outside. Passing beneath the portcullis and murder holes, he'd taken an arrow in the shoulder and his mount had taken three. The beast barely seemed to notice, protected by its scales, while Luther had bled copiously, and was now in agony.

The pursuit broke off quickly. When Luther saw them disappear, he knew what they were thinking. "The two foreigners don't stand a chance. They'll die in the desert."

At first, they were hopeful. The abzulim were harnessed for travel, with full saddlebags and waterskins. But the reserves disappeared quickly under the merciless sun. For two days they rode north, looking for signs, for the landmarks described in his grandfather's runes. How could Luther even believe this nonsense? Hah! If he ever found the joker who'd engraved those words, copying the old legends, he'd have him roasted on a spit and eat him with a good, cold Aragonian wine!

He knew it was the delirium talking, that the heat was fogging their minds. His companion was nodding off sixty feet behind him. But behind him... what was that whirlwind that had been following them for several leagues? Why was it getting closer?

Why had it just swallowed Thufir?

"No!" the knight shouted, throwing himself from his abzul and drawing his scimitar. He charged to his friend's defence. But other whirlwinds converged, and Luther stumbled. His head smashed against a rock.

When Luther awoke, he was alone in the desert. His mouth was puffy, his eyes swollen closed. He rose painfully, leaning on his weapon for support. His friend was gone. And his mount, all their provisions and water. So this was it. Death by thirst and the killing sun.

Unless... Down there... Was that a city shimmering on the horizon. He stumbled towards it.

A shape shimmered out of the desert haze. Someone was approaching. An emissary from the mysterious city?

"Who are you?" the man from the desert asked.

"Luther Magnusson," Luther gasped, through parched lips. "Knight of Grunwald, seventh walker of the North."

"Welcome, stranger. You're not the first to claim such titles."

"My grandfather? Ingmar Bjornson was here? Aether be praised!"

"No. We killed your grandfather on his ship, not in the desert."

Luther's blood boiled. In a second, he charged at his ancestor's murderer. Against all his expectations, the man lofted gracefully into the air, and Luther saw he had no legs, but floated on coils of uncanny smoke.

*"You're no man! You're a demon! Heretic! Murderer!"*

*"Your anger is... understandable. But your grandfather summoned us. He begged to be submitted to the question. When he he didn't know the answer, we had no choice but to sink his ship. I suppose you've come for the same reason?"*

*"Where's my companion?"*

*"With one of my brothers. Having the same conversation as we are. Stranger, will you submit yourself to the question? If you answer correctly, I will let you pass. If you do not, the desert will be your tomb."*

*Luther looked around at the endless sands. What choice did he have? He would honour the memory of his ancestor. He nodded.*

*"So. My question is simple, and you have until sunset to answer. What is your name, you who were the last but one to answer us correctly?"*

# THE DJINN, SPIRITS OF THE DESERT

Born from the agony of Tiamat, the Goddess of the Primordial Ocean slain by Marduk, the dragon who became a god, the djinn are demons to some, divine beings to others. All agree that they are unpredictable spirits, sometimes cruel, sometimes benevolent, who must be treated with respect and fear.

Although each people has its own understanding of the djinn, no-one doubts their magical nature—a fact of which these capricious desert tricksters never fail to take advantage...

## On the Origin of the Djinn

### In the Beginning

The Jazirati are the only people to fully integrate the djinn into their myths. Other peoples identify them with other beings from their own tales.

According to legend, when the young gods fought the old, Tiamat, Goddess of the Primordial Ocean, created a horde of bloodthirsty monsters to defend herself. She threw these at Marduk and his warriors. These monsters were the very first djinn. They were powerful, but devoid of intelligence, created to spread chaos and destroy life. In spite of their attacks, Marduk, son of Enki, defeated Tiamat and plunged his spear into her heart. The goddess fell, but her death agony lasted several days, during which her mind birthed a new generation of djinn. This second generation were very different from their elders. Drawing on the life energies leaking from Tiamat's dying body, they received strength, intelligence, maliciousness, and power, depending upon which of the goddess' thoughts were giving them birth. With a keen awareness of their identity and a limitless lust for life, they spread throughout the world to satisfy their curiosity. None of them understood that their very origins made them the immediate and natural enemies of the One Thousand and One Gods ruled by Hubal.

## The Hunt For the Djinn

During his war against Tiamat, Marduk annihilated almost all of the first generation of djinn, although some hid when they saw their mother laid low by the god's blows. Many of Marduk's friends had fallen victim to these monsters, and the god had developed a boundless hatred towards the offspring of the old goddess. Thus, when he saw Tiamat giving birth to thousands of new children during her death-throes, Marduk took up arms to track them down and eliminate them from the face of the earth.

At first his task was easy. The new-born djinn were ignorant of their enmity, even innocent, and Marduk slew a thousand with no resistance. But the children of Tiamat soon understood the danger, and decided to protect themselves. While some formed an army to fight the vengeful god, others sought shelter, a place to escape Marduk's wrath.

It was a djinn called Fals who discovered how to enter the **mirages**—those phantasmal worlds which exist alongside our own and that were born from the dreams of the god Apsu. Some scholars think that djinn and mirages have a similar origin, which would explain Fals' discovery and the djinn's undoubted affinity for these mysterious realms. Fals sacrificed his freedom to become a portal to the mirages, and the exodus of the djinn began. In the meantime, the army led by the djinn Jad Rabb al-Bakht held Marduk at bay; but the wrathful god was invincible, and massacred the djinn

arrayed against him. In desperation, Jad threw down his weapons and asked the god, eyes filled with tears, what justified such butchery. Marduk was speechless: he had thought the djinn soulless monsters, but here was one grieving for the death of his people! The god realised his mistake and his madness. Weeping, too, he invited Jad to parley.

## The Great Truce

Jad and Marduk parleyed for days. Eventually they reached an agreement.

According to the terms of what became known as the Great Truce, the gods recognised the djinn's right to exist in total liberty within the magical worlds of the mirages, and granted them a more limited freedom even in the mortal world. The djinn could travel to the mortal world, but would have to follow certain rules limiting their actions. Finally, the Great Truce stipulated that the djinn may never intervene directly in human history. They might guide, inspire, and mentor exceptional mortals, but acting directly to affect the flow of events was forbidden to them.

In exchange, the djinn were promised a place in Hubal's court, for those of their number who behaved and gained the respect of humanity. Jad Rabb al-Bakht was named God of the Djinn, leader of his people and protector of humanity, while Fals became God of Fugitives and Guardian of Mirages. Many theologians today believe many Saabi gods were originally djinn.

# On the Nature of the Djinn

While it's hard to generalise about beings as protean as the djinn, they have a common nature and origin constraining them.

## The Afreeti—First-born of the Djinn

It's important to differentiate between the two generations of djinn. Although the second generation is made up of sensitive and intelligent minds, the first are monsters created by Tiamat who escaped destruction at Marduk's hands.

This first generation of djinn, known as **afreeti**, are creatures of little intelligence, moved only by malevolence and hunger. They're primitive beings that supposedly have no soul. They roam the world, killing everything in their path, until a hero slays them in turn. Few people even know these monsters are really djinn, so different are the two generations. Most importantly, the afreeti respect none of Marduk's rules.

The monsters born of Tiamat possess few supernatural powers. Nevertheless, their skin can be as hard as bronze, their fangs as sharp as steel, their muscles as powerful as the best Aragonian stallion. Their appearance often reflects their natures: they are chimer-

ic beings, monsters of myth and legend. Cruel minotaurs, swamp hydras, cannibal cyclopses, fierce harpies, three-headed wolves: all these are examples of the afreeti spawn of Tiamat.

## The Spirits of the Desert

The djinn that everyone knows about, the genies and spirits of the desert, are the second generation of Tiamat's spawn. They draw their life energy and nature from the body of their mother, their

---

## The Rules of the Great Truce

Most djinn prefer to live in **mirages** (page 298), leaving only out of interest or necessity. Some, though, prefer the mortal world, exploring it to satisfy their curiosity and thirst for contact. The gods laid down certain rules to ensure the djinn do not abuse their power over humans.

The first rule, breaking which would end the Great Truce, is the **Rule of Non-Interference**, an absolute ban on intervening in human history. No djinn may lead a mortal army, create a kingdom, or kill a rightful monarch. Actions such as these would affect the fate of the world and run counter to human free will, which the gods will not tolerate.

The second rule, which gives rise to the djinn's reputation for capriciousness, is the **Rule of Trials**. When a djinn interacts with a mortal, he may force him to submit to a trial, such as a riddle or physical test. The trial must be achievable—the djinn may not make impossible demands—and the djinn must grant any mortal succeeding in the trial a favour or service matching its difficulty. A simple riddle might be rewarded with a djinn answering a single question about the nature of the universe, while an epic fight against a legendary monster might end up with the djinn becoming the bonded servant of the victor for several months. These trials are the truth behind the legends of djinn granting the wishes of virtuous men and women. Note that the second rule may never contradict the first: a djinn serving a human may help that human win a war through his advice or protection, but may not lead his armies or fight in battles directly.

The third rule is the **Rule of Hospitality**. If a mortal enters the dwelling-place of a djinn—usually a shimmering mirage—the latter must provide him with food and lodging as long as the mortal respects his duties as a guest. Many djinn stretch this rule to its limits, imposing strict codes of conduct in their palaces, breaching which enables them to easily expel undesirable guests.

Jad Rabb al-Bakht, as God of the Djinn and Protector of Mortals, himself guarantees the Rules of the Great Truce.

---

souls forged from the confused death-agony thoughts of the goddess. They are complete beings, with body, mind, and soul. They are able to distinguish between good and evil (though they're somewhat more flexible about these concepts than mortals), and are aware of their place in the cosmic scheme. Magical creatures of divine essence, they have many natural magical powers.

A djinn's most common powers include polymorphism, the ability to create illusions, the power to read minds, and a limited aptitude to fashion reality. Some claim they can also possess the bodies of human beings; this belief is especially widespread among the Quarterians.

The appearance of djinn is extremely variable, and even an individual djinn will change its shape. Among mortals they often appear humanoid, like a chubby, jovial man or an attractive young woman with a veiled face; their distinguishing feature is their lack of legs, their lower body instead tapering away into a soft, moving mist. Indeed, it's a stipulation of the gods that the djinn aren't able to assume a fully human form. The more mischievous—or malevolent—djinn take on terrifying, nightmarish forms. Some appear as elemental beings, tornadoes of fire, sandstorms, refreshing rains, or even gentle breezes. Others may appear as animals, particularly desert creatures such as snakes, scorpions, and jackals, often of prodigious size.

## Djinn Society

The djinn do constitute a people, but they are a disunited one. Nevertheless, they do recognise a common leader—the god Jad Rabb al-Bakht—and a core of common laws. Their society is far from anything mortals have created.

The two most important djinn are Jad Rabb al-Bakht and Fals. Jad is God of the Djinn, the ruler of this people and its guarantor before the gods. This is why he is so strict regarding the Rules of the Great Truce: he remembers the battle against Marduk all too well, and nothing in the world would make him want to see the Truce broken. He is completely intransigent on this point, and does not hesitate to punish disobedient djinn in person. Jad dwells in a mirage reflecting the heavenly palace where he receives his most important vassals among the djinn.

Fals is Guardian of Mirages, and decides which of his peers may move between these marvellous realms. He can prevent any djinn from finding and entering mirages. His essence is imprisoned in the interstices between the mortal world and the world of mirages; this allows him to be present in all mirages at once, but also restricts his freedom: Fals is unable to travel to the Court of Heaven, and cannot even leave the desert.

Not all djinn are equal in power. The most powerful surround themselves with a court aping human habits, and gather their vassals in domains. This "djinn nobility" is recognised as such by Jad, but he demands that no djinn may possess such power without accepting the responsibilities that go with it. As a result, djinn society is organised like a kingdom, with a benevolent sovereign and his many vassals charged with maintaining the Rules of the Great Truce among their subjects.

Of course, there are some independent djinn who don't recognise any of this. They prefer to roam the desert, or retreat into secret mirages and have as little to do with their peers as possible. Jad Rabb al-Bakht tolerates these loners as long as they don't break any of the Rules of the Great Truce or otherwise attract the anger of the gods. Those who do break the rules are called **marids**, and are the outlaws of the djinn.

# MIRAGES

Legend says that bold travellers in the deep desert may sometimes glimpse ghostly, magical realms, the dwelling places of fabulous creatures such as djinn. Anyone who finds a **gateway** to such a realm is assured of great riches—but finding them is not easy. Many adventurers have perished wandering endlessly through Jazirat's burning deserts; gateways to these wondrous lands are rare, and lethal traps guard their entrances. These realms are called **mirages**.

## On the Nature of Mirages

Sages have long pondered the nature of mirages. What is their purpose? Are they real? Few know their nature: only the rare few who have entered a mirage and returned to tell the tale can provide credible reports, and unfortunately most of their written testimonies are hidden or have crumbled with time.

All we have are conjectures of dubious accuracy. Most of what we do know comes from legends. When Apsu, the primordial god, was slain in his sleep, he carried on dreaming, and his dreams became mirages. Legend does not say if Apsu ever truly realised he was dead.

Some sages say Apsu's dreams differ. Some are simple and inconsequential; others are strange, terrifying, and dangerous.

## On the Differences Between Mirages

It's difficult to categorise mirages. That said, legends seem to recount four broad types.

### Temporal Mirages

Rarest of all, temporal mirages may be visions of the past, or the future, or what the future might be. They can portray the past or future of a person, tribe, or people, but also of a place, unconnected to any other element. Gateways to temporal mirages of the future are sometimes easily found, as the gods seem to use them to send messages to mortals. Temporal images of the past sometimes show a very specific event, perhaps to reaffirm the truth, but sometimes perhaps to offer the possibility to right a wrong committed long ago. Often, though, temporal images of the past are little more than nostalgic visions of a bygone time.

### Chaos Mirages

These mirages are the most unsettling, and one looks for meaning in them in vain. Entering a chaos mirage can be extremely dangerous, as there is no way to know what you may encounter or what the environment may be. Sometimes, though, such a mirage may provide a traveller with a pleasant, if incomprehensible, stay. It's not unknown for chaos mirages to drive travellers insane, as they try to find their way out of nightmare landscapes, witnessing things that human beings were never meant to know.

### Mirages of Almaqah

Mirages of Almaqah appear by moonlight. Legend says they are peopled with undead, ghosts, and evil spirits. They are the most dangerous mirages. Some are a window to a past of blood and fury, others are simple visions of horror capable of shaking the sanity of the bravest of mujahidin. They are extremely dangerous to enter; those doing so may face cursed creatures and be cursed themselves, transmitting their curse onwards after they emerge. Sages say these mirages came into being when Almaqah the Moon Lord, faithful servant of Hubal, turned some of Apsu's dreams into traps for evil creatures. Monsters are attracted and trapped in these mirages, keeping them from the world of men.

## Ephemeral Mirages

Ephemeral mirages are so-called because the gateways to them are temporary, often fleeting. They may change overnight. There may be a thousand leagues separating subsequent gateways to the same mirage. Sometimes it isn't the gateway that changes, but rather the method of entry. It's not uncommon for those straying into an ephemeral mirage to fail to leave before such a change occurs, thus being imprisoned forever. Some believe the risks are worth it, for ephemeral mirages are veritable Edens, oases of lush greenery, where water, that rarest of treasures in the desert, flows in abundance. Such mirages are usually peopled with magnificent nymphs, ready to welcome the tired traveller. It's also said that these mirages hide magnificent treasures and artefacts, stored in sumptuous marble palaces and protected by fierce guardians. Ephemeral mirages are the dwelling places of djinn.

# Common Features of Mirages

Although all mirages are different, they have common features.

## False Gateways

The desert contains many mirages, not all of which lead to magical lands. Some are simple tricks of the eye, illusions in the heat shimmer of the horizon. These "false gateways" are common enough that they sow doubt in the minds of those who would deliberately try to find ways into the magical lands of the true mirages. Sometimes the desert regions where they occur are deliberately avoided by the nomads, because they know they'll see there mirages which will lead them astray, to nowhere except their inevitable deaths. Very often these false gateways are surrounded with false clues—phantasmal paths, mysterious odours, imaginary winds. The desert tribes avoid mirages like sailors flee from the sirens' song.

## Mirage Spots

It may seem obvious, but bear in mind mirages are only found in the desert, and only when the sun shines in a cloudless sky. The Mirages of Almaqah are an exception; in their case, it's moonlight that reveals them to view.

## The Reality of Mirages

Everything that happens in mirages is real (with certain exceptions). If you die in a mirage, that death is definitive and irrevocable. On the other hand, some mirages can undo what has already become reality. Temporal mirages, for example, may let you travel back in time and intervene in past events.

# Illusory Items

It's rare, but not impossible, to bring back objects from a mirage. Some items are known, to a greater or lesser degree. Some are magical items described on page 335; those typically linked to mirages are given below.

## The Fable Shells

Fable Shells are actually shells, even if some have been carved into the shape of more exotic items, such as fangs or carapaces of dead animals. They allow the wielder to hear an "echo" from a specific mirage. The nearer the bearer is to the mirage in question, the clearer the noises coming out of the shell will be. Anyone seeking a mirage should equip themselves with a Fable Shell if they're to be successful.

## Illusion Paintings

Some people are unable to describe what they have seen or experienced in a mirage. They sometimes start painting—perhaps even without knowing it, and in realistic ways—to try and convey the places they have visited. Their paintings often incorporate optical illusions: a door painted on a wall at the end of a corridor, a window through which you can see a marvellous garden. These paintings are gateways to the mirages, which only work when certain conditions are met. Legend tells of the works of Occidentian painter Almossi, several of whose optical illusions have been gathered into a collection together with ancient tales and legends, explaining how to reach the places depicted within. The book, known as *Liber Illusio*, seems to be as unreal as the places it describes.

## Dust of Illusion

Dust of Illusion is sand said to come from an ancient palace of many colours, from the first mirage Apsu created. The mirage is so old that even Apsu forgot about it in his tormented dreams and, little by little, its substance became lodged in our reality, succumbing to the ravages of time. Everything within the mirage was destroyed, including the many-coloured palace. It's said a passing pilgrim gathered some dust from what had been the palace's walls, sealing it in magical bottles capable of protecting their contents from the passage of time. In this way he gathered significant quantities of this sand, which has strange magical properties, depending on its colour. One colour renders any object on which it is sprinkled invisible; another colour renders an object as light as a feather, or allows an individual to walk on air.

## Two Mirages

### The Oasis of the Floating Palace

❖ **Place:** Somewhere in the Aramla El-Nar.
❖ **Mirage Type:** Ephemeral Mirage.
❖ **Gateway and Conditions:** To enter this mirage, legend says there is a path carved around the side of some particularly sharp, rocky peaks in the Desert of Fire. The path eventually reaches a precipice overlooking a vast drop. There you must pray, until the djinn reveal the gateway. You may pray for a few minutes, or a few days... or you may pray forever, never succeeding, depending on the guardians' mood. You must have a Heroism score of 4 or higher to enter. If the djinn allow entry, the traveller steps out into thin air over the precipitous void—an invisible bridge leads to an adjoining rocky peak!

**Description:** A traveller fortunate enough to find himself inside the mirage sees a vast, Saabi-style palace on a huge stone floating in the air. Smaller stones float around it, above and below the level of the palace. Between each such floating "island" are exquisite stone arches which link to luxuriant gardens, pools, or large courtyards. The Oasis of the Floating Palace is the abode of the djinn Nafis, who helps those on pilgrimages. The help he provides is often surprising. As the saying goes: "Bring your own questions, Nafis will give his own answers."

Usually Nafis will give advice to deserving individuals (undeserving individuals won't have got this far). Petitioners may stay a few days in this paradise to regain their strength, sleep, and enjoy the aerial ballets the sylphs perform above the floating plateaus. At a time of Nafis' deciding, the djinn dismisses the travellers and the gateway to this mirage will be forever closed to them.

### The Mirage of the Haunted Caravan

❖ **Place:** On the old trade route from Carrassine to the city of Esperine.
❖ **Mirage Type:** Mirage of Almaqah.
❖ **Gateway and Conditions:** This ancient road is cursed, and on nights of the gibbous moon it's said to be travelled by a strange and uncanny caravan. The foolhardy traveller who takes this road at such a time sees nothing unusual before encountering its procession. By then it's too late: he's already inside the mirage.

**Description:** All components of the caravan—wagons, animals, and drivers—are surrounded by a whitish aura. Some ride fantastic creatures like elephants with dark, cracked hides and milky-white tusks; the skin of the drivers is husky and dry, as if from a long sojourn in the desert without water. All bear arms and, though their posture and clothing may hint at a readiness to fight, their eyes belie that impression: a deep and resigned weariness broods in their gaze.

A traveller entering the mirage feels compelled to accompany the caravan, actually a detachment from an ancient army that was betrayed by its leaders.

Yr'kri was a powerful and talented general. He led his men to many victories. Hailing from the now-lost city of Esperine in northern Jazirat, the general led its armies against their perennial foe, the city of Carrassine. Esperine was ruled by a powerful caste of merchant princes, who noticed that the constant fighting between Carrassine and Esperine was damaging the city's economy. They signed a surrender with Carrassine without telling Yr'kri, who they knew would be fiercely opposed. Determined not to leave the Esperine general alive, the leaders of Carrassine demanded the location of Yr'kri's army. The cowardly Esperines withdrew their supply lines from the general's troops, and revealed his position to his foes.

For days on end General Yr'kri waited for food and water. Believing his supply lines had been cut by enemy attack, he ordered his army to turn back. The forces of Carrassine, fresh and rested, harassed Yr'kri's army for days. They finally cornered them in a stone circle and massacred them all.

A traveller trapped in the Mirage of the Haunted Caravan is doomed to relive the events from the moment Yr'kri gave the order to turn back to the army's final demise trapped in the stone circle. He will experience his own death, waking up hours later at sunrise, alone and filled with a profound and uneasy sadness. Whatever he does, he will be unable to change the hapless army's fate. Nevertheless, legend says there's a way to break the Haunted Caravan's curse—perhaps by finding the heirs of the merchant princes who betrayed Yr'kri...

# AGALANTHIAN RUINS

The Agalanthians have invaded Jazirat several times in their history, each time holding the peninsula for long periods. The land still bears the scars, social, technological, and otherwise. As well as their currency, language, and measuring system, the invaders left many abandoned ruins the length and breadth of Jazirat; whether deep in the desert, in Capharnaum, or on the Kh'saaba high plateaus, the Agalanthians founded outposts, villages, fortresses, and temples, traces of their presence. Time and wars have done their job, and most are little more than piles of rubble, fallen columns, collapsed sections of wall. But some still contain secrets, forgotten centuries ago...

# The Ruins

No one knows exactly how many Agalanthian ruins there are in Jazirat, or where they are. Ancient Agalanthian maps may lead explorers to certain sites, but no official census has ever been made.

Many ruins lie under countless feet of sand. Dunes move, and sandstorms drastically reshape the landscape. A single stone may appear overnight, indicating the remains of an entire temple, fort, or even city beneath.

# Magic in the Ruins

Many Agalanthian ruins have strong magical auras. The sorceries of centuries of chiromancers permeate their stones.

## The Phargos Oasis

*The fortified village of Phargos was founded by the Agalanthian Republic during their first occupation of Jazirat, millennia ago. It was built around an oasis deep in the Desert of Fire, a fort of a hundred civilians and a defense against desert rebels. Its garrison included many soldiers and myrmidons, so the village was essentially barracks and stables, surrounded by a solid wall.*

*In recent decades, the village—abandoned ever since the invaders left—has been recovered by a lesser tribe linked to the Ibn Tufiq Abd-al-Tarek. These feared desert raiders have chosen Phargos as a secret hiding place, cleaning and renovating the buildings, integrating elements of Saabi architecture into Agalanthian walls collapsed by time.*

*There's another reason the tribe settled here. When Alik Ibn Tufiq Abd-al-Tarek, then the chieftain's eldest son, discovered these ruins, he explored them with his closest companions. Deep underground, beyond traps and animated skeletons, they found a raised stone covered in Agalanthian glyphs, which pulsed with a purple light when they approached. Alik was the first to touch it; not only were his wounds immediately healed, a fighting fury coursed through him, and he was ready to battle any foe.*

*Anyone touching the Agalanthian glyph stone becomes a potent fighter for several hours. Once per day, they recover 3D6 HP and gain a +1 Heroism bonus lasting 1D6 hours. The tribe conducts a ritual at this stone whenever they leave on an expedition.*

# Ritual Residues

Powerful Chiromantic rituals, repeated over years in certain ruins, have left magical imprints with random effects that no one can predict or understand. At a site where people were healed in antiquity, today you might find a spring with regenerative properties; where warriors' weapons were blessed, a ruin may bestow strength and hardness on any blades.

This magic may be beneficial or malign. Some ruins are enchanted with deadly spells of protection; others saw terrible tortures and their stones are impregnated with pain. Woe to the travellers venturing into these places: laying a hand on a stone may fill their body and mind with the agony of centuries of suffering. Few emerge intact from such a harrowing ordeal.

# Magical Items

Agalanthian Heroes often possessed items blessed by the gods or imbued with chiromantic power. During the wars that ravaged Jazirat, many such items were abandoned in these ruins, perhaps deliberately buried in the tombs of their owners, perhaps left on bodies that fell in battle. If you're brave enough to venture into the ancient tunnels slumbering beneath the sands, you may emerge with a gladius with uncanny powers, or a shield with astonishing protective strength.

Mulad Ibn Malik Abd-al-Hassan is one of the rare and courageous explorers to return alive from robbing an Agalanthian tomb. His tale is a dark one: there are times even an Ibn Malik can do nothing. His employer was slain during an ambush by Aragonian warriors and, despairing, Mulad sought refuge in a ruined desert tomb. When he emerged three days later, he was in a pitiful state, but bore in his hands a gladius whose glyph-filled blade shone in the sunlight like a thousand stars in a summer sky. Since then,

Mulad has used his sword's light to blind his opponents in combat and escape from tough situations.

# The Dead and the Undead

So many have died over the centuries of invasion, domination, conquest, and retreat—so much pain, so much suffering! Not all the spirits of the dead have found rest; some still haunt the ruins they inhabited in life. Foolhardy adventurers have confronted these tortured beings, trapped between life and death, but the terror they inspire discourages saner folk from even approaching certain ruins.

These **undead** are often dangerous, made violent by horrible deaths. After an eternity of suffering, they hate all Saabi, blaming them for their fates. Some are calmer, and may even provide good counsel, or information about historical events. Sorcerers often try to approach these revenants to communicate with the world of the dead. Unfortunately, other dangers in the ruins usually preclude anything more than a tentative approach.

# Traps and Mechanisms

The Agalanthians once possessed an advanced knowledge of mechanisms, and this is seen in their ancient constructions. From complex locks to hidden doors, their artistry can be found in ruins, often still operational despite the passage of centuries. These un-

---

## Al-Hisn al-Mahjur, the Forgotten Fort

*On a dry and rocky overhang in the middle of the desert stand the ruins of what was once one of the largest forts in the Agalanthian Empire. Built to train troops in harsh conditions, it's spartan and functional, devoid of decoration. Its walls rise high above on the exposed rock; but no one enters its precincts. Legends says anyone who goes in never comes out; people have watched their companions climb its walls (the heavy gate seems blocked from within) and disappear forever. There are tales of strange screams from behind the walls; some people have even recognised the voices of friends who left to explore the fort in search of lost treasure.*

*The craziest rumours describe what's to be found behind the walls. Of course there are stories of spectres and ghosts of the past, buried treasures and terrible traps; but there are also tales of artefacts that use the power of dragons. There are always reckless adventurers keen to try their luck, hoping to be the first to penetrate the mystery of Al-Hisn al-Mahjur.*

*An ancient report, lost among the scrolls of the sage Eddi Ibn Aziz somewhere in the warrens of Sagrada (or is it Carrassine?), identifies an arsenal beneath the fortress. Protected by traps devised by devious Agalanthian engineers, its hidden vault contains magical gladii, lighter and easier to handle than normal blades. Next to it, haunted by the wraiths of the tortured, there's an ancient cultic place where the Agalanthians once spoke to their gods. The sanctum vibrates with mystic energy, and it's said you may reach the domain of the gods if you pass through a portal there. The most protected chamber, further underground still, contains, it is said, a dragon egg.*

---

## Assawari Halawui—the Columns of the Halawui

*At the foot of the mountains of Kh'saaba springs a bright blue watercourse, the Halawui River, which crosses the whole desert before entering Capharnaum. The gorge it flows through is a strategic passage between Kh'saaba and the rest of Jazirat, a fact which the ancient Agalanthians understood well, installing there an important garrison. Today almost nothing remains of this fortress which rose high in the rock face, except for two immense columns on either side of the river. Each is twenty feet in diameter and one hundred feet tall; they have resisted the passage of time, the desert winds, sandstorms, landslides, erosion, and the wars of the Jazirati. Their white stone is covered in ancient writings, forgotten except by Agalanthian sages. Some say they are chiromantic formulas, waiting to be recited, which will activate magical barriers to block the pass.*

*Higher up the cliff, in what remains of the fortress, tunnels penetrate deep into the rock. There lurk the malevolent spirits of Agalanthian war chiefs who died in desperate battles, who will do anything to prevent intruders from reaching the fortress's sanctum. There, behind traps and unknown perils, stands a basin containing pounds of sand from the Pilgrim's Comet.*

dergound complexes, spared by sandstorms, house the most beautiful relics of this Agalanthian craft, and any adventurer braving those depths will have to deal with the traps protecting them. The Agalanthians wanted to prevent their treasures falling in the wrong hands, and equipped their treasure chambers with deadly devices: floors that open onto pits of sharp spikes, sliding blades, collapsing ceilings, and more. There are many different mechanisms, deadly for those who don't deactivate them. Some may no longer function; ropes may be gnawed, poisons may evaporate, and many have long since been triggered by careless or clumsy intruders. Any guard beasts of course are long dead—unless some unknown sorcery has transformed them into undead.

## Treasure

Many Agalanthian forts and villages were abandoned in haste during the liberation of Jazirat. Some may still hide wealth buried by the fleeing invaders. The dangers recounted above are enough to dissuade most treasure hunters: only the bravest or the craziest venture into the surviving Agalanthian underworlds.

Recently a mighty Tarekid warrior emerged from an Agalanthian tomb bearing the crown of an ancient lord and sacks brimming with artefacts. He won't talk about the ordeals he suffered in those depths, or what happened to the ten companions he went in with, but since then his life has become a dizzying round of excess, and he spends fortunes every day.

# THE ONE THOUSAND AND ONE GODS

### ...give or take a star or two

## De Stella Rerum—the Reign of Stars

The gods exist. This is a fact, a truth unquestioned for millennia. But what are they, and where do they come from? What is a god?

The sage and philosopher Aristopheles Sapios Polato formulated a theory stating that a god is but a stage of existence in the cosmic order. According to him, man is born a child, becomes a youth, an adult, an old man, and finally a dead man, bones and dust. But it need not be so, and some forces, like fate, magic, free will, courage, and self-overcoming can modify life's course. A normal human being does not see the possibilities before him; he is content with following the path laid out by his parents, his family, the world he lives in. Some, however, one day see a door open before them, and

dive through it, body and soul. A peasant chooses to defend his lands against raiders and becomes a local hero; his destiny changes, a neighbouring lord offers to fund his militia to protect the region; war is declared, the local hero becomes troop leader, faces infernal creatures. He becomes a lord, loved and feared. One day, he leaves to hunt a roc that is threatening the herds and never returns. The people whisper that he's dead, but then rumours spread that the gods have taken him as one of their own, and that he has become a minor godling protecting the earth and those who farm it for their food. If enough people remember him, offering him respect, reverence, and eventually worship, his divine nature will be strengthened still further, and he'll become a known and powerful god. Maybe one day he'll even equal Hubal, or take Hubal's name and become one of his new aspects.

People like this are extraordinary. Unknowingly they bear within them a spark of divinity; they are the bastard offspring of the gods. The cosmic dragons choose the best of them, those who seem most likely to accomplish great deeds, to shine in war or poetry, magic or knowledge. This is the very definition of the Dragon-Marked.

If the Dragon-Marked choose well, if they listen to the gods or challenge them in the right way and at the right moment, they can transcend their mortal fate. Embracing the Dragon Mark means leaving the rank and file, rising above ordinary mortals, questing to enter the Kingdom of Heaven to wrestle immortality from the gods.

Such, at least, is the theory of Aristopheles Sapios Polato.

The theory is true. Mortals can become gods. Sometimes the dragons sense these uncommon births when the child is in the womb, and the child is born with the Dragon Mark. At other times, the dragons sense no such thing, and the child is born normally, apparently to face a mundane destiny. But then, later in life, he starts to shine, to come into his own. For such mortals the Dragon Mark appears spontaneously, apparently from nowhere.

So what does the Dragon Mark do? In itself, nothing: the Dragon-Marked already carry the spark of divinity within them. But it is an indication of potential greatness, a promise that this individual may one day open the Orichalcum Gates to the very Kingdom of Heaven.

## Gods, Dragons, and Mortals

It has been this way since the dawn of time. Humans are born, and sometimes they become gods. This was the celestial order established by the First Gods. They were never human; their origins are obscure even to themselves. These First Gods—and their demonic foes—are the parents of the pantheons of the known world: Hubal, Hubal-Uzza, and Tiamat among the Jazirati; Kalos, Nerea, and Cthonos among the Agalanthians. The great gods of the other peoples—Aether, Mira, and Shirad—are late-comers, merely aspects of the First Gods.

The First Gods peopled the cosmos by creating the Builders of Worlds: the dragons. These mighty beings were the first to worship and serve them; their task was to inhabit the world the First Gods had created and continue to fashion it. Things changed quickly: after a few aeons, the dragons became aware they were slaves, and three quarters of their number rose up and tried to destroy the First Gods, their masters. The fighting was desperate, and the Kingdom of Heaven almost fell; but the First Gods were part of the fabric of the cosmos, and could not be defeated by the beings they had created themselves. Regardless of their magical power, the rebellious dragons proved wanting before the might of their creators.

The thousands of dragons who had rebelled against the First Gods were punished. They were transformed into vile creatures that already existed on the Earth, beings almost devoid of magical power and with few natural defences, that staggered on two legs, hairless, scrawny, naked and larval. Thus were the traitorous dragons cursed with human form.

Even as they mixed with humans, the rebel dragons remained superior. They became guides, leaders, and sages. Some even became local deities—for good or ill. From that moment on, the history of these fallen dragons becomes entwined with that of humankind, and it is impossible to separate the two.

Those few dragons who had not rebelled against the First Gods were named the Great Dragons. They were given greater powers and greater responsibilities. Even so, despite their loyalty, the First Gods never fully trusted them again, and removed from the Great Dragons their ability to reproduce. Henceforth, their eggs would never hatch, but would remain forever eggs, pregnant with dreams and fancies, the mystical potential for what might have been—the **imaginary worlds**. Some of these eggs contained imaginary worlds

so vibrant, so filled with energy and richness, that they began to shine in the Vault of Heaven, forming new constellations. It's believed that the more worlds a dragon has among its unhatched eggs, the more stars are in its constellation, extensions of its power and identity. The dragons with the most stars are the most powerful.

Following the Rebellion of the Dragons, the First Gods understood that they were not invincible, and would have to protect themselves better if their supremacy was not to be threatened again. After appointing the Great Dragons to be the Guardians of the Gates of the Kingdom of Heaven, the First Gods decided the time had come to multiply. The imaginary worlds of the dragon eggs were growing in power and number, and required their own gods themselves if they were not to endanger the cosmic balance. The First Gods made the imaginary worlds into domains for their offspring to rule.

Thus the First Gods reproduced among themselves, giving birth to new beings of divine essence. They soon found that reproduction was nothing without the pleasure of mating—without variety, change, and originality. In their desire, they looked to humankind. Coupling with human men and women, enjoying the games of love and seduction, the gods continued their theogony, birthing lesser divine beings in great numbers. These were not gods in themselves, but bore divine blood, and could become gods if they lived extraordinary lives. In a way these divinities were the first Dragon-Marked, the great heroes of human history. They are the Jazirati Prophets, as well as Mogda, Sarah Bat Caleb, General Yassine, Saint Gerda, and Agalanth himself. They numbered in the hundreds during the first centuries of human civilisation. Today some are considered exceptional human beings, or heroes, like Sarah or Agalanth; others,

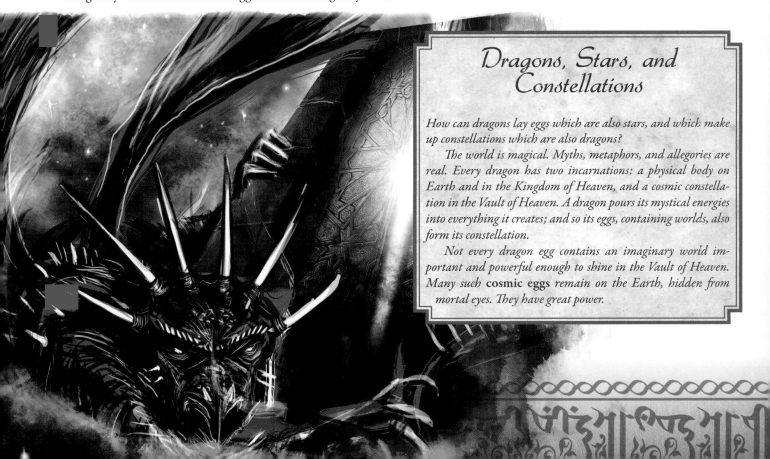

## Dragons, Stars, and Constellations

*How can dragons lay eggs which are also stars, and which make up constellations which are also dragons?*

*The world is magical. Myths, metaphors, and allegories are real. Every dragon has two incarnations: a physical body on Earth and in the Kingdom of Heaven, and a cosmic constellation in the Vault of Heaven. A dragon pours its mystical energies into everything it creates; and so its eggs, containing worlds, also form its constellation.*

*Not every dragon egg contains an imaginary world important and powerful enough to shine in the Vault of Heaven. Many such* **cosmic eggs** *remain on the Earth, hidden from mortal eyes. They have great power.*

like the Prophets Hassan, Tarek, and Salif, have been elevated by history to the rank of demi-gods.

The gods had entered the vicious circle of human conquests, manipulations, and heavenly ascension. It was a game of which they would never tire.

## Allegiances

The gods coupled with one another, with men and women, and sometimes with dragons, whether fallen or faithful. The very existence of Marduk, born millennia ago and both a dragon and a god, suggests the power which could be obtained via such mixing. But Marduk, son of Hubal and the dragon Sal'Hyam'Ensaali, was the only dragon ever to attain such a level of power. All who followed remained lesser deities.

The gods of the Jazirati and Agalanthians mostly coupled with humans. It was an obsession for them, an addictive game they could not do without. They had hundreds of offspring: humans

with divine powers who became heroes of good and evil. Soon the supremacy of the First Gods was threatened again; but none of the gods was prepared to stop their dalliances, and few could find it in themselves to slay their children. Everywhere in the world, humans grew to power and renown; everywhere they became lesser gods. Soon there were gods of rivers, mountains, singing creeks, bread, weapons, war; and a thousand peoples to worship them, to seek their protection, to propel them into the pantheons of the highest gods. A thousand peoples, a thousand deities; a thousand wars.

## The Dragon Mark

The divine "arms race" was everywhere, but the gods would not refrain from their games of seduction. In response, the Great Dragons, guarantors of the divine order, established a way of monitoring the descendants of the gods so that their divine gifts would not rage uncontrolled and unchecked within creation. They tracked down births of divine ancestry, followed nascent godlings, and tried to nurture and guide them.

This was harder than it looked. All it took was for one godling to have his own children for more potential gods to be born. Gods that in turn would give birth to more superhuman beings, and so on, in an inescapable theogonic proliferation that would leave divine beings everywhere. One child of a god may never be more than a farmer; but his child or grandchild might one day rise to rival Kalos, Aether, Hubal, or Shirad.

The solution the dragons proposed was to mark certain descendants of the gods. The dragons would watch every birth in a lineage of divine blood, and make a magical mark if the child seemed capable of rising to its destiny. As a result, regardless of how it may be seen locally, the Dragon Mark always indicates divine ancestry. A Dragon-Marked may be the child or grandchild of Hubal, or a hundredth-generation descendant of a lesser god of some mountain stream; each bears the same divine spark that can lead him to the Kingdom of Heaven.

After debating the solution the dragons proposed, the gods grudgingly accepted. Since then, the Dragon Mark has led to all manner of manipulations, intrigues, and conflicts of influence between the dragons and the gods, as each of them tries to offer his own favourite—or his own blood—the better fate. And a few Dragon-Marked (a very few), have become gods themselves, achieving the mythical **apotheosis** sung of by the Agalanthian philosophers.

---

### Heredity and Bloodlines

*A Dragon-Marked is born because a god asked a dragon to watch over a bloodline with which that god once had a child. The dragon watches over each birth in that bloodline to see if the child has inherited the god's divine spark. If it has, the dragon marks the child before it is born. One of the Dragon-Marked has something like a one in five chance of having Dragon-Marked offspring. This means that there are lineages of Dragon-Marked on the Earth.*

*A character whose father was a brilliant sage, whose grandfather was a powerful sorcerer, whose uncles were invincible warriors, may hail from a Dragon-Marked bloodline. In such bloodlines, at least one Dragon-Marked is born per generation. However, it's also possible for Dragon-Marked to be born into families where the dragons have not seen a divine spark for generations. Such Dragon-Marked births come as a great surprise.*

*Sometimes, in very rare cases, a god may ask a dragon to watch over a bloodline that was once the recipient of special lore. In such cases, the Dragon Mark goes beyond the physical; it's a question of the inheritance of talents and knowledge. A black-smith who received from a god the gift of forging magical weapons may pass this knowledge to his apprentices and in doing so make them Dragon-Marked.*

*Strangely, most Dragon-Marked bloodlines were broken in the 55th century, some five hundred years ago. Overnight, dragons simply stopped granting the Dragon Mark. Just as surprisingly, the Dragon-Marked started appearing again at the end of the 5950s, just under fifty years ago.*

## One God, Many Gods

The religions of *Capharnaum* organise their pantheons in pyramidal hierarchies, with a single great divinity at the top ruling over all. This god is Hubal among the Jazirati, Shirad among the Shiradim, and Aether among the Quarterians.

In truth, these three gods are the same. Hubal was one of the First Gods, worshipped and feared in his most fearsome aspect by the very first humans. In time, history gave other faces to the god—some by simple evolution, others because other gods were identified with him and "became Hubal". One aspect, Hubal-Shirad, was worshipped as the only god by some Jazirati, who split themselves off as a separate social group. These became the Shiradim, and they made a single almighty god from a god who before had a thousand faces. Later came Jason, who chose the goddess Mira as his mother and invented a new divine father for himself, in the form of Aether. Those who accepted this god, invoked by Jason seemingly out of nowhere, associated him gradually with the worship they had formerly offered Shirad or Hubal, so that in the end Jason had fashioned for himself a divine father in the image of the greatest god.

There are other gods which are shared between pantheons, common to the Agalanthians and Saabi, the Quarterians or Shiradim. One example is Nerea, Goddess of Fertility and the Sea, who is also Mira, Jason's heavenly mother. Finally gods such as Kalos, Bacchoros, or Demetra seem to be unique, and share neither identity nor powers with deities of other pantheons.

### Gods, Mortals, and Power

How can a human being become a deity? How can a god have several names and faces? The answer lies in the ancient punishment of the dragons.

At the beginning of time, when the traitor dragons were cursed to become human, the Great Dragons who had remained loyal to the gods lost the ability to reproduce. The **cosmic eggs** they laid were doomed never to hatch, but contained within them imaginary worlds, like dreams or nightmares, the product of the ancient draconic power of **evocation**.

The traitor dragons never lost this power. Rather, they gave it away. They bestowed upon humans part of the power they had wielded as Builders of Worlds, renouncing it themselves forever. They gave humans the ability to manipulate the world with their emotions, faith, wishes, and beliefs. Ordinary men and women can harness this ability by becoming **sorcerers**. Magic is a way of harnessing the draconic power of evocation, a gift from fallen dragons rebelling against the gods.

The most important consequence of the gift was not magic, but the human ability to influence the form and magnitude of the gods themselves by their worship. This ability—called **faith**—is a phenomenon beyond the control of gods, dragons, and mortals alike. It is the faith of mortals that magnifies the power of a god beyond measure; the stronger a god is believed to be, the stronger he is; the more a demon is imagined as evil, the more evil he becomes.

This is why the greatest of gods have many aspects. Hubal is perceived in many different ways in many different regions, and so has many different forms, multiplying his powers. These manifestations still remain the same god; each shares the same memories, even though his goals and powers may differ.

This means a Dragon-Marked hero known by the whole of Capharnaum as the "Wrath of Hubal" could quickly become a new incarnation of the god. Hubal himself would become more powerful, and the Dragon-Marked would partake of his power. He would even share some feelings and memories of the different aspects of the god—usually in his dreams—until the time came for his own apotheosis.

# MONSTERS AND ADVERSARIES

*T he man sitting by the fire pointed to a tent.*

*"You'll find the one you're looking for in there," he said.*

*The Sagrada caravanserai was huge, but everyone seemed to know who I was there to meet. The tent was spacious, but in the flickering firelight I saw how old the curtains and hangings were. I entered without waiting, drawing aside a heavy canvas bleached by the sun and the desert wind. My eyes adjusted to the gloom, and then I saw him, by the fire, unmoving as if asleep. I waited a moment, and then began in what I hoped was a confident voice: "Honourable Abu al-Qasim Mansur Ibn al-Zabriqan Ibn Salamah Il-Namari, I am—"*

*He raised his hand to interrupt me. His voice was hoarse, fatigued by the years. "Your name doesn't matter. I know who you are. They told me you were coming. Sit down and have some tea."*

## The Creature Write-ups

This section contains write-ups of a variety of creatures found in Jazirat. The statistics are for typical specimens, and represent a good challenge for inexperienced characters. Some are stronger than others, and you're encouraged to adapt them to your needs.

Many creatures use skill specialisation, especially for combat (see page 74). Creatures larger or smaller than human beings receive modifiers to damage and defence, as described in the **Capharnaum** bestiary **Fables & Chimeras**.

**Soak** scores already have any Armour Values added. They also include, instead of Heroism, a value called **Legend Points**. These are used exactly like Heroism, as follows:

❖ For calculating the character's Soak. Soak = CON + Legend.
❖ For asking Urim and Turim (see page 77).
❖ For determining the maximum number of swagger dice the creature can take (page 49).
❖ For making attribute rolls.
❖ For adding to damage on a Double Attack (page 54).

**Initiative** is likewise adjusted for several parameters (creature size, aggressiveness, natural agility, and so on), and therefore may not match the character creation rules. **Damage** scores are also pre-calculated and include STR; you only need to add the attack's magnitude. **Magic Resistance** is equal to INT x 6 (max 30); you can also make rolls of INT + Willpower where appropriate.

*I obeyed. Raising my head, I shuddered at the sight of his dead eyes. After a silence, he opened his toothless mouth.*

*"I was told you were interested in the creatures of these lands, that you wish to accompany the caravan on its dangerous journey. And so you thought old Abu would tell you everything he's learned in his long years and countless travels. You don't need to answer. I'm tired, and in any case it's better you know what you're getting into, and that you spread the word about Abu al-Qasim Mansur, the mad naturalist."*

*Settling himself more comfortably, the old sage began his tale.*

## Abzul

The *abzulim* are lizards as big as two full-grown oxen. You know, of course, that they're originally from Al-Fariq'n? Some say they're the offspring of fallen dragons, and indeed they resemble the dragons depicted in murals and frescoes all around the world.

Abzulim vary in colour from white to black, passing through green, blue, and mauve. Legend says there were abzulim with blood-red scales of a terrifying ferocity, but they seem to have already been extinct when these creatures died out in antiquity.

Yes, that's right! The abzulim once vanished from Al-Fariq'n, many centuries ago. They only reappeared with the visit of Khalil

Abd-al-Salif to the tribe of the Ungara (see page 249). That tribe had been entrusted with two spherical stones by one of their *kahini*, which turned out to be *abzulim* eggs! Khalil discovered that the saurians could form a mental bond with a human mind, in a communion the Ungara call the Walad Badiya.

You may not know this, but abzulim don't exist in the wild. A young abzul won't even survive birth if it doesn't bond with a human, and the death of the abzul or its bonded human always leads to the death of the other, through suicide or grief—or madness.

No one knows how the abzulim reproduce. They seem both male and female, laying three or four eggs every ten years. If you keep them in water, the eggs can be preserved for centuries without hatching! But the Ibn Khalil only permit a person driven by the Walad Badiya Fever to take an egg from the water, bury it in burning sand, and cause the abzul to hatch. And don't think you can pretend to have the Fever! The abzul will be stillborn, and the Ibn Khalil will slay you out of hand! The clan protects its eggs jealously.

Abzulim eat almost anything. They can even go without eating or drinking for weeks. That's not the case for their bonded companions!

### Abzul

| STR: 8 | Max Init: 5 |
|---|---|
| CON: 7 | HP: 70 |
| DEX: 4 | Soak: 12 |
| INT: 2 | Passive Defence: 11 |
| CHA: 1 | Magic Resistance: 12 |
| | Legend: 3[1] |

❖ **Skills:** Athletics 4, Endurance 5, Fighting (Bite) 2 (5).

❖ **Attacks /Active Defences:** Bite[2] 9/4 +18 damage, Bash[3] n/a +(STR+5) damage; -3 Active Defence due to large size.

❖ **Armour:** Thick Skin (AV: 2).

❖ **Area Found:** Among the Walad Badiya.

❖ **Notes:** 1: Once per game session, an abzul can provide 1 Legend point as a Heroism point to its companion.

2: If ridden by anyone other than a companion, a rider must make a difficulty 15 DEX + Riding roll to remain in the saddle when the abzul makes a bite attack.

3: Any human-sized character within (abzul's DEX / 2) paces of an attacking abzul must make a difficulty STR + Athletics roll to avoid taking damage equal to the abzul's STR +5.

## Handling Abzulim in Your Game

An abzul should be considered a non-player character with its own stats and personality, which under normal circumstances is run by the player who plays its rider. However, Al-Rawi can and should take advantage of the presence of an abzul in the game, as such a creature necessarily has an impact on adventures.

The empathic bond between an abzul and its rider primarily concerns emotions and sensations, not thoughts. An abzul sensing danger will transmit a sense of urgency and imminent peril to its bonded rider, but will be unable to communicate the danger's exact source. Al-Rawi may also award bonus dice to the rider's rolls when in the abzul's presence whenever the player describes his character taking actions in concert with his abzul.

## Animated Skeleton

Maybe you think that necropolises are quiet places where the bodies of the dead in peace for eternity. Let me tell you—not all those bodies rest in peace!

Once again, I had broken my oath to myself to never venture into ruins. But what can you do? Curiosity is a terrible affliction to one who believes themselves wise. I had accompanied an expedition of fifteen explorers to the ruins of a temple deep in the desert. We had avoided any perilous encounters, and I had come to believe—poor deluded soul!—that good fortune was on our side.

The feeling of doom returned as soon as we reached the ruins. Their architecture was unknown to me, filling me with an indefinable unease. The symbols of death decorating the pillars which still stood could mean only one thing: that we were in a necropolis, the last resting place of many hundreds of the dead. My companions seemed not to share my apprehension, telling each other tales of treasure. We dismounted our camels and went to inspect the entrance to a temple whose state of preservation was almost miraculous, leaving a single guard to watch over our beasts.

We were no more than twenty paces from the opening when the sand around us seemed to writhe. Then human bones thrust from the ground, skeletons emerging armed with scimitars and ancient blades. I felt I would faint, filled with the desire to flee, but my companions reacted swiftly. Weapons in hand, they charged the uncanny guardians. I was surprised at the speed with which they hacked down the monsters. I was reassured, but I confess I was reluctant to go further.

## Animated Skeleton

| | |
|---|---|
| STR: 2 | Max Init: 3 |
| CON: 3 | HP: 30 |
| DEX: 3 | Soak: 5 |
| INT: 2 | Passive Defence: 12 |
| CHA: 2 | Magic Resistance: 12 |
| | Legend: 1 |

- ❖ **Skills:** Athletics 3, Endurance 3, Fighting 3.
- ❖ **Attacks /Active Defences:** Suyuf 6/3 +10 damage.
- ❖ **Armour:** No living tissue (AV: 1).
- ❖ **Area Found:** Ruins, underworlds.
- ❖ **Notes:** Animated skeletons are considered Valiant Captains in combat: a Critical Success puts them automatically out of the fight. They fight tirelessly.

The skeletons had been animated by I don't know what magic. They were nothing more than bones, some gnawed or broken, but they stood and moved their heads and arms. I saw no tendons connecting their bones, but they walked, if clumsily, and their empty eye sockets clearly saw. It was the first time I had seen such a thing.

My companions had dispatched these guardians without trouble. Once a leg was smashed, they fell, still waving their weapons; they only stopped when their skull was detached or staved in. I even saw a severed bony hand that still grasped its sword and struggled to attack as long as its owner still acted, too.

The battle done, we continued, warier than before. On the threshold of the temple, we heard screams from the guard who had remained behind. A skeleton had appeared behind him and had skewered him where he stood. Our mounts were thus in danger, and several of my companions rushed back, dividing our group.

It was at that moment that more skeletons appeared from the sands. Many more, almost beyond number. For every one that fell beneath the blows of my companions, another two appeared. Fatigued, we started to falter; several of the expedition already bore wounds. I ran through an opening to escape that terrible scene, and hauled myself on the back of a camel and fled. From a distance, I watched my companions die helplessly.

A dark sorcery animates these skeletons, whose sole purpose is destroying anything that lives. I have never found a trace of such necromancy in the works I have read, but some sages say all it takes

is one act of sacrilege to make the buried bodies rise. When small in number they are no danger for an experienced adventurer; but in multitudes they can make even the greatest soldier fall.

## Animated Statue

You may know my fear of abandoned ruins far from settled lands. You may even think I'm a coward, afraid of ghosts and the dark. But you may change your mind after this story!

I had accepted, under the influence of an excellent liqueur, to accompany a small expedition into the desert looking for ruins. We were seeking the mythical Qatra, a Jazirati city from before the Saabi era, which legend says was the site of the largest pleasure palace ever known. Our guide possessed a map he had been given, he said, by a sage. By a liar more like!

In a few days, we had arrived at some ruins in a deep gorge. They were well-preserved, and several statues, spared by the elements, formed what looked like a guard of honour for our approach. My first surprise was that the statues looked more like Agalanthian sculptures than monuments of our own; but I had to cut short my study to follow my impatient companions. After tying our camels, we entered a corridor leading deep into the cliff. For a moment my fear of ruins faded before the majesty of the edifice before us.

We proceeded several dozen paces into the depths of the rock face. A heavy door barred our way, but not for long, given the ardour of the explorers. The next chamber was even more magnifi-

## Animated Statue

| | |
|---|---|
| STR: 14 | Max Init: 6 |
| CON: 11 | HP: 110 |
| DEX: 2 | Soak: 22[1] |
| INT: 2 | Passive Defence: 10 |
| CHA: 1 | Magic Resistance: 12 |
| | Legend: 2 |

- ❖ **Skills:** Athletics 2, Endurance 8, Fighting (Brawling) 2 (5).
- ❖ **Attacks /Active Defences:** Brawling[2] 7/2 +14 damage.
- ❖ **Armour:** Stone (AV: 9).
- ❖ **Area Found:** Ruins, temples.
- ❖ **Notes:** 1: Double Soak against heat-based attacks.

  2: Animated statues always try and make Brutal Attacks at 19/14 + 20 damage.

  **These creatures are unaffected by lighting conditions and always move towards the closest target without fail.**

cent, faced in blood red stone veined with black. More than a score of statues identical to those outside stood along the walls. There were several openings in the walls, and my associates hurried past them to the far end of the chamber while I tarried by the nearest statue. It was also in a style close to Agalanthian, barely taller than a man, perhaps seven feet, and absolutely perfect in its representation. It was a warrior, but its face left me ill at ease; it seemed filled with an evil will. Then, when I turned to follow my companions, I saw my worst nightmares were sweet dreams compared to the reality of this place.

For, at the moment my companions reached level with one of the passages, the statue nearest to them started to move. Yes—like it was flesh and bone!—the statue moved noiselessly to bar their way. I cried a warning as several more statues started to move. It was as though stone had become flesh, so natural were their movements—and yet so unnatural for stone! Some statues bore stone swords, others had only their fists. My acolytes stepped back, but the statues had cut off their retreat. A shiver ran down my spine when I saw the statue I had been examining also begin to shift.

My associates were now engaged in combat. No doughty warriors they, yet some knew how to handle scimitar and spear. Quickly stepping backwards, I saw the fight was not fair: their blades did not even scratch the stone, or did so barely, whereas the blows struck by the statues broke bones and crushed organs. One by one my companions fell; I stumbled backwards as my own statue approached with heavy steps. I turned as quickly as I could and fled to the surface.

Everything was calm outside. I untied a camel and rode away with all speed. The statue seemed not to have pursued. I reached our previous camp and waited two days, but none of my companions returned.

You have doubtless heard of such animated statues. But how disconcerting it is to see these things move, such a contradiction of all that we know! Imagine your house leaving its foundations for a stroll—that is the feeling which churned my stomach as I beheld them, or even worse. My studies told me little more about these abominations. They are said to be the leftovers of an ancient civilisation, and the guardians of ancestral shrines. A powerful magic lets them move and act as if alive and flesh and blood. However, they are bonded to a place, and cannot leave. This point is certainly true, for one never finds such statues striding across the desert.

A blacksmith from Sagrada once told me the steel of his weapons could cut through stone. When I told him my story, he even boasted his creations would destroy those stone monsters. He was reluctant to test his words himself, it must be said. Beware these creatures, quick despite their weight, and shun the places they guard! In my opinion, no weapon forged by mortals can slay them.

## Chimera

Do you ever ask yourself what the Agalanthians did for us? Yes, they tried to conquer us, again and again, killed us and burned our cities—that's all true. But, more than that, they gave us their culture—and their chimeras.

The deserts aren't the only places where you can find these legendary creatures. Most avoid people and live far away in the wilderness. They followed the Agalanthian armies into impenetrable mountains or trackless wastes. I've only ever seen one chimera, near Sagrada. I wasn't even in a caravan; I was going to see the great library.

I'd stopped in a village, a place blessed by the gods, good land and well-watered. The crops were fine, the women had wide hips and promised many pleasures. There couldn't have been more than fifteen houses in the whole village. To my surprise, the villagers welcomed me with weapons in hand. They weren't hostile, but it was clear they were afraid. I was getting ready to address them when one shouted the alarm. I turned and saw one of the strangest creatures I'd ever seen.

The chimera was less than thirty paces away. I still don't know how it could have got there without being noticed. It was big, maybe five feet at the withers. Its body was that of a huge goat, its head that of a lion, like those you find to the west. Its tail was a snake, hissing and coiling. The strangest was the extra goat's head in the middle of its back. I'd heard some of these monstrosities had followed the Agalanthian armies into Jazirat, but it was the first time I'd ever seen one.

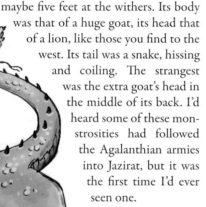

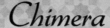

## Chimera

| | |
|---|---|
| **STR:** 8 | **Max Init:** 7 |
| **CON:** 12 | **HP:** 120 |
| **DEX:** 5 | **Soak:** 14 |
| **INT:** 3 | **Passive Defence:** 16 |
| **CHA:** 1 | **Magic Resistance:** 18 |
| | **Legend:** 1 |

- ❖ **Skills:** Athletics 5, Endurance 4, Fighting (Fire Breath, Lion Bite) 2 (5), Intimidate 5, Notice 8.
- ❖ **Attacks /Active Defences:** Fire Breath 10/5 +8 damage[1], Lion Bite 10/5 +14 damage, Snake Bite 7/5 +10 damage[2].
- ❖ **Armour:** Thick hide (AV: 1).
- ❖ **Area Found:** Anywhere.
- ❖ **Notes:** 1: Fire breath spreads in a cone 6 paces long and 1 pace wide at its end. It can hit every creature in the area of effect. The chimera won't use its breath attack against a target fighting in melee, but it is its favoured attack at the beginning of combat.

  2: Snake venom: Deadliness 3, Incapacitation 3, Rapidity 6.

  **If at least two targets are in range, the chimera will make two bite attacks (lion and snake) in a single action (one is effectively a Free Attack). However, any single target may only be attacked by one attack in a single action.**

The peasants charged the monster, yelling insults. I later learned the beast had appeared a few weeks earlier, attacking lone peasants irrespective of age or sex and eating them. I felt a pang in my heart, thinking the peasants were going to destroy such a strange creature, leaving nothing for me to study, but as it happened things became far worse than I could have imagined. About a dozen men surrounded the beast, keeping a respectful distance from its impressive jaws; but the creature didn't look impressed, it roared and snaked its tail while slowly turning. The first man attacked, but with its three heads it was impossible to take it by surprise.

The snake head flashed and bit the peasant in the arm. He collapsed screaming. Then the goat's head breathed a gout of flames. Yes—it's true! I really saw fire spouting from its mouth! The flames hit two other peasants, who screamed in pain while the fire consumed them. There then followed utter carnage, as the lion teeth shredded, the flames burned, the snake bit left and right, and all the while hooves trampled the fallen who tried to stand. I couldn't help myself: I seized my horse and fled to find a military camp. When I returned with an escort, there was nothing left of the village. The houses were burned, and the half-eaten corpses were scattered over the ground. Not even the children had been spared.

I think that some massacres blamed on raiders may be the work of these monsters. Even the scorpion-men avoid them. Some claim the Agalanthians brought them deliberately to infest our lands—although they also say such mighty beasts would never let their offspring be captured.

## Dabbat

It was like a small earthquake, imperceptible at first, but growing stronger. It was the first time I'd felt it since taking to the road. The caravan I had joined wasn't large—perhaps fifteen caravaneers and twice as many camels. We were carrying precious cloths, spices, and other delicate goods from Carrassine to Beth, north of Kh'saaba, and were four days from our destination. We had stopped in a dry valley in the desert, sheltered from the winds by high cliffs, a frequent stopping place for caravans.

My companions were busy putting up the tents while I stretched myself after a long journey in the saddle. It had been more than three moons since I'd last travelled, and my muscles

## Dabbat

| STR: 10 | Max Init: 6 |
|---------|-------------|
| CON: 10 | HP: 80 |
| DEX: 4 | Soak: 12 |
| INT: 2 | Passive Defence: 9 |
| CHA: 2 | Magic Resistance: 12 |
| | Legend: 1 |

- ❖ **Skills:** Athletics 5, Endurance 7, Fighting (Bite) 3 (6).
- ❖ **Attacks /Active Defences:** Bite 10/4 +24 damage[1], Spit Acid 7/4 Special[1], Tail Bash 7/4 Special[2]; -6 Active Defence due to huge size.
- ❖ **Armour:** Scales (AV: 1).
- ❖ **Area Found:** Jazirat.
- ❖ **Notes:** 1: Dabbat venom acts as a powerful acid, causing 3D6 damage to the target during the action in which he was hit, and then 2D6 the next action, and 1D6 the action after that. For a bite, the venom is Deadliness 5 Incapacitation 1 Rapidity 6.

  2: The dabbat uses its tail to knock down prey. Up to (magnitude) adjacent human-sized targets may be struck. Targets must make a DEX + Athletics roll to remain standing, against a difficulty equal to the result of the attack roll. The tail bash does no damage.

felt it. The others didn't seem to be aware of the trembling I'd felt beneath the ground, absorbed as they were in their various tasks. That's when the beast broke from the sand. It was a **dabbat**—one of those legendary serpents that live beneath the desert. Most likely attracted by the steady thump of the camels' hooves, it had left its lair to join us.

Sand flew into the air as the monster emerged just two paces from my companions. Its head rose ten feet above the ground: it must have been three feet wide, a dark mouth with four fangs, each as long as your hand. Its forked tongue darted in and out; its eyes were small and black, set well back in its head. On either side, two small holes marked its nose, and a four-inch horn rose behind the nostrils. The dabbat was brown in colour, darkening to ochre with red-blood scales. Its underside was lighter.

Said drew his weapon, while others retreated in fear. The giant serpent left him no time to close; like lightning, it grabbed the unfortunate in its huge maw and swallowed him down to his belly. Said's scream was short: I heard his ribs snapping in the dabbat's jaw. The monster lifted its head higher, and swallowed the hapless caravaneer in one. I could see the shape of his body undulating down beneath the monster's skin. Several of the men collected themselves and readied weapons—a sharp stick, a scimitar—and then charged to avenge their friend. The serpent began flailing from side to side to keep them at bay. I can still see those proud soldiers holding their own; but the beast had emerged fully from the sand, its body at least twenty paces long, its tail sliding quickly forwards.

The attack was as sudden as it was powerful. The serpent supported itself on a loop of its mid body, and swept its tail in a circular motion, bashing three men who fell heavily. Its maw then spat a jet of green fluid over a fourth bedouin. He turned towards me, and my heart froze when I saw his melting flesh and right eye rolling free. The fifth warrior fared no better, the dabbat's fangs seizing his arm and tearing it off without effort, leaving a splash of blood on the sand. The tail still lashed, striking the men on the ground again, breaking their bones. Then it rose up, and its head turned to me. I was petrified. Then it dove into the sand in pursuit of a group of fleeing men, and I escaped. A few days later I reached a village. I never saw or heard of any survivor from that caravan again.

I've heard many things about these creatures. It's claimed they live beneath the sand, sleeping until vibrations wake them. Some say they were created by the djinn to keep mortals away. All I know is that we didn't stand a chance against the dabbat, it appeared out of nowhere and it butchered as many as it could. Some villagers near the desert told me they'd found the corpse of one of these serpents, and when they opened its stomach they found the remains of a suit of armour and a scimitar. They say these creatures can spit acid or inject it with a bite. Many alchemists would doubtless pay dearly for a flask of such venom, but don't risk it: the reward is not worth your life.

# Djinn

So you want to know if I've ever met a djinn? It's a common enough travellers' tale around the campfire, but most such stories are just drivel for audiences thirsty for nonsense. The djinn rarely show themselves to travellers, and interfere little with the mortal world. And a good job too! But, to answer your question: yes, I have...

As was my custom, I was travelling with a caravan from Carrassine to Kathrat. We were surprised by a sandstorm, as sudden as it was violent, far from shelter. One of the worst I had experienced. When it was over, I was alone, the caravan impossible to find. My camel soon succumbed to the wounds the storm had caused, and I thought my end was near.

That's when he appeared. About a dozen paces away, watching me with dark eyes, an enigmatic smile on his lips. A man with a round belly, moon-faced, hairless but for a braid a few inches long at the back of his head, bound by a leather cord. He was naked to the midriff, where he wore red canvas trousers which ended in

misty swirls where his legs should have been. A djinn, the first I'd ever seen. I was frightened, but his person radiated an aura of calmness and friendliness. I fell to my knees, more out of exhaustion than devotion.

He watched me for several minutes, saying nothing, making no gesture. Finally, in desperation, I begged his aid. He answered slowly, his voice soft and warm, telling me I still had much to accomplish, and that he thought me a good man. In accordance with the pact which binds the djinn to the lands of men, he agreed to help by answering one question if first I answered his. All too happy, I agreed. He then asked his question, which was a riddle. Exhausted though I was, I was surprised by the riddle's simplicity and answered quickly. He smiled when I asked him where I could find the caravan, and raised his finger in the direction I should go. Then he vanished, as mysteriously as he had appeared.

Two hours later, I found the surviving members of the caravan. I don't know why the djinn helped me, but their ways are mysterious. They may not act directly in human affairs, and always ask for something in return for their aid: the answer to a riddle, a story, sometimes a song.

Of course, not all djinn are as benevolent as the one I met. There are some that aren't interested in human affairs and wouldn't lift a finger to help, and others that are evil through and through. In fact, there are three kinds of djinn: the true djinn; the ancestral djinn, also called afreeti; and the marids, djinn who refuse the rule of Marduk and who are the most evil of all. It's hard to tell djinn and marid apart by just looking, as their appearance varies according to their whim. Most of the time they look like well-proportioned humans with a benevolent aura, or sometimes fearful or even despairing. They don't touch the ground, and seem buoyed by a swirling mist which tells everyone what they are.

The marids are destroyers of life and tormentors of men and women, although even they don't do so directly—even if their power would doubtless let them do so. Instead they corrupt the weak or greedy to carry out their plans for them. Some say there are marids who have allied with humans, making the latter more powerful and so more capable of helping them in their evil plans. Both true

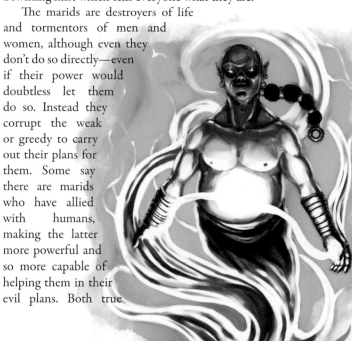

# Djinn

STR: 6

CON: 9

DEX: 6

INT: 8

CHA: 5

Max Init: 9

HP: 90

Soak: 15

Passive Defence: 18

Magic Resistance: 30

Legend: 6

- ❖ **Skills:** Athletics 6, Endurance 6, Fighting 6, History & Peoples 3, Sacred Word 6, Storytelling 4, Survival (Desert) 2 (7).

- ❖ **Attacks /Active Defences:** Bastard Suyuf 12/6 +16 damage (+19 2-handed).

- ❖ **Armour:** None.

- ❖ **Area Found:** Jazirat.

- ❖ **Notes:** Like the Dragon-Marked, djinn and marids have one dragon die. They may also use magic in an instinctive way; each has at least one specific power. The list below gives some examples. You may create other powers to suit your campaign.

**Elemental Fury (permanent, no Sacred Word roll):** The djinn creates a wind that becomes increasingly violent, capable of knocking a target to the ground, of provoking huge waves at sea, or monstrous sandstorms in the desert. Wind strength increases rapidly and becomes problematic after 2 rounds, rendering all combat impossible after 5. The area of effect is a square a number of paces equal to the djinn's INT x 50 on each side.

**Gaseous Form (permanent, no Sacred Word roll):** The djinn can transform his body into the consistency of gas, like a ghostly shape made of mist. In this form, he is invulnerable to attack, and may cross any non-airtight barrier. He may make no physical attacks while in gaseous form. It takes one action to go from solid form to gaseous form or back.

**Hallucination:** The djinn can control minds to create illusions on an INT + Sacred Word against a difficulty of 9, +1 per 10 additional targets. The illusion may be a simple image of an oasis that moves farther away as you get closer, or a huge palace with every kind of luxury, bang in the middle of the desert. The only restriction is that the djinn can't simulate animal or human life (however, he can create the illusion of plants). The difficulty of the INT + Willpower roll to resist the illusion is equal to the result of the djinn's Sacred Word roll.

**Healing (permanent, no Sacred Word roll):** The djinn can heal other people's wounds and diseases. He can't heal himself. Healing restores 6D6 HP to the target, who may only benefit once per day, and lowers all disease or poison attributes by -3 (see page 68).

**Immolation (permanent, no Sacred Word roll):** The djinn can create fire on any surface, flammable or not. The fire has a maximum width of (INT x1) paces when created, and the djinn may try to set fire to an individual as a ranged attack on a roll of 10/6. Damage to living targets is +10. The flames persist for 3 actions, inflicting 1D6 damage per action.

**Lightning (permanent, no Sacred Word roll):** The djinn can throw a bolt of magical lightning up to 100 paces. The attack roll is 10/6, damage is +20. The attack requires two actions.

**Shapechange (permanent, no Sacred Word roll):** The djinn can take 1 action to assume another physical form; this is not an illusion, but a true shapechange. The power can be used any number of times, but the djinn cannot become larger than twice his normal size or smaller than a quarter of his normal size. He may assume any form, whether an animal or a individual he knows. The result must always be tangible: the djinn may not become incorporeal. The djinn acquires the natural abilities of any creature whose form he assumes (fangs, wings, etc), and may use them with a dice roll of DEX + Legend.

**Teleportation (permanent, no Sacred Word roll):** The djinn can move instantaneously to any place up to (INT x 50) paces away. Teleportation requires 1 action, with no chance of failure.

djinn and marids live in mirages. They can appear and disappear without trace.

All my research supports the saying that "if you cross paths with an afreet, your life is but a memory". These ancestral djinn are primitive creatures compared to the marids and true djinn. All afreeti share common features: their power, their rage, their destructive ability, and their complete lack of regard towards Marduk's laws. Unlike their more evolved kin, they move on the ground without artifice, they can't change shape, and they most often have the appearance of demonic creatures like one-eyed giants or large humanoids with scaly red skin. My studies told me the largest can be up to ten paces tall, although in general they are around ten feet. No one knows what they eat or what their habitat is; they seem to move constantly, day and night, tireless, with no specific goal. Maybe they avoid humans and busy areas for reasons I can't fathom; if your path ever leads you towards one, then don't be a fool: choose your life before your hunger for knowledge.

What? You want to know the djinn's riddle? Very well, it's this: "Ahmet needs a candle every night to go to his bed. With five used candles, he can make a new one. Knowing he began with twenty five, how many nights will his candles last?"

# Ghul

My first encounter with a ghul was when I was travelling with a small caravan to Al-Mamlakah Jabali. The caravan master had employed a handful of old veterans of the war against the invaders as guards. It was unusual to see warriors accompanying such a small caravan, but it reassured me.

The attack took place in the morning, while we were asleep. The shout of a sentry woke me, and I hurried from my tent. The first thing I saw was the sentry's body, hurled through the air in ungainly flight. The creature that had thrown it was thirty paces away: big, ten feet tall, massively built. It looked like a man, but was more bestial and primitive. Its face—if I can call that ignoble muzzle a face—was notable for its large jaw, filled with sharp teeth, and the small horns protruding from its skull. The ghul (for such it was) wore rags, a loincloth and coat ravaged by time, as if the creature had a perverse inkling of modesty. I now believe that they are a parody of human form, a joke by the demons that created these monsters. It was carrying a huge lumpen bone of some animal or other that it was clearly employing as a club.

The creature ripped open a tent with one hand, at the same time striking a massive blow to the head of the unfortunate within trying to flee. The first two guards arrived, hastily armed and armoured; for a moment, I thought they would beat the monster, its lumbering slowness contrasted so much with the soldiers' grace. But the ghul hit the first guard, who stumbled backwards from the impact, only to collapse, vomiting blood. The second guard struck the ghul on the leg, but the blow seemed to have no effect, and the monster grabbed the soldier's weapon arm and unblinkingly crushed his shoulder with a terrible crunching sound. I grabbed my few belongings and took shelter near the camel enclosure.

I could still hear screams as the ghul put the three other guards out of action. I fled, only looking back when I thought myself safe. I saw the other caravan members trying to escape death. Some succeeded, but others could not keep ahead of the ghul's gigantic strides.

I have since studied ghuls in the largest libraries of the land, and with the greatest sages. It's said they were once equals of the afreeti, but could never enter the mirages. They have haunted the deserts since, killing all humans they meet and feeding on their flesh. They can survive without food and water for several weeks, but can also spend three days devouring a huge number of victims. They can regenerate their wounds rapidly. They do not speak, or create anything but the rags they wear. Their demonic origin is clear:

## Afreet

| STR: 8 | Max Init: 10[1] |
|---|---|
| CON: 18 | HP: 180 |
| DEX: 8 | Soak: 24 |
| INT: 2 | Passive Defence: 20 |
| CHA: 2 | Magic Resistance: 12 |
| | Legend: 3 |

- ❖ **Skills:** Athletics 6, Endurance 10, Fighting (Bite, Claws) 6 (9), Survival (Desert) 5 (8).

- ❖ **Attacks /Active Defences:** Bite 17/8 +22 damage, Fist or Claws 17/8 +16 damage, Massive Suyuf 14/8 +24 damage.

- ❖ **Armour:** Thick hide (AV: 3).

- ❖ **Area Found:** Jazirat.

- ❖ **Notes:** 1: Because of its high Max Init, an afreet will almost always act before the Dragon-Marked. Rather than concentrating on one character, an afreet will often alternate between targets. Often it'll open its attacks with a Charge Attack.

**Afreeti don't usually use magic, unlike other djinn, but some individuals have a single power. They can take several shapes, and often have bestial characteristics (fangs, claws, and so on) which they fight with. Some have hands and can use manufactured or improvised weapons.**

horns, eyes like flaming almonds, and I don't know what else. I found some writings saying ghuls could assume human form, but surely that is just a legend.

# Golem

I carefully avoid the ruins you find along the trade routes. Not out of fear, but so as not to defile the last resting place of one of the faithful. The few rare times I have made exceptions have not gone well. I remember once I accompanied a small caravan whose master boasted that retrieving unusual objects from such ruins was his specialty.

We had stopped near the remains of a mausoleum of unknown origin. It didn't take long for the master's followers to open a passage leading deep into the tomb. I took a step back when the light entered the dark tunnel and I saw the whitened remains of a man. Doubtless one of the builders of the edifice. Ignoring my forebodings, we climbed down to explore the place.

The chamber we found was filled with debris, dust, and a dozen skeletons. A corridor led away, beneath the desert sands. We were about to enter when we heard the sound of metal scraping stone. I stepped back while my companions raised their scimitars or torches. The noise grew louder, and a nameless terror grew in my heart. Finally, the thing itself appeared: a grotesque parody of a human being, a creature made of metal, more than eight feet tall. Imagine the suit of armour of an infidel Westerner walking all on its own! Its head was carved with the features of a man, fixed for eternity in a hateful, fearsome expression. Two horns had been sculpted on its temples.

You have doubtless heard of **golems**—creatures animated by dark magic. Metal, clay or wood, these puppets are enchanted for evil purposes, or perhaps simply to protect the tomb of someone powerful. It is said that the secrets of breathing life into golems have been lost, but rumours in Jergath whisper some still have this forbidden knowledge. I've heard many tales about these creatures: all speak of their power, invulnerability, and implacable devotion to their task. A golem of clay is invulnerable to blunt weapons, its mass absorbing blows; golems of wood are invulnerable to cutting weapons other than a stout axe—they are even invulnerable to fire. Golems of metal withstand most attacks without showing any sign of damage. All can continue to act even if their head is cut off; their senses appear to be magical, and even the deepest darkness hides nothing from them. To stop a golem for once and for all, you must find and destroy the piece of parchment hidden inside the creature's body on which are written the formulae giving it its travesty of life. At least so I've heard.

The monster facing us was made of metal. My companions did not hesitate, and threw themselves into the attack, but their weapons just slid off its surface. Even when a blow struck a more vulnerable part, it seemed to have no effect. The golem sustained a dozen blows before going on the offensive. Without warning, one of its massive fists shot forward, lightning fast for something that size. Hassan didn't stand a chance: his head exploded like an overripe

## Metal Golem

| | |
|---|---|
| **STR:** 9 | **Max Init:** 5 |
| **CON:** 8 | **HP:** 80 |
| **DEX:** 3 | **Soak:** 11+9[1] |
| **INT:** 2 | **Passive Defence:** 12 |
| **CHA:** 1 | **Magic Resistance:** 12 |
| | **Legend:** 2 |

- ❖ **Skills:** Athletics 3, Endurance 3, Fighting (Brawling) 4 (7).
- ❖ **Attacks /Active Defences:** Brawling 10/3 +20 damage[2].
- ❖ **Armour:** Special.
- ❖ **Area Found:** Palaces, temples.
- ❖ **Notes:** 1: Non-magical damage against a metal golem is reduced by Soak + STR, and not just Soak. So, a golem of this type reduces damage by 20 points instead of 11.

  2: A golem will try to make Brutal Attacks at 16/9 +26 damage. Also, on any Critical Success, it inflicts 20 damage then grabs its target. Thereafter, the target must make a difficulty 18 STR or DEX roll every action to escape the hold, or suffer 12 points of damage per action.

  **Golems are magically animated creations:** they have no essential organs. However, each has hidden inside its body a piece of parchment which animates it. Finding this parchment and removing it will destroy the golem. The parchment is always accessible (it was placed at the end of the golem's creation process), but is often hidden in a hard-to-reach place. It's a difficulty 15 INT + Notice roll to notice where the parchment is hidden, and a difficulty 21 DEX + Athletics roll to remove it.

fruit. Prudently, I retreated. The caravan master, filled with an incomprehensible fury, dealt several blows that would have dismembered a man—again without effect. He didn't even have time to breathe: gripping him in a bear hug, the golem squeezed him until his rib cage burst.

I climbed up the rope. I could still hear the screams of my last two companions who hadn't had the time or presence of mind to follow me. Even today, I still hear the cracking of their bones when the golem caught them, their agonised screams. Only because I ran did I keep my life.

## Katanes

Our lands hold many secrets and dangers, but most monsters prefer to live in the wilderness, far from the habitations of people. Not so the *katanes*! What? You've never heard of them? How strange! Well, you've certainly passed one in a city street without noticing. How's that? Let me tell you...

I had been living in Fragrance for several months, tired of my constant travels and their inevitable encounters. I had set myself up as a scribe for hire and a *rawi*, and had taken the opportunity to surround myself with willing and comely women. Don't laugh! I was still a handsome man at the time! I lived peacefully, soothed

by their sweet embraces. But perhaps I am not fated to live in peace for long.

I had spent the evening in a tavern in Old Fragrance, relating some adventures and drinking a little fig liqueur. I was preparing to leave, when my gaze was drawn to a tall, well-built man with an angular face and dark eyes. He was dressed like a rich merchant. He had approached two dancers who had charmed us earlier with their art; he played calmly with a gold coin while he was talking. I don't know what drew my attention to the scene, perhaps I simply wished to be in his place? When he left with the two women, I

couldn't help following them, my curiosity piqued by some strange foreboding.

He plunged into the deserted streets, arms around the waists of his companions, who laughed gaily at his jokes. The threesome suddenly turned into a dark alley. I stopped a moment, hesitating, then followed after.

A few dozen paces ahead, an abominable spectacle awaited me. Both women lay on the ground, unconscious; there was no trace of the man I had followed. Instead, a creature black as night was leaning over the two unfortunate girls. A little larger than a sheep, its body was lean and slender, although powerfully muscled, and ended in a short tail. It was on all fours; its head was rounded, with large, red eyes, and its mouth gaped revealing a frightening set of teeth like a multitude of daggers. The creature plunged its teeth into the first woman's bared throat; blood flowed, and I heard a sickening sucking. I staggered, kept myself from falling by leaning against the wall. A horrified cry escaped my lips.

The katanes, its teeth never leaving its prey, raised its head towards me. I saw the neck of its victim twist as her backbone

# Katanes

**STR:** 6

**CON:** 7

**DEX:** 5

**INT:** 5

**CHA:** 4

**Max Init:** 6

**HP:** 70[1]

**Soak:** 14

**Passive Defence:** 17

**Magic Resistance:** 30

**Legend:** 5

- ❖ **Skills:** Athletics 6, Elegance 5, Endurance 5, Fighting (Bite) 3 (6), Flattery 3, Sacred Word 6[2], Stealth 4.

- ❖ **Attacks / Active Defences:** Bite 11/5 +12 damage[2].

- ❖ **Armour:** Thick hide (AV: 2).

- ❖ **Area Found:** Capharnaum.

- ❖ **Notes:** A katanes is a shapeshifting creature which avoids direct combat as much as it can, using cunning to reach its goals. It has the powers described below. A katanes can only live by drinking the blood of its victims. It loses (CON x 1) HP for every seven days it does not feed. It recovers HP as soon as it sucks blood from a target, regaining a number of HP equal to the damage caused.

**1:** Maximum HP can be exceeded by drinking blood, up to a maximum of (CON x 15) HP. A typical katanes may have as many as 105 HP if it has drunk enough

blood in the last seven days. Seven days after the most recent feeding, it will start to lose HP. A katanes which cannot drink human blood will eventually perish.

**2:** A katanes only uses its Sacred Word skill for its own powers; it uses no other magic.

**Mental Control:** A katanes can mentally control a number of individuals equal to its INT. At first, it induces a feeling of trust, even sexual attraction, to isolate its target from other humans. Then, it renders its victim completely passive, and attacks without resistance. Mental control requires a roll of INT + Sacred Word (11/5 for a typical katanes); the target may resist with a single INT + Willpower roll.

**Shapechange:** A katanes may change its appearance by making a difficulty 9 INT + Sacred Word roll. The appearance is necessarily human, but sex and age may vary. The transformation is instantaneous and of unlimited duration. Katanes usually assume their natural form to attack, although they may attack while in human form using weapons.

**Spider Climb:** A katanes can climb any vertical surfaces, either in human or natural form, no matter how smooth. They use DEX + Sacred Word instead of Athletics for such manoeuvres.

snapped. The monster looked me in the eye and I saw there as much cruelty as challenge. I turned and ran as fast as my legs could carry me.

In my haste, I hit upon a guard patrol a few hundred feet further. My stammering explanations led them to think I was drunk, but still they decided to follow me. My screams had attracted onlookers, and it was as a small troupe that we discovered the bloodless bodies of the two women. The guards concluded they were killed by a marauding desert dog—a fanciful explanation that was more reassuring than my own. My heart thumping, I returned home. As I had left the macabre scene, I had been seized by a feeling that I was being watched. I had looked all around me until my gaze had fallen on a woman who stood apart from the group. Her eyes were an intense black, and I shivered when I saw the same expression of cruelty and challenge. I returned home in a rush, packed my bags, and left for the desert the next morning.

My subsequent research told me little about the **katanes**. I am one of the few to have encountered one and lived to tell the tale. They feed on the blood of their victims, the only food which sustains them. They can fast for several days, feasting on human blood once or twice a fortnight, but must drink at least ten pints when they do. They can assume any human form, man or woman, child or elder; they usually adopt a shape most pleasant to their chosen prey, as if they could read it in their minds. Usually they strike by surprise, but are fearsome predators in combat. These monsters live in all inhabited places, preferably where there are so many people that their evil deeds remain unnoticed. They seem to be solitary, but at least one tale I read spoke of two of them joining forces and hunting together.

# Lamassu

Of course, I haven't just explored Jazirat. I've travelled to the North, East, and West as well. One of my most memorable encounters took place near Khalawat in mystical Nir Manel. I was accompanying a group of what you might call grave robbers. It wasn't really voluntary; these gentlemen had misled me regarding their intentions, knowing I had already visited the ruined shrines of Khalawat. They were holding me against my will, as those shrines are reputed to hold much treasure.

We were visiting one such place when the lamassu appeared. The brigands were roughing me up after I had explained yet again that I had no idea where any treasure was, and I thought my time had come, when a voice shouted: "Enough!" It was a deep voice, sonorous and powerful. My tormentors turned and I espied the owner of the voice.

The creature that had spoken had the body of a massive winged black bull, larger than even the largest of the beasts of Aragon. Its head was that of a man, with a long, braided beard, whose eyes flashed with anger. "You dare desecrate this holy place? I am its guardian. Flee, or face my wrath!"

My companions scoffed at these words, and two of them rushed forwards. The guardian reacted quickly, charging and using his great mass to hurl the brigands to the ground. He gave them no time to get back up, but crushed them beneath his hooves, killing them without mercy.

The numbers were against him. Four more robbers had drawn their weapons, and were spreading out while approaching the monster. The lamassu then unfolded his wings and beat them powerfully, rising up into the air and picking up altitude to escape his attackers. The bandits were already rejoicing at the guardian's flight, but it did not last. The lamassu reached the top of his ascent, then veered to one side and flew back at us. It was a wonder to see: so massive, yet so agile in the air. Taken aback, the thieves prepared to meet the attack, but the creature did not land. It seemed to gallop across the sky, its hooves pounding the air. Its feet struck two of the scoundrels before they could dodge, and they fell like stones, their skulls crushed.

The leader of the group hid behind a wall, but that didn't stop the lamassu. He ploughed into it, sending a shower of rocks and the hapless bandit into the air. Then he fell on the man where he landed as he was flailing for his dropped weapon. The man-bull showed no mercy, but rose on his hind legs then dropped the main bulk of his forequarters on my tormentor. I must confess I was as happy to see my gaolers defeated as I was worried to learn my own fate. I decided to run. The lamassu could have overtaken me easily, but merely watched as I moved away.

## Lamassu

| | |
|---|---|
| **STR:** 10 | **Max Init:** 7 |
| **CON:** 10 | **HP:** 100 |
| **DEX:** 4 | **Soak:** 17 |
| **INT:** 5 | **Passive Defence:** 14 |
| **CHA:** 3 | **Magic Resistance:** 30 |
| | **Legend:** 5 |

- ❖ **Skills:** Athletics (Flight) 4 (7), Endurance 8, Fighting (Hooves) 4 (7), Survival (Desert) 2 (5).

- ❖ **Attacks /Active Defences:** Hooves 11/4 +27 damage, Trampling 8/4 +31 damage; -3 Active Defence due to large size.

- ❖ **Armour:** Thick hide (AV: 2).

- ❖ **Area Found:** Nir Manel.

- ❖ **Notes:** A lamassu may only use one type attack in a given action. However, he may roll a single trample attack against multiple targets in his path; each potential target must make a CON + Endurance roll as an active defence or be thrown to the ground, taking full Trampling damage; on a success, the target takes only half Trampling damage.

  **For example:** A lamassu charges three individuals and rolls a 19. Each target succeeding on a difficulty 19 CON + Endurance roll is simply struck and takes half damage; otherwise he is struck, thrown to the ground, and suffers full damage.

If you encounter a lamassu on your travels, know that they always protect a place that is sacred to them, and which they will let no one desecrate. They are both intelligent and brave. No fight seems to frighten them, but they use all their cunning and the full power of their muscles and mass. Lamassu are more agile in the air than on the ground and, though they are slower than birds, they have the same grace and agility when borne by the winds. I was told some places attracted more than one lamassu, and that the largest group ever encountered included eleven of these creatures. Normally, however, they are solitary beings. There seems to be no female of the species, and thus their number presumably diminishes, although they may live for hundreds of years.

## Nasnas

There are creatures you laugh at even though you know nothing about them. Creatures like the demonic **nasnas**, which children would throw stones at if they saw one at the circus. But you should never trust appearances.

The first time I saw a nasnas, we were crossing the Pass of Kerleth, west of Kh'saaba. I was travelling with a rich merchant who, feeling his end approaching, had gathered a small entourage and set out to see the wonders of the Caravan Kingdoms. It was when we were upon the rubble-strewn flats of Kerleth, our employer, the guide, five guards, and myself; we had traded our camels for horses and were having a quiet stop.

We heard a loud voice declaring unintelligible words. The speaker soon emerged from behind a rock. My first instinct was to laugh: it was a ridiculous creature, a one-legged torso with a single arm, head, and supporting tail. It was grotesque, but something made me ill at ease. The nasnas was entirely hairless, its skull with a small bony ridge, prominent teeth like little daggers, its oversized arm with a hand big enough to grasp a man's head in its palm. The creature seemed as surprised as we were.

For a moment, the demon hesitated. Then it shrieked something in a language none of us could understand, and its tone was anything but friendly. The guards did not take it seriously, since it seemed so clumsy on its single leg. Out of bravado, one threw a stone at the creature, but missed. Fast as lightning, the creature caught it in its hand. I saw the dust that the stone had been trickle out of the half-opened fist. The guards were surprised. Then even more so when the nasnas attacked.

It leapt, supporting itself on its tail, bounding effortlessly across the twenty paces that separated us. The guards had no time to react before one was grabbed by the neck, which was crushed in seconds. The nasnas threw the flopping body at the two other guards, who fell on their backs. One guard—a little faster—struck the demon, but the thick hide of its skull was barely marked by the blow. Balancing on its leg, the creature lashed its tail, hurling the foolhardy guard to the ground. The last guard standing feinted with his blade, but the monster turned the weapon with the back if its hand, then smashed its fist into the guard's torso.

## Nasnas

| | |
|---|---|
| **STR:** 8 | **Max Init:** 6 |
| **CON:** 8 | **HP:** 80 |
| **DEX:** 5 | **Soak:** 12 |
| **INT:** 2 | **Passive Defence:** 14 |
| **CHA:** 2 | **Magic Resistance:** 12 |
| | **Legend:** 2 |

- ❖ **Skills:** Athletics 3, Endurance 5, Fighting (Brawling) 3 (6).
- ❖ **Attacks / Active Defences:** Brawling 11/5 +10 damage, Tail[1] 8/5 +12 damage.
- ❖ **Armour:** Thick hide (AV: 2).
- ❖ **Area Found:** Kh'saaba.
- ❖ **Notes:** 1: Nasnas only use their Tail attack against targets they deem harmless, since it deprives it of one of its supports. In the action following a Tail attack, the nasnas suffers a -2 DEX penalty.

  **Jumping:** A nasnas may make a tail-assisted jump across great distance. It leaps (STR x 1) paces upwards and (STR x 2) paces in length without effort.

He collapsed, spitting blood. Using its advantage, the nasnas leapt into the air again, landing on a fallen guard, whose ribcage burst with the shock.

Our guide had fled already. Our employer was desperately trying to mount his horse, but his rotund girth hampered him. I wanted to help, but the demon leapt from the remains of the crushed guard and appeared right next to him. I saw the fear in the old man's face. He died without screaming when the tip of the nasnas's tongue—a bone shard sharp as a spear—pierced his abdomen and ran him through. My horse chose that moment to bolt, carrying me away from the slaughter. When I turned my head, the nasnas had killed the horses and was finishing off the guards.

Since then I've seen nasnas three more times, but I've never got close. Some people say they're descendants of two-headed djinn that couldn't stand each other and decided to separate, each taking one head, leg, and arm. I think that's just a story. Nevertheless, nasnas are aggressive and defend their territory. No one has ever survived long enough to analyse their language, and no nasnas has ever been caught alive. They're intelligent and fearless; they don't charge into melee like bloodthirsty beasts, but use subterfuge to attack small groups of warriors.

## Raiders, Bandits, and Other Scoundrels

The desert holds many dangers, my friend, from sandstorms to treacherous ground to the most fabulous monsters. The greatest danger, though, is an entirely different beast: man! In every caravanserai you can hear tales of the dark deeds of the desert raiders. Almost everyone here has lost a family member, friend, or acquaintance to their attacks.

The raiders roam the desert in gangs of twenty, thirty, a hundred or more, often accompanied by slaves, kidnapped women, ne'er-do-wells and hangers-on. I was told the largest gang belonged to Yazid Ibn Abi Hakim, with more than six hundred bandits and just as many followers. They live off attacking caravans and enslaving the survivors. The fate of the womenfolk is terrible; the raiders keep them in their tents before they're sold in the slave market.

The raiders never chase caravans. No, they wait quietly, maybe near an oasis, for tasty prey to arrive. They don't attack absolutely every caravan; some don't look rich enough, and they don't want to dissuade everyone from travelling their way. When they do go raiding, they spend at least three days attacking every caravan they come across. Then they ride deep into the desert, back to their camp or another oasis.

There's not a lot of difference between the desert raiders and the Al-Fariqani pirates, or those from the floating city of Anvaros. They're just as bloodthirsty, and the way they work is similar. It's common knowledge that many merchants from the cities actually trade with the raiders, who pretend to be honest caravaneers when they approach settlements.

## Group of Babouche-Dragger Bandits

| | |
|---|---|
| **STR:** 2 | **Max Init:** 3 |
| **CON:** 2 | **HP:** None |
| **DEX:** 3 | **Soak:** 3 |
| **INT:** 1 | **Passive Defence:** 11 |
| **CHA:** 1 | **Legend:** 1 |

- ❖ **Skills:** Athletics 2, Endurance 2, Fighting 2, Survival 2.
- ❖ **Attacks / Active Defences:** Suyuf 5/3 +12 damage, Recurved Bow 5/3 +9 damage; +1 bonus die per group member after the first.
- ❖ **Armour:** None.
- ❖ **Area Found:** Anywhere.

## Valiant Captain Raider

| | |
|---|---|
| STR: 2 | Max Init: 3 |
| CON: 3 | HP: 30 |
| DEX: 3 | Soak: 5 |
| INT: 2 | Passive Defence: 12 |
| CHA: 2 | Legend: 2 |

- ❖ **Skills:** Athletics 3, Endurance 3, Fighting 3, Survival 3.
- ❖ **Attacks /Active Defences:** Suyuf 6/3 +13 damage, Recurved Bow 5/3 +10 damage.
- ❖ **Armour:** None.
- ❖ **Area Found:** Anywhere.

If you ever see raiders, run away as fast as your mount can carry you! Leave everything behind, never look back. That's how I've survived. Many of my companions weren't so lucky.

## Roc

Of all the legendary birds, one is by far and away the greatest: the roc. The caravan I was travelling with was following the northern edges of the desert in the direction of the small village of Emlebak. It was a medium-sized caravan of fifty camels and thirty men. I was drifting to sleep in the saddle as the sun sank towards the horizon—we would be setting camp soon—when my eyes were drawn to a shadow crossing the desert. A huge shadow. I raised my eyes, expecting to see a cloud.

In the sky flew one of the most majestic birds I had ever seen. Its head resembled that of the griffon vulture; its tail tapered in a single feather of unusual length. Its plumage was ochre, except for the white-feathered tips of its wings. Not too extraordinary? Wait a moment.

The bird was *huge*. Its wingspan must have been thirty paces. Its body alone was fifteen paces long. Its talons were bigger than a man. With a shout, I alerted my companions, while the bird wheeled soundlessly above us. It seemed to notice us when the caravan started to disperse. It made a long turn, and then returned in our direction. It furled its wings like a bird of prey on the stoop, and dived. As it passed overhead, its talons grasped one of our camels, lifting it effortlessly off the ground. As it rose into the air, the rider fell, smashing into the ground.

One of the soldiers notched an arrow and shot at the creature. The arrow hit its mark, and the bird gave a strident shriek. But it

## Valiant Captain Champion

| | |
|---|---|
| STR: 3 | Max Init: 4 |
| CON: 4 | HP: 40 |
| DEX: 4 | Soak: 10 |
| INT: 2 | Passive Defence: 14 |
| CHA: 2 | Legend: 3 |

- ❖ **Heroic Virtues:** Bravery 3 (2), Faith 2 (1), Loyalty 6 (3).
- ❖ **Skills:** Assassination 5, Athletics 4, Endurance 3, Fighting 5, Intrusion 4, Stealth 6, Survival 4, Thievery 4 .
- ❖ **Attacks /Active Defences:** Suyuf 9/4 +13 damage, Recurved Bow 9/4 +10 damage.
- ❖ **Armour:** None.
- ❖ **Area Found:** Anywhere.
- ❖ **Notes:** Most raiders are Babouche-Draggers. For each group of 6 Babouche-Draggers, there will be one Valiant Captain. The leader of a large gang (30 raiders or more) will probably be a Champion.

kept its prey. Quickly it rounded on us again. With its free talon it caught an unfortunate soldier, who it dropped from a height of fifty paces or more. And so it continued, the roc falling on the runaways, until finally it grabbed another camel. I escaped its attentions by taking shelter beneath the shadow of a rocky overhang.

These gigantic birds are not rare, and they do not shy from attacking caravans—even large ones. They carry their prey away to their eyries. Female birds lay a clutch of up to five eggs every two years, only half of which hatch. A sailor once told me that, dropped in a roc's nest (he had unfortunately remained attached to the horse a roc had seized as prey), he had found piles of diamonds the creature had accumulated. I don't know whether the man could be believed—he seemed more interested in the wine I was offering. But take heart! Rocs rarely attack human beings, which they seem to find meagre pickings. Horses and camels, on the other hand, they dive on eagerly, and woe betide you if your mount is chosen! Some of these monsters have even attacked boats, perhaps mistaking them for the great fish of the sea.

## Roc

| | |
|---|---|
| **STR:** 18 | **Max Init:** 8[1] |
| **CON:** 26 | **HP:** 260 |
| **DEX:** 4 | **Soak:** 36 |
| **INT:** 3 | **Passive Defence:** 6 |
| **CHA:** 1 | **Magic Resistance:** 18 |
| | **Legend:** 3 |

- ❖ **Skills:** Athletics 5, Endurance 4, Fighting (Talons) 3 (6), Notice 6.

- ❖ **Attacks /Active Defences:** Talons 10/4 +34 damage[2], Beak 7/4 +32 damage; -9 Active Defence due to enormous size.

- ❖ **Armour:** Thick hide (AV: 2).

- ❖ **Area Found:** Edges of the deserts.

- ❖ **Notes:** 1: The relatively low Max Init is due to its clumsiness on the ground and inability to hover.

  2: If a roc rolls a Critical Success, it will grab and hold its target. The target must make a difficulty 21 STR or DEX + Heroism roll to escape the grab, or be carried away to wherever the bird wishes.

  **Most of the time, human-sized targets or smaller don't interest a roc; only while defending itself or its nest will a roc attack a human. When fighting on the ground the roc can only use its beak.**

# Scarab Beetle Swarm

So, you want to know why I hate abandoned tombs? No, it isn't heartlessness—it's fear. It was just such a place where I witnessed one of the most abominable things that can happen in our lands. Even thinking of it fills me with horror. But you have to know this, it could save your life.

I was young, younger even than you, and I was accompanying one of my uncles on an expedition he had organised with one of his, shall we say, "associates". There were about fifteen of us, and we were travelling to some abandoned ruins said to hold vast treasures. The ruins were deep in the desert, leagues away from any trade route. Unimpressive to look at: just some pillars sticking out of the sand. The entrance was blocked, and it took us more than ten hours to dig it out. It was a simple sealed slab, opening onto a dark chamber six paces below. With some rope, we climbed down.

The entrance chamber was huge, its walls covered in colourful paintings. There was no obvious treasure, but the beauty of the place excited us beyond measure. Several corridors had been blocked by large stones, but we were undaunted. It took several hours to open the first passage, which led to chambers of jars filled with cereal, oil, and salt. The second passage was more interesting, and led to a cluster of smaller chambers, the last of which contained a mound of gold. Yes—a mound of gold, the height of a man and two paces wide! I was on my guard at the sight of the warning glyphs on the walls, but my companions rushed in unheeding, plunging their hands into the pile.

There was a noise I could not easily identify, like a muffled scratching on stone. I made to shout at my companions to run, when I saw with horror the small black creatures issuing from the walls. Beetles—the largest maybe three inches long—in their thousands. They moved at an incredible speed, like a black tide flowing towards my companions. I screamed, but there was no time to react: the beetles fell upon them, devouring them, pouring into their mouths, feasting on their eyes. When I saw my uncle, his face eaten away, his eye hanging from its empty socket, my bowels gave way, and I took to my heels, hoping my companions would hold the swarm at bay. I thought I heard insects pursuing; I reached the entrance; I got out; I dropped the slab to close the tomb. Then I threw up everything I'd eaten for the last three days.

The return journey was a nightmare. How could I face my uncle's wife to tell her of his terrible end? Nothing had stopped the beetle swarm; weapons had been useless. Fleeing was the only recourse; all other choices meant death. I tried to find references to these creatures in other writings, but my searches were fruitless. Had no one survived an encounter with them until now?

## Scarab Beetle Swarm

STR: -

CON: $5^1$

DEX: 10

INT: 1

CHA: 1

Max Init: 6

HP: $50^1$

Soak: $5^1$

Passive Defence: 20

Magic Resistance: 6

Legend: 0

- ❖ **Skills:** n/a.
- ❖ **Attacks /Active Defences:** Bite 10/20 +10 damage.
- ❖ **Armour:** Special[1].
- ❖ **Area Found:** Anywhere.
- ❖ **Notes:** 1: A tomb beetle swarm is treated as a single creature. An average swarm contains 5000 beetles and covers 5 square paces on the ground, with 5 points of CON. For each additional 1000 beetles, increase CON by +1 and the area covered by +1 square pace. Attacks against the swarm do no damage unless they are area attacks (flames, sprays of poison, etc.).

**Any target in the path of a scarab beetle swarm suffers a bite attack.**

## Scorpion Man

We had left the oasis only two days before, slowed by an infuriating wind which insinuated itself into our clothes and burnooses. Women, some caravaneers say, bring bad luck to caravans, and we were escorting a dozen to a harem down South!

When the wind finally dropped, I saw the monsters not far from our caravan. There were ten of them. Their head, arms, and torso were those of a man, but their abdomen was that of a scorpion, with eight chitinous legs and a long tail arched over its back—a tail which ended in a sting as big as a dagger! At the front of this repulsive body, two huge pincers jabbed in all directions. The muscular human body which topped this bestial abdomen was bronzed by the sun and entirely hairless; there was no humanity in their eyes. Each stood seven feet tall, and their animal body was bigger than any horse. I estimated each should weigh about a thousand pounds.

The most imposing of these monsters advanced towards our caravan and, in a strangled guttural voice I could barely understand, demanded that the women of our caravan should be handed over to him and his fellows, who would then let the rest of us go in peace.

From my studies I knew that scorpion men look for human women to bear their young. There is no female to their species, but somehow they are capable of carnal relations with our women. The tales I had read were terrifying, relating the horrors their captives undergo. Most are driven mad when their bellies swell and the filthy creatures grow within them; many would prefer death to the fate which awaits them, but the scorpion men permit no such easy release. Six months later, the evil young burst forth, sometimes two or three, and no mother survives; the stings of these frenzied sons finish off any who might otherwise endure.

This disgusting species does not deserve to live under our skies. They gather in tribes of ten to fifty individuals, in underground caves. They are skilled at burrowing and tunnelling, and seem impervious to pain. One captured scorpion man is said to have survived more than thirty days without eating or drinking, in the desert sun. Finally, he became insane and committed suicide with his own sting.

The rare naturalists who have managed to get close to the scorpion men report that their society is based on the law of the strongest. Violent combats oppose pretenders to the tribal chief. Death in these bouts is rare, but defeated chiefs must leave the tribe. Children are raised by the whole group without any notion of kinship; a scorpion manchild reaches his adult size at age 8. Their life expectancy seems to be more than fifty years. Some unscrupulous caravans trade with this people, exchanging gems or precious metals for weapons, tools, cloth, and sometimes even women.

But back to our tale. Yusuf, the leader of the caravan guards, laughed scornfully as he drew his scimitar. We trusted the thirty soldiers accompanying us; they had proved their skill and determination during an attack by raiders when approaching the oasis, killing six of the bandits without loss or even wounds. Three guards charged the one they thought to be the scorpion man leader, but these creatures are quick; he had already drawn two scimitars, and moved his pincers at the same time. Before our soldiers were close enough to strike, the head of one flew into the air, snipped off by one of the pincers. The two other soldiers perished an instant later beneath the monster's blades.

That was the signal for the other scorpion men to charge, sowing death and desolation. Yussuf succumbed without even wounding one of the monsters. Seeing that all was lost, and despite the begging of the women, I resolved to flee.

## Scorpion Man

| | |
|---|---|
| STR: 5 | Max Init: 6 |
| CON: 7 | HP: 70 |
| DEX: 6 | Soak: 11 |
| INT: 3 | Passive Defence: 16 |
| CHA: 2 | Magic Resistance: 15 |
| | Legend: 2 |

- ❖ **Skills:** Athletics 4, Endurance 5, Fighting (Blades, Pincers, Polearms) 1 (4), Intimidate 3, Survival (Desert) 3 (6).
- ❖ **Attacks /Active Defences:** Pincers 10/6 + 15 damage, Suyuf 10/6 +16 damage, Spear[1] 10/6 +14 damage, Sting 7/6 +6[2].
- ❖ **Armour:** Chitinous carapace (AV: 2).
- ❖ **Area Found:** Jazirat.
- ❖ **Notes:** 1: Spear attacks are always Brutal Attacks.
- ❖ 2: Poison: Deadliness 5 Incapacitation 1 Rapidity 6.

**Scorpion men can use two weapons without meeting the usual prerequisites. They attack two targets with their pincers (one pincer attack per target), and a third with their weapons, in the same action, for a total of three attacks. If they use their sting, however, they may make no other attack that round.**

## Sea Serpent

You know of my aversion for travelling by water when I cannot see the shore. But do you know I once travelled the sea? Not much, for sure, but nevertheless I've visited the city-states of Agalanthia; I've even seen once-great Therema. It was during one of my voyages that my fear of the sea was born.

I was accompanying a captain of one of those pirate ships that dares brave the elements. He wished to make one more voyage before retiring or dying. He had made twelve such journeys that had made him a rich man, but he had frittered away his gold on a dissolute life. So he decided to make a thirteenth.

We were sailing not far from Etrusia. The sea was calm, and for once my stomach was, too. We had the good fortune to happen upon a school of flying fish, those strange creatures that leap from the waters and soar for great distances. Several had ended their flights on our boat, so I took advantage and was drawing and studying them.

I was settled at the front of the boat, sitting with my stylus and tablet on the figurehead that served as my seat. It was the ideal place to sit on hot, calm days; from there I could observe the sea and the prow cleave the waves, without getting in the way of the crew. I was daydreaming when my eyes were drawn to a piece of flotsam floating a few paces from the ship. I quickly espied other debris on the surface of the sea; doubtless the remains of a vessel, and a good-sized one if I was any judge.

I called the captain, who watched the horizon with worry as soon as he set eyes on my discovery. He ordered full sail. I wanted to quiz him further, when my attention was distracted by a dark shape passing under the ship. It was huge, sixty paces long, three paces wide.

My cry alerted the captain. He rushed to the poop deck, barking orders, and the crew stepped up the pace. I had rarely seen such agitation. Out of precaution, I left my perch to take shelter by the railing. I scanned the sea, not knowing what to look for, but with growing fear. The captain had taken the helm and was manoeuvring to leave with greater speed. It was then I saw the underwater shadow again. The thing seemed to be circling us, drawing closer each time. My fear turned to terror when I saw part of the monster emerge from the wave: an immense reptile, with gracile fins all along its bulk. The shadow vanished when the creature dived.

Our respite did not last. Seconds later, with a sound like a waterfall, the head of the serpent spewed from the water. Huge, greenish scales, encrusted with shells, a maw half-open revealing teeth as long as your arm, a snake tongue darting in all directions. The head towered ten paces above us, and I screamed with the sailors in terror. The monster dove at us, passed just under the ship with a shudder, then lifted it into the air and sent it falling downwards with a crash. The crew had seized spears and were preparing to defend their lives, but the monster gave them little time.

## Sea Serpent

| | |
|---|---|
| **STR:** 20 | **Max Init:** 8[1] |
| **CON:** 28 | **HP:** 280 |
| **DEX:** 7 | **Soak:** 36 |
| **INT:** 2 | **Passive Defence:** 9 |
| **CHA:** 1 | **Magic Resistance:** 12 |
| | **Legend:** 3 |

- ❖ **Skills:** Athletics 5, Endurance 8, Fighting (Bite, Body Smash) 2 (5), Notice 4.
- ❖ **Attacks /Active Defences:** Body Smash 12/7 +35 damage, Bite 12/7 +38 damage[2]; -9 Active Defence due to enormous size.
- ❖ **Armour:** Scales (AV: 5).
- ❖ **Area Found:** The sea.
- ❖ **Notes:** Human-sized targets suffer a body smash attack when the sea serpent passes beside them. The serpent attacks ships by lifting them up or smashing them. It will only bite if it wants to eat a victim.

**1:** Max Init is relatively low, explained by the fact that it's too big to act rapidly against human opponents, and does not remain in one place long enough to make more than a single attack.

**2:** Bite damage is for targets not swallowed whole. If the serpent attacks with a Critical Success, any target up to twice human size is swallowed whole. Survival in the serpent's gut is at most a couple of rounds.

When the sea serpent resurfaced it was directly beneath the ship. It threw us high into the air, above the waves. The hull broke with the shock and sailors fell into the sea; I clung onto the timbers for dear life. When the boat fell down again and turned on its side, the creature tore the aftcastle away with its maw.

All was lost. The sea serpent swallowed the two sailors who had been in the aftcastle with the captain. I grasped at split timbers floating in the wreckage. I heard the screams of the drowning, struggling in the water. The sea serpent made three more passes, picking off the survivors, swallowing limbs and timbers alike.

Why did it spare me? I still have no idea. Perhaps it had sated its infernal hunger. But when evening came I was alone on the ocean, drifting in the debris, bereft of hope.

I was rescued by an Agalanthian ship, babbling like a madman. They were to sell me into slavery, but I escaped at the first opportunity and made my way to Jazirat.

The sea serpent is the terror of every sailor, matched only by the fearsome kraken. No ship can rival its speed or resist its attack; death awaits any vessel crossing its path. They say the Occidentians lost five ships of men and horses during their crossing to Carrassine. I've read hints that it might be possible to survive several days in the belly of such a beast, but I fear those are just tall tales, and that a few minutes of agony is all that awaits those swallowed by those terrifying jaws.

## Sila'at

As you'll discover, the only refuge in the desert is the oasis. They're often protected, and you can sleep peacefully there. At least, most of the time; pay heed to my next lesson.

We'd reached an oasis and were not alone; about a hundred caravaneers were staying there. Night had fallen and groups had gathered musicians and storytellers. There were women among us, including some travelling with the caravans, but one surpassed in beauty anything I had ever seen in the desert.

She was talking to three men, clearly merry with drink. I was close enough to hear her voice, although I could not make out the words. She was a beauty, her perfect curves barely hidden by her veils in the torchlight. Her voice was bewitching, and I could not help but follow her group as it strolled away. It seemed extraordi-

## Sila'at

| | |
|---|---|
| STR: 4 | Max Init: 5 |
| CON: 5 | HP: 50 |
| DEX: 5 | Soak: 9 |
| INT: 4 | Passive Defence: 15 |
| CHA: 5 | Magic Resistance: 24 |
| | Legend: 4 |

- ❖ **Skills:** Athletics 4, Endurance 4, Fighting 3, Flattery 5, Music 3, Poetry 4, Sacred Word 4.
- ❖ **Attacks /Active Defences:** Claws and Fangs 8/5 +10 damage.
- ❖ **Armour:** None.
- ❖ **Area Found:** Desert.
- ❖ **Notes:** The sila'at is not a good fighter, and avoids combat, preferring to use cunning and mind control. She feeds exclusively on human flesh, usually men, but she'll devour women, too. Her powers of seduction only work on targets attracted to women. She has the following powers:

**Charm:** The sila'at can charm anyone attracted by her beauty, controlling up to (INT x 1) persons at a time. A charmed person does anything to please the sila'at, even offering his throat to her fangs. A charmed person witnessing her feeding will remain charmed and take no action to flee or help the victim, although he'll remember what happened (it's rare for a sila'at to leave witnesses). Charming a target requires an INT + Sacred Word roll, resisted by the target's INT + Willpower. A charmed person will remain charmed as long as he is within sight of the sila'at, or until the sila'at releases him from the charm, or until the sila'at dies. Charmed individuals will take no offensive action, and the sila'at may not use them as bodyguards. Charming does not require concentration and is instantaneous.

**Human Appearance (permanent, no Sacred Word roll):** The sila'at may take the illusory form of a woman of great beauty. This will always appear to be the same woman to a given target, although the same sila'at may appear to be different women to different targets. Even if these differences are mentioned, those observing her will tend to disregard them, focussing instead on her great beauty. The illusion can't be cancelled, but it will fall away whenever the sila'at is feeding.

nary to me that such a beauty should wish to pass time with such a gaggle of drunkards.

They moved to a place away from the rest. I could hear their laughter and low voices. But when I drew closer the spectacle I beheld turned my stomach. The three men sprawled over the ground, and the woman kneeled next to them. The men were laughing, their movements spasmodic, as if they were losing themselves to drink. Then the woman—or should I say creature—began to change. Her eyes turned fiery red, her face distended, eyes stretching like almonds, her nostrils tightening into slits, her wide lips gaping in a massive jaw. I saw the whole thing by torchlight, and it filled me with horror. The monster had now completed its transformation: a hairless head with elongated skull, no ears or nose, slanting eyes shining evilly, a fang-filled maw.

The **sila'at**—such is the name people give these monsters— plunged its teeth into the first man's throat. He did not react at all, and his companions continued to laugh. The monster raised its head when I cried out with terror, and its eyes met mine. A grin split its loathsome face.

I fled, screaming, alerting the caravaneers. When I had regained my calm, I explained what I had seen, and a group of us returned to the macabre scene. The three men were dead, their throats torn out, their hearts missing from their chests. But of the sila'at there was no sign; nor did I see the beautiful woman.

There are many legends about these creatures. Some say they can only survive the day in human form, and that their voice will charm the most hardened of men, rendering them docile like sheep to be slaughtered, but that their power has no effect on women.

Some women can be too beautiful, my friend. Beware their enchanting powers.

## Simurgh

It was on my last trip to southeastern Jazirat, near the capital of the Kingdom of Kathrat, that I encountered a **simurgh**. I was traveling in the company of my faithful Ramazan, who had followed me for many years. The day was drawing in, but we still had far to go. We were looking for a good spot to camp, when a deep male voice called to me. I looked round to see who spoke.

It was perched on a large branch, about two paces from the ground, in a tree not far away. The bird—if I can call it that—was as large as a great eagle. Its plumage was bright, coloured red, orange, and yellow, and its feathers had black tips. Its talons were red. Most astonishing of all was its head, which was that of a man with a long beard and long black hair, and skin browned by the sun. It smiled at me and, for the first time in years, I felt confident and relaxed.

### Simurgh

| STR: 4 | Max Init: 4 |
| CON: 5 | HP: 50 |
| DEX: 4 | Soak: 9 |
| INT: 10 | Passive Defence: 14 |
| CHA: 8 | Magic Resistance: 30 |
| | Legend: 4 |

- ❖ **Skills:** Athletics 4, Endurance 4, Fighting 3, History & Peoples 8, Instruction 6, Music 3, Sacred Word 6, Storytelling 6.

- ❖ **Attacks /Active Defences:** Claws 7/4 +8 damage.

- ❖ **Armour:** None.

- ❖ **Area Found:** Jazirat.

- ❖ **Notes:** Simurgh are friendly to travellers, although strange. They seek knowledge, and are eager to listen to the tales of those they meet. In return, they tell a tale themselves. They usually do not answer questions, but will provide a single answer to one question that will be enigmatic but always true. They're never aggressive and will flee if attacked. However, they are not defenceless if they must defend themselves, and will not hesitate to retaliate if given no choice.

  **Appeasement (permanent, no Sacred Word roll):** Creatures in a 30-pace radius around the simurgh feel peaceful and calm. It requires an opposed INT + Willpower roll to take any offensive action.

  **Power of the Word:** A simurgh may use the words of creation to undo what was done and thus irrevocably destroy anything which exists on the Earth. This is a simple difficulty 12 INT + Sacred Word roll, and removes from existence a single individual target. There is no way to resist this. In return, the simurgh suffers damage equal to the target's maximum Hit Points, and so may die as a result. A simurgh will only use this power in extremis, and will be forever haunted by the feeling of emptiness left by the destruction of a living thing—assuming they survive.

  **The Tree of Truth:** Not a power, but secret knowledge of a real tree, which exists somewhere in the world, the quest for which is the mark of true Heroes. Only the simurgh know its location, and they protect it fiercely. The fruit of the Tree of Truth compels those who eat of it to tell only the truth until the next moon—they may not lie, even by omission. None can escape this, not even the Gods.

The creature tilted its head to the left, then to the right, as it asked me questions, rolling its eyes in its sockets. It asked me who I was, where I came from, where I was going, and many other things. I answered as best I could, without protest. After a time it paused, then began to relate to me tales of the distant past which had happened in the place we now stood—when, according to the creature, it had been young. I did not want to interrupt its nostalgic reverie, nor did I move, fearing it would depart. It spoke on, for a long time, and I felt that Ramazan, who had returned from his search for a campsite, stood behind me and listened too, without making a sound.

Finally, it fell silent, having described the magnificent spectacle of the setting sun over the walls of the Madina Al-Muhit and the River of Abundance. It flapped its wings. Before it took flight, I asked it: "Who are you?" It furled its wings again and said, with a smile: "I am the one that brings the word that sets you free." And, with that, it took wing.

I've never seen a simurgh again, and I will regret that to my dying day. These creatures bring learning, they are the incarnation of knowledge. I have never heard tell of them being anything other than friendly to strangers. However, it's difficult to converse with them: they choose a story that they tell in exchange for another tale, or for your answers to their questions, however insignificant they may seem.

## Spectre

The moon was peaceful, playing on the sea, and I watched the waves breaking on the rocks. I was a son of the desert, and there I was contemplating the unfathomable deep off the coast of Sagrada. I had never been drawn to navigation, fearing too much for my health, but the spectacle of the sea had always driven me into a state close to bliss. I don't know how long I had been there, when the voice of the guide on my next voyage distracted me. He had come to talk about his choice of itinerary and, on the way, he had found a little house that seemed abandoned. He seemed excited by his discovery, which I did not understand, until he took me by the hand and led me to the place. Strangely, I had passed the building by without noticing it. It was a simple wooden hut hardly bigger than our tents, obviously abandoned.

A shiver of fear ran through me when my companion showed me what had excited him. Through the bare window I saw an interior filled with amphorae, rolls of fine fabrics, cutlery of precious metals. I could not believe my eyes. Stunned, I stared at my guide, who clearly thought himself incapable of bearing away these treasures alone, and so had come to elicit my aid. I told him my misgivings, but the man would not listen, dragging me unwilling to the wooden door. He entered quickly, I following mechanically, my willpower blunted by his haste. Everything inside looked real.

The door slammed behind us, and panic rose in my breast as I tried to re-open it in vain. My companion seemed dazed, contemplating the riches, unaware of the danger which threatened us. The temperature dropped, and I felt the evil presence before I saw it: the master of the place, a creature almost transparent but for the shimmer in its appearance which made it visible. It floated at the other end of the room, gathering the darkness around it. The guide's torch guttered, although I felt no wind.

My eyes were locked on the apparition. Vaguely human, its legs trailed away into shadow. Its face was gaunt, its eye-sockets empty, its lips yawning in a toothless chasm, like a sick or dead old man. It moved his arms softly like it was trying to communicate, but its mouth made no sound.

Then my guide committed an act of madness. He leapt on the creature, knife in hand—he didn't want it to keep its treasure! The blade passed through the spectre without resistance or wound. The guide took a step back, surprised; then the revenant's ghostly hands clutched at his temples, and it pulled the mouth of the horrified guide to his, drinking his life energy in a shining golden torrent that flowed between them. My companion's skin wrinkled, and he aged at a staggering speed.

I threw myself through the first opening I could find—the window—fleeing to the outside. I returned the next day, in daylight, with guards, but we found nothing but the body of an old man I could barely recognise. The wooden house had gone.

These creatures are called **spectres**, and are lost souls trapped in our world. Something prevents their passage to the lands beyond, perhaps a horrible crime that forever closes the gates of the afterlife, perhaps a burning desire to avenge their own murders. They are only encountered at night, and often recreate a scene from their

# Spectre

**STR:** -
**CON:** 12
**DEX:** 5
**INT:** 3
**CHA:** 2

**Max Init:** 7
**HP:** 120[1]
**Soak:** 18[1]
**Passive Defence:** 14
**Magic Resistance:** Special
**Legend:** 1

- ❖ **Skills:** Athletics 3, Endurance 4, Fighting (Embrace) 1 (4), Sacred Word 2.
- ❖ **Attacks /Active Defences:** Embrace[2] 9/5 + special.
- ❖ **Armour:** Intangibility[1].
- ❖ **Area Found:** Anywhere.
- ❖ **Notes:** 1: The spectre is an intangible creature, and cannot be hit or damaged by weapons made on Earth (if you have a weapon forged in a mirage, that might be another story...).

  2: A spectre's embrace may affect a material target (normally, the creature is insubstantial, passing through all physical matter). If the spectre succeeds on its attack roll, it embraces its victim, who can no longer act freely and loses (spectre INT x 4) Hit Points per round while its life energy is drained. A victim killed in this way looks withered and prematurely aged. The spectre remains immaterial throughout the embrace, and only magical attacks may damage it.

  Spectres are souls trapped on earth that desperately seek to escape to the beyond. They beg everyone they meet past to attract a victim. They always expect something from the living but, incapable of communication, they finish by killing without pity, man, woman, old person or child. No living being can touch them, nor any mortal weapon wound them. Some exorcisms may force them into the shadow realm, but the requirements are almost impossible to fulfil, and I have never heard of a ritual that succeeded. Expect no pity from these monsters, keep as far from them as you can, and avoid any house or building that should not be.

for help, but their inability to communicate drives them into a murderous rage which few escape. They haunt specific locations, from which they cannot go farther than a few hundred paces (INT x 50 paces). They may use their powers at will whilst in their domain.

**Icy Wind (permanent, no Sacred Word roll):** A spectre is surrounded by ice-cold draughts which announce its arrival. These blow out candles and make larger fires dance. They lower the ambient temperature noticeably.

**Illusion:** A spectre may create visual illusions of non-living objects and places to fool its victims by making a difficulty 9 Sacred Word roll. The illusion may be modified at will, and cannot be resisted.

**Magic Resistance:** Spectres are highly resistant to magic, including all spells that aren't normally resisted (such as healing). When magic is cast on a spectre, it rolls CON + Sacred Word to resist, and every die rolled is considered a dragon die (ie every six is rerolled and accumulated).

**Speed Through Matter (permanent, no Sacred Word roll):** A spectre moves slowly through the air, but through solid matter it may move 8 to 10 times faster than normal human speed. This may look like teleportation, but it's actually very rapid movement: the spectre vanishes into the ground (or a rock wall, etc) and almost immediately emerges further away, often right in front of its next victim. Its range of movement is limited to (INT x 50) paces from the central point of its domain.

# Waswas

The wind had now risen, although our trip had been hot and calm, raising columns of burning sand. We had camped in a small oasis by a modest permanent settlement, and an impromptu party had started where everybody took part. Watchfires, regularly fed, provided illumination, and I had set myself a little apart to enjoy the sweetness of solitude.

Imperceptibly, something changed. Hard to explain; as if a wind-born voice was whispering in my ears. Soft and bewitching words I couldn't hear, in a hypnotic cadence. Imagination and the wine were doubtless playing tricks on me; I shook myself and sought to regain my former serenity. But the voice came again, this time with a grating sound. Then it fell silent; that's when the first brawls began.

It started with two musicians. Shouting, they threw themselves at one another, before their companions' dumbfounded gaze. Then other fights started, while other calmer heads tried to cool them down. A few paces away, a man drew a dagger and plunged it several times into the body of his travelling companion, then hurled

# Waswas

| | |
|---|---|
| STR: 3 | Max Init: 6 |
| CON: 6 | HP: 60 |
| DEX: 6 | Soak: 8 |
| INT: 5 | Passive Defence: 16 |
| CHA: 2 | Magic Resistance: 30 |
| | Legend: 2 |

- ❖ **Skills:** Athletics 4, Endurance 5, Fighting (Fists) 1 (4), Survival (Desert) 2 (5).

- ❖ **Attacks /Active Defences:** Fists 10/6 +6 damage.

- ❖ **Armour:** None.

- ❖ **Notes:** A waswas is a creature of shadow encountered only at night, when darkness hides it from its victims. It can create overwhelming emotions that obliterate coherent thought in those who do not resist. However, it's not particularly effective in combat, so avoids direct conflict.

A waswas can't be attacked by someone who failed to resist its mental powers, as these effectively mask the creature's presence. All waswas have the powers described below.

**Angry Whispers:** A waswas whispers words causing anger in those who hear up to a range of 50 paces and affecting up to (INT x 1) targets. The words exacerbate existing emotions, such as jealousy or disappointment, to the point of violence in the form of a murderous rage. The waswas makes an INT + Legend roll, resisted by the target's INT + Willpower; for multiple targets, you can roll per target or make a single roll for the waswas which all targets must resist. The duration of the effect is (7 – target's INT) hours, with a minimum of 1 hour.

**Soul Absorption:** A waswas feeds on the souls of the dying (those with 0 HP or less). It must make physical contact with its victim. No roll is required, and the process takes one full round. A person whose soul has been absorbed may never achieve Apotheosis.

**Terror:** If a waswas fails to create anger in a target, it may try to terrify him, forcing him to flee. The waswas may only target one person per action, making an INT + CHA roll against the target's INT + Willpower. A target successfully resisting will never again be affected by the powers of this waswas. A target failing to resist will be terrified and will flee as rapidly as possible for at least one hour.

himself yelling into the fray that the party had become. I understood nothing; the sight before me made no sense. And then I saw the creature.

It was hardly visible in the night. It was staying away from the fires. In shape it was a little like a hermit, robed in a mantle of darkness which floated on the wind. It drew closer to the man who had been stabbed, bleeding out on the ground, and I could not tear my eyes away. It leaned over him, and gazed into his dying eyes with eyes that glimmered red.

Time seemed to hang. Milky swirls of mist rose from the body of the unfortunate, which the creature seemed to inhale, and the body contorted in abominable spasms. Finally the movements ceased, and the creature stood up. Its eyes met mine, and a nameless terror came over me. I fled as fast as I could.

When I returned a few hours later, things were quieter. More than thirty were wounded and six were dead, five of whom had a strange mark at the base of their foreheads, like a burn made with a brand. One of the bodies was that of the stabbed man. No one could explain what had happened, the anger and hatred that had moved them had vanished as mysteriously as it had come.

I've long searched for an explanation for their madness. In a far off land, I met a sage who told me of the **waswas**, a demon that whispers in the wind and corrupts the mind, setting son against father, wife against husband, friend against friend. It can influence weaker minds and foment murderous rage, before feasting on the souls of the unfortunates that succumb to its charms before they die. The sage claimed it was a real creature, and that one who could fight its power might kill it. For this reason it avoids showing itself, keeping to the shadows and taking advantage of the chaos it creates to accomplish its foul deeds. The sage told me that his village had been decimated after a waswas made it its hunting ground. Solitude is a light burden when it spares you from such infamy.

# Zauba'a

It's getting late, my friend. I'm old, and I need my sleep. Are you sure my prattling on hasn't bored you? No? Well, since you insist, let me tell you of one last encounter.

I was a young man and I was approaching the Kingdom of Kh'saaba. I was travelling with a small caravan, and our trip had gone well, without the slightest danger. We were camping one last time in the desert before the more fertile lands of the kingdom began. It was still daylight. While we were putting up the tents and quenching our thirst with hot tea, our watchman cried the alarm. He had spotted a strange dust cloud approaching.

It was a stunning spectacle. The rest of the desert was calm, but fifty paces from us a whirlwind raised a tiny sandstorm. It couldn't have been more than three feet across at the base, and less than ten paces high. It swirled the sand up into the sky and dropped it several paces away. What worried me, however, was that the whirlwind was getting closer, but at a variable speed, stopping every now and then, then quickly restarting.

Jarid, the oldest caravaneer, looked nervous, and barked orders for us to move what we could out of the camp. We did as he said, but the whirlwind changed direction and followed us, accelerating when we did. Panic set in.

Jarid picked up a stone and threw it at the whirlwind, cursing loudly. Of course, it did nothing. Or at least so I thought—but then the whirlwind stopped. Encouraged by the unexpected turn of events, everyone else copied Jarid. Soon the ridiculous spectacle began of a dozen caravaneers stoning a motionless whirlwind. I was laughing with the rest, but my laughter was short-lived, and gave way to fear. The whirlwind was growing. I was sure of it. Then for an instant I seemed to see a flash like eyes surrounded by lightning shine out from the whirling sand. Taking a few steps back, I saw my companions still hard on the attack, while the whirlwind was now twice its original size. The violence of the gusts increased, and then the tornado suddenly bore down on the group of caravaneers. Although more than a dozen paces away, I was thrown to the ground by the violence of the wind, and blacked out.

When I came to, hours later, I was half-buried in sand, and there was no trace of my companions or our caravan. Calm had returned and I was alone, without mount or water. I wandered, thinking my end had come. I owe my life to a group of Saabi horsemen who happened upon me en route to one of their forts.

So what was the whirlwind? I only found out years later. It was a **zauba'a.** That tells you nothing. It's not surprising, as few who encounter them survive. They're primitive, elemental beings, linked to the winds. They roam the desert, but some losses at sea might also be explained by their presence. It's said the zauba'a seek out

## Zauba'a

| | |
|---|---|
| STR: 8 | Max Init: 6 |
| CON: 8 | HP: 80 |
| DEX: 8 | Soak: 9[1] |
| INT: 1 | Passive Defence: n/a |
| CHA: 1 | Magic Resistance: 6 |
| | Legend: 1 |

❖ **Skills:** Fighting (Whirlwind only) 10.

❖ **Attacks /Active Defences:** Whirlwind 18/8 +8 damage[1].

❖ **Armour:** None.

❖ **Area Found:** Kh'saaba.

❖ **Notes:** 1: Only weapons with a direct link to the Earth element can injure a zauba'a. Rocks and stones can affect it, but metal weapons cannot. An arrow with a flint head can cause damage. Some bedouins have spears with flint heads which can be useful against these creatures—although it's not likely they know.

The zauba'a is an elemental creature linked to the wind. It can be found on land but also at sea. At sea, it can sink any ship it encounters; on land, it's found mostly in the desert, where it blows the sands in its very strong winds, the main source of its danger.

**Whirlwind:** A zauba'a's attack is a fast whirlwind that would merely knock you to the ground if it wasn't carrying a cargo of abrasive sand and stones. The zauba'a can affect any creature within two paces of its centre. Its attack does a base 8 damage in the action of the attack, and then 4 additional points for each subsequent round of exposure. The blast can also unbalance a target, which must make a STR + Endurance roll against a difficulty of 18 plus the magnitude of the attack (difficulty 18 + mag) or be knocked down. A character caught directly inside a zauba'a (for example, trapped against a cliff face) immediately suffers 8 points of damage per round, and is subject to the asphyxiation rules (page 68).

the company of travellers, but that—alas!—their very nature is incompatible with living things. Some say they have a pact with the djinn to destroy all mortals. Whatever the truth, they are dangerous. Their winds can lift a fully-laden camel, their abrasive sands can burn the skin, infiltrate the lungs, prevent you from breathing. The only defence is to flee—especially if you can leave an offering behind you to delay them. Are they intelligent? I don't know. But I can assure you that the zauba'a I encountered followed our every move, and seemed to take time to watch and analyse what we were doing. Can they be fought, or destroyed? No one knows for sure, and I for one would never take the risk—although an old madman I once talked to said that only stone weapons can damage a zauba'a. But who would be reckless enough to attempt such a thing?

# Chapter Nine

# Melpomene – Gamemastering Capharnaum

## The Maze

**T**hufir waited until the last sunbeam touched the horizon before giving his answer to the djinn. For two hours, he had tracked his brains over the riddle, turning it over and over in his mind, trying to find its solution. He had quickly dismissed the logic trap. "The last but one..." If Thufir gave the name of the last but one person to have solved the riddle, that person automatically became the one before the last but one, and so Thufir would lose. But that was an obvious trick. No, what the djinn was asking was the name of the last person to have answered the riddle—who would then become the last but one as soon as Thufir found out his name. But who could that have been? He remembered the words of the Sheikh of Jibreen: "My dynasty was founded five centuries ago... we have never failed in our task!" So the last person to come here had done so before then. Was he one of the Prophets, whose tomb was supposed to lie ahead? If so, why did the djinn ask for only one name? And why did the scroll mention "a twice-sacred sanctuary"? But then—last of all—there was the secret that simplified the riddle, the well-kept secret known only to the distant guardians of the memory of Hammad, to which Thufir belonged...

"I am Jason! Jason Quartered!" he shouted, as the day-star disappeared.

Jason hadn't died facing King Pelorius! He had joined the desert djinn, and Hammad had become his disciple!

The djinn transformed itself into a whirlwind, enveloping Thufir and lifting him off the ground. Was he wrong? Was he about to die for having followed a miserable Orkadian knight on this fool's quest?

Hope flooded into him when his feet touched the ground.

"You have become the answer to the riddle. You are long-awaited. For with you a new age begins."

The djinn vanished as it had appeared, leaving Thufir at the foot of a cliff cloven by a narrow gorge. Behind him, the desert stretched away out of sight. Luther was out there somewhere. Of course he had answered wrongly: the knight had been raised in the Quarterian faith and Jason was his prophet. For him, the martyr has died in the duel with King Pelorius, and no part of his holy life had ever brought him to these lands. Convinced he would never see his friend again and determined to complete the quest in his honour, Thufir started down the defile.

He walked for several hours in a maze of ravines, in which sometimes flowed a stream of refreshing water through ingenious irrigation channels. Who maintained these workings? Thufir saw no signs of civilisation other than abandoned buildings, caves carved into the cliff walls, dwellings without dwellers and tombs without corpses. Human hands had worked these stones, but the inhabitants were long gone, and had left nothing behind. Lost in the labyrinth, he saw no living soul, except for a few mountain goats which he milked, a lamb he quickly slaughtered and roasted over a makeshift fire. After that, the traveller slept.

The next day Thufir entered a verdant wadi, hidden at the heart of the maze of stone. A river flowed there, with cascading pools amidst palm trees, and its slopes held a sober and elegant city. Thufir was poet as much as assassin, and the beauty of the place moved him to tears. A forgotten paradise, inviolate for more than five hundred years; perhaps the cradle of civilisation that the hermit Ezekiel Bar Itzhak had believed lost for millenia. So this was the explanation of the apparent antiquity of the papyrus over the runes it held! Its civilisation had not been forgotten in time, but in space. Here men and women had lived in secret, and—Tarek's moustache!—did so still, to judge by the smoke rising from a group of houses!

*Thufir hesitated, preferring instead to visit the majestic temple towering on the other side of the valley. The tomb of the Prophets! Their treasure! He was sure—he wanted to know! And the inhabitants of this sacred wadi would hardly allow him access to their holy of holies.*

*He began to climb the hundreds of steps. Half-way, he realised he was being followed: behind him silhouettes hurried up the stairs. He quickened his pace, but was unused to the exertion. The desert had drained his strength.*

*He reached the temple just ahead of his pursuers, passing through the smooth marble of its monumental entrance. Above, a fabulous mosaic graced the temple's dome, but this was no time for study. He dashed into an alcove and drew his blade.*

This chapter is especially for you, Al-Rawi, and reveals some of the secrets of *Capharnaum* for you to use in your campaign. If you're not intending to game master *Capharnaum*, we recommend you read no further...

# Magical Items

Sorcerers are powerful, their fates exceptional, their actions extraordinary. However, the spells they wield do not belong to them, but rather derive from a source of power beyond their wildest imaginings. Magic—mysterious, age-old—impregnates all things. It's in the air you breathe and deep in your blood. And yet it eludes our gaze, wherever we might look.

Only the wisest are aware of the harmony that unites the time-eroded material world and the eternal, divine force the sorcerers shape. And yet it is real; and sometimes it happens that this magical force condenses in such concentrated form that mortals can see it and be dazzled by its power. Some such "condensations" are what mortals call **magical items**, and in this section we'll examine how they come into being, what powers they possess, and how can they be used, as well as providing some examples.

## An Overview of Magical Items

Magical items are items which contain enough magical power to provide their wielder with certain abilities, either permanent or requiring activation. Their appearance and powers vary enormously, but over the centuries scholars have managed to identify some common features.

### The Creation of Magical Items

New magical items may be created in two ways. The first—and most natural—is for magical powers to appear spontaneously in an item. This phenomenon remains a mystery, despite centuries of

### The Legend of the Sand Merchant

*An old Jazirati legend tells that a fabulous creature roams the trade routes and cities of the world after dark, in search of magical items. This creature, said to be immortal, hungers for magical power, the only thing to give it sustenance. Even as it feeds, it grows hungry again, and its appetite increases, leaving it with no way to survive other than to break the magical items it steals and devour their essence.*

*This creature is known as the Sand Merchant, although no description of its appearance exists. Indeed, its arrival in a settlement is always preceded by a whirlwind of silver sand, preventing any from opening their eyes and seeing its form.*

research; in some unknown manner, perhaps overnight, a common item you have long had in your possession may suddenly reveal itself to have magical or supernatural powers. Some theorise that such items have always been magical, but that their magic only comes to the fore at the moment it is noticed. Perhaps it is touched by a certain person, or perhaps a certain event occurs, or perhaps simply a certain time has come, and the item becomes magically active. Before this moment, the latent power in an item appears to be undetectable; there is no known way to identify an item which will one day become magical, or to predict when it will do so.

Of course, some items have such starred histories that they may more easily attract magic. A sword which wins a decisive battle, a pendant worn by a cursed queen, a dragon scale given in dowry at the founding of an empire; items such as these seem to have a greater chance of becoming magical items than a simple soldier's chamber pot or a mortared stone in the west wall of your workshop...

The second way magical items may be created is for them to be fashioned by one of the *artepharatim*. This guild of crafters, largely unknown even to other sorcerers, preserves ancient Shiradi teachings. Unfortunately, their oral traditions have led to much being lost, and their manufacturing techniques today are less sophisticated than of old. They belong to the Shiradi tribe of the Pharatim; few in number, they are artists, devoted to their work. The dream and duty of every *artepharat* is to create a powerful and unique magical item—an **artefact**—the fruit of a lifetime devoted to magic.

Even when a sorcerer manages to find an artepharat (no easy task), there's no guarantee a request to create a magical item will be granted. Like any artist, the artepharatim are sensitive, with great and delicate souls. They assure themselves of their client's good faith and honesty before agreeing to work for them, sobered by the histories of their guild which tell of the times their arts have been put to evil use. Even today, magical items exist which are used in acts of great evil, so these great-hearted watchmen have reason to be cautious.

## The Power and Effects of Magical Items

Magic is a complex natural phenomenon, and no one really understands its workings. When the gods decide the time is right for a new magical item to come into existence, only they know what it's powers will be. Some items are benign, filled with light, improving everyday life, or perhaps performing some unusual, incomprehensible, or even seemingly pointless task. Others have unimaginable power, and can ravage entire civilisations in inexpert hands.

Potentially, magical items can do anything. One may be a gourd which is always filled with water; another may be a sword that parries every blow, or a heated camel saddle, or a grain of sand upon which is etched a map of the heavens. Nor does the shape or size of a magical item seem to have any bearing on its powers; a tiny item may have vast power, while a magical palace may do very little at all.

## Indestructible!

*Many magical items have a common physical property: under normal circumstances, unless otherwise indicated, they are indestructible. Such a magical item will not wear out, become rusty, break, catch fire, or suffer any of the usual wear and tear which afflicts mundane items. It's said that powerful sorcery or even other magical items are the only things that can harm these items.*

Despite this, there are a few rules (or perhaps guidelines). Magical items are rare, and powerful ones rarer still. Finding the Mirror of Heaven may be the quest of a lifetime—or even more than one. Sometimes a wandering adventurer may unearth a magical item of great power, where he was just looking for a little water, or a roof for the night; but such instances are rare, and are usually the result of intervention by the gods themselves.

And, of course, finding a magical item is often not enough. You must also know how to use it.

## Activating Magical Items

In theory, magical items can be used by anyone, sorcerer or not. That's one of their great advantages. However, few magical items give up their powers readily, and most require at least some conditions to be fulfilled before they can be used.

Magical items can have almost any form, so it's difficult to generalise. Some items may just require touching to work; some may require a special sign to be traced on them with a finger; others still require a word to be spoken, or will only function during certain weather conditions or at a certain time of day. Other items have more complex conditions still, things which are impossible to fathom simply by watching or examining them.

Unfortunately, magical items don't come with an instruction manual. At least, not usually. Many an ambitious sorcerer has ended up with an item of apparently stupefying power, with absolutely no idea of how to use it. That's why from time to time you find magical items exhibited in glass cases, perhaps in the collections of rich merchants or sorcerers, incapable of accessing their dormant power.

Some magical items don't require activation, or simply operate obviously. In such cases, only damage or destruction may stop their operation. If an amphora which serves a different wine each meal is broken, it may no longer perform its function. However, some permanent magical items continue to work even when shattered into pieces. See the "Indestructible!" text box for more.

# Defining a Magical Item

A magical item is defined by two attributes: **Power** and **Complexity**, the latter being a function of the former. An item's Power is a score between 1 and 5, and defines the extent of the item's magical powers. Complexity represents the difficulty to master and employ those powers. If a magical item requires activation to be used, using it requires an INT + Willpower roll against a difficulty equal to the item's Complexity. If the item's power is permanent, no roll is needed; all you need to know is how to wield it.

A magical item's **Power** score is divided between the **magical abilities** possessed by that item. Each magical ability has its own score. Put differently, a magical item's Power is equal to the total of all its magical ability scores.

*For example: a magical item with Power 5 might have three magical abilities: one with a score of 3, and two with a score of 1. Alternatively, it may have two magical abilities: one with a score of 3 and the other with a score of 2. And so on.*

Table 9-1: Magical Item Abilities provides a non-exhaustive list of magical abilities, together with their scores. Al-Rawi, you can use these when defining your own magical items. Magical abilities only function when the magical item is held by its wielder, or is in his possession, or is otherwise close to him. You can increase the duration, range, or other parameter of a magical ability (such as changing hours to days, a house to a palace, and so on). In such a case, you should also increase the magical ability score by +1. No single magical ability score may exceed 5. You can't do the opposite; you can't get a magical ability at lower power by reducing its score.

A Power 1 magical item is weak, with just one magical ability, and a rather common one at that. A Power 2 item has two weak magical abilities, or one a bit stronger. A Power 3 item may have three weak magical abilities; an average one and a weak one; or one significant magical ability; and so on.

There is no precise rule for determing the cost of a magical item, as prices vary enormously depending on situation. Remember that all magical items are rare and precious, and rarely come onto the market (this is especially true of the more powerful items). Even when they do come up for sale, they're coveted by many people, and often traded at exorbitant prices.

# Example Magical Items

The following ready-to-use magical items can be inserted into your campaign as is, or you can use them as templates to create your own (or if your players do—see page 339). Of course, there are **many** more.

| TABLE 9-1: MAGICAL ITEM POWER AND COMPLEXITY | | |
|---|---|---|
| **POWER** | **COMPLEXITY** | **DESCRIPTION** |
| 1 | 15 | A common magical item which can be bought or stolen from any market, if you know where to look. You can detect such an item with a difficulty 21 Detecting Magic roll (see page 121). |
| 2 | 18 | A moderately powerful magical item which can be bought on the black market or stolen from an experienced sorcerer. You can detect such an item with a difficulty 18 Detecting Magic roll (page 121). |
| 3 | 21 | A powerful magical item which can be bought on the black market or stolen from an experienced sorcerer. You can detect such an item with a difficulty 15 Detecting Magic roll (page 121). |
| 4 | 24 | A very powerful magical item which can be stolen from the collection of a rich sovereign or a particularly powerful sorcerer. You can detect such an item with a difficulty 9 Detecting Magic roll (page 121). |
| 5 | 27 | A legendary magical item (an artefact), usually in the possession of a supernatural being. It can be found in a magical place, provided the artefact itself *wants* to be found, in which case the most unmagical character can easily perceive its magical power. Such magical items have their own will and consciousness and are masters of their own fate—which may include you, if you're lucky (or unlucky...) enough to come across one. |

| TABLE 9-2: MAGICAL ITEM ABILITIES | |
|---|---|
| MAGICAL ABILITY SCORE | MAGICAL ABILITY (SELECT 1 FOR EACH ABILITY) |
| 1 | +1 bonus die on a skill roll or in a given situation: running faster, carrying heavier loads, appearing more charming, voice carrying farther. Force a flower to open at night. Emit a small light from your hand. Act as a magnet for small items. Change the hour hand on a pendulum clock just by looking at it. |
| 2 | +3 bonus dice on a skill or attribute roll. Force a plant to grow twice as fast as normal. See in the dark as if in twilight. Dissolve any fabric upon contact. Create a light fog over about a hundred square paces. Heal all the wounds and diseases of a living being. |
| 3 | Gain a score of 3 in a skill you don't know. Walk on quicksand for a few minutes. Look like any other person for several hours. Transform a metal weapon into wood, or vice-versa. Cause a house to collapse. Create an intense emotion in a person. |
| 4 | Animate a statue for a few hours or days, depending on its size. Walk through walls. Be able to eat sand and rocks. Locate any person whose name you know. Resurrect a dead individual. Instantly wake up a whole city. |
| 5 | Cross the desert without drinking a drop of water. Breathe while buried in sand for several weeks. Assume the appearance of a mythical creature or god for a few days. Dry up a vast expanse of water (several million waterskins). Become one of the Dragon-Marked. |

## Dagger of Sharpness

- ❖ **Type:** Permanent.
- ❖ **Power:** 1.
- ❖ **Complexity:** 15.
- ❖ **Location Found:** Certain markets in large cities.
- ❖ **Price:** 10 gold talents.
- ❖ **Powers:** These relatively common magical items have widely different appearances, depending on where they're bought. They're the work of the artepharatim (page 336). Wielding a Dagger of Sharpness gives you a bonus die on any roll to use it. The dagger is also a little more resistant than a non-magical version, and takes twice as long for the blade to go blunt (and require sharpening).

## Dancing Buckler

- ❖ **Type:** Activated (a simple thought).
- ❖ **Power:** 3.
- ❖ **Complexity:** 12.
- ❖ **Location Found:** The private collections of powerful sorcerers or great warriors.
- ❖ **Price:** 100 gold talents.
- ❖ **Powers:** Dancing Bucklers are rare and hard to find. They defend their owners at all costs. They have two magical abilities. Firstly, when tied to a wielder's arm, a Dancing Buckler moves the arm so it parries incoming blows unerringly, regardless of their source or the skill of the wielder. Secondly, a Dancing Buckler can block the passage of any substance, even including divine or orichalcum weapons, and never takes damage. This magical item would have a higher Power score were it not for its singular disadvantage of relying on its wielder's physical strength: a Dancing Buckler, for example, cannot save its wielder from a wall collapsing on top of him if he doesn't have the strength to hold the wall back himself. That said, many a seasoned soldier has been saved from the clutches of death more than once by a Dancing Buckler.

## Flying Carpet

- ❖ **Type:** Permanent.
- ❖ **Power:** 3
- ❖ **Complexity:** 21.
- ❖ **Location Found:** In a long-forgotten basement, dungeon, or store.
- ❖ **Price:** 20 gold talents.
- ❖ **Powers:** A flying carpet is a rectangular carpet or rug a little over three feet wide by about six feet long. Richly and beautifully decorated, it has the traditional tasselled fringe and four pompoms at the corners. A user may manipulate these pompoms to "pilot" the carpet using an INT + Survival roll. Only two people may ride a flying carpet at any one time.

## The Frivolous Quill

- ❖ **Type:** Activated (use the quill to trace a cross on a map at the target location).
- ❖ **Power:** 5.
- ❖ **Complexity:** 27.
- ❖ **Location Found:** Unknown.
- ❖ **Price:** Priceless.
- ❖ **Powers:** The rare scholars who know of the existence of the Frivolous Quill search for it in vain. It's said anyone using the Quill can move to any place in the world in the blink of an eye. Legend says using the Quill is fraught with danger, since although the user seems to move instantaneously, in reality he steps through multiple mirages before arriving at his destination—a journey which itself is not without risk...

    The Frivolous Quill is said to be the feather of an immortal bird called the *Trah'Eikt*, which is able to fly through other dimensions and universes. Anyone who could find and ride such a legendary beast would have untold power.

## Magic Lamp

- ❖ **Type:** Activated (by rubbing three times).
- ❖ **Power:** 4.
- ❖ **Complexity:** 24.
- ❖ **Location Found:** Beneath the sands of the Desert of Fire.
- ❖ **Price:** 20 gold talents.
- ❖ **Powers:** This oil lamp of metal or often leather is similar to its non-magical peers, except that it holds within it an imprisoned djinn. The djinn may only leave when the lamp is activated; once free, it must reward its saviour by granting him three wishes. The djinn must do everything in its power to fulfil the wishes, although it is possible that a wish may exceed its powers. Once the three wishes have been granted, the djinn regains its freedom, leaving the magic lamp to await a new occupant. To imprison a djinn inside the lamp, it must either be physically constrained, or tricked with a difficulty 24 CHA + Unctuous Bargaining roll.

## The Mirror of Heaven

- ❖ **Type:** Permanent.
- ❖ **Power:** 5.
- ❖ **Location Found:** Somewhere at the bottom of the Halawui River.
- ❖ **Price:** Priceless.
- ❖ **Powers:** The Mirror of Heaven is a circular portable mirror about six inches in diameter, with a short ivory handle sculpted with tiny but realistically detailed epic scenes. The mirror itself is dappled with stardust. It has only one magical ability, of rare power: after nightfall, it reflects the Kingdom of Heaven, allowing an observer to watch the activities of the gods in the heart of their domains. Even so, the vision is overwhelming to mortal eyes, and prolonged use of the Mirror of Heaven (for more, say, than seven consecutive nights) renders the user blind.

## Sundowner

- ❖ **Type:** Permanent.
- ❖ **Power:** 1.
- ❖ **Complexity:** 15.
- ❖ **Location Found:** There's a sundowner embedded in the wall of every building in Jergath the Great.
- ❖ **Price:** 20 gold talents.
- ❖ **Powers:** Sundowners are fist-sized stones which shine with colours which change throughout the day. They give off a bright white light during the day, turning dark green at twilight, and becoming increasingly black (and emitting no light) at night, before turning green again before dawn. Jergath's inhabitants are adept at judging the precise hour of the day from the nacreous sheen of the sundowner. They can also be used for judging the perfect time for a spot of larceny...

# Players Creating Magical Items

Magical items are rare and powerful, and never found with any regularity. However, player characters with skill and dedication may attempt to enchant their own.

The arts of enchantment are not what they were. At best, a character who joins the Guild of the Artepharatim may learn to create magical items with a Power of no more than 3, and which may have no magical ability with a score greater than 2. To create a magical item, begin by determining the Power score it will have. Creating such an item requires a CON + Sacred Word skill roll, against a difficulty equal to the magical item's Power, multiplied by 10 (Power x 10). From start to finish, the process of enchanting a magical item takes a number of months equal to the item's Power, multiplied by 2 (Power x 2 months). If the roll is successful, the Power score of the item created should then be shared among its magical abilities.

# THE DARK SIDE OF MAGIC

In **Chapter Four: Terpsichore – Magic and Sorcery**, we suggested that the indiscriminate use of sorcery by characters was not without consequence. This is an aspect of *Capharnaum* which has great roleplaying and dramatic potential, and so we present the rules for it here, away from your players' eyes. Al-Rawi, we reveal to you the truth of...

## The Shaytan

The rules for magic presented on page 117 are powerful and apparently without limit. However, they're not the whole story. There is, in reality, a grim and perilous downside to the use of magic by mortals, one which may cost a sorcerer his very soul.

In the heart of every sorcerer there grows a demon—the **shaytan**. The most commonly accepted theory among those few sorcerers who become aware of this phenomenon—or who became aware and committed their theories to writing before being definitively possessed—is that the *shaytan* is a form of divine punishment. In going against the will of the gods and following the dictates of their own egos, the dragons created magic and placed it in the world, enabling gifted mortals to manipulate their environment at will. In return, the gods chose to inflict upon those transgressors a slow and terrible punishment which still exists today. Some gods—like those of the Agalanthians—did not agree; chiromancers do not develop *shaytan* from wielding magic (nor, interestingly, do the users of the Kitaba Nader of the Bint Mimun—see page 256).

If partly true, this explanation is not the true origin of the *shaytan*. The dragons did indeed gift mortals with magic following their rebellion, giving them access to the draconic power known as *evocation* (see page 306). However, the gods did not limit the magic which mortals might perform.

A god named Shaytan, imprisoned in the underworld by his peers at the dawn of time, seized this moment to increase his own power and avenge himself on the gods. He took advantage of a flaw in the workings of sorcery to release demons from the underworld, using the magical power which circulates between the worlds when a spell is cast.

Because of its nature, the insidious threat of the shaytan is known only to a few sorcerers at any one time—usually those who have passed the point of no return, but have not yet succumbed to its nightmarish power.

Each time a character attempts to wield magical power, his body is altered, regardless of whether the attempt succeeds or not. The alteration takes the form of tattoo-like markings emerging upon the sorcerer's skin, in colours that change and extend a little with each sorcerous attempt, each of which is a tiny act of rebellion against the ban of the gods. Hypnotic arabesques, these mystical symbols are however merely the consequence of something much more serious: the gradual destruction of the sorcerer's humanity.

Over time, spell by spell, a sorcery-wielding character develops a new identity—a second magical personality which will, if unchecked, eventually replace his own. This new entity, gradually coming to awareness deep within the sorcerer, is a demon of a very special sort: the *shaytan* (pl. *shayatin*). Malevolent and determined, the shaytan will play countless evil tricks on the hapless sorcerer before he begins to suspect what is happening to him. By that time, usually, it is too late...

In game terms, whenever a character successfully makes a Sacred Word skill roll to cast a spell, his *shaytan* gains 1 Adventure

---

### Should I Tell My Players About the Shayatin?

*Over time, and with experience,* Capharnaum *players will of course become aware of the existence of the shayatin, even if the characters they're playing may not. To begin with, however, we recommend keeping this aspect of the rules a secret as much as you can (it may not always be possible, of course); discovering the reality behind sorcery can be both exciting and terrifying, and provide some great role-playing moments. Until your players know what's going on, you can manage their shaytan yourself, using the accumulated AP to gradually define their abilities.*

*Later, when your players are more experienced, you can delegate the management of the shaytan to your players, letting them attempt to mitigate its development and define its abilities. Playing a sorcerous character and his shaytan counterpart is a great roleplaying challenge, and can be awesome fun!*

---

Point (see page 78). Likewise, whenever a character fails at such an attempt, his *shaytan* gains a number of AP equal to the magnitude of failure.

Al-Rawi, or optionally the player, should spend the AP accumulated by the shaytan on its abilities, as discussed below and using the rules described in **Chapter Two: Thalia – Word and Deed** (see page 79).

Al-Rawi: never forget that the shaytan growing in a sorcerer's heart is a malevolent demon, an entity in its own right, with its own goals, desires, and world view. Its main motivation is to complete its protracted birth, taking over the sorcerer's body and annihilating the sorcerer's mind and soul, giving birth to an independent and utterly unique demonic creature.

### Abilities

A shaytan has five **abilities**—Apparition, Nightmare, Orchestration, Possession, and Verve—each with a score from 1 to 6. It may use these abilities to take independent actions, as described in "Shaytan Attacks", below. The effects which a shaytan may achieve with its abilities depend directly on the ability score, as indicated in the ability descriptions below. Ability rolls are made combined with the sorcerer's Sacred Word skill (shaytan ability + Sacred Word) against a difficulty equal to the sorcerer's Intelligence, times 5 (INT x 5). A shaytan may neither swagger nor light up constellations on its ability rolls.

**Shaytan ability roll = (shaytan ability + Sorcerer's Sacred Word) vs sorcerer's INT x5**

## Apparition

The first of a shaytan's abilities is **Apparition**. The shaytan manipulates, in a minor way, the reality of the sorcerer they are possessing, creating illusions only the sorcerer can see. The illusion encompasses all the sorcerer's senses, and lasts for a number of minutes equal to the magnitude. Once its effects dissipate, the sorcerer returns to reality and any wounds suffered disappear, items apparently lost or destroyed are still in his possession and intact, and so on.

| TABLE 9-3: APPARITION | |
|---|---|
| **ABILITY SCORE** | **POSSIBLE APPARITIONS** |
| 1 | Creates an illusion of a single small inanimate object: a stone, a clay pot, a plank, etc. The volume of the object may not exceed two pints. |
| 2 | Creates an illusion of a single medium inanimate object, or up to five small objects. The total volume may not exceed ten pints. |
| 3 | Creates an illusion of a large inanimate object or a small living being: a small house, or a plant, rodent, etc. The size of the living being may not exceed six inches. |
| 4 | Creates an illusion of a complex inanimate object or a medium living being: a large dwelling made up of several furnished rooms, an animal like a dog or a cat, or even a tree. |
| 5 | Creates an illusion of several complex objects of medium size, or a single human being: a small village made up of hovels, a young woman, a warrior, etc. |
| 6 | Creates an illusion of thousands of small objects, or a group of animals or humans: a sandstorm, a herd of camels, half a dozen people. |

## Nightmare

The shayatin are, by nature, creatures of dream, and dream manipulation is an innate talent—unfortunately for sorcerers! A shaytan may use the **Nightmare** ability to manipulate its host's dreams, leading to loss of concentration, low morale, and generally weird behaviour. A shaytan may create nightmares so realistic that the hapless victim considers them premonitions and behaves accordingly.

A nightmare's impact is determined by its duration and how often it repeats, regardless of its actual contents. A nightmare lasts a number of seconds equal to the Nightmare ability score multiplied by the magnitude, which equates to the same number of hours within the nightmare, and the shaytan may create such a nightmare once every (7 – Nightmare score) days. On the day following the nightmare, all the sorcerer's dice rolls face a difficulty increase equal to the magnitude of the Nightmare roll.

## Orchestration

With this ability, a shaytan may influence and even control its host's thoughts. It may make its host think of something specific, or not think of a thing; or it may influence one of its decisions in any direction. On a successful Orchestration ability roll, a shaytan may act according to the table below. The sorcerer may not otherwise resist the effects of Orchestration, as at that moment he believes the thoughts are his own.

| TABLE 9-4: ORCHESTRATION | |
|---|---|
| **ABILITY SCORE** | **THOUGHTS INFLUENCED / CONTROLLED** |
| 1 | Insignificant. The shaytan may eliminate or create thoughts the sorcerer doesn't really care about, and that have no priority in his head or life. |
| 2 | Minor. The shaytan may cause the sorcerer to forget something he's thinking about right at that moment, embarrassing him. This won't prevent him from sleeping, but it can give the sorcerer weird thoughts or humiliate him in public due to forgetfulness. |
| 3 | Significant. The shaytan may create or eliminate significant thoughts, making the sorcerer miss a meal or forget that he came to his laboratory to prepare a potion for a regular client; or giving him aggressive thoughts in the middle of a meditation session. |
| 4 | Major. At this ability score, the sorcerer may seem to be losing his mind. He may stop in the middle of a sentence without even remembering he was speaking; he may think of changing his profession to something completely unrelated to magic; he may decide to insult an important dignitary or otherwise experience great trouble controlling himself. |
| 5 | Overwhelming. The shaytan may manipulate the sorcerer's main flow of consciousness, his ideas, worries, ambitions, everything that might destabilise him. It may cause the sorcerer to forget half a day and replace it with memories of something the sorcerer has never done in his entire life. |
| 6 | Complete. The shaytan has complete control over the sorcerer's thoughts. It may make him believe he's a simple Agalanthian shepherd, cause him to forget to breathe, and more. Note obviously that the shaytan has no actual interest in killing its host, as this would cause its death, too. |

### Possession

With this ability, the shaytan may temporarily take control of the sorcerer's body. This lasts a number of minutes equal to the Possession ability score multiplied by the magnitude (Possession x magnitude), during which time the sorcerer is conscious and fully aware, but has absolutely no control over his body's actions, and absolutely no idea of who or what is controlling him. The sorcerer may make a CON attribute roll against a roll of the shaytan's Possession ability + his own Sacred Word skill to reduce the duration of possession by a number of minutes equal to his magnitude. In any case, once the possession is over, the sorcerer regains control of his body.

### Spell Stealing

Spell Stealing is the most powerful of the shaytan's abilities, and the most dangerous for the sorcerer. It's the equivalent of the Sacred Word skill for a shaytan, and is used by shaytan to cast spells.

Whenever a sorcerer fails to cast a spell (page 118), the shaytan may "steal" the unrealised magical effect, and release it later using its Spell Stealing ability. It may do this again and again: the failed magical effect essentially becomes a fixed spell which the shaytan may use.

The shaytan has no originality in its ability to use magic; it may only reproduce those effects it has stolen from its host's failed spell-casting attempts. Note that this requires you, Al-Rawi, to maintain a list of possible stolen spells. Do this judiciously; you shouldn't feel obliged to note *every single time* a sorcerer fails to cast a spell. But, when a sorcerer character fails to cast a spell whose effect is one you can imagine his shaytan one day using back on him, then jot down a few quick words to remind you. Little by little, a shaytan will develop an arsenal of magic it has stolen from its host's failed spells.

A shaytan may cast a stolen spell whenever it's possessing its host (using the Possession ability above). To do so, it must make a Spell Stealing ability roll against a difficulty of 15. The power of the spell to be cast is determined by the shaytan's Spell Stealing skill score: a score of 1 allows the shaytan to cast minor spells (creating a little water, etc), while a score of 6 might make the whole of Jazirat shake for a few seconds.

*For example: A player's reckless sorcerer character decides, in a fit of rage, to set a village on fire. As his Sacred Word skill score is low, he fails in his attempt, and the spell is not cast. Al-Rawi sees this as a good shaytan Spell Stealing opportunity, and jots down "setting a village on fire".*

*As the sorcerer is relatively inexperienced, his shaytan is not yet properly developed, and can't really benefit from the failed spell. A few years later, however, the sorcerer has progressed, and his shaytan now has a Spell Stealing ability score of 4. If it successfully possesses the host sorcerer, the shaytan may set a village on fire by succeeding at a difficulty 15 Spell Stealing roll.*

## Shaytan Attacks

In theory, a sorcerer's shaytan may attempt to exercise control over its host at any moment. In practice, it does so at moments of great stress or distraction, when the sorcerer's own willpower is compromised and it has a greater chance of success. Al-Rawi, we encourage you to be creative about these moments: a good opportunity may be at a dramatic moment in an adventure, when the sorcerer is asleep or possibly rendered unconscious. Additionally, Critical Failures on rolls to resist magic or even cast spells might be ideal opportunities for a shaytan to assert itself; you can even award the shaytan one or more bonus dice in especially propitious circumstances. Don't feel you have to do this at times when it might frustrate your game or interrupt otherwise exciting action, but it can be cool to hook the shaytan into moments of great tension and make the players really afraid of the sorcerer rolling a Critical Failure at a decisive moment!

## Losing Control

Little by little, a sorcerer's shaytan takes control of its host's life, eventually replacing them completely. This moment is reached when all the shaytan's ability scores reach 6. At that moment, the shaytan totally overcomes and absorbs the sorcerer's mind. His body becomes that of a shaytan, and the new creature departs to lead its demonic life elsewhere in the world. The former player character becomes an NPC.

Note that, even if you decide to let a player determine how his sorcerer character's shaytan spends its AP, it's always you, Al-Rawi, who decides what the shaytan does. When a shaytan takes control of a sorcerer character, his player is just a hapless spectator, with no control over what happens to his character.

Fortunately, there are two ways to mitigate this loss of control:

### Tattoos

A shaytan's development is always accompanied by the appearance and growth of tribal tattoos which eventually expand to cover the sorcerer's whole body. Once a character has realised these tattoos are linked to the growth of his shaytan, he can gauge—very ap-
proximately—how far the shaytan has advanced, as the proportion of his body covered by the shaytan tattooes is roughly equal to the sum of the shaytan's abilities multiplied by 3% (shaytan ability total x 3%). Thus, when the shaytan has attained full power, the tattoo will cover 90% of the sorcerer's body. As a rough guide, a character with a shaytan tattoo covering 75% of his body is barely playable; at 90%, it's time to make a new character.

The shaytan tattoo can have any appearance. It's up to Al-Rawi and the player to decide its shape and colour, based on the character's origins.

### Regression

A sorcerer may cause his shaytan to lose power. This is a long, hard struggle that usually doesn't end in victory, but which nevertheless allows a certain respite. Each of *Capharnaum's* peoples has its own approach: the Saabi make offerings to the Muses (usually of poems, fruit, meat, cloth, and so on); the Shiradim meditate; and the Quarterians pray.

Whatever his origins, a sorcerer may cause a shaytan ability to reduce by 1 point for every continuous period of 24 hours dedicated entirely to doing so, to the exclusion of all else. No sorcerer may spend more than one day a month regressing his shaytan's abilities in this way, and in any case a shaytan's regression is limited as follows:

| TABLE 9-5: SHAYTAN REGRESSION | |
|---|---|
| CURRENT SHAYTAN ABILITY TOTAL | MINIMUM TOTAL AFTER REGRESSION |
| 0 to 6 | 0 |
| 7 to 12 | 7 |
| 13 to 18 | 13 |
| 19 to 24 | 19 |
| 25 to 30 | 25 |

As you can see, regression is sometimes impossible (a shaytan ability score total of 7 permits no regression, for example). In such cases, you must wait for the shaytan's abilities to increase above the current threshold minimum before making a regression attempt.

# Secrets of the Peoples of Capharnaum

The realms of *Capharnaum* are not static places, and there are conspiracies and secrets everywhere. Individuals jostle for power, peoples rise and fall, and secrets hidden for years, decades, or even centuries bubble to the surface and threaten the status quo. Here are some of the secrets of *Capharnaum* in the year 5997.

## The Assassins of the Salonim

The Oath of Salone (page 269) taken by the followers of the Sacred Heart of Shirad has some disturbing implications. Of course, everyone knows that the Salonim physicians swear never to harm the people of Shirad; however, not everyone knows that, in swearing to never *allow* harm to come to the people, some Salonim employ their knowledge of human physiology to become expert assassins defending the interests of their people.

It was Mogda himself who first interpreted the second part of the Oath of Salone to justify the existence of assassins who would preventively strike down all those who might threaten the people

of Shirad before they could do harm. During his reign, the faction called **the Bloodmoons** was formed—a nickname referring to the mark in the shape of a crescent moon the assassins leave in the palm of their victims' hands. Mogda wished for the Shiradim never to fear enslavement or extermination again. He believed it was essential for them to strike known enemies before they could act.

As expert healers and physicians, the Salonim know the arts of poisoning and the vital points of the human body. It was easy to recruit assassins from among their number, and the Bloodmoons have continued to exist until the present day, performing in the shadows the dirty work necessary to the protection of the Shiradim. Trained in the arts of combat by high-ranking Ashkenim, the Bloodmoons nevertheless rely more on their medical knowledge to perpetrate their deeds: poisoning or striking lethal blows remain their preferred techniques. They can easily make these murders pass for accidents or natural deaths if discretion is required.

Generally, only high-ranking Shiradim are aware of the existence of the Bloodmoons. They know how to contact its members to order an assassination, which they do only after closed-door sessions where all other options are examined. The Shiradim never dispatch a Bloodmoon on a mission lightly.

That said, the Bloodmoons have been called on more often of late. The rulers of Shiradim communities in Capharnaum are consolidating their power, and eliminating irritating obstacles.

In addition to the standard path abilities of the Sacred Heart of Shirad, Bloodmoons may also use their Science skill instead of their Assassination or Fighting skills. Note that this doesn't allow them to take an assassination or weapon specialisation in their Science skill; this is one drawback of the Bloodmoon way (see "Specialisation and Expertise" on page 74).

# GAME MASTERING ADVICE

*Capharnaum* is an epic game of characters with great destinies. Each scenario, each session should be filled with adventure, suspense, twists, betrayals, glory, riches and passions. Al-Rawi, in this chapter we'll give you a few tools to do this. The following essays are just advice, and should be taken as such; there's nothing better than your own experience and knowledge of your players to breathe life into your adventures.

## Your Player Characters

The player characters in your games should be in the thick of events. The most important thing that happens in your game is always what happens to them. It hardly matters what this book or future supplements say; don't hesitate to rearrange the *Capharnaum* setting and its components to enrich the environment in which your players' characters act.

### Background and Relationships

After a few sessions of play, ask your players to say a little more about their characters' backgrounds—the stories of their families, where they come from, their homes. Most characters hail—at least to some degree—from illustrious bloodlines, and may have famous ancestors, domains to manage, local political and economic events to sway. Don't neglect the characters' personal relationships, either: whether friends or simple acquaintances, one day the people the characters know may get the Dragon-Marked out of trouble.

Fleshing out your characters this way lets your players better understand the characters they're playing. Additionally, it'll also give you an array of cool details you can bring into your games during play, or maybe when designing adventures. There's an unknown or missing father? Well you can have him appear in an adventure! A sister who converted to a different religion? Use that to create tension, and play on the clichés and themes of cultural and religious differences. An elderly relative dies and there's a vast domain to share between several siblings? Intrigues and conspiracies galore!

Al-Rawi, you can also take the initiative and create compelling non-player characters (NPCs) to enrich (or plague!) the lives of your PCs. A playful neighbour, a frequently visited merchant, a mad old woman who harangues the neighbourhood, a lyric poet who follows a PC everywhere and documents his deeds, a harlot who's got more emotionally involved with a PC than was planned, a cousin who's always getting into trouble: all these give life to your game, and make your players' involvement that much deeper.

### Personalities, Point of View, Motivations and Triggers

If you want to define a character (whether PC or NPC) even more, you can use a **personality quiz**. There are plenty of these on the internet and in psychology magazines, from party guessing games ("if you were an animal, what animal would you be?") to true questionnaires designed by psychologists.

Start off by asking the players how his character would answer the following questions:

- ❖ What do you think of religion, and of the differences between religions?
- ❖ What do you think of your people (your blood), and those of other peoples?
- ❖ What do you think is the role of the Dragon-Marked?
- ❖ What do you think of the rulers of this city? What would the ideal political system for you be?
- ❖ What are your main motivations? In the short and long term?
- ❖ What things do you respect, fear, or envy? What makes you angry?

### The Dragon-Marked Party

Your player characters will likely have many adventures together. The ideal is to build a cohesive party with a really good reason for braving death side by side. *Capharnaum* isn't a game which pulls characters together only for specific missions, nor is it a game which presents you with a ready-made pretext for getting the char-

## The Secret Movers of Events

Throughout this book, we've presented many of the important figures of the realms of **Capharnaum**, with descriptions of their deeds, beliefs, and plans. In most cases these represent reasonably common knowledge. They may not, however, be the whole story. Here are some of the secrets about the world's movers and shakers.

### Shayna Bat Eli, Leader of the Bloodmoons

Shayna Bat Eli is a travelling midwife in the prime of life. She has brought many children—Shiradim and Saabi alike—into the world, and has helped their mothers to recover quickly.

Secretly, Shayna is the leader of the Bloodmoons (page 344), and can dispense death as easily as she helps give life. Her cover as a travelling midwife allows her not to remain too long in one place, and to easily cover her tracks. Only her most loyal lieutenants remain in contact with her, to inform her of missions received and accomplished and take their orders.

Shayna has a steely temperament. When she was younger, she really was a midwife, but did not belong to the Salonim. While living with a Shiradim tribe on the edge of the desert, Saabi raiders attacked the village in an orgy of rape and murder. Shayna was enslaved and suffered a thousand humiliations, before being rescued by a Shiradi counter-raid. A mysterious old man took her in to heal her, and talked for days about the threats facing the children of Shirad, and of the necessity to wipe them out before tragedies like the one she had experienced could happen again. The old man was the leader of the Bloodmoons, and Shayna became his disciple and heir.

Shayna does her best to protect her people. When given a mission for her assassins, she ensures it's in the interests of the Shiradim. Woe betide whoever would use the Bloodmoons for their own agenda. Shayna can be merciless. She has long buried within her the

softness and sensitivity of the midwife she once was.

### Julius Nona Selens, Archon of Therema

The story of the Archon of Therema (page 277) is one of the city's best kept secrets. Julius's true name, known to almost no one, is Julia. At birth, Julia's twin brother died, and the sacred eagles refused to eat the infant's corpse. The priests saw this as a sign that the existing archon's line had lost divine favour, and a new heir had to be chosen from among the patrician bloodlines. In response, the Archon gave his daughter to the priesthood, and announced that he was adopting the son of an extinct Heroic family, Julius Haestes Selens.

In reality, the "daughter" the Archon surrendered to the priests was that of a servant, and the adopted son was none other than his true daughter, in disguise. Julia grew in fear, learning the ways of power, growing up as a boy and then a young man, with only her father, the eunuch Vortis, and the palace chiromancer Nesphes Tremens (page 277) as her confidants. After her father's death two years ago, the masquerade has been getting harder to maintain: with adolescence, Julia's nubile body is forcing "Julius" to wear baggy clothing and even ceremonial masks. The young Archon has so far managed to avoid comments, claiming to be in mourning for his noble father, but Julius knows the charade cannot last—all the more so as custom is increasingly demanding the Archon take a wife...

Julia has asked Vortis the Eunuch to find her a husband who will agree to reverse roles with her. She knows the risk she's running, but believes it's the only way for her to return to public life and set in motion the reforms that will restore Therema to its glory.

### Vortis the Eunuch

A devoted servant of the Thereman throne, to the point of caring little who sits on it, for Vortis only the security of the city matters. This aging diplomat has conspired with all the rulers of the Agalanthian city states and even those of Capharnaum to develop a basis for a completely new form of government: the bureaucracy. For these visionaries, the age of heroes and conquests is over, and people should now aspire to peace and prosperity. The current goal of the bureaucrats is to quell political unrest and the ambitions of the powerful by isolating them little by little from power using disinformation and luxury. They organise ministries and offices to distance the nobles from their subjects and lessen the confidence of subjects towards their rulers, directing that confidence instead towards competent ministers such as themselves. They work to prevent wars, preferring indirect actions like cutting food supplies and spreading disease, and try to discourage exploration and heroism by portraying foreign countries as barbarian lands unworthy of attention. The Agalanthian cities' introversion is largely due to the bureaucrats that now lead them. With Julius, the current archon, Vortis is now preparing the second stage of his project: to eliminate the archon of Therema and to let the ministries run the Senate from behind the scenes. He knows he has little time to waste, as his health has been deteriorating; he suspects the hand of Nesphes Tremens, the archon's chiromancer, but does not dare oppose him. Who could go against a man who claims to speak to the spirit of the very city?

## King Edrick of Lothringen, Elector of Orkadia

In reality, Emperor Jorg of Orkadia knows only part of the truth about Edrick of Lothringen, his vassal (page 292). Edrick does indeed hate him—but for obscure reasons having to do with his father's death. He wishes only to overthrow the Emperor and his supporters. Not expecting Jorg to die any time soon, Edrick has decided to hurry things along by requesting the help of King Simeon IV of Occidentia. In the guise of friendship, the Occidentian king has agreed to station mercenaries on Occidentian soil who are in fact paid for by Edrick. In this way, Edrick's army now has more than a thousand horsemen and 1500 footsoldiers stationed in Occidentia, enough to take by force the positions held by the Emperor's loyalists, especially in a surprise attack. Edrick continues to reinforce this army, and hopes to have two thousand horsemen and five thousand footsoldiers in six months. Of course, such a force is astronomically expensive, and Edrick is forced to squeeze his people, who are beginning to become rebellious.

## King Simeon IV of Occidentia

Faithful to Aether, King Simeon (page 288) has been shaken by the secrets revealed to him in the deserts of Jazirat. However, urged on by his desire for power, he has turned the situation to his advantage, obtaining the support of the Quarterian Magister in the events to come. Once he has resolved his internal problems at home, the King plans to take advantage of Aragonian weakness to begin a territorial conquest at the expense of the Orkadian Empire, who he suspects still has links with the Occidentian revolt.

## Optional Rule: Contacts

Here's a short set of rules to handle character **contacts**.

Each contact is defined by name, profession, culture, and geographical location.

There are two kinds of contacts: **acquaintances** and **allies**. An acquaintance can give information to a character, or provide access to a resource, as long as doing so doesn't deprive or hurt him in any way. An ally, on the other hand, can get involved in a character's business, going and asking for information, putting himself in danger to obtain a resource, getting into trouble.

Favours you get from contacts should be reciprocated. You can't ask another favour from a contact until you've paid him back for the last one.

Characters can acquire new contacts by adventuring. Al-Rawi, you can simply declare a character has a new contact, or you can let players acquire contacts by spending Adventure Points (AP). It costs 5 AP to acquire a new acquaintance, and 15 AP for a new ally. You can also turn an existing acquaintance into an ally for 10 AP.

Note that, as per page 42, the number of contacts for beginning characters is determined by adding Loyalty + Solidarity, as as well as any contacts indicated in the Legend tables on page 35.

## Examples of Contacts

Here's a quick list of contacts if you suddenly need one during play. Feel free to create your own!

| TABLE 9-6: EXAMPLES OF CONTACTS | | | |
|---|---|---|---|
| **NAME** | **PROFESSION** | **ORIGINS** | **PLACE** |
| Sdek Ibn Lhomar | Herbalist | Saabi | Sagrada |
| Matthias Bar Shimon | Physician | Salonim | Carrassine |
| Suad Bint Labiadd | Poisoner | Saabi | Jergath |
| Klionykos Lius Arkus | Playwright | Thereman | Fragrance |
| Eustache the Mad | Armourer | Occidentian | Sagrada |
| Sayid Ibn Idrissi | Militia Captain | Saabi | Carrassine |
| Iwan Shamir | Pirate | Unknown | The Inner Sea |
| Mustafah Ibn Yussef | Caravaneer | Abd-al-Salif | The Desert of Fire |

acters together. To provide a certain credibility to your game, you should try and answer: why are the player characters together? Why are they staying together?

Here are some possible answers.

### The Plot Demands It

This is the simplest and most common answer. Your player characters are brought together by chance, because the plot of the scenario you're playing requires it. This isn't always the most elegant solution, and it isn't always possible to justify.

### The Characters Were Created at the Same Time

Creating all or part of your party of characters at the same time can really help bond them together. Each player describes to the group the character he wants to play, then all the players work with Al-Rawi to create a coherent background which connects all these characters together. For example, you could create a party of characters who are members of the same family, former classmates,

brothers in arms, business partners, and so on. This means your characters know one another before starting play. This is a good solution, but it can require some work.

### Character Backgrounds or Personalities

Characters can have backgrounds or personalities which unite them. This can be one of the most effective solutions, but it's also the least likely unless you communicate with one another a lot when creating your characters.

### The Deus Ex Machina

In this case, the circumstances of the meeting between the characters is defined by a third party, who may be mentor, guide, support or—on the contrary—a recurring nemesis.

### The Dragon Mark

All the player characters are Dragon-Marked. Some higher agency—the dragons, gods, or simply fate—has brought them together at this precise moment, and they have to figure out why.

### All of the Above

These justifications (and all the ones we forgot to mention...) aren't exclusive. You can use a bit of one and a bit of another. What's important is that your player characters have a reason to be together that they can believe in.

## Creating Your Own Scenarios

### Types of Scenario

#### Adventure

*Capharnaum* is a *world* of adventure! Everything, from the game system to the setting descriptions, has been structured to provide an epic framework for roleplaying, loaded with opportunities for adventure and scenario hooks. Head off in search of long-forgotten Agalanthian ruins, cross djinn-haunted deserts, face raiders and creatures lurking in caves, encounter demons, dragons, and even gods. You can download a free introductory adventure for *Capharnaum*, "The Tears of Ampharool", at www.drivethrurpg.com.

#### Exploration

Strongly linked to adventure scenarios, exploration scenarios focus on the discovery of a place and its inhabitants. These are classic "dungeons"—often "palaces of wonder" in *Capharnaum*. Underground complexes, traps, puzzles, riddles, guardian monsters, and rescuing princes and princesses—all these elements can be part of a *Capharnaum* scenario.

---

### Optional Rule: The Party Reserve

*You can emphasise the importance of your player characters as a coherent **party** of adventurers by using the optional **Party Reserve** rule.*

❖ *The Party Reserve is a pool of bonus dice.*
❖ *Any player in the party can transfer one of his Adventure Points into the Party Reserve as a bonus die.*
❖ *Each bonus die in the Party Reserve can be used once, in any action taken by any member of the party.*
❖ *All members of the party should agree on the use of a Party Reserve bonus die—or at least a majority should. If necessary, you can vote on it.*

---

### Intrigue

Political and economic intrigue scenarios focus on the relationships between clans, tribes, and peoples. The northern region of Jazirat, Capharnaum, particularly lends itself to intrigue scenarios, so many and varied are the forces at work there. Quarterians, Saabi, Shiradim, and Agalanthians all meet, exchange, trade, plot—and conspire.

### Investigation

Investigative scenarios are very possible in *Capharnaum*, particularly in urban environments. This book provides maps and descriptions of four large cities and dozens of smaller towns, ideal locales for investigations with twists and turns and plenty of interpersonal drama.

# INSPIRATIONS

Here's a non-exhaustive list of the books, movies, comic books, video games, and music which we think are great inspirations for playing *Capharnaum*. There are of course many, many more—what are yours?

## Literature

*The Tales of the One Thousand and One Nights* by Anonymous (the translation by Sir Richard Burton is fantastic!)
*Alamut* by Vladimir Bartol
*The Crusades Through Arab Eyes* by Amin Maalouf
*Eaters of the Dead* by Michael Crichton
*The Guillaume d'Orange Cycle* and *The Song of Roland* by Anonymous
*The Iliad* and *The Odyssey* by Homer
*Julius Caesar* by Shakespeare
The *Khokarsa* series by Philip José Farmer
*The Lions of Al-Rassan* and *The Sarance Mosaic* by Guy Gavriel Kay
*The Manual of the Warrior of Light* by Paulo Coelho
*Roman Blood* and its sequels by Steven Saylor
*The Rose of the Prophet* by Margaret Weiss and Tracy Hickman
*Salammbo* by Gustave Flaubert

## Comic Books and Graphic Novels

*The Five Storytellers of Baghdad* by Fabien Vehlmann and Frantz Duchazeau
*The King of the Jellyfish* by Thierry Ségur and Igor Szalewa, from a novella by Pierre Bettencourt
*Murena* by Phillipe Delaby and Jean Dufaux
*300* by Frank Miller

## Movies, TV Series, Animated Movies and Cartoons

All the great movies featuring the work of animator Ray Harryhausen, and particularly:
*Clash of the Titans* by Desmond Davis
*The Golden Voyage of Sinbad* by Gordon Hessler
*Jason and the Argonauts* by Don Chaffey
*The Seventh Voyage of Sinbad* by Nathan H Juran
*Sinbad and the Eye of the Tiger* by Sam Wanamaker

*Aladdin* by John Musker and Ron Clemments
*Alexander* by Oliver Stone
*Azur & Asmar: The Princes' Quest* by Michel Ocelot
*Ben Hur* by William Wyler
*Cleopatra* by Joseph L. Mankiewick
*Gladiator* by Ridley Scott
*Hidalgo* by Joe Johnston
*Kingdom of Heaven* by Ridley Scott (choose the Director's Cut version!)
*The Last Days of Pompeii* by Sergio Leone, Mario Bonnard
The countless adventures of *Maciste*
*The Mummy* and *The Mummy Returns* by Stephen Sommers
*The Passion of the Christ* by Mel Gibson
*The Prince of Egypt* by Steve Hickner, Simon Wells, Brenda Chapman
*Prince of Persia: The Sands of Time* by Mike Newell
*Quo Vadis* by Mervyn LeRoy
*Rome* (HBO) by Kevin McKidd, Ray Stevenson, Polly Walker and Kenneth Cranham
*Spartacus* by Stanley Kubrick
*The Ten Commandments* by Cecil B. De Mille
*The Thief of Baghdad* by Clive Donner
*The 13th Warrior* by John McTiernan
*300* by Jack Snyder
*Troy* by Wolfgang Petersen
*Ulysses* by Mario Camerini
*Zaina: Rider of the Atlas* by Bourlem Guerdjou

## Music and Soundtracks

*Alexander* by Vangelis
*Au Cabaret Sauvage* by Lo'Jo
*Brotherhood of the Wolf* by Joseph Loduca
*Caravans* by Mike Batt
*Children of Dune* by Brian Tyler, Adam Klemens
*Concerto d'Aranjuez* by Joaquín Rodrigo
*Everything* by Dead Can Dance
*Duality* by Lisa Gerrard
*Dune* by Toto

*Gladiator* by Hans Zimmer and Lisa Gerrard
*Hidalgo* by James Newton Howard
*The Iranian Classical Tradition* by Djamchid Chemirani et al
*Kingdom of Heaven* by Harry Gregson Williams
*Lawrence of Arabia* by Maurice Jarre
*The Legend of Zorro* by James Horner
*The Mask of Zorro* by James Horner
*The Mummy* by Jerry Goldsmith
*The Mummy Returns* by Alan Silvestri
*Passion (Last Temptation of Christ)* by Peter Gabriel
*Passion of the Christ* by John Debney
*The Prince of Egypt* by Hans Zimmer
*The 13th Warrior* by Jerry Goldsmith
*300* by Tyler Bates
*Troy* by James Horner

## Video Games

*Assassin's Creed* (Ubi Soft)
*God of War 1 and 2* (SCEA – Santa Monica)
*Prince of Persia 3D* (The Sands of Time, Warrior Within and The Two Thrones) (Ubisoft)
*Titan Quest* (THQ Inc. developed by Iron Lore Entertainment)

# STAGING ADVICE

## Setting the Mood

*Capharnaum* is a roleplaying game of ancient world adventure set in a fantasy version of the Mediterranean Sea and focussing on its ancient, classical, and mediaeval civilisations, particularly those of the Arabian Peninsula. Its general atmosphere is loosely "Middle Eastern". You can reinforce your descriptions and your players' immersion by using some of the following elements:

❖ A low table with pouffes and cushions.
❖ Coloured hangings.
❖ Dates and figs, dry or fresh.
❖ Burners and incense.
❖ For music, choose from the inspiration list above.
❖ Mint tea, maybe poured from traditional middle eastern brass teapots and served in tea glasses.

## How to Play NPCs

Al-Rawi, when you can, act in character. Speak in the first person, play out the voice and language of an NPC as you'd imagine them. Highlight turns of phrase with flourishes in your best accents—

Hispanic for Aragonian, Frankish for Occidentians, Germanic for Orkadians, Middle Eastern for Jazirati, and so on. Don't go overboard, unless you've a gift for accents, but little touches here and there can really convey the atmosphere. Other times, you can just deliver the character's lines and end with "he says with a strong accent from Carrassine's northern districts". That works just as well. You'll often be working with stereotypes and archetypes in *Capharnaum*—noble knights, wily merchants, evil sorcerers, fanatical priests. Describe their attire and expressions, their social peculiarities, and don't be afraid to lay it on a bit thick to make them memorable. *Capharnaum* is an epic game of adventure, larger than life!

## Keep Your Players Happy

One last piece of advice: as we've said, *Capharnaum* is an epic game, and your players will be expecting to head off on amazing adventures, discover unknown cities, obtain the favours of sumptuous courtesans or handsome seducers in far-away lands, and prove their mettle against creatures of legend. Don't hold them back—give them what they want! Obviously not too easily, but don't be afraid to think big, describe epic events, and give the players the thrill of this epic setting. You don't have to give it all away for free—it's fine to make the adventurers work hard for their glory!—but don't frustrate their desires for greatness. The characters are Dragon-Marked, and should want to change the world. Let them tell big stories—they'll pay you back.

# Afterword

When I picked up the first edition of the French-language role-playing game *Capharnaüm—L'Héritage des Dragons* at the Paris Games Fair in 2009, I knew I'd found something special. First of all, it was a gorgeous book—that's why it had caught my eye, among all the other RPGs on sale that weekend. When I leafed through its pages my excitement grew—clearly here was a setting of amazing depth, crafted with unmistakeable passion. As I read on, standing there, fascinated, I realised that *Capharnaüm—L'Héritage des Dragons* had solved that age-old RPG conundrum of how to design a playable game chock-full with historical depth and themes, but which didn't get bogged down in an obsession with real-world historical accuracy, and which didn't trample underfoot cultural and religious sensitivities which are still very much with us today.

Because *Capharnaum* is a game packed with historical and cultural themes, without being a historical game. It's a game where you can play "what if?" with the great questions of our own past, but in a fantasy world which reflects and refracts our own, but very obviously is not our own. It's a great sandbox where you can run amok and riff off historical and cultural conflicts, without disrespecting the real-world forces which have shaped our societies. But, even more than that, it's a game where "the Orient", "the Middle East", isn't presented as something foreign and exotic, something

*other*, but is the heart of the world, the norm, the home where most of your characters come from. The conventional European focus of fantasy RPGs is displaced, the tropes of mediaeval fantasy become the things that are foreign—and we, as game masters and players, get the chance to view and understand the world from a different and compelling perspective, at a time in our real-world history when that understanding is more necessary than ever. From a human point of view, *Capharnaum* is an ambitious game, full of humanity and the desire for acceptance and coexistence.

For me, it was irresistible. I wanted to play this game. More, I wanted to translate it and bring it to the English-speaking world.

Fast-forward five years, and Mindjammer Press was publishing our flagship *Mindjammer—The Roleplaying Game* and talking with non-English language publishers about producing translated editions. Here in France, where I live, I suddenly found myself talking with Studio Deadcrows, a fantastic group of RPG gamers and designers based in the Mediterranean city of Montpellier. Not only were they interested in publishing *Mindjammer* in French—but they were the writers and publishers of my beloved *Capharnaum*, which had now grown into a magnificent product line of supplements and adventures, each as exciting and as detailed as the core book itself! And so a deal was struck...

The book you hold in your hands today is the fruit of the dreams of many people: François Cédelle and Raphaël Bardas, creators and coordinators of *Capharnaum* and its universe, and their team of writers; of Boris Courdesses, artist and imagineer of this beautiful setting, and his team of cartographers and illustrators; Stephan Barat, publisher and manager of the Studio Deadcrows team, who saw the opportunity for collaboration on *Mindjammer* and *Capharnaum*. And of course my own dream—almost ten years old, now—to bring this gorgeous and inspiring game to you.

None of this would have happened without the *Capharnaum* Kickstarter which Mindjammer Press ran in late 2017. Kickstarters are humbling experiences: people come up to you and say they believe in you and what you're doing, and back up that belief with their hard-earned cash, investing in a product because they trust what you're doing and want to see it become a reality. *Capharnaum* was my second Kickstarter, and it left me as breathless as the first—the near five-hundred backers of the campaign had allowed me to realise this dream. They didn't know the game or the system or setting, but they were willing to give us a chance. With great trust comes great responsibility, and I hope we've met your expectations with this game. I hope you'll love it as much as I do.

Producing this book has been a labour of love. For the past six months I've worked on the initial translation by José Luis Porfirio, restructuring, retranslating, rewriting, incorporating elements from the second French edition, and hopefully polishing it into something which you'll love reading. The concepts in *Capharnaum* are beautiful, profound, inspiring and, as much as my humble skills permitted, I wanted the language to express that, too. But perhaps the most exciting part of producing *Capharnaum* has

been working with the awesome Jason Juta, artist, art director, and layout guru at Mindjammer Press. As soon as the *Capharnaum* Kickstarter unlocked the stretch goal of funding colour art for the game, we knew we could do something special. The original French version of the game featured evocative art in sand and sepia tones, and yet I had a dream of producing the game in colour. Jason would be colouring the original artwork by the talented French illustrators who'd produced the original game, adding pieces of his own and, with good fortune and the blessings of the spirits of the sands and seas, we would achieve something special.

Jason has succeeded beyond my wildest dreams. I hope you'll agree—the artwork and layout here is beautiful. It complements the original French version and updates it for the present day, looking forward to the future of new products appearing in the *Capharnaum* line. We're translating the existing French supplements and publishing new material, and hope that, just as *Mindjammer* has become our flagship science-fiction RPG, *Capharnaum—The Tales of the Dragon-Marked* will become the flagship fantasy RPG of Mindjammer Press. Many adventures lie ahead...

So, all of us, French and English, dreamers and gamers, would like to thank you for making this game possible, and for joining us in the fantastic and fascinating world of *Capharnaum*. Empires will shake, kingdoms will fall, and the very gods themselves will tremble before the epic adventures of the Dragon-Marked.

The world was made by dragons. Its destiny will be decided by their children.

All hail the Dragon-Marked!

Sarah Newton
*Normandy, France*
*June 2018*

# APPENDICES

## The Temple of Truth

"Luther!"

"Thufir? Is that really you? Why didn't you come and see us first?"

"I didn't know you were here... My friend—I thought you were dead! I came to the temple in your honour. I wanted to finish your quest! I didn't think your new friends would let me..."

"Don't worry. We've got here at last. These people don't speak our language. Not the one we speak today. But they're peaceful! If I understand them correctly, they've been waiting here for centuries for someone to come. They welcomed me like a prince yesterday evening. They were about to show me their temple..."

"How did you get here? How did you answer the djinn's riddle?"

"I didn't even need to think about it! Listen, there's something you don't know. I didn't tell you the truth when you noticed how impossible the dates were when I tried to tell you the Prophets had written those runes. Well, some monks in my kingdom recently identified Jason as their author, and after the date of his martyrdom! It was... an uncomfortable discovery, shall we say. The Quarterian Magister has burned heretics for less. So they entrusted me with the knowledge, and I came to find this place, following in the footsteps of my grandfather. Ah, if only he'd known, he'd've been able to answer the riddle of the djinn who sank his longship. But how did you guess?"

"Hah! Because you're not the only liar here, my friend! I belong to a secret society that has always known Jason didn't die, but sought sanctuary with the djinn. When you translated the runes and mentioned a holy place protected by desert spirits, my brothers and I decided to help you."

"I suppose that makes us even. Let the spirits beware! Do you think this is the tomb of the Prophets?"

"I don't know. I don't see any tomb. But look at that mosaic..."

Luther raised his eyes. High above, a character clad in gold flew across the temple's dome, showing the heavens blazing with dragon breath. His head turned backwards, his body straight, he seemed to have paused in his ascent. From the sword in his left hand as from the three canes in his right, blood fell to the earth below, on the hundreds of corpses he was leaving behind. All around the base of the dome paintings of men and women grimaced, twisted faces of people wounded, tortured, flayed, their bonds removed. Luther's head spun.

Thufir had walked up to the wall and was calling back to him.

"Come and look at this. You'll need to see this to believe it."

Luther approached and looked at the part of the painting his friend was pointing at.

"It looks like..."

"Yes. It's us. You and me, the white and the brown, the blonde-haired and the black. That's the Quarterian cross on your left break, the salamander on my right thigh. That can't be chance. We were destined to come here."

"We're the only ones in all this crowd of people who aren't in agony. We don't even look wounded. We look ready for battle, ready to climb a mountain of corpses..."

"I wonder who the rest of these unfortunates are?"

"Maybe they're like us. The Dragon-Marked..."

# Travel and Distance

When travelling the lands of Capharnaum and beyond, you can usually make the following average speeds every day. Note that unexpected events, heading off-road and into uncharted territory, poor weather, and many other factors can modify these times and distances.

Here are some travel times and distances for the most used trade routes.

| TABLE 10-1: TRAVEL TIMES AND DISTANCES FOR PRINCIPAL TRADE ROUTES | | |
|---|---|---|
| **TRADE ROUTE** | **DISTANCE** | **TIME** |
| **FRAGRANCE – JERGATH** | | |
| The South Route | 1323 leagues (3969 miles) | 150 days |
| The Halawui Route | 1500 leagues (4490 miles) | 178 days |
| The Copper & Turquoise Road | 2122 leagues (6366 miles) | 226 days |
| **CAPHARNIAN CITIES** | | |
| Fragrance – Sagrada | 289 leagues (867 miles) | 26 days at 10 leagues / day |
| Sagrada – Carrassine | 322 leagues (966 miles) | 29 days at 10 leagues / day |
| Carrassine – Zarbeth | 344 leagues (1032 miles) | 31 days at 10 leagues / day |
| Fragrance – Kawimsha | 222 leagues (666 miles) | 20 days at 10 leagues / day |
| Kawimsha – Albagdir | 333 leagues (999 miles) | 38 days at 8 leagues / day |
| **THE SOUTH OR INCENSE ROUTE (THROUGH THE DESERT OF FIRE)** | | |
| Sagrada – Zarbeth | 289 leagues (867 miles) | 26 days at 10 leagues / day |
| Zarbeth – Alayahba | 356 leagues (1068 miles) | 54 days at 6 leagues / day |
| Alayahba – Jergath | 389 leagues (1167 miles) | 44 days at 8 leagues / day |
| Alayahba – Jergath (the direct route)[1] | 256 leagues (768 miles) | 38 days at 6 leagues / day |
| **THE COPPER & TURQUOISE ROAD (THE WEST COAST OF JAZIRAT)** | | |
| Carrassine – northern point of the Bay of Dragons | 422 leagues (1266 miles) | 48 days at 8 leagues / day |
| Northern point of the Bay of Dragons – Ishankti | 511 leagues (1533 miles) | 58 days at 8 leagues / day |
| Ishankti – Jergath | 578 leagues  (1734 miles) | 65 days at 8 leagues / day |
| Ishankti – Balzabaar | 189 leagues (567 miles) | 22 days at 8 leagues / day |
| **THE ROAD TO THE CITIES OF THE SOUTH (VIA THE HALAWUI RIVER)** | | |
| Longer than the Incense Route, this is sometimes very pleasant, but also much harder in places, with cliffs, detours along the river meanders, and so on. | | |
| Sagrada – south of the Lazurine Sea | 444 leagues (1322 miles) | 57 days at 7 leagues / day |
| South of the Lazurine Sea – Opona | 222 leagues (666 miles) | 29 days at 7 leagues / day |
| South of the Lazurine Sea – Muhyl | 511 leagues (1533 miles) | 66 days at 7 leagues / day |
| South of the Lazurine Sea – Madina Al-Muhit (Kathrat) | 489 leagues (1467 miles) | 63 days at 7 leagues / day |
| Muhyl – Jergath | 256 leagues (768 miles) | 29 days at 8 leagues / day |
| Muhyl – Madina Al-Muhit (Kathrat) | 233 leagues (699 miles) | 24 days at 9 leagues / day |
| Madina Al-Muhit – Opona | 322 leagues (966 miles) | 37 days at 8 leagues / day |

1: This route takes many short-cuts and often goes off the beaten track. It is much more dangerous; you travel at a slower pace, but the overall distance to be travelled is shorter.

| TABLE 10-2: AVERAGE TRAVEL TIMES | |
|---|---|
| **METHOD OF TRAVEL** | **DISTANCE COVERED** |
| A caravan following roads | 6-11 leagues (18-33 miles) / day |
| Difficult terrain (deserts, etc) | 6 leagues (18 miles) / day |
| Average terrain (wild coasts, broken lands, canyons, etc) | 9 leagues (27 miles) / day |
| Easy terrain (plains, grasslands, etc) | 11 leagues (33 miles) / day |
| Lone camel or small mounted group travelling without a caravan | 30 leagues (90 miles) / day |

# THE GRAND BAZAAR

## Price Lists for Capharnaum

### Warning

Prices in this list are averages for Jazirat—real prices will vary from city to city, and even merchant to merchant. Use the prices below as bases, but adapt them to the characters' bargaining skills (depending on the magnitudes of Unctuous Bargaining rolls) and the players' roleplaying. Prices may also vary depending on the quality of the goods (see page 42):

❖ Poor quality: half price.
❖ Average quality: price shown.
❖ Very Good quality: x2 price.
❖ Superior quality: x5 price.
❖ Exceptional quality: x20 price.

## Spices, Currency, and Coinage

*1 gold talent (GT) = 1 ounce of saffron (OS)*
*= 10 silver talents (ST) = 10 ounces of cumin (OC)*
*= 100 copper talents (CT) = 100 ounces of cardamom (OCM)*

## In the City

| TABLE 10-3: MONTHLY SALARIES | | |
|---|---|---|
| **PROFESSION** | **COIN** | **OUNCES OF CUMIN** |
| Architect | 35 GT | 350 |
| Bell Dancer | 40 GT | 400 |
| Calligrapher | 14 GT | 140 |
| Charioteer | 18 GT | 180 |
| Craftsman (generalist) | 12 GT | 120 |
| Craftsman (specialist) | 20 GT | 200 |
| Farmhand | 8 GT | 80 |
| Gladiator | 14 GT | 140 |
| Mercenary, famous | 26 GT | 260 |
| Mercenary, lone | 16 GT | 160 |
| Officer | 28 GT | 280 |
| Physician | 30 GT | 300 |
| Renowned Artist | 30 GT | 300 |
| Sailor | 12 GT | 120 |
| Scribe | 12 GT | 120 |
| Senator | 60 GT | 600 |
| Servant | 10 GT | 100 |
| Soldier (guard) | 18 GT | 180 |
| Trader (any kind) | 18 GT | 180 |
| Tutor | 20 GT | 200 |
| Weapons Master | 30 GT | 300 |

## Table 10-4: Slaves

| Item | Coin | Ounces of Cumin |
|---|---|---|
| Child | 1 GT | 10 |
| Younger Female Slave | 5 GT | 50 |
| Older Female Slave | 2 GT | 20 |
| Younger Male Slave | 6 GT | 60 |
| Older Male Slave | 3 GT | 30 |

## Table 10-5: Services

| Service | Coin | Ounces of Cumin |
|---|---|---|
| Bath-house | 8 CT | 0.8 |
| Circus, Theatre, Show, or other Spectacle | 4 ST | 4 |
| Consult a Physician | 4 ST | 4 |
| First Aid | 2 ST | 2 |
| Forger | 2 GT | 20 |
| Fortune Telling | 1 ST | 1 |
| Get a Massage | 3 ST | 3 |
| Hire a Messenger | 2 ST | 2 |
| Hospitalisation (per day) | 6 ST | 6 |
| Repairs to Armour, Tool or Weapon | 4 ST | 4 |
| Sewing and Patching | 2 ST | 2 |
| The Services of a Prostitute | 5 ST | 5 |
| The Services of a Paper Virgin | 1 GT | 10 |
| A Shave and / or a Haircut | 1 ST | 1 |

## Table 10-6: Food, Drink, and Accommodation

| Item | Coin | Ounces of Cumin |
|---|---|---|
| Common Room (per night) | 5 CT | 0.5 |
| Room (per night) | 3 ST | 3 |
| Suite (per night) | 6 ST | 6 |
| Beer (pint) | 5 CT | 0.5 |
| Exotic Alcohol (bottle) | 1 GT | 10 |
| Tea (glass) | 2 CT | 0.2 |
| Wine (bottle) | 2 ST | 2 |
| Feast | 5 ST | 5 |
| Good Meal | 3 ST | 3 |
| Today's Special | 1 ST | 1 |
| Eggs | 2 CT | 0.2 |
| Fish | 6 CT | 0.6 |
| Jerked Meat | 6 CT | 0.6 |
| Meat (beef, mutton) | 8 CT | 0.8 |
| Poultry | 6 CT | 0.6 |
| Vegetables | 3 CT | 0.3 |
| Cereal Biscuits | 5 CT | 0.5 |
| Dried Fruits & Vegetables | 3 CT | 0.5 |
| Honey (1lb) | 1 ST | 1 |
| Pastries | 5 ST | 5 |

## TABLE 10-7: WEAPONS (SEE ALSO PAGE 58)

| WEAPON | COIN | OUNCES OF CUMIN |
|---|---|---|
| Axe, Orkadian | 4 GT | 40 |
| Axe, Throwing | 5 ST | 5 |
| Bow, Jazirati Recurved | 15 ST | 15 |
| Bow, Long | 9 ST | 9 |
| Bow, Short | 5 ST | 5 |
| Choora | 6 ST | 6 |
| Crusader Sword | 3 GT | 30 |
| Espada Valladena | 4 GT | 40 |
| Falkata, Aragonian | 2 GT | 20 |
| Flail, Military | 2 GT | 20 |
| Gladius, Agalanthian | 1 GT | 10 |
| Jambiya | 8 ST | 8 |
| Javelin | 4 ST | 4 |
| Kaskara, Jazirati | 2 GT | 20 |
| Khanjar | 1 GT | 10 |
| Khedama, Saabi | 24 ST | 24 |
| Kopis, Agalanthian | 22 ST | 22 |
| Lance, Quarterian | 2 GT | 20 |
| Mace, War | 1 GT | 10 |
| Sayf | 12 ST | 12 |
| Shimshir, Saabi | 3 GT | 30 |
| Sling | 8 CT | 0.8 |
| Spatha, Agalanthian | 2 GT | 20 |
| Spear, Hoplite | 24 ST | 24 |
| Spear, Rumh | 6 ST | 6 |
| Suyuf, Capharnian | 3 GT | 30 |
| Trident, Agalanthian | 4 GT | 40 |
| Whip, Aragonian | 6 ST | 6 |
| Yatagan, Capharnian | 2 GT | 20 |
| Two-handed Weapons | +30% | +30% |
| Bastard / Hand-and-a-Half Weapons | +10% | +10% |

## TABLE 10-8: ARMOUR (SEE ALSO PAGE 64)

| ARMOUR | COIN | OUNCES OF CUMIN |
|---|---|---|
| Buckler Shield | 1 GT | 10 |
| Heavy Armour | 3 GT | 30 |
| Light Armour | 8 ST | 8 |
| Myrmidon Armour | 10 GT | 100 |
| Piece of Armour | 2 ST | 2 |
| Round Shield | 5 ST | 5 |

## TABLE 10-9: JEWELLERY

| ITEM | COIN | OUNCES OF CUMIN |
|---|---|---|
| Bracelet | 8 ST | 8 |
| Crown | 30 GT | 300 |
| Diadem | 10 GT | 100 |
| Earrings | 6 ST | 6 |
| Fibula | 4 ST | 4 |
| Necklace | 2 GT | 20 |
| Ring | 5 ST | 5 |
| Torc | 12 GT | 120 |

## TABLE 10-10: PERSONAL GROOMING

| ITEM | COIN | OUNCES OF CUMIN |
|---|---|---|
| Make-up | 1 ST | 1 |
| Mirror | 2 ST | 2 |
| Oils & Bath Soap | 8 CT | 0.8 |
| Perfume | 2 ST | 2 |
| Razors | 1 ST | 1 |

| Table 10-11: Clothing | | |
|---|---|---|
| **Item** | **Coin** | **Ounces of Cumin** |
| Complete Set of Workaday Clothes | 4 ST | 4 |
| Complete Set of Travelling Clothes | 8 ST | 8 |
| Complete Set of Urban Clothing | 1 GT | 10 |
| Complete Set of Luxury Clothing | 10 GT | 100 |
| Agalanthian Toga | 3 ST | 3 |
| Asaba Headband | 6 CT | 0.6 |
| Babouches Slippers | 2 CT | 0.2 |
| Belt | 1 ST | 1 |
| Boots | 16 CT | 1.6 |
| Cape | 9 CT | 0.9 |
| Cloak | 8 ST | 8 |
| Fez | 1 ST | 1 |
| Gloves | 1 ST | 1 |
| Hat | 2 ST | 2 |
| Jellaba | 1 ST | 1 |
| Keffiyeh | 5 CT | 0.5 |
| Qamis Shirt | 1 ST | 1 |
| Quarterian Robes | 3 ST | 3 |
| Qumbaz Vest | 2 ST | 2 |
| Religious Robes | 1 GT | 10 |
| Sandals | 8 CT | 0.8 |
| Shawl | 2 CT | 0.2 |
| Sarwal Large Trousers | 1 ST | 1 |
| Talet Large Robe | 2 ST | 2 |
| Taquia Cap | 8 CT | 0.8 |
| Thawb Tunic | 2 ST | 2 |
| Turban | 4 CT | 0.4 |
| Veil | 5 CT | 0.5 |

| Table 10-12: Tools | | |
|---|---|---|
| **Item** | **Coin** | **Ounces of Cumin** |
| Brush | 1 ST | 1 |
| Canvas (per square pace) | 4 ST | 4 |
| Carpentry Tools | 7 ST | 7 |
| Cooking Gear | 5 ST | 5 |
| Farming Tools | 5 ST | 5 |
| Fishing Gear | 2 ST | 2 |
| Hunting Gear | 3 ST | 3 |
| Knives | 1 ST | 1 |
| Ladder (10-15 ft) | 1 ST | 1 |
| Paint (one colour) | 3 ST | 3 |
| Painting | 25 ST | 25 |
| Parchment Holder | 3 CT | 0.3 |
| Pestles & Mortar | 6 ST | 6 |
| Physician's Kit (10 uses) | 1 GT | 10 |
| Picture Frame (2ft x 3ft) | 1 GT | 10 |
| Pottery Equipment | 4 ST | 4 |
| Spade, Rake | 7 CT | 0.7 |
| Surgical Kit (10 uses) | 2 GT | 20 |
| Woodcutter's Axe | 9 CT | 0.9 |
| Writing Kit | 4 ST | 4 |

| TABLE 10-13: ADVENTURER'S GEAR | | |
| --- | --- | --- |
| ITEM | COIN | OUNCES OF CUMIN |
| Backpack | 1 ST | 1 |
| Blanket | 4 CT | 0.4 |
| Candle | 1 CT | 0.1 |
| Compass | 12 GT | 120 |
| First Aid Kit | 2 ST | 2 |
| Hourglass | 1 ST | 1 |
| Lantern | 1 ST | 1 |
| Oil (1 pint) | 5 CT | 0.5 |
| Oil Lamp | 5 ST | 5 |
| Pouch | 5 CT | 0.5 |
| Purse | 4 CT | 0.4 |
| Rope (50 ft) | 8 CT | 0.8 |
| Saddlebag | 5 CT | 0.5 |
| Shovel, Pickaxe | 5 CT | 0.5 |
| String | 1 CT | 0.1 |
| Spyglass | 10 GT | 100 |
| Torch (burns for 2 hrs) | 2 CT | 0.2 |
| Waterskin (2 pints) | 3 CT | 0.3 |

| TABLE 10-14: ART, MUSIC, & WRITING MATERIALS | | |
| --- | --- | --- |
| ITEM | COIN | OUNCES OF CUMIN |
| Astrolabe | 30 GT | 300 |
| Clay Tablet | 5 CT | 0.5 |
| Drum | 2 ST | 2 |
| Gold Leaf | 5 GT | 50 |
| Harp | 3 GT | 30 |
| Ink (1 pint) | 3 ST | 3 |
| Lute | 9 ST | 9 |
| Lyre | 2 GT | 20 |
| Mandolin | 1 GT | 10 |
| Nay (Jazirati flute) | 6 ST | 6 |
| Papyrus (1 page) | 2 CT | 0.2 |
| Parchment (1 page) | 2 CT | 0.2 |
| Pen | 7 CT | 0.7 |
| Quarterian Flute | 5 ST | 5 |
| Santoor | 15 ST | 15 |
| Scroll | 1 ST | 1 |
| Sistrum | 6 ST | 6 |
| Wax Tablet & Stylus | 3 ST | 3 |
| Wax & Seal | 2 ST | 2 |
| Zarb | 2 GT | 20 |
| Zither | 1 GT | 10 |

| TABLE 10-15: ROGUES' TRAPPINGS | | |
| --- | --- | --- |
| ITEM | COIN | OUNCES OF CUMIN |
| Game of *Dhamet* | 5 CT | 0.5 |
| Game of *Owaré* | 6 CT | 0.6 |
| Game of *Senet* | 1 ST | 1 |
| Glass-cutting Diamond | 9 ST | 9 |
| Lockpicks | 1 GT | 10 |
| Pendulum | 7 CT | 0.7 |
| Set of Tarot Divination Cards | 5 ST | 5 |
| Six-sided Die | 2 CT | 0.2 |
| Weighted Die | 8 ST | 8 |

## Table 10-16: Poisons

| Item | Coin | Ounces of Cumin |
|---|---|---|
| Amanite | 4 GT | 40 |
| Arsenic | 20 GT | 200 |
| Black Saffron | 3 GT | 30 |
| Datura | 25 ST | 25 |
| Hemlock | 9 ST | 9 |
| Penitent's Mint | 8 GT | 80 |
| Poor Man's Spice | 4 ST | 4 |
| Quicksilver | 35 GT | 350 |
| Rakshasa | 8 ST | 8 |
| Sylvite | 10 GT | 100 |

## Trade Goods & Merchandise

### Table 10-17: Animals

| Animal | Coin | Ounces of Cumin |
|---|---|---|
| Camel | 15 GT | 150 |
| Cat | 15 ST | 15 |
| Elephant | 80 GT | 800 |
| Exotic Bird | 15 GT | 150 |
| Goat | 24 ST | 24 |
| Guard Dog | 8 ST | 8 |
| Horse | 10 GT | 100 |
| Lion | 24 GT | 240 |
| Monkey | 5 GT | 50 |
| Mule, Ass, Donkey | 2 GT | 20 |
| Ox | 9 GT | 90 |
| Pet Snake | 6 GT | 60 |
| Tiger | 30 GT | 300 |
| Warhorse | 25 GT | 250 |

## Table 10-18: Ornaments and Containers

| Item | Coin | Ounces of Cumin |
|---|---|---|
| Amphora | 8 CT | 0.8 |
| Barrel | 1 ST | 1 |
| Basin | 3 ST | 3 |
| Bowl | 1 CT | 0.1 |
| Carpet | 4 ST | 4 |
| Cask | 5 CT | 0.5 |
| Casket | 5 ST | 5 |
| Censer | 1 ST | 1 |
| Clay Pot | 1 CT | 0.1 |
| Cloth (1 square pace) | 6 CT | 0.6 |
| Cooking Pot | 8 CT | 0.8 |
| Flask | 8 CT | 0.8 |
| Goblet | 1 CT | 0.1 |
| Hookah | 3 ST | 3 |
| Mosaic (1 square pace) | 4 ST | 4 |
| Statue | 5 GT | 50 |
| Statuette, Clay | 5 CT | 0.5 |
| Statuette, Metal | 6 ST | 6 |
| Strongbox | 1 ST | 1 |
| Tajine | 6 CT | 0.6 |
| Teapot | 2 ST | 2 |
| Trunk | 9 CT | 0.9 |
| Urn | 2 ST | 2 |
| Vase | 1 ST | 1 |
| Vial | 5 CT | 0.5 |

## Table 10-21: City Structures & Constructions

| Item | Coin | Ounces of Cumin |
|------|------|-----------------|
| Apartment Building | 1000 GT | 10,000 |
| Barn | 35 GT | 350 |
| City House | 650 GT | 6500 |
| Forge | 120 GT | 1200 |
| Plot of Land | 25 GT | 250 |
| Shop | 300 GT | 3000 |
| Workshop | 100 GT | 1000 |

## Table 10-22: Outdoor Structures & Constructions

| Structure | Coin | Ounces of Cumin |
|-----------|------|-----------------|
| Aqueduct (per league) | 10 GT | 100 |
| Bivouac Tent | 5 GT | 50 |
| Bridge (per pace) | 3 GT | 30 |
| Irrigation Works (per acre) | 1 GT | 10 |
| Peasant Hut | 85 GT | 850 |
| Well | 40 GT | 400 |
| Windmill | 140 GT | 1400 |

## Table 10-19: Spices (per ounce)

| Item | Coin | Ounces of Cumin |
|------|------|-----------------|
| Black Pepper (*Felfel khal*) | 1 CT | 0.1 |
| Caraway (*Keruiya*) | 3 ST | 3 |
| Cardamom (*Hal*) | 1 CT | 0.1 |
| Cinnamon (*Karfa*) | 5 ST | 5 |
| Coriander (*Kasbur*) | 9 ST | 9 |
| Cumin (*Kammn*) | 1 ST | 1 |
| Dragonblood | 5 GT | 50 |
| Ginger (*Skinjbir*) | 8 ST | 8 |
| Gum Arabic (*Merka*) | 4 CT | 0.4 |
| Laurel (*Rend*) | 7 CT | 0.7 |
| Marjoram (*Merdekuch*) | 6 ST | 6 |
| Mint (*Naana*) | 4 CT | 0.4 |
| Nutmeg (*Guzt Ettib*) | 5 ST | 5 |
| Saffron (*Za'Faran*) | 1 GT | 10 |
| Sesame (*Jeljlane*) | 7 ST | 7 |
| Thyme (*Zaatar*) | 3 CT | 0.3 |
| Turmeric (*Querkub*) | 5 CT | 0.5 |

## Table 10-23: Large Structures

| Structure | Coin | Ounces of Cumin |
|-----------|------|-----------------|
| Castle | 6000 GT | 60,000 |
| Cathedral | 7000 GT | 70,000 |
| Chapel | 600 GT | 6000 |
| Fort | 500 GT | 5000 |
| Fountain | 240 GT | 2400 |
| Monument | 110 GT | 1100 |
| Palace | 8000 GT | 80,000 |
| Plaza or Paving (per acre) | 40 GT | 400 |
| Ramparts (per league) | 100 GT | 1000 |
| Temple / Church | 3500 GT | 35,000 |
| Watchtower | 100 GT | 1000 |

## Table 10-20: Incense (per 4 oz)

| Item | Coin | Ounces of Cumin |
|------|------|-----------------|
| Agalloch | 3 ST | 3 |
| Benzoin | 6 ST | 6 |
| Myrrh | 1 GT | 10 |
| Olibanum | 8 ST | 8 |
| Sandalwood | 1 ST | 1 |
| Styrax | 4 ST | 4 |

## Transportation

### Table 10-24: Ships

| Ship | Coin | Ounces of Cumin |
|---|---|---|
| Bagala (200 tons) | 1200 GT | 12,000 |
| Cange (60 tons) | 500 GT | 5000 |
| Felucca (20 tons) | 20 GT | 200 |
| Trireme | 2000 GT | 20,000 |
| Zarug (100 tons) | 800 GT | 8000 |

### Table 10-25: Overland Transport

| Item | Coin | Ounces of Cumin |
|---|---|---|
| Chariot, Small (80HP) | 8 GT | 80 |
| Chariot, Large (160HP) | 16 GT | 160 |
| Saddlery | 1 GT | 10 |
| Sedan Chair | 4 ST | 4 |

### Table 10-26: Booking Passage

| Travelling by... | Coin | Ounces of Cumin |
|---|---|---|
| Caravan | 4 GT | 40 |
| Merchant Ship | 10 GT | 100 |

## Magic

### Table 10-27: Magical Resources

| Item | Coin | Ounces of Cumin |
|---|---|---|
| Ritual Paraphernalia | 2 ST | 2 |
| Spell Book | 50 GT | 500 |

### Table 10-28: Chiromancy Tablets

| Tablet | Coin | Ounces of Cumin |
|---|---|---|
| Against Wind and Tide | 24 ST | 24 |
| Blessing of Good Fortune | 12 ST | 12 |
| Carry Pregnancy to Term | 24 ST | 24 |
| Cure This Disease | 36 ST | 36 |
| Curse of Misfortune | 12 ST | 12 |
| Destroy Clouds | 48 ST | 48 |
| Destroy Wall | 38 ST | 38 |
| Find the Path | 24 ST | 24 |
| O Joy, Light Up His Face | 24 ST | 24 |

### Table 10-29: Magical Items

| Item | Coin | Ounces of Cumin |
|---|---|---|
| Dagger of Sharpness | 10 GT | 100 |
| Dancing Buckler | 100 GT | 1000 |
| Draconic Marvel | 1000 GT | 10,000 |
| Flying Carpet | 20 GT | 200 |
| Magic Lamp | 20 GT | 200 |
| Orichalcum Item | 200 GT | 2000 |
| Sundowner | 20 GT | 200 |

# Capharnaüm
## The Tales of the Dragon-Marked

Name

Path

Blood

Status

Occupation

Strength

Constitution

Dexterity

Bravery

Heroism

Intelligence

Charisma

Faith

Loyalty

Max Init

Soak

Dragon Dice

Adventure Points

**Passive Defence**

First Weapon

Damage

Second Weapon

Damage

Third Weapon

Damage

**Armour**

**Hit Points**

### The Adventurer
- Athletics
- Riding
- Storytelling
- Survival

### The Poet
- Acting
- Music
- Oratory
- Poetry

### The Rogue
- Assassination
- Intrusion
- Stealth
- Thievery

### The Sorcerer
- Prayer
- Sacred Word
- Sacrifice
- Willpower

### The Labourer
- Agriculture
- Craft
- Endurance
- Solidarity

### The Prince
- Elegance
- Flattery
- Save Face
- Unctuous Bargaining

### The Sage
- History & Peoples
- Instruction
- Notice
- Science

### The Warrior
- Combat Training
- Command
- Fighting
- Intimidate

# Path Abilities

Level _____

# Magic

## Sacred Word

⬤ Create   ⬤ Transform   ⬤ Destroy

| Element | Type | Element | Type |
|---------|------|---------|------|
| | | | |
| | | | |
| | | | |
| | | | |
| | | | |
| | | | |
| | | | |
| | | | |

# Character Portrait

# Equipment

Wealth Level ⬤ Money _____

_____

_____

# Personal Legend

# GLOSSARY

**Abzul:** Saurian steed of the Walad Badiya, famous for their mental bond. From Al-Fariq'n; said to be the offspring of fallen dragons.

**Aether:** The supreme god among the Quarterians.

**Afreeti:** Foul and monstrous offspring of the dying Tiamat, Mother of Monsters.

**Agalanth:** Mythical hero of the Agalanthiad. He wandered all over the known world and gave birth to the Agalanthian people.

**Agalanthians:** People who once ruled the world, as much by force as through the arts and sciences. After being a Republic and an Empire, they are now in full decline, fighting one another to assert the power of their city-states.

**Agalanthian Schools:** Universities or sects devoted to one discipline (fencing, magic, diplomacy, etc.) with an important political or cultural impact among the Agalanthians and within Capharnaum.

**Al-Kimyat (pl. Al-Kimyati):** Jazirati magicians who manipulate the alchemy of words and arts in a sorcerous art known as the *tamasheq*.

**Al-Muhit El-Mandab:** The Ocean of Lamentations.

**Al-Ragon:** Formerly the southern half of the Quarterian Kingdom of Aragon; for the past couple of years it's been under Saabi occupation, ruled by King Jalal.

**Amir:** A high Saabi noble rank belong to the three Great Tribes, ruling fiefs containing several cities.

**Ancient Arts:** The nine forms of art gifted to mortals by the divine Muses. They are central to the Saabi magical practice of *tamasheq*.

**Aragon:** One of the three Quarterian Kingdoms. Proud and brave, the Aragonians are also famed for being born horsemen.

**Aramla El-Nar:** The Desert of Fire, the great desert at the heart of Jazirat.

**Archetype:** Body of trades or templates used to define what a character does. Includes: Adventure, Labourer, Poet, Prince, Rogue, Sage, Sorcerer, Warrior.

**Ashkenim (singular: ashken, feminine: ashkene):** The most warlike of the three tribes of the Shiradim. Their warriors specialise in a dancing combat style that is both graceful and formidable.

**Babouches:** The traditional slippers worn by the Saabi.

**Bint Mimun:** A matriarchal clan of the Tarekids also known as the Horned Vipers and renowned for their "Paper Virgins", the sacred prostitutes of Kh'saaba.

**Blood:** Your geographic origin: the people you belong to, your tribe and clan. Example: Saabi, Quarterian, Shiradim, Agalanthian.

**Book of Essences:** Also called the Kitaba Nader, this is a form of mystical body alchemy used by the Paper Virgins.

**Califah-al-Sahla:** Also called the Caravan of Purification, this caravan of the Tarekids travels throughout Jazirat on a holy mission to bring the decadent back to the pure faith.

**Calliope:** The Muse of the ancient art of Epic Poetry, used in the *tamasheq* of the Ibn Tufiq.

**Campeador:** The "country nobility" of the Aragonians, and expert horsemen. See also *hidalgo*.

**Capharnaum:** An ancient and cosmopolitan region in northern Jazirat, the heart of conspiracies, intrigues, and extraordinary and supernatural events since the dawn of time.

**Caravan Kingdoms:** Jazirati kingdoms smaller and less influential than mighty Kh'saaba. Most are limited to nomad tribes; some swear allegiance to Kh'saaba.

**Carrassine:** A city in Capharnaum specialising in trade and mercenaries. Its nine legions and star-shaped ramparts have rendered it historically impregnable. It is also the only place the dragonriders of the Walad Badiya settle down.

**Chimera:** Monstrous hybrids of serpent, lion, and goat, said to have followed the Agalanthian armies into Jazirat.

**Chiromancers:** Agalanthian sorcerers capable of manipulating fate by making clay tablets. Considered trivial – you can buy tablets at the market to regrow your hair or make an adulterous wife return to her husband. Nevertheless, this form of sorcery can be frightening and powerful.

**Choora:** An easily concealable dagger with a straight triangular blade, preferred by women.

**Clio:** The Muse of the ancient art of History, used in the *tamasheq* of the Ibn Rashid.

**Council of Princes:** The ruling council of the city of Carrassine.

**Covenant:** A form of voice-centered magical spell cast using the *tasannu* of the *sephirim*.

**Djinn:** Powerful magical spirits of the desert, constrained by a Great Truce with the god Hubal. They live in mirages, and are capricious. See also *marid*.

**Dragon:** Titanic, godlike beings who serve the Gods and guide the fates of mortals on Earth—particularly the Dragon-Marked. They dwell in the sky in the form of constellations.

**Dragon Mark:** A birthmark in the shape of a dragon's claw, located on the left shoulder blade just behind the heart, marking an individual as a Dragon-Marked.

**Dragon-Marked:** Rare and extraordinary mortals marked for a special destiny, watched over by dragons and the gods. They may be treated as heroes, watched with suspicion, or even persecuted.

**Erato:** The Muse of the ancient art of Lyric Poetry, used in the *tamasheq* of the Bint Mimun.

**Espada Valladena:** A relatively light longsword with a basket hilt, used by the *campeadors* of Aragon.

**Etrusia:** An Agalanthian island housing one of the most powerful city states of this people. Etrusia is a centre for magic and winemaking.

**Euterpe:** The Muse of the ancient art of Music, used in the *tamasheq* of the Ibn Malik.

**Falcata:** The sabre of the warriors of Aragon.

**First Gods, The:** The original gods of the world and parents of its pantheons; the dragons are (or were) their servants. They include Hubal, Al-Uzza, and Tiamat among the Jazirati and Kalos, Nerea, and Cthonos among the Agalanthians.

**First Path:** Simply the first special ability you acquire (usually during character creation) by virtue of belonging to a path. There are six path abilities in each path, each more powerful than the last.

**Fragrance:** A city in Capharnaum founded by the Agalanthians. A city of the arts marked by the proximity of the East.

**Golden Sight:** Also called the *nasar dahab*, this is the mystical ability of the Ibn Yussef to know the heart's value of things.

**Hammad:** The mystical weaponsmith who forged the famous Sword of Hammad, stolen by the Quarterian Crusaders.

**Hassan:** See *Prophets*.

**Hassanids:** The tribe of the descendants of Hassan. The Hassanids, or the Abd-al-Hassan ("Servants of Hassan") guarantee the military and political order among the Saabi. The noble families making up this tribe are the nearest to the King of Kh'saaba.

**Hero:** A term for the Dragon-Marked used among the Agalanthians.

**Hidalgo:** The courtly nobility of Aragon, more urbane and sophisticated than the *campeador*, but generally less accustomed to the rigours of the field.

**Holy Crusade, The:** Invasion of Capharnaum ten years ago by the Quarterians questing for the *Mirabilis Calva Reliquiae*, the Sacred Skull of Jason the Martyr. Although the Quarterian armies mostly departed three years ago, many Quarterians remain in Capharnaum. The city of Sagrada in particular is entirely under Quarterian control.

**Hubal:** The main Jazirati god, he has many aspects, of which Hubal-Shamin, God of Storm and the Fertilising Rains, is the most important. His temples and shrines are everywhere and his deeds and legends beyond number. In Carrassine he is called Hubal-Hadad.

**Ibn Aziz:** A clan of the Saabi tribe of the Salifah, they oversee organised crime in Jazirat. In each city the clan is led by a Prince of Thieves.

**Ibn Khalil:** A dark-skinned clan of the Salifah who originated in Al-Fariq'n. Renowned for the Walad Badiya dragonriders and their enormous *abzulim* steeds.

**Ibn Malik:** The clan of the Hassanids which provides the rulers of the Saabi and the generals of its armies.

**Ibn Mimun:** See *Bint Mimun*.

**Ibn Mussah:** A clan of the Hassanids which provides advisors, politicians, and ambassadors to the rulers of the Saabi.

**Ibn Rashid:** A clan of the Hassanids which provides bodyguards, protectors, and sometimes assassins for the great and the good of the Saabi.

**Ibn Tufiq:** Also known as the Desert Jackals, these are the fanatical leaders of the Tarekids. They are rigid tradionalists, and incredibly intolerant.

**Ibn Yazid:** A newly "recreated" clan of the Tarekids led by the firebrand Yazid, who aims to purify Jazirat of its sinful ways.

**Ibn Yussef:** The travellers and merchants of the Salifah, either caravaneers or sedentary business men and women in the cities. The greatest among them are gifted with the *Golden Sight*.

**Jalal Ibn Khalil Abd-al-Salif:** King of Al-Ragon, formerly the southern half of the Quarterian Kingdom of Aragon.

**Jambiya:** A recurved dagger and survival tool of the Saabi.

**Jason Quartered:** A man who became a god when he survived death by quartering. His legend inspired an entire civilisation and gave birth to the Quarterian faith.

**Jazirat:** A huge and mostly arid peninsula located at the heart of the known world. It is divided into three regions: Kh'saaba, the Aramla El-Nar desert, and Capharnaum.

**Jazirati:** An inhabitant of Jazirat whose religion is that of Hubal and the 1001 gods.

**Jebel:** A mountain, often the bare and rocky kind found in and around the Aramla El-Nar.

**Jellaba:** The long, hooded cloak worn by the Saabi.

**Jergath the Great:** Located in the fertile region in southern Jazirat, this city was built in one night by the god Hubal-Jergath the Dragon. It is the capital of the holy Kingdom of Kh'saaba.

**Jergathine:** See *Sagrada*.

**Kahan (pl. Kahanim):** In the Shiradi tradition, both a sage and a spiritual guide.

**Kahini:** A priest of the Saabi.

**Kaskara:** A type of long gladius used in Jazirat.

**Khanjar:** A dagger with an undulating blade, designed for penetrating between the chinks in armour.

**Khedama:** A single-edged sabre used in Kh'saaba. Extremely common—most peoples use something similar.

**Kh'saaba:** An opulent kingdom in southern Jazirat, Kh'saaba is a great military, commercial and magical power. It is ruled by High King Abdallah from his court at Jergath the Great.

**Kitaba Nader:** See *Book of Essences*.

**Kopis:** A sabre in common use among the troops of Agalanthia. Similar to the Saabi *khedama*.

**Krekhin:** The inhuman barbarian horde of the *Krek'kaos*. Savage, violent, and extremely hostile. They're said to travel in wagons pulled by giant bears.

**Krek'kaos, The:** Vast northern wastes, frozen and inhospitable, inhabited by the inhuman *Krekhin*. Throughout history great calamity has repeatedly poured forth from the Krek'kaos. There are monsters here, and a great evil which never sleeps.

**League:** The major measure of distance in *Capharnaum*, the distance an average person walks in one hour. Roughly 3 miles (5 km).

**Macchabah (pl. macchabim):** In Shiradi tradition, a macchabah is a mystical warrior inspired by the god Shirad.

**Magisterium:** The Holy City of the Quarterians, in the Western Kingdoms.

**Marduk the Dragon:** One of the most important Saabi gods and protector of Carrassine.

**Marid:** An evil djinn who does not obey the Great Truce of Hubal.

**Medina:** in the Jazirati tongue, madina means the town, the centre of the city as opposed to the suburbs. The term distorted in time, and at present, in the common tongue of Capharnaum, it may mean sometimes a town, sometimes a district, and is pronounced "medina".

**Melpomene:** The Muse of the ancient art of Tragedy, used in the *tamasheq* of the Ibn Aziz.

**Mirabilis Calva Reliquiae:** A holy relic for the Quarterians, it is, supposedly, the skull of Jason. The Quarterian crusade to recover it is at the heart of the recent wars that shook Capharnaum.

**Miracle:** The term for a magical spell cast by the Quarterian thaumaturgists. It takes the form of a prayer-like supplication to Aether, Jason, or Mira.

**Mogda:** A Saabi statesman who converted to the Shiradi religion to guide the slaves towards their holy land of Capharnaum. The Shiradim consider him a founding father.

**Mujahid (pl. mujahidin):** For the Jazirati, a mujahid is an inspired warrior, in turn Hubal's military arm, poet, and knight. The responsibilities and religious commitment demanded of the mujahidin varies from tribe to tribe.

**Myrmidons:** Agalanthian elite warriors wearing insectoid armour. It's said the order was created by the God of Hell, Cthonos himself.

**Myrmidon Armour:** A finely crafted suit of articulated heavy plate armour in use among the Agalanthians, and the signature of their myrmidon elite troops. It gives its wearer an almost insectoid appearance, and is much less cumbersome than conventional heavy armour.

**Occidentia:** A Quarterian nation culturally and politically more advanced than its neighbours. It was the instigator of the Holy Crusade. Its king is Simeon IV, called "The Proud".

**Orkadia:** One of the three Quarterian realms, to the northeast of Occidentia. The Orkadians are fierce warriors, enemies of the Agalanthian Empire and the barbarians of the Krek'kaos.

**Ounces of Cumin:** Spices are a common currency in Jazirat, often more available than silver or gold. One ounce of cumin (OC) is worth the same as a coin called a silver talent (ST), and will buy a decent meal at a caravanserai.

**Pace:** The standard Capharnian unit of length, commonly used in movement and in combat. Two steps by the average person, a distance of roughly 5 feet.

**Paths:** Mystical, philosophical or martial disciplines described by the *Prophets*. The sects that follow these precepts and teach their disciplines are also called paths. Belonging to one of these paths is considered a great honour among Jazirati nobles, and conveys special abilities. Other peoples have similar institutions, variously called schools, academies, and orders.

**Pharatim (sg. Pharati):** One of the three Shiradi tribes, the Pharatim are the guardians of Shiradi knowledge. In the days of yore this tribe wrote down the Commandments of Shirad.

**Polymnia:** Muse of the ancient art of Writing and Mime, used in the *tamasheq* of the Ibn Yazid.

**Prophets:** The Jazirati popular heroes Hassan, Salif, and Tarek, founding fathers of the Kingdom of Kh'saaba and preachers of the Paths.

**Quarterians:** A people in the West worshipping Jason the Quartered God and His Holy Father, Aether Almighty. Ten years ago the Quarterians invaded Capharnaum on a crusade to recover a holy relic, the skull of Jason Quartered. Although they left the region devastated, peace seems to have returned.

**Quarterian Academies:** Universities or sects devoted to one discipline (fencing, magic, diplomacy, etc.) with an important political or cultural impact in the West and within Capharnaum. See *Paths*.

**Quarterian Kingdoms, The:** The kingdoms of the West worshipping Jason the Quartered God, comprising Aragon, Occidentia, and Orkadia.

**Quarterian Magister, The:** Leader of the Quarterian Church and the representative of Aether on Earth. The current Magister is Deogratus I.

**Raiss:** The lowest rank of Saabi nobility, just above the common folk. In the desert a raiss rules a nomad camp.

**Rumh:** A halberd with a long bamboo haft, used by both footsoldiers and horsemen. It's as common as the scimitar.

**Saabi:** The main Jazirati people, those living in the Kingdom of Kh'saaba and revering the Three Prophets. There are Saabi throughout Jazirat, including in the Aramla El-Nar and cities of Capharnaum.

**Sagrada:** Once called Jergathine, it was founded by Mogda to challenge Jergath the Great. It is the largest city in Capharnaum.

**Salif:** See *Prophets*.

**Salifah:** The tribe of the descendants of Salif. The Salifah, or the Abd-al-Salif ("Servants of Salif") are mostly nomads. Although noble, they are more attached to trade and travel and prefer to rule through business rather than politics.

**Salonim (sg. Saloni):** One of the three Shiradi tribes, the Salonim live and die by the science of life. Sage physicians, they are sought after even in the West when local science has reached its limits.

**Sarwal:** The wide trousers traditionally worn by the Saabi.

**Sayf:** The short scimitar in common use among the city guards of Capharnaum.

**Sephirim (sg. Sephir):** A sorcerer in the Shiradi oral tradition.

**Sheik:** An "honorable sage", the highest noble title available to any noble not from the three Great Tribes (the Hassanids, Salifah, and Tarekids). In the desert, a sheik rules a caravan or oasis, and has several raiss beneath him.

**Shimshir:** The long scimitar used in Kh'saaba and the pride of the Saabi mujahid. Also called a shamsheer.

**Shirad:** The One But Many God, worshipped by the Shiradim. The Saabi claim him as an aspect of Hubal.

**Shiradim (sg. Shiradi):** Although native to Jazirat, this people is not considered Jazirati because of their religion. For long periods of their history they were the slaves of the Agalanthians and then the Saabi. Armed with an unshakeable faith, they managed to prevail despite their many persecutions and hardships, and have turned Capharnaum into the fertile land it is today. They are considered experts in the fields of science and commerce.

**Spatha:** The long gladius used by Agalanthian troops.

**Strategos (pl. strategoi):** The general of an Agalanthian army. Sometimes called a "strategist".

**Suyuf:** The long scimitar used in Capharnaum.

**Sword of Hammad:** A fabulous sword forged by the legendary weaponsmith Hammad. Stolen by the Quarterians during their Holy Crusade; the Saabi have invaded Aragon in the far west to get it back.

**Tamasheq:** The Tarmel Haja combination magic of the Saabi al-kimyati. It uses a form of spell called a working, based on one of the Ancient Arts.

**Tarek:** See *Prophets*.

**Tarmel Haja:** A Jazirati term used to describe a widespread form of sorcery known as "combination magic". The term is used by almost everyone in Capharnaum to refer to magic.

**Tarekids:** Tribe of the descendants of Tarek. The Tarekids or the Abd-al-Tarek ("Servants of Tarek")

are the defenders of the Jazirati faith. Refusing the luxury of cities that deadens the soul, they live amidst the purity of the desert and are Kh'saaba's military arm. The Abd-al-Tarek mujahidin horsemen are the most feared of all, no doubt because of the fervour of their faith.

**Tasannu:** The form of magic practised by the *sephirim* of the Shiradim. It's focussed principally on the use of the voice to articulate *covenants* (similar to prayers) with Shirad, the One But Many God.

**Terpsichore:** Muse of the ancient art of Dance, used in the *tamasheq* of the Ibn Khalil.

**Thalia:** Muse of the ancient art of Comedy, used in the *tamasheq* of the Ibn Mussah.

**Thaumaturgists:** Sorcerer-priests practicing miracles, the only form of magic permitted in the Quarterian Kingdoms.

**Thawb:** The long robe worn by the Saabi.

**Therema:** The old Agalanthian capital, this huge city is now half-ruined, partly sunk following a devastating earthquake three centuries ago. It's famed for its theatres as well as for its elite troops, the Myrmidons.

**Urania:** Muse of the ancient art of Astronomy, used in the *tamasheq* of the Ibn Yussef.

**Walad Badiya:** Dragonriders belonging to Ibn Khalil of the Salifah tribe. Linked by a mystical bond to their draconic *abzulim* steeds, these enigmatic warriors are terrifying in battle.

**Wazir:** A high-ranking Saabi nobleman, commonly an advisor in a king's court (and usually in the High King's court in Jergath).

**Western Kingdoms, The:** The three Quarterian Kingdoms of the West: Aragon, Occidentia, and Orkadia.

**Yatagan:** The common single-edged sabre used in Capharnaum.

# Kickstarter Backers

**Mindjammer Press would like to thank:** A V Jones, A. DIAZ, Ada Fairweather, Adam Boisvert, Adam Dray, adamsmith, Adrian Breau, Adrian Czajkowski, adumbratus, Akiazoth, Albert Cukingnan Jr., Alex Draconis, Alex Villemure, Alexander Chang, Allan Prewett, Alpharalpha, Alton C. Capps, ANALOG GAMES, anderland, Andre Heidt, Andreas Wichter, Andres G Aguirre, Andres Zanzani, Andrew Fones, Andrew Foxx, Andrew Lotton, Andrew Martinez, Andrew Moreton, Andrew Peregrine, Andy Sangar, Anestis Kozakis, Angry Goblin, anonymous1453, anton.g.cox, Aramis, Austin, Azlunde, Ben Zorn, Benjamin Welke, Bernard Gravel, Bil Corry, Bill Robertson, billk, Björn, Brad Kane, Bram Dyckmans, Brennan Dawson, Brett Bozeman, Brian Greene, Brian Koonce, Bruce Curd, Bruce Gray, Bruce Turner, BRW Games LLC, Bryan Considine, Bryant, Bryant Durrell, buckwheats, Cable, Cabochard, Campaign Coins, Cardinal, Carl Gilchrist, Carl Walter, Cary Harrison, Casey Loehrke, CB Ash, Charles Alston, Charles Crowe, Charles Evans, Charles Pugsley, CharlesDM, Chris Bekofske, Chris Dalgety, Chris George, Chris Little, chris pugh, Chris Skuller, Chris Slowinski, Chris Turner, Christian Thier, Christoph Wagner, Christopher McDonough, Christopher P. Crossley, CK Cowan, Claudia Fabrizek, Clint Doyle, Clint Williams, Conan McKegg, Craig, Craig "Stevo" Stephenson, Craig Bishell, Craig Senatore, Craig Wright, Cristian Andreu, d70, Dale Andrade, Daniel, Daniel C. Barton, Daniel Markwig, Daniel Wilks, danielyauger, Darkulic, Darryll Smith Walker, Darth Peregrine, Daschickster, Dave Harrison, Dave Poppel, David Alford, David Andrews, David B. Semmes, David Dalton, David Eber, David Grophland, David Lewis, David Paul, David Ryack, David Stephenson, Derek Kinsman, Dillon Burke, Dominique Poulain, Don Arnold, Donald A. Turner, Doug Grimes, Drew Wendorf, Dustin Schwartz, Ed Kowalczewski, eibaan, Ella Woodhouse, Eric Blair, Erich L., Erich McNaughton, Erin Ratelle, Etienne Olieu, Evgeny, Fabrice LETARD, Farkas Tivadar, fiend, Francis Helie, Frank Bath, Frank Tonn, Frits Kuijlman, Fuchs, Gabriel Garcia, Gallant Knight Games, Geoffrey Allen, Geoffrey Davis, GK Coleman, glyptodont, Gonzalo Dafonte Garcia, Gonzalo Durán, Gordon Hefner, Graham Owens, Greg Gilmore, Greg Maroda, Hannu Kokko, Hans-Henning Wenkel, Herman Duyker, Holger Hansch, imredave, infomorph, Jack Gulick, Jackson Brantley, Jacob Conerly, James Culshaw, James Gavin, James Robertson, James Wood, Jameson Mulroney, jamie, Jamie Revell, Jamie Wheeler, Jan Artoos, Jan Hendrik Gravert, Jared Kenjamin Fattmann, Jason, Jason Childs, Jason Haynes, Jason Pasch, Jason Smith, Jason Yacalis, Jeb Boyt, Jeffrey Kreider, Jennifer Fuss, Jens Hoelderle, Jere Manninen, Jeremy Baker, Jeremy Wasik, Jerome Devie, Jerry G Prochazka, Jesper Cockx, JG Cully, Jiester "Smartkid" Traifalgar, Jochen Linnemann, Joe Stacey, Joerg Baumgartner, John "johnkzin" Rudd, John A W Phillips, John Absher, John Cohen, John M. Kahane, John M. Portley, John Shimmin, John Snead, John W. Luther, Johnny Casady, Jon Terry, Jonas Karlsson, Jonathan Bowen, Jonathan Finke, Jonathan Korman, Jonathan Ly Davis, Jonathon Dyer, Jonny Knowles, Joran aus den Schatten, Jordan, Jordi Rabionet Hernandez, Jörg S., Jort Douwe Feenstra, José Luis Porfirio, Joseph Provenzano, Joshua Lake, J-P Spore, Julian Hayley, K.Lenae, Karl Kreutzer, Karl Rodriguez, karl vestin, KarlTheGood, KarstenZ, Kathryn V. Fields, Keith, Kenneth Tedrick, Kergonan, Kevin A Swartz MD, Kevin Bender, Kevin Flynn, Kevin Grubb, kroner, Ku Hap, Kurt Ellison, kustenjaeger, KylarDragonFang, Kyle Rimmer, Lawrence Alman, Lee Graham, Lenurd the Joke Gnome, Leslie Wilson, Liam Murray, Lloyd Rasmussen, Lois M Zaleski, Loren the GM, Lorenzo Bandieri, Louis S Gowers, Luca Beltrami, Luke Cunningham, Luke Florer, M Vamp, Marc Bevan, Marco Rower, Marcus Anderson, Marek Benes, Marek Hendziak, Marius Johnsen, Mark Buckley, Mark Edwards, Mark Giles, Mark Shocklee, Mark Solino, Marko Soikkeli, Martin Greening, Martin Legg, Martin Schramm, Martin Trudeau, Mathias Green, Matt Dowd, Matteo Signorini, Matthew B, Matthew Russo, Mauno Joukamaa, Mauro Adorna, Max Kaehn, Mel Hall, Mendel, Michael Bowman, Michael E Best, Michael Feldhusen, Michael G, Michael Hill, Michael M. Brislawn, Michael Pruitt, Michael Siegel, Michael Sim, Michael Stuff, Michael Thompson, Michael Tree, Michael Vincent Ogaz, Michael Wibberley, Mike Weber, Mirko Froehlich, Morgan Weeks, Nathan Reetz, Nathaniel Gullion, Neil, Neil Smith, Newton Grant, Nicholas Peterson, Nicholas Rowe, Nick, Nick Riggs, Nigel Clarke, Nigel Phillips, Njall - Cayne Corp. Shareholder 6.66, Noah Salady, Norarat Pitisant, Obadiah Psalter, Obsidianherz, Occam, Okas Leinert, Olav Müller, Oliver Steiger, Olli Matilainen, Ols Jonas Petter Olsson, Omar Ismail, Orko the Dragon-Marked, Ornithopterx, Otherland Buchhandlung, P Tracy, Pablo "Diacrítica", Pablo Domínguez Castro, Pablo Pérez Gómez, Paco Garcia Jaen, Patrick Chapman, Patrick Healey, Patrick P., Paul Inman, Paul Mitchener, Paul Watters, Paul Weimer, Pavel Gurov, Pedro Garcia, Pegana, Peter Holland, Peter Klein, Peter Petrovich, Philip Rogers, Philippe Marcil, Phillip Bailey, Phillip McGregor, Piotr Nowakowski, R.G., Rabah Abu Khadra, Raf Bressel, Ramón Domingo Herreras, Ratat0skr, Raúl Sánchez Ruiz, Raymond Fowkes Jr., RedneckRedge, Reise, Reise, René Schallegger, Rich Riddle, Richard Auffrey, Richard Greene, Richard Harrison, Richard Rivera, Richard Woodfield, Rob James, Robert G. Male, Robert L Bridges, Robert Newman, Roberto Hoyle, Roberto Mandrioli, Rod Meek, Roland Bahr, Ron (Khaalis) Owen, Ronald Miller, Ross Rice, RPG Crunch, Russell Ventimeglia, Ryan, Ryan Dukacz, Ryan Wilson, Ryan Wymer, S.W. Hannan, Sabrina Klevenow, Saigo, Sam Dannemiller, Sam Hing, Sam Osborne, Samuel, Samuel Farro, Sandfox, Sean Nicolson, Seleem Choudhury, Seth Hartley, Shadowsmith, Shane Mclean, Shaun Beckett, Shaun Burton, Shomari Kirkwood, Simon Brunning, Simon Early, Simon Harding, spacht, Stefano Monachesi, Stephan Szabo, Steve Arensberg, Steve Dulson, Steve Snow, Steve Thompson, Steve Turner, Steven Lord, Steven Warble, Storn Cook, Teilzeithelden, TGabor, Thalji, The Freelancing Roleplayer, The Rangdo of Arg, The Rosenthal Family, Thomas J., Thomas Ladegard, Thomas Powell, Thomas R., Thomas S., Thomas Shey, Tim Baker, Tim Ellis, Tim Ryan, Timolution, Timothy Carroll, Tobias, Tobias, Todd C, Todd Stephens, Tom, Tom, Tom Shen, Tracey Willis, Trip Space-Parasite, Tyler Brunette, Vedrin, Victor Serrano, victorpc, Victory Condition Gaming, Ville Ojanperä, Ville Vuorela, Vincent Arebalo, Vojtech Pribyl, vshadow, W Ryan Carden, W!, W. L. Munn, Wade Geer, Waelcyrge, Warren Nelson, Wieteke Bruinenberg, Will Triumph, Xander Schrijen, Yaitza Hernandez.

*All hail the Dragon-Marked!*

# INDEX

## CHAPTER FICTIONS

## GAZETTEER

## PATHS

## PERSONALITIES

# REFERENCE SHEETS

## TABLE 2-1: DIFFICULTIES

| DIFFICULTY | DESCRIPTION | EXAMPLES |
|---|---|---|
| 6 | Simple | The default difficulty for most easy tasks. You may not even need to roll for this. *Reciting verses you know well, kicking open a rickety door, urging a Saabi horse to gallop down an empty road, picking the pockets of a distracted chatterbox.* |
| 9 | Average | The default difficulty of a professional-level task, and hence for most dice rolls. *Repairing your own armour, lifting more than your own weight, writing a long letter, evaluating a precious stone at first sight, stealing from a market stall on a quiet street.* |
| 12 | Difficult | An action worthy of a specialist. *Forging a weapon of quality, succeeding in a feat of athletics, organising a festival for an entire city quarter.* |
| 15 | Heroic | Now we sort the wheat out from the chaff! *Crossing a street by jumping from one roof to another, winning a running race against a dog, juggling with sabres, riding back to front and shooting arrows from the back of your horse, dropping 30 feet onto a shop awning.* |
| 18 | Insanely Heroic | These actions are recklessly heroic, and have serious consequences! *Sleeping with the king's wife while the king is sleeping next to you, winning a running race against a horse, dropping 60 feet onto a shop awning.* |
| 21 | Fabulous | People will be talking about you in a hundred years' time! *Persuading the king who's just woken up next to you and his wife to let you carry on, winning a running race with an abzul, diving from a clifftop into a rocky river.* |
| 30+ | Legendary | Actions beyond the reach of ordinary mortals! *Pole-vaulting over a 60-foot high rampart, juggling excitable snakes while blindfolded, stopping a bolting horse on a slippery surface using only one hand.* |

## TABLE 2-5: DEFENCE MODIFIERS

| CONDITION | DEFENCE MODIFIERS |
|---|---|
| Target in partial cover | +3 |
| Target in near-full cover | +6 |
| Target prone | -6 |
| Target with back turned | -3 |
| Target on lower ground, inferior position | -3 |
| Target on higher ground, superior position | +3 |
| Target dodging and weaving | +3 |
| Target making a headlong dash | -6 |
| Attacker attacking in darkness | +3 |

## TABLE 2-6: RANGED ATTACK PENALTIES

| RANGE | PENALTY TO THE RESULT |
|---|---|
| Short | No change; attack at your full ability. |
| Medium | -3 result penalty. |
| Long | -6 result penalty. |
| Extreme | -12 result penalty. |

## TABLE 2-3: DESCRIBING MAGNITUDE

| MAGNITUDE | SUCCESS | FAILURE |
|---|---|---|
| 0 | Marginal Success | Marginal Failure |
| 1 | Normal Success | Normal Failure |
| 2 | Good Success | Stinging Failure |
| 3 | Very Good Success | Painful Failure |
| 4 | Memorable Success | Memorable Failure |
| 5 | Exceptional Success | Catastrophic Failure |
| 6+ | Critical Success | Critical Failure |

## TABLE 2-11: OPPONENTS

| | |
|---|---|
| Champions | Use the normal combat rules. |
| Valiant Captains | On a Critical Success, a Valiant Captain is dead, knocked out, taken out of the fight, etc. |
| Babouche-Draggers | No HP. Attack in groups of 6. 1 bonus die for each Babouche-Dragger after the first. One Babouche-Dragger is taken out for each point of magnitude on a successful attack. If half or more of a Babouche-Dragger group is taken out, the rest run away. |

## Table 2-2: Figuring Magnitude

| Result on Magnitude Die | Addition to Magnitude |
|---|---|
| 1 | +0 |
| 2 | +1 |
| 3 | +1 |
| 4 | +1 |
| 5 | +1 |
| 6 | +2 |

## Table 2-4: Duration of Combat Actions

| Name | Duration | Description |
|---|---|---|
| Talk | 0 actions | |
| **Attack Actions** | | |
| Normal Attack | 1 action* | DEX + Fighting. |
| Brutal Attack | 2 actions | STR + Fighting, +6 damage. |
| Charge Attack | 3 actions** | STR or DEX + Fighting, +10 damage; -6 Passive Defence. |
| Ranged Attack (Bow) | 2 actions | DEX + Fighting. |
| Ranged Attack (Thrown) | 1 action | DEX + Fighting. |
| **Defend Actions** | | |
| Active Defence | 1 action | DEX + Athletics or Fighting; a skill roll. |
| Passive Defence | 0 actions | DEX + Athletics + 6; a static value, no dice roll. |
| **Magic Actions** | | |
| Cast a Spell | 1 action* | INT + Sacred Word. |
| Break a Tablet | 1 action | No dice roll required. |
| **Move Actions** | | |
| Combat Move | 1 action | DEX in paces (5 ft). |
| Unengaged Move | 1 action | DEX x 2 in paces; -6 Passive Defence. |
| **Other Actions** | | |
| Aiming | 1 action | +1 bonus die. |
| Disengage | 2 actions | DEX + Athletics or Stealth. |
| Draw a Weapon | 1 action | No dice roll required. |
| Help or Hinder | 1 action | See description. |

*you may only take one of these actions per round.

**your Charge Attack takes place at your Initiative order in the following round.

## Table 2-7: Critical Success and Critical Failure Effects in Combat

| Critical Result | Effect |
|---|---|
| Critical Success on Attack | The damage the attacker does ignores the defender's Soak. |
| Critical Failure on Attack | The defender acts before the attacker on the next round, and gains 1 bonus die. |
| Critical Success on Active Defence | The defender acts before the attacker on the next round, and gains 1 bonus die. |
| Critical Failure on Active Defence | The damage the attacker does ignores the defender's Soak. |
| Critical Success on Attack vs Critical Failure on Active Defence | The damage the attacker does ignores the defender's Soak. The defender is disarmed, knocked to the ground, and at the attacker's mercy. |
| Critical Failure on Attack vs Critical Success on Active Defence | The defender turns the attacker's attack back on him, causing the attacker to suffer the damage he would have inflicted on the defender. The defender acts before the attacker on the next round, and gains 1 bonus die. |

## Table 2-10: Armour

| Armour Type | Armour Value[1] | Weight (lb) | Cost (oc) | Description |
|---|---|---|---|---|
| Shield, Buckler or Targe | +1 | 10 / 20 | 5 / 10 | +1 bonus die to Active Defence rolls. |
| Partial Armour | 1 (2) | 4 | 2 | A helm, pieces of mail, leather doublet, epaulettes, etc. |
| Light Armour | 3 (4) | 20 | 8 | A helm, plus leather armour (may be studded), or ring or plate mail. |
| Heavy[2] or Myrmidon[3] Armour | 6 (7) | 60 | 30 / 100[3] | A helm, plus solid plate armour over mail. |

1: AV in brackets are if a shield is also carried.

2: All rolls of Assassination, Athletics, Intrusion, Riding, Stealth, and Thievery are one step harder (+3 difficulty).

3: Myrmidon armour (page 65) costs 100 OC. It does not suffer the skill penalty of other forms of Heavy armour.

## TABLE 2-8: MELEE WEAPONS

| WEAPON | DAMAGE | DESCRIPTION | WT (LB) | COST (OC) |
|---|---|---|---|---|
| **SHORT AND NON-LETHAL WEAPONS** | | | | |
| Aragonian Whip | DEX +3 | 3-pace reach, non-lethal damage. | 4 | 6 |
| Choora | STR +4 | Triangular-bladed dagger, easy to conceal. | 4 | 6 |
| Jambiya | DEX +3 | Curved dagger, parry bonus. | 4 | 8 |
| Khanjar | STR +3 | Wavy-bladed dagger, -3 AV. | 4 | 10 |
| Kick | (STR x2) +3 | Non-lethal damage. | n/a | n/a |
| Punch | STR x2 | Non-lethal damage. | n/a | n/a |
| **LONG WEAPONS (-3 attack / Active Defence in restricted spaces; Normal Attack at 1 or 2 paces)** | | | | |
| Agalanthian Trident | STR +8 | Break weapon / disarm. | 10 | 40 |
| Hoplite Spear | STR +10 | +1 bonus die vs Charge. | 10 | 24 |
| Quarterian Lance | STR +8 | +12 mounted charge damage bonus. | 10 | 20 |
| Rumh | STR +8 | Poleaxe; "whip" attack: +1 bonus die vs Babouche-Draggers. | 10 | 6 |
| **ONE-HANDED WEAPONS** | | | | |
| Agalanthian Gladius | STR +8 | +6 Passive Defence with 2 weapons; +1 bonus die to attacks or Active Defences. | 4 | 10 |
| Common Axe | STR +8 | -3 Active Defence penalty. | 4 | 0.9 |
| Crusader Sword | STR +8 | Two-edged hvy longsword; +1 bonus die vs Babouche-Draggers. | 4 | 30 |
| Espada Valladena | STR +6 | Longsword with basket guard; knockout attack. | 4 | 40 |
| Falkata (Aragon), Khedama (Kh'saaba) or Yatagan (Capharnaum), Kopis (Agalanthia) | STR +6 | Two-edged straight sabre; +3 damage on Brutal and Charge Attacks. | 4 | 20/26/20/22 |
| Military Flail | STR +8 | -3 Active Defence; +1 bonus die vs Babouche-Draggers. | 4 | 20 |
| Orkadian Axe | STR +10 | Double-bladed war axe; -6 Active Defence. | 4 | 40 |
| Sayf | STR +4 | Short scimitar; possible Free Attack on failed attack roll. | 4 | 12 |
| Spatha (Agalanthia), Kaskara (Jazirat) | STR +8 | Longsword; -3 Active Defence unless STR & CON 4+. | 4 | 20/20 |
| Suyuf (Capharnaum), Shimshir (Kh'saaba) | STR +8 | Long scimitar | 4 | 30/30 |
| War Hammer | STR +10 | On Critical Success, break weapon or -3 penalty bruising. | 4 | 10 |
| **BASTARD WEAPONS** | | +2 damage if used two-handed. | +2 | +10% |
| **TWO-HANDED WEAPONS** | | +4 damage. | +4 | +30% |

## TABLE 2-9: RANGED WEAPONS

| WEAPON | DAMAGE | MINIMUM RANGE[1] | SHORT / MEDIUM (-3) / LONG (-6) / EXTREME (-12) RANGE (5-FOOT PACES) | WEIGHT (LBS) | COST (OC) |
|---|---|---|---|---|---|
| Javelin / Throwing Axe | STR +8 | 2 | <12 / na / 12-24 / 24+ (Max = STR x 6) | 2 | 4 / 5 |
| Knife | STR +6 | 2 | <12 / na / 12-24 / 24+ (Max = STR x 6) | 2 | 1 |
| Sling | STR +1 | 2 | <12 / na / 12-24 / 24+ (Max = STR x 6) | 2 | 0.8 |
| Jazirati Recurved Bow | STR +7 | 7 – DEX | <36 / 36-72 / 72-120 / 120-150 | 8 | 15 |
| Long Bow[2] | STR +9 | 9 – DEX | <36 / 36-72 / 72-120 / 120-150 | 9 | 9 |
| Short Bow | STR +6 | 5 – DEX | <18 / 18-36 / 36-72 / 72-90 | 6 | 5 |

[1] *Range is in 5-foot paces. Minimum range is 2 paces.*  [2] *+2 bonus dice when aiming.*

| Table 4-1: Magical Effect Parameters | | | | | | | | | |
|---|---|---|---|---|---|---|---|---|---|
| Mag | Duration | Range (paces) | Targets | Area / Volume[1] | HP | Att | Virtue | Skill | Dmg / AV[2] |
| 0 | 1 action | 1 | 1 | 1 | 5 | +0 | +0 | +0 | +/-1 |
| 1 | 1 round | 5 | 2 | 2 | 10 | +/-1 | +0 | +/-1 | +/-2 |
| 2 | 1 minute | 10 | 5 | 5 | 20 | +/-1 | +/-1 | +/-2 | +/-3 |
| 3 | 15 minutes | 50 | 10 | 10 | 30 | +/-2 | +/-1 | +/-3 | +/-4 |
| 4 | 1 hour | 100 | 20 | 20 | 40 | +/-2 | +/-1 | +/-4 | +/-5 |
| 5 | 4 hours | 500 | 50 | 50 | 50 | +/-3 | +/-2 | +/-5 | +/-6 |
| 6 | 1 day | 1000 | 100 | 100 | 60 | +/-3 | +/-2 | +/-6 | +/-7 |
| 7 | 1 week | 1 league | 200 | 200 | 70 | +/-4 | +/-2 | +/-7 | +/-8 |
| 8 | 1 month | 2 leagues | 500 | 500 | 80 | +/-4 | +/-3 | +/-8 | +/-9 |
| 9 | 1 year | 10 leagues | 1000 | 1000 | 90 | +/-5 | +/-3 | +/-9 | +/-10 |
| 10 | 1 lifetime | 20 leagues | 2000 | 2000 | 100 | +/-5 | +/-3 | +/-10 | +/-11 |

1: The area unit is the square pace, the volume unit is the waterskin (2 pints), except for rare or precious materials, in which case the unit of measurement is the ounce.

2: Applies to increases or decreases in weapon damage or armour value.

Al-Rawi may modify the difficulty of the Sacred Word roll for any effects which are not represented in the above table.

| Table 4-3: Spell Difficulty Modifiers | |
|---|---|
| Situation | Difficulty Modifier |
| Noisy environment: Tavern | +1 |
| Noisy environment: Crowd | +2 |
| Noisy environment: Battlefield | +3 |
| Caster's Faith at 0 | +3 |
| Narrowly-defined element | -3 per element |
| Broadly-defined element | +3 per element |
| Improvising an element | +6 per element |
| Supplementary element | -3 per element |
| Per step of duration concentrating* | -1 |
| Complete silence | -1 |
| Place of worship | -1 |
| Burning incense (al-kimyati) | -1 |
| Wearing ritual apparel (sephirim) | -1 |
| Burning a candle (thaumaturgists) | -1 |
| Performing an act of faith (fasting, etc) | -1 |
| Sacred ground | -2 |

*Uses the steps of duration on Table 4-1: Magical Effect Parameters, ie 1 action is -1 difficulty, 1 round is -2, 1 minute is -3, etc..

| Table 4-4: Detecting Magic | |
|---|---|
| Magnitude | Detection |
| 1 | The character detects the presence of magic, and is able to determine whether its source is a spell, or the presence of a sorcerer or magical creature. |
| 2-3 | As above, and the character may determine which people's magic he is detecting (Saabi tamasheq, Shiradi tasannu, Quarterian prayers, etc), whether or not the magic is being used by a human being, and whether the magic is benevolent, malevolent, or neutral. |
| 4-5 | As above, and the character may accurately locate the source of the magic in relation to himself. He also gains a vague impression of the magic's nature and effects (heat if it's connected to fire, suffocation if connected to death, and so on). |
| 6+ | As above, and the character knows the target's location, the effects of the spell or exact nature of the creature, and how powerful the magic is. |

### Table 2-12: Examples of Major Wounds

| Roll 1D6 or choose | Major Wound | Effects | Major Wound Type[2] |
|---|---|---|---|
| 1 | Partially or Fully Severed Limb[1] | Lose 1-3 points of DEX. | Open Wound. |
| 2 | Maimed Limb | Lose 1-3 points of DEX. | Broken Bones. |
| 3 | Damaged Muscles | Lose 1-3 points of STR. | Open Wound and / or Bludgeoning. |
| 4 | Head Trauma | Lose 1-3 points of INT. | Open Wound and / or Bludgeoning. |
| 5 | Disfigurement | Lose 1-3 points of CHA. | Open Wound. |
| 6 | Perforated Organ | Lose 1-3 points of CON. | Open Wound and / or Bludgeoning. |

1: *Attribute loss from a fully severed limb is always permanent. Attribute loss from a partially severed limb becomes permanent if it is not successfully stitched (page 71)—the limb is amputated.*

2: *The most common major wound type associated with this major wound. See "Healing, Medicine, and Surgery" on page 70 for how to treat it.*

### Table 2-16: Heroic Virtue Gains and Losses

| Heroic Virtue | Gains (stars) | Losses (stars) |
|---|---|---|
| Bravery | ❖ Saving a life: +1<br>❖ Saving a stranger's life: +2<br>❖ Disregarding your own safety to save a stranger's life: +3<br>❖ Facing certain death in a disinterested way and living: +4 | ❖ Lying to save your skin: -1<br>❖ Leaving someone in danger: -2<br>❖ Placing someone else in danger to save your skin: -3<br>❖ Surrendering for fear of dying, begging or asking for mercy: -4 |
| Faith | ❖ Making a ritual sacrifice: +1<br>❖ Talking about your faith or gods in an important speech or debate: +2<br>❖ Dedicating a poem, song, mosaic, etc, to your gods: +3 to +4, depending on duration and quality of work<br>❖ Converting a village, neighbourhood, caravan, troupe, etc, to your faith: +4 | ❖ Letting someone disparage your gods (either through words, deeds, artworks, etc) without trying to make them repent: -1<br>❖ Letting someone preach another faith without contradicting them, however gently: -2<br>❖ Disrespecting a precept of your faith: -3<br>❖ Refusing to die for your faith: -4 |
| Loyalty | ❖ Proudly displaying your people's colours in an enemy land: +1<br>❖ Turning against your peers to defend your own people or other Dragon-Marked: +2<br>❖ Dropping everything to go and support one of your people several days from here: +3<br>❖ Killing a loved one (not a PC!) for the sake of your own people: +4 | ❖ Hiding your allegiance in an enemy land: -1<br>❖ Preferring a foreigner to your own people (unless it's one of your Dragon-Marked companions): -2<br>❖ Refusing to help one of your people for any reason at all: -3<br>❖ Refusing to give your own life for your people: -4 |

# What Do You Use Heroism For?

❖ **To calculate your character's Soak.** Soak = Constitution + maximum Heroism.

❖ **To consult Urim and Turim, the Stones of Fate.** See page 77.

❖ **To determine the maximum number of swagger dice you may take in a single dice roll.** Maximum number of swagger dice = current Heroism.

❖ Some paths also use Heroism.

❖ **To make an attribute roll.** Roll = attribute + current Heroism.

❖ **To make a Double Attack.** Your current Heroism score is a damage bonus in a Double Attack (page 54).

❖ **To avoid environmental and encumbrance penalties.** Costs 1 point of Heroism, lasts an entire day. See pages 67 and 78.

❖ To avoid a major wound (page 67)

## TABLE 2-18: SUMMARY OF ADVENTURE POINT AWARDS

| Event | AP Award |
|---|---|
| Completing an adventure | 1 |
| For being virtuous | 1 x your highest heroic virtue |
| Creative use of the rules | 0-5 |
| Immersive roleplaying | 0-5 |
| After a Challenge (1-2 session adventure, <2 hrs) | AP total x 1. |
| After a Tale (3-4 session adventure, <24 hrs) | AP total x 2. |
| After an Epic (5-6 session adventure, >24 hrs) | AP total x 3. |

## TABLE 4-11: ENCHANTMENT INSCRIPTION DIFFICULTIES

| Condition | Difficulty (or modifier) |
|---|---|
| Moderately difficult enchantment[1] | 9 |
| Difficult enchantment | 12 |
| Heroic enchantment | 15 |
| Insanely heroic enchantment | 18 |
| Fabulous enchantment[2] | 21 |
| Per unspecified element, declared loudly when the tablet is broken. | +5 |
| Per element replaced by a drawing or paraphrase. | +3 |
| Per extra detail requested | +3 |
| Per additional target | +3 |
| To target a group of ten or so people | +9 |
| Per point of Faith | -1 |

## TABLE 4-2: MAGICAL ELEMENTS

| Broadly-defined Elements (+3 diff) | Normally-defined Elements | Narrowly-defined Elements (-3 diff) |
|---|---|---|
| Animal | Feline | Cat |
| The Elements (air, etc) | Fire | Flame |
| The Elements (air, etc) | Earth | Sand |
| The Elements (air, etc) | Water | Ice |
| Plant | Tree | Palm Tree |
| Food | Meat | Beef |
| Sense | Sight | Night Vision |
| Weapon | Bladed Weapon | Scimitar |
| Living Being | Human Body | Heart |
| Person | Man / Woman | You / Me / Amir |
| Person | Adult / Child | You / Me / Amir |
| Treasure | Jewel | Ruby |
| Truth / Falsehood | Telling the Truth / Lying | A Lie |
| Attribute | Strength | Lifting ability |
| Health / Unhealthiness | Recovery / Injury | Healing / Wound |
| Cloth | Clothing | Boots |

1: See Table 2-1: Difficulties (page 46). Note that chiromancy enchantment difficulties differ from spells of the Tarmel Haja.

2: There are enchantments of greater power and difficulty, but they are usually in the hands of priests of Cthonos (page 144), certain archons (page 270), or the scolaria. Few chiromancers can inscribe enchantments of such power.

## Table 1-1: Archetype Skills

| Archetype | Skills |
|---|---|
| The Adventurer | Athletics, Riding, Storytelling*, Survival. |
| The Labourer | Agriculture, Craft, Endurance*, Solidarity. |
| The Poet | Acting, Music, Oratory*, Poetry. |
| The Prince | Elegance, Flattery*, Save Face, Unctuous Bargaining. |
| The Rogue | Assassination*, Intrusion, Stealth, Thievery. |
| The Sage | History & Peoples, Instruction*, Notice, Science. |
| The Sorceror | Prayer, Sacred Word, Sacrifice, Willpower*. |
| The Warrior | Combat Training, Command, Fighting, Intimidate*. |

## Table 1-18: Wealth Levels

| Wealth Level | Label | Description | Starting Money (Oz of cumin) |
|---|---|---|---|
| 0 | Impoverished | An impoverished character with poor quality equipment. | Unctuous Bargaining x 10 |
| 1 | Struggling | A struggling character with average quality equipment. | Unctuous Bargaining x 50 |
| 2 | Well-to-Do | A well-to-do character with good quality equipment. | Unctuous Bargaining x 100 |
| 3 | Rich | A rich character with very good quality equipment. | Unctuous Bargaining x 500 |
| 4 | Filthy Rich | A filthy rich character with superior quality equipment. | Unctuous Bargaining x 1000 |
| 5 | Extraordinarily Rich | An extraordinarily rich character with exceptional quality equipment. | Unctuous Bargaining x 5000 |

# Character Creation Checklist

*Step One: Blood and Path (page 8)*

    *a. Choose your **blood** (your geographic origin) from page 13, and note down the attribute and skill points it gives you on your character sheet.*

    *b. Choose your **path** (the discipline you follow) from page 17, and note down its attribute and skill point bonuses, as well as your first path ability and its parameters, on your character sheet.*

    *c. If the blood and path you've chosen are unconnected, see "Rebels, Dissidents, Mixed-Bloods, Cousins and Traitors" on page 11.*

*Step Two: Heroic Virtues (page 22)*

    *a. Distribute 10 points between Bravery, Faith, and Loyalty, with a minimum score of 1 and a maximum of 6.*

    *b. The average of your Bravery, Faith, and Loyalty, rounded down, is your Heroism score. This is usually 3 for beginning characters, unless your scores were modified in Step 5 (page 35).*

*Step Three: Attributes (page 23)*

    *a. Assign 1 point to each of your five attributes (Strength, Constitution, Dexterity, Intelligence, Charisma).*

    *b. Then, allocate 6 additional points between them, and add any bonuses gained from your blood and path in Step 1. No attribute score may exceed 4 at this point.*

*Step Four: Archetypes and Skills (page 25)*

    *a. To begin with, increase the following skills by +1: Endurance, Prayer, Unctuous Bargaining, and Willpower.*

    *b. Then, rank the eight archetypes in descending order of relevance to your character. Increase the skills belonging to those archetypes by +3, +2, +1, +1, +1, and then +0, +0, +0 respectively.*

    *c. Total up the scores in each of your skills, including any bonuses acquired in Step 1 (page 8). If any skill score exceeds 5 at this point, reduce it to 5 and set aside the excess points to use as **freely distributed points** in Step 5 (page 35).*

*Step Five: Finishing Touches (page 35)*

    *a. Freely distribute 5 points among your skills, adding no more than 2 points to any one skill, and with no skill exceeding 5.*

    *b. Roll for your Legend, rolling twice on the Legend table for your blood, once on the Legend table for your main archetype, twice on Table 1-16: Legendary Archetypes, and once on Table 1-17: Legends of the Dragon-Mark.*

    *c. Create a back story for your character, incorporating your Legend roll results.*

    *d. Determine your contacts and acquaintances.*

    *e. Calculate your Soak, Hit Points, Max Init and Passive Defence.*

    *f. Determine your equipment and your Wealth Level.*

| TABLE 2-19: ADVANCEMENTS | | |
|---|---|---|
| **ADVANCEMENT** | **AP COST** | **COMMENTS** |
| Increase a skill by +1 | New skill score x 10. | |
| Increase an attribute by +1 | New attribute score x 20. | |
| Acquire your second path ability | 40 | You must have a score of at least 2 in all your path skills.[1] |
| Acquire your third path ability | 50 | You must have a score of at least 3 in all your path skills, and a Loyalty score of at least 3.[1] |
| Acquire your fourth path ability | 60 | You must have a score of at least 4 in all your path skills, and a Loyalty score of at least 4.[1] |
| Acquire your fifth path ability | 70 | You must have a score of at least 5 in all your path skills, and a Loyalty score of at least 5.[1] |
| Acquire your sixth path ability | 80 | You must have a score of at least 6 in all your path skills, and a Loyalty score of at least 6.[1] |
| Acquire a second dragon die | 50 | You must have a Heroism score of at least 5.[2] |
| Acquire a third dragon die | 100 | You must have a Heroism score of at least 6.[2] |
| First specialisation or expertise in a skill | 0 | During play, you must wait until an advancement milestone. |
| Second specialisation | AP to increase skill score by 2. | The skill score doesn't increase; you gain the specialisation instead. |
| Second expertise | AP to increase skill score from reduced level by 5 points. | See page 74. |

1: You must also be accepted by a master of your path. See below.
2: You must take a truly heroic action to activate the new dragon die. Your Heroism must remain equal to or above this threshold. See below.

| TABLE 2-14: POTENCY OF DISEASE, POISON, OR VENOM | |
|---|---|
| **ATTRIBUTE TOTAL** | **POTENCY** |
| 6 | Common, low Potency. |
| 8 | Average Potency. |
| 10 | Rare and potent. |
| 12 | Extremely rare and highly potent. |

| TABLE 2-15: SIDE EFFECTS | |
|---|---|
| **ROLL 2D6 OR CHOOSE** | **SIDE EFFECT** |
| 2-3 | Vomiting |
| 4-5 | Itching |
| 6-7 | Skin discolouration |
| 8-9 | Pustules |
| 10-11 | Fever |
| 12 | Temporary blindness |

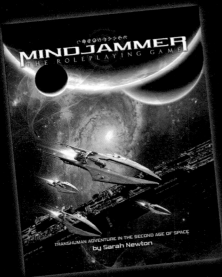

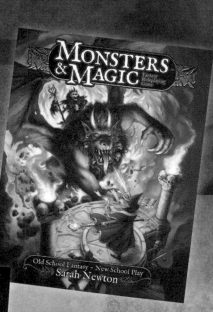

Jazira

AL-MAMLAKAH JABALI

ALBAGDIR

Arm of Tiamat

THE INNER

SEA

FRAGRANCE

CARRASSINE

KAWIMSHA

Claws
of Othoros

Eastern
Mires

Samsara
Camel Trace

Master Elalin

Bar Nissim's Noreolef

Gulf of
Oxyrynchus

SAGRADA

Canharnaum

Nejat Plain

VILLAGE OF
THE PROPHETS

Jebel Nisrox

Falcons Cove

Omphax

Linkere
Plateau

Trail of Emeralds

Azurine Sea